SAMUEL BECKETT

A Biography

SAMUEL BECKETT

Deirdre Bair

JONATHAN CAPE
THIRTY BEDFORD SQUARE LONDON

British Library Cataloguing in Publication Data

Bair, Deirdre
Samuel Beckett.
1. Beckett, Samuel – Biography
2. Authors, Irish – 20th century – Biography
828'.9'1209   PR6003.E282Z/
ISBN 0-224-01461-7

Printed in Great Britain by
Lowe & Brydone Printers Limited, Thetford, Norfolk

For VON
        — who shared it
For KATNEY and VONN SCOTT
        — who grew up with it

CONTENTS

Illustrations follow pages 114, 370, and 562

PREFACE

In 1971 I was a doctoral candidate in search of a dissertation topic, and I wrote a letter to Samuel Beckett (I blush now to think of it) asking to write his biography. He replied with the courtesy and patience that has characterized all my correspondence with him, offering to meet me if I came to Paris, telling me he doubted it would be worth my while. We met in November, 1971, with Beckett stressing how important his privacy is to him, but at the same time urging me to follow my inclinations. He would not help me, he said, but he would not hinder me, either. I told him it would be impossible for me to undertake such a massive project on the strength of that statement; as a scholar, I needed to have access to family records, correspondence, manuscripts, and had to be able to conduct interviews. He repeated that he would neither help nor hinder me and I was free to do as I wished in the matter.

We spent more than two hours in this fashion—talking about art, life, Dublin, Joyce, theater, my family, chess, teaching (his and mine), museums, whatever, always returning to my regret that I could not undertake a biography on so tenuous a remark, and he insisting that he would neither help nor hinder, but I was free to do as I wished in the matter.

He would "neither help nor hinder." It was a remark I would hear over and over for the next six years, as I conducted about three hundred interviews, corresponded with another hundred persons, and had telephone conversations with fifty or so more (for some reason I can't bring myself to add them all up). I would like to think that his "neither help nor hinder" remark was his way of giving me the necessary freedom to write an objective, independent biography. He added at the end of our first conversation that he was sure I was out to do a serious job of good scholarship, that he would not read the book before or after it appeared, and that he was sure I would understand his reasons.

In very nearly those words he wrote that letter over and over again to persons who asked him if they should grant me interviews or provide me with correspondence and other materials. I would like to think that it was his way of guaranteeing my access to sources and materials I would need.

Samuel Beckett was kind enough to see me whenever I went to Paris, even though I soon realized how much pain and embarrassment my questions caused him. He introduced me to his family and wrote letters on my behalf and all the while, I am sure he did not want this book to be written and would have been grateful if I had abandoned it.

I wrote the biography of Beckett because I was dissatisfied with existing studies of his writings. I felt that critics tended to try so hard to place Beckett in whatever particular theory or system they espoused that they ignored those works that did not fit, thus creating unexplainable gaps and blatant flaws. It seemed to me that many of the leading Beckett interpreters substituted their own brilliant intellectual gymnastics for what should have been solid, responsible scholarship; that they created studies that told more about the quality of the authors' minds than about Beckett's writings. This exasperating situation made me aware of the need for a factual foundation for all subsequent critical exegesis.

Thus, I began to write a biography, intending to concentrate on the life of Samuel Beckett's mind, to find out as much as I could about the circumstances that led to the writing of each work, to place these works within the framework of his daily life. I felt that my book had to fall somewhere between Samuel Johnson's dictum that biography must be all that is seemly to know of a man's life and Lytton Strachey's impertinent adage, "Discretion is *not* the better part of biography." "Warts and all" is the phrase used to describe the current biographical approach: the only warts I intended to show were those which produced or were produced by the writing. "Warts" for their own sake would not do. I felt a responsibility to cover the details of his life without ever losing sight of the shape and direction of the writing; to comment on his writings as they appear in the story; to characterize him, his relationships, his friends, and the many people who appear in his life.

I wrote this book to be a useful tool for scholars of Beckett's writings. I also wrote it in the hope that it would encourage many more people to read Beckett's novels and see his plays. I believe he is one of the truly great writers of our time, and (although Samuel Beckett does not need my championship) I would like everyone else to think so, too.

This is the first biography of Samuel Beckett, and weighty as it is, it is still incomplete. Although it was six years in the making, lack of time prevented me from dealing fully with such major episodes in Beckett's life as his involvement with theater in Germany. For every person I interviewed, there were at least two or three who were inaccessible to me—their statements must be gathered. This is a contemporary biography, and because of the feelings of persons close to Beckett, there are some areas best left unwritten at this time. If I have inadvertently offended anyone with what I have written, I apologize.

Many persons were friends of this book, and I would like to thank them here. My family gave me much-needed support: Helen, Leo, Judith and Vincent Bartolotta; Linda and Wayne Rankin; Catherine Montecarlo. Carl D. Brandt, whose patience has sustained me. Thomas A. Stewart, for his sensitivity to the content and his editorial judgment. Nancy MacKnight went to Paris with me. Mary Brucker made it possible to go the first time. Nancy Milford made my way smooth at the beginning. Lawrence S. Freundlich and Tom Maschler believed in this book from the first. Jean Reavey and the late George Reavey generously gave me access to their important collection of Beckett correspondence and memorabilia. Laurence Wylie gave me all his information about Samuel Beckett in Roussillon. Vivian

Mercier read the manuscript. Elaine Rosenberg, A. J. Leventhal and J. D. O'Hara gave me intelligent, provocative conversation. Joseph Reed gave me a place to work and a valued association with Wesleyan University, and Kit Reed shared creative insights. John Unterecker and William York Tindall encouraged the dissertation that became this book. John and Marge Hiller knew it better than I did by the time they finished typing and proofreading. Brian and Bridget Coffey provided information, comfort, encouragement and friendship. For hospitality, I am indebted to Marilyn Letsche Rush, Mary Kling, Juan and Dolores Pala, Anthony Johnson, James and Tania Stern, Joan Mitchell, Patricia Dunton, Josette Hayden, Marion Leigh, Michael and Anne Chisholm Davie, Mary Manning Howe, Mr. Lawrence of Cheshire, Patricia and W. Roger Louis, Beatrice and Alec Reid, Charles and Elizabeth Renauld Edwards, and many others. Elizabeth Ryan and Margaret Farrington allowed me to read Beckett's letters to Thomas McGreevy. Members of Beckett's family were kind and patient during my repeated interviews. Louis leBrocquy allowed me to use his portrait of Beckett. Barney Rosset was incredibly generous with the Grove Press files. Jean and Alan Schneider made me welcome in their home for long conversations about Beckett's theatre. Patrick and Monica Henchy extended kindnesses in Dublin, at their home, and at the National Library. I wish also to thank David Farmer and the other members of the staff of the Humanities Research Center of the University of Texas.

Much of the research for this book was conducted with the aid of fellowships and grants-in-aid from the American Philosophical Society, the American Council of Learned Societies, the Connecticut Commission on the Arts, the University of Pennsylvania, and especially the Danforth Foundation, who believed in women long before it became fashionable, with their (alas, now defunct) program of Graduate Fellowships for Women.

Deirdre Bair

August 11, 1977
Woodbridge, Connecticut

SAMUEL BECKETT

CHAPTER ONE

1906–23:

"YOU MIGHT SAY I HAD A
HAPPY CHILDHOOD . . ."

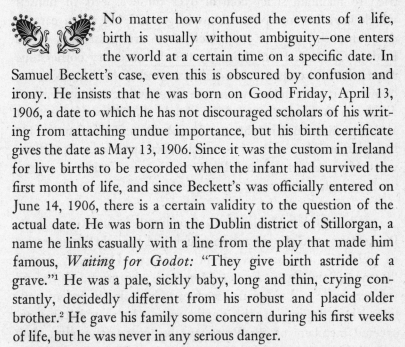No matter how confused the events of a life, birth is usually without ambiguity—one enters the world at a certain time on a specific date. In Samuel Beckett's case, even this is obscured by confusion and irony. He insists that he was born on Good Friday, April 13, 1906, a date to which he has not discouraged scholars of his writing from attaching undue importance, but his birth certificate gives the date as May 13, 1906. Since it was the custom in Ireland for live births to be recorded when the infant had survived the first month of life, and since Beckett's was officially entered on June 14, 1906, there is a certain validity to the question of the actual date. He was born in the Dublin district of Stillorgan, a name he links casually with a line from the play that made him famous, *Waiting for Godot:* "They give birth astride of a grave."[1] He was a pale, sickly baby, long and thin, crying constantly, decidedly different from his robust and placid older brother.[2] He gave his family some concern during his first weeks of life, but he was never in any serious danger.

He has been known to pass off the inconsistencies in accounts of his birth with the remark that his cautious parents waited two months before officially registering it, first because they were concerned for his well-being, and later because they simply forgot. However, members of the family who remembered Samuel Beckett's parents find this explanation uncharac-

teristic of the carefully regulated life they lived, a life dominated
by respect for all forms of authority and compliance with all its
dictates.

Beckett himself calls these curious areas of disagreement
"one further embarrassment in this legend of my life."[3] On rare
occasions he has commented with uncharacteristic relish that he
"likes all these lies and legends—the more there are, the more
interesting I become."[4] Then, as if he has revealed too much and
to disparage what was probably a truthful statement, he intones
as if by rote a solemn speech which evades it entirely: "I was
born on Friday the thirteenth, and Good Friday, too. My father
had been waiting all day for my arrival. At eight p.m. he went
out for a walk, and when he returned, I had been born."[5]

In the years since he became world-famous, Beckett has
tried to maintain strict control over those aspects of himself
which have become public knowledge, and has taken care to
determine the manner in which they are presented. Good
Friday, April 13, 1906, thus becomes the necessary cornerstone
upon which to construct the public legend of his life. Whether
or not it is true, he mentions the date with carefully feigned
diffidence to scholars and critics. Should they then seize upon it
as being important, he shrugs offhandedly and dismisses it. He
has planted the seed of symbol, correspondence, parallel—
whatever—and for Samuel Beckett, their confusion is amusement enough.

When he left Dublin in 1937 to live permanently in Paris,
Beckett reversed the migration which had brought his ancestors
to Ireland in the late seventeenth century.[6] Originally named
"Becquet," they were French Hugenots who moved to Ireland
for economic and religious freedom. They also hoped to continue their dealings in the poplin trade. As they became respected members of the Protestant business community, they
moved from the crowded linen industry into the construction
and building trades.

Samuel Beckett's grandfather, William Frank Beckett, a
builder-contractor, amassed a considerable fortune by the
mid-nineteenth century, most of it from real estate and land
holdings which he sold or leased with the stipulation that he

receive all building contracts for work on the land involved. His business prospered and when he married Frances Crothers, he moved to the then-fashionable suburb of Ballsbridge, and the impressively substantial house called Earlsfield at 7 Prince William Terrace. There, on July 22, 1871, their eldest child and Samuel Beckett's father, William Frank, Jr., was born. Three other sons, Howard, James and Gerald, were born in swift succession.

Howard Beckett was plagued throughout his life by injuries incurred during World War I when he fought in the British army in France, but he lived a long and quiet life as a Dublin businessman. Gerald and James were the only members of their generation to receive a university education. Both were champion swimmers and sportsmen as undergraduates at Trinity College, and both men later became prominent physicians who were known throughout Ireland.

The fifth child and only daughter, Frances, was originally called "Fanny" to distinguish her from her mother, but her adoring brothers soon nicknamed her "Cissie," a name by which she was known all her life. Cissie Beckett became a high-spirited woman, a talented painter strangely out of place in a family so complacently settled in the Anglo-Irish business world, and it was she who first gave rise to the now-common Dublin gossip that there was always "a wild artistic streak" in the Beckett family that resulted in "at least one Bohemian per generation."[7] In 1904 tongues wagged in proper Dublin society when she persuaded her father to send her to Paris to study art. Two years later she created a genuine scandal when she married William Sinclair, the dashing, penniless son of a Jewish antiques dealer. The marriage was an embarrassment to her parents and brothers, especially William.

Willie (as he was known to his siblings; he became "Bill" to his wife and business associates) left school at the age of fifteen to enter his father's business. Although his father was made unhappy by his decision not to attend Trinity, Bill insisted on an active, vigorous life and chafed at scholarly work. He was grossly out of place in a drawing room, but in his element on a construction site or an athletic field. Bill Beckett had become a balding, round-faced, ruddy-complected man with a booming voice and a penchant for backslapping that literally knocked the wind from many of his brawny buddies. He stood just under six feet in height, but his powerful torso and thick bull neck made him seem much shorter. He was a man of voracious appetites who consumed prodigious amounts of food and drink, and although first impressions often made him seem a buffoon, he possessed a shrewd head for figures and keen business acumen.

Bill soon tired of taking orders even though his father was grooming him for succession. He persuaded the senior Beckett to loan him money to purchase a partnership in a quantity surveying firm owned by an elderly man named William Medcalf, located at 6 Clare Street in Dublin. Medcalf died shortly after the partnership, which had become known as Beckett & Medcalf, was established, but Bill retained his name because it carried prestige and continued to bring in business.[8]

Now, ironically, Bill suddenly found himself confined to a suite of dark and dingy office rooms and the monotonous, meticulous daily work of poring over architects' drawings to estimate the amount of materials necessary to construct a building. Quantity surveying is one of the highest-ranking professions one can enter in Ireland without a university degree, and for an ambitious man such as Bill Beckett, the financial rewards were considerable. By the time he was thirty, he had acquired a substantial amount of money, which continued to increase throughout his lifetime.

In keeping with the custom of the time, Bill lived at Earlsfield with his parents until he was thirty years old. He seemed unaware that he was considered one of Dublin's most eligible bachelors. He centered his life around his business, sports, and membership in several of Dublin's better men's clubs, for he was well aware of his station and would not have thought of drinking in any ordinary pub. He was an avid sportsman, passionately devoted to horse racing and golf. As if to throw off the confinements of his sedentary work, he swam year-round in the turbulent waters of the Irish Sea and spent nearly every Sunday of his life walking briskly through the hills and valleys surrounding Dublin.

If there were women in his life, he kept them well hidden. It was not until he was hospitalized for a mysterious illness—

variously called influenza, pneumonia or fatigue, it seemed to have no beginning and no end and was probably a euphemism for severe depression—that his family and friends were aware that he had gone through a wrenching emotional experience.

Bill had fallen in love with the daughter of William Martin Murphy, a prominent Catholic industrialist who had received a certain amount of fame for his part in seeking the downfall of Charles Stewart Parnell.[9] Murphy and his family were alarmed by this relationship with a Protestant and took steps to end it. When their efforts seemed doomed in the face of Bill's persistent courtship, a melodramatic renunciation was staged at the girl's mother's deathbed, where the young woman was forced to swear on a Bible that she would never marry a Protestant, and then was hastily married to the elderly, widowed physician who attended her mother. Bill seemed outwardly unconcerned by this marriage, but he became severely depressed, and within a short time was hospitalized by the first illness of his life.

Mary Jones Roe, his nurse at the Adelaide Hospital, was told by mutual friends to take care of Bill because they would like each other. She was a Protestant, but her family was on a slightly higher social level than his because they were landed gentry.[10] Her father was Samuel Roe of "The Roes of Roe Hall" (as they were always called, to distinguish them from other branches of the family), the leading family in Leixlip, County Kildare, owners of the only grain mill in the village and looked up to by the farmers and peasants to whom they dispensed largesse with a profound sense of duty.

Samuel Roe had fathered a large family, and his grown children were scattered from Australia and Hawaii to central Africa and England. Although he was still nominally in charge of the family grain business, he did no actual work there, snobbishly preferring to list his profession as "gentleman."[11]

Mary Roe (called "Molly" by her family and "May" by the Becketts) was born the same year as Bill, 1871. She was educated at the Moravian Mission School in Ballymeena, where her high spirits and penchant for the unusual made her a constant discipline problem. In later years, she was fond of telling her nephews and nieces that she had been expelled for talking to a young man over the back fence, a legend they had no reason to doubt.[12] By nursing at the Adelaide Hospital she was once more demonstrating her stubborn streak of independence: there was no need for the daughter of a gentleman to work, especially one who was well known in Dublin as the generous benefactor of several important charities. May should have been content to remain at home and, as an unmarried daughter, to accompany her mother on visits to the sick and other errands of mercy throughout the village. Instead, as she saw her twenties rushing by and her thirtieth birthday approaching with alarming rapidity, she decided to put her skills to more formal use and set off for Dublin where she shocked everyone by taking a job and getting a salary for work someone of her station should have been content to do as charity.

May was tall and thin, with the same pale blue eyes and white-gold hair her second son would inherit, and it was she who bequeathed him the hawklike nose and imperious bearing. Her piercing stare and reserved austerity in dress and demeanor gave an initial impression of coldness and severity to all who met her, and even as a young woman she adopted plain dark dresses and tailor-made suits of mannish cut, which she wore all her life in indifference to fashion. She kept her hair tightly coiled against her head, fastened with savage-looking iron pins, hiding it first beneath her nursing cap, then under a succession of fashionable hats—her one vanity. She was an intensely moody woman whose wild sense of humor and great store of impersonations and jokes caused her to veer from gales of laughter to tears, bewildering herself as well as others by her mercurial swings of temperament.

When the forceful and determined May barged into Bill's hospital room and ordered him to stop malingering, he was immediately smitten. Her sharp, biting wit was the perfect foil for his earthy, jovial humor. They complemented each other in ways that were important to them both: he was fond of walking and athletics; she liked gardening and animals. Neither had any overt intellectual interests. Most importantly, both were Protestant, and though she secretly considered her family above his, their social class was similar. Within weeks they were engaged, and on August 31, 1901, they were married. The license showed that May was "a spinster of full age" and the daughter of a "gentleman." Bill gave his father's occupation as "contractor" and his age as "full." While Bill gave his own occupation as "contractor," May, who was still working as a nurse, left that space blank. The marriage was witnessed by her aunt and his father and took place in the Church of Ireland.[13]

They lived temporarily in a small house in Pembroke Road, Ballsbridge, near Earlsfield, until the great house, Cooldrinagh, named by May for her family's manor in Leixlip, was completed in the extremely fashionable suburb of Foxrock. Bill's increasing affluence brought him a certain amount of influence, and he arranged shortly after the house was built for *The Irish Builder*, an important trade publication, to print a photo, a blueprint of the house, and a rendering by its architect, Frederick Hicks.[14]

Situated to the south of Dublin, facing the Wicklow Mountains, Cooldrinagh is an imposing three-story Tudor house, shingled and shuttered and placed attractively in the midst of several acres of garden, with wide verandas facing south and west, screened by mimosa and verbena. The house was secluded behind high brick walls topped by higher shrubs and trees which made it seem far removed from the busy main thoroughfare just over the walls. The grounds contained a croquet lawn and tennis court as well as several large gardening sheds, outbuildings, hen house, and stables for the donkeys May loved to keep. Part of the surroundings were carefully groomed by May and her gardener and there were large kitchen, cutting and vegetable gardens, all of which provided bounteous harvests for the Becketts with enough left to share with friends. The rest of the estate was kept in its natural wooded condition, and when she was in one of her black rages, May went there to fling rocks and fallen branches from one part to another in sporadic attempts to clear it as well as her mood. She called this part of the grounds "the other side of my disposition."[15]

There was little individuality displayed inside Cooldrinagh and little indication of May's personality.[16] The furnishings were the trappings of the times, no different from those in the home of any other prosperous Dublin businessman. There was an imposing array of dark mahogany furniture, a powerful

gloom of large overstuffed chairs, patterned rugs on dark wood
floors and heavy velvet draperies. The atmosphere was one of
controlled decoration, of comfort and durability rather than
style; yet because it was such a large house, the furnishings actually seemed spare. Flowers and plants from the garden provided the only softening effect in the decor. There were no
books to speak of, and visual decorations were limited to occasional family photographs and inconsequential landscapes and
still lifes.

From the beginning, May and Bill settled into the comfortable, superficially companionable life which characterized the
thirty-three years of their marriage. She proclaimed proudly
that she devoted herself to her husband, her sons, her house,
garden and church—in that order.[17] She had always been sensitive and somewhat withdrawn, but marriage, instead of softening her tall, gaunt figure, made her appear even more aloof and
severe. She did not like large gatherings or social events, and
with the exception of Sunday afternoon tennis parties or high
teas given for relatives and her few close friends, she rarely
invited people into her home.[18] Early in their marriage, Bill
tried to entertain his business associates and friends at dinners in
Cooldrinagh, but these were so stilted and uncomfortable that he
soon confined his frequent entertainments to weekday nights at
one of his clubs. On these nights he usually telephoned and
spoke to his sons before they were put to bed; often they did not
see him from weekend to weekend, except briefly at breakfast.

May was often alone in the evenings but not lonely. She
usually sewed and sometimes glanced through the newspapers
before retiring to her room. She claimed that reading put her to
sleep or made her nervous and she had little interest in theater or
art. Early in their marriage she and Bill took separate bedrooms,
using her insomnia as an excuse, but actually because she had
scant interest in the physical aspects of marriage. She did have
difficulty sleeping through the night, and there were often
periods when she paced the floor of her room or wandered
through the darkened house as silently as one of the ghosts
which she swore haunted it. Like her namesake, May, in the play
Footfalls, which Samuel Beckett wrote almost seventy years

later, she removed the carpets in some areas of the house because she ". . . must hear the feet, however faint they fall."[19]

Bill was a sound sleeper and her nocturnal wanderings seldom disturbed him. In the mornings, when she glowered with headache and fatigue, recounting her latest proof that ghosts did indeed keep her company on her nocturnal prowls, he dismissed her gloomy imaginings with a hearty guffaw that left her angry, irritated and cross for the rest of the day. There was no catching up on lost sleep while he was at the office, for she was imbued with the Protestant work ethic and spent her days either supervising her two house servants or working alongside the man who tended the gardens and the animals.

May loved donkeys and kept them for years, even after her children were grown and living away from Cooldrinagh. She was an espouser of causes, an especially dedicated antivivisectionist and a member of several societies for animal lovers. She had no fear of animals, and vented her rage on anyone who mistreated them. Once when she saw a tinker beating a pathetic half-starved donkey, she abandoned her usual reticence and upbraided him vehemently in the middle of a crowded public road. When the tinker paid no attention to her curses and imprecations, she bought the donkey on the spot, took him home and kept him for years.

The donkey, named Kisch by her sons, was supposed to stay on the part of the grounds that was wild and wooded. May loved Kisch dearly and sent to nearby Bray for the finest trappings from a shop that specialized in elaborate harnesses and expensive equipment. However, Kisch, who was both independent and stupid, grew stubborn as he grew old and refused to stay where May wanted him, preferring the succulent morsels in her garden instead. After several forays into her prize strawberry bushes, she tearfully gave him to a mountain man in nearby Wicklow. Poor Kisch came to a bad end when he wandered into a turnip patch and ate so many that he quite literally blew up when his stomach burst. May usually began in laughter and concluded in tears when she told the tale of his demise.[20]

Each afternoon throughout her life she asked her manservant to hitch up a little cart behind the then-current donkey.

She drove it herself, inviting her children, then her grandchildren, and finally any children living in the neighborhood to ride up and down the lanes with her before tea. When there were no children to join her, she rode alone, making no excuse or apology for her obvious enjoyment.

She kept a succession of Kerry Blue Terriers who were so mean that she was constantly separating fighting dogs and calming unhappy owners whose dogs had lost to hers. In one memorable fight she strode into the midst of several biting dogs, lifted the smallest one high over her head to protect him and walked through the others, who snarled and leaped at her thighs as they strained to reach their victim.[21] Toward the end of her life she acquired a Pomeranian so mean that when she died no one in the family would take him. They gave him to her maid, who was afraid of his nasty ill-temper but so devoted to May that she took the dog to honor her memory.

Family photos show May time after time at dog shows, regally erect, holding a straining Kerry Blue at the end of a taut leash, her craggy profile shown to best advantage beneath a skull-hugging black cap, her angular figure outlined in a mannishly tailored suit. Later photos show her carrying a small Pomeranian childlike in her arms, gazing at the dog with just a hint of softness touching her eyes and the corners of her mouth, a softness seldom apparent in photos in which she appears with other humans.[22]

May was always more at ease with animals than with people, from whom she deliberately distanced herself. With the exception of her own family and one or two nursing companions, she had formed no friendships before her marriage. To some it seemed as if, upon entering this new station in her life, she deliberately cut all the social ties of her previous one. To her neighbors in Foxrock, May appeared generous and kind, as long as she was able to maintain a certain psychic distance from them. First to arrive in their times of need, she dispensed her largesse with clinical detachment and rushed to the seclusion of Cooldrinagh as soon as she could. Her only genuine warmth and kindness surfaced when she found someone who shared her love of gardening, with whom she could swap plants and cuttings. Several of her neighbors, much older than she, considered her a boon companion because of this shared interest, and to them, when the talk was of new varieties or methods of cultivation, she seemed vivacious and voluble.[23]

May consciously directed her considerable energies toward becoming her idealized version of an exemplary wife and mother, and deliberately worked to appear as a model of restraint and decorum. Consequently, she often suffered from severe tension headaches, dark depressions and thundering rages. These sporadic ruptures of the mold into which she had forced herself resulted in periods of retreat and hostile silences behind her bedroom door. Bill simply left the house during these tense times, finding outlets for his hearty joviality in long walks or at his clubs. The other inhabitants of Cooldrinagh, the servants and children, retreated behind softly closed doors to private places where they hoped her icy rage would not reach them. Her moods were inscrutable to all who knew her, so that it became established procedure for her husband and children to lead lives of reaction within Cooldrinagh—to act only after they had first determined May's mood, and then to act judiciously for fear it might change instantly.

Although most of May Beckett's generation is now dead, those persons still alive who knew her are slightly sheepish and abashed, both puzzled and embarrassed, when they speak of her; as if she possessed all the qualities they had been taught to admire in a woman, but nevertheless, were made uncomfortable by those qualities as manifested in her.

Bill Beckett, too, for all his seeming joviality and willingness to tolerate the stormy scenes created by his wife, was not without a streak of stubborn cruelty that often took the form of a relentless insistence on physical perfection in his sons and compliance with outward forms of genteel behavior by his wife.

Bill's relationship with his wife was totally ambiguous: while he lived, she treated him with barely veiled animosity and spoke to him in a voice tinged with sarcasm; after he died, she spent the rest of her life grieving for him, as if she had been unjustly deprived of the passionate core of her being.

Into the atmosphere of Cooldrinagh, superficially serene but fraught with tension, two sons were born who insisted all their lives that theirs was a happy childhood.

On July 26, 1902, May gave birth to her first child, Frank Edward, in Cooldrinagh. He had his mother's fine, white-blond hair, pale blue eyes and angular facial features, but as he grew he became a well-formed, husky child whose hair darkened and whose body soon took on the stockiness of his father's. Like Bill, Frank was tall but seemed shorter because of his girth. At a very young age he developed severe myopia, and like his younger brother wore glasses for the rest of his life.

Four years later, on April (or May) 13, a second son and last child, Samuel Barclay, was born in Cooldrinagh. In appearance, this was truly his mother's child. From birth he was thin, with the same angularity and sternness of bearing, the cold blue eyes and fair hair.

Years later, when asked to describe his childhood, Beckett called it ". . . uneventful. You might say I had a happy childhood . . . although I had little talent for happiness. My parents did everything that could make a child happy. But I was often lonely. We were brought up like Quakers. My father did not beat me, nor did my mother run away from home."[24]

This remark is typical of the kind of biographical statement Beckett chooses to make about himself, one which juxtaposes images of a happy childhood with teasing hints of loneliness and unhappiness, and which concludes with what should be a positive statement undercut by the insertion of a tone of lurking, brooding melodrama. Why, one wonders, of all the images that he could have used to describe his life, did he choose to say that his father did not beat him nor his mother run away from home? These are hardly images to convey an idyllic existence. Perhaps the interior realities of the situation did indeed belie the exterior trappings of the perfect childhood.

Although separated by four years, Sam and Frank were closer than usual. It was a camaraderie of equals as soon as Sam was old enough to toddle after Frank, yet to most of their friends it seemed that Sam was the elder because he was always the leader in their games and exploits.[25]

Life at Cooldrinagh for the Beckett boys was an ongoing series of afternoon teas where the neighborhood children congregated because May told the funniest stories and served the best jam cakes. There were donkey rides, croquet on the lawn, and tennis on their own court. By the time they were twelve, they had won all the local tennis championships and only had each other for opponents because most of their friends were terrified of the deadly accurate shots aimed straight for their heads by the coolly smiling Beckett boys. To save their own court for serious play, Sam and Frank coerced their friends into playing bicycle polo on a neighbor's court, thus incurring his wrath and serious beatings from their mother.

May always served sumptuous Sunday teas right at the edge of the tennis court during the summer, but in winter they were transferred indoors, away from the hovering swarms of wasps and bees who made eating her home-made jam cakes an exercise in bravery and determination.

Sam and Frank went bird-nesting in the vacant fields across from Cooldrinagh, they teased the dogs and donkeys and were often scolded for falling into one of May's flower beds in pursuit of a wildly thrown ball. One of Sam's favorite games was to climb to the top of one of the pine trees that towered over the house and to throw himself down, arms and legs spread-eagled, willing himself to fly, until the very end of his free fall, when he hoped fervently that one of the broad lower branches would stop him before he slammed into the ground.[26] It was a game that frightened even Frank, who told May out of fear for his brother's life. Frank's tale horrified her and led to one of the many ferocious beatings she dealt to deter her younger son from dangerous games and practices. Nevertheless, he continued, suffering constant scrapes and bruises, but miraculously never breaking any bones. He seemed to set out deliberately to provoke his mother's anger, as if to test the supremacy of her will or his, as he invited her beatings by inventing one foolhardy scheme after another, earning him the lifelong nickname of the "Family Jonah."[27] One of the worst beatings came when he dropped a lighted match into a can of gasoline as he peered intently into it to see what would happen. Fortunately, the can was nearly empty and his only damage was a pair of badly singed eyebrows. May beat him so hard that her hand swelled and she was forced to finish with a substantial stick jerked from a low-hanging branch of one of the already offended pine trees.

From the very beginning of Beckett's development as a rational human being, May was determined to conquer his stubborn refusal to be reached, his unwillingness to show all the ordinary emotions, from fear to affection. And he was just as determined to maintain his independence from her domination. The battle of wills between mother and son began when Samuel Beckett was little more than three years old, and it continued, through periods of rage and depression, for the length of May Beckett's lifetime. There is perhaps an ironic reversal in this relationship which could explain Beckett's statement that his father never beat him and his mother did not run away from home—May beat him constantly, while Bill was never there. In a sense Bill was the parent who had run away, but still the children idolized him.

All the Becketts were strong swimmers, especially Bill's brothers, Gerald and James, who were held up to the younger generation as models to be emulated.[28] Bill taught his sons to swim with competitive fearlessness, and luckily both boys were strong and athletic and approached the water with gusto. The Forty Foot, a swimming area immortalized by Joyce in *Ulysses*, was Bill's favorite. The name is misleading—the height from diving board to water is actually ten feet—but still it was the place where Bill taught his sons by throwing them into the water before they knew how to swim a single stroke, for he had a streak of genuine cruelty hidden behind a facade of masculine bravado. It showed when he forced the two little boys to match his prodigious athletic feats in ways which strained their bodies beyond a reasonable limit of endurance. But Sam and Frank had inherited a combination of qualities from both their parents which resulted in seemingly fearless behavior, an indifference to physical pain and a refusal to exhibit emotional behavior normal for boys their age—they never cried or complained, but stoutheartedly tried to imitate everything their father did, for they adored him.

John Manning, a childhood friend, remembers how Bill took him and the two Beckett boys to the Forty Foot when Sam could not have been more than five years old. Looking straight ahead without pausing, Bill announced that he was going to dive and that he expected the boys to follow—all this without first inquiring if young Manning even knew how to swim. Frank followed Bill's dive impassively, then Sam. Manning, in tears, forced himself to dive only because he could not bear the shame implied in a refusal to jump.[29]

When Sam was three, his aunt Cissie and two of her friends, Dorothy and Beatrice Elvery, neighbors of the Becketts in Fox-rock and students of William Orpen and Walter Osborne at the Dublin Metropolitan School of Art, were competing for the Taylor Art Scholarship, a coveted prize in Dublin. Dorothy Elvery persuaded May to pose with Sam in a setting she called "Bedtime." To spare her subjects repeated sittings, she took a photograph and painted from it. In Dorothy Elvery's photograph, Beckett is kneeling at his mother's knee on a small white pillow, dressed in a long white nightshirt.[30] Beckett recalled the scene in *How It Is:*

> . . . and my mother's face I see it from below it's like nothing I ever saw

> we are on a veranda smothered in verbena the scented sun dapples the red tiles yes I assure you

> the huge head hatted with birds and flowers is bowed down over my curls the eyes burn with severe love I offer her mine pale upcast to the sky whence cometh our help and which I know perhaps even then with time shall pass away

> in a word bolt upright on a cushion on my knees whelmed in a nightshirt I pray according to her instructions that's not all she closes her eyes and drones a snatch of the so-called Apostles' Creed I steal a look at her lips

> she stops her eyes burn down on me again I cast up mine in haste and repeat awry

> the air thrills with the hum of insects

> that's all it goes out like a lamp blown out[31]

On Sunday mornings, May and the boys walked the short distance from Cooldrinagh to the Tullow Parish of the Church of Ireland, where the family, as befitted its status, owned a pew. Bill accompanied his family sporadically, usually on holidays, preferring to spend his Sunday mornings walking through the Wicklow Hills or playing on a nearby golf course. He was particularly fond of the short, nine-hole course at Carrickmines, and when the boys were older Sam often accompanied him, but only on Saturdays.[32]

May gave an impression of religious rigidity to her neighbors and fellow parishioners; she took her sons to services, said short bedtime prayers and an occasional grace before dinner with them, but her own feelings were governed by the rote performance of ritual observance and not by any true belief. This dichotomy between practice and belief bothered the constantly curious Sam from his earliest memories of religious practice, but the placid, docile Frank accepted all the outward manifestations of his mother's religiosity, acquiring in the process a devout Protestant belief that sustained him throughout his life, though much of his devotion seemed to bear the stamp of duty.[33] As an adult, he was a trustee of Tullow Church, where he donated his time, money and the services of the family business to the parish.[34] He attended church regularly all his life and practiced private devotions scrupulously, but his wife and children accompanied him or not, depending on their mood, and were more casual in their expressions of faith and belief.[35]

As for Samuel Beckett, the last religious experience of any importance he remembers was the first Communion which followed his Confirmation.[36] He considers the organized profession of belief "only irksome and I let it go. My mother and brother got no value from their religion when they died. At the moment of crisis it has no more depth than an old school tie."[37]

The late Beatrice Orpen, who was a prominent painter in Dublin, sat with her family in the pew opposite the Becketts at Tullow Church, and remembered Sam frowning at her week after week during services. Years later she discovered that "his dissatisfaction was nothing personal—it was toward the whole cosmos rather than with me in particular."[38]

Still, critics and scholars have refused to accept Beckett's insistence that he cares nothing for the trappings of organized faith and insist that he is profoundly religious, even stating with assuredness that he reads the Bible daily.[39]

"I am aware of Christian mythology," Beckett replies. "I have had the Bible read to me as a child, and have read the writings of others who were affected by it and who used it in one form or another. Like all literary devices, I use it where it suits me. But to say that I have been profoundly affected by it in daily reading or otherwise is utter nonsense."[40]

In truth, May was more concerned about the manners and morals of her sons than she was about their immortal souls, and religious profession was simply part of their socializing process. When they were little more than babies, they were expected to perform all the social amenities before guests, with handshakes, bows, and genteel replies to questions about their age and general state of being. Frank usually answered with the good humor and agreeable politeness that characterized all social encounters throughout his life, but Sam was often taciturn and sullen, his responses governed by his mood of the moment. He received many severe beatings from his mortified mother for his refusal to bow politely to visiting dowagers.[41]

May zealously culled their language of anything which might in any remote way give offense or indicate bad manners. After a long and intense search she finally found a suitable nanny, one whose standards were close to hers, to look after them. The woman was so prissy that she refused to write the word "bottom," preferring the euphemistic "btm," which she abbreviated even when speaking.[42] Beckett commemorated her in "Serena I," a poem he wrote in London during the mid-thirties, with the line, "the burning btm of George the drill . . ."[43]

In 1914, when Sam was eight and Frank twelve, the three children of May's brother, Edward Price Roe, came to live at Cooldrinagh. Roe owned an African coffee and tea plantation in Nyasaland (now Malawi). His wife had died suddenly, and though he remarried shortly after and decided to stay on in Africa, he wanted his children to receive a proper English education. May and Bill took them in, and Mollie (thirteen), Sheila (eleven), and Jack (nine) lived in Cooldrinagh as part of their family until they were adults.[44]

Mollie and Sheila shared a room on the middle floor of the house where May and Bill each had a bedroom. Frank, Sam and Jack had the top floor, a large dormitory room with a separate playroom and bath. The entire floor was cluttered with cricket bats, tennis rackets, golf clubs and a motley assortment of boyish treasures. All three boys were generally too active for the sedentary pastime of reading, and they were never encouraged by their elders to do so. There were few books other than school books in their aerie and they all belonged to Sam.

He kept them on a small shelf above his bed, and by the time he was ready to leave for boarding school, he had amassed quite a few as, to his family's surprise, he had become an avid reader. Quite independently of any exposure to literature he received in school, Beckett developed respect for writers as well as their writings. Neatly placed on the shelf beside his books was a small bust of Shakespeare. Later he acquired a larger bust of Dante, which he kept on the windowsill because he liked the way the light changed as the sun moved across the crags and crannies of Dante's hawklike visage.[45]

Although he accumulated his share of things, he quietly contrived for all the clutter to be in other parts of the room, away from his bed and bookshelf, which he arranged with Spartan simplicity and order. Gradually he began to retreat more and more into his corner, so that a definite aura existed of "Sam's place" within the confines of "the boys' room." He kept very few possessions in his area, but these were never touched by the other boys. He chose the times when he would join them in games or conversation, and he also decided when he had had enough. Then he would return to his space, where the other boys never came, as if invisible walls formed a barrier between them that made communication impossible once Sam had left their part of the room and retreated into the inner world which encompassed him in his own part.

Though the Roe children called them "Aunt" and "Nunc," May and Bill had, in effect, become the parents of a family of five children. With three servants to assist May in running the house, there was no need for her to delegate actual tasks to the children, but there were some areas in which she had to impose order and discipline. All the children took piano lessons, and practice time was doled out on the queue system: whoever got there first played.[46] When this system foundered because the boys, bigger and tougher, monopolized the piano, May set up a rigid practice schedule and insisted they all follow it.

All five children took lessons from Miss Beatrice Skipworth, one of four impoverished spinster sisters who lived in nearby Monkstown. This presented a problem for May, as Miss Beatrice Skipworth secretly tippled from the sherry bottle. May's natural inclination was to yank the children away from an environment she considered fraught with the evils of drink— even though only the merest wisp of the scent ever reached the children, and when it did they were largely unaware of it. But May was the sort of woman who felt deeply sorry for the poverty of the Skipworth sisters' lives, and so she continued the lessons as one of her social responsibilities. Years later, when all five children were long gone from Cooldrinagh, May continued to send small amounts of money regularly to the Skipworth sisters and to remember them at Christmas, for she was a generous woman to those who were truly in need.[47]

Of all the children, Beckett was the most dedicated and diligent in practicing the piano, but he was also the most heavy-handed and mechanical player. Miss Beatrice Skipworth complained constantly throughout the lessons to the other four children that Sam was "all technique and no feeling," and she always reserved him for last, as if girding herself for the ordeal. As she complained, he sat stoically in her waiting room, peering with nearsighted intensity at back copies of *Punch* dating from half a century earlier.

One day, in more despair than usual, she asked him what he wanted to do when he grew up.

"Play," he replied grumpily.

"Music?" she asked, beaming to think that she had created interest even though talent was lacking.

"No," he said with asperity. "I want to play cricket for Later she overcame her natural antipathy to his playing by Ireland."[48]
doing her housework while he took his lesson. As Beckett pounded the piano, she would shout instructions down the stairs in her booming voice, for she was always careful to arrange chores just barely within earshot.

May spent a great deal of her time finding ways to entertain the five children.[49] On wet days she held painting competitions, rewarding the painter of the best picture with a penny or an extra slice of cake at tea. Often she painted right along with them, so there were five children on hands and knees on the floor, engrossed in large sheets of brown paper and slopping pots of watercolors, and next to them May, in the same position, painting with the same intensity. She could make the children laugh so hard they clutched their sides in pain, and most of the time she laughed along with them. On the other hand, she could be temperamental, and her moods zigzagged crazily from hilarity at their pranks and misbehavior to demands for strict silence and immediate obedience. While there was a great deal of laughter at Cooldrinagh, the children were just as often reduced to tears by May's scathing temper. Many times they hid in their rooms trembling from her latest onslaught, which came without warning as her mood changed suddenly for no apparent reason.

Frank, easygoing like his father, was more amenable to obedience and duty; his altercations with his mother were fewer and less intense, and he recovered more quickly from them. But Sam, who had the same fierce sense of independence as May, was less malleable. As he grew older, many of their arguments and disagreements were resolved more by cease-fires than settlements, as neither would submit to the other's will.

For the most part, the parents' devotion to the children's welfare was the dominant emotion in the household, but careful attention to physical well-being, concern for the proper expression of manners and discharge of duties were hardly the equivalent of a natural, spontaneous expression of love. Bill and May's was a marriage of opposites, held together by a strong sense of duty and position, and by a deeply sublimated affection. In an era when husbands and wives had definite roles within marriage, May and Bill were fully conscious of these roles and not only fulfilled them in public but permitted them to dominate their private lives as well. In the evenings when he was at home, Bill would heave the bulk he had accumulated over the years into his favorite chair, fuss with his pipes and settle down with one of the never-ending stream of "potboilers," as he liked to call the popular novels he devoured. Each night he might manage to read five or six pages before sleep overtook him, and when he had finished one book in this cursory manner and gone on to another, he liked to boast that he could not remember what he had read and said that no one book was different from the others in any significant way that he could discern. As he sank each evening into a gentle snore, with reading glasses slipping down to the end of his nose, his large belly distended over his unbelted and unbuttoned trousers, he emitted sounds ranging from a gentle snore to a raucous belch.

May usually sat opposite him in a high, straight chair, fidgeting with an unread newspaper. Often she paced nervously and stealthily through the ground floor rooms of the house after the children had gone to bed, checking the back door innumerable times to make sure it was locked, turning over each pot to make sure the maid had scoured the kitchen utensils to her satisfaction, pausing to investigate every creak and sigh as the big house settled for the night.

Eventually she would cease her pacing long enough to direct a sharp barb at her still-sleeping husband, and then she would creep up the stairs for one final look at the children, where her gaunt apparition, hovering ghostlike over their semi-sleeping forms was often the cause of nightmares and subsequent fears of the darkness.

Then she would finally retire to her own sparely furnished bedroom and shut the door firmly, enclosing herself in another celibate night of restless napping punctuated by more ghostly walks through the sleeping house. A separate bedroom was a convenient excuse for evading what she would have called her "nuptial responsibilities."

As the boys grew older their parents gradually assumed consistent roles in their lives: May became the stern, unyielding parent, strongly disciplining the least infraction, a veritable slave to manners, morals, status and class. Bill was the blaze of humor who burst upon them in the evening, to regale them with the latest sporting scores or the "men's talk" of his club; who prodded them toward physical well-being and athletic excellence. While May saw to their piano lessons, Bill made sure they hiked in rough weather and swam in stormy seas. The Beckett boys grew hard and tough, buffeted as they were between their increasingly rigid mother and their ever loving, always laughing father. For her, they had unequivocal respect; for him there was love, indeed adoration, for the "sweating, swearing, farting, belching red-faced mountain of a man,"[50] whose homecoming each evening was the special event of their day. And for Sam, and to a certain extent Frank as well, there was guilt for loving their father so much when their mother told them repeatedly how disgraceful was his behavior; there was shame that they loved him who was so bad and hated her who was so good and therefore deserving of their love. These emotions, instilled in Samuel Beckett when he was very young, became the source of severe mental anguish that plagued him for the greater part of his adult life and found their way repeatedly into his writings.

Having Mollie and Sheila in the house added another dimension to the boys' early family life. The two girls were like sisters to them, and they developed an ease in the presence of young women, from whom they were more or less separated when they went to boarding school until they had graduated from the university. Boys who had hitherto come to Cooldrinagh to play with Sam and Frank now gravitated to the veranda where the two pretty Roe sisters sat with their games and sewing. Both Mollie and Sheila were confidantes of Sam, but he and Sheila were especially close. A relationship of quiet affection and understanding developed between them which has lasted throughout their lives, and Sheila's home outside London has been a refuge to which he has often gravitated.

Samuel Beckett's education began when he was five years old and followed his brother to the private academy of Miss Ida Elsner. She and her sister (who was such a silent partner in the school's operation that even her Christian name seems consigned to the oblivion in which she lived most of her life) were two elderly German spinsters who had operated a kindergarten from their home in Stillorgan for many years, and when Beckett wrote the novel *Molloy*, he immortalized them.[51]

The Misses Elsner conducted rigidly disciplined classes where children were expected to sit still and pay attention and where individuality was a trait to be tempered, if not stifled. Discipline came first, learning second. It was exactly the sort of education May and Bill wanted for their sons, as long as it would prepare them from the beginning to take their place when the proper time came as responsible citizens in Dublin society and the family business.

Then, each boy went in turn to Earlsfort House School, a preparatory day school for boys at Number 4 Earlsfort Place, Dublin. Earlsfort House School was founded by Alfred Le Peton, who styled himself "Professor of French" and boasted that his students would have a bilingual education from the beginning of their studies in his school.[52]

Monsieur Le Peton was one of a considerable number of French men and women who were employed in Dublin as teachers and governesses, for there was a remarkable appreciation of French culture in many upper-class Dublin families,[53] and children whose families were on the fringes of this class often benefited indirectly because of this affinity for France. May and Bill, who were in this second category, wanted their children to have French lessons because it implied that their education was one of refinement. The boys learned the basic elements of the French language at Earlsfort House School, but neither developed any real interest in it at this time. Monsieur Le Peton was simply one of their teachers, French one of their subjects, no more, no less.

Le Peton continued the discipline first encountered at Miss Elsner's academy. He ruled by the liberal application of corporal punishment, and the sight of the tense, wiry headmaster lovingly stroking his thin leather gloves brought fear to their hearts, for they knew it meant that someone was about to be severely caned. The slightest departure from form or the least hint of an infraction of the rules was grounds for a severe beating, and Le Peton was often guilty of choosing scapegoats to prod and bully, to pick on mercilessly whether or not they had misbehaved.[54]

Neither of the Becketts was ever beaten: Frank because he was docile and agreeable and never misbehaved; Sam because he shrewdly chose to misbehave when Le Peton was not there to observe him. His behavior seemed just shy of arrogant insolence; he was so self-contained and insular that other, smaller boys boasted that Le Peton would not dare to touch Sam Beckett, while the older boys shrugged as if to say there was no reason to waste time beating a boy who could not or would not allow himself to be reached by it.

Each day Sam and Frank rode their bicycles to the Foxrock Station, where they boarded the Dublin and Southeastern Railway (dubbed by all the boys "The Dublin Slow and Easy") into the Harcourt Street Station.[55] The Protestants of Dublin comprised the greater part of the population of the southern suburbs so that this train was filled with prosperous business and professional men on their way to work and their sons on their way to school. The riders of the Dublin Slow and Easy were proud of the saying that one could ride from the south end of the line into the heart of the city without having to speak to a Catholic except for the train conductors, who did not count.[56] This is no doubt an exaggeration, but it gives some idea of the character of the community in which the Becketts were brought up. "West Briton" was how most of their acquaintances described themselves, and it was always said with pride.[57]

The Easter Rebellion of 1916 occurred while Sam and Frank were at Earlsfort House, but it caused little upheaval in their lives other than keeping them from school. Bill prudently stayed away from his office for several days and was luckier than many Dubliners who had been caught at the Fairy House racecourse and were stranded for as long as two or three days before they could find their way home. Sam, then ten, and Frank, fourteen, were vaguely aware that something exciting was happening in Dublin, but in Foxrock nothing more than an occasional report of the fighting troubled their placid existence until Bill took them to the top of a hill from which the fires in the city could be seen clearly. He and Frank laughed at the spectacle, which had taken on a holiday atmosphere for the throng of onlookers, but Sam was so deeply moved that he spoke of it with fear and horror more than sixty years later.[58]

The rebellion seems to have touched the Beckett family as something akin to an irritating wildcat strike. Less violently loyal to the crown than some of the Dublin Anglo-Irish, May and Bill looked to their neighbors and whatever newspapers found their way to Foxrock for information about events in Dublin. The fact that a Free State was about to be created did not cause them to worry as much as some of their neighbors, who feared instant rebellion and insurrection from their Catholic cooks, gardeners and chambermaids, and a general disruption of their life-style. In fact, except for political changes in Dublin itself, very little was altered in the day-to-day existence of most Foxrock families; their relations with servants and local shop-keepers went on as they had before.[59]

Sam left Earlsfort House School in 1919 at the age of thirteen and in the Easter term of 1920 followed Frank to Portora Royal School in Enniskillen, County Fermanagh, Northern Ireland. He and Frank were the only two boys in their generation of the extended Beckett family to attend Portora, which was not in any sense a "family" school. May and Bill chose Portora because, of all the Protestant boarding schools in Ireland, it ranked with Campbell College in Belfast as the best, and because it was more fitting in terms of their social standing to educate the boys at an Irish school than an English one. May and Bill were not in the upper class, which put down its sons for an English public school at birth, and sending them to Portora was as close to this as they could come.

At Portora both boys received a solid educational foundation which served them well when they entered Trinity College. It was a school which relied heavily on tradition and the "old boy" spirit, where games were an important part of education, and where both boys excelled in several different sports. Nevertheless, it left no lasting impression on Samuel Beckett, nor does he remember his time there with fondness. While his many kindnesses and generous responses to appeals from Trinity College are well known in Ireland, he has not responded to one single appeal from Portora since leaving the school.[60]

When Beckett arrived at Portora, Frank was already established as a solid rugby and cricket player; like his father before him, he was more at home on the playing fields, where his devotion to the team and his willingness to practice made up for what he lacked in natural grace and ability, than in the classroom, where he had to work diligently to earn barely creditable grades. By the age of fifteen Frank had become a paragon of the Anglo-Irish schoolboy: one who could be counted upon to put the good of the school first and any personal feelings second.

Frank was shy and awkward off the playing fields, but always smiling and eager for friendship. He was also more anxious to please his teachers than his younger brother, who gave an impression of indifference to them all.[61] Frank accepted authority, unlike his brother, whose lifelong struggle with his own individuality and the need to express it began in earnest at Portora.

Beckett was reserved when making friends, preferring to take stock of a situation before committing himself, and he moved about Portora much as he had in his bedroom at Cooldrinagh. When he wanted to join in the escapades of his classmates, he was so charming and quick-witted that he immediately became their leader, but just as quickly he could retreat into a mysterious inner privacy, leaving the other boys puzzled and dismayed by his withdrawal and stony indifference.

By the time he was fourteen Beckett had become a slim young man whose pleasing appearance enhanced his natural poise and grace, so that he was capable of carrying on conversations with the masters and their wives which were far above the usual schoolboy expression. Still, he seemed to be troubled by the ease with which he moved in social situations and often became so deliberately taciturn that his housemaster scolded him for being sullen and stubborn.[62] Despite his natural ability in sports and games and his quick intelligence, he never fit into the schoolboy community with ease. He could not keep that part of his personality which was aloof, reserved and questioning from asserting itself, so that no matter how hard he tried to be like the other boys, he never completely succeeded.

On paper, at least in official school records, his was a successful preparatory school career, one which prepared him suitably for the university, and ultimately for life among his family and their friends in Foxrock and Dublin. In his very first term at Portora he won a place on the First XI, the varsity cricket team, of which Frank was the captain. *Portora*, the school magazine, called him an "elegant left-handed bat,"[63] and gave a detailed description of the bowling, fielding and captainship of "Beckett i" (Frank), commenting in an aside that "Beckett ii" (Sam) "can bat well at times but has an awkward habit of walking across the wicket to all balls."

In later years, Beckett tried to explain away his place on the varsity cricket team during his first term with the casual remark that "it was not difficult to be visible when one's brother captained the team."[64] There is a modicum of truth to the statement, for the entire enrollment at Portora during his time there was never more than 120 boys. However, he soon became known as a brilliant, flashy player, albeit undependable. *Portora* said he ". . . has some really stylish strokes, but he ought to put more force into them. . . . His bowling is not up to expectations from last year's form, his length being erratic. An excellent field who tries hard."

By the time he was in his last year at Portora, he was the star bowler on the team. Cricket fans find it intriguing that Beckett batted left-handed but bowled right-handed:

> Anyone who is a bowler in cricket is of especial interest. The bowler is the one with the brains, thrust back upon his own resources. He must judge everything—the distance, the players; he must concentrate on how to quell the batsman (the victim, if you will). There is an element in the bowler which strikes some people as low cunning; certainly there is shrewdness involved. But it's also mathematics, logic, precision. All this is involved in Sam's attitude toward the game, and I think quite possibly in his attitude toward life as well. But never forget that he simply loves the game with a schoolboy enthusiasm that has never diminished.[65]

In fact, Beckett probably holds the distinction of being the only Nobel Prize winner to be listed in *Wisden*, the cricketer's Bible.[66]

During Michaelmas term, 1921, he was elected to the Literary and Scientific Society, supposedly the honor society, but his election was based more on excellence at sports than on grades. In general, his were mediocre this term, but he was one of three students who won a school prize for French composition. On November 12, 1921, he took part in a debate on what *Portora* called "the somewhat hackneyed subject of woman's emancipation," opposing the motion that "women ought no longer to be permitted to hold any position such as membership in Parliament, barristership at law, or any other important public post." Beckett and another boy ". . . succeeded in proving themselves capable ladies men, but in spite of their violent and eloquent statements, they were defeated by a majority of ten votes."

In Trinity term, 1922, *Portora* notes that Beckett was awarded his cricket cap even though a measles epidemic swept the school and caused the cancellation of several matches. This was also the term in which he boxed for the first time and was so good that he became light heavyweight champion. *Portora* commented: "In this event, Beckett was a fairly easy winner, showing good speed and footwork and using both hands to effect."

His success in boxing was almost certainly responsible for his appointment as captain of the Connaught House swim team, for he was only fair, never placing higher than third in the frequent competitions to swim across "the Straight," where Loch Erne met the Erne river. Each time, Beckett's dismal showing was explained away by *Portora* as a result of his "lack of training."

In 1922 he was made a junior prefect because of his athletic prowess, though this award, too, was supposed to follow more from scholastic ability. The following year, in *Valete, Portora*'s farewell column of Michaelmas term, 1923, Beckett is listed among the students who had been accepted to Trinity College, Dublin. He was also listed as senior prefect of form VI, captain of the First XV (varsity rugby), and captain of the First XI (varsity cricket). He entered Trinity without honor or prize, and his grades were the reason for his low standing.[67] In his third year at Portora, Beckett's grades were average or above in four of his ten subjects: Latin, arithmetic, algebra and trigonometry. His French was decidedly mediocre—two hundred out of a possible four hundred—and his English, history, geometry, physics, and chemistry were slightly worse. His grades declined in his last year at Portora, with only three of his subjects—arithmetic, geometry and English—normal or above. His Latin had dropped to 184, which was far below normal, and his French remained at the midpoint of two hundred.

Beckett seems to have had little interest in his studies at Portora, and his grades reflected this attitude. His name does not appear on the honors board in the main hall (which includes his fellow Portoran, Oscar Wilde) among the list of scholars who distinguished themselves in the Junior or Senior Exhibition examination. The best that can be said of his academic career is that it was competent.

Besides his moodiness and periods of withdrawal, he had several keen interests which set him apart from the other boys.[68] He (and Frank as well) continued to take piano lessons at Portora; special arrangements had to be made to allow them to practice, which was so unusual that it was remembered by classmates almost fifty years later as one of the most distinctive facets of Beckett's years at Portora. Sam was also wildly enamored of Gilbert and Sullivan, and studied and memorized all the scores of the operas, which he sang as well as played. He was an avid bridge player, with the kind of memory that kept track of every card and hand, and remembered hands in games long past. He coaxed and cajoled the other boys into playing with him, and didn't hesitate to use strong-arm tactics when persuasion failed. However, his scientific and mathematical studies showed no trace of the logic or memory which he brought to his bridge games. He simply did not like these sub-jects, and took advantage of every opportunity to show his disdain.

Most of his classmates do not remember that Beckett showed any interest in writing, or that he ever wrote for *Portora*. However, one article signed "Bat" was almost certainly written by him.[69] It is entitled "Some Home Truths About the Ancients," and is a splendid example of the snotty, pseudo-sophisticated style of writing that passed for schoolboy humor. A satirical piece about Julius Caesar, it was probably intended as well to poke fun at the master of Connaught House, Arthur Thomas Murfet,[70] who taught classics and was often the butt of Beckett's jokes and drawings.

Murfet had a long pointed nose on a small round head perched precariously atop a gangling body dressed in dapper clothing. He suffered from painful boils and was an object of derision to the boys, who mocked his appearance and deport-ment. When he was older, his eccentric mannerisms inspired affection, but at this time, when he was still a young man, he was the object of many cruel jokes. An idealized plaster bust of one of the headmaster's sons was in the dining hall, and Beckett led his friends in decorating it with a tweed cap, weskit, bow tie and a sign that read "Mickey," Murfet's nickname among the boys.

One of his roommates remembers that Beckett was "withdrawn and sometimes moody, but he had a keen sense of the ridiculous and could be as relentless in teasing teachers who were bad disciplinarians as any other schoolboy."[71] This is reflected in his behavior toward Murfet and his two French teachers, Miss Tennant and Miss Harper. Miss Tennant called him "Inky Sam" because his papers were sloppy both in form and in content.[72] She was a firm disciplinarian who demanded strict obedience, so that Beckett, who gave little thought to the preparation of his papers but was well aware of the severe punishment Miss Tennant directed toward boys who misbehaved, paid more attention in her classes than in any other. Miss Tennant spoke French with a strong North-of-Ireland accent, and she soon dispelled the influence of Monsieur Le Peton's flawless Parisian. From that time on, Beckett's French has been heavily tinged with the Irish accent he learned from her. When she left to be married, poor Miss Harper, the gentler soul who replaced her, had all she could do to keep Beckett under control, and she and Mr. Brueil, the English master, were often provoked to "a pitch of rage which must have brought [them] to the point of a coronary on many occasions."[73]

As the years passed, Beckett became increasingly moody, so that his fluctuations in temper caused him to become an enigma to his classmates. His teasing was different from the harmless, good-natured sport of his classmates. For the most part, Beckett stood on the sidelines and watched their rough-and-tumble escapades, but when he joined in, the teasing often took a frightening, vicious turn.

Mr. Tetley, the mathematics and science master, was the particular bane of Beckett's existence and the victim of many cruel jokes. Beckett drew pictures of Tetley bending over with his head peering right side up between his legs, his buttocks overly large and prominent.[74] He was careless about where he drew these caricatures and often sat in the classroom turning out one after the other in reckless abandon, as if daring the master to catch him. Whenever Tetley did confiscate them, he was shocked and hurt, and this was so apparent to the other boys that they were united in their shame against Beckett. His classmates were astonished by his audacity and frightened by his thoughtless cruelty. To allow something so devastating to the master's ego to be so casually confiscated showed a side of his personality that deeply disturbed the other boys, for whom fairness and right conduct were tenets of faith not easily breached.

In the poem "For Future Reference" written in Paris in 1930 and published in the same issue of *transition* as C. G. Jung's essay "Psychology and Poetry," Beckett relived his years at Portora and his abrasive relationship with Tetley in order to define and accept the meaning of the experience.[75] Tetley's science laboratory was in the basement, below the lecture room, and Beckett begins the poetic version of his almost irrational hatred of Tetley with a veiled description of descending there for an experiment. Beckett was always in trouble for confusing experiments because he paid no attention to chemical abbreviations and often mistook one for another. At one point, he deliberately poured a beaker of sulphuric acid down a sink and was severely punished for the incident because it was assumed that no student could have made such a stupid mistake accidentally.[76]

Tetley was also the swimming coach of Connaught House, a tough taskmaster who insisted on excellence from all his swimmers and passionately wanted to win the school championship each year. He was particularly hard on the talented but uninterested Beckett, who spent little time actually training, even though he and Charles Jones began every school day with an early morning swim across the Narrows of Loch Erne, no matter how inclement the weather. Beckett describes the Narrows as representative of the way to freedom, away from the exhortations of the swimming master's demands that they swim faster and farther. The poem moves through feelings of success in eluding Tetley to feelings of despair that the bullet-headed, rat-faced master has found a way to reach them after all. This is followed by another dream of escape from the unrelenting demand to strive for excellence, but the truth of the episode was probably told in *Portora:*

Swimming season opened very late due to the adverse weather conditions . . . the senior long race, 540 yards approximately,

was won by G. R. Wilson . . . S. B. Beckett, who was swimming strongly until the end, had to abandon the race due to
lack of training.[77]

The poem ends with reference to an altogether different
image, that of a caged parrot, the snowy floor of his cell burning
the roof of the mouth of the speaker, possibly a reference to
Beckett's playing of the birdcalls in the Prize Day performance
of Haydn's *Toy Symphony* during his last year at Portora.
Classmates remember how Beckett drove everyone mad after the
concert by imitating the birds with his own voice.[78]

Once the obscurities of this poem are pierced, it can be
considered as Beckett believes it to be, "mere juvenilia,"[79]
aimed at getting even with an unpopular instructor. But there is
an element of fear and loathing in the relationship of the student
and the master which one feels immediately upon first reading
without any prior knowledge. The swimming conveys a curious
contrast between two sensations: calm floating in womblike
tranquillity and the anguish of one who is relentlessly driven to
continuous painful movement. In the last two stanzas, the wistful expression of longing to be unnoticed and thus free is
abruptly ended by the contrasting image of the parrot, a tropical
bird upon a snowy floor, burning at dawn on the roof of his
mouth—perhaps the hangover imagery of a young man in
Paris,[80] but more likely the painful sensation of a young boy
frustrated because he is unable to rebel against a situation in
which he is forced to obey, much like a bird in a cage. The idea
that it might be based on birdcalls from a musical performance
adds an ironic note to the ending, which, if secret, must have
been amusing as Beckett listened to explications several years
later in Paris, in another world.

In the schoolboy world of Portora, where grace on the
playing field counted for more than ability in the classroom,
Samuel Beckett was respected, if not well liked, by his classmates. He was instilled at Portora with the idea that his education should lead to life as a high-ranking public servant, government official or businessman. When he left Portora, there was
no reason for his classmates to see him in any other role. He was
a "regular" boy, someone most likely to graduate from Trinity
to take up life in Foxrock among the carefully cultivated lawns

and Sunday tennis parties. For him, Portora was a way station in life, one he had to pass through in order to go on to the next one. He kept his own counsel, was popular (as good athletes and handsome boys usually are), but he did not make any really close friends there. The classmates who continued on to Trinity with him are unanimous in feeling that their friendships with Beckett developed after they left Portora. Everyone seemed to know Beckett there, but no one knew him well.

When Beckett received the Nobel Prize in 1969, Mrs. Mary Rogers, wife of Portora's then-headmaster, prepared a file for the many inquiries the school received about Samuel Beckett. Based on the information about him in *Portora* and on comments from his classmates, Mrs. Rogers wrote:

> As a schoolboy at Portora from 1920-23, he was successful in all the ways most schoolboys long to be . . . he made his mark in the school aristocracy, becoming senior prefect in 1923. Yet he does not seem to have remembered his school days with any pleasure. Perhaps because he was too successful a schoolboy. . . . Perhaps he regarded it as ironic nemesis that *Waiting for Godot* should have been the school play at Christmas, 1961, and that it was so successful a production that the company were invited to repeat it at the Dublin Theatre Festival where praise flowed from the English and Irish press . . . yet no invitation, no matter how pressing, induced him to visit the performance or give it his blessing in any way. The same has been true of further Beckett productions of *Endgame* and *Embers*. It is true, one can hardly visualize him going round Portora signing autograph books like a pop star. It is his scrupulous honesty perhaps that has made him disdain success, and he has had the example of that other Portora Oscar Winner, Wilde, who revelled in it and loved being lionized, but hated and dreaded the work that were its preliminaries. Beckett has not wanted to be distracted from his labours as the spokesman for disenchanted men, and so it is natural that we can speak our pride in him while he has none in us.[81]

CHAPTER TWO

1923–28:

"CONTINUOUS AMAZEMENT AT THE STRANGER IN THEIR MIDST"

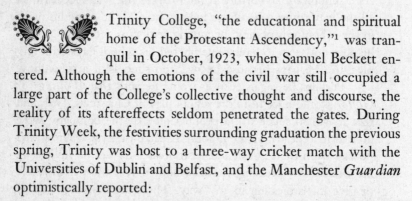 Trinity College, "the educational and spiritual home of the Protestant Ascendency,"[1] was tranquil in October, 1923, when Samuel Beckett entered. Although the emotions of the civil war still occupied a large part of the College's collective thought and discourse, the reality of its aftereffects seldom penetrated the gates. During Trinity Week, the festivities surrounding graduation the previous spring, Trinity was host to a three-way cricket match with the Universities of Dublin and Belfast, and the Manchester *Guardian* optimistically reported:

> That such a programme, in which the three Irish Universities took part, was successfully carried out, is a symptom of the comparatively peaceful state of the country, and perhaps an augury of restored goodwill and consequent prosperity in the future.[2]

Although Trinity is situated on the main stream of north-south traffic through Dublin, the college weathered the political strife surprisingly unharmed and, for the most part, unchanged in its political outlook even after 1921. For every ardent proponent of the newly formed Irish Republic, there were scores of others, smugly apolitical and bent on pursuing studies which were sometimes undertaken for their own sake, but usually, as in Beckett's case, as a suitable hiatus and gift of leisure before entering the family business.

Beckett was only seventeen at entrance (because his education began a year earlier than usual), almost a full year younger than most of his classmates. When he came to Trinity, his record was so mediocre that he had to take the Junior Exhibition examination, required of students whose ability to do college work was questionable, and in his case, his youth was questioned as much as his ability.

Beckett's tutor at Trinity was Dr. Arthur Aston Luce, D.D., the eminent philosopher, authority on the writings of Berkeley and Descartes, and author of the Donellen Lectures on the Philosophy of Bergson. Dr. Luce was not actually responsible for teaching or keeping a formal record of Beckett's grades, but acted more as an overseer, as the person Beckett was supposed to turn to for advice and assistance in all matters pertaining to his studies; but like most students, Beckett turned more to the professor in his major field for such needs. The tutor's function was to make suggestions, give advice and, in rare cases, admonitions and punishments. Meetings were usually prearranged formalities, usually mere visits with tea or sherry and polite conversation.

Beckett's relationship with Dr. Luce was more distant than was usual because he lived at home during his first two years and came to Trinity only for classes. This was not uncommon, for Trinity had more students than housing, and those who lived within commuting distance were urged, if not actually required, to live at home.

Also, according to Dr. Luce, Beckett was "one of the ninety and nine just persons who have very little need of a college tutor."[3] To him and to others, Beckett was "a simple, untalkative schoolboy" who did not engage in small talk, did not go out of his way to make friends beyond the small circle of boys who came with him from Portora, had very little contact with women, and whose greatest delight was cricket.[4]

He seems to have spent his first two years at Trinity dabbling in various courses and earning only an occasional note from Luce to "keep your terms."[5] This carried an extra meaning besides the usual enjoinder for a pupil to improve his grades; in Beckett's case, it was an admonition to one who had been cutting classes excessively and therefore had to take and pass examinations in order to receive credit. Usually attendance and recitation sufficed to earn passing marks, so that having to take examinations carried a certain stigma.

Dr. Luce remembers how Beckett floundered during this time:

> He kept his terms and all that, but it was evident in his first two years that he hadn't found his metier. Nobody who knew him thought he would become so distinguished because his first two years were actually quite dismal—it wasn't until he was twenty and in his third year that he blossomed. He even took a second in his French examination and that is most thoroughly undistinguished. It's amusing now to think of it.[6]

Dr. Luce kept small file cards for each of his tutees on which they were expected to list relevant information about their previous education and their families. Beckett listed his father's occupation as "architect," thus elevating Bill Beckett a step in Dublin society; for his own future profession he wrote "law and chartered accountant."[7] He probably did this because he had no idea when he entered Trinity what he wanted to do other than enroll in a general liberal arts curriculum and play cricket. He drifted from course to course, attending Professor Wilbraham Trench's lectures on Shakespeare; but instead of concentrating on the subtleties of *Macbeth*, he paid more attention to composing complicated, doodle-decorated lists of how many times Trench would say "at all" throughout each lecture. For Beckett, the course was a waste of time, and when he attended lectures at all, he usually left in a state of extreme agitation and boredom.[8]

Gradually Beckett found himself attracted to the study of modern languages. It was an unusual choice. Modern languages were usually the special province of women, while men were expected to follow the classics, mathematics, or engineering.[9] Trinity was the first university in the British Isles to admit women as full-time students and candidates for degrees, but they were usually shunted to the professors who were most grudgingly agreeable about letting them attend classes. Men seldom enrolled in modern language courses and almost never were degree candidates. Beckett had attended Walter Starkie's Italian lectures and was beginning to come under the influence of the professor of French, Thomas B. Rudmose-Brown, and to concentrate exclusively on those two languages and their literatures. In Rudmose-Brown he found a mentor to whom he could give unqualified admiration, respect and, ultimately, affection. Rudmose-Brown was Professor of French at Trinity from 1901 to 1942, a Scotsman from Aberdeen with an astonishingly wide range of linguistic knowledge, and an authority on Racine, Corneille, Ronsard and Scève.[10] He also taught Vielé-Griffin, Le Cordonnel, and Larbaud, Fargue, and Jammes, who became Beckett's friends when he moved to Paris.

Rudmose-Brown lived with his wife in Malahide, at the end of a long tram ride from the college, and both were considered in Trinity vernacular to be "characters," i.e., eccentric. Theirs was a stormy relationship and students who made the long tram ride to Malahide for tea found it a fertile subject of gossip. Rudmose-Brown was a massive man, his huge frame crowned with an aureole of white hair, his red face flaming from too much drink, an imposing figure as he moved slowly about the college squares. Depending on the student's relationship with him, Rudmose-Brown could be either fiercely intimidating or, as one of his friends said, "serenely detached, standing out in relief against the background of many years."[11]

Beckett was fascinated with Rudmose-Brown as much as the literature he taught. His wild oratorical style when reading French poetry aloud, his severe, disciplined knowledge of the classics, and his almost religious devotion to popularizing current French poetry opened new avenues of thought. On Sunday afternoons Rudmose-Brown held open house for friends and Trinity students, and Beckett usually made the trek to Malahide, often dragging reluctant classmates and friends with him.[12]

"Old Ruddy" or "Ruddy-nose,"[13] as Rudmose-Brown was called by his students either in affection or terror, was an inspiring lecturer who demanded dedication and excellence from his students. By the time Beckett, in his third year at Trinity, took Rudmose-Brown's course in Dante's Divine Comedy, he was well on his way to bringing up his academic record from nondescript to honors. At the conclusion of his third year, at ceremonies on Trinity Monday, he stood fourth in his class and received one of the coveted Foundation Scholarships in Modern Languages.

When Beckett was a student at Trinity, only seventy men were eligible to become Foundation Scholars (women who would have won were simply called "non–Foundation Scholars"), and then only after four to thirteen days of rigorous testing. The Foundation Scholars were so called to distinguish them from other prize recipients because theirs was the most important undergraduate award and carried a number of coveted privileges:

> They have their commons free of charge and their rooms for about half the usual rate. For Arts Fees they pay only one guinea per quarter, and this liability ceases after the quarter in which they pass the Examination for the Degree of Bachelor in Arts. They hold their Scholarships either until the end of the June quarter following the date at which they become or might have become Master in Arts, or until the end of the June quarter of the fifth year following their election, whichever period terminates first. Scholars elected . . . in and after 1926 receive a quarterly salary of £5.[14]

Three students stood higher than Beckett in modern languages, and in its account of the winners, the *Irish Times* wrote:

> Samuel Barclay Beckett, the fourth scholar in Modern Languages of this year, was educated in the Portora Royal School and matriculated in 1923. Among his college distinctions may be mentioned first of first class honours in Italian and first class honours in French, English Literature and Modern Literature, French Term Composition Prize, a Senior Exhibition and a first class "Little Go" [the required Senior Exhibition examination].[15]

He had come far since his diffident beginning at Trinity, and as he began his final year, he had gained a reputation for brilliance, albeit unorthodox.

His last year at Trinity was marked by a decided personality change which greatly puzzled his family. He no longer rushed home to Foxrock every weekend and when circumstances required his presence, was strangely quiet and uncommunicative.

By the end of his second year, when he moved into rooms at 39 New Square,[16] Beckett began to acquire some of the veneer of a college undergraduate, a veneer which was often scratched during May Beckett's weekly excursions into Dublin. She used these trips as an excuse to spy on his living conditions, but mostly to bring him food, for she worried about his health.[17] He was embarrassed by her ministrations and the hilarity it caused among his cousins, but May was grimly determined to remain part of every aspect of her son's existence away from Cooldrinagh. He was just as determined to lead his own life, and so she often returned to Foxrock angry and humiliated by his polite but cold formality and the haste with which he dispatched her from his rooms. Still, her weekly trips with the food baskets continued, partially prompted by her curiosity, but also by her genuine concern for his well-being.

Unlike Bill and Frank, Beckett had never been a hearty eater. His tastes at table were simple; if he missed one meal he would not go out of his way to eat before the next one. Always thin, he seemed to have become thinner since going to Trinity, and May worried that his strenuous athletic schedule on top of his studies might injure his health. But the real reason for her visits was that Beckett, since moving to Trinity, had withdrawn from his family, holding the greater part of himself secret. His genuine affection for his father and brother and his studied devotion to his mother remained the same, but there was a part of himself which he no longer shared. He answered their questions about how he spent his time with vague accounts of long hours of cricket practice and even longer periods of time in the library, but he told them nothing more of his social life than accounts of Sunday afternoons at Rudmose-Brown's, or an occasional evening at the home of one of Dublin's many hostesses. All of this pleased May, for she was eager that both her sons be accepted in this society, but her ambitions for her younger son were especially strong. Bill tended to ignore his wife's carping because both his sons had brought him great honor and pleasure through their athletic endeavors. Bill's unwillingness to listen to his wife's fears about the changes in Beckett's personality made conversation with him a safe haven during dutiful visits to Cooldrinagh and cemented the bond of friendship and affection between father and son that exacerbated the growing inability to communicate between Beckett and his mother. She was thrust, mostly by her own action, into the role of spiteful questioner who resented his newfound freedom and was more determined than ever to fit him into the role she envisioned for him.

And indeed his athletic career—a source of such pride to his father—was spectacular; when he won the Foundation Scholarship at the end of his third year, he also won his "pink" in cricket,[18] which for the first time took second place to academics in his life. Making the first team at Portora probably did have as much to do with the smallness of the school as his ability, but at Trinity it was quite another matter. This was an era of great cricket, when being on the team depended on superb skill and playing ability.

He gave up rugby as a varsity sport at Trinity and turned instead to golf, becoming a stalwart of the Dublin University Golf Club (usually abbreviated as D.U.G.C.), won the prize for the best eighteen holes in his second year with a score of seventy-seven,[19] and in 1926, he was elected D.U.G.C. representative (along with another student and Dr. Luce) to the Dublin University College Athletic Council,[20] a position he held until his graduation.

At the same time, he was one of a hardy band of motorcycle enthusiasts who called themselves the Dublin University Motorcycle Club and careened madly about the countryside in the Wicklow Hills. Beckett was no stranger to motorbikes and motorcycles, having owned several since his early teens.[21] He was a reckless driver and had been involved in several serious accidents before enrolling at Trinity, but had ruined the machines without harming himself. In helmet and goggles, he flew over the narrow roads and ditches, stony-faced and grim, impervious to the dangers that lay around every curve in the landscape. When his bikes became too badly wrecked to repair— Beckett had no patience for anything but minor work—he passed them on to John Manning, whose widowed mother could ill afford such luxuries as motorcycles.

Manning's mother, Mrs. Susan Manning, was a lifelong friend of Bill and May, and her three children, Christabel, John, and Mary,[22] had been friends of both younger Becketts since childhood. Mrs. Manning held regular evenings to which Frank and Sam and other eligible young men from Trinity were invited. In her home there was talk of politics and music, but especially of theater. Mary Manning was an aspiring playwright and actress whose friendship with Samuel Beckett grew when both became a part of the small society of the Drama League which met intermittently at the old Peacock Theatre.[23] "Entertainments" were usually a major part of Mrs. Susan Manning's "at homes," with guests taking part in impromptu dramatic and musical presentations. Dublin was a city of music at this time, with a flourishing Musical Society and an orchestra conducted by Michele Esposito, the pianist-composer, whose name, in common Dublin parlance, was always prefaced by "the great." During the winter months the Musical Society gave frequent concerts, many featuring Esposito in a trio whose other members were the violinist Simmonetti and the cellist Clyde Twelve-trees.

Naturally, all this interest in music gave rise to parties in which singing, playing and listening to music were important. Mrs. Walter Starkie, the mother of Beckett's professor, kept a celebrated salon. Her two younger daughters, Murial and Chou Chou, played piano while several well-known local ladies sang and Walter Starkie, Jr., played his violin. Many of Dublin's leading cultural figures came to Mrs. Starkie's, among them Jack Yeats, A. E., William Butler Yeats, Sarah Purser, James Stephens, and Oliver St. John Gogarty.[24] As Walter Starkie's pupil in Italian, Beckett was invited to these evenings and, under duress because of this relationship, he attended several times before he was able successfully to decline additional invitations.

He was beginning to dislike large social gatherings, a dislike which became more pronounced with every passing year. However, these evenings were important because they showed him that there was an intellectual life beyond Dublin. The latest developments in theater on the continent and in England were argued about, and talk grew heated as someone was always present to defend the Abbey as the world's best theater. Walter Starkie, however, was especially excited by continental theater, and it was he who first introduced Beckett to the works of Pirandello in his lectures at Trinity.[25]

Dublin, much smaller than London or Paris, was a manageable city in that all of its artists and writers knew each other, and from this time on Beckett came to know most of them. It is difficult to determine in many cases just when these friendships began because he was almost always encountering them in the "evenings" and "at homes" which were a regular part of Anglo-Irish intellectual life. If there were coteries, the city was small enough that each knew the doings of the others. And if there were "characters" (a favorite Dublin expression), their doings and sayings, comings and goings were repeated from clique to clique, losing none of their flavor in the drama of repetition. There were many small salons and groups, all touchy, argumentative and political, some even with a genuine mission and zeal for dispensing and producing culture. In such a small town there was ample opportunity to build up family histories and characters, to speak of ancient insults and glories as if they were current and continuing.

This artistic society was the one to which Beckett gravitated in his last year at Trinity, so that he was more withdrawn than ever from the Foxrock world of Sunday teas and tennis parties. He listened politely to his father's talk of business and sports, but offered little in response. He and Frank still played an occasional game of tennis or took long silent walks on the Glencullen Road from the back of the Pine Forest to Sally Gap, Beckett's favorite walk in all of Ireland[26] and one which he described repeatedly in his later writings. Their talk was perfunctory and superficial; the closeness of their earlier life had dissipated. Frank was working with his father now that he had graduated from Trinity, and was living once again in Cooldrinagh while waiting to go to India, where he was to join the Indian Civil Service, building bridges in isolated mountain passes.[27]

Beckett's remoteness toward his family was noticed by others as well: R.B.D. French, one of Beckett's classmates and later lecturer at Trinity, remembers:

There was always a slight sense of remoteness about him, even as an undergraduate. I don't think anyone then really knew him well. He simply was not what is called a "public character." He became known by degrees in Dublin, but then his only prominence was as a cricketeer. He seemed to be a man that everyone knew of but no one knew well.[28]

Dr. Luce recalls that Beckett

. . . kept pretty much to himself here. I think if he had made anything of a splash in college I should have had some recollection and I really have no recollection of his personality at all. I don't think he was a witty or humorous student. He kept to himself altogether.[29]

He went to parties, but no one who was with him seems to remember any sparkling conversation emanating from Beckett. Though he went to great trouble to take the long, uncomfortable tram ride out to Rudmose-Brown's house, he usually stood in the corner when he got there and watched while others talked. Except for occasional private conversations with Rudmose-Brown, which amounted to little more than those of any professor with one of his brighter students, Beckett seldom spoke.[30] When he went to casual drinking parties in someone's rooms or in homes far removed from the formal salon circuit, he was remembered as a tall, awkward, shy young man who usually stood against the wall all night long with his great head hanging down, speaking seldom but always staying until the very end.[31]

These parties were part of the reason he kept his private life a secret from his family. May had rigid ideas about suitable companions and proper behavior, and she would have disapproved of the people who were his friends and the parties he attended. It was easier to avoid scenes and arguments by keeping this information from her. There had been frequent angry confrontations between the inflexible parent and the stubborn son, and now that Beckett was partially independent of the family attitudes and prejudices, it seemed wisest not to tell her more about himself than was necessary.[32]

Some of his Trinity friends were welcome at Cooldrinagh, but never informally or on short notice. They were invited by May on formal note cards after she had been asked to do so by Sam, for specific dinners, teas or weekends, and they were expected to reply accordingly. Usually invitations were issued to fellow Portorans or Trinity friends of respectable background, similar to his own.[33] Other friends, members of the artistic or

Bohemian circle of the university, would have been entertained at Cooldrinagh had Beckett asked, but he knew the frigid reserve they would encounter from his mother. On the rare occasion when he did bring someone "not the right sort"[34] to Cooldrinagh, May managed to be polite, but her displeasure was evident.[35]

Just about the time that Beckett, during his last year at Trinity, became an integral part of the coterie surrounding Rudmose-Brown, he began to drink heavily, usually a brand of stout brewed at Cork called Beamish,[36] and he became a regular customer at Madame Cogley's cabaret, a pub near Trinity College. Madame Cogley was a Frenchwoman married to an Irishman; she had literary pretensions and welcomed a clientele with the same. Artists made charcoal sketches of the great, the near great, and the would-be great for a few shillings, while poets read their latest poems and spirited discussion roared round the heads of all who tried to hear them. Padraic O'Connor, the Galway poet famed in Dublin pub circles for drinking his stout heavily laced with black pepper, was often there, as were Liam O'Flaherty, F. R. Higgens, and Austin Clarke. Even Louis MacNeice, who did not live in Dublin, made a point of stopping at Madame Cogley's on his visits to the city.[37]

Davy Byrnes's Pub, then a simple tavern and not the elaborate tourist favorite it has since become, was another of Beckett's favorites. At Davy Byrnes's, he often met Cecil Salkeld, the painter and friend of his aunt Cissie and her husband, Boss Sinclair. John Weldon, who wrote as Brinsley MacNamara, and Francis MacNamara, who became the father-in-law of Dylan Thomas, held court there, along with most of the leading literary and political figures in Dublin. Although he was too young to be of this generation, Beckett was exposed to it simply by being in the same place at the same time. In later years he has often been written of as being an integral part of it, but this is only true in the sense that he may have been among the crowd when one or another of its members uttered a famous witticism.

In a town as relatively small as Dublin, one might wonder why May and Bill knew nothing of their son's pub-crawling. Quite simply, their friends and business associates never frequented these places. Bill's lunchtime world of private dining clubs and evenings at his yacht club were far removed from late-night binges in the pubs and shebeens of Dublin, and so there was no reason for them to find out as long as Beckett was discreet enough to be able to get himself back to his rooms at Trinity without untoward incident. Nevertheless, there were disquieting hints dropped here and there in casual conversation of outrageous behavior which Beckett later transposed to the stories comprising the collection *More Pricks Than Kicks*,[38] but the parents were too conscious of the rules of decorum to pry into their son's affairs openly, and he took extreme care not to fall into conversational traps where the subject might arise.

The painter William Orpen described the situation succinctly in his book, *Stories of Old Ireland and Myself*:

> If they [Dubliners] wanted a drink and a talk, they would hide themselves somewhere in the places in Dublin for . . . the lower middle classes who can't afford a club. You must understand that no respectable middle-class man in that city can be seen going into a pub. That is against all the social laws of middle-class Dublin. It cannot be done. A drink in a club with your equals is right enough, but in a "pub," where there may be others below your class, is quite impossible for the self-respecting middle-class man.[39]

Drinking and the theater supplanted cricket and other sports as Beckett's favorite pastimes, and in Dublin there was ample opportunity for both. The city was fairly bursting with theater in the 1920's. Amateurs gave performances ranging from informal readings to full-scale productions, and there seemed to be an audience for them all. Professional groups gave such a variety of entertainment that Dubliners were fond of boasting that their theater excitement was the equal of anything offered in London or Paris.

Sean O'Casey, Lennox Robinson, Lady Gregory and Denis Johnston alternately shocked and thrilled audiences at the old Abbey Theatre, and Beckett was among them for several of O'Casey's first-night performances.[40] He liked the gripping reality with which O'Casey conveyed life in a segment of Dublin society entirely foreign to one who had grown up in Foxrock, but his admiration for O'Casey's genius was tempered by his even greater admiration for Pirandello and the drama that electrified audiences in Germany and Paris. Irish realism was admirable as far as technique was concerned; but for theme and form Beckett leaned toward European experimentalism.

As the Abbey was the home of Irish nationalism, the Gate was the home of experimental European drama (prompting one wag to describe the difference between the Gate and the Abbey as "the difference between Sodom and Begorrah!")[41] and the Queens Theatre was the center of melodrama in Dublin. Beckett was more likely to be found in the Queens on a regular basis— especially after an early evening start in the pubs. At the Queens, he developed a lifelong fascination with pratfalls and slapstick. Vaudeville was still popular in Dublin, and Beckett went often to the Theatre Royal and the Olympia. He was fascinated with the developing cinema as well, and never missed a film starring Charlie Chaplin, Laurel and Hardy (who became the "hardy Laurel" in the novel *Watt*),[42] or Harold Lloyd. Later, when the Marx Brothers began to make movies, Beckett saw every one.

The curious thing about his theater-going was that it was solitary. After drifting into a classmate's room or spending an hour or two in a pub, he would quietly disappear. Later, he might mention casually that he had been to see a film or a play, and would often launch into detailed, technical discussions of the dramatic unities—of "how it worked."[43] He seems to have studied the works he saw as much as or more than he enjoyed them.

By the time Beckett won the Foundation Scholarship in 1926, he had to face the sobering fact that he was more than just a bright student with a gift for languages, for his studies had opened his mind to new ways of thought. Rudmose-Brown, eyeing Beckett as his possible heir at Trinity, urged him to spend the summer before his senior year in France exploring the culture of the country first-hand. May and Bill were agreeable as it seemed a just reward for his improved scholarship. They, however, did not view the trip as possible preparation for a career, but only as a holiday.

In June, 1926, Beckett went alone to Tours to begin a bicycle trip through the chateau country. At a pension named Le

Petit Belmont, he met a young American, Charles C. Clarke, who decided to join him on the tour.⁴⁴ They spent a leisurely month bicycling through the countryside, visiting monuments and museums, and making a respectful pilgrimage to the place where the poet Ronsard had been buried at Prieure de Saint-Cosme.⁴⁵ The following summer Clarke returned to Europe and spent several weeks at Cooldrinagh, which served as home base for long bicycle trips he and Beckett took through County Wicklow.

This brief visit to France marked the beginning of Beckett's serious fascination with that country. It was strengthened upon his return to Trinity in September, 1926, when he met Alfred Péron. Trinity's Department of Modern Languages supported an exchange agreement with the École Normale Supérieure under which an outstanding Irish graduate would go to Paris for two years to be the English *lecteur*, while an equally outstanding French graduate would hold the position of lecturer in French at Trinity for the same period of time.

Alfred Péron, a 1924 graduate in *Lettres* from École Normale, received the appointment for the years 1926–1928. Beckett met him through Rudmose-Brown, and a friendship developed which was to last until Péron's death in 1945. Péron, dark and slender, with an air of disarming elegance, was handsome, witty, intelligent, and both accessible to and popular with his students. He became fixed at the center of a very loving coterie which included Rudmose-Brown, Beckett, W. Stuart Maguinness, Ethna MacCarthy and Oliver McCutcheon.⁴⁶

Beckett invited Péron to Cooldrinagh on several occasions, and he was received with pleasure by May and Bill, who found him an admirable young man. Péron set their minds at ease concerning Beckett's increasing interest in France and his desire to return there as soon as possible. They were concerned that Beckett had, like so many other Irishmen, succumbed to the earthier pleasures of the French; but as long as he associated with a man so cultured and refined, with such impeccable manners, May and Bill were reassured that Beckett's interest continued to be in all the best things and not the worst.

France had opened the floodgates of Beckett's speech and imagination, and Péron, with his first-hand knowledge of art and literature in Paris, was often at the center of conversations in which Beckett and his friends expressed their yearning to be back there. At Péron's urging, Beckett became more sociable and developed interests in groups which did not meet on playing fields. He became the librarian of the newly formed Modern Languages Society, but had so little regard for what was supposed to be an honorable position that he spent most of his time inviting his friends to take whatever books were helpful to their own study.[47]

Because of Péron, the Modern Languages Society became the meeting ground for Rudmose-Brown's coterie, who made it "their club." It marked the first time during his four years at Trinity that Beckett actively sought membership in a group. He still needed to slink away periodically for solitary binges in the nondescript shebeens that lined the alleys around the college grounds, but more and more of his time was taken up with Péron and the others, who were all brimming over with the sheer intellectualism of their studies. There was an aura about them which made academic work come alive for Beckett. Now, instead of mere exercise necessary in order to amass enough credits to graduate, he found real pleasure in animated discussions about literature and theater.

It was in this atmosphere that Beckett persuaded his friends to go along with a hoax still remembered in Dublin.[48] He delivered a long, scholarly paper to the Modern Languages Society about a literary movement called "Le Concentrisme," led by one Jean du Chas, which was supposedly revolutionizing Parisian intellectual circles with its Rabelaisian humor and bawdy writing. He persuaded several of his friends to support the paper by reading other "examples" of "Concentrismiste" writing. The body of the membership, all serious scholars, spent the remainder of the meeting diligently discussing the possible literary merit of this shocking new school of writing. However, "Le Concentrisme," which existed only in Beckett's imagination, was never heard of again after that evening, except for Jean du Chas, who became, in abbreviated form, one of the characters in *More Pricks Than Kicks*.[49]

Time and again in Beckett's writings, he seems to have had the need to revile learning, to castigate those who respect knowledge for its own sake, and this incident is probably the first public demonstration of this attitude. In this instance it cannot be dismissed as a collegiate prank because of its scope. The Modern Languages Society was an honored, respected organization, and membership was not taken lightly. That Beckett could have played such a trick was a serious affront to the others who had elected him one of their number. It amounted to a public slap in the face and was only considered humorous many years later, when time had softened the memories of the persons involved.

The incident also points out the curious split in Beckett's personality at this time: he thoroughly enjoyed his studies during his final year at Trinity, he loved France and was anxious to return and, most importantly, for the first time he was able to carry on several friendships concurrently, without the curious need to compartmentalize, to see only one person at a time and then on his terms. He was growing comfortable in the role of university student and burgeoning intellectual, but it was this comfort that was the source of mental anguish. For May and Bill were snug and satisfied at home in Foxrock that soon his university days would be ended and he would come along obediently to take his place beside Frank, in business and in Cooldrinagh. Time was running out on his student days, but coming to terms with the adult world of his family was something he preferred not to think about. It was easier to get rousingly drunk than to plan his future, and this was the course of action he took most often.

Bill Beckett bought an automobile that year, a Swift, and Beckett drove it around Trinity very badly but with enormous style. He shifted gears with sweeping, dramatic arm movements, and involved his entire torso in negotiating turns. He made blowing the horn a musical art and parking was an exercise in dance and mathematics with an occasional fillip from the latest Mack Sennett comedy.[50] One evening, after several hours in a favorite pub, Beckett was negotiating the Swift through the streets around Merrion Square with more difficulty than usual because of the large amount of liquor he had consumed. The Swift rolled over a curb and stopped only inches from one of Dublin's leading legal figures, Judge Eugene Sheehy, out for a stroll to

escape his wife's regular Thursday "evening." Beckett received a
severe dressing down from the judge, who lectured long and
eloquently on the dangers of reckless driving.[51] This was not his
first or only brush with the law; several times he lost the use of
the car for legal infractions and several times Bill simply forbade
him to drive it, which reduced him to the motorcycle when he
had one in running condition or, most humiliating of all, to an
ordinary bicycle. By now rumors of his erratic behavior were a
matter of grave concern to his parents, but for the most part
they remained silent, thinking that it would soon come to an end
with his graduation from Trinity.[52]

He, however, began to give them hints that this might not
happen. When he was in their company, he usually tried to talk
about poetry and philosophy. He was elated with his study of
Dante and tried to convey some of his enthusiasm, but these
conversations usually proved entirely confusing to them. Their
attitude toward their second son was one of "continuous amazement at the stranger in their midst."[53]

He had become an omnivorous reader. He read Descartes
voraciously and filled three large loose-leaf notebooks with his
own thoughts and impressions as well as excerpts from critics
and biographers.[54] He referred continually to French poetry
for ideas he adapted to his own use in criticism and, later, in his
beginning attempts at writing poetry. From Vielé-Griffin, he
moved on to Rimbaud, Baudelaire and Apollinaire, finding in
them techniques of allusiveness and arcane symbolism that suited
his own style. Max Jacob, who years later spoke of Beckett as a
writer who deserved a wider audience,[55] was at this time read
avidly by the student Beckett.

But most of all, he found himself returning again and again
to the fifth canto of the *Inferno*, "the never ending flight of
those who sinned in the flesh, the carnal and lusty who betrayed
reason to their appetite."[56] This is the canto which figures most
often in Beckett's writing: Dido, Semiramis, Cleopatra, Helen
and others, all swept away by passion; also the tragic canto in
which Dante is overcome by the sad story of Paolo and Fran-
cesca.

No doubt Beckett's own personal situation had something

to do with his preference for this above all other reading matter. He had always been more at ease and self-assured around women than many of his contemporaries, probably because of the influence of Mollie and Sheila Roe. He had become almost incredibly handsome, arrogantly poised and graceful; thus it was no surprise when so many of the women students at Trinity became infatuated with him. He infuriated them by being aloof and seemingly unmoved by their open and at times blatant declarations and invitations. The only woman who mattered to him was Ethna MacCarthy, also a student in modern languages and later to become one of Dublin's leading pediatricians.[57] She was a remarkable woman, free and unfettered, who not only ignored the strictures by which properly brought-up young women were supposed to conduct themselves, but who literally flew in the face of convention by deliberately behaving outrageously. She smoked in public, wore bright red, low-cut dresses and went unchaperoned to parties, pubs, and public meetings. Worst of all, she was seen brazenly entering men's rooms at Trinity in broad daylight to drink sherry and smoke cigarettes. She was several years older than Beckett, and while he followed her around like a friendly puppy, she responded by treating him as a faithful pet, someone to be patted on the head and thrown an occasional kindly bone.

MacCarthy probably allowed a relationship to develop because she was a generous woman. It was something in which she acquiesced for its brief duration because she knew how much Beckett wanted it, but she decided when it had lasted long enough and cut it off with surgical ruthlessness, shutting her ears to his pained entreaties. To her credit, she ended it graciously and thus retained his friendship for the rest of her life. But all through his years at Trinity and for some time after, he adored her and wrote love poems for her, calling her "The Alba," and inserting her as the love object in *More Pricks Than Kicks* and the still-unpublished novel, *Dream of Fair to Middling Women*.[58]

His only other relationships with women parallel the euphemisms for masturbation and the brief therapeutic encounters with prostitutes or willing acquaintances he alludes to in *More Pricks Than Kicks* and *Dream of Fair to Middling*

Women. There was such a strong feeling of shame attached to these, however, that his verbal and written self-castigation was especially harsh.

However, at this time his only writing consisted of whatever was necessary for his studies. Because he had won a moderatorship, or postgraduate scholarship, and because it was by definition a research prize, some writing was expected of him, although none was required. He thought he would prepare the equivalent of a senior thesis on the French writer Jouve and the group called the Unanimistes to satisfy the moderatorship. The only writing he had done to this date which was independent of his studies was a translation of Rimbaud's *Le Bateau ivre*,[59] and even that was more a scholastic than creative exercise.

Meanwhile, Rudmose-Brown, who had been pleased with Beckett's success the previous year in France and the obvious change it had wrought, was urging him to repeat the trip the following summer. He was also urging Beckett to think very seriously about preparing through graduate study to join the Trinity faculty in French. The idea was appealing, for Beckett certainly had demonstrated a flair for languages; he had won the Foundation Scholarship on the basis of his scores in Italian and Spanish as well as French. Now he was becoming interested in German, which he considered an "architectural" language.[60] Though he had evinced no previous interest in any discipline which required a systematic approach, Beckett found himself fascinated by the regularity, precision and rigid structure of the German language, so different from the Romance languages he had studied.

Becoming a professor at Trinity certainly seemed more attractive than entering the family business, but Frank was now in India, and the logical place for Beckett, in his parents' minds, was at his father's side, at least until Frank returned. While May chattered incessantly on the subject, Bill was strangely silent, and it is difficult to assess his role in these family confrontations.

He simply took it for granted that Frank would take over the business. Frank was given no option, and when he staged what was probably the only rebellion of his life by demanding to go into the Indian Civil Service, he was told by Bill coldly and dispassionately that he could have three years, no longer.[61]

With Beckett, however, it was a slightly different matter. He and Bill seemed to treat each other with polite deference, careful to skirt subjects which they did not have in common. Bill, whose education ended at fifteen, was puzzled by Beckett's interest in languages, but pleased by his excellent grades and scholarship. It was much easier for them not to talk about anything but sports, and so there was great affection and camaraderie in this area of common interest. Bill would most likely have voiced his disappointment at his younger son's choice of career had Sam stated at this point that he wanted to become a writer, but a son who decided to spend his life as a professor of languages was really not so alarming. Bill might have been privately puzzled, but the position carried enough prestige that he need have no shame if any of his colleagues on the Dublin–Greystones line inquired casually about what his younger son planned to do with his life. Life as a university professor seemed the best solution for Samuel Beckett at that time; besides it offered the opportunity for annual visits to the continent.

During the summer of 1927, at Rudmose-Brown's urging, Beckett went to Europe a second time, but this time to Florence. He spent most of his time in museums and churches, looking at paintings and familiarizing himself with spoken Italian. He was there a bit longer than one month and returned to Foxrock just in time for Charles Clarke's visit.

Following his two trips to the continent, Beckett began to wear a French beret, to pepper his speech with Gallicisms his parents couldn't understand—actually becoming a bit of a snob, as undergraduates often are before parents who might not have enjoyed the same educational advantages.

In the fall of 1927 he returned to Trinity and on December 8, was granted his B.A. degree. He stood first in his class in modern languages and received the large gold medal given for outstanding scholarship. The award carried with it a stipend of fifty pounds, which he used to meet expenses the following year in France.

Rudmose-Brown, still guiding Beckett towards a career at

Trinity, saw to it that he was named *lecteur* for the years 1928–1930 at the École Normale Supérieure. The appointment, however, did not begin until October, 1928, and Beckett found himself with nine months to fill before going to Paris. Again, Rudmose-Brown stepped in and helped him to secure an appointment in Belfast at Campbell College, Portora's rival school, where he taught French for the first nine months of 1928. He considered himself lucky to get any position at all in the middle of the academic year, but he remembers his time in Belfast as "grim."[62]

During his years at Trinity he had developed the habit of sleeping late in the morning, and could only arouse himself (or more likely, be aroused) with great difficulty. Now, at Campbell, he missed breakfast and part of his first class with such frequency that the headmaster grew purple with rage at the mere sound of his name. Beckett was uncomfortable cooped up in a schoolroom with a group of staring, squirming boys and took them outside whenever he decided the weather permitted, even though the ground was soggy or rain drizzled upon them. He received a series of notes from the headmaster suggesting that the school was not a playground for night-blooming debutants who spent their mornings lolling in bed and their afternoons reading effete poetry on wet grass to bewildered students.[63]

Beckett marked his students' papers with such caustic and acerbic comments that any creative or critical instinct they might have developed was nipped in a very early bud. Many papers carried such scathing negative comments that the headmaster wrote his own comment upon them, asking the student and his parents to disregard Beckett's opinion.[64]

These incidents were usually followed by a lecture from the headmaster. After one particularly nasty series of remarks, the headmaster entreated Beckett to take his teaching more seriously, for he had been entrusted with the education of young men who were "the cream of Ulster."

"Yes, I know," Beckett replied dryly, "all rich and thick."[65]

Beckett never intended to ask that his appointment be renewed, and the authorities at Campbell College were relieved to be spared the embarrassment of dismissing someone who had come with such high recommendation from the eminent professor of French at Trinity. When the term ended, Beckett returned to Cooldrinagh just long enough to pack his belongings for his first year in Paris at the École Normale. He persuaded his parents to pay for a month's holiday with his aunt Cissie and her family in Kassel, Germany, and left in early September. Cissie's branch of the family was one with which May and Bill had had little contact over the years, and they were not especially happy that Beckett wanted to visit them.

He might not have been so insistent about going to Germany had he not met Cissie's daughter, Peggy, the previous winter when she was in Dublin to stay with their grandparents.[66] Peggy Sinclair was a cool, green-eyed beauty who always wore green and was openly artistic and unorthodox in her behavior. Beckett was entranced; she was such a fascinating, quicksilver creature that he wanted to know more about her and the branch of the family that no one in Cooldrinagh seemed willing to speak about.

Her mother, Cissie Beckett, was the youngest child and only daughter of a prosperous Protestant businessman who had grown up in an Anglo-Irish society where it was believed more "classy" to be Protestant than Catholic.[67] One can imagine the consternation in her family when she announced that she wanted to marry William A. Sinclair, who was half-Jewish.

Cissie was an unlikely candidate for a Bohemian life, with her businessman father, two brothers on their way to becoming prominent physicians, and a third, Bill, becoming every bit as rich and successful as their father. Yet she persuaded her parents to allow her to enroll in art classes at the Royal Hibernian Academy, where she was considered to be a promising artist. Because of her friendship with the Elvery sisters, whom the Becketts considered a very good Anglo-Irish family, she was allowed to go to Paris in the summer of 1904 with Dorothy and Beatrice and Estella Solomons to practice drawing.[68] They moved into a wretched hotel on the boulevard du Montparnasse, near the quarter of Paris where Samuel Beckett later made his home, and spent their mornings drawing from life at Colorossie's and their afternoons sightseeing.[69]

When they returned to Dublin, Cissie resumed her art

studies and found herself drawn into the circle of Beatrice Elvery, Estella Solomons and Bea Orpen, who were known as "the three Graces."[70] This group also included, among others, William Orpen, Oliver St. John Gogarty and William Sinclair.

William A. Sinclair, called Boss (a term of respect in Dublin indicating an all-round good fellow), was a large man with a flamboyant personality and considerable charm. During the day he worked with his brother, Henry Morris Sinclair, in the Nassau Street Antiques Shop which had been left to them by their grandfather. Sinclair hated the job, according to his friend Orpen, "like poison":

> At heart, "the Boss," . . . was an artist. . . . he loved things so much that he hated to let them go—so as a dealer he was a failure. But as a friend he was a glorious success.[71]

At night, Gogarty, Orpen and Sinclair were often seen driving through Dublin on their way to a billiards parlor in Gogarty's butter-colored Rolls-Royce, one of the first in Ireland.[72] According to Orpen, Sinclair gloried in billiards played amidst the smoke, drink, sweat and dirt of a back street bar, but he gloried in the physical beauties of Ireland as well. Even in winter, he scrambled down the Hill of Howth each morning at dawn for his daily plunge into the rough waters of Dublin Bay. He was a great walker, and relished the heat, cold, hills and sea with equal enthusiasm.[73]

The dashing Sinclair was soon attracted to Cissie, a quiet, plain young woman of great good nature, and there was no stopping the marriage. Cissie's demeanor may have been docile, but her mind was independent and spirited, and she refused to be dissuaded from this unseemly marriage. Her parents simply gave in under the pressure she exerted. Thus the popular only daughter of the prosperous Protestant businessman married the penniless Jew of great charm, good looks, and no profession.[74]

Boss and Cissie moved into a tiny cottage on the Hill of Howth, while Boss and his twin brother tried to make their living by sharing the proceeds of the shop. Boss had become an expert on antiques and paintings by old masters, and was beginning to develop a sound knowledge of modern art. By 1913, barely eking out a living, he and Cissie moved on to a larger, more ramshackle cottage in Howth where they took in all the penniless poets, writers, painters and revolutionaries who passed through Dublin.

Lord and Lady Glenavy (Beatrice Elvery), who lived nearby in more sedate circumstances, recalled that the Sinclairs often kept open house for

> all the freaks and oddities of Dublin. A sort of permanent party seemed to be going on there, with endless talk and drink and intermittent music and dancing. It was lively, warm, and human, with children tumbling all over the place.[75]

Most of the children were Sinclairs, as Cissie gave birth to five in fairly quick succession, which left her no time to continue painting.[76] Boss found that the antiques shop was not able to support his twin, let alone his growing family, and the poverty in which they lived grew less genteel and more real.

Rumbles of nationalistic feeling began to dominate artistic activity in Dublin, and the new morality and all-pervading aura of Irish chauvinism made Cissie and Boss feel increasingly isolated from the mainstream of Irish intellectualism. In an effort to revive his failing antiques business and to turn his knowledge of modern German art into a marketable commodity, Boss decided to move his family shortly after the end of World War I to Germany, where he hoped to inject a new vitality into the business by shipping German antiques and paintings to the shop in Dublin and writing articles and monographs on emerging forms of art and rising new artists.

His good friend, the painter Cecil Salkeld, had gone to Kassel sometime earlier and was living there in comfortable circumstances. At Salkeld's urging, Boss and Cissie packed up their family and went off. At first they managed to live with some degree of financial stability. Boss produced an intelligent monograph on new forms of German painting, and the antiques he sent to Morris in Dublin sold consistently.

Thus, Beckett had not seen much of Cissie and her family while he was growing up, for they had been in Germany while he was at Portora and Trinity. When he was still very young and living at home, the Sinclairs either were not invited or else declined May's tennis parties and high teas. Cissie and the Boss

tolerated such entertainments only on the most familial, ceremonial occasions, and May and Bill would have been sadly out
of place sitting on the floor drinking wine from jelly glasses in
the house on Howth. May and Cissie were equally strong-
minded and independent women, and there does not seem to
have been much in either of their lives to inspire any friendship
or understanding beyond what family ties demanded.

Beckett had been anxious to go to Germany for more than
a year, ostensibly because he was interested in becoming fluent
in the language, but actually because he wanted to see Peggy
again. May and Bill were in a quandary; they were far from
happy about their son suddenly dropping into the Sinclairs'
Bohemian existence, but they were equally unhappy about the
thought of him on his own in Weimar Germany.

Germany between the two wars was well known for license
and sexual freedom, but this was even further exaggerated by
the Irish propensity toward elaboration. In Ireland, Germany
was known quite simply as a land of sin, sex and debauchery,
and every German citizen was considered a participant. May and
Bill had heard these stories, and they chose the lesser of the two
evils: they sent Beckett to Kassel for the month so that he would
at least have some sort of family supervision, no matter how
casual. There was something comforting in Cissie's known
qualities, and they carefully overlooked the many possibilities of
unsuitable behavior in her home which they would normally
have shunned or feared.

When Sam arrived in Kassel, he found the Sinclairs living
the same sort of life they had led in Dublin; again there was a
large shabby house with plump pillows on the floor, paintings
stacked here and there or hung unframed on simple white-
washed walls, very little furniture, no rugs, and certainly no
matching cutlery or table service. Life was casual, meals were
simple, people came and went as they pleased and conversation
was intense and often brilliant. It was a far cry from the carefully appointed rooms of Cooldrinagh, heavy with massive furniture and Oriental rugs, dark with thick draperies drawn
against the daylight; where dinners were served elegantly and
punctually on fine silver and fresh napery, with flowers cut
routinely from the garden; where polishing, waxing and other

chores were performed by the three in service in a smooth, unvarying routine.[77]

It was an introduction to a new world for Samuel Beckett, one that he had not begun to imagine even in the confusion and clutter of his rooms at Trinity or on his own in France and Italy. Except for one or two classmates at Trinity, the Sinclair household was his first sustained experience with persons to whom a life of the mind was more important than physical comfort and respectability. He was fascinated with all the Sinclairs, especially Peggy, and one month with them was not nearly long enough. He returned to Kassel for ten days during his Christmas holiday, and this marked the beginning of the long series of visits to Germany which he made throughout the 1930's.

When September ended and it was time for him to go to Paris, he went reluctantly, counting the months until he could return to Kassel and Peggy. In Paris, on the rue d'Ulm, he began two years at the École Normale Supérieure which changed the direction of his life. He entered a world of brilliant Frenchmen and poverty-stricken young Irish exiles desperate to make their mark in a world far removed from the rigid strictures they felt imposed on them by the literary society of the Irish Free State. Through them he met James Joyce, with whom his name has been linked from that time onward.

CHAPTER THREE

1928–29:

"THE SPLENDIDLY MAD IRISHMAN"

Beckett arrived in Paris anxious to sort out the bombardment of sensations which had beset him in Kassel. The attitude of "continuous amazement" with which his family regarded him was one with which he now regarded himself as well. No one, not even he, seemed to know what to make of his mercurial moods, sudden fluctuations of temper and deepening desire for solitude.

But when he arrived at his quarters on the rue d'Ulm, he discovered at École Normale Supérieure—the bastion of ultra-respectability, superior intelligence and highest prestige in the French educational system—that the solitude he had hoped for was not to be had. The rooms usually assigned to the English *lecteur* were still occupied by his predecessor, Thomas McGreevy.

Beckett's appointment to École Normale for the two-year period, 1928–1930, came upon the recommendation of Rudmose-Brown and was considered a preliminary to a position at Trinity for which Rudmose-Brown was seriously grooming him. Beckett had agreed to write the thesis on Jouve because he was expected to return from Paris with a publishable scholarly treatise to secure his appointment. Unlike Beckett's, McGreevy's appointment to École Normale had not been given for a specific time, and he could have stayed on as long as he liked. However, through the auspices of James and Nora Joyce, he had just been appointed to the staff of the art magazine *Formes,* and so he good-naturedly relinquished the set of rooms reserved for the official Trinity *lecteur* and moved upstairs into another, smaller apartment. Despite their inauspicious meeting, Beckett and McGreevy quickly became friends; in fact, McGreevy became Beckett's closest friend, and for the rest of his life Beckett's only confidant.

McGreevy,[1] born in 1896 in Tarbert, County Kerry, was ten years older than Beckett and already had distinguished credentials. A graduate of University College in Dublin, he had been an officer in the Royal Field Artillery during World War I and was wounded twice in the Battle of the Somme. While recovering, he learned French with amazing rapidity and facility, and since French culture appealed to him, he enrolled in Trinity College when the war ended and took a second degree with honors for an essay on the French Revolution. For several years following his graduation from Trinity, he wrote a series of articles about the pictures in the National Gallery for the publication *New Ireland,* and this made him decide to seek a profession within the art world rather than as a diplomat, as he had been urged to do after the creation of the Irish Free State.

His appointment to École Normale in 1926 was a surprise to many prominent persons in Dublin, for McGreevy was active in both the Dublin Arts Club and the Drama League, and with Lennox Robinson and Christine Keogh, had been instrumental in founding the Central Library for Students. He had been a man-about-Dublin in the four years between his graduation from Trinity and his École Normale appointment. Beckett had heard of him, but the ten-year difference in their ages made McGreevy part of an entirely different group of people from those Beckett knew. The lifelong friendship which was to last until McGreevy's death in 1967 had its real beginning in Paris.

Because he was older than most of the *lecteurs* at École Normale, McGreevy quickly moved away from student groups and sought out the most famous Irishmen in Paris for his companions. He became a central member of Joyce's coterie, and soon became another of the continuing procession who helped him, but he was one of the few who became an intimate of Nora Joyce as well. At their home, he met almost everyone who passed through Joyce's life in the late 1920's and early 1930's, and became a good friend of Sylvia Beach, Nancy Cunard, and especially Richard Aldington, who called him "a paradox of a man if ever there was one. He looked like a priest in civvies."[2]

McGreevy was a puckish creature who insisted on writing his name in hotel registers in Irish—at that time almost the total extent of his knowledge of the language. His patriotism for Ireland was intense and verbal, but he always traveled with a British passport, excusing the gesture with the feeble remark that a man of his standing could not be expected to use a passport from "a wee little country like that."[3] Though he spent most of his time with witty and skeptical Frenchmen whose satire demolished his every prejudice and superstition, McGreevy swore that he sincerely believed that "all men of genius were Irish." Shakespeare, he solemnly insisted, came from County Cork.[4]

McGreevy was the catalyst who brought many people together. He was responsible for authors finding subjects as well as publishers; he arranged for jobs or loans, served as confidant, and often extricated friends from all sorts of legal or personal entanglements. He urged his young friends to write while he himself, busy talking and arranging their affairs, wrote very little. He had all the gifts of a writer, but his creative impulse was just as easily satisfied by conversation. One of the better-known examples of his seeming unconcern occurred with a poem he wrote about driving a cab through Dublin, placing himself in the midst of imaginary or historic scenes and encountering persons on the streets and lanes with which they were associated. He showed the poem to Joyce, who said very little about it, but shortly after, it turned up in *Finnegans Wake* in the paragraph containing "Wachtman have look seequeerscenes, from yonsides of the choppy . . ."[5] When McGreevy heard what Joyce had done, he laughed and shook his head and called him "the crayture," pleased to have been of help.[6]

His poems and the two volumes of criticism he wrote during the 1920's and 1930's show more than occasional flashes of brilliance, but the rabid anti-British hostility which dominated his later life is apparent even in these relatively early writings. His study of T. S. Eliot, the first book-length critical appraisal of the poet, is marred by excessively emotional anti-British sentiment, and his study of Richard Aldington is seriously flawed because of it.[7]

Brash, peppery, opinionated—this was the short scrappy Kerryman who thickened his brogue in sheer perverse glee at the sight of the bewildered Beckett towering above him, dazed by still another of the continuing procession of diverse people who sought out McGreevy every day. Beckett's first response upon meeting McGreevy was to retreat behind the barrier of Foxrock behavior his Anglo-Irish upbringing had instilled and to adopt the natural reticence normally shown toward Irish Catholics. But McGreevy would have none of this: they were both *Irishmen*—in all that the word implied now that independence was an established political fact—furthermore, they were both TCD men (as Trinity graduates call their university) and most importantly, they were both poets. McGreevy thought scholarship was "fine, fine," but (with finger pointing in the air for emphasis and exaggerated brogue impossible to convey on paper) "sure and it's poetry, isn't it, that makes an Irishman's heart dance and sing and be merry! What else have we got now, I'm after asking!"

He was irrepressible, irresistible, and it was impossible not to like him. Beckett was swept up into the fast-running current McGreevy generated and was soon carried along in it all over Paris. Nevertheless, he continued the habits and attitudes he had manifested in Ireland, especially those which had become exaggerated to the point where they bothered him because he was powerless to change them. He was a deeply troubled person who, had it not been for McGreevy, would have been viewed by all who knew him as a severely alienated young man, uninterested in and disengaged from the society in which he found himself. McGreevy's perpetual motion and chatter were valuable to Beckett because they cloaked his solitude and despair; they made his silence and morbidity seem the pseudosophisticated behavior of a young man new in Paris and slightly unsure of himself.

Richard Aldington, McGreevy's close friend, was one of the first to meet Beckett, and he described him as

. . . the splendidly mad Irishman . . . who wanted to commit suicide, a fate he nearly imposed on half the faculty of the

École by playing the flute—an instrument of which he was far from being a master—every night in his room from midnight to dawn.[8]

Suicide as an intellectual exercise had first intrigued Beckett at Trinity, when he eagerly cornered anyone who came to his rooms for long, rambling, gloomy discussions on all aspects of the subject—from the great men who had committed suicide in strange ways to the infinite variety and multiplicity of reasons for wanting to do so. He himself, given to protracted periods of depression, wondered aloud for hours on end about the value of ending life. These conversations were boring to some of his friends, but others found them so disturbing that they actively sought ways to avoid going to Beckett's rooms.[9]

Beckett tried to continue these conversations in Paris with anyone who would listen, but the young Frenchmen at École Normale had a more world-weary outlook than his Dublin companions and they were very quickly bored by what most of them considered his affectations. When they all tired of listening and went off to bed, Beckett entertained himself for the rest of the night with melancholy dirges on his flute.

Beckett's proclivity for rising in the early afternoon became an established habit on the rue d'Ulm. McGreevy, too, often slept into the afternoon; his students usually found him in bed when they arrived after lunch for lessons. Beckett was in the habit of calling on McGreevy shortly after he awoke and usually hung about on the fringes of these animated discussions while McGreevy held court from the comfort of his large bed in the middle of the room.[10] Beckett's usual reason for calling at this time of day was to take McGreevy to a cafe for breakfast; afterwards, he went directly to his research and writing while McGreevy jaunted about Paris to make sure "the world was where [I] left it the night before."[11]

There was only one *Anglicist* in the *promotion* of 1928, and Beckett, as *lecteur* in English, was supposed to give him private lessons.[12] The first lesson was arranged with great formality, as Beckett invited Georges Pelorson to come to his rooms one morning in October at 11 a.m. Pelorson arrived at the appointed hour, knocked on the door for a very long time and finally walked in. There he found Beckett sound asleep, unwilling to get up and give the lesson. When they met later that day, Beckett apologized but said they would have to arrange meetings in the evenings, as mornings were impossible.[13]

Beckett was at a loss as to how they should go about learning each other's language. They sat in a student cafe awkwardly trying to avoid each other's eyes, until Beckett suggested off-handedly that they read *The Tempest*, sharing the parts between them. For the next few months Pelorson and Beckett met sporadically in a cafe to read *The Tempest* in a gradually lessening formality, Pelorson in quickly improving English, Beckett in an easier but strongly accented French. They became good friends when they discovered that both were interested in the same writers. Beckett wanted to talk about Joyce, while Pelorson, who knew many of the Surrealist poets, wanted to share his ideas. They spent evenings in the famous cafes of Montparnasse, the Dôme and the Coupole, watching out of the corners of their eyes to see what famous persons were sitting at the other tables. Beckett had been a heavy drinker since Trinity, but whiskey was expensive in Paris so he drank white wines, somewhat ostentatiously ordering the same brands as Joyce.

He had met Joyce during his first month in Paris. McGreevy, who saw Joyce every day, had telephoned to ask if he could bring a young friend from Dublin to the flat that evening. Joyce said yes without thinking but as soon as he put down the telephone, he regretted the invitation because eleven people were coming to dinner and McGreevy and Beckett brought the total number of persons at the table to thirteen. Joyce tried to persuade someone to leave, to the amusement of several guests who did not know him well, but his intimate friends realized that he took simple superstitions in deadly earnest and was serious about wanting someone to go.[14] Apparently someone did leave before McGreevy arrived with Beckett, for the initial meeting was without incident.

Beckett knew of Joyce's reputation through Dublin gossip, and he had already read *Ulysses*. He was fascinated by the technique and considered it an important and influential novel. He was eager to meet Joyce, for McGreevy, unlike some of the other young Irishmen who ran the multitude of errands Joyce dreamed up for them, spoke glowingly of him as the one original genius and greatest writer of the twentieth century. But more than that—McGreevy had the uncanny knack of spotting talent before it was developed, and he was convinced that Beckett would become as great as Joyce. He was as proud to introduce Beckett to Joyce as Joyce to Beckett, and naturally this was all very thrilling for Beckett.

The first meeting between the two men was uninspiring: Joyce sat slumped in a deep chair, his thin legs twisted awkwardly around each other, replying laconically to conversation as it whirled around the eddy formed by his chair in the center of the room. A cigarette dangled from his long thin hand, which was weighted down by a ring with an enormous stone, and he seemed oblivious of the ash which grew longer and longer before it finally dropped onto his extraordinarily flower-patterned waistcoat.[15] Beckett sat in silent fascination, trying not to stare while McGreevy, with his boundless energy, chatted nonstop. Beckett was awed by Joyce, and Joyce was intrigued with the handsome young man with pale blue eyes myopically vague behind small round glasses whose thinness was accentuated by his tight, ill-fitting French suit.

In rapid-fire succession, McGreevy gave Beckett's pedigree, his Foxrock upbringing, Trinity education, ability on the cricket field and academic honors. Joyce was delighted to find that Beckett had recently come from Dublin and could tell him almost everything he wanted to know about the city and the people. The relationship of the two men, twenty-four years apart in age, developed slowly but steadily after this meeting, as Beckett seized every opportunity to accompany McGreevy to the Joyce flat. Soon he was going independently, but only when he had been invited to call; and indeed, until their last meeting, they called each other "Mr. Joyce" and "Mr. Beckett."[16] Sometimes the two met accidentally at a restaurant or cafe when Joyce was with someone Beckett knew, and Beckett was asked to join them. Occasionally there were meetings at the homes of Nancy Cunard, Richard Aldington or Mary Reynolds, all friends of McGreevy and soon of Beckett as well.

Yet for all that has been written about the immediate compatibility of the two men, their relationship during the years 1928 to 1930 was not really one of friendship. Joyce's affection was given to his family with such intensity that he had very little left for outsiders. He was a man who had little need for relationships except when they could be useful to him.

This attitude was difficult for Beckett to understand, for as Joyce gradually took over his life and turned him into a man-of-all-work, Beckett formed an intense emotional attachment and expected that Joyce would do the same. He did not realize that he was not the first person Joyce had tried to insinuate into his life. In Zurich there had been Frank Budgen, who for a time gave the total, unqualified allegiance Joyce demanded. In Paris, Robert MacAlmon filled this need for a short while, but MacAlmon was his own man, with his own books to write and his own driving need to be the center of an attentive circle of admirers. Besides, MacAlmon was flippant with Joyce instead of being respectfully obedient, and he thought the intricacies of Irish politics were too silly to be taken seriously. He had no time, either, for Catholic thought, which left very little in the way of agreeable topics of conversation for Joyce. When they talked about writing, MacAlmon usually became argumentative and belligerent, which always offended Joyce. In a sense, then, Beckett offered Joyce a relationship he had not had since he left his brother Stanislaus in Trieste. But (important for Joyce) unlike Stanislaus, Beckett was not surly when silent.

Joyce was quick to appreciate Beckett's intelligence and wit, and soon had him performing errands and doing research on a routine basis. Theirs was the relationship of a professor and his trusted research assistant. Joyce had the habit of incorporating anything that interested him into what was then known as *Work in Progress* but was later published as *Finnegans Wake*. He began to ask Beckett detailed questions about Dublin, his family and his education, and some of Beckett's replies went directly into the book. This puzzled Beckett, who was beginning to formulate his own ideas about writing. Joyce caught Beckett's puzzlement with

> You is feeling like you was lost in the bush, boy? You says: It is a puling sample jungle of woods. You most shouts out: Bethicket me for a stump of a beech if I have the poultriest notions what the farest he all means.[17]

Much later in the book, and much later in their relationship, Joyce inserted an aptly sarcastic paragraph about Beckett:

Sam knows miles bettern me how to work the miracle. And I see by his diarrhio he's dropping the stammer out of his silenced bladder since I bonded him off more as a friend and as a brother to try and grow a muff and canonise his dead feet down on the river airy by thinking himself into the fourth dimension and place the ocean between his and ours, the churchyard in the cloister of the depths, after he was capped out of beurlads scoel for the sin against the past participle and earned the factitation of codding chaplan and being as homely gauche as swift B.A.A. Who gets twickly fullgets twice as allemanden huskers. But the whacker his word the weaker our ears for auracles who parles parses orileys. Illstarred punster, lipstering cowknucks. 'Twas the quadra sent him and Trinity too. And he cantab as chipper as any oxon ever I mood with, a tiptoe singer! He'll prisckly soon hand tune your Erin's ear for you.[18]

Another time Joyce wanted to insert a story about a kind-hearted Irish soldier in the Crimean War who could not bring himself to shoot a defecating Russian general until he picked up a chunk of turf to finish the act. "Another insult to Ireland," Beckett remarked dryly. Joyce used his exact words, as they were what he needed to nationalize the story.[19]

Besides Beckett's intelligence and wit, one of the reasons Joyce was so eager to establish him in the role of amanuensis was the snobbish pleasure it gave. All the other young Irishmen who helped him were, like himself, Catholics educated at University College, lower middle class, strangers to the world of tennis parties, men's clubs, Trinity Week and the Horse Show. Their families seldom spoke to a Protestant, let alone entertained one. Joyce had been shabbily poor for most of his life, ashamed of his own socially impoverished background at the same time as he was fiercely proud of it. He bore a hidden frustration that his education had been at University College and not Trinity. Always intrigued by the trappings of the rich and the near rich, he was fascinated by Beckett's background. Beckett, whom Adrienne Monnier described as "a new Stephen Dedalus, striding all by himself along the strand,"[20] was immensely flattering.

Joyce's eyesight was failing again, and he depended on

Beckett as a willing but unpaid servant; Richard Aldington, among others, referred to him sarcastically as "James Joyce's white boy."[21] One of the most oft-repeated fallacies is that Beckett was actually Joyce's paid secretary. This has always annoyed Beckett, to the extent that he stresses that he was never officially in Joyce's employ:

> I was never Joyce's secretary, but like all his friends, I helped him. He was greatly handicapped because of his eyes. I did odd jobs for him, marking passages for him or reading to him, but I never wrote any of his letters.[22]

In truth, Beckett did no more nor less than any of the other young Irishmen in Paris who were drawn into Joyce's orbit. The difference is that they have not subsequently become as famous as Beckett, and so their dedicated services have not been as well publicized.

To the dismay of some of his friends, Beckett began to imitate Joyce's mannerisms.[23] He dangled his cigarettes carelessly from limp-wristed hands. Although he was nearsighted, his eyes were not then seriously troublesome, but he held books and papers up close to his glasses in the same attitude of languid exhaustion that Joyce affected in order to cover his very real inability to see clearly.

Beckett even wore pointed-toe patent leather pumps that were too small because he wanted to wear the same shoe in the same size as Joyce, who was very proud of his small, neatly shod feet.[24] Joyce had been vain about his feet since his youth, when poverty forced him to go about Dublin in a pair of white tennis shoes, the only footwear he owned. It is impossible to know if Joyce was even aware of Beckett's slavish gesture, for his eyes were so weak that he saw very little. What is intriguing about this imitative gesture is the sacrificial element involved in the picture of Beckett, suffering terribly from huge corns and terrible calluses, walking only with great pain. He must have pulled off his shoes in much the same way as his character Estragon pulls off his horrible misshapen boots in the first act of *Waiting for Godot* with a sigh of infinite relief.

There were other, more valid reasons for the affinity between the two men: both were Romance linguists, having read

French and Italian in their universities. Both men pondered their role as Irishmen abroad in the larger world. Both had a serious interest in all forms of arcane knowledge, so that Beckett eagerly searched for new information to feed Joyce's voracious appetite. There was also the natural superstition which both men credited to their Irish background, and which both took seriously to varying extent. Both were superstitious about the number thirteen. Beckett simply considered it lucky, since it was his birthday and, when doubled, his brother's.[25] Joyce was ambivalent about it—he finished writing *Ulysses* in 1921, which added up to thirteen, and he considered this a good omen, but his mother had died on the thirteenth. He was genuinely afraid of the thirteenth day of each month—it was ultimately to become the day of his own death—and his fear of thirteen at table has already been noted. A number of his friends engaged in discussions of the number thirteen with Joyce, and he was deadly serious about the importance of numerology and would not stand for humorous comments.[26]

Joyce was more than a master for Beckett, he was a social mentor as well, and by watching him carefully, Beckett learned much about the vagaries of life in Paris. Joyce had developed several poses which helped him to cope with sophisticated Parisian society since the time he had made several gauche remarks at a party given by a prominent hostess and brought down a rain of humiliation upon himself. He learned that silence looked like knowledgeability,[27] and he sat on the edge of groups until people turned to him for conversation. Eventually Joyce, who was not at ease in large groups of relative strangers, began to lead his literary life at home, avoiding salons and large parties unless the group had been formed expressly for the purpose of making him its center. Politeness, silence and reserve became his favorite social defenses, and he used them with consummate skill.

Beckett, too, had found since his days at Trinity that literary evenings bored him and that compartmentalizing his friendships gave him a certain amount of control over the tenor of a meeting, which he needed in order to function with ease. When he saw Joyce's success in his independent behavior, Beckett imitated it and discovered that he also could dispense with the niceties of social convention. He saw that it was possible for him to take from society as much conviviality as he wanted while still keeping his distance. In time he honed this practice to a fine point of protective privacy that far outdistanced Joyce.

But in all this catalog of comparisons and affectations, one fact looms above all: Beckett sincerely considered Joyce to be one of the greatest writers of this century, if not of all time. His respect and admiration were boundless and his reverence has not wavered. In 1969 he admitted that Joyce had become "an ethical ideal" for him. "Joyce had a moral effect on me," Beckett said; "he made me realize artistic integrity."[28]

Joyce wrote amidst the terrible pain of failing eyesight, uncertain financial status and disturbing emotional problems within his family. This ability to write each day no matter what the circumstances of his personal life had tremendous effect on Beckett, who was just beginning to think that he, too, could be something more than a professor and critic. Years later, he still marveled at Joyce's ability to write every single day of his life, and complained of the torment of being at the mercy of a muse who came and went with capricious irregularity.[29]

From their first meeting in the fall of 1928, Beckett found himself bound up with the fortunes of the entire Joyce family. First, of course, with Joyce, who shortly before Beckett came to Paris had suffered another of the collapses that seriously impaired his vision throughout his life. The attack, which doctors blamed on "nerves" rather than something organic,[30] left him unable to see print and heavily dependent on others. Beckett stepped into the void by reading to Joyce and taking his dictation for passages of *Work in Progress*.

Then, in November, Nora Joyce's doctor determined that she needed a hysterectomy. Joyce became so upset by the threatened separation from his wife that he insisted on having a bed placed in her hospital room.[31] Beckett became the family messenger and dutifully trotted back and forth between the Joyce apartment and the hospital.[32]

So much of his time had been taken up with the Joyces and their continuing problems that when the impending holiday season crept up on him in mid-December, he was virtually unable to return to Cooldrinagh because the Joyces required his services. He told his disappointed family that his commitments in Paris were so pressing that he could not stay long enough in Ireland to make the journey worthwhile,[33] but his real reason was because he wanted to go to Kassel instead.

That fall, his attraction to Peggy had intensified. When he arrived in Kassel, he discovered she was much the same as he had left her: headstrong, willful, imperious and beautiful. She bewildered Beckett with her perpetual energy and bursting health. Peggy was intelligent and as capable of returning banter as initiating it, and she spoke her native English with such a strong German accent that Beckett called her his "Irish Fräulein"[34] She could tell jokes in several languages, and playing word games and flirting during piano duets were her standard behavior. She practiced her wiles on the steady stream of young men of many nationalities who came to the house to call on her and her three sisters, but with her first cousin her teasing took on a slightly different tone; she was more gentle and less appraising than she was with her other suitors. Beckett's emotional turmoil increased as Peggy flitted about, first enticing him into performing on the piano while she sat beside him and sang, then disappearing for hours on a shopping expedition, taking another man along to carry her packages.

He was twenty-three years old, but none of his relationships with women had prepared him for coping with Peggy. Until now most of the young women he knew had been family friends, proper young women from the same Dublin background to whom he gave little more than polite condescension. At Trinity, he had suffered terribly from his unrequited crush on Ethna MacCarthy, but then so had just about every other man in his class.[35] He had been seen in pubs with the "not-so-nice ladies" (a Dublin euphemism). Occasionally his friends saw him in their company, skulking about the darker streets and lanes, but he insisted when they questioned him later that he had only been escorting them, as any gentleman would, to the Westland Row Station and the train ride home.[36] In his few months in Paris he had seen enough of cafe life to learn more about women than he had heretofore imagined, but for all that, his actual relationships with them were neither serious nor deep.

Now Peggy had him in her thrall, and he was powerless

when confronted with the force of such vivacity. Beckett was much like his fictional character Belacqua Shuah, named for Dante's slothful inhabitant of purgatory, who became the hero of the unpublished novel *Dream of Fair to Middling Women*, written in Paris in 1931–32.[37] In it, he calls Peggy the "Smeraldina-Rima" because of her deep green eyes and her passionate love of green clothing. He called her everybody's darling, young and lovely and so funny, with her off-color jokes that amused her sisters. Although she acted as though she could not play the piano, she was able to improvise both in playing and singing. When she was in form, the words tumbled out in a convulsive stream and she had everyone, even her own family, literally rolling on the floor with tears streaming from their eyes. Everyone thought she should have been in vaudeville, especially her mother, who laughed harder than anyone.

News of Beckett's infatuation with Peggy drifted back to Foxrock, where it was received glumly; Bill was noncommittal, but May was furious. Sam was too young, she said, to think seriously about anyone, especially his first cousin. More to the point was Peggy's half-Jewish background. Bill Beckett had been forbidden by his parents to take even a passing interest in a Catholic. Now his son was seriously involved (so it seemed to them in Dublin) with a girl whose heritage was Jewish, even though no formal religious practice had ever occurred in the Sinclair family. May and Bill's only consolation lay in the brevity of the holiday, and they felt somewhat easier when Beckett returned to Paris shortly after the beginning of 1929.

Immediately the Joyce family preempted Beckett's free time. Sometime during the previous fall Joyce had mentioned in passing that Beckett might contribute an essay to a collection he was planning as a reply to critics of *Work in Progress*. Now he made the offer seriously. Beckett was probably a last-minute substitute for someone else, because Joyce had written to Adrienne Monnier on September 3, 1928 (before he had met Beckett), mentioning "eleven articles plus one other by Stuart Gilbert, bringing the total to twelve"[38] (which there were when the book was printed with Beckett's article).[39]

Beckett spent the better part of the first few months of

1929 writing his essay for *Our Exagmination Round His Facti-fication for Incamination of Work in Progress,* and subsequently it appeared as the first essay in the volume. Dante was one of the strongest bonds between Joyce and Beckett, and Joyce, who assigned the subject matter of each essay, suggested that Beckett was the best equipped to explicate his debt to Dante. He then instructed Beckett to discuss his other favorite Italian writers as well, and their influence upon him. Beckett had not yet read Giordano Bruno and Giambattista Vico, so his first and most time-consuming assignment was to read the Italian originals and discuss them with Joyce. Joyce was at pains to instruct Beckett not only to show his indebtedness to them but also to make it plain that he had moved beyond them to create his own particu-lar work of art. The title of the essay, "Dante . . . Bruno. Vico . . Joyce," was mutually agreed upon. Joyce wanted a title which would not only indicate the separation of the writers in physical time but would also suggest that the first three cul-minated in the pinnacle of *Work in Progress.* Beckett explained the punctuation as follows: "From Dante to Bruno is a jump of about three centuries, from Bruno to Vico about one and from Vico to Joyce about two."[40] Many of the ideas contained in the essay, particularly the interpretations of Bruno and Vico, came directly from his conversations with Joyce, who was eager to guide his protégé to the correct version, but the language and structure of the essay are Beckett's own.

It is a curious essay. Its language is fussy, pedantic and pompous, reminiscent of a paper prepared by a beginning aca-demic with a penchant for verbal virtuosity. There are passing references to Conti, Bacon and Bossuet, and analogies from Dickens and Shakespeare—references which seem to be there more for the sake of displaying erudition than advancing argu-ment. Beckett quotes from the Italian of each of his three authors and from Dante's Latin as well, and the quotations he selects to illustrate his principles are perceptive and to the point. His exuberant admiration for Joyce permits him no expression short of hero worship, and he thumbs his nose at a public too vulgar and unenlightened to appreciate *Work in Progress:* "And if you don't understand it, ladies and gentlemen, it is because you are too decadent to receive it."[41] But this after all is what the essay was intended to be: not only an apologia, but an affirmation of Joyce's genius and the excellence of his new writing.

Beckett's essay, as the first published work of a twenty-three-year-old graduate student, shows promise. It demonstrates his ability to manipulate language, to extract the essence of a writer's thought and to use it to elucidate a critical theory. When he wrote it, Beckett was preparing for a university career, and it is an excellent beginning. His gushing admiration for Joyce may be embarrassing at times to present-day readers, as it is to him,[42] but more important in this essay are the oblique references to what would later become his own literary credo: the reduction of life and humanity to its simplest, most basic function and form. It is almost too easy now for scholars to examine Beckett's writings and to chronicle the development of his ideas. Beckett did not consciously formulate these theories until much later in his life, and so one must turn to the first sentence of the essay for a warning as well as a summation: "The danger is in the neatness of identification."[43]

Our Exagmination did not generate the wide readership and interest that Joyce wanted, but there were several reviews. One year later Frank O'Connor, writing in the *Irish Statesman*, said:

> I have before me a book of essays on his [Joyce's] latest work by some of the young people who have come under his influence. Two or three of these essays—I am thinking in particular of Samuel Beckett's, Eugene Jolas', and Thomas McGreevy's—are very interesting, and with a little more detachment would have been first rate criticism; others are merely dull.[44]

Beckett's essay appeared in June, 1929, in *transition*, the influential review published by Eugene and Maria Jolas.[45] They had moved to the center of Joyce's devoted group and had become his most ardent supporters, giving him the unswerving homage of true believers, insinuating themselves among those who offered Joyce "unqualified allegiance,"[46] such as Paul and Lucie Léon, Stuart and Moune Gilbert, Louis Gillet, Nino Frank, and others.

Many of the persons who had been close to Joyce now

began to move away from his dominance and influence for one reason or another. MacAlmon's ego could not tolerate being second to anyone else's. McGreevy had been forced to realize that he must leave the École Normale if he were to try to make a decent living through his writing. William and Jennie Bradley, who had previously seen the Joyces several times weekly, were annoyed by Joyce's increasing egocentrism and gradually drifted away.[47]

The new group which formed around Joyce offered him the unquestioning leadership and idolatry he demanded. He was at the center of their lives; they saw him often and most likely did not see each other except when with him. Beckett was still on the periphery of this new coterie, still sitting silently on the fringes of any group that included Joyce. How peripheral his role was at this time can be gauged by the memory of his presence that persons who are now his friends have—most of them do not remember Beckett as being among Joyce's friends until much later.[48]

If they remember Beckett at all, it is as an interesting young intellectual from Dublin. His obvious intelligence, as demonstrated by his essay, and his occasional comments about philosophy and literature made him something more than another of the talkative Irishmen who filled the cafes with grandiose schemes for great works which were never written except in their own minds. For Beckett was becoming a worker. While others in Joyce's circle spent most of their time trying to be seen in his company, Beckett began to be absent for conspicuous periods. When he reappeared, it was simply understood that he had been off somewhere writing and a place was made for him in the group without comment.[49]

He tended to resume conversations as if there had never been an absence or a break, conversations that were usually a continuation of the themes which preoccupied him at École Normale, especially suicide and all its aspects. There were historical events which made this question especially intriguing, as it was a period during which poets seemed to be committing suicide in large numbers—Mayakovsky, Yesenin, Radiguet, Crevel, Hart Crane and Harry Crosby among them. In Paris itself the list could have been expanded to include unknown poets from all over Europe and America. Their deaths offered so many possibilities for one such as Beckett to interpret.

In fact, in another circle, Henry Miller, Walter Lowenfels, and Michael Fraenkel were forming a "Death Movement" which prophesied the death of the modern age and the beginning of a new society dominated by pure art as the only viable way out of the morass the post-Schopenhauer Western World had become. To answer the question of why there was no mass suicide as the necessary purge before the art-dominated society could begin, Fraenkel wrote *Werther's Younger Brother*[50] about a man who was unable to follow Goethe's hero and commit suicide and thus was forced to endure the horrific aftermath of World War I without finding any way to exteriorize it, either through suicide or that other possibility—verbal experimentation by way of Joyce, Gertrude Stein, and *transition*.

Beckett knew both Fraenkel and Lowenfels, and had had a number of conversations with Lowenfels about art, writing and death, which were to continue as long as they knew each other in Paris.[51] Beckett was concerned that Lowenfels understand from the outset of their discussions that he had not disavowed Schopenhauer, as Lowenfels urged. Schopenhauer's ideas would become in later years the philosophical foundation of much of Beckett's thought and the system with which he felt most at ease, but at this time, his thoughts were still far-reaching and chaotic. He worried about the impossibility of language and the repeated failure to communicate on any meaningful level. He was coming to the Schopenhauerian conclusion that, since the only function of intellect is to assist man in achieving his will, the best role for himself would be the total avoidance of any participation in a world governed by will. The doctrine suited him but at the same time made him uneasy. He coped by returning to Descartes and mindlessly filling the pages of his notebooks with Descartes' thoughts and sayings.

The idea of Beckett as a talented young man of literary promise gained credence when the Jolases published his short story "Assumption" in the same issue of *transition* that bore his essay on Joyce.[52] There were other magazines in Paris—*This Quarter* and the *New Review* were probably the most important—but *transition* was the most prestigious. Beckett's appearance twice in the same issue did much for his literary reputation. The editors took notice of his promise in the biographical information following his story: "For future reference: Samuel Beckett, an Irish poet and essayist, is instructor at École Normale Supérieure in Paris."

"Assumption" is Beckett's story of a young man of extreme sensitivity who yearns for a woman. Told in a vocabulary which labors toward erudition and a syntax strained to the point of incomprehensibility, "Assumption" concerns a young man who is afraid to speak the words welling up within him. He bottles up his emotion until he is visited by "the woman," and when she leaves he is helpless to maintain his silence. He pours forth "a great storm of sound" and dies. Sexual and religious images are intermingled in strained passages in which the man dies, then becomes God, is first revived, then battered and torn, until he can no longer bear it and yearns to be united with a vague eternal force. The habit of using snatches and phrases from one work in subsequent writings is one Beckett developed with this, his first printed fiction. He writes here of the "birdless, cloudless, colourless skies," which he uses later in a sonnet to the Smeraldina in *Dream of Fair to Middling Women*. Most likely, "Assumption" had some basis in his relationship with her, that is, with Peggy Sinclair.

At its best, "Assumption" is one step above juvenilia. Again, themes from the later writings are to be found here: the protagonist, an artist, struggles with sound and silence, and after long struggle is forced to utter his sound, which brings death—in this case, release or repose.

Samuel Beckett's complicated relationship with James Joyce was further compounded because of a relationship that developed with Joyce's daughter, Lucia. He had been introduced to Lucia the very night he met her father—and her mother and brother, Giorgio, as well. There were a number of other young women present that evening, Irish, American and French, but Beckett told several friends later that he found Lucia the most striking.[53] She was slender and graceful, with her mother's features and dark hair and brilliant blue eyes. She was sensitive about a small scar on her chin and a squint (strabismus) which she had unsuccessfully tried to have corrected by surgery.[54] At twenty-two, Lucia was one year younger than Beckett and, like him, was in a state of emotional uncertainty. He was awkward and unsure of himself with the women he had met in Paris, especially those around Joyce. She was also awkward with men, but she was anxiously seeking an involvement or an alliance, always with marriage in mind. Her life as Joyce's daughter had not been tranquil, as her family had wandered from Trieste to Zurich to Paris, and her education had suffered from all these moves. Throughout her life, she had taken lessons in drawing, singing and seven different forms of dancing,[55] but after varying periods of intense concentration and practice, she found some excuse to forgo each one.

Lucia made no friends of her own in Paris, nor for that matter had she made any in the schools she had attended. She was naturally shy, but she was also convinced she had hideous physical deformities, her father's protests to the contrary notwithstanding. Lack of fluency in the languages of the cities in which her family temporarily resided was a further stumbling block to friendships: by the time she had learned one language, her family was ready to move to another country and another language. In Zurich, for example, she had missed an entire year of school because she did not know German. Then, too, there was the eccentricity of her background. The middle-class families of her classmates viewed her as an oddity, this daughter of the man who wrote the book that had caused so much comment. They were not anxious to promote or encourage friendships between their daughters and Lucia.

The few friendships she formed were usually with persons who were her father's friends first, for Joyce hardly ever accepted invitations that did not include his family. From her earliest years Lucia was accustomed to dining nightly with her parents, her brother and her father's friends. The women with whom she did strike up a lackadaisical relationship were either young married women with families, such as Maria Jolas, or women who were busy making a name for themselves, such as Kay Boyle. There were no young, unmarried women whose approximate age and background resembled Lucia's.

She was a lonely young woman in the midst of so much

artistic activity. Everyone else seemed to be writing, painting, publishing or composing. Everyone else was living alone and seemed to be independent of family. None of this mattered to her brother, Giorgio, who was not possessed by the same fierce intensity to create that his sister felt. He had a fine bass voice and was content to allow Joyce to arrange occasional recitals for him. Most of all he wanted to marry Helen Kastor Fleischman, and he was beginning to draw away from the tightly knit family circle into a life of his own. His father's friends held no real interest for him.

Joyce loved both his children very much, but he had been a somewhat indifferent father because he was so preoccupied with his writing. He said he wanted his children to be independent, but still he bound them to him through hint, evasion and subtle suggestion that they were powerless to ignore. Nora Joyce was a dutiful mother, but her attitude toward her children was reserved and did not include much open physical affection. Joyce had a childlike dependence upon his wife and demanded all her attention, affection and care. What emotional residue she had left, she gave indifferently to her children.

Though Joyce's attention was sporadic, his affection was less stinting, and Lucia received more warmth from him than she did from her mother. She was devoted to her father, but adored Giorgio, just two years older than she. She was resentful and confused about his forthcoming marriage, afraid the close bond between them would be severed. Though she and Helen were friends after the marriage, she railed against her before, calling Helen "the gigolo" who was taking her brother away.[56]

All these circumstances were exacerbated by the fact that there was nothing for her to do at this time. Her artistic hopes had come to naught, and there was no question of her taking a paying position. Her sporadic education only pointed out the inadequacies of her preparation for anything. She was a nubile young woman, and she began to fasten her affections onto Beckett, who in a sense was her rival for her father's time and attention.

Her parents began to be aware that something was seriously wrong with Lucia, although her father could not yet face the fact. Her mother began to criticize her openly, and with some justification, for Lucia had become sloppy in her dress and personal hygiene. Nora would admonish her (sometimes publicly) to "be more like ——," naming one after another of the constant succession of young women who flittered like bright decorative butterflies on the fringes of the Joyce family. But nothing seemed to affect Lucia, who moved dreamlike and defiant through the flat, fixated more and more on Beckett.

He, with his all-encompassing devotion to "Shem" (his and McGreevy's private name for Joyce), was unaware of Lucia's attitude toward him for a much longer time than an observant man should have been. Some of Joyce's group thought Beckett deliberately ignored Lucia in the hope that her crush on him would dissipate before it affected his relationship with her father; others saw his behavior as evidence that Beckett had a crush of sorts on Joyce and didn't want it disturbed.

Both these opinions have some validity, for Beckett's emotional development was somewhat arrested. He had adopted Joyce as a surrogate father and had become so closely identified in his own mind with the older writer that there was a certain amount of fear in his reaction to Lucia: if he upset her or made her angry, he feared he might lose Joyce.

Joyce was intrigued by Beckett's mind but he still kept him at a distance. Once he actually told Beckett "I don't love anyone but my family," implying that "I don't like anyone but my family either."[57]

Undeterred, Beckett continued to identify himself even more openly with Joyce. In *Our Exagmination*, he wrote, "And now here am I, with my handful of abstractions . . . and the prospect of *self extension* [italics mine] in the world of Mr. Joyce's *Work in Progress*."[58] First he affected Joyce's manners, then he aped his dress. He had become so close to Giorgio that many persons remarked how much they were "like brothers." Now, in what was for Joyce the ultimate adulatory gesture, Beckett consciously began to pattern his writing after his. He gave Joyce all the love and devotion he gave to his own father, but with a difference: there was no need with Joyce to hedge, hide or apologize for being a poet.

All the while, Beckett was running errands and performing chores that kept him in constant view of Lucia. Beckett found her a fascinating young woman, albeit one he would rather have studied from a distance than from the delicate, highly involved situation in which he found himself. When Beckett was around, her behavior was nervous, hyperactive and sometimes silly. What she thought was witty, flirtatious chatter was really erratic speech; she leaped from one unconnected thought to another, forcing anyone listening to follow with difficulty as she skidded from one unreality to another. Beckett watched her, fascinated by aspects of the father's mind running rampant in the daughter.

One night, after dining quietly with the Joyce family, Beckett went to a party at a small Left Bank flat where he sat in a corner on the floor talking excitedly about Lucia to a mutual friend.[59] He thought Lucia was becoming insane, and watching the process of disintegration from so close a distance made him feel like someone watching a charmed snake: he was mesmerized by her behavior but powerless to intervene. He speculated excitedly whether her madness would lead to suicide. He thought Lucia's reckless intelligence might veer too far one day and self-destruction become the only possible resolution of the conflict within her tortured mind. The possible manifestations of her behavior fascinated him.

Beckett had been in Joyce's party when Giorgio made his public debut as a singer on April 25, 1929, and on May 28, he was among the celebrating group that watched Lucia, costumed as a shimmering silver fish, dance in an international competition at the Bal Bullier. Though she did not win a prize, she won the audience's affection and they cheered loudly for "l'Irlandaise."[60] It was Lucia's last moment of glory as a dancer. Shortly after, she began to have the usual doubts about her ability and stamina, and by November of that year she had given up dance completely. She was ready for something, or perhaps more accurately, someone, to fill her life.

Beckett's frequent afternoon visits extended into dinner invitations more often now. One evening he and some others in Joyce's coterie were invited to dine with Ezra Pound at one of Joyce's favorite restaurants, Les Trianons, in the Place de Rennes. Pound, who had decided to behave that night as an irascible old man,[61] may have been miffed at being forced to dine on Joyce's favorite territory. Enraged by what he considered a climate of sycophancy among the Joyce group, Pound turned to Beckett and demanded in withering tones whether he was writing the next *Iliad*, or perhaps another *Divine Comedy*. Beckett reacted as Joyce would have done had he been the one attacked: he said nothing. Silence was to become his most effective weapon against critical attack in the years to come; it was a technique he perfected at the foot of a master.

Twenty-four years later, Beckett recollected this incident in a letter to a Joyce scholar: "The only time I remember having met Pound was one evening at dinner with the Joyces in the Trianons, Place de Rennes. He was having great trouble with a fond d'artichaut and was very aggressive and disdainful."[62]

As the academic year at École Normale drew to a close, Beckett made plans to mollify his family with a brief visit before spending the rest of the summer with the Sinclairs. But when he was invited with a select few to attend a luncheon celebration of the publication of the French translation of *Ulysses*, he delayed his departure from Paris until July. Adrienne Monnier was the hostess at a hotel in a remote country village selected only because of its name—the Léopold in Les Vaux-de-Cernay. The occasion was only one of the many celebrations Joyce's friends were constantly arranging for his entertainment. The luncheon took place on June 27, 1929, slightly late, as the book had been published on February 2, Joyce's birthday, and so the reason for celebration was enlarged to include the twenty-fifth anniversary of Bloomsday, June 16. Mademoiselle Monnier hired a bus to take the guests from her bookshop in the rue de l'Odéon to the tiny village just beyond Versailles. Besides the Joyce family and Beckett, guests included McGreevy, Edouard Dujardin, Paul Valéry, Philippe Soupault, Jules Romains, Léon-Paul Fargue, Sylvia Beach, and Helen Kastor Fleischman.[63]

A printed menu was given as a souvenir to each guest during the sumptuous luncheon, which featured pâté Léopold, proceeded through five other courses served with vast quantities of appropriate wines and ended with coffee and a generous selection of liqueurs.[64] Beckett and McGreevy, the only Irishmen present besides Joyce, both imbibed freely and began to call loudly for speeches. Joyce was horrified by what he termed their typical drunken Irish behavior, and Mademoiselle Monnier, sensing his embarrassment, ended the luncheon discreetly. After a spurt of picture taking, she loaded her charges into the bus to return to Paris.[65] Beckett, egged on by McGreevy, persuaded the driver to stop at various wayside cafes until the stops grew more frequent and of longer duration. Mademoiselle Monnier and Valéry grew angry and demanded that the driver proceed to Paris without stopping. Finally, even Joyce lost patience with them, and wrote later: "[Beckett had to be] ingloriously abandoned by the wagonette in one of those temporary palaces which are inseparably associated with the memory of the Emperor Vespasian."[66]

In semidisgrace, Beckett avoided the Joyce flat and changed his plans for the summer. He could not face Dublin at once, so he decided to go to Kassel for the greater part of his holiday, then to Cooldrinagh for a brief, late-summer visit before the fall of 1929 and the beginning of his second year at École Normale Supérieure.

By mid-July, Beckett was with the Sinclairs, helping them pack for their annual holiday in one of the smaller resort towns along the Baltic Sea. Summer, traditionally the time for light reading, found Peggy tearfully engrossed in Theodor Fontane's novel, *Effi Briest*. Beckett read it too, but with more detachment than Peggy, who wept and suffered as Effi's infidelity ended her marriage, and as subsequent catastrophes culminated in the tuberculosis that ended her life.

By the time they reached the Baltic, Peggy was buried in *Effi Briest*, and she wept more tears for Effi than she did for herself and her confusing relationships. What makes it especially poignant and ironic now is that within the next two years Peggy Sinclair died of tuberculosis.

Beckett had an uneasy summer with Peggy, for May and Bill had protested, both about the developing relationship and the length of his visit. In Kassel, Peggy alternately gave him effusive devotion or teased him openly with other suitors. Several proclaimed their passion while he was there, and she seemed willing to favor at least one of them, a young German, who, to Beckett's dismay, had her parents' approval. Her cousin's passion flattered Peggy but for the most part left her unmoved, for she was not yet ready to commit herself.

Almost thirty years later, Beckett wrote about the summer of 1929 in one of his most autobiographical writings, *Krapp's Last Tape:*

> Scalded the eyes out of me reading *Effie* [sic] again, a page a day, with tears again. Effie . . . (Pause.) Could have been happy with her, up there on the Baltic, and the pines, and the dunes. (Pause.) Could I? (Pause.) And she? (Pause.) Pah! (Pause.) Fanny came in a couple of times. Bony old ghost of a whore. Couldn't do much, but I suppose better than a kick in the crutch.[67]

and:

> . . . gooseberries, she said. I said again I thought it was hopeless and no good going on and she agreed, without opening her eyes. (Pause.) I asked her to look at me and after a few moments —(Pause)—after a few moments she did, but the eyes just slits, because of the glare. I bent over her to get them in the shadow and they opened. (Pause. Low.) Let me in. (Pause.) We drifted in among the flags and stuck. The way they went down, sighing, before the stem! (Pause.) I lay down across her with my face in her breasts and my hand on her. We lay there without moving. But under us all moved, and moved us gently, up and down, and from side to side.[68]

The holiday ended with nothing settled between Beckett and Peggy, and he went back to Dublin to face his family. May received him in pained silence and let him know that his refusal to spend all his free time in Cooldrinagh had upset her.[69] Bill trod carefully to avoid confrontation with May. He was pleased to see the maturity his son had developed during the past year and was happy to have another man in the house to share his interests and conversations (Frank was still in India), but dared not express these emotions too openly for fear of incurring his wife's steely rage. May could sustain her anger and silence for inordinately long periods of time when she did not get her way, and Bill did not want Beckett's holiday to be depressing if he could help it. He was lonely, overworked and tired; having his son around to talk about horse racing, to play golf, and take long walks was so pleasant that Bill was anxious to have the visit proceed without incident.

Frank had been in India for more than a year, the only white man for miles, constructing a railroad through isolated mountain regions. He seldom corresponded and, when he did write, gave every indication that he wanted to stay permanently in India. May was furious at his defection, and had been ordering Bill to insist that Frank come home as soon as his original period of service ended. It had been a troubled time for Bill, who was naturally disappointed to think that Frank would desert the business, but who also realized that Frank was twenty-seven years old and should be allowed some freedom in deciding what to do with his life.

May succeeded in involving Sam in these discussions. They were uppermost in her mind, and she tended to harangue until she got her way. Her constant reiteration had its effect: with great reluctance, Bill wrote to Frank, ordering him to come home at the end of his contracted time. Silently, Frank obeyed. Within the year he became firmly settled in Clare Street and worked there uncomplainingly until his death in 1954.

Beckett coped with his mother's temper by being out of the house as much as possible. He spent time with his uncle Gerald's children, Ann, John and Peter, and took refuge in piano duets, playing Chopin and Schubert badly but with gusto.[70] He amused them with watered-down tales of his student life in Paris, and his friendships with Joyce and McGreevy. As they listened to his tales, wide-eyed and eager to get to Paris themselves, it seemed that he spoke longingly of his life there and could not wait to return.

He was proud of his friendship with Joyce and wanted May and Bill to know of it, but he had to be very careful: not only was Joyce the author of a book banned in Ireland, he was born a Catholic and his family had been low on the Dublin social ladder, and Beckett's associations with the raucous Irish Catholic element in Paris would have disturbed his parents. Beckett was careful in his description of these friendships; he told his parents that he had been privileged to have been introduced to Mr. Joyce, for whom he had performed several small services connected with his latest writing. He showed them his essay in *Our*

Exagmination which, though they did not understand it, made them proud. It seemed to them that he was performing creditably under the terms of his scholarship.

At the end of his visit, May was especially pleased, as she thought that Frank would return to Cooldrinagh within the next year and there was no reason to doubt that Sam would follow in due course. She thought she had managed once again to bind them both to her, and this time it seemed as if the bonds would hold securely.

CHAPTER FOUR

1929–30:

"A YOUNG MAN WITH THE ITCH
TO MAKE AND NOTHING TO SAY"

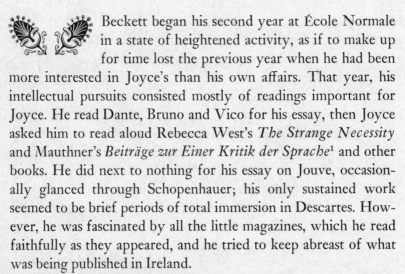 Beckett began his second year at École Normale in a state of heightened activity, as if to make up for time lost the previous year when he had been more interested in Joyce's than his own affairs. That year, his intellectual pursuits consisted mostly of readings important for Joyce. He read Dante, Bruno and Vico for his essay, then Joyce asked him to read aloud Rebecca West's *The Strange Necessity* and Mauthner's *Beiträge zur Einer Kritik der Sprache*[1] and other books. He did next to nothing for his essay on Jouve, occasionally glanced through Schopenhauer; his only sustained work seemed to be brief periods of total immersion in Descartes. However, he was fascinated by all the little magazines, which he read faithfully as they appeared, and he tried to keep abreast of what was being published in Ireland.

Beckett had begun to write poetry seriously shortly after his arrival in Paris and now considered himself equally at home in the disciplines of poetry and criticism. This reflected the influence of McGreevy, who thought of himself as a poet first and an essayist and critic after. McGreevy's struggle to write a poem every day most likely tempted Beckett to try it himself, but thoughts of poetry had been with him since Trinity. Dublin, after all, was a city of poets, and Paris was filled with eager Irish practitioners. What is ultimately important about his early creative writing is that poetry is the form that first attracted him.

One of the earliest poems dating from 1929 is "Sanies II,"[2] which owes much to Beckett's reading of French poetry, especially Valéry and Rimbaud. That summer in Dublin, he had quoted Valéry at length to his friends, who felt once again that he was ahead of them in his intellectual development and his knowledge of contemporary currents. They envied him his time in Paris and the relative ease with which he could obtain such writings, which were hard to come by in Catholic Dublin.[3]

Rimbaud, whose dictum was "we must be absolutely modern," was being rediscovered in Paris in the late twenties and early thirties. The Surrealists especially were following him closely, and this phrase had special significance for them. Walter Lowenfels described the impact of Rimbaud on the poetic temper of the time:

> To be alive, to be young, to be with it, to be swinging, you had to know what time it was . . . socially, scientifically, and above all, verbally. You had to write out of a consciousness that had absorbed the experiments that had preceded our generation. We had a consciousness of an avant-garde tradition.[4]

Thus, as he began his second year in Paris, Beckett found his interests divided between the exhilaration he felt in conversations with all the writers he had come to know, and the reverential respect for learning that he encountered among the scholars at École Normale. He was leaning toward the first group, with whom he felt most relaxed and companionable, but the sense of responsibility instilled in him by his family pulled him strongly toward the scholars and critics.

Because he had not taken a philosophy course at Trinity College,[5] which he felt was a serious defect in his education, he set out on what he thought was a systematic schedule of readings. He turned to Descartes first, completed the reading begun the previous year, and moved on to Arnold Geulincx (1624–69), the Belgian follower of Descartes. Beckett first heard of Geulincx in Dublin and had been deeply affected by his idea that a thinking man must realize that he can only achieve true independence in his own mind, that the only thing he can control is his own mental state. Therefore, man should waste no energy or time trying to control the external world, which includes his own body, as it often refuses to be controlled by his mind. In Geulincx's words: *ubi nihil vales, ibi nihil velis*—where you are worth nothing, you should want nothing. The reasonable, sensible man, if he follows Geulincx, does not act against passion, but is indifferent to it. Geulincx's philosophy had the most powerful and lasting effect on Beckett of anything he had read to date. So impressive was it that he made it the key of his novel *Murphy*, written in 1935.[6]

There was a more immediate effect, albeit a subtle one. Beckett had always been distant and withdrawn, traits generally interpreted by others as reserve due to his breeding and upbringing. From Joyce he had learned the skillful use of silence as an effective reply to criticism. Now, from Geulincx, he learned how passivity could be an instrument to gain his will. He wanted desperately to see his work published—he even described himself as "a young man with the itch to make and nothing to say."[7] But if he engaged in any sort of activity to insure publication, it was done so discreetly that no trace of it remains. He never pushed his own work, but allowed others to do it for him, and throughout his life, he has not deviated from this attitude.

Meanwhile in Dublin, a satire that he had written during his summer holiday appeared pseudonymously in the November issue of the Trinity College Weekly, *T.C.D.*[8] "Che Sciagura" was inspired by a quotation from Voltaire's *Candide,* in which the Eunuch, finding himself before the beautiful nude heroine, says "O che sciagura d'essere senza coglioni," or "What a misfortune to be without balls!" A satire on the ban of contraceptives by the Republic of Ireland, the title is another example of Beckett's use and reuse of material: "What a Misfortune" is the title of one of the stories in the 1934 collection, *More Pricks Than Kicks;* it is also Malone's lament on losing his stick, "quel malheur," in *Malone Meurt* (*Malone Dies*), the novel published in 1951.

"Che Sciagura" received one review, the report of the *T.C.D.* Editorial Subcommittee for Michaelmas term, 1929: "Che Sciagura . . . was extremely clever, though fortunately a trifle obscure for those who do not know their Joyce and their

Voltaire."⁹ Among those who did, Beckett's reputation as a clever fellow was enhanced.

Lucia Joyce was pleased to see her father resume his long conversations with Beckett that fall because it meant she had more opportunities to see him. Occasionally, when her advances became too obvious, or when he found himself trapped, he invited her to the theater, to dinner or to a party. Usually he invited others to go along with them as a possible hedge against Lucia's ardent expression of her feelings, for she was embarrassingly frank. Not having had friends her own age, she was unschooled in the art of flirtation and coy banter, and because of her deteriorating mental condition, it was impossible for her to be anything but honest. She still fascinated Beckett, but more as a case study than a possible love interest.

Then, too, there was the problem of his relationship with her father. Joyce, though still addressing him as "Mr. Beckett," was displaying what amounted to considerable affection. Beckett would never take Giorgio's place in Joyce's affections; in Beckett, Joyce saw, if not a son, then a devoted disciple who brought pleasure and intellectual stimulation into his life without any of the demands necessitated by a familial relationship. Beckett was always available; no errand or task was too insignificant for him, and whenever he was with Joyce, he was content to allow Joyce to initiate the tone and content of the meeting. It was the ideal mental climate for Joyce and he thrived on it.

Both men were prone to long silences and their conversations were usually suffused with "sadness, Beckett mostly for the world, Joyce mostly for himself."¹⁰ The severe and almost painful sensitivity to the world which dominates Beckett's mature fiction was struggling for expression even at the beginning of his career, but at this time he was so heavily under Joyce's influence that he was unable to find his own voice and he thought any possible method of creation must have its basis in Joyce's artistic credo.

Joyce was seeking to bend and shape the English language into new forms and meanings, to create new words from existing words, to make established sounds and syllables do new duty in new combinations. Beckett interpreted this technique in his *Our Exagmination* essay:

> Here form is content, content is form. You complain that this stuff is not written in English. It is not written at all. It is not to be read, or rather it is not only to be read. It is to be looked at and listened to. His writing is not *about something: it is that something itself* [Beckett's emphasis]. . . . When the sense is sleep the words go to sleep. When the sense is dancing, the words dance.[11]

Yet when it came to expressing his own ideas within the Joycean framework, he often found himself "verbally constipated,"[12] a wry, though aptly chosen phrase which he meant to do more than describe his creative condition, for increasingly, as the words became more difficult to deliver to his satisfaction, ailments multiplied and physical constipation became his most prevalent problem.

Beckett's attempts to imitate Joyce's seemingly casual technique of writing led to what Beckett viewed as an intolerable loss of control over the finished product. What seemed to others Beckett's eccentric behavior was in reality his response to situations over which he did not have complete control. But even more than he needed to control his relationships with people, he had a fierce need to be in total, absolute control of his writing. To him, Joyce's method of creating was fascinating and upsetting. The story of Beckett taking Joyce's dictation has often been repeated: in the middle of a session, someone knocked on the door and Joyce said "come in." Later, when Beckett read back the passage, Joyce was puzzled by the words "come in" and wondered how they came to be there. When Beckett insisted that he had said them, Joyce thought for a moment and decided to retain them, as for him, "coincidence as collaborator" was quite all right. The episode unnerved Beckett.[13]

When he found himself unable to capture random words and phrases to express his feelings of the moment, he experimented with surrealistic methods (especially apparent in the poetry he wrote during the years 1930 to 1935). But this proved unsatisfactory: he found himself trying to imitate the stream-of-consciousness technique, taking straightforward expressions and phrases and making them elusive (and at times pompous) by the accretion of layers of language, consulting dictionaries to find archaic forms and unknown variants of established words he then substituted for the common forms that first came to his mind.[14]

Early on in his writing he rejected the techniques of Eliot and Pound, which he described as "wholesale borrowing from others," calling them "jewel thieves" and heaping scorn on their methods.[15] He also rejected Joyce's technique of coining new words from combinations of those already existing.

Yet in spite of the difficulties he encountered in trying to follow Joyce, he doggedly kept on. Perhaps he thought a breakthrough in his own technique lay just around some mental corner; perhaps he was too involved in the day-to-day activity Joyce generated in his life to think clearly about it. He found his efforts to write poetry becoming increasingly tentative, halting and thwarted. He blamed it on too much drink, not enough sleep, and no sustained periods of time to concentrate.[16]

To further complicate his life, in December, 1929, Joyce invited him to work on the French translation of *Anna Livia Plurabelle*, to that date the most celebrated section of *Work in Progress*. Beckett was delighted by the opportunity, but still not sure of his command of French, and he asked Alfred Péron to assist him. He brought him to meet Joyce, and Péron passed Joyce's test and became Beckett's collaborator.[17] Péron's two years at Trinity had given an Irish cast to his English, which delighted Joyce, and the two men subsequently became friends. Joyce's friendships, like his work, grew by accretion and were seldom formed through his own volition, for the life he led was hermetic in many ways.

When he had committed himself to the new translation Joyce commissioned, Beckett steeled himself for a Christmas visit to Foxrock. He had been suffering from a lingering cold throughout the fall, and the rough sea passage to Ireland did little for his health. When May saw how thin and tired he looked, she alternated between fits of worrying and feeding him hearty meals. He stayed in Foxrock just long enough to observe the social amenities, and then went to Kassel. The strain of his relationship with Peggy was a factor contributing to his general inability to concentrate, and he wanted to come to some sort of agreement with her.

He arrived in Kassel in desperate physical condition and took to bed with the flu, where he suffered jealously as Peggy flitted from party to party. By New Year's Eve, 1930, he was determined to have it out, and he dragged himself from bed and followed her and the rest of the family from one night club to another, where she allowed him neither time nor privacy for any resolution of their situation. If anything, she was more determined than ever to keep him dangling, for she was becoming seriously interested in a quiet young German who tolerated her antics while pursuing her doggedly. Dejected, depressed and still suffering from a cold, Beckett boarded a train and slept most of the way back to Paris huddled in a cold compartment—an inauspicious beginning to 1930.

While Peggy led Beckett on a merry chase, Lucia Joyce pursued him with determination. In his confusion, he decided the best way to avoid a difficult situation was to retreat from it. He began to spend most of his time in cafes—the Dôme, the Coupole and the Select, when he could afford their prices; the cheaper cafes near the rue d'Ulm with McGreevy and Aldington; or the Café Mahieu on the boulevard St. Michel when Aldington wanted him to meet "a lady worth impressing."[18] There they often found Alan and Belinda Duncan, whom Beckett had first met at Joyce's. Alan Duncan was the son of a well-known Dublin hostess with a celebrated literary salon and he had been W. B. Yeats's secretary during his trip to the United States. Now he lived in Paris on an army pension and his salary from Lamb's Travel Agencies. Joyce adored Belinda Duncan, who could match him drink for drink, and he paid her his ultimate compliment by inserting her into *Finnegans Wake* as the "little hen of the dorans."[19] The Duncans tried to woo Joyce from the elegant Fouquet's on the Champs Élysées, but Joyce did not like the Mahieu's ambience and continued to go his own way.

There was also the small sleazy bar popular with Americans in the rue Mouffetard which Beckett made the setting for his poem "Sanies II,"[20] but the younger, poorer Irishmen congregated in a "local" on the rue Gay Lussac near École Normale called the Café du Depart. Cafe sitting was a way of life simply because most of them lived on the edge of poverty. Cafes were warm in winter, as their rooms often were not, and meeting there meant that no one was required to play host. Brian Coffey aptly described cafe life:

> One went to a cafe and came back from the cafe. One didn't do much else besides one's work, and much of that was done in the cafe. In fact, many of those times were intolerably dull for the lot of us. In conversation we never talked about personalities. There were none of the awful discussions about relevance and sincerity as there are today. We would discuss, for instance, Heidegger on being. But for the most part we sat and stared into space, because what else is there to do if one is hoping to write and nothing comes from inside? It's no good trying to construct on a given plane. One waits. And Sam has waited very often for very long periods of time before anything has come.[21]

At the end of one of these very long and silent afternoons, Beckett turned to a companion and said listlessly, "Sunshine is an overrated virtue."[22] It was the sort of pronouncement, or cafe-philosophy, in which he indulged himself, punctuated frequently with languid sighs of boredom.

All the cafes he frequented were somewhat loosely connected with the literary world, but the nearest Beckett came to actually seeking the atmosphere of writers was during the time he went to the Café de la Mairie on the place St. Sulpice, where Paul Eluard liked to do his writing.[23] In this cafe, the men's toilet was a source of amusement, separating the casual visitor from the initiates. Middle Eastern, with a hole in the floor and two depressions for the heels, it was triangular and built into a corner. It had a large overhead water closet which sent down gushing torrents to drench those who did not know the secret—that the door must be opened before pulling the chain or the hapless victim would emerge sopping wet down his entire front.

Djuna Barnes, one of the few women with whom Beckett has maintained a lifelong friendship, immortalized this facility in her novel *Nightwood*. Beckett liked to take visitors (male) from Ireland to the Café de la Mairie, both to show them the demented toilet and to let them know that Djuna Barnes was his friend.[24]

Of course, the most frequent topic of conversation during his second year in Paris—besides money—was poetry. It had been Beckett's only form of creative expression throughout the fall, now that he had for all intents and purposes abandoned his scholarship essay on Jouve.

In the fall of 1929 McGreevy introduced him to another Irishman who did much over the next few years to further Beckett's ambitions to be published. George Reavey had been part of the Cambridge *Experiment* group and had come to Paris from Cambridge to study French literature and write poetry. To augment his meager income, he took a job tutoring the son of an English newspaper magnate and lived during the week in a chateau near Fontainebleau, coming into Paris only on weekends. Some of Reavey's poetry had already been published while he was an undergraduate at Cambridge, and in Paris he began immediately to seek outlets for his writing. He had much of the same fervor for promoting the work of his friends as McGreevy, and he made sure that other young Irishmen were introduced to all possible sources of publication.

Through Reavey, Beckett met Samuel Putnam, the American who was Edward Titus's associate editor of *This Quarter* magazine.[25] Putnam had an ambitious venture of his own under way which later became the poetry anthology called *The European Caravan*.[26] He had conceived a scheme of publishing English translations of the new poetry being written in Europe listed according to the country of the poet's birth. Reavey, fluent in Russian, was preparing those translations, and he suggested to Putnam that Beckett might prepare the Italian section. Even though he received only nominal payment, Beckett was delighted to do the translations, as they represented one more publication he could show at Trinity College the following fall. He was seriously beginning to be worried about facing Rudmose-Brown without an honors essay, as each passing week found him drifting further away from any work at all on Jouve. To return to Dublin with only the *Our Exagmination* essay was tantamount to admitting that he had wasted two years. But most of all he was delighted, as any twenty-four-year-old would be, to find his work appearing in the prestigious little magazines published in Paris.

Three of Beckett's Italian translations appeared in the April-May-June, 1930, issue of *This Quarter:* "Landscape" by Raffaello Franchi, "The Homecoming" by Giovanni Comisso and "Delta" by Eugenio Montale. Credit for the translations was attributed to S. B. Beckett, as he was then signing his name.[27]

Like most of the people who worked with the abrasive Titus, Putnam soon quarreled and left to found his own magazine, the *New Review.* He invited Reavey to become an associate editor, thus insuring Beckett's continuing publication.

Putnam lived in the Parisian suburbs with his wife and son, and came in by Metro each night to visit the cafes of Montparnasse. Often, coming up the steps in front of the Carrefour Vavin, the stop in front of La Coupole, he saw

> . . . certain young Irishmen, friends and admirers of Joyce: Thomas McGreevy, Samuel Beckett, George Reavey, and others, the Dublin intellectuals being in the habit of gathering at the École Normale, where McGreevy and Beckett were instructors. Beckett and Reavey were often seen on the Boulevard du Montparnasse . . .[28]

heading toward the Closerie des Lilas to play billiards. Beckett had always been a keen player, but in Reavey he found a companion of equal skill and passion. They played for hours, each silently enmeshed in his own thoughts, sometimes communicating bits and snatches of new poems composed as they played.[29]

In this lackadaisical manner the winter of 1930 passed, and as spring arrived, bringing with it Beckett's imminent departure for Ireland, Lucia Joyce began to make her intentions unavoidably obvious. Each time he had gone to the Joyce flat that spring, Lucia had been at the door to greet him, detaining him until he simply broke away from her and, flustered and embarrassed, entered the room where Joyce waited for him.[30] Lucia had made no secret of her feelings to her father; after a series of relationships with men Joyce found unsuitable, it pleased him to see her fasten her affections on Beckett. He wanted to believe that his daughter's problems would be solved once she was settled into an enduring relationship with a man. And of course, Beckett, already almost a son, was ideal.

The situation was becoming highly charged for Beckett, who was terrified that an emotional explosion by Lucia would upset his all-important relationship with her father. Lucia was not an unattractive woman, and he was flattered that the daughter of Joyce found him interesting, but these feelings were superseded by a genuine feeling of horror that someone he looked upon as a sister found him sexually attractive. Lucia's feeling for him was almost, he confided to a friend, like incest.[31]

Meanwhile, rumors about the two of them were the hottest gossip among the Paris cognoscenti. Some swore that Beckett actually proposed to Lucia Joyce on bended knee and then asked her father for her hand in marriage.[32] Others insisted that Beckett was frightened by Lucia's advances but too passive to resist them and too worried about the loss of access to Joyce to do anything to stop them.[33] This latter group was closest to the truth.

Passivity in many forms has been the distinguishing characteristic of all Beckett's relationships with women throughout his life, and he carried it to the extreme with Lucia. He decided to play a waiting game, to do nothing overt for as long as possible in the hope that her feeling for him would dissolve, just as her interest in other men had.

In May, Lucia tried to force a resolution to the situation by inviting Beckett to lunch in a small Italian restaurant opposite the Luxembourg Gardens where they had dined previously with her parents. Lucia had taken great pains with her usually sloppy appearance: she had had her hair fixed especially for the occasion and was wearing makeup and a new dress.

Beckett did not want to be alone with her, and so he persuaded Georges Pelorson to go along. The unwitting Pelorson knew nothing of the crisis Beckett anticipated, and accepted the invitation for a free lunch. They waited for Lucia outside the restaurant and watched as she came up the street smiling at Beckett. When she discovered that he had invited Pelorson to join them, her face fell and she began to quiver. She composed herself and allowed the two men to escort her into the restaurant, where Beckett carefully seated her on the banquette and sat opposite, on a chair next to Pelorson.

As the meal progressed, the silence thickened. Pelorson was appalled as he watched Lucia staring into space, haphazardly slinging an occasional bite of food into her mouth. Her lipstick grew smeared, her mascara blurred, the carefully done hair grew disarranged. She became a ghastly caricature, like a painted mannequin that had been left out in the rain. After barely touching her food, she stood up slowly as if in a trance, then ran out of the restaurant and down the street. By the time they settled the bill and ran after her, she had disappeared. Beckett and Pelorson parted in mutual embarrassment. For a long time after, they took pains not to discuss the luncheon, but Beckett typically offered no explanation or apology.

The awful moment had come at last, the one he had been dreading. He told Lucia that he only came to the flat to see her father and could not continue to see her. Lucia behaved erratically for a time, then grew depressed, and both her parents were terrified at what would happen to her. Nora was furious with Beckett, whom she accused of leading Lucia on, ingratiating himself into her affections under false pretenses. Joyce, in tones of icy rage, informed Mr. Beckett that he was no longer welcome in his home or his presence. The break that Beckett had feared became a reality.

He was desolated by his loss of Joyce and turned to Mc-Greevy for advice and comfort. McGreevy understood all too well the terrible trap Beckett had fallen into and urged him to believe that time would heal the rift with Joyce. He convinced Beckett that Lucia's behavior was so unstable that soon even her father would have to face it, and would have to believe that Beckett had behaved throughout an intolerable situation with the honesty and integrity that characterized all of his relationships. Beckett could do little more than nod his head sadly and hope that McGreevy was right.

McGreevy knew how depressed Beckett was by what he had begun to call "the bust-up with Shem."[34] The result of his efforts to cheer him up was Beckett's first separately published work, the poem *Whoroscope*, printed by Nancy Cunard at her Hours Press in late summer, 1930.

On the afternoon of June 15, Beckett was in his room on the rue d'Ulm, desultorily going through a sheaf of notes on Geulincx, when McGreevy mentioned that Richard Aldington was disappointed by the lackluster quality of the one hundred or more poems he had just read—all entries in the contest, cosponsored by him and Cunard, for the best poem on the subject of time. None, Aldington said, was worthy of the ten-pound prize, let alone publication by the Hours Press.

Jokingly, McGreevy suggested that Beckett dash off a poem to take his mind off Joyce and get it over to Cunard's shop on the rue Guenegaud before midnight when the contest officially ended. Beckett laughed, but when McGreevy left he thumbed through his notebook on Descartes, and as he read, an idea for a poem began to form in his mind.

Beckett's stipend from École Normale was long gone by this time, and his allowance from home never seemed to be enough, so the ten pounds loomed large as he thought about the contest. His reading of Descartes had occupied his mind off and on for the past academic year, and although he wanted to write something, he had not yet decided what would be the best genre. The thick notebook he filled was kept in lieu of actually writing—he himself called it a paltry excuse for not really working—and he was growing impatient about not being able to organize these notes into something creative.[35]

In 1959 Nancy Cunard wrote the history of the Hours Press, and she asked Beckett to tell her the circumstances in which he came to write the poem:

> *Whoroscope* was indeed entered for your competition and the prize of I think 1,000 francs. I knew nothing about it until the afternoon of the last day of entry, wrote first half before dinner, had a guzzle of salad and chambertin at the Cochon de Lait, went back to the École and finished it about three in the morning. Then walked down to the Rue Guenegaud and put it in your box. That's how it was and them were the days.[36]

He wrote the manuscript in longhand on stationery filched from the Hotel Bristol, Carcassone.[37] Six pages and ninety-eight lines long (length was limited to one hundred lines), with only two or three minor word changes in the manuscript, the poem seems to have been almost completely thought out before Beckett committed it to paper. The circumstances of his entering the contest may have been frivolous and haphazard but not the poem itself, which was the culmination of several years of study. That it appeared as a poem was due, of course, to the contest; had it not been for that, the result of his research would most likely have been another monograph such as his study of Proust, which appeared the following year.[38]

Time was the subject of the contest, but time seems present in Beckett's poem only in the pun of the title—which combines the Greek *horo* (hour) with Descartes' superstitious refusal to tell his birth date so that no astrologer could cast his nativity and thus predict his death—and in the last line, "starless inscrutable hour." The poem deals with the life of René Descartes, Seigneur du Perron, and the life of a man, loosely speaking, as an aspect of time. It follows Descartes to the court of Christina of Sweden, where he died from being forced to rise early and go out into the harsh Swedish winter.

Beckett was in the process of reading Adrien Baillet's *Life of Descartes*,[39] and *Whoroscope* follows Baillet's life so closely that it is more a prose monologue than poetry. To further enhance this effect, Beckett incorporates a technique of the Symbolist poets—choppy lines of uneven length and almost no rhythmical pattern. He makes a bow toward Joyce with puns such as "prostisciutto" (ham/harlot) and "Jesuitasters." And he uses arcane information in an effort to maintain the poem's obscurities. *Whoroscope* begins with two questions: "What's that? An Egg?"—referring to Descartes' habitual breakfast omelette of eggs hatched from eight to ten days. It proceeds with "by the Brothers Boot it stinks fresh . . ." —an esoteric reference to the two brothers who refuted Aristotle, included in the poem only because the refutation occurred in Dublin. The passage reflects Joyce's influence, too, his insistence that poets should use the personal and particular, which for him meant Dublin. In this instance Beckett was delighted to learn later that with the Brothers Boot, he had discovered something that Joyce did not know had taken place in Dublin.[40]

In general, *Whoroscope* is a witty, superficial exhibition of esoteric knowledge. Baillet's *Life* is condensed into ninety-eight lines of verbal ingenuity that demonstrate the author's close association with his subject but his affectionate disdain for it as well. However, as John Fletcher points out,[41] the poem has overtones of Beckett's future themes, namely, his preoccupation with the revolting (blood, rotten eggs), and the manner in which the philosopher's thought moves through the poem by association.

When Nancy Cunard found the poem in her box, she was puzzled but enthusiastic:

> . . . across the cover of a small folder was written *Whoro-scope*. Beneath was the name Samuel Beckett. His name meant nothing to either Aldington or myself. The poem on the other hand, meant a very great deal, even on the first, feverish read-through. What remarkable lines, what images and analogies, what vivid coloring throughout! Indeed what technique! This long poem, mysterious, obscure in parts . . . was clearly by someone very intellectual and highly educated.
>
> Our enthusiasm was great, and the fact of its having arrived at the last moment made it all the sweeter.[42]

Actually both Cunard and Aldington were so puzzled by the poem's obscurities that they barely recognized what it was about. They sent for Beckett in great haste in the early morning of June 16, and he rushed to the rue Guenegaud. When they found out how quickly the poem had been written, they were astonished and pleased with this proof that Beckett was someone of genius. They decided to give *Whoroscope* the prize, but realized that notes, after the manner of *The Waste Land*, were a necessity for the edification of the common reader; so, as quickly as he had written the poem, Beckett sat down and appended twenty notes to it.

Whoroscope appeared in midsummer, 1930. Bound in a scarlet cover, some of the three hundred copies contained a white printed slip glued to the front cover which read:

> This poem was awarded the £10 prize for the best poem on time in the competition judged by Richard Aldington and Nancy Cunard at the Hours Press and is published in an edition

of 100 signed copies at 5 s. 200 unsigned copies at 1 s. This is also Mr. Samuel Beckett's first separately published work.[43]

With a feeling of pride and accomplishment, Beckett sent several books to Dublin, hoping that it would be reviewed in some Irish publications. He distributed copies around Paris, including (at McGreevy's urging) one to Joyce, who grudgingly agreed to McGreevy's enthusiasm for it.[44]

In a letter to his parents, however, he said vaguely that he had had a new poem published. He sent no copy. They thought little of it until Georges Pelorson, who had since been sent to Trinity as École Normale's exchange lecturer, called on them shortly after his arrival in Dublin.[45] Pelorson was unprepared for the elegance and formality of Cooldrinagh, so unlike the diffident shabbiness of the casual fellow he knew in Paris. In an awkward pause, he commented that May and Bill must certainly be very proud of the new book, and he knew he had committed a terrible blunder when May's countenance changed as she asked one probing question after another. Pelorson sensed from both parents' reaction that they would disapprove of the book and he was correct. May wrote immediately to Beckett, furious that he had not told them all the details of the poem's publication, and demanded that he send a copy at once.[46]

When the family copy arrived at Cooldrinagh, Frank (who had just returned from India) and Mollie Roe read it with puzzled incomprehension. May read the title disapprovingly, glanced through it, quietly closed the book and left the room without speaking. That evening, when Bill had finished dinner and settled into his chair, he asked to see it. There was the same disapproving glance at the title, the same incomprehension as he thumbed through it. Frank offered to read the poem aloud so that all could listen and perhaps make sense of it.

"Never mind," Bill said, putting the book on the table beside his chair. He and May left the room while Frank and Mollie sat there not knowing what to do. Frank put the book on a high shelf in the drawing room and it was not mentioned again.

Bill and May suffered no immediate embarrassment over the book. They made no mention of it to their friends, and no one spoke to them about it, for few people in Dublin even knew it had been published. No bookseller would risk the ire of the

Catholic Church by stocking a book with such a title, and no publication reviewed it.

In Paris, it was much the same. All the little presses and literary groups bought each other's work, but most of the copies were passed freely (and free) from one to the other. Years later Beckett fell into the habit of giving away the unsold, leftover copies to scholars or professors who came to see him in Paris.

Whoroscope fulfilled none of his expectations: only a handful of people knew that it had even been published and few of them had read it. It was not scholarship, and its value to his career at Trinity was negligible. It did not give him widespread recognition in Paris, but it was a critical success among those who already knew him. And perhaps what he most hoped to effect with it—a reconciliation with Joyce—did not come about. All the excitement of winning the prize and rushing to publication seemed to have dissipated into few copies sold, no reviews and the bewilderment and hurt of his family.

Nevertheless, it was a milestone for Beckett. It was, after all, a *published book*. He had written quickly and written to his satisfaction. He had no reason to doubt his ability to repeat the achievement. It was an enormous boost to his self-respect and his belief in himself as a writer.

Whoroscope also marked the beginning of Beckett's friendship with Nancy Cunard, which lasted until her death in 1965. Her faith in Beckett's genius never faltered, and from the beginning she gave him whatever help she could to establish his literary reputation. Aldington, too, began to take Beckett seriously for the first time. Aldington was riding the crest of success with his war novel, *Death of a Hero*, published the previous year, and he was generous in giving young writers money, praise and introductions to publishers. He and McGreevy were the best friends of Charles Prentice, one of the editors at Chatto and Windus, and they urged Prentice to allow Beckett to write the volume on Proust in the Dolphin series. Prentice, impressed with *Whoroscope*, agreed, and Beckett suddenly found himself with another commission. He was delighted—it was just the sort of publication to make his return to Trinity a success. More than ever, *Whoroscope* seemed to him a talisman of good things to come.

Beckett's eagerness to accept the Proust commission was quickly dispelled by the realities of his existence. His term at École Normale was officially ended, and unlike McGreevy, Beckett was a formal *lecteur* and therefore obligated to vacate his rooms by mid-July. His stipend was also ended; his only income, from his parents, amounted to little more than cigarette and wine money. His family wanted him to come home for the summer as soon as he was free. In May he had written to them saying that he wanted to stay with the Sinclairs in Germany until shortly before he was due to begin to teach at Trinity. May replied to his letter in haste, stating firmly that there would be no money from home to support pleasure trips to Germany. As usual, he vacillated when her letter arrived, hoping that if he did nothing, something would come along to resolve his situation. That "something" was *Whoroscope*, which gave him ten pounds toward the trip to Kassel. However, the idea of another published book was more exciting than a visit to a noncommittal young woman, and he decided to stay in Paris to write *Proust*.[47]

He tried to explain to his parents that there were valid reasons for his staying on past the end of term: he spoke of the physical difficulty of transporting the sixteen volumes of *À la Recherche du temps perdu* in what he called the "abominable edition of the *Nouvelle Revue Française*"[48] with all his other baggage to Dublin. The process of clearing his rooms at École Normale was an arduous task, as he suffered the scholarly agony of which papers to save and which to throw away. He ended up by packing everything, and from then on he has saved every scrap he has ever written, whether unpublished, incomplete or abandoned. Then there was the very real possibility that once his belongings were placed on the ferry dock in Ireland the customs officials would not allow many of the books he needed to write *Proust* into the country. Also, he complained that he could not possibly commit himself to the strenuous intellectual effort such a book would require while living among his family and adhering to their daily schedule. He begged them to understand the necessity for time, seclusion and most of all, money, so that he could stay on in Paris.[49] His efforts to sway them were unconvincing, for May wrote that his small allowance would continue to come to him, but not one cent more.

He was just about to concede defeat and return to Dublin when Aldington came to his rescue. Exasperated by what he considered an insignificant financial impediment, he agreed to finance Beckett's continued stay in Paris until the book was written. Beckett, overjoyed, promised profusely that he would pay back the loan with royalties from the sale of *Proust,* which he was able to do as the book sold well.

He began the assignment with eagerness, but soon found it "difficult," one which he afterward said he "hated."[50] Aldington and McGreevy had gone off on a motor trip to southern France and Italy, and Beckett camped out in their rooms. Each day he went to the Café de l'Arrivée,[51] just opposite the Luxembourg Gardens, where he wrote most of it. When writing became too tedious, he took long walks through the beautiful park until he was able to face it again.

The essay on Proust that resulted from this period of enforced solitude and concentration marks the high point of Beckett's critical writing, even though it is read more often by those interested in Beckett than in Proust. It shows how much Proust influenced Beckett and is probably his first attempt to formulate a literary credo of his own. The essay reveals Beckett's literary conscience in its formative phase, when the ideas that were to shape his mature fiction were still twenty years or so in his future. There is no doubt that the ideas he propounds here are those to which he himself adhered, for his sympathetic treatment of Proust indicates a shared communality of thought. However, with hindsight, it is much too easy to see the mature Beckett revealed in this essay and to ignore the subject—Proust and his multilayered novel—for this essay is still today one of the finest introductions to it.

Throughout the essay one is aware of a smoothness in the writing, the ease with which Beckett glides from idea to idea. The syntax is clear, flowing and lucid, definite progress from the schoolboy preciosity of "Dante . . . Bruno . Vico . . Joyce." The vocabulary is intelligent and restrained, avoiding the verbal pyrotechnics that characterize the earlier essay. Though the present-day reader is almost constantly aware of Beckett's presence in this essay as phrases illustrative of his mature writing seem to leap off the printed page, there is a constant, clear-sighted view of Proust.

Proust sold well and received excellent reviews, among them one from the London *Daily Telegraph*, which said: "Proust is a master who deserves criticism as intricate and careful as his own work. Mr. Beckett here proves himself a real interpreter . . . an excellent work, for Mr. Beckett is a very brilliant young man."[52]

Although Beckett completed the book by late summer, 1930, it was not published until the following year when he was teaching at Trinity. In Ireland, *Proust* received what Beckett called "silent praise,"[53]—if it was not ignored, snide remarks were made about it.

In Cooldrinagh, after the debacle of *Whoroscope, Proust* was received with pride and respect. May and Bill found it too specialized for pleasurable reading, but the language was at least straightforward and civilized, and the English reviews were a point of pride: they placed it on a more prominent shelf in their bookcase.[54]

Proust has never been translated into French, and Beckett, as his own translator, says it never will be. He feels that translation into Proust's native language would be a pretentious action, more of an insult than a tribute to the man he considers one of the two geniuses of the twentieth century.[55] Perhaps Beckett's own words best explain his feeling about *Proust:* several years ago, a copy surfaced in a second-hand bookstore in Dublin with comments and emendations in Beckett's handwriting scattered throughout. On the title page Beckett has written: "I have written my book in a cheap flashy philosophical jargon."[56] This is a harsh self-judgment, but he believes it.

In September he sent the manuscript of *Proust* to Chatto and Windus, and just before his departure for Dublin, Nancy Cunard invited him to contribute a poem to a book of Henry Crowder's music she planned to publish. As Walter Lowenfels described her then, Nancy Cunard was

> tall, very thin, a childlike blonde face. African bracelets on her arms, a petition for the Scottsboro boys in her hands.

I have only realized during the past few years that among all of us in the avant-garde in Paris Nancy was by far the most advanced. She was doing something about the central issue of our time, the Negro people.

Yet I don't ever recall a discussion with Nancy on the "issue." She was the most personal person I knew. She didn't talk about issues, she did things. She had close Negro friends and she wore African ornaments; also collected and showed friends African sculpture.[57]

Cunard was one of the few persons Beckett met during his life who could persuade him to go places and do things that he did not want to do, and to follow her with good grace. Cunard was known for her predatory relationships with men, always the pursuer and never the pursued; so that many of their friends believed that her relationship with Beckett was sexual—she as the aggressor and he as the passive respondent to her desires. However, their relationship was totally asexual; it was one of devoted friendship, in which each would have done anything the other wanted or needed, a friendship based entirely on an emotional bond.[58] Cunard never really understood Beckett's writings, but she was one of his strongest champions all her life. He was puzzled and exhausted by her constant involvement with causes, issues and oddball characters, but he loved her spunk and verve, her decisiveness, originality and outspokenness. And because she had been kind to him at a time when others found him an object of derision, nothing she would ever do would sway him from absolute loyalty to her.

Cunard and Beckett, physically much alike, were studies in contrast. Both were tall, blond and slender, with piercing blue eyes. Cunard was a dynamo in motion, never seeming to sit still, busy with myriad social causes and publishing projects. Her speech was staccato, her emotions never seemed to fall below extreme intensity. Beckett, just the opposite, was quiet to the point of stillness. His speech, if one could call it that, was a series of sighs punctuated by occasional whispered phrases. He moved slowly, when at all. He had no projects that anyone knew of, and was seemingly ready to take on any assignment that was offered.

Cunard had joined McGreevy as the second committed believer in Beckett's genius, and with her particular nervous intensity, she poked and prodded him into a semblance of sociability. She insisted that he accompany her as she made her rounds nightly through her Paris haunts and brooked no refusal. To Harold Acton, he seemed curiously misplaced, like an Aztec eagle being pecked at by a covey of small chirruping birds. On one particularly drunken occasion, when the music blared while Cunard danced frenetically, Beckett sat slumped over a table among the empty glasses and overflowing ashtrays. Suddenly he raised his head and proclaimed loudly, "Christ in heaven, what am I doing here!"[59]

Henry Crowder, a black American jazz pianist, was Cunard's lover and her assistant at the Hours Press. Crowder was a talented composer as well, and made his living playing and singing in the cabarets and boîtes of Montparnasse. Cunard wanted to publish a book of songs with music written by him, and since he was a notorious procrastinator, she began a search for "poems that would inspire" him.[60] Beckett, Aldington, Lowenfels and Acton all told Crowder that he was free to choose any of their poems he liked, and this spurred him to concentrate on the book. All the poems were set to music within a four-week period and published the following December as *Henry-Music*.[61] The book cover featured one of Man Ray's most striking photographs, showing Cunard's arms, covered to the elbow with her collection of rare African ivory bracelets encircling Crowder's neck like a collar.[62]

Beckett composed a seventeen-line poem called "From the Only Poet to a Shining Whore," which he subtitled "For Henry Crowder to Sing." Crowder described the score as "slow and sonorous,"[63] and he sang and played it regularly at the Dôme, his principal place of employment. He was especially fond of it and recorded it along with Cunard's "Equatorial Way."[64]

With *Proust* at the publisher's and *Henry-Music* in production, one last literary chore remained before Beckett ran out of excuses to stay in Paris. This was the translation into French of *Anna Livia Plurabelle*, which he and Péron had begun early the previous spring. They had been meeting several times a week to work on the complicated text, which required the creation of a new form of the French language, and it was slow, tedious work.[65] Often their sessions ended with the two men going their separate ways, their minds too befuddled to yield the desired word, which hovered teasingly just beyond their reach. Hours or even days later, it would suddenly come, and their next meeting would begin on a crest of enthusiasm which almost without fail gradually slowed to the same confusion in which they had ended the previous session. Both men kept at the job doggedly, and by late August, 1930, they completed a first draft of the French text. They were discouraged with the result and despaired of ever completing it, especially since Beckett could no longer postpone his return to Ireland. When Beckett left, Péron was entrusted with the final polishing of the text, and since Beckett was still persona non grata to Joyce, they agreed that Péron should present the manuscript to him. Joyce seemed satisfied with it and sent it to the printer, where it reached the stage of galley proofs[66] and was scheduled to appear in a coming issue of the *Nouvelle Revue Française*.[67] At this point, Joyce casually asked three of his friends—Philippe Soupault, Paul Léon and Ivan Goll—for their opinions. They began by suggesting one or two minor changes which led first to a phrase, then a sentence, then a complete block of text being discarded and replaced. After some heated discussion, Joyce agreed that the entire manuscript needed revision, and asked Soupault, Léon, and Eugene Jolas to rewrite it completely. By the time it was published the following May, it was an entirely different manuscript from the one which Beckett and Péron had worked so hard to finish.

Soupault has since given the impression that the part Beckett played in the translation was minimal and that Péron was an occasional minor commentator.[68] Nevertheless, Beckett and Péron did the difficult, time-consuming first translation. How much of their text was revised is not known, for the manuscript disappeared among the papers of James Joyce. When he speaks of this translation now, Beckett simply says that he and Péron did "three-quarters," and that it was afterwards transformed.[69]

He was obviously disappointed that Joyce had not accepted the version upon which he and Péron had labored so long and faithfully. He could not help but consider it a personal affront that rankled. But by the time the translation was published, Beckett was immersed in the life of a university instructor at Trinity College. The events of his literary life in Paris were part of an existence that seemed irretrievably lost and therefore best not thought about; the contrast between his life there and his life in Dublin produced comparisons too painful to contemplate.

CHAPTER FIVE

1930–31:

"... LOST THE BEST"

Beckett's fellowship to École Normale Supérieure stipulated that he would return to Trinity College to serve as an instructor in French for three years. He was expected, also, to bring back a work of significant scholarship, a publishable treatise—the essay on Jouve he had agreed to write when he received the moderatorship research prize. But he had consigned it to an unwritten oblivion more than a year before. Not having written it was a black mark against the academic aspirations he was assumed to possess—one barely made up for by the essay on Proust—but he was still able to receive the Master of Arts degree at the next commencement simply by paying a fee for the diploma and then claiming it, which he did.[1]

Rudmose-Brown was disappointed that Beckett had returned without the essay, but rather than chastise him, saw to it that Beckett was given a position as lecturer in modern languages, which made him the most important of Rudmose-Brown's seven assistants. No doubt he did this in an effort to shore up Beckett's wavering commitment to an academic life, but also because he liked Beckett and wanted him as close as possible.

As a lecturer, Beckett held a three-year appointment with a salary of two hundred pounds which was supposed to be increased annually until it reached 350 pounds. At the end of the

William Beckett (photo supplied by Reading University Library)

May Beckett, ca. 1947 (courtesy Caroline Beckett Murphy)

Frank and Sam Beckett, ca. 1908 (courtesy Caroline Beckett Murphy)

Beckett and his mother, ca. 1908 (photo by Dorothy Kay, supplied by Reading University Library)

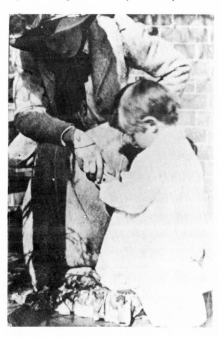

Cooldrinagh (photo by Deirdre Bair)

Beckett at Portora Royal School, 1921
(courtesy Portora Royal School)

Beckett (third from right) on the Portora cricket team, 1923 (courtesy Jerome Lindon)

...ckett with Thomas McGreevy in ↑
...ndon in the early 1930s (cour-
...y Elizabeth Ryan and Margaret
...rrington)

...icature of Professor T. B. Rud- ➤
...se-Brown, published in *T.C.D.*,
...9 (courtesy Reading University
...rary)

Great Moments in Great Lives—No. II.
L'Après-midi d'un Faune.

Beckett drawn by Sean O'Sullivan, early 1930s (courtesy Mariah B. Rowe)

Pegeen Guggenheim, ➤ George Reavey, Geer van Velde, Gwynned Vernon Reavey, Beckett, and Lisl van Velde at Peggy Guggenheim's country house, Yew Tree Cottage in Sussex, 1938 (courtesy George Reavey)

James Joyce, sketched by his daughter Lucia, ca. 1930 (courtesy Society of Authors and the Poetry Collection of the Lockwood Memorial Library of SUNY at Buffalo)

Illustration from a ➤ German rotogravure, which Beckett thought should be used on dustjacket of *Murphy*. Caption reads, "What! You are giving up your Queen? Sheer madness!" (courtesy George Reavey)

Beckett with Frank and Suzan at Ussy, 1952 (courtesy Caroli Beckett Murphy)

← Beckett at Yew Tree Cottage, 19 (courtesy Peggy Guggenheim)

Beckett at The Shottery, late 19 (courtesy Caroline Becke Murphy)

← Edward, Caroline, and Sam Beckett, ca. 1948 (courtesy Ca line Beckett Murphy)

A picnic on Killiney Hill, 1947. Back row: Jean Beckett, Mollie Roe, Susan Manning, Sheila Roe Page, May Beckett. Front row: Edward Beckett, Caroline Beckett Murphy, Susan Howe, Fanny Howe (courtesy Mary Manning Howe and John Manning)

May Beckett and Sheila Page at Cooldrinagh, early 1940s (courtesy Caroline Beckett Murphy)

Robert Pinget, Beckett, and Claude Simon outside the offices of Les Editions de Minuit, early 1950s (courtesy Jerome Lindon)

Beckett in the pond he made at The Shottery just before Frank's death, 1954 (courtesy Mary Manning Howe)

three years he would be eligible for reelection to the faculty, this time ad vitam, aut culpam (i.e., with tenure).² A suite of rooms was one of the fringe benefits of the appointment, and in September, 1930, Beckett moved into 40 New Square, directly opposite the rooms he had lived in as an undergraduate.³

May and Bill were delighted and relieved to have him back in Dublin and carefully avoided mentioning what they considered his past intransigencies (*Whoroscope* prominent among them). They saw the three years Beckett owed to Trinity College as a pleasant holiday period in his life, a fitting climax to an academic career, at the end of which they still envisioned him taking his place beside Frank in the Clare Street office. However, there were uneasy moments in Cooldrinagh, intimations that he would not be satisfied with life in Dublin.

For one thing, he had come back from Paris wearing French clothing, and showed no inclination to discard it. He had abandoned the baggy, durable tweeds beloved by the Irish for tight-fitting French suits, but because he had had little money, the suits bought in Paris were made of sleazy material and the workmanship was shoddy. Possibly his clothing would have inspired an occasional comment and then been dismissed as the affectation of a young man who wanted his friends to know that he had been to the continent, but the beret with which he completed the outfit was too much for Irish sensibilities. Those who knew a few words of French spoke privately of Samuel Beckett as "a bit *farouche*."⁴

The painter Sean O'Sullivan caught "the young poseur"⁵ one night in a pub with a charcoal sketch of Beckett in a tight-fitting French jacket and beret. Beckett was furious when he saw O'Sullivan passing it around amidst the laughter and derision of local Irishmen who had not been to Paris. Several years later O'Sullivan remembered the angry look on Beckett's face and drew a large, more formal charcoal portrait capturing his tight-lipped disapproval, but without the beret.⁶ O'Sullivan initially drew the portrait hoping to dispel some of the superior disdain with which Beckett faced Dublin, but it did not have the desired effect.

It was as if, upon returning to Dublin after two years in Paris, Beckett saw his native land for the first time, and what he saw horrified him. Dublin was nationalistic in the extreme, and politics dominated almost every conversation, leading Beckett, in despair, to declare that if all the people who claimed to have been in the General Post Office during the uprising had really been there, the building would have burst at its seams.[7] He deplored the insularity of Irish literature and was caustic in his ridicule of writers who wrote in Gaelic. Most of all, he hated gossip, wherein fifty-year-old incidents were dredged up as if they had just occurred moments before, and where family feuds were remembered and recounted until they had lost all vestiges of reality.

He was convinced that Dubliners could not tolerate the independence of his mind and spirit. Beckett stubbornly peppered his conversation with Gallic witticisms, avoided "evenings" or "at homes" or other pseudoliterary activity,[8] and managed to let everyone know how boring and provincial he found Dublin. When his friends spoke enthusiastically of Valéry and Rimbaud, whom they had just read, Beckett scornfully told them they should be reading Apollinaire, Breton and Crevel, of whom they had not yet heard. When he had gone away, they sometimes spoke with shame and spite of what they considered his secret pleasure in being different from them,[9] a deliberate artistic affectation at variance with what they all knew to be his inherent decency. Most of these people were generous enough to realize that he was frustrated by Dublin, by Trinity College and by teaching, and that he missed the casual life he had led for the past two years in France.

On one occasion in Sean O'Sullivan's studio, when his friends were praising the work of an up-and-coming Irish realist painter, Beckett, who had been silent so far, suddenly derided the painter as "A Veronicist who would wipe the face of Christ with a sanitary towel," and stomped angrily out of the studio.[10] Most of the people in the room were Catholic and were shocked at his ferocity. In the end they dismissed the remark with "Sam will get over it," and a shake of the head.

He checked his behavior carefully when he was in Cooldrinagh, however. To the family, he appeared more silent than usual, but they attributed this to occasional moodiness, now more pronounced than ever. They thought he was working too hard at Trinity, that teaching took what little spirit for conversation he possessed out of him.[11]

He made his mother very happy when he asked her to help him furnish his rooms at Trinity but she would have been saddened to know that he did so only because he didn't want to be bothered. New Square had been built in the graceful Irish Georgian style of architecture, but in 1931 there was still no electricity in the students' rooms and no central heating. On a central wall there was a brick fireplace in which he burned turf for heat. May gave him two large armchairs which he placed on opposite sides of the fireplace, facing it. Between them was a large round table, covered with a green cloth, and on it a huge white china oil lamp with a flower-painted glass dome. He had a gas jet for cooking simple suppers, and the fireplace had a fender where he kept his teapot warm.

Beckett saw Georges Pelorson, then in his second year at Trinity, almost daily. It became routine for them to dine in each other's rooms on an unvarying menu of omelette (Pelorson's specialty) or scrambled eggs (Beckett's). After dinner they sat in armchairs in front of the turf fire, drinking whiskey, reading and talking.

They were rereading Proust because Pelorson was interested in the process of translation, but for the most part Beckett read French poetry, intending to keep his name alive in Paris by preparing translations for the little magazines. He worked steadily for several months on St. Jean Perse's *Anabase*, but finally abandoned it because he despaired of putting it into publishable form. He had gone back to Rimbaud's *Illuminations* because of discussions with Dublin friends. He believed there was a real need for an English translation and felt that a good English rendering of the poem was vital for its understanding. At one point, in Rimbaud's poem *Barbare*, Beckett was struggling with the word *douceur*, which was especially difficult to translate because he found it to be the kind of abstract for which there is no proper English equivalent. Pelorson had been out with friends one evening, and as he was returning to his rooms quite late, saw Beckett's light and decided to stop for a visit. As he walked in, he saw Beckett, sunk in his armchair with an empty whiskey bottle on the floor and a glass dangling from his hand. Without moving, Beckett said "Mozart." He had found his equivalent for *douceur*, he explained. *Zart* in German has connotations of sweetness, and Mozart, for him, was sweet. Apparently, in the sober light of dawn he thought better of it, because he abandoned the translation.[12]

Of all the French writers he read during this time, the one who had the most influence on his own later writing was Jules Renard, the novelist and diarist. For Beckett, Renard was a man who had found the secret of the perfect approach to life: how to live completely within himself, to examine himself minutely, to write about this examination and yet to inhabit the outer world with tranquillity and contentment. Renard eschewed literary groups, avoided the avant-garde, lived in the same small town his family had always lived in—was even the mayor as his father had been. And yet, for twenty-four years, all the while he was writing novels and plays, he kept a journal which grew to 1,267 pages.

Renard had trained himself to be absolutely honest in his journals and it was the last entry which has had the most sustained and moving effect upon Beckett. Renard had been ill and confined to his bed for some time. In the entry of April 7, 1910, he wrote:

> Last night I wanted to get up. Dead Weight. A leg hangs outside. Then a trickle runs down my leg. I allow it to reach my heel before I make up my mind. It will dry in the sheets.[13]

It was this cold, hard, exacting look at oneself which struck Beckett, so that the first time he read this passage he spent hours repeating it over and over as he sat in his armchair sipping whiskey in front of the fire. It was the same sort of piercing exactitude with which he made Malone examine himself in *Malone Dies*. Beckett took notes from Renard's *Journal*, many of which he memorized and used in discussion to illustrate points he wished to make about his own writings, so that a close reading of Renard's *Journal* and Beckett's postwar fiction shows many instances of Renard's influence.

One of the techniques Beckett most admired and talked about was Renard's casual, commonplace reference to natural functions. "He always speaks so well about chewing and pissing and that kind of thing," Beckett said to Pelorson one night in his room. "It's funny when you think of all the trouble that a playwright takes to get his characters on and off the stage. It's so simple, you see: when you think this man might want to pee, you simply make him leave for that!"[14] It was a technique that Beckett used later with great success in *Waiting for Godot* and *Krapp's Last Tape*.

These pleasant evenings with Pelorson soon became Beckett's only social contact, and McGreevy, who was still in Paris, worried about the effects of so much isolation on his friend's already pronounced tendency toward brooding introspection. McGreevy knew how much Beckett needed an older figure of authority and trust in his life, especially since the crushing blow of the breakup with Joyce. With this in mind, he arranged for Beckett to meet Jack B. Yeats, the painter and writer, brother of the poet William Butler Yeats.

Jack B. Yeats was sixty years old when Beckett met him, but in spite of the difference in their ages, the similarities in their artistic outlook and temperament made them fast friends until Yeats died in 1957. Yeats was the first of a number of celebrated artists who became his close friends, all of whom, according to Beckett, struggled to deal with the problem of creativity and the artistic vision in ways similar to his own.

Beckett received his first invitation to Jack B. Yeats's "Thursdays" through McGreevy, who sent a letter of introduction from Paris. After their first meeting, Beckett wrote a long, effusive letter to McGreevy, who conveyed the sense of it back to Yeats when he wrote that Beckett ". . . was completely staggered by the pictures and though he has met many people through me he dismisses them all in his letter with the remark 'and to think I owe meeting Jack Yeats *and* Joyce to you!' "[15]

Jack B. Yeats lived at 18 Fitzwilliam Square in a large first-floor apartment where he held "afternoons" each Thursday. Guests were invited to drink Malaga with a twist of lemon and to talk about art and literature. The guest list changed each week to include those friends who were in Dublin at the time, but among the regular visitors were Terence DeVere White, Austin Clarke, Padraic Colum, and Joseph Maunsell Hone.

Yeats's Thursdays were a peaceful experience for the most part, a tranquil time lasting until twilight, with serious talk and quiet conversation interspersed with occasional low laughter.

In both his painting and his writing, Yeats looked westward toward Sligo, where he grew up. Its plain country people and wild, passionate landscape never failed to inspire him. The people and their customs were his models, and he placed them at the center of everything he created. He was not a churchgoing man, nor did he seek to impose his own beliefs on others, but he was strongly moral, and the upright character of the people of Sligo filled him with an affirmation of life.

For Yeats, the ability to represent the simple life of the Irish people came naturally, because it was the life he had always loved and lived. He felt that nationality gave dignity and purpose to the artist and was fundamental to his understanding of himself.

On the other hand, Beckett's only contact with the simple life was with the people he had met in neighborhood cafes during his two years in Paris. Talking to the maid, the gardener and the postman at Cooldrinagh hardly qualified for an intimate knowledge of how the simple folk lived in Ireland. As for the glorification of nationality, he was appalled by its extremes, especially in such things as the Censorship Act of 1927 or the four-year-long boycott that closed the libraries in County Mayo because the librarian happened to be a Protestant.[16] He viewed the growing militancy of the Catholic Church in its effort to censor art as an unbearable affront to his personal liberty, and unlike Yeats, found it increasingly impossible to continue to work in a society that had just removed the last remaining nude from the National Gallery.[17] Beckett had no pride in his Irishness; national identity meant nothing to him. Yet he hoped to find his place in Ireland, and his friendship with Jack B. Yeats gave him an opportunity to observe someone entirely rational who was perfectly content in an irrational society.

Jack B. Yeats was an elegant, formal gentleman, a courtly reminder of times past, who always dressed in a style of dark suits that had been fashionable many years before. He wore huge black ties or scarves fastened with a beautiful emerald pin, was elegantly thin and wore a heavy ring which weighted down his slender hand. At home he liked to wear a pale gray dressing gown—all, as his biographer Hilary Pyle has noted, "things so inseparable from him that they seem like accretions of personality rather than things worn."[18]

He was a quiet man who disliked pubs, so Beckett usually visited him at his studio directly across the hall from his flat. He visited there to avoid Cottie (Mrs. Yeats), a charming woman whose pleasant chatter he considered a distraction and an intrusion on his time with her husband. When he was with Jack B. Yeats, Beckett wanted all his attention and grew petulant when he had to share it. Soon he stopped going to the "afternoons" altogether because he resented the presence of all the other people whose friendships Yeats sincerely enjoyed.[19]

Beckett was looking once again for a surrogate father, as he had looked to Joyce in Paris. He was most comfortable when he had one trusted friend, older than himself, whom he could respect, idealize and, in a sense, love. In both attempts to gain such a father figure he was thwarted and frustrated, because both Joyce and Jack B. Yeats kept their primary love for their families and gave their friendship to many others besides Beckett.

Just as he sought Jack B. Yeats's company, Beckett avoided introductions to his brother, whom he regarded as pompous and posturing, fatuously slobbering over all the wrong aspects of Ireland and Irish society.[20] Beckett actually met W. B. Yeats only once, during a brief encounter in Killiney, where he was disgusted with the way W. B. Yeats simpered over his wife and made an inordinate fuss with his children.[21]

It had often been noted among Irish writers and critics how strong the strain of metaphysical irony is in Jack B. Yeats, predating Beckett by some twenty-odd years. Yeats's humor, tinged with irony and enigma, and the ability of his characters to persevere with pragmatic optimism in the face of often grim distresses have been suggested as possible precursors of Beckett's postwar fiction. What these writers and critics fail to consider, however, is the strong strain of moral affirmation that runs through Yeats's writing and is its strongest characteristic. The popularity of Yeats's writing in Dublin was significantly hindered by his constant head-on confrontation with the ugly side of life, as his readers refused to see the portrayal of sickness, suffering and despair for what it meant to him—the necessary foil for affirmation of life's goodness. Beckett was aware of the blackness in Yeats's writing, but he realized what it was and knew what purpose it served, and when he wrote about Yeats, he praised him.

But Yeats was not so effusive in his praise for Beckett's writing. Although Samuel Beckett was one of Jack B. Yeats's dear, good friends for the rest of his life, Yeats considered Beckett's writing "amoral."[22] He neither approved of the direction in which Beckett's writing took him, nor did he enjoy reading it.

However, Beckett's friendship with Jack B. Yeats provided a haven of tranquillity in the abrasive and often abusive atmosphere of literary Dublin. Seeing Yeats as often as he could Beckett managed to make a temporary peace within himself, to withstand Dublin society for a little while longer.

His major problem was, quite simply, his students. He disliked teaching. As one of the seven instructors under Rudmose-Brown, he was responsible for forty students and, like the other six teachers, was assigned to beginning courses in language and literature. Because modern languages were the special province of women, most of his students were female. One of his students remembers him as

> A very handsome young man. We were thrilled with him the first time we walked into his class. Very handsome indeed he was, but he had a distracted look, his blue eyes trying to avoid us—as if to say "well I have this bunch in front of me now, I must try and do something for them." Not in an unkind way, because one felt he was—"shy" might be the word for it. He faced us all with a distracted air, or abstracted might be the better word. But one felt he didn't enjoy lecturing. He didn't seem to be very good, nor did he want to be, at communicating. I think he just felt that he was going to give us what he felt about these poets and writers and didn't want to worry about it otherwise. At that time we were not aware that he had written anything but we did think he was brilliant.[23]

Beckett hated lecturing, feeling that he had no knack for it: "I did not enjoy all those women, mooning about. They were a great problem and I was sorely tempted to ask them all to get out, to leave the room."[24] He used his repugnance at the thought of standing in front of a room filled with giggling young women, which he likened to exhibiting himself, as an excuse to drink heavily the night before each class in an effort to blot the coming ordeal from his mind.[25]

His teaching technique was highly unorthodox. Instructors were required to take the roll at the beginning of each class, but Beckett stopped doing it after the second lecture. He did nothing to encourage his students to pay attention or to take his lectures seriously. It didn't matter to him if they talked, read something else or stared out the window. He was always present in the classroom before the students, staring out the window, with his back turned. When they had stopped bustling and were silent, he usually continued to stare out the window for a very long time. Finally, he would turn to face them and deliver a sentence perfectly crafted but puzzling. He spoke without notes and never seemed to have anything but the work to be discussed in front of him. Most of his students found they were able to take verbatim notes of his lectures, because when he was finished with the delivery of one sentence, he would turn again to the window, wait another long time, almost as if he had forgotten they were there, and then suddenly turn and speak again. It went on like this in every lecture.

For example, his entire lecture on Symbolism, given during a fifty-minute class period, consisted of the following cryptic comments:

Rimbaud, Verlaine and Baudelaire were the precursors of symbolism. Baudelaire provided the text in "Correspondence." Verlaine the music. Rimbaud the dislocation of verse as affected by the Symbolists. Romanticism plus irony equals symbolism. LaForgue invented composite words like "éternulité." He died at the age of twenty-seven. It was fashionable to die young, and to be pessimistic. Some hold him to be a poet without genius or spleen. Others think him a worthy follower after Baudelaire. He was overshadowed by Rimbaud. LaForgue had no poetic development as he grew older. He is called a whiner by some. There is recurrence of motif in every one of his poems.

Reminiscences of Rimbaud in his work. A symbolist because he is concerned with evocation of mood.[26]

No matter how much Beckett disliked teaching, he still managed to convey his regard for the Symbolists and the love for Racine and Corneille which he had learned from Rudmose-Brown. Occasionally, he deigned to recognize the students' bewilderment, and in the interest of clarity he drew amusing sketches on the blackboard; once, to illustrate a point in Racine's *Andromache*, he drew the characters chasing each other around the circumference of a circle.[27]

Beckett lectured in English but sometimes lapsed into French; when his students raised their hands in confusion because they could not follow him, he slipped back into a carefully enunciated English, which was his way of mocking them—supposedly French scholars and knowing so little French. This was only momentary, however, for he was too courteous to pursue this track for longer than a sentence or two. Afterwards, perhaps because he was embarrassed at his irritation with students who were, after all, only beginning their studies, he spoke very quickly and kindly for several minutes at a time.

He produced a fair amount of confusion among his students, especially in some of the young women who were anxious to get to know their instructor better. He discouraged any contact with them, and as soon as the class hour was ended, he bolted from the room. He gave them the lecture they had paid for and that was all. As far as he was concerned, if students wanted advice or assistance, he felt they should see their tutors or the professor of French.

Trinity was a small university where everyone knew each other and classroom gossip was a favorite topic of conversation. Some eyebrows were raised by Beckett's teaching, but Rudmose-Brown explained away his protégé's arrogance by saying that he was simply having a difficult time settling down during his first semester. Rudmose-Brown was not overly concerned. He knew that Beckett was a brilliant man and expected that he might become a somewhat eccentric professor. He had read all of Beckett's published work to date, and he had read *Proust* in proofs. He was willing to put up with eccentricity in the hope that it might be tempered with time.

By December, 1930, Beckett was fed up with teaching and beginning to fall prey to unusual physical ailments that accompanied his most severe mental depressions. He had persistent boils in awkward places, the most troublesome forming on the back of his neck just where his shirt collar rubbed it, and also in his genital areas. He had colds, runny nose and flu that did not let up, and he had serious problems with insomnia.[28]

He was yearning to get out of Dublin and wanted to flee to Kassel as soon as the Christmas holiday began. His family was naturally disappointed that he didn't want to spend his entire holiday with them, but made little protest because they hoped that time away from Dublin would effect some change for the better in his desperate physical appearance.

He had become so sloppy they hardly knew him. His trousers were stained and spotted with remains of food and spilled liquor. He wore a filthy pullover sweater on top of a shabby shirt he had bought in Germany the year before and seldom washed. His old battered green raincoat had a pocket permanently distended by the bottle of stout he carried in it, and his boots were threadbare. He looked more like one of the bums who haunted the quays than one of Trinity College's rising young luminaries. If going to Germany would snap him out of this erratic behavior and bizarre appearance, even May, with her overwhelming need to keep her sons at her side, wanted him to go.[29]

On his way to Kassel, Beckett stopped in Paris, where Nancy Cunard gave him copies of the newly published *Henry-Music*. He visited other friends briefly, and then was on his way.

He found Peggy in a petulant mood, flitting from one place to another, never seeming to sit still long enough for conversation, but angry with him for being reserved and distant. There was something wrong but he was at a loss to discover what it was. Eventually he discovered that it was she who now hoped for some resolution to their situation just as he was hoping to avoid one. Quite without his being aware of it, he was over his infatuation for her. He was so wrapped up in himself, life in Dublin and the career at Trinity that he hated, that he had no emotional energy left for Peggy. He was content to let matters ride, while she wanted to provoke him into some lasting declaration.

To her it seemed that Beckett was having second thoughts about their relationship, but actually he was having *first* thoughts, if there is such a term. His infatuation with Peggy's green eyes and disarming manner had quieted. He found that he was not willing to exert the energy needed to continue the relationship. The only sort of woman he wanted was someone who would fill his occasional physical needs; someone calm, who would make his tea and see that his socks were laundered, not someone who dragged him to half the nightclubs in Germany all the while demanding passionate verbal proof of his undying love and affection, which she did not feel bound to return. He decided to bow out to her German suitor. The time during which he chased Peggy and wanted her desperately had only served to convince him that women were not worth the effort. He believed that love, if there was such a thing, soon gave way to apathy, and therefore, passivity was the best attitude on his part. It lessened by far the complications and expenditures of emotional energy.

For Beckett the holiday was draining and did nothing to alleviate the condition in which he had arrived from Dublin. The Sinclairs, their friends, and their daughters' friends seemed to be on a continuous party as they moved from one nightclub and cabaret to another. Beckett could not keep up with them and took to his bed for several days when his cold grew worse and he developed a severe intestinal disturbance. The boil on his neck grew so large and painful that he could barely turn his head from side to side. He called it "the baby anthrax"[30] and when he returned to Dublin it had to be lanced for the first of many times.

His family was dismayed to see him return from Kassel worse than when he had departed, but little could be done or said. He returned to the rooms on New Square and girded himself for the coming term.

One adjunct duty from which Beckett could not escape was the annual drama festival performed by the French group of the Modern Languages Society. As one of the lecturers, he was

expected to assist in the creation of the work as well as the production, of which Georges Pelorson was nominally in charge.
The previous year, while Beckett was still in Paris, Pelorson and
the others had staged Giraudoux's *Siegfried et le Limousin*,
which had been a great success. They wanted to do something
equally ambitious in 1931, and hoped that Beckett would be able
to give them some idea of what was new and exciting in the Paris
theater. Beckett could think only of a melodrama called *La
Souriante Madame Vevey*, which the other instructors quickly
dismissed as a "stupid imitation of *Madame Bovary*."[31] Beckett
liked it because it was about an ineffectual woman who killed
her husband in sheer boredom, but the idea was dismissed by the
others almost as soon as he mentioned it because the annual performance was always given in the Peacock Theatre, where a
high degree of propriety surrounded performances given before
the entire university community and important townspeople as
well. They wanted none of Madame Vevey, and decided the
next best thing to a popular play was an original play. Beckett
then came up with the idea of a parody on Corneille's *Le Cid*,
which he called *Le Kid*. As he described the plot, with elaborate
suggestions from Pelorson, who quickly caught the spirit of the
idea, the others agreed that it was hilariously original if not intellectual.

Le Kid was written to correspond to the classical dramatic
dictum that all drama should be completed within a twenty-four-
hour period of time. The set was constructed with a huge alarm
clock with movable hands painted onto a backdrop at the rear of
the stage. Pelorson sat next to it, atop a large ladder. As the
hours of the play passed, he moved the hands of the clock.
Beckett, as Le Kid's father, Don Diegue, portrayed a very old
man with a long white beard holding a small alarm clock in his
hands. Don Diegue had a long soliloquy and Beckett wrote it
to be the funniest scene in the parody. As Beckett talked,
Pelorson, at the rear of the stage, began to move the hands on
the clock, slowly at first, then faster and faster. Beckett kept
turning around to glance over his shoulder at Pelorson, and as he
did so, he increased the tempo of his speech. Suddenly the alarm
clock in his hands began to ring. He silenced it and spoke faster,
but it rang again. Meantime at the rear of the stage, Pelorson was

turning the hands with greater and greater speed, racing up and down the ladder to do so. By this time, Beckett was shouting at full speed and his speech had degenerated into a series of nonsense phrases and syllables, wilder and wilder, with less and less coherence, until after a time it didn't matter what he said because the audience was roaring with laughter and the only sound they could hear was the shrill of the alarm clock. It was a speech so distinctive in rhythm and delivery that years later members of *Le Kid*'s audience remember the uncanny feeling they had when they first saw *Waiting for Godot* and heard Lucky's speech.[32]

The audience thought the play a howling success, but Rudmose-Brown was furious. He sent for Beckett and Pelorson after the performance and upbraided them severely for what he called their cavalier attitude to a serious undertaking. Beckett, who still had a severe head cold, was exhausted by his performance and dejected by Rudmose-Brown's characterization of the affair as "frivolous, irresponsible and juvenile."[33] He wanted to go back to his rooms and sleep the night away, but there was another performance to get through that evening. This was the performance attended by newspaper critics and by most members of the university community, and it was a disaster. Beckett had to be dragged onto the stage. By this time he no longer found it funny and spoke his lines in a deadpan monotone. No one laughed, and most people were incensed by what they considered a tasteless parody of a great play. The kindest review of the performance appeared in the Trinity College magazine: "None of the actors was outstanding, but all were capable."[34]

By March, his ubiquitous illness had settled into his shoulder, giving him a painful case of pleurisy. He began to miss his classes and spent his days as well as nights in bed, in total darkness, with all the shades pulled. Not even the publication of *Proust* on March 5, 1931, could relieve the deep gloom and dispel the whispers of his friends that it was "really all in his head."[35]

In mid-March, during the Trinity spring vacation, he was so debilitated that May and Bill thought several weeks in Paris might restore him to health. He went eagerly, in time to attend the *Séance consacrée à James Joyce* given by Adrienne Monnier in La Maison des Amis des Livres on March 26.[36] The program, arranged by Mademoiselle Monnier, was one of elaborate homage to Joyce, almost religious in its reverence. Mademoiselle Monnier began by talking about Joyce's influence in France. Next, Philippe Soupault gave a talk about the method, technique and labor of translation of *Anna Livia Plurabelle*, omitting all but passing reference to the others who had worked on it, and Mademoiselle Monnier concluded the program by reading the translation.[37]

If Beckett reacted to Soupault's talk and the subsequent reading, it was not evident to anyone there because it was completely upstaged when Édouard Dujardin, whose book Joyce claimed was his inspiration for *Ulysses*, slapped Robert MacAlmon. The rest of the evening was spent by guests clustered into small groups trying to calm those who took the affront seriously.[38]

Beckett spent the rest of his vacation trying hard to place some of his poems to keep his name alive in Paris. Samuel Putnam was about to publish *The European Caravan* and he accepted four of them.[39] "Hell Crane to Starling," a twenty-five-line poem, is loosely based on Dante's *Inferno*, taking its title and little else from Beckett's favorite fifth canto. "Casket of Pralinen for a Daughter of a Dissipated Mandarin," seventy-five lines, was about the disastrous New Year's Eve party he had just been to in Kassel, and the "daughter" of the title is the Smeraldina (Peggy). He used this material the following year in another form when he wrote the still unpublished novel *Dream of Fair to Middling Women*. "Text," a poem of sixty-nine lines, is a meditation on Tiresias and Manto, whose story appears in the twentieth canto of *Inferno*. "Yoke of Liberty," thirteen lines long, is based again on Dante, the *giogo della libertà*, which is quoted several times in *Dante . . . Bruno . Vico . . Joyce*.

Putnam lists the poems as published by "courtesy of the author," Samuel B. Beckett (who received no payment for their publication). Putnam printed the blurb Beckett gave him:

> Samuel Beckett is the most interesting of the younger Irish writers. He is a graduate of Trinity College, Dublin, and has lectured at the École Normale Supérieure in Paris. He has a great knowledge of Romance literature, is a friend of Rudmose-

Brown and of Joyce, and has adapted the Joyce method to his poetry with original results. His impulse is lyric, but has been deepened through this influence and the influence of Proust and the historic method.[40]

Beckett was also mentioned when the book was reviewed in the *Saturday Review of Literature:*

> It is difficult to say much of the English and Irish sections. Mr. Putnam has apparently been hard put to it to find among the islanders representatives of the new spirit who are worthy of inclusion . . . so he has been obliged to include some very small people . . . notably . . . Beckett.[41]

Beckett met several times with Jacob Bronowski, one of the editors, to discuss further translations, but Putnam ran out of money and was forced to abandon the project.[42]

Beckett moved about Paris with great vigor, recovered from everything but lingering twinges of pleurisy,[43] and this visit marked one of the few times that news of Samuel Beckett was ever listed in the social columns of any newspaper. Wambly Bald, who wrote a Paris column for the Chicago *Tribune*, said on April 7: "Another Irish poet now among us is Samuel Beckett, instructor at the University of Dublin. His book on Proust has just been published in London."[44] Bald also wrote that Beckett had "taken tea with Gertrude Stein," but he was mistaken; it was George Reavey who had gone to Stein's flat on the rue de Fleurus; Beckett was too busy with publishing arrangements to do much socializing.

He arranged with Putnam for "Text" to appear in the winter issue of the *New Review,*[45] and for another poem, "Return to the Vestry," to be published in an earlier issue.[46] Beckett was not satisfied with "Return to the Vestry," but any publication was better than none at all; however, he has never allowed it to be reprinted and would prefer that it be forgotten.

With these arrangements completed, Beckett returned to Trinity to complete the spring term and remained in Dublin to teach during the summer term. For the first time in several years, he did not go abroad during his summer holiday, but spent the time concentrating on ideas that were forming for a novel. However, he wrote very little of what became *Dream of Fair to*

Middling Women until the following year. For the most part he concentrated on poetry, spending much time on Rimbaud, as Edward Titus had agreed to publish his translations in *This Quarter*.

In June an unsigned dramatic parody appeared in *T.C.D.*, called *The Possessed*, which Beckett had written earlier that year when he wrote the script for *Le Kid*.[47] Only 380 words, *The Possessed* was reviewed by *T.C.D.*:

> In the Joyceian medley, *The Possessed*, its anonymous author performs some diverting verbal acrobatics, but in the manner of a number of *transition*'s offspring, is too allusive to be generally comprehensible.[48]

News of Beckett's friendship with Joyce was jealously bruited about Dublin at this time, and so comparisons and allusions of this sort were not uncommon. All the Irish writers and poets who had recently returned from Paris furthered the comparisons between Joyce and Beckett because they all insisted that the only way to arrange a meeting with Joyce was through his secretary, Beckett.[49] The irony of misapprehensions such as this did little to improve Beckett's relationships with others or his regard for his native city.

In late summer, when the Trinity term ended, he joined Frank on a walking tour of Connemara. It was the first time in several years that the brothers had spent any significant amount of time together.[50] Frank had always been a quiet person, but his years in India made him even more retiring than his brother. With their beloved Kerry Blue bitch, they set off for several weeks of tramping across Ireland. After the debilitating winter that he had just spent, Beckett found the jaunt especially renewing, even though it failed to bring back completely the comfortable camaraderie he and Frank had always had between them. Much had happened since both were at Trinity, and their present lives had little in common. They had no mutual interests besides sports, and each often found the other staring surreptitiously in puzzlement at his brother, the stranger.[51]

Until September, 1931, all of Beckett's published work, with the exception of the slight pieces in *T.C.D.*, had been pub-

lished outside Ireland. Now, James Starkey (who wrote as
Seumas O'Sullivan) published Beckett's poem "Alba" in the
September issue of the *Dublin Magazine*. Starkey's wife, the
former Estella Solomons, was a member of a prominent Jewish
family in Dublin and had been Cissie Beckett Sinclair's friend
and fellow student at the Dublin Metropolitan School of Art.
Starkey founded the *Dublin Magazine* in 1923, and published it
until his death in 1958. It was to Dublin what *transition* was to
Paris, and publication in its pages meant one was considered a
serious literary personality in Dublin intellectual circles.

Beckett wrote "Alba," a seventeen-line poem, for Ethna
MacCarthy. It is an early version of the poem of the same name
which was published in his first complete volume of poetry,
Echo's Bones, in 1935. The poem loosely relies on Dante as its
source but owes its title and form to the Provençal aubade—the
first line is "before morning you shall be here."

Publication of this poem brought Beckett closer to the
Starkeys, and he was occasionally lured into gatherings at The
Grange, their home in the Dublin suburb of Rathfarnum. On
Sundays the Starkeys held their salon, at which Estella presided
over sumptuous teas, after which her guests usually stayed on
into the evening. A. J. Leventhal recalled:

> There must be many who will never forget those Sunday after-
> noons on Morehampton Road where Stella presided over the
> teacups. One generally met writers for the magazine and it was
> remarkable how often these turned out to be Trinity graduates.
> Not all, however, for there was a lively group of contributors
> from the National University. A cultural ecumenism was al-
> ready sprouting in the Starkey drawing room. These afternoons
> were a continuation of similar gatherings at the Grange, Rath-
> farnham, where the couple lived before settling down in their
> Dublin residence. Sam Beckett, whose Aunt Cissie Sinclair was
> a fellow art student of Stella's, remembers meeting AE there,
> though it was never the right season for a game of croquet with
> the Sage of Rathgar.[52]

The Starkeys were charming but conventional hosts:

> No one sat on the floor. . . . The cake was ceremoniously
> passed round. There was almost an air of ritual. One came and
> left at the right hour. Not that there was the slightest possi-

bility of the serenity of the afternoon being disturbed by the suggestion of a dance or a game of cards. On the other hand, no one offered to read his verses or a story to this very critical audience. There was talk. About the arts. All of them. Occasionally an acid remark about a new book or play gave an astringent taste to the conversation. Gossip as such would have been left to the servants, had there been any. But gaiety in speech was not wanting.[53]

For several years Beckett remained on the fringe of this sedate literary atmosphere, until his eccentric behavior became too much for the shy, retiring Estella. He was barred from the house when Beatrice, Lady Glenavy, asked him for a lift back to Dublin in his father's car, which Bill had willingly lent for a visit to the Starkeys. "No," Beckett replied, "I don't want to."[54] And he didn't. This ill-mannered behavior cost him dearly with Starkey as well, who from that time on took what seemed to Beckett a spiteful delight in finding his writing too avant-garde for the conventional literary taste of *Dublin Magazine* readers.[55]

The Starkeys loved masquerades and costume parties, and often asked their Sunday guests to join them in games and charades. Beckett was a reluctant participant because he detested these entertainments. Perhaps the company intimidated him at the Starkeys, for he was not nearly so reserved among his Trinity classmates and students.

One of his colleagues at Trinity was the daughter of the Protestant archbishop of Dublin. She invited a large contingent from the Modern Languages Society to an evening party at her home, and suggested that everyone there do an imitation. Beckett shocked everyone when he sprang to his feet, grabbed the archbishop's hat, twisted it into a Napoleonic shape and gave an impeccable imitation of Benito Mussolini. Back and forth he strutted in front of the amazed assemblage while he shouted in a hodgepodge of real and invented Italian. His audience was shocked that Beckett should choose a political figure, for he was apolitical and walked away from any conversation that veered into politics. He felt that artists had no business concerning themselves with anything but art, and politics—anathema for him—was the least of his concerns. Also, they were shocked by his willingness to entertain, which was totally unexpected. Any humor they found was quickly dispelled, however, for the moment he finished the imitation, he flung the hat back onto the bannister and stalked out of the house.[56]

Once again Dublin was in the grips of winter, and Beckett was deep in the doldrums. Each day meant facing his students, who were no longer content to accept his eccentric lecturing and often accosted him afterwards, demanding explanations for his provocative statements. The students had already given him two sarcastic "valentines" in an earlier issue of *T.C.D.*:

S-. B-CK-TT: I wish he would explain his explanations.
—BYRON

and

S. B-CK-TT: An exhausted aesthete who all life's strange poisonous wines has sipped, and found them rather tedious.
—J. C. SQUIRE[57]

They had lost any respect they might have had for his teaching, and he fluctuated between fits of terror and total unconcern at what they might write, say or do next. His thoughts were on Paris, on writing poetry and even on Peggy Sinclair, whom he had not seen for such a long time that she had once again become intriguing. Most likely, the "Irish Fräulein" represented Germany in general, where life as he had experienced it was the exact antithesis of Dublin. The thought of spending two more years at Trinity troubled him; and the same sort of gloom which had preceded his illnesses the previous year encompassed him.

His poetry took an especially black turn. His depression and uncertainty are apparent in "Eneug II," a poem written during this time and not published until *Echo's Bones* several years later. The poem relies on the Biblical event of Veronica wiping the face of Jesus for its central image, but is mainly a collection of poetic lines which Beckett used the following year in the unpublished novel *Dream of Fair to Middling Women*. The narrator of the poem is "sweating like Judas," and is

tired of dying
tired of policemen

feet in marmalade
perspiring profusely
heart in marmalade

. . . .

the old heart the old heart
breaking outside congress
doch I assure thee
lying on O'Connell Bridge
goggling at the tulips of the evening . . .[58]

The poem aptly reflects Beckett's sentiments in his indecision and anxiety about his position at Trinity and Dublin life in general. He compared himself to Judas because he felt like a betrayer. He wanted to turn his back on his family and friends and flee, and he was ashamed of himself for it. He wanted to get out of Dublin, with its censorship, its overwhelming smugness that glorified mere artistic competence veiled in a countenance of social respectability instead of respecting true talent and genius. He knew he could never write freely in such a culture and also that no matter what he wrote, it would not be considered on its merits because of his personality.

Also, he hated the idea of standing in front of a classroom dispensing knowledge when he felt insignificant and unlearned and had no interest in amassing great quantities of facts to spew out upon his hapless students. Those eager faces, all just slightly younger than he, looking to him for knowledge, frightened him. The insularity of Ireland and the eagerness of his students rubbed his nerves raw. He became unable to decide even whether to get up in the morning, to eat his breakfast and meet his classes, or to sleep away the day, to emerge at nightfall and slither into the nearest pub.

By the end of November he had taken to his bed permanently, lying rigidly in the fetal position facing the wall. He lowered the blinds and spent his days in darkness with the blankets pulled over his head. Nothing and no one could get him to move. His parents were summoned and they came immediately, bringing the family doctor with them. The episode was kept as quiet as possible and very few people besides the college authorities and his family knew what had happened. Those involved quickly invented excuses to explain his behavior, for they refused to accept the fact that he had had a very serious break-down. He was too tired, they said, he had been working too hard, devoting too much of his frail energies to his students and trying to write poetry at the same time. What he needed, they decided, was a vacation, and since the term was ending, May and Bill agreed that he would benefit from a visit to the Sinclairs. Once they were able to break through his mental barriers to tell him, Beckett showed enough improvement to leave his bed and move about his rooms.[59]

His mental anxiety had taken the physical form of a feeling of choking and suffocation, and he convinced himself that if he could get back to the continent, where he would be able to think, he could resolve his problems and alleviate these symptoms.

On the morning of December 8, 1931, his Master of Arts degree was granted. Long after the commencement ceremony was ended, Beckett still wandered around the campus in formal dinner dress and academic robe. When any of his classmates asked him why he had not changed his clothing, he replied abstractedly that it seemed silly to do so when he had to attend the formal dinner at 8 p.m. that evening in the college commons.[60] On December 15 the term ended and he was on his way to Kassel. Shortly after he arrived, he wired his resignation to Trinity officials. He had completed less than half of the three-year appointment. Rudmose-Brown was astounded by Beckett's action, but he recovered quickly and appointed A. J. Leventhal to finish Beckett's appointment.[61]

In the years since his resignation, Beckett has regarded Trinity with the bittersweet reflection of one who sincerely regrets that he was unable to find a place for himself there. He seems to remember the Trinity College of the playing fields and pubs, the genuine intellectual relationships he enjoyed, the friendships made there that have endured throughout his life. He seems to ignore the unpleasantness of teaching and the strictures of the academic profession; he has created a tabula rasa within himself. Officially, he has stated on a number of occasions that he found it impossible to stand in a classroom dispensing knowledge when he himself knew so little.[62] This is no doubt partially true, but it has to be taken with the same caution as any of the few public statements about himself that Beckett has made over the years.

This was the explanation he offered his family, but they could not accept it. May was furious. Her bitterness and anger reached him in letter after letter. Bill was mystified by this younger son who refused, now that college was behind him, to come home "to pull his weight in the business," but he refused to cut him off completely. Each month, Bill sent a chilly note with money enclosed—not much, but enough to keep Beckett in cigarettes and liquor and to pay for his few physical needs.[63]

Beckett's friends were surprised by the resignation, but when they thought about it, all agreed that it was not unexpected. There was no scandal associated with it; in fact, not many persons other than his family and a few friends knew anything about it. It was received by the college authorities and processed in the routine manner, and was duly recorded in the college magazine several months later: "Mr. S. B. Beckett, M.A. has resigned his Lectureship in French and is at present in Dresden [sic]. He was one of the contributors to the *Exagmination of the Factification of a Work in Progress* [sic] and was the author of an essay on Proust."[64]

Only two people were unable to accept the resignation: Rudmose-Brown, deeply disappointed that Beckett had not been able to settle down to become a great professor as he believed he could have been, and Beckett himself. Beckett said he "lost the best" when he resigned from Trinity College, and spent the following years "not knowing what to do."[65] He said he had "betrayed" his colleagues by resigning and had "disappointed his family and friends by his ingratitude and desertion."[66] Not wanting to break with his own family completely, and not able to strike out on his own financially, he compromised by staying with the Sinclairs until he was able to face family and friends again. His Christmas, 1931, visit to Kassel stretched over the first six months of 1932, until he saved enough money and gathered his courage to go to Paris. He could not bring himself to face his parents until the following autumn, and then he only returned to Dublin because he had been expelled from France.

CHAPTER SIX

1931–32:

"I'LL BE HERE TILL I DIE,
CREEPING ALONG GENTEEL ROADS
ON A STRANGER'S BIKE"

In an anguish of indecision and remorse, Beckett prolonged his Christmas visit with the Sinclairs. He spent the greater part of each day sleeping, rising late in the afternoon to prowl about the house, which had become strangely hushed because of the unspoken fear of its occupants. Boss Sinclair was in tight straits financially and was worried that his Jewish ancestry would present serious problems as time went on. He and Cissie began to plan to leave Germany within the year, but were frustrated by their four daughters who were a great concern now that they were all of marriageable age. Peggy especially worried them, for she was listless and feverish, and was only a shadow of the vivacious beauty she had been. A series of German doctors diagnosed her illness as fatigue and prescribed rest, mountain air and wholesome food. The Sinclairs all wanted to believe this diagnosis, and so Peggy's pallor was explained away as "too much holiday spirit"[1] and she was allowed to sleep quietly while her parents hovered nearby, praying that tuberculosis had not touched her.

The Sinclairs were too concerned about their own problems to pay much attention to Beckett as he slouched through Boss's library, lackadaisically picking up one of Balzac's novels or a tattered copy of Jane Austen. Cissie was too worried to give him any advice—help he had come to depend upon—for she had become a surrogate mother and he placed great value on her most casual remarks about the direction of his life.

Cissie represented all the lightness of his own mother's personality without any of May's dark anger. Unlike May, Cissie and Boss were quick to point out that giving birth gave them no special ownership of the souls of their children. They watched as their daughters formed alliances that worried and distressed them, but they confined their negative opinions to humorous or caustic comments and hoped that time and common sense would make them change their minds.

In the few years they had come to know him well, Beckett had become like another child. They, like his own parents, had been troubled when he and Peggy seemed so smitten with each other, but they trusted time and were rewarded when the romance fizzled. Cissie was discreet in all her dealings with her nephew, and she allowed him to vent his rage by listening to his outbursts and calming him without derogating his parents. She had great belief in his talent while he had very little, and she was one of the first to tell him that he could make a living as a writer if he would dedicate himself to serious work.

Beckett needed this sort of attention once again as he prolonged his days in Kassel, but Cissie was too preoccupied to do much more than listen absentmindedly. Still, he stayed on, unwilling to return to Ireland, unready to face Paris. By the end of January, however, he decided to go to France. Joyce's fiftieth birthday was to be celebrated on February 2, and he hoped that the occasion would lead to an invitation that would restore him to Joyce's circle. If no invitation was forthcoming, he reasoned that he could still reestablish contact with the various publishing outlets in Paris and thus begin a writing career in earnest. The news from Cooldrinagh was not good, and he had to face the fact that he could not return to his family unless he was self-supporting, and that might take a long time.[2]

Sylvia Beach wanted to celebrate Joyce's jubilee year and planned a party for the occasion, but Joyce was not up to it. He was depressed by his father's death the previous December, and concerned because Lucia was showing further symptoms of instability. His friends decided to hold a quiet dinner in the apartment of Eugene and Maria Jolas, but on the afternoon of the party, Lucia, who had been depressed, suddenly became violent and threw a chair at her mother, accusing Nora Joyce of interfering in her relationship with Samuel Beckett.[3] Giorgio took Lucia to a *maison de santé* that afternoon, and the dinner, though subdued, was held as scheduled.

Beckett had not been invited, and when he heard what had happened to Lucia, thought it best to avoid Joyce altogether.[4] Nevertheless, he did move back into contact with some of Joyce's circle, which led to several appearances of his name and his work in *transition*. In March, Eugene Jolas published the manifesto *Poetry Is Vertical*,[5] and Beckett was one of the signers.

Poetry Is Vertical most likely resulted as the culmination of countless hours of conversation brought on by the publication in an earlier issue of *transition* of a manifesto by a group of Americans who were in favor of materialism and scientific progress.[6] The Jolas manifesto took its theme from the epigraph by Léon-Paul Fargue:

> On a été trop horizontal, j'ai
> envie d'être vertical.

The manifesto was signed twice by Jolas, once under his own name, and once as Theo Rutra, a pen name he used when he wanted to write something to beef up *transition*'s pages or to state an opinion he thought someone in his editorial position should not have held.[7] Other signers included Carl Einstein, the German ethnologist who was the precursor of Lévi-Strauss and cofounder with Georges Bataille of *Documents;* Hans Arp, already well known for his sculpture; James Johnson Sweeney, the museum director and art critic; and McGreevy, Pelorson and Ronald Symons.

Beckett's bibliographers consider it difficult to decide how far the manifesto represents his opinions at that time, but they assume that since it is his only known public artistic statement it must be considered seriously, since "we may assume that he does not sign anything lightly."[8]

However, one must consider Beckett's circumstances in 1932. He had just resigned from Trinity and was in disgrace with college officials and his family. He had no income of his own. He was twenty-six years old, and though he had published two slim books, neither they nor his other publications had brought him any significant income or recognition. It is highly likely that he signed this manifesto because he was eager to re-insinuate himself into Paris literary circles. In conversation forty years later, Beckett dismissed his signature as "not worth talking about,"⁹ and he probably should be taken at his word. He was no doubt honored to be asked to sign this manifesto, but he did it as much for the publicity it brought him as for his belief in it.

Beckett's short story "Sedendo et Quiescendo" was also published in the same issue of *transition*.¹⁰ The title comes from the statement by Belacqua in Dante's *Purgatorio*, *"Sedendo et quiescendo anima efficitur prudens"*—sitting quietly the soul acquires wisdom. Jolas classified this story with three others by Kafka under the heading of "anamyth" or "psychograph"; "the first being a fantastic narrative reflecting preconscious relation-ships, the second a prose text expressing hallucinations and phantoms."¹¹ Beckett rewrote the story several months later and included it in *Dream of Fair to Middling Women*.

In April, Samuel Putnam published another prose fragment called "Text,"¹² and again Beckett incorporated it into *Dream of Fair to Middling Women*. Like "Sedendo et Quiescendo," "Text" is derivative and highly imitative of Joyce's *Work in Progress*. Beckett had no doubt that both these stories would be brought to Joyce's attention, and perhaps he wrote in such an obviously imitative style in the subconscious hope of pleasing him. A word of praise from Joyce would have done much for Beckett, both directly, to help further his chances for publica-tion, and indirectly, to give him the peace of mind he craved since their previous unpleasant parting. However, these stories were both written very quickly, under pressure, and with the strong desire for immediate publication, and perhaps he wrote them as he did because Joyce's was the first technique that came to mind.

There was a ferment of literary activity in Paris during 1932, and magazines proliferated. In weeks, Beckett found that he was able to place almost everything he had written up to that time. He began to believe that to make his living as a writer was not impossible after all. The fact that these magazines paid little did not deter him; he was certain that publication in the little magazines would soon lead to remunerative appearances. He began to think seriously about how to make money as a writer. He knew that he must have a novel at least in progress, but he also needed a body of shorter, more immediately publishable material. Also, to meet his financial needs, he had to continue to seek translation assignments. To this end, he called upon Edward Titus, who planned to publish a Surrealist issue of *This Quarter* sometime during the fall.[13]

Titus was delighted to give Beckett twenty-one poems by French Surrealists because he had been having difficulties with André Breton, coeditor of the series, who wanted absolute control of the issue. Titus was not about to allow his authority to be dispersed and was relieved when Beckett, whose translating ability he was sure of, freed him to deal with Breton on administrative rather than literary matters. In March, 1932, with only a short time to complete the translations and with his money running out, Beckett returned to Germany and the Sinclairs, where he planned to work steadily on his own writing as well as the translations until he had enough of both to return to Paris. By May he had finished the translations, written several poems of his own and had an idea for a novel as well.

With a certain amount of trepidation, he left the Sinclair house and found lodgings in Paris. He had money coming from Titus and expected to be able to obtain enough translations to pay for his room and board. Bill had secretly begun to send Beckett small amounts of money at regular intervals, and though he was ashamed of himself for taking it, his need was so great that he had no choice. "Sam must never want," Bill was heard to remark from time to time, but always out of earshot of his wife.[14] While May waited grimly for her son to return home, beaten because he could not survive financially, her husband was surreptitiously sending just enough money to keep this from happening.

"Dear old Father," Beckett called him, "Sweet man, what a fellow. . . ." And as his love swelled toward his blustering, bewildered father, so too did his feeling of guilt at having betrayed him.[15] He arrived in Paris filled with determination to make good, to make his father proud of him. He took a room in the Hotel Trianon[16] on the rue de Vaugirard near the boulevard St. Michel and set out immediately to get more commissions from Titus, whose office was at 8 rue Delambre, just above the Rosebud Bar. Titus was in the habit of conducting most of his business in the Rosebud, which soon became one of Beckett's favorite meeting places.[17] Titus knew he had chosen wisely as he read through Beckett's translations of poems by Breton, Eluard and Crevel. However, Beckett's hopes for further assignments were dashed when Titus murmured vaguely about "something by Rimbaud" for an issue in the fall, and Beckett left the office empty-handed.

Bloomsday, June 16, was about six weeks hence, and though no formal celebration was planned, Joyce's friends all planned to give him presents. Beckett wrote a poem called "Home Olga," a ten-line acrostic based on the letters of Joyce's name. The title had its apocryphal origins in Dublin, where a certain Irishman was supposed to have summoned his wife by bellowing the phrase whenever he wanted to quit a dull party. Joyce's intimates used it when they were trapped in similar situations and wanted to leave and regroup at a more congenial cafe agreed upon in advance.[18]

Joyce thought the acrostic "all right," and Beckett moved once again into Joyce's circle, but this time more cautiously. He was determined not to have any further trouble over Lucia, and so he appeared at the Joyce apartment only on the most businesslike occasions, when he had no other alternative. However, Joyce soon took advantage of him and Beckett began to run errands in much the same way as he had before. His friends were dismayed at a situation they felt could only repeat itself, ending in disaster, but they said little about it to him. Beckett had such an air of reserve that no one was willing to volunteer even a hint that he should modify his behavior, for he met all comments, no matter how slight, with a cold stare and blank visage. He brooked no criticism of anything he did, and usually dropped the intrusive offender forever.[19]

It is surprising that Beckett had such a strong effect on people who were all busily engaged in furthering their own careers and meeting with a certain amount of success in doing so.

He was hardly someone to fear or envy at that time. The few clothes he had brought with him from Dublin were falling apart. He lived in a shabby furnished room and seldom had the price of a decent meal, let alone could he provide hospitality for anyone else. His life appeared to be a shambles. In short, he had nothing anyone could possibly want, nor could he provide introductions or perform services. He must have governed the behavior of others by the sheer force of his personality. Turbulent within, to the world he presented an exterior so calm and composed that most people were in awe at the strength of character he exhibited. When something went wrong, he never showed his temper; instead he broke out in boils which he told no one about except McGreevy.[20] He could barely bring himself to visit Titus and the other publishers and did so only because of dire necessity, but he never tried to ingratiate himself with them. If they wanted to give him a commission or publish something he had written, all was well; if not, he would depart abruptly, when a few words of polite chatter on his part might have made them change their minds. He had taken Geulincx to heart: he would control his own fate without pandering to the outside world, no matter how dearly it cost him.

However, there were people in Paris who were not in Joyce's circle and did not care to be, and who had no qualms about criticizing Beckett's behavior. Henry Miller was one of these. Walter and Lillian Lowenfels gave a party in their small apartment on the rue Denfert-Rochereau one night, and Miller, who had been drinking, crossed the room abruptly and told Beckett that he had too much talent to waste it imitating Joyce.[21] Beckett made no reply, but quietly left the party.

Lowenfels and Michael Fraenkel had begun a publishing venture several years earlier called *Anonymous*, in which they hoped to establish art, not the ego of the artist, as the ideal:

> In an age when morale is collapsing, *Anonymous* is a discipline for disciplined artists. By remaining anonymous, the artist dedicates to all creation what is most important—his own creative efforts. He merges his individual creative consciousness in the total creative consciousness of the world. All art becomes the joint manifestation of every individual artist.[22]

Beckett met Lowenfels through McGreevy, just as *Anonymous* was coming to an end. McGreevy jokingly suggested that Beckett was a likely candidate for publication in such a movement, for most writers were hungry for recognition during an era when everyone seemed to be publishing and refused to support it. Lowenfels, a brash, cheerful American, was too poor to frequent the cafes of the quarter now that his publishing venture had failed. He had grown fond of Beckett, "That crazy Irishman,"[23] and gave him an open invitation to his flat. Beckett frequently called unannounced because he found the chatter, confusion and eager optimism of Walter and Lillian Lowenfels soothing.

On one such afternoon, Beckett, who was once again sighing in imitation of Joyce, slouched into the Lowenfels flat and sank into a corner, where he sat, "tall, thin, looking like a forest ranger in a Western."[24]

Lowenfels expounded on his theory of anonymity at great length, especially in the relationship of art to the desolate condition of society. Beckett, according to Lowenfels, nodded, but said nothing:

> Finally I [Lowenfels] burst out, "You sit there saying nothing while the world is going to pieces. What do you want? What do you want to do?"
>
> He [Beckett] crossed his long legs and drawled: "Walter, all I want to do is sit on my ass and fart and think of Dante."[25]

This might have been an honest answer in 1929 when Beckett was new to Paris and firmly ensconced in École Normale Supérieure, but it wasn't now. Beckett simply could not afford anonymity, no matter how much it corresponded to his philosophical beliefs; if he wanted to remain in Paris in 1932, he had to earn his living, and to do so, he had to make a reputation for himself.

In May, 1932, just after he had settled at the Trianon, he began in great haste to write a novel called *Dream of Fair to Middling Women*.[26] Still unpublished, it is Beckett's first substantial fiction, and is often referred to as an earlier version of *More Pricks Than Kicks*, the collection of stories published in

1934. However, it should be regarded as a separate entity. Although he transfers themes, episodes and characters with very little change to *More Pricks*, there are large portions of *Dream* which he does not incorporate into the later work. Once again he did not abandon much of it; the portions of *Dream* not incorporated into *More Pricks* appear in an occasional line or paragraph here and there throughout his later writings. Characters, descriptions, phrases, evocations—even the famous first line of *Waiting for Godot*, "Nothing to be done"—almost all of the manuscript appears at one point or another in his subsequent published work.

Unfortunately, Beckett refuses now to allow *Dream* to be published. He considers it "immature and unworthy,"[27] his way of dismissing blatant, undisguised autobiography. The problem with the manuscript is not so much that its revelations about the young Beckett are embarrassing to the mature man, for he has consented to the publication of many works that he once swore would never appear; the problem is that *Dream* viciously satirizes many people who have remained lifelong, steadfast friends. His sarcasm is tinged with venom in many of the characterizations, and he is well aware that many persons who were seriously offended by caricatures of themselves in *More Pricks* would be deeply hurt to find themselves portrayed with even greater savagery in this earlier work.

In his early writings, Beckett seems to have had a need to turn on everyone in his life—from his mother, father and brother, "the blue eyes of home,"[28] to the most casual acquaintances at École Normale Supérieure. He even inserted verbatim a letter from the sadly ailing Peggy, who wrote English phonetically as she spoke it with her heavy German accent.[29] Not only did he incorporate her letter into *Dream*, but he later retained it as "The Smeraldina's Billet Doux" in *More Pricks*. Cissie and Boss were horrified when they saw what he had done and cut him off completely, forbidding him the one haven left in his life. Yet he seems to have had little remorse for deeds such as this, complaining only of the loss of visiting privileges, as if someone else, a complete stranger, had committed the transgression.[30]

If Beckett was ruthless in combing his own life for material for *Dream*, he had good authority for the technique. His early writings all seem to try to follow Joyce's dictum that a writer must first write of what he himself knows best. In a letter to Arthur Power, another Irish writer, Joyce wrote:

> You are an Irishman and you must write in your own tradition. Borrowed styles are no good. You must write what is in your blood and not what is in your brain. . . . For myself, I always write about Dublin because if I can get to the heart of Dublin I can get to the heart of all the cities of the world. In the particular is contained the universal.[31]

This was the sort of conversation Joyce often had with Beckett and the other young Irish writers, telling them to cull their own biographies, examine their own relationships and write about the people they knew. There would be time enough later to worry about the intellectualization of the work.[32]

The main character of *Dream* is Belacqua, named once again for Dante's indolent Florentine lutemaker. The book is narrated by a fictional Mr. Beckett (who is not named until midway through the book). Both Belacqua and the fictional Beckett are stand-ins for the real Beckett—their adventures are his adventures, their thoughts are his, their acquaintances are his.

Because the novel is unpublished, it may be worthwhile to present a detailed summary of the plot, since much of it is either incorporated as it stands or with only slight modification into other published writings. *Dream* is an episodic novel, following Belacqua (the barely fictionalized Beckett) from childhood to École Normale Supérieure, back to Trinity, where it records his impatience with teaching and life in Dublin. Except for the first episode, the book is loosely divided between biography and Belacqua/Beckett's intellectual musings. Biographical details frame many of the episodes, but the focus is either philosophical theory, literary criticism or personal evaluation.

Chapter one is purely biographical: nine lines long and containing two childhood vignettes, it begins with Belacqua, an overfed little boy, peddling his bicycle after a delivery van. Some years later Belacqua is seen climbing trees in the country and sliding down ropes in a gymnasium in town. The second chapter begins with Belacqua sitting on a pier with the

Smeraldina and ends when he is surprised by a wharfinger who ejects him from the premises, leaving him to hobble away on painful feet. Belacqua is next seen saying his prayers, a blessing his mother taught him followed by the Lord's Prayer. In bed, still thinking of the Smeraldina, he has a wonderful night mis-quoting Dame Julien of Norwich ("Sin is behovely but all shall be well . . .") as he masturbates.

Next, he recounts an episode from his 1926 vacation in France in order to slide into a diffuse allegory about China to make an artistic statement—in this case, arguing, like Stendhal, that the best music is that which becomes inaudible after a few bars, the best object one which becomes invisible and the best narrative that which is not stated.

He introduces his family only for the purpose of saying good-bye to them, thus beginning another, related pattern in *Dream*—the habit of introducing characters only to summarily dismiss them. His father shrugs his shoulders, wishes him luck and pays the bills. His mother wishes him to be happy, which he interprets as an insistence to be merry instead of taciturn.

The Smeraldina is the central female image of the first half of the novel. He places Smerry, as he sometimes calls her, in a "very vangardful" school on the outskirts of Vienna, and he describes her body elaborately, calling it "all wrong."[33] He analyzes their relationship in what seems to be a purgative ex-perience, then moves into his mind for a painstaking, detailed analysis of himself.

At this point the narrator intrudes, breaking into the story of Smerry and Bel to say that while he was making his usual moan about one thing or another, his family was just as he had left it—calm, blue-eyed, clean and gentle.

Belacqua leaves Smerry for a teaching position in Paris, where he is besieged by the exterior world in the form of two male friends, Lucien and Liebert, one or both with homosexual inclinations, and one predatory female, the Syra-cusa. Despite their interruptions and imprecations, Belacqua persists in his de-termination to "womb-tomb" his mind, to withdraw into him-self, free of all outside interference. He spends long hours in his bed, curled up alone in the dark, thinking about the best method to obtain nullity of being. He muses on the book he will write, in which he will ". . . state silences more competently than ever a better man spangled the butterflies of vertigo." In what is probably the most powerful and meaningful statement in the book in the light of his mature fiction, Belacqua/Beckett writes, "The experience of my reader shall be between the phrases, in the silence communicated by the intervals, not the terms of the statement."[34]

Belacqua has a literary conversation with Lucien and Liebert about D'Annunzio, Racine and Malherbe (three of Beckett's favorite writers), and says that, as one can experience Proust's *madeleine*, one cannot experience a *margarita* in D'Annunzio because he writes a uniform, horizontal flow, without the particular accidence of style that would give such an experience meaning. However, Belacqua continues, Racine and Malherbe write in styles pitted and sprigged with no end of opportunity for the evocation of such an experience. Perhaps, Belacqua/Beckett concludes, only the French can do it: "They have no style, they write without style, they give you the phrase, the sparkle, the precious *margaret*. . . . Perhaps only the French language can give you the thing you want."[35] Beckett paraphrased this passage more than twenty years later when he told a scholar that he wrote in French *"parce qu'en français c'est plus facile d'écrire sans style"*—because in French it is easier to write without style.[36]

Typically, throughout this entire manuscript, whenever Beckett makes a serious statement, he denigrates it. Immediately following this thoughtful analysis of writers he admires, he entreats his readers not to be too hard on Belacqua because he was studying to be a professor. This kind of flippant undercutting occurs throughout much of Beckett's subsequent writing as well, as if he would reveal too much of himself if the serious statement were allowed to stand.

Later, as he lies on his bed, Belacqua's mind wanders back to Dublin, recalling a letter from his mother telling him that she has bought turf for the fire from two little boys who stole it off the bog, and now the room in which the family spends its evenings is more snug than ever. He describes his mother, drowsing over the newspaper but lying awake when she went to bed. John (his name for Frank) comes down from his solitary aerie at the top of the house for a late night cup of tea, and his father sits reading the ever-present potboiler until he falls asleep.

"The Smeraldina's Billet Doux" is next in sequence followed by Belacqua during Christmas vacation, ill with fever and colic and confined to his room in Paris. He has decided not to go to Germany, but entreaties from Smeraldina's Mammy persuade him that he should, and he finds a miffed Smerry waiting for him. She won't listen to his protestations of illness and insists that he celebrate the New Year at parties and nightclubs. A nightmare evening follows, with visions of dancers, drinkers, smoke-filled rooms, ghouls and harridans, juxtaposed with Belacqua's impressions of them all. Parts of what became the poem "Sanies II" are followed by "Text," some references to Rimbaud, and a series of allusions to *Whoroscope*. Bel and Smerry snipe at each other with increasing venom until her father, "The Mandarin" or "The Jew" (as he calls Boss Sinclair), comes into the bar and engages Bel in conversation. After a series of insulting exchanges, he calls Belacqua a "low-down, low-church Protestant high-brow,"[37] but Belacqua insists that he is worse—meaner, baser and dirtier. The evening ends disastrously as Smerry leaves Bel stranded and goes off with another man. They meet at breakfast the next morning, when Belacqua/Beckett comments that all things can be made to end like a fairy tale, even the most unsanitary episodes. He last sees her through a veil of nausea as he heads back to Dublin. Beckett as narrator reflects upon Belacqua's infatuation, and in a passage reminiscent of *Krapp's Last Tape*, recalls

> . . . where underneath them the keel of their skiff would ground and grind and rasp and stay stuck for them, just the pair of them, to skip out on to the sand and gather reeds and bathe hands, faces and breasts . . .[38]

—before [he] "so expelled her, for better or worse, from his eye and mind."[39]

But before he reaches Dublin, Beckett has Belacqua pause in Paris long enough to tidy up the characters there. Beckett considers the possibilities open to him, then discards them all, saying he is tired and neither deus enough nor ex machina enough to bring their situations to a successful resolution. From this he glides into a discussion of the conventional novel, and seems almost relieved at his decision to free himself of the necessity to further his own plot. He defines his view of fiction through Jane Austen ("the divine Jane!") and Balzac (who he says writes only of "clockwork cabbages" without a life of their own). Beckett, in terms of Balzac, discusses suicide. Balzac's characters, he says, could never entertain such thoughts because Balzac has spelled out their every move for them. Beckett seems proud that he has so little control over his own characters, and insists on looking for ways in which Balzac's characters might commit the act, even though he thinks they are not free to do it.

Literary criticism gives way to the inside of Belacqua's mind once again, and memories of how he ruined his feet: Belacqua abandoned by the others on a walking tour when his boots have mangled his feet; Belacqua buying other boots in Germany and begging Smerry to listen carefully to the clerk because he himself cannot understand the language; and Belacqua's final comment that now he wears shiny patent shoes (like Joyce) and no longer needs ugly, deforming boots.

The first half of *Dream* ends with the narrator on the boat returning to Dublin in the usual manner—with a hurting conscience—thinking of the kind of book he will write. Then he abandons seriousness and closes this section as Belacqua, in gathering dusk and a veritable torrent of Joycean language, is abandoned by Beckett to his palpitations, adhesions, effusions, aganesia, womb-tomb and aesthetic of inaudibilities.

The second half of *Dream*, shorter than the first, has the Alba as the central female image. Belacqua is settled now in his rooms at Trinity College, where there is much drinking and perambulating. He holds long conversations with friends, and hides from students who pursue him, demanding to know what he meant by what he said in class.

The Alba, patterned upon Ethna MacCarthy, is a forceful young woman, independent of mind and behavior. She drinks brandy, takes pills, meets men in hotel bars and is intellectually Belacqua's equal. She is upset when a mutual friend tells Belacqua that she has casually asked about him because, as she correctly guesses, Belacqua will come to see her and she does not share his infatuation. Indeed Belacqua does come, and there are several increasingly gauche conversations in which Belacqua tries to explain a literary theory as a way to bring them closer and only succeeds in increasing the distance between them. After more drinking and mooning about, he attends a party given by a literary lady-about-town because the Alba is supposed to be there. He is roaring drunk, sopping wet from rain and quite late when he arrives. As he stands in the doorway with his great head hanging down and his clothes dripping, the Alba, seated among the guests listening to a musical interlude, sees him and entreats all those in her row to move over and make room for him. Shortly thereafter they leave the party and Belacqua takes the Alba home in a taxi for which she pays because he has spent all his money on drink. With only minor revisions, this section became "A Wet Night" in *More Pricks Than Kicks*.

Dream then hurries to a close. Actually, Beckett wrote two endings; in both, Belacqua recovers from too much brandy and exposure to the cold Dublin night and decides simply that he will move along now because he feels like it.

Beckett wrote *Dream* very quickly, in only a few weeks, because he needed money and wanted immediate publication. When he finished, he discovered that it was too long for the little magazines and would not lend itself to serialization without extensive revision. No book publisher in Paris would take such a work written in English. No Irish publisher would risk a work which referred at one time or another to rape, masturbation, wet dreams and illicit affairs. Beckett realized that his only hope for publication was in London, but he had no money to go there, nor did he know anyone to whom he could send the manuscript for personal attention. In fact, he was so poor that he could not even afford the postage to mail the manuscript unsolicited. There was still the nagging problem of how to face his family, and events suddenly transpired to make the decision for him. On May 6, 1932, Paul Doumer, President of France's Third Republic, was assassinated by a Russian fanatic. Following Doumer's death, the French police mounted an intense effort to check the identity papers of all aliens residing in Paris.

Beckett did not have a valid *carte de séjour*, which meant he could not register legitimately in any hotel; nor did he have the money to leave the country voluntarily, so he left the Trianon and spent several nights hiding out in the Villa Seurat, sleeping on the studio floor of the painter Jean Lurçat, while he tried to amass enough money to go to London. Almost immediately he thought of Edward Titus. He had finished most of a first-draft translation of Rimbaud's *Le Bateau ivre* (in *Dream*, Beckett as narrator says of Belacqua: "And Rimbaud, the Infernal One, the Ailing Seer. . . . You know of course, don't you, that he did him into the eye into English?"). He took the translation to Titus, who liked it and agreed to print the finished version in the October Surrealist issue of *This Quarter*, along with the other translations Beckett had already completed. Titus was known for not paying at all when he could get away with it, but Beckett made it clear that he could not finish the poem unless he had a guarantee of payment. He asked Titus for one thousand francs, but after much haggling, settled for the eight hundred Titus offered to pay in advance.[40]

Beckett finished the translation at Villa Seurat in a few days, but Titus delayed printing it for one reason or another until he was no longer publishing *This Quarter*, and the manuscript disappeared somewhere among his papers when he closed shop. From the very first, Beckett's habit had been to make three of everything he wrote—the original for himself, the first copy for the publisher, and the second to keep for safety's sake or else to be given to anyone who wanted it. In this case, he gave the second copy to Nuala Costello, one of the young Irish women in Joyce's circle who was fond of Beckett. His own copy was subsequently misplaced, and all copies of this translation were presumed lost until more than forty years later when Costello found hers folded between the pages of a book.[41]

With money in hand, Beckett bade a sad farewell to McGreevy, who was reduced to escorting visitors through Versailles in order to make enough money to live.[42] He was giving serious thought to relocating in London in the hope that literary journalism would be more profitable there,[43] and he urged Beckett to do the same, but Beckett's main reason for wanting to go to London was to find a publisher for *Dream* and thus sweeten the homecoming to Dublin he knew he could not delay much longer, and which he knew would be painful.

But no publisher would take *Dream*, and he wrote a scathing letter to George Reavey in Paris to describe their rejections:

> The novel doesn't go. Shatton & Windup thought it was wonderful, but they couldn't. They simply could not. The Hogarth Private Lunatic Asylum rejected it the way *Punch* would. Cape was écoueure [sic] in pipe and cardigan and his Aberdeen terrier agreed with him. Grayson has lost it or cleaned himself with it. Kick his balls off. They are all over 66 Curzon St. W. 1.[44]

To add injury to insult, Beckett was forced to cut short his stay in London when his last five-pound note was stolen from Jacob Bronowski's apartment on Ampton Street (by ". . . a coinmate, poor fellow, whose need was greater than mine . . .") where he had cadged free lodgings while he made his rounds of publishers. There was nothing left but to return to Dublin.

After an initial burst of violent anger, May settled into grim silences which she broke only long enough to demand to know when Beckett would find a job. There was a humiliating confrontation, in which Bill and Frank, besieged by May, admitted that there was little Beckett could do besides take care of correspondence or assist with routine arithmetical calculations. May stopped pestering about the business, but still insisted that Beckett had to go to work as soon as possible.

Beckett tried to explain patiently that he wanted to be a writer, and that writing took enormous amounts of time during which it might appear that he was doing nothing. He begged their indulgence for a little while longer, saying he needed time to rewrite his novel. If he did not succeed in finishing it in a reasonable amount of time, then . . . and he left the rest of the sentence unsaid, because he simply had no idea what he would resort to then.

This explanation was good enough for Bill, but not for May. She insisted that the only money he should receive from the family was one pound per week, and Bill honored her edict.[45]

Beckett was in Dublin less than a month when the old familiar feelings of sadness, boredom and frustration set in, but this time there was no way out because he had no money.

George Reavey, who had been energetic about promoting Beckett's earlier poems, wrote from Paris offering to try informally to place them. Beckett replied languidly that he might try to excavate a poem "one of these dies diarrhoeae." He was bitter about the possibility of payment, supposing it would not come in money, but "in honor and glory." "So much piss," he concluded rancorously. But he did have an idea for a poem: one written after the manner of Marcel Schwob, as if he were peering through an incipient cataract at the Crystal Palace and Primrose Hill. He thought it would be long and sad, and hoped that it would do him great credit when put into "Dublin stutter."[46] This poem became "Serena I," which Reavey published in the collection *Echo's Bones* several years later.

Beckett ended this letter on a note of self-pity, saying, "I'll be here till I die, creeping along genteel roads on a stranger's bike."[47] Reavey replied with news of a possible way out of Dublin. Titus had been asked by the publishing firm of William Heinemann, Ltd., to judge a contest for the best short story of the year, which would then be printed in *This Quarter*. The fifty-guinea prize would have gone a long way toward supporting Beckett in Paris, and he wanted very much to win it. He adapted some of the writing from *Dream* into the short story which became "Dante and the Lobster" and was later published as the first one in *More Pricks Than Kicks*. He was disappointed when he did not win, but was consoled when Titus published the story anyway in the December, 1932, issue. Since there seemed to be no escape from Ireland in his immediate future, he set to work in earnest to make something publishable of *Dream*.

CHAPTER SEVEN

1933:

". . . MY FATHER DIED WHEN I WAS A BOY, OTHERWISE . . ."

While Beckett was determined to shape *Dream* into a publishable manuscript as soon as possible, May was equally determined that he should quickly get a job.[1] Every day she gave him the employment sections of the Dublin newspapers, entreating him to "at least apply" for whatever was advertised, no matter what the position. In what she thought was subtlety, May dropped hints about jobs she claimed her friends had told her about, only to succeed in arousing Beckett's animosity and stubbornness. Frank said nothing about Beckett's employment prospects, but he was so far removed from family discussion that he rarely spoke, and then only in monosyllabic asides. Bill adopted a hearty joviality to mask a deepening concern that he would have to support a wastrel son for the rest of his life.

No matter how politely these conversations began, they disintegrated into nasty verbal battles, with May in tears, Bill red-faced and raging, Frank silent and embarrassed, and Sam, as usual, white with unspoken anger. In an effort to alleviate these painful confrontations, and as a possible spur towards gainful employment, Bill allowed Beckett to turn the unused top floor of the Clare Street offices into a small studio where he could go each day to write, as if he were going to a real job. May bit her tongue and confined her entreaties to the weekends when he was at home or evenings when she saw a particularly promising advertisement in the newspapers.

Life for Beckett quickly settled into a boring routine. To May's distress, he did not arise early with Frank and Bill, but stayed in bed until early afternoon. Then he dawdled over tea, wandered around the house aimlessly, and finally dressed haphazardly for the train ride into Dublin. Once in the city, he shuffled into Clare Street after fortifying himself with stout in a nearby public house, took care of correspondence and set out for yet another public house. He took to staying in Dublin several nights each week when he missed the last train or was not sober enough to face his family, sleeping on a cot he had installed in Clare Street.

May grew increasingly angry and ashamed of him, and when she could no longer contain her anger, she set out to do something about it. To explain to her friends that Sam's sloth was the necessary prelude to his becoming a writer was difficult, for none of them had ever heard of the little magazines in which his work had been published in Paris, and she was not proud of *Proust* or *Whoroscope*. In her eyes, it was imperative that Beckett do some "legitimate" work while she waited for him to be transformed magically into an established and respected writer. If, she reasoned, he put his time to good use while he was waiting, there would be no need for her to make shamefaced apologies to her friends.

Without consulting him, she arranged for six young women, daughters of her friends, to take French lessons with young Monsieur Beckett, newly back from Paris, ex of Trinity College.[2] The six gathered weekly in each other's homes on a rotating basis for what was to be informal conversation and formal reading from the French classics. Week after week the giggling girls waited long past the hour of the lesson for Beckett to arrive. At first they had been thrilled by the idea, for they remembered how handsome Beckett had been as a Trinity undergraduate. Now, however, they were not attracted to the disheveled mess before them, but thought of him as an object of pity and a humorous break in an otherwise dull week. As the lessons went on, they thought him uproariously funny. He wore the same grubby trousers each week. He had taken to wearing a dirty raincoat several sizes too large for his thin frame. In one pocket he carried the week's text, in the other a large bottle of stout. He was usually fresh from a pub and full of drink-inspired conviviality. As they chatted, he pulled the stout from his pocket and drank it. He seldom spoke French, except in sarcastic derision, but the young ladies had a wonderful time anyway and were reluctant to see the afternoons come to an end. After several such bizarre sessions, their mothers grew uneasy about the instructor's unorthodox behavior and overcame their fear of May Beckett long enough to cancel the lessons, to their daughters' dismay.

It was becoming difficult for Beckett to rely on old Trinity friends for companionship, as they had all dispersed in one way or other. Some went to teach or study in England. Some had married and were no longer free to spend every night in the company of their old companions. The newer, younger crop of graduates from University College were still about, and he made do with their company, even though as a Protestant graduate of Trinity College, he sometimes considered them his social inferiors.

A number of these younger men were genuinely friendly, eager to exchange knowledge and to discuss their writing, but others made only the slightest effort to veil derisive disrespect for the man they considered the prime example of a lazy ne'er-do-well.[3] With few exceptions, Beckett was without friends, and it was a new and difficult situation for him to accept. Since his days at Portora, he had always been the center of a group of admirers. He may have been reserved and stinting when it came to giving his friendship, but his ability in all things from athletics to academics had made him someone others gravitated to, so that companionship had always been easily available. Now his contemporaries had moved on, while Beckett was still living the life of a Bohemian student, although at twenty-seven, an aging one. When he was with friends from Trinity, Beckett acted as though nothing had changed since their university days, even though they were uncomfortable around him as he drifted aimlessly in an alcoholic fog.[4]

The younger group of men had not known him in the earlier phases of his life, and to them he was someone who had been "spoiled by Paris," a common expression in Dublin literary circles, given its special meaning by Joyce. To have one of

Joyce's intimates among them in Dublin to observe firsthand gave an added dimension to the expression, and they were often so sarcastic in their conversations that Beckett usually avoided them.

He began to lead a solitary existence, with his only excitement coming in letters from McGreevy, still in Paris. This was the beginning of his lifelong correspondence with McGreevy, and in the more than three hundred extant letters which he wrote until McGreevy's death in 1967, Beckett poured out all the agony, anger and uncertainty of his existence. McGreevy became his safety valve, his lifeline to the world outside Dublin, his alter ego. McGreevy was the only person to whom Beckett has ever been absolutely truthful, to whom he told his innermost, deeply secret thoughts. In many cases, these letters parallel Beckett's creative writings, for he transfers passages from them into his fiction and drama, from the briefest image and scantest phrase to whole paragraphs. These letters to McGreevy are important documents, as they show clearly how Beckett's writing evolved and matured.[5]

As his solitude deepened, his illnesses multiplied. He had persistent colds, flu and chills. The doctors diagnosed bursitis in his left arm and shoulder, and the "anthrax" on his neck swelled time after time until it either burst or had to be lanced, spewing foments of pus which left him incapacitated for days. His mother grew so alarmed by these illnesses that she stopped pestering him to get a job and began to minister to his health: modest quantities of stout were brought to Cooldrinagh and Beckett was exhorted to drink his fill, as May believed that stout promoted a large appetite and was a precursor of good health. He joked to McGreevy that an ill cyst had blown him something good at last.[6]

Loneliness and boredom were bad enough, but worse was his inability to write. As he endured long days with nothing to show but an occasional phrase or snatch of verse, his frustration grew, until he found himself spending most of his time walking (his remedy for coping with and possibly inviting the muse) or sitting in one pub after another until he abandoned any attempt at schedule or routine in disgust.

Later, he would use these long frustrating walks—from one

end of Dublin to the other, through the Wicklow Hills, along country lanes and past deserted railway stations—in his writing, in descriptions of the countryside or of his thoughts while pacing; but at this time, these walks only inspired a thirst for liquor which drew him into the handiest pub.

In Paris, one could sit in a cafe for hours, with a half-empty glass, staring into space, and no one thought anything of it. In Dublin, someone who did not down his glass with regularity and offer occasional invitations to others to join him in drink and conversation was considered "a bit daft." While others, in eloquent Dublin pub talk, bemoaned the fickle muse who ignored their efforts, Beckett kept silent. For the most part he sat and stared and thought, for it took an enormous amount of whiskey to loosen his tongue enough for him to expound his ideas, and then only in congenial company. He sat slumped over a drink, waiting for his muse to come, while others around him attributed his silence to moodiness or snobbishness. It was during this time that he began mentally to divide creative persons under two labels: those who kept their own counsel and waited for their muse, and those who did not, for whom he had great contempt and whom he subsequently called noncreative writing machines.[7]

Beckett was anxious to produce something that would earn him enough money to be able to leave Dublin. Shortly after the publication of "Dante and the Lobster" in December, 1932, he had received several further humiliating rejections of *Dream*, but rather than abandon it, he decided to use it as the point of departure for a collection of stories, to which he now pinned his hopes for publication.

This seemed the safest way to use certain parts of the manuscript, for now that he was in Dublin he realized how much *Dream* revealed of himself and of all the people with whom he was in frequent contact once again. He knew that as long as he lived in Dublin, he could not bear the scandal *Dream* would cause if it were published. He had no desire to be an object of literary gossip, and so began to delete all offensive portions. He did not stick to this resolve, because he decided at once that the most immediately salvageable segment was the Smeraldina's letter, which became "The Smeraldina's Billet Doux," and which subsequently cost him banishment from the Sinclair household. Next, he wrote "A Wet Night," incorporating the lady-about-Dublin's party that comprises most of the second part of *Dream*. This, again, was the literal recall of an actual event, with all the characters blatant caricatures of people who were supposedly his friends. "Ding-Dong," the tale of Belacqua's meeting a woman in a pub who sells seats in heaven for "tuppence apiece, four fer a tanner,"[8] comes next, with its heavily autobiographical descriptions of Belacqua's peregrinations about Dublin when he was a student at Trinity College. To these Beckett added "Dante and the Lobster," his account of an ordinary Italian lesson with Vera Esposito, his teacher and the daughter of the famous Dublin musician, Michele Esposito.

These gave him a total of four stories, which he showed to Seumas O'Sullivan, hoping to have at least one printed in the *Dublin Magazine,* but O'Sullivan refused, saying he admired them, but that his fictional taste was admittedly behind the times, the only place where he could be happy. This excuse angered Beckett.[9] He toyed with the idea of sending one of them to the *Adelphi* magazine, but abandoned the idea as ridiculous. He let it be known that he was willing to forgo payment and would give any of the stories to the first person who would publish them, for he realized that his chances of selling them as a book were slim unless they appeared first in magazines. But he had no takers. He also knew that he would need at least four or five more in order to have enough pages for a book, but he was stymied in his efforts to write.

By this time it was Easter, 1933, and he had to stop writing during the long holiday weekend because Bill and Frank went to Wales for a walking holiday, leaving him alone in Cooldrinagh with May. As the holiday dragged on, he knew he had to get away from the house before he and she crossed swords in argument again. On Holy Saturday, he got up early and sped away on his motorbike through Malahide, around the estuary to Portrane, and back to Foxrock by way of Swords.[10] From this came the poem, "Sanies I," a re-creation of his thoughts during the ride, which was published later in *Echo's Bones.* Easter Sunday passed in a blaze of boredom, but on Monday he bowed to social amenity and took his mother to The Botanic Gardens. Both tried hard to be agreeable, and the afternoon passed without incident in an atmosphere of enforced good will and feigned interest in the exhibits.

The following day, when Bill and Frank returned, Beckett and his father took a long walk in the Wicklow Hills. While Bill, swearing and sweating, stopped to rest under pretense of admiring the view, Beckett gently explained Milton's cosmology. Many years later he recaptured the tenderness his father inspired in him in a scene incorporated into *From an Abandoned Work*. Beckett was concerned about the rapidity of Bill's aging, but he also knew the futility of admonishing him to cut down on the strenuous exercise and hearty diet his father insisted upon. Beckett was overcome by the rush of affection he felt for his father, who seemed to be the only person in the world besides McGreevy who appreciated his plight. His father was doubly dear to Beckett because he gave love and sympathy wholeheartedly, even though he had no real understanding of his son.

With the holiday over at last and his mind devoid of ideas for further stories, Beckett began to read. His friend, Joseph Maunsell Hone, the Irish writer and journalist, suggested Plutarch's *Lives* and Berkeley's *Commonplace Book* for inspiration. Beckett began to use the Trinity library, and soon became a familiar figure as he sat hunched over a book, his shabby raincoat draped on the back of his chair.

Between May and September, when he sent a total of ten stories to Charles Prentice, his and McGreevy's friend at Chatto and Windus, Beckett wrote seven stories: six that, with the four mentioned above, complete the collection published as *More Pricks Than Kicks;* and "Echo's Bones," which the editors decided not to include and which has never been published.[11]

These last six stories are probably the most purely fictional writing that Beckett has ever done. Unlike the first four, they depend very little on actual events or people. He called them "bottled climates" and said they came into being without any conviction on his part, only because he would have perished from boredom had he not written them.[12]

Belacqua is again the name of the protagonist. A descendant

of "the grand old Huguenot guts," Belacqua reads Dante, has been abroad briefly, peppers his speech with comments and allusions in French, German and Italian. He makes "a great play with [his] short stay abroad."[13] Belacqua finds interruption both threatening and unacceptable. He is obsessed with exactitude, is a heavy drinker and either evades or agonizes over all his commitments, excusing his bizarre behavior by saying that "he had been drunk at the time, or that he was an incoherent person and content to remain so, and so on."[14]

In the first few pages of "Ding-Dong," the unnamed narrator gives the most explicit biographical explanation to be found in all the stories of Beckett as he was at this time. In the descriptions of Belacqua's comings, goings and stayings, Beckett's own inner torment, indecision and dissatisfaction with his life are readily apparent. He discusses Belacqua's belief that if he moved constantly from place to place, the Furies could not find him:

> [These] little acts of motion did do him some good as a rule. It was the old story of the salad days, torment in the terms and the intervals a measure of ease.

But Belacqua, "being by nature however sinfully indolent, bogged in indolence, asking nothing better than to stay put," finds no real peace in either course. Belacqua, whom Beckett places and describes in Dublin society with a certain amount of precision, is curiously apart from it, yet through moral cowardice and lazy indifference, he is also unable to break away from it. Like Leopold Bloom, Belacqua makes his appointed rounds, but there is a deliberate distancing in *More Pricks,* unlike the sense of day-to-day Dublin life that *Ulysses* conveys. Belacqua lives in and for his mind; still he moves within a fiction that depends to a large extent on an actual place to further the plot and to add depth and meaning to the central character. In these stories, there is none of the technique of interiority divorced from physical landscape that characterizes Beckett's later writings in French.

Beckett relates these ten stories of Belacqua in a style that ranges from pedantic pomposity to ironic wit. They are arranged chronologically and show no explicit link; there are often abrupt transitions between them, and they differ in theme, tone and style. At the same time there is a natural progression from one to the other, so that all ten might be read as the chapters of a picaresque novel. Beckett uses the same technique here as in the postwar French *Nouvelles*, that of a series of *aperçus* which present to the reader the perception of one existence.

Style is Beckett's overriding concern in *More Pricks*. In all the stories there is the by-now unmistakable accretion of obscure, learned and personal detail, but there is also a definite stylistic development. Each story shows a care for craftsmanship lacking in the flamboyant, flippant *Dream*, so that while all the earlier stylistic posings are here, they are made to do work, to further the plot. Even his arch flippancies have their place. Where there is humor, there is mockery, usually interjections by the narrator, designed to cut Belacqua and friends down to a certain manageable size. The learned erudition of the narrator and Belacqua both are often undercut by sarcasm, and if there is any compassion it is frequently bizarre. Belacqua shows stronger feeling for the death of the lobster than for the little girl who is run over, and Lucy's accident is dismissed in several cavalier sentences.

Beckett treats death with casual irony—Belacqua dies in a burst of humor, much like a practical joke gone wrong; but death is there all the same, black and frightening. The book is peopled with cripples: Belacqua has "his ruined feet and spavined gait," there is pathetic Lucy and the legless creature who comes from the Coombe each day to beg outside the Bank of Ireland, and countless others crippled mentally as well as physically. Beckett's continuing fascination with down-and-outers is here, but it is not the one which sometimes inspires empathy in readers, as do the later heroes in his French fiction. Beckett is concerned with style to the detriment of thought and feeling.

No doubt this had something to do with his unhappy mental state, but his boundless admiration for Joyce and his eagerness to be part of the Parisian publishing world also played a large part. While the various revolutions of the word which had swept through Paris in the 1920's had either come to a crashing end or else quietly fizzled out, Beckett, isolated in Ireland, was still trying to tailor his writing for publications that no longer existed. It was difficult for him to be away from the mainstream of experimentation, even though the stream, unknown to him, was now a mere trickle. He chafed at not being able to keep up to date, writing wistfully to McGreevy that he had heard of Céline's *Voyage au bout de la nuit* and admired the title, but had not been able to get a copy of the book in Dublin.[15]

The stories in *More Pricks* were written in what he called a desperate itch to grub up his guts for publication,[16] and from the beginning he called them superficial and, like Belacqua, "not serious."[17] In later years he was embarrassed by them, called them juvenilia and refused to have them reprinted. He only relented in 1966, when the requests from scholars who wanted to read the book grew to such a large number that he allowed his English publisher to reissue it *hors commerce*. Shortly after, he agreed to general publication of a trade edition.

By mid-May, 1933, when Beckett was hard at work on *More Pricks*, he was in a state of acute anxiety. The "anthrax" erupted two more times, each time totally incapacitating him. He had disturbing dreams, one after another every night. He imagined himself racing downhill on his motorbike toward Rudmose-Brown who was standing on a step at the bottom waving desperately for him to stop. In another, he was in a panic as he tried to begin a long walk by the sea with Jack B. Yeats but was constantly frustrated by missing trains and not being able to get there.[18]

His only relief came in drink, which he paid for with the pound-a-week allowance his father gave him. Once, when he stumbled home in the early morning, he barged into the pantry enraged, broke all the plates and crockery, and threw a large pudding out the back door into a hedge of veronica.[19] He was punished by having his allowance reduced to ten shillings a week, which barely bought him cigarettes. His presence in the house disrupted and depressed the entire family, and this only deepened his feelings of guilt and hostility, and led to a further outbreak of boils and afflictions.

In May, when he was in the depths of a depression, he received word from the Sinclairs that Peggy had died peacefully in her sleep at Wildungen.[20] The news was a shock. Only a week before, he had been told that Peggy was well enough to lie out in the sun and there was a good chance that she would be completely cured of the tuberculosis. Peggy, at the time of her death, was happily engaged to a young German, so that her relationship with Beckett was (and had been for a long time) only that of two cousins who were fond of each other. Nevertheless, Peggy's death brought him to a crisis in his feelings about himself. He envisioned time fleeing, leaving him stranded in an Ireland he had grown to despise; himself a wastrel son in the prime of his life, yet dependent as a baby on his parents' generosity, and lately, their mere tolerance.

He was secretly planning to gather his courage to ask his father for enough money to go away again, this time to Spain. To bolster his courage, Beckett began to spend all his time studying the Spanish language.

Another blow from the outside world buffeted this ephemeral daydream: a Mr. Sean Cagney of the Irish Tax Bureau had begun to write threatening letters demanding payment of back taxes, which he claimed would amount to five guineas a week for a prolonged, undetermined period of time.[21] Beckett was unable to prove that he had received next to nothing in payment for his writing to date, and the functionaries in the tax offices could not believe that a man of his age had no regular occupation or taxable income. Beckett made several exhausting trips to the tax offices, but still he was threatened with court suits because he could not convince Mr. Cagney that he had nothing taxable. Attempts to keep all this from May failed, and her anger was once again suffused with shame, a deadly two-edged weapon she used with piercing accuracy against him.

Now Beckett began to suffer from severe headaches which, even though he spent most of his time recumbent in a dark room, gave no sign of letting up. He was seeking for some outlet or interest (but not an occupation) that would bring him enough money to leave Cooldrinagh. He developed a sudden, intense interest in Colorado, because the sound of the name conjured up visions of majesty and romance. Denver and the Grand Canyon struck him as particularly appropriate for a long rhythmic poem, and he began to daydream about going there. He soon abandoned this fantasy to concentrate once again on

Spain, which seemed more easily attainable, and just as he finally gathered his elusive courage to ask his father for the money, Bill Beckett suffered a serious heart attack on June 21.

He was put to bed at home and ordered to remain absolutely quiet for at least a month. Along with hired nurses, his wife and sons took turns caring for him. Bill had never been ill a day in his life, and the sight of the great mountain of a man, totally dependent on his family, beyond wanting food or companionship, was a terrible shock. Yet to Samuel Beckett, it was strengthening as well. His father needed him, and he accepted nursing duties with alacrity, tenderly bathing and shaving, reading, sitting quietly at his father's bedside for hours on end. He accepted the doctor's admonition that all the family would have its work cut out when Bill was over the initial crisis. Bill would never be able to roam the hills or swim throughout the winter, nor could he eat and drink voraciously again. The family would have to see to it that he stuck to a strict diet and took only prescribed amounts of exercise.

Bill's illness gave Beckett a feeling of being needed for the first time in his life, and he relished the warmth with which this feeling suffused him. Beckett allowed himself to indulge in eager, childish fantasies of what life would be like when Bill recovered.

On the morning of June 26, the doctor examined Bill and told Beckett and May that he was making remarkable progress toward recovery. Beckett was so elated that, to celebrate, he dressed in his brightest clothes before going in to spend the day with his father. Scarcely had the doctor gone when Bill collapsed. For the rest of the day he suffered terribly, until four o'clock in the afternoon when his heart stopped beating. At the age of sixty-one, William Beckett died of a second massive heart attack.[22]

The immediate fear within the family was that May's emotional equilibrium would shatter. Beckett was thus forced to remain strong, now drawing on the inner reserves of strength he had used throughout his father's brief illness to comfort his mother. It fell to Beckett to answer the endless stream of letters of condolence, to attend to well-wishers, to take care of May's daily needs. Frank, inundated at the office, now had the matter of settling Bill's estate added to his normal work load, and was only in Cooldrinagh long enough to sleep each night. But May was indomitable and made all the arrangements herself to bury her husband in Redfern Cemetery on the Greystones side of Bray Head, between the mountains and the sea he loved so dearly.

May's brother came from England to be with her, and suddenly Beckett found his central position in the household usurped. As May's external strength grew, his weakened. All he could do was remember how Bill had joked during the last two days of his illness, when it seemed he would get better, saying he would never work another day in his life but would go instead to the top of Howth where he would "lie in the bracken and fart," or his last words, "What a morning!" and "fight, fight, fight!"[23]

May turned the house into a mausoleum, with her mourning centrally enshrined on an altar of gloom.[24] She kept the curtains drawn each day. No one was allowed to play the piano, except for the mournful dirge "Crossing the Bar" once each evening. Dinner was a study in dignity and reverence, which Beckett thought completely and utterly false. He was horrified that his father, who would never go near a cemetery when alive, was to be enshrined—once May chose between granite and limestone for the monument and gorse and heather for the shrubbery. Settling Bill's estate became May's overriding obsession for the rest of the summer, and so Beckett was unable even to hint at leaving Dublin until the legal requirements had been completed. In the meantime, to keep his own emotional balance, he had to get away each day from Cooldrinagh, which he felt May had filled up to the eaves with the vile worms of melancholy observance. He lied, and told her that he had advertised for pupils and had been successful in acquiring many, when in truth he had only one, the dumpy little daughter of the master of a national school. For teaching her French he received five shillings an hour, which he usually spent by midafternoon in the nearest pub. Otherwise, he passed his days in the stuffy little room on the top floor of the Clare Street offices, finishing the stories in *More Pricks* and brooding. He was not sleeping well; each night irrational panic beset him, causing his heart to pound wildly. A new cyst had formed on the palm of his hand which did not respond to lancing and made writing or typing difficult and painful. It required great care not to let anyone in the family know that he was doing next to nothing.

May was concerned that she might not be able to afford to live in Cooldrinagh once Bill's will went through probate, and she goaded Frank to put the estate in order as quickly as possible. At the same time, each night after he finished work, Frank had to devote long hours to studying for examinations for membership in the Surveyor's Institute. His normally genial disposition had given way to harried crossness, as he struggled to balance all the aspects of his professional life with the demands engendered by his family. May's brother had gone back to England; in his stead, her niece, Mollie Roe, had come to stay for the rest of the summer. With someone else to care for his mother, Beckett found a sense of relief and freedom, but at the same time it exacerbated his feeling of not being needed or useful. All he could do to fulfill May's vision of him as one of her two grieving sons was to show up each night on time for dinner and to try not to make too much noise opening the one bottle of stout he was allowed now that they were all in mourning.[25]

He poured out his venom in long letters to McGreevy, and was especially unhappy and lonely because Cissie and Boss had come back to Dublin but would not receive him. They had escaped from Nazi Germany with little more than their toothbrushes, and had taken a small house on Howth near the place where they had lived many years before.[26]

The only person in Dublin to whom he could confide some of his feelings was Dr. A. G. (Geoffrey) Thompson, a friend from his Trinity days. Thompson was working at the Rotunda Hospital, where he shuttled between classroom cadavers and women giving birth. To Beckett, Thompson described life in the Rotunda as a shock which required a certain amount of mental accommodation after the rarefied atmosphere of Trinity's medical school classrooms.[27] Beckett replied that his father's sudden death also required mental accommodation on his part, and he was unable to come to terms with it. Beckett began to seek Thompson when he was not on duty, at first for the congenial company, and then, as their conversations grew more intense, for the medical information that Thompson was able to impart. Beckett was fascinated with physical deformities, fantasized about what he called "deadbeats" and asked endless questions about the abnormalities of the people he saw. One woman in particular was especially fascinating: a victim of panpygoptosis, or Duck's disease. Within the year, Beckett described her with textbook precision when he created Miss Rosie Dew in *Murphy*:

> Duck's disease is a distressing pathological condition in which the thighs are suppressed and the buttocks spring directly from behind the knees, aptly described in Steiss's nosonomy as Pan-pygoptosis. Happily its incidence is small and confined, as the popular name suggests, to the weaker vessel.[28]

Thompson, thrust as he was into the midst of disease and death, was not averse to discussing hospital life with a friend eager to listen and to ask intelligent questions. As Thompson was considering psychiatry as a career, he listened intently as Beckett, at first abstractly but then specifically, described his own physical problems and mental uncertainties.

Beckett, in his questioning, was attempting to assess illness and deformity in terms of religion and philosophy and to explain the two medically. At one point Beckett insisted that all of life was a disease, with babyhood its beginning. Man, to him, was the prime example of the mortally ill, for man began as a helpless infant, unable to attend to himself, and most of the time ended in the same manner. In man's beginning and end there was im-mobility, and each man was thus at the mercy of all others. It was a grim philosophy, and one which Thompson, a young doctor eager to comfort mankind, could not accept. Beckett insisted with glum solemnity that Thompson's efforts were well-meaning but useless, for the fate of mankind was to begin dis-eased and to progress inexorably through further stages of suffering to a painful end. There seemed to be no point upon which the two men could agree, and Thompson was relieved that the strain of argument which threatened their friendship was mitigated by Beckett's increasing need to discuss his own symptoms. These, Thompson was certain, could be cured by a change of residence, for he believed (although he did not say) that Beckett's illnesses were psychosomatic.

In September, 1933, Bill's will went through probate. He had named May, Frank, Beckett, and his brother, Dr. Gerald P. G. Beckett, as executors. In a will dated March 5, 1923, Bill bequeathed his estate to May for her lifetime. Frank and Sam were to be supported until they were educated, with the proviso that this period of time should not last beyond their twenty-fifth year. Upon May's death, the estate was to be divided equally between them.[29] Since Bill died when Frank was past thirty and Beckett twenty-seven, May legally controlled the estate, which was valued at £42,395, or approximately $106,000—an estate of considerable size in 1933.

Frank had his own income as manager of and now heir to the firm, but Beckett was humiliatingly dependent upon his mother for every penny. When he was alive, Bill had said repeatedly that "Sam must never want, Sam must be provided for,"[30] but according to the will, any money he would get would be doled out by May, according to her whim or inclination. Fortunately there was another clause in the will which allowed each heir to ask at any time for an annuity, which Beckett did, hoping to receive enough to live outside Ireland as soon as he was convinced that his mother was capable of living by herself. He also asked to renounce his trusteeship, and thus, Frank and Dr. Gerald Beckett became the only two trustees in a legal ceremony on September 12, 1933, when Beckett and his mother resigned in their favor.[31]

The entire Beckett family was amused that Dr. Beckett was named a trustee, since he was known among them as the brother with the least concern for the value of money.[32] As his children came of educable age, his method of financing them was to sell off his property piece by piece. No one was more relieved than he when Frank actively took over the management of the estate, leaving him a trustee in name only.

Once the legalities were settled, May rented a small house on the sea just beyond Dalkey Harbor, hired moving vans and transported from Cooldrinagh her own bed, much of her favorite furniture, her dogs and all their paraphernalia, and Beckett—leaving Frank behind to watch over the house. Beckett was miserable living with the sea crashing relentlessly just outside the door. It frightened and exhausted him, and he grew to hate it.

For May, the euphoria of so much activity did not last once the change had been effected, and she fell back into the whining and crying with which she had passed her time in Cooldrinagh. Beckett was thankful she had only rented the seaside house for a month, and that by mid-November they would be back in Foxrock, where May would be forced to take more interest in her surroundings simply for the sake of appearance among her neighbors and friends. In the meantime, he worked diligently at "Echo's Bones," which was to be the "recessional story" (as he called it)[33] for the collection *More Pricks*. Chatto and Windus had just agreed to publish the book the following May. The contract buoyed him considerably, but not for financial reasons. He had been paid twenty-five pounds, less a 25 percent advance on royalties; however, the money had to be paid to the relentless Mr. Sean Cagney to settle the tax claim.[34]

With no money left from the advance and less than two hundred pounds annually from his share of the estate, Beckett decided the only way he could get out of Ireland was to find gainful employment somewhere else. In a moment of what he called "gush," he applied for a job as an assistant curator in the National Gallery of England, and asked Jack B. Yeats and Charles Prentice, his editor, to send letters of reference.[35] As soon as he applied he began to have doubts about his action, but they were short-lived because almost by return post he received a letter telling him that his application would not be considered. It was the first job he had applied for since resigning from Trinity College, and he had not even survived the first winnowing. Even though he was relieved, it was still a devastating blow to his ego.

Then he conceived the idea that he should apprentice himself to an advertising firm in London and began to watch the newspapers for openings. When nothing appeared for which he was qualified, he thought of enrolling in a school which taught advertising copywriting, if he could find such an institution in London. Slyly, he reasoned that it was not only a way of postponing employment, but it was practical enough that he might be able to persuade his mother to finance it. This, too, came to nothing, and he was forced to confront the frightening realization that if he were to go to London, it would be on his own, without prospect of employment, supported only by his annuity and whatever he could earn. He decided to put it out of his mind for the time being because he could not face up to it, and with the excuse of helping his mother through her first Christmas without his father, he delayed his decision until the new year.

CHAPTER EIGHT

1934:

"DEPRESSED . . . IN A CONFUSED STATE"

 What finally brought Beckett to London was his health.[1] During the last months of 1933, his physical deterioration had reached the point where the Beckett family physicians were baffled by the cysts and boils which refused to respond to medication, and the colds, flus and aching joints that often kept him bedridden for days.

Geoffrey Thompson was convinced that the eruptions were psychosomatic. Beckett, in his conversations with Thompson, had unleashed torrents of anger and venom he felt towards his mother, his situation within the family and within Ireland. Thompson feared Beckett was on the edge of total incapacitation unless something drastic happened immediately to reverse the symptoms.

Suddenly, dramatically, the illnesses took a new turn. Beckett would awaken in the middle of the night, drenched with perspiration, his heart pounding erratically, unable to breathe or to extricate himself from the blind panic which threatened to suffocate him. He tried to avoid sleeping because he was afraid to dream. The resultant insomnia led to further complications: he was unable to empty his bladder and his constipation became so severe that Thompson, who until then had tried to mitigate his diagnosis, was forced to tell Beckett the truth, that he was suffering from severe anxiety complicated by depression. He insisted that Beckett enter psychoanalysis immediately, as a way of exorcising whatever demons had brought him to this sorry state. Thompson spoke convincingly of the benefits of analysis, but Beckett was not ready to open his emotional recesses to a stranger and continued to rely on their informal conversations, as he was unable to make any decisions.

Finally the night tremors became so severe that Beckett could relax only if Frank slept in the same bed, to hold and calm him when he was in the grips of nightmarish terror. May was terrified that he was having a nervous breakdown before her eyes, but she continued to hope that sleeping pills, large quantities of food and stout, and long walks through the countryside would overcome his steady downward slide. She admitted defeat only when Frank blew up in an uncharacteristic display of temper. Solid and patient, bearing the burden of his brother as though it, too, were a part of all the responsibility that he would have to shoulder now that Bill was dead, Frank finally rebelled. He told his mother he could no longer run the business during the day, study for examinations in the evening and spend his nights nursing his brother. He was exhausted, and the resignation with which he had previously shouldered all his mother's demands had reached the breaking point.

Frank's rebellion placed May in the midst of a dilemma from which she could not emerge without terrible loss. If Sam were to enter analysis in Dublin, it would soon become common knowledge to all her friends and would be only another in the never-ending stream of mortifications he caused her. However, if she permitted him to go to London for treatment, no one in Dublin need know, but she would have to relinquish her control over him and face her own anxieties alone in Cooldrinagh. May and Frank had never been particularly close, beyond what the rules of propriety between mother and son demanded, probably because Frank operated so completely in the mold set by his father. May expected no complications in her relationship with Frank, and until his abrupt refusal to care for Beckett, she had received none. With Beckett, however, it was an entirely different matter. She was still determined to break him, to make him accept the life she envisioned for him. Now, if she allowed him to go to London, she was in a sense cutting the bonds that bound him to her.

By mid-January, 1934, however, May had no choice. She reluctantly gave Beckett the necessary money to permit him to live in London for six months, during which he was to enter into analysis and continue to try to establish himself as a writer.

Tom McGreevy was in London also, and Beckett had hoped to share a flat with him, but McGreevy's financial situation was so bleak that he was forced to move into the home of Mrs. Hester Dowden, where he lived rent-free in exchange for helping with household chores and acting as general handyman. Mrs. Dowden was the widow of the celebrated Trinity professor, Ernest Dowden, and was herself a well-known automatist.[2] She lived in a large house at 15 Cheyne Walk on the Chelsea Embankment, with numerous animals and an assortment of odd people who came and went, some as paying guests and others who simply stayed till Mrs. Dowden tired of their mooching and asked them to leave. McGreevy was embarrassed by his penurious position and excused his residence with a halfhearted attempt to joke, saying he had gone to live there for "1000 pounds in the bank and the sake of a good address."[3] McGreevy was chief critic of *The Studio*, an art magazine, and gave occasional lectures in art history at the National Gallery. He reviewed sporadically for the *Connoisseur* and the *Times Literary Supplement*. But, as Beckett was soon to learn, literary journalism was hardly enough to make a decent living, and McGreevy's titles were infinitely greater than the income they brought him.

Shortly before Christmas, 1933, Beckett moved into a furnished room at 48 Paulton's Square, just off the King's Road in Chelsea.[4] He was there only long enough to deposit some of his books and clothing and to make preliminary investigations into the possibility of psychoanalysis before he went home for the holidays.

He arrived in Cooldrinagh with a new vitality and sense of well-being that they had never seen before. Even though his stay in London had been brief, the change it wrought in him was astonishing to May and Frank; to them he seemed almost magically cured, so much so that May could not keep herself from speculating aloud whether he should bother to go back now that he was so much better. His good spirits could not withstand that sort of talk and it was not long until he fell back into the familiar and frightening lethargy. By January 20, 1934, when he finally tore himself away from his mother's entreaties to stay, he was in the same condition as if he had never been to London at all. Frank, who had to make a business trip to England sometime during the month, quietly scheduled his affairs so that he could escort his brother, because Beckett seemed barely capable of managing on his own.

Once back at Paulton's Square, Beckett couldn't decide what to do first: make arrangements for beginning analysis or investigate the publishing introductions McGreevy had arranged for him. Being away from Cooldrinagh made him feel so good that his first inclination was to pursue the latter, but as soon as he thought about what was necessary to establish contact with strangers whom he feared would only rebuff him, he was overtaken by the same irrational fears that had beset him in Dublin, and he realized that analysis would have to come first.

With introductions and recommendations from Geoffrey Thompson, Beckett set out for the Tavistock Clinic, the bastion of the British psychoanalytic movement. There, he began therapy with Dr. Wilfred Ruprecht Bion, who was his analyst for more than two years. Bion, only slightly older than Beckett and just beginning his medical career, believed strongly in the theories of Melanie Klein, especially projective identification and the interplay between the paranoid-schizoid and depressed positions. He worked at that time mostly with patients who were diagnosed as psychotic, as did all the younger doctors at Tavistock. Bion has since become a recognized authority on group psychology,[5] but at the time he treated Beckett, he practiced a one-on-one doctor-patient relationship.

Beckett was a new kind of patient for Bion, and the analysis proved to be meaningful for both men. Bion brought an intelligence into the discussions, which as often as not touched upon the abstract creative process as upon Beckett's personal problems. This was an era when artists and writers were all strongly influenced by Freud and Jung. In fact, so many writers and artists of this period were either undergoing analysis or writing their own criticisms of psychoanalytic publications that Ezra Pound, a staunch unbeliever, hooted in derision that he was the only sane writer left in Europe.[6] Beckett himself had read Jung's essay on

"Psychology and Poetry," which appeared in *transition* in 1930. He knew that most of the Surrealist poets—Breton, Aragon, Eluard, Soupault and Crevel—practiced automatic writing in their poetry, and Breton had actually had experience as an analyst. The playwright Henri-René Lenormand had stated publicly that he tried to create tragedy based chiefly on psychoanalytic knowledge of character.

This familiarity with the literary aspect of psychoanalysis was probably the primary moving force in the ease with which Beckett accepted the idea that he should enter analysis.[7] He had known for a long time—since his days at Portora—that he was not fitting into the world of his family and their friends, but he was powerless to make himself do so. Even his intellectual flirtations with suicide were, he suddenly realized, more than random thoughts about coping with the dilemma of life. All these thoughts, especially when reinforced by the actual presence of people he knew who had been in analysis and who seemed happier for the experience, made the idea attractive to him.

Nevertheless, if he had not had such frightening, debilitating physical experiences, he most likely would not have gone into it. Probably the most important aspect of Samuel Beckett's self is and always has been best described by the word "control." Until this time he had always been the one in any of his relationships to decide how close he would allow others to come to him. He was the one to arrange meetings or engagements, and these were always in public places from which he could easily and gracefully escape. He rarely invited friends to his family home, or later to his rooms and apartments, because then he would have been forced to entertain them, perhaps long after he was tired of their presence or bored with them. And consistently, in conversations and interviews with persons who claim to have been his lifelong friends, the realization comes that it has always been Beckett who set the pace and direction of the friendship. For a person such as Beckett who has raised personal privacy almost to a religious fetish, it must have been extremely difficult to begin a professional relationship in which total and absolute openness about every aspect of his life was the only ground rule upon which the relationship could be established.

He had gone through a period of rage, as evinced by the

drunken scene in which he destroyed all the crockery and threw the pudding into the bushes. Rage gave way to panic when he realized that years were passing and he was still living at home, a wastrel son. Panic in turn gave way to frustration, which brought with it horrible physical symptoms that resembled impotence. He could no longer urinate and suffered severe flashes of pain in the lower abdomen and pelvic regions. These, finally, were what brought him to analysis. He gained a certain amount of relief upon hearing Geoffrey Thompson describe his symptoms as typical of causing somatic nightmares and anxieties, but nevertheless, they were so physically painful that these intellectual explanations were of little real comfort.

As he was beginning analysis, several publications appeared bearing writings he had done much earlier, and these did a great deal to cheer him up and give him the impetus to begin to write again seriously. Nancy Cunard's anthology *Negro* appeared in January, with nineteen translations he had prepared from the French originals.[8] Most of these had been done between the time of his resignation from Trinity and his brief stay in Germany and Paris. They range from prose articles on jazz and Louis Armstrong to chronicles of imperialism and history in places like Haiti, the Congo and Madagascar. They are solid, impersonal translations, undistinguished by any individual touch. Nothing in them would draw attention to Beckett as translator.

In February, the acrostic "Home Olga," which he had written for Joyce in 1932, appeared in the American magazine *Contempo*.[9]

More Pricks Than Kicks was published on May 24, and received generally favorable reviews except in Ireland. Typical of the kind of comment the book engendered there is the review signed by N. H. in the *Dublin Magazine* which called it "so unblushingly highbrow as to overawe all but the plain man, who . . . will close the book promptly suspecting acute cleverness."[10] He admits grudgingly that it is "a book that glitters and will make holiday for the highbrow." And he concedes that "Mr. Beckett is an extremely clever young man, and he knows his *Ulysses* as a Scotch Presbyterian knows his *Bible*."

Actually, the book's title is Biblical, from Acts 9:5: "I am

Jesus whom thou persecutest; it is hard for thee to kick against the pricks." In Beckett's usage, martyrdom may figure, but the pricks are also sexual. The title itself was enough for the book to be banned in Ireland without even having been read by the censors.[11] For Beckett, being banned in Ireland was the same as being praised, but another sort of faint praise came from Paris which pleased him even more. He sent a copy of the book to Joyce, and in a letter to his daughter-in-law, Joyce wrote:

> Beckett has brought out his book *More Pricks Than Kicks*. . . . Haven't time to read it. But looked at it here and there before quitting Paris. He has talent, I think . . .[12]

Joyce's personal appraisal of *More Pricks* was echoed by most of Beckett's friends, but critical appreciation marked the extent of the book's success.

The jacket blurb called the collection of stories ". . . brusque and defiant—that rare humour the last weapon against despair"—a line calculated to appeal to an English reading public beset by economic woe and already troubled by warlike rumblings from the continent. It concluded, "*More Pricks Than Kicks* is a piece of literature, memorable, exceptional, the utterance of a very modern voice." It was apparently too modern for popular English taste: printed in an edition of fifteen hundred copies, only five hundred were sold.[13]

With so little success coming his way after *More Pricks* had been published, Beckett had no alternative but to concentrate on critical writing for income. In April, McGreevy's book of poems, called simply *Poems,* appeared. McGreevy was so destitute that even though his publisher had given him a substantial number of free review copies, he could not afford the postage to send them out. Seumas O'Sullivan had agreed to feature the book prominently in the *Dublin Magazine*'s July issue, and McGreevy, who could not risk an unkind appraisal, asked Beckett to write the review. The title, "Humanistic Quietism," was selected by O'Sullivan, but the content is entirely Beckett's. Naturally, he was enthusiastic in his praise for McGreevy, but again, there is a literary statement which expresses Beckett's belief as well, the remark that "All poetry, as discriminated from the various paradigms of prosody, is prayer."[14]

McGreevy was a friend of T. S. Eliot's, and he showed Beckett's review to him in the hope that it would lead to reviewing assignments for *Criterion*. Beckett never really knew Eliot, but like most Irish poets of his generation, he disliked the kind of poetry that Eliot wrote. This dislike carried over to the man as well, and no doubt it was mutual, as both men were quiet, courteous and careful when meeting someone new. Beckett made a perfunctory call on Eliot; Eliot was not impressed, and nothing came of it but one assignment, a five-hundred-word review of Leishmann's translation of Rilke's *Poems*, which Beckett castigated for its ineptness.[15] It seemed as if Eliot, satisfied that he had made a polite gesture toward McGreevy's young friend, felt he had no further obligation, and Beckett, hampered by pride, stubbornness or the simple inability to ingratiate himself with persons who could give him work, never called on Eliot again.

Next, McGreevy introduced Beckett to Desmond Mac-Carthy, who was known as the one man who could help beginning writers more than any other. This, too, came to nothing, even though Beckett felt more at ease with MacCarthy than he had with Eliot.

Then McGreevy inquired at the *Spectator* for Beckett, and was responsible for sending two more book reviews his way.[16] "Schwabenstreich," a review of *Mozart on the Way to Prague*, by Eduard Moerike, was published in March. Beckett called the book "not merely a betrayal of itself; it is a violation of its subject," and the only good he could say was that it was "at least short, which is nowadays so rare a quality in a literary work that one cannot refrain from commending [it]."

In June, the *Spectator* carried his "Proust in Pieces," a review of *Comment Proust a composé son roman* by Albert Feuillerat. He criticizes Professor Feuillerat for seeking to impose ". . . the sweet reasonableness of plane psychology à la Balzac," upon Proust, and says, "It is almost as though Proust should be reproached for not having written a social *Voyage of the Beagle*."

Before he gave up completely on literary journalism, Beckett wrote four other reviews which were published in the *Bookman*. Under the name Andrew Belis he wrote an article called "Recent Irish Poetry," which was published in the summer issue.[17] The pseudonym was necessary for several reasons, the most important that this issue also carried his short story "A Case in a Thousand." Also the article made statements which were bound to rankle many persons in Dublin whom Beckett could not afford to offend. He still believed, even though the evidence was quite to the contrary, that he would be able to make a substantial income from literary journalism, and he thought it best to write under several names so that editors would be more likely to pass commissions his way and the public would not grow tired of seeing his name.

In the article on Irish poetry, Beckett divided contemporary poets into two classes: antiquarians and others, with the former in the majority. Of these, he has nothing kind to say. The latter, who "evince awareness of the new thing that has happened, namely the breakdown of the object . . . [the] rupture of the lines of communication . . ." receive his praise. These are the artists, Beckett states, who are aware of the vacuum which exists between perceiver and the thing perceived, an early portent of *Film*, where the printed script begins with Beckett's observation, esse est percipi:

> [The artist] may state the space that intervenes between him and the world of objects; he may state it as a no-man's land, Hellespont or vacuum, according as he happens to be feeling resentful, nostalgic or merely depressed.

As antiquarians, Beckett includes James Stephens, Oliver St. John Gogarty, Austin Clarke, Brian O'Higgins and others. The latter group includes McGreevy, Brian Coffey and Denis Devlin—already his friends—and Niall Sheridan, (Percy) Arland Ussher and Niall Montgomery, soon to become so.

The other three reviews all appeared under his own name in the last published issue of the *Bookman* in December.[18] He wrote an honest but appreciative review of Pound's *Make It New*, in which he declared that Apollinaire's *Chansons du mal-aimé* was more valuable than the entire output of the Symbolist writers. He summed up Pound's book as "a galvanic belt of essays, education by provocation, Spartan Maieutics."

"Papini's Dante" was his title for *Dante Vivo* by Giovanni Papini. He describes Papini as having written ". . . Marginalia . . . [for] the reduction of Dante to lovable proportions." Because of his admiration for Dante, Beckett was somewhat unjust in his accusation that Papini misrepresents Dante, once again revealing his own preferences in otherwise objective writing.

Beckett called his review of Sean O'Casey's *Windfalls* "The Essential and the Incidental," and dismissed the stories and verse as inferior to O'Casey's farces. Beckett calls O'Casey

> a master of knockabout in this very serious and honourable sense—that he discerns the principle of disintegration in even the most complacent solidities.

He cites *Juno and the Paycock* as O'Casey's best work thus far, because "it communicates most fully the dramatic dehiscence, mind and world come asunder in irreparable dissociation." It is quite likely that Beckett put his admiration for these qualities in O'Casey's writings to good use when he himself turned to drama.

Beckett's intention in moving to London had been to support himself with journalism while doing his own creative writing, but intention and reality were very far apart. In the first eight months of 1934, he published seven book reviews, one article, one poem ("Home Olga") and the collection *More Pricks Than Kicks*, the last two previously written. In eight months he had been able to write only one four-line poem, "Gnome," and one short story, "A Case in a Thousand." O'Sullivan published "Gnome" in the same issue of *Dublin Magazine* in which Beckett's review of McGreevy's *Poems* had appeared. Beckett said he was inspired to write it by Goethe's "Xenien," and that it was typical of his attitudes toward himself at this time:

> *Spend the years of learning squandering*
> *Courage for the years of wandering*
> *Through the world politely turning*
> *From the loutishness of learning.*[19]

The only other poetry he was able to produce was the finished version of "Serena I," which he first began to write in 1932, but which was not published until 1935 in *Echo's Bones*.

His analysis, moving along at a sustained pace, was causing him to think about himself in new ways, and this is perhaps one reason why his output was so limited. It is also perhaps partially the reason that someone as reticent as Beckett should have revealed so much of himself in these reviews, which were ostensibly impersonal writings. Each contains at least one personal statement or idea more in keeping with Beckett's concerns than with the book he is reviewing, and all show a writer still groping toward a viable creative statement for his own work. John Fletcher correctly notes that Beckett is "guilty of a certain arch flippancy, and betrays an oddly defensive manner in this as in other pieces of journalism."[20] This "flippancy" was probably a subconscious camouflage he affected to conceal the true tenderness of his personal feelings and emotions, but it was also an intellectual rejection of writing that seemed to him flawed. He has never been able to abide fuzzy thinking, in his own work or others', and much of what he reviewed seemed to have its basis for being in the crass roots of commercialism.

The other creative work, "A Case in a Thousand," seems in many respects to be Beckett's way of using his analysis creatively. It is the story of a Doctor Nye, and an encounter between him and his old nanny, Mrs. Bray, whose son is hospitalized with empyema. Although there is no clearly defined reason given in the story for or against surgery, the time has come when Dr. Nye must decide whether or not to operate, and he is unable to reach a decision. To facilitate it, Dr. Nye grasps the boy's wrist and stretches out full-length alongside the boy on the bed, where he falls into a trance.

The relationship between Dr. Nye and Mrs. Bray is fraught with unstated feelings, but the reader is told only that Dr. Nye had loved her when he was a child. She has been sitting silently by her son's bedside, and when she sees Dr. Nye in the trance, she forces herself to look at her son instead, then shuts her eyes completely.

When the moment passes and Dr. Nye has "reintegrated his pathological outlook," he is irritated to discover that Mrs. Bray has seen the entire episode. Abruptly, his irritation becomes regret that he has no peppermint creams to offer her, as he remembers how much she liked them when he was a child. He makes the decision for lung surgery, and a surgeon (aptly named Bor) is called in to perform it. The boy dies. Dr. Nye goes off to take a short holiday at a seaside resort. When he returns, he is told that Mrs. Bray has begun to spend every day on the embankment across the canal from the hospital, where, carrying an umbrella and a shooting stick, she appears to be keeping a vigil. At the end of this day, as she is crossing the canal to go home, Dr. Nye confronts her on the bridge, and tells her he has been wanting to ask her something. She replies, wondering if it is the same thing she has been wanting to ask since she saw him on her son's bed. Then she relates something from his youth that the narrator decides need not be enlarged upon.

The story ends abruptly with Dr. Nye presenting Mrs. Bray with a small box of peppermint creams and leaving to perform a Wassermann test on an old school friend.

The story contains the same equivocal erotic attitudes toward women first introduced with Belacqua in *Dream* and *More Pricks*. Dr. Nye's fascination with Mrs. Bray as a mother-sweetheart, his longing for his childhood and the curious womb-like evocation of the bizarre incident of the bed all seem to be clumsy attempts to integrate his real-life attitudes towards his mother with his fiction. In Beckett's subsequent fiction and drama, Dr. Nye will give way to the single-name narrators and these themes will occur repeatedly in more subtle forms, but here they are only strangely disquieting.

In early June, 1934, Beckett decided to take up George Reavey's offer to publish a collection of his poems in the Europa Press. Reavey, still living in Paris, had gone into the publishing business in a small room just above a Russian bookstore at 13 rue Bonaparte. From there he sent letters to all his friends, inviting them to submit their writings—and their money as well—to help defray publishing costs. Reavey had extended an invitation to Beckett earlier in the year, but Beckett ignored the offer because he was sure that he could find a commercial publisher for his work. He was confident that *More Pricks* would sell well enough that Chatto and Windus would want to keep him as one of their authors, but this did not happen. Rather than expose himself to rejection by other commercial publishers, Beckett decided to allow Reavey to bring out the poems even though he would have to pay for them. He reasoned that he could send what he hoped would be a highly successful "slim volume" with excellent reviews to many publishers, who would then compete in inviting him to allow them to publish his next book.

In giving Reavey the go-ahead, he expressed his feelings for his rejection by Chatto and Windus in scathing terms, calling them "Shatupon and Windup."[21] He invoked all the whores of Olympus to be favorable to the venture, and said that it didn't much matter what happened to the poems once printed—he could always wipe his auxiliary lips (i.e., anus) with them in the saddest winter of his "fecontent," punning on fecal matter and discontent. Like most of his scatological correspondence, he wrote this letter in French, and it became his habit when corresponding with friends to communicate his angriest, most venomous thoughts in a foreign language—usually French, but sometimes German.

Depressed, and in what he was to call later "a confused state,"[22] Beckett began to gather his poems. The thirteen he selected were written during a period of years in a variety of places and circumstances which Beckett noted in his own volume beneath eleven of the poems.[23] In the order in which the poems appear, the notations are as follows: "The Vulture," Beckett writes, is "not without reference to Goethe's Den geiergleich etc." "Enueg I," the poem he wrote when Peggy Sinclair was dying, bears his notation "Canal Dublin at Portobello Bridge and thence west one day that . . ." "Enueg II," with its Judas image, was written during the time of his resignation from Trinity, and has no notation. "Alba," his poem of homage to Ethna MacCarthy, he notes as "39 Trinity College Dublin," his rooms when they were both students and where they sometimes held trysts. "Dortmunder" he calls simply "Kassel revisited." "Sanies I," the poem he wrote during Easter weekend, 1933, carries the note "Exitus Redditus this evening Montparnasse 1957," which probably refers to Dr. Jacob Schwartz,[24] the dealer to whom he sold the book. "Sanies II" is his recollection of the Café Mahieu and carries the notation "École Normale Paris 1929." "Serena I," he calls "London/ World's End," and "Serena II" is "Glencullen—Prince Williams's Seat Enniskerry"—his favorite walk in all of Ireland and the one he was most likely to take when setting off from Cooldrinagh.[25]

These nine poems were written before and during 1934, and were supposed to comprise the total content of the volume, but Reavey did not work as fast as Beckett would have liked, and as time dragged on, he wrote and added the last four poems to the book. "Serena III" bears the notation "James Barry," but has a decidedly Irish setting, as it retraces another walk Beckett often took late at night in Dublin when he was drunk and depressed. "Malacoda," the poem about his father's death, gave him an inordinate amount of trouble to write, and he worked over it almost to the date of printing. In a small neat hand at the end of it, he has written the word "father." Under "Da Tagte Es" he has written "Walther von der Vogelweide," with the final syllable of the last name encircled and followed by a question mark. "Echo's Bones," the last poem and the one which gave the volume its name, bears his note "Echo's Bones were turned to Stone. Ovid's Metamorphoses?"

These poems vary in length from four to seventy-six lines. Unlike *Whoroscope*, each is intensely personal, often elliptic and obscure, but they all show a conscious striving for perfection. For example, the six poems that carry Provençal titles— Enueg, Alba and Serena—show the care and exactitude with which Beckett worked to imitate the older forms. His debt to Dante appears in "Malacoda," who is both Dante's deceitful demon (*Inferno* XXI.76) and Beckett's name for the undertaker (also deceitful) at his father's funeral. In the three derivative poems, "Echo's Bones," "Da Tagte Es" and "The Vulture," he has made his own personal statement while once again adhering to the form of the originals.

The poems in *Echo's Bones* have been relatively neglected by critics because Beckett has not bothered to note when he wrote them or offer any biographical explanation to make them more accessible. They are often dismissed as immature and derivative. They are heavily dependent on other writers, for form, idea and style, as if Beckett is hesitant to eschew imitation and allow his own voice to be heard. None of the poems has the abrasive pedantry of *Whoroscope;* some of the images are shocking, some painful; others range from seamy to delicate. Nevertheless, as examples of his life and his attitudes during the years in which they were written, they are personal statements marked by intelligence and sensitivity. It is not a volume to dismiss lightly.

Beckett seems to be of two minds about *Echo's Bones.* To Lawrence Harvey he said they were "the work of a very young man with nothing to say and the itch to make." Harvey writes that Beckett "deplores their self-consciousness and display of literary and artistic erudition, which he terms 'showing off.' "[26] But several years later Hugh Kenner wrote that the poems in *Echo's Bones* "seem to constitute the only early work he values at all."[27]

This second view seems truer of the two; Beckett has many other poems, published and unpublished, which he has refused to allow anyone to collect and publish in the years since he has become famous, and yet he always allows *Echo's Bones* to be translated and to appear in as many editions as his publishers wish to bring out.

Once he had decided on private publication, his problem was to find the money to pay for printing costs. He decided to move out of Paulton's Square and go home to Cooldrinagh for what was outwardly a holiday, but in truth an economy measure. He arrived on August 2, 1934, after a rough crossing during which he was almost incapacitated by persistent urinary and bladder pains, to find his mother in a state of nervous irritation brought on by the exuberant high spirits of Sheila Roe Page's two children,[28] who, with their mother, had come for a holiday.

May Beckett still kept the house in a state of deep mourning, even though her husband had been dead for more than a year.[29] She had worn black since Bill's death, and would continue to do so until the end of her life. She kept the curtains drawn, spoke in a hushed voice and insisted on reverential behavior from everyone who entered Cooldrinagh, as if her husband's body still lay in the next room. She took the sound of the children's laughter, their games and their happiness as a personal affront. Although she tried to convey what Beckett called an attitude of "luf and hom," her impatience showed, and Mrs. Page was anxious to end the visit as quickly as possible before the children created too many "flicks in the sacred mausoleum."[30]

Beckett found all this highly amusing, and boasted to McGreevy that the analysis had helped him enormously to deal with situations like this. He was delighted to see that he could maintain the necessary distance from the situation to be able to find amusement in his mother's behavior without being drawn into any overt display of petulant behavior of his own. He found himself actually capable of being nice to people, no matter who they were or what they wanted from him, and he was pleased that the privacy he had always maintained could now be put to positive use as a protective covering that would allow him to appear to be taking part in the life of Cooldrinagh while actually keeping himself separate from it.

Nevertheless, this detachment must not have been as successful as he boasted, for in the very same letter, he wrote that the only measures which alleviated his physical disabilities were large quantities of "dope" (probably sleeping pills) and sleeping in the same bed with Frank. Long conversations during walks with Geoffrey Thompson helped also, for Beckett was finally able to accept Thompson's diagnosis, that the night panics and irrational fears were indeed psychoneurotic. Once he had accepted this diagnosis, he was in a hurry to get back to Bion to go on with the analysis, but he had taken a cheap excursion ticket and was obligated to stay in Ireland until mid-September.

Armed with the confidence that he could meet people, Beckett spent a fairly social time during this month, which inevitably caused some dissension with his mother. He spent long solitary afternoons in the National Gallery, made discreet visits to the Dublin pubs, where he behaved so circumspectly that his former confreres wondered what had happened to change him, and kept himself on an even keel by talking to Thompson. He wrote to Cissie Sinclair asking her to see him, and was astonished when she sent her consent personally via Boss, who appeared on the doorstep of Cooldrinagh fortified by a long session in the Bailey Pub. May was furious—first because she disapproved of all the Sinclairs and especially disliked Boss, but also on this occasion because of Boss's high spirits and drink-inspired conviviality. His rollicking invasion of the sepulchral confines of Cooldrinagh was her excuse to go into one of her whining, self-pitying tantrums. These poses always worked to bind Beckett to her, even though acceding to her demands always produced white-hot rage and shame in him that he bottled up unsuccessfully until he exploded in some form of physical violence.

May began to attack his defenses. She seized on the idea of renting Cooldrinagh for an extended period and taking a flat in London. Although she said she would live alone there, Beckett knew this was only a prelude to an eventual request for him to move in with her; but since leaving Cooldrinagh meant that Frank could have a life of his own, he was reluctant to dismiss it out of hand.

There was no question that he felt a terrible guilt at leaving Frank with full responsibility for their mother. He wrote to McGreevy of the desperation of Frank's acceptance of everything that happened in his life without ever taking any sort of action to be in control of his own destiny. Beckett watched his brother secretly, horrified to see a man who was so unaware of himself that he seemed to exist only to fill the needs of anyone who wanted to use him. Beckett's guilt at contributing to his brother's sorry state was mitigated by his ferocious desire to be in control of his own life, to overthrow the demands of May once and for all.

May did not give up easily, and when whining and begging failed, she resorted to reason and marshaled all her arguments to persuade him to stay. But he was not deterred, and on September 2, when his ticket expired, he sailed back to London. For the first time he was completely on his own there, for McGreevy was on an extended visit with his mother and sisters at their home in Tarbert, County Kerry.

Living at Paulton's Square had not been pleasant for Beckett; the landlady was brusque and it always seemed to Beckett that she considered him an intrusion, even in his own room, so he decided to strike out and find new lodgings. He read the newspaper advertisements for furnished rooms until he came upon one that cost the same as Paulton's Square.

The house at 34 Gertrude Street in the World's End district, was run by Mr. and Mrs. Fred Frost—he a retired
chauffeur, and she, called Queeney, a former maid;[31] their son,
Fred Frost, Jr., a dentist's mechanic, served as general handyman
around the house. Mrs. Frost was Irish, born in Athlone, and she
swept Beckett up into the family as if he were not only a long-
lost countryman but a dear relative as well. Beckett had the run
of the kitchen and fell into the habit of taking his tea there, with
Mrs. Frost encouraging him to eat as much of her homemade
jams and jellies as he liked and to read the family copy of the
Weekly Telegraph as long as he wanted. When he asked hesitantly for a reading lamp, Fred, Jr., rigged one in his room,
while Mrs. Frost encouraged him to play the tuneless piano in
the front parlor. Beckett liked Mrs. Frost, calling her a "mother
on draught," because he could turn her ministrations off or on at
will. He had only to say he was feeling low, and she would
appear with a cup of Sanatogen (a popular tonic) or hot tea, and
when he said he preferred Lapsang souchong instead of Lipton's, she invited him to keep his tin in the kitchen, even though
she had never heard of it and thought it a bit fancy. His room
was large, airy and full of light, and his only complaint was the
frequent sounds of connubial bliss that filtered down through
his ceiling during the day from the tenants above, a waiter at the
Cadogan and his parlormaid wife. He felt so comfortable that he
expected he would be able to turn to his writing with ease. The
Bookman editors had told him before his holiday that they
might be interested in an article discussing censorship in Ireland,
and although he would have preferred to be writing fiction, he
dutifully set his hand to it.[32] Nothing much seemed forthcoming, however, and by the time he was ensconced in Gertrude Street, he had no enthusiasm for it, even though he kept
trying dutifully.

Since McGreevy was not there to do it for him, he had to
telephone the *Bookman* office himself and did so in a highly
anxious state, only to find they had no reviews for him. The
rejection provoked a long letter to McGreevy full of revulsion
for them and for the Irish social scene he had just left. He railed
against the mechanistic age in which he found himself living and
praised what he called the deanthropomorphization of the artist.

He was in complete accord with painters who chose to portray human beings as blobs of color and form because he thought this intensified the dehumanization of mankind, emphasizing how hermetic and alone he really was. People, he thought, were totally alone; there was no community of thought and feeling, only the inner man had any importance. Each was as alien to all others as to a protoplast or God, incapable of loving or hating anyone but himself, or of being loved or hated by anyone but himself.[33]

These were bitter thoughts, and as the year drew to an end, his bitterness increased. He was convinced that analysis had brought him as far as he could go, and, disappointingly, that was not far enough. He still suffered from a variety of aches and pains; he was often very lonely. Occasionally he went to Mrs. Dowden's, where he had become friendly with some of the people who lived in her house, but they, like him, were often moody and petulant, and going there usually produced so much anger and hostility that he decided he would be better off staying away, especially when Mrs. Dowden's maid contrived excuses about the piano tuner's instructions and would not allow him to play the wonderful grand piano, one of his few pleasures. All he had to look forward to was compiling *Echo's Bones*, a hollow pleasure since he had to forgo so many creature comforts to pay for it. He liked to go to concerts and movies, but these were pleasures he had to give up for the time being. He could only go to art galleries and museums on free afternoons or when the rate was reduced. He even had to give up his Lapsang and dinner out and make do with Lipton and sausage and egg in Queeney's kitchen. Worst of all, he could no longer spend long hours in the Seven Bells, his "local," but only went into pubs when he happened across someone who would pay.

Occasionally he had a brief therapeutic encounter with women, usually from the neighborhood, all of whom he melded into the composite character of Celia when he wrote *Murphy* the following year. There was a more serious, lasting episode with a woman who became pregnant (but not by him), which became the basis for the story *Premier Amour* (*First Love*), written in 1946 but withheld from publication until 1970, "when the woman in question was dead."[34]

But mostly he was lonely, disappointed and faced with long stretches of empty time because he could not write. He turned again to Schopenhauer, read Nietzsche and contemplated the futility, sterility and boredom of his life, while waiting and hoping for something to happen.

CHAPTER NINE

1935:

"TIME TO PULL THE PLUG ON LONDON"

 At the end of August, 1935, Queeney Frost raised a celebratory cup of tea in Beckett's honor to commemorate the one year he had been lodging in Gertrude Street. Silently and fervently, Beckett prayed that he would never again have a year like the one he had just lived through.[1] The worst of it began with his annual Christmas visit to his mother. May assaulted him with whining and tears, then retreated behind hostile silences; as usual, he was powerless to act when she was this way. She was disappointed to see him in much the same physical state as during his previous visit. She decided the analysis was a dismal failure, then implored him to pull himself together, stand on his own two feet, and prove himself a man![2] "Pauvre madonna," he thought, but said nothing, knowing all comment was useless.[3]

In the midst of her imprecations, he received an adulatory letter from a Dublin man named John Coghlan who had read *Proust* and wanted to know if Beckett had written anything else. This letter thrilled May, and she took it away from him; it was tangible proof that he was a writer after all. Beckett snickered and sent the man a copy of *More Pricks* knowing it would shock him and silence the mouth of praise.[4]

Yet the letter so cheered him that it gave him the courage not only to withstand May's diatribes but to try to explain to her that living in London was a necessity and not a luxury. But

again it was useless. Since Bill's death, May seemed bent on two
things: maintaining his memory, so much so that her friends had
grown weary of her company; and keeping Beckett with her in
Cooldrinagh. As if she had to prove something to the friends,
neighbors and relatives who had deserted her, May maintained
the standard of living she had enjoyed while Bill was alive, and
was living far beyond her income.[5] Beckett could not talk to
Frank about this because he came home late each night to sleep a
few hours and slipped off early in the morning without seeing
anyone but the cook, who made his breakfast. Frank managed to
avoid the confrontations between Beckett and May by spending
long hours at the office, then going to dance halls and pubs.
Beckett worried that Frank was drowning himself in work and
drink, but his own precarious hold on health and freedom kept
him from initiating the sort of conversation that might have
effected some change in all their lives.

To get away from May, Beckett went to Howth for a
weekend with Cissie and Boss, with his mother's screams ringing
in his ears. Boss and Cissie were still not entirely over their anger
with Beckett for using Peggy's letter, but once they had seen the
wretched condition he'd been in ever since Bill's death, it was
impossible for two such good and gentle people to withhold
their affection and understanding. Once again their home became his refuge. There he had an anxiety attack that left him
virtually paralyzed, and terrified all the Sinclairs. He managed to
crawl back to Cooldrinagh where he came down with what was
officially diagnosed as pleurisy.[6] Even though it kept him in bed
for a week, it improved his state of mind because he was always
better when he could blame his ill health on something having
physical origins. In fact, his entire disposition improved so much
that he was actually brave enough to go into Dublin.

One of his first acts was to visit Rudmose-Brown, ill in
Richmond Hospital. Rudmose-Brown sent him on an errand to
Trinity College, his first time there since his resignation. It gave
him the courage to go regularly to the College library. He began
to walk through the crowded, crooked streets of central Dublin,
seeing them as he had never seen them before. Street scenes filled
him with poetic images and renewed a longing to write that he
thought had left him forever.[7] He was struck especially by

Dominic Street, where the pale winter sunlight trickled down on the eighteenth-century houses with their conglomeration of chimney pots and stacks and on the people he saw there, whom he called the human comedians. He found the space and light, after the darkness and misery he equated with London, to be truly magnificent.

Yet the sights he saw were not really beautiful: in fact, they were the ordinary sights that he had formerly despised. He was full of contradictions about Dublin, neglecting his usual fastidious sensibilities to revel in the prodigious smells of the streets and the people who inhabited these warrens. He was saturating himself with sensations and images because he did not know how much longer he could last in London; but he did not know either if he could maintain his precarious hold on sanity if he came back to Dublin.

When he tired of walking through the city, he climbed the hills of Glencullen to the old lead mines, where the air was so still that sounds carried from the houses in the valley far below and he could see the distant sea before him, and behind, the pink and green sunsets he loved and found only in Ireland.

Throughout this holiday he had been halfheartedly setting up a study in an unused bedroom in Cooldrinagh. A carpenter had put up shelves for his books, and he had moved some of the things he loved from his bedroom in the hopes of making the study a more pleasing place to write. These small acts increased his nighttime torments instead of soothing them, so that he lay awake in panic waiting for daybreak and escape from his sweaty, rumpled bed.[8] Nevertheless, he kept trying to create a quiet place to work.

He had begun to write a story during the fall of 1934 in London. It was about a young man, a down-and-out intellectual similar to himself, who lived in the World's End with a prostitute he had picked up off the street there. During the course of the year, it gradually evolved into the novel *Murphy*. He had written the first sixteen hundred words in London, but since coming to Cooldrinagh he had written nothing. Still, he had an intuitive feeling that he would be able to pick it up again soon and finish it, no matter where he was living.

At the end of January, 1935, his cheap excursion fare ticket expired and he returned to London and Gertrude Street, following Bion's instructions not to stay with his mother one day longer than the duration of the ticket. He had serious doubts about continuing with Bion, and seemed to find inordinate pleasure in tabloid accounts of poor unfortunates bled white by shyster analysts, but nevertheless he made arrangements to resume as soon as possible.

The usual feeling of relief and vitality that accompanied his departure from Cooldrinagh lasted through his first week in London, and then the familiar feelings of worthlessness, sordidness and incapacitation beset him. On February 8, 1935, he noted that he was about to complete his one hundred and thirty-third session with Bion, a never-ending "squabble."[9] Every time he thought he was improving, his heart pounded erratically, he was unable to breathe and he suffered agonizing pains in his chest. He was sure he had angina pectoris, and would die any moment, victim of the same disease that had killed his father. When he confided these fears to Thompson, he received only an enigmatic smile and a polite, murmured denial.[10] He wanted to consult a physician but was embarrassed and afraid he would be told all his symptoms were psychosomatic.

McGreevy, still in Tarbert, was disturbed by Beckett's long, neurotic letters, and begged him to take the time to write an accurate, detailed account of all that had happened to him during his analysis and whatever else he felt might be of use in sorting out his true feelings. Beckett's reply filled six large sheets of paper with densely packed handwriting.[11] No doubt Beckett meant to write a thoughtful, cogent letter, but what he actually wrote is a confusing jumble of ideology and jargon that was not likely to please either man. McGreevy, a devout Catholic, had written of how much his faith sustained him, urging Beckett to try to believe in something. Beckett wrote back in a sarcastic vein, saying he had quite given up hope of ever finding a god to believe in, and had been unable to accept in its stead the Protestant (as opposed to orthodox Catholic) goodness that McGreevy urged upon him. He had tried to be good, Beckett said, but the sweats, shudders, furies, rages and rigors of a burst-

ing heart had not been lessened by goodness. Instead, he hoped
to find a persona within himself, among his own features and
entrails, which would provide him with a rationale for being.

Because all else had failed him, he could find no relief in
anything but what he called baroque solipsism. He also called
himself a Puritan and, in the most important part of his self-
analysis, said Puritanism comprised the simple, straightforward
and dominant part of his personality, but that he had agreed to
allow this part to be necessarily disrupted by analysis because he
could no longer function. He wrote:

> For years I was unhappy. Consciously and deliberately ever
> since I left school and went into TCD, so that I isolated myself
> more and more, undertook less and less and lent myself to a
> crescendo of disengagement of others and myself. But in all
> that, there was nothing that struck me as odd. The misery and
> solitude and apathy . . . were the elements of an index of
> superiority; guaranteed the feeling of arrogant "otherness"
> which seemed as right and natural and as little morbid as the
> ways in which it was not so much expressed as implied and ob-
> served and kept available for a possible utterance in the future.
> It was not until that way of living, or rather negation of
> living, developed such terrifying physical symptoms that it
> could no longer be pursued, that I became aware of anything
> morbid in myself. So that, if the heart had not put the fear of
> death in me, I would still be boozing and dreaming and lounging
> around feeling that I was too good for anything else.

He went on confusedly, equating his heart with a puddle
that had to be drained by repeated forays into his own prehis-
tory. In a rather sinister note, he concluded that remaining alive
might prove intolerable if the analysis should fail, but said he had
faced this fact and had been able to cope with it. He concluded
gloomily that he spent most of his time with Bion and the rest
walking.

Murphy, at this point, was horribly stalled. His mood was
not lightened by the cheerful letter his mother wrote, saying
brightly that she was quite sure he was probably brimful of ideas
for books, all just bursting to come out of him.

Because he needed money, he made another try at literary
journalism, calling on Cyril Connolly, who thought it best that

he "suffer a bit more, perhaps with a job as a dishwasher," to give him the needed experience to become a true writer.[12] He sent part of what he had already written of *Murphy* to the English publisher Lovat Dickson, who rejected it immediately. He thought of asking Edwin Muir to help him find translating assignments, but rejected the idea, as well as the thought of asking Desmond MacCarthy to help him again. He chafed because he had asked Brian Coffey to send him poems by Eluard and Jarry, which he thought of translating, but the books had not yet arrived.

To occupy his time, he began to frequent the local lending library where he decided to work his way through the English classics. He read *The Mill on the Floss*, thought Eliot's treatment of infancy commendable and was struck by how much Dickens took from her. He thought Jane Austen had much to teach him, but was disgruntled with what he called her insistent use of the cult of the home.[13] He read Ben Jonson's plays, which he found superb but of little value to him personally. Abruptly he decided that all English literature was based on banality, typification and simplification which amounted to nothing more than a mere listing of the vices and virtues. From Austen to Aldington, he proclaimed, English literature was straight out of the Chester Cycle. He turned to Balzac, marveling in *Cousine Bette* at Balzac's bathos of style and thought, claiming such a book could not possibly have been written seriously, but must surely be parody.

When not reading, he went to museums and galleries. He was entranced with Dutch painting (to McGreevy's disdain) and wanted to see all that he could. For a short time he even thought of buying some good reproductions for his room before common sense and a dwindling bank account stopped him. He had already succumbed to a small watercolor by Jack B. Yeats, for which he paid thirty shillings in a junk shop off the King's Road—for him a purchase of such expense that he scarcely survived until the next installment of money from Dublin.

An embarrassing and somewhat frightening note was injected into his aimless existence when Lucia Joyce came to London. In January he had received a rambling six-page letter from her from Zurich,[14] the language of which convinced him she had been in analysis. What most upset him was her reference to "My father the James Joyce," who she claimed had just told her the bad news of Peggy Sinclair's death, which she had actually known of since it had happened seven months before. Beckett was in an awkward situation and decided the best reply would be none at all.

At the end of February Lucia sent a note asking him to meet her in Grosvenor Place, where she was staying with her aunt in a small rented flat. She told him she was there en route to Ireland, and that it was important for her to see him at once. The memory of the break she had caused between him and her father was still fresh in Beckett's mind, and he had no intention of giving Joyce any further cause to be angry. Again, he did not reply to Lucia's letter, but made detours all over London, hoping not to encounter her. Lucia persisted, and when letters went unanswered, she began to telephone the Frosts, who grew skilled at telling her Beckett was out. After several months of erratic behavior, she grew tired of pestering him and stopped calling. He sensed correctly that something was terribly wrong with her and congratulated himself on having avoided involvement in her unhappy situation.

In late April he returned to Cooldrinagh to see whether or not he could live there permanently. He had fallen into the unfortunate pattern of running to Cooldrinagh whenever he ran low on money or whenever he could not cope with the hostility and rejection which he felt were all that he encountered in London. Bion opposed his going back to his mother whenever he was miserable, but Beckett never seems to have given Bion's dicta too much importance. (In retrospect, it seems that he followed only those of Bion's suggestions that he wanted to hear.) Nevertheless, he went doggedly on with analysis, and planned this visit to last exactly one month because Bion insisted he could not tolerate a longer time without suffering a serious setback.[15]

Because he was interested in determining if he could make a place for himself in Irish literary circles, he spent much of his visit trying to rekindle old acquaintanceships. There was a more particular reason for his doing so, however: Beckett was anxious to lay the groundwork for favorable reviews of *Echo's Bones* in all the Irish publications when it was officially published on

November 23. A. J. Leventhal entertained him, and there he forced himself to make pleasant conversation with Sean Kavanaugh and Leslie (Yodeiken) Daiken. He managed a courtesy he did not really feel when Arland Ussher told him he was translating *Utopia* into Gaelic, for Beckett believed that putting modern literature into a dead language was, at best, futile. He even went to the theater, something he had not done in Dublin for years; he went to Jammet's, the fashionable literary restaurant, but it was an unpleasant experience and he vowed he would not repeat it.

T. S. Eliot was in Dublin lecturing in conjunction with the performance of *Murder in the Cathedral* by the University of Dublin Players. Beckett attended the first lecture but avoided everything else because he resented Eliot's flippant remark that Joyce was "an unconscious tribute to a Catholic education acquired at a time when few people were educated at all."[16]

He was delighted when he called on Jack B. Yeats to find that Cottie was in bed with a cold, leaving him all alone with her husband. Yeats had just completed a new painting called *Morning*, a small canvas Beckett described succinctly as "almost a skyscape. Wide street leading into Sligo looking west as usual with a boy on a horse. £30."[17] It was a case of passion at first viewing, and he wanted it badly. What stood between him and it, of course, was the sum of thirty pounds. Beckett made no secret of his feelings, but Yeats was noncommittal. Beckett thought of asking to pay for it in installments, but did not even have the few pounds with which to make the down payment, and he dared not ask May or Frank for the money since he already owed them a considerable amount. When he and Yeats met by chance a week later in the National Library, Beckett hinted once again, but still Yeats said nothing. To show Yeats how much he appreciated all his painting, Beckett brought the King's Road watercolor to the studio and asked him to name and date it. "Probably the fish market in Sligo," Yeats said vaguely, and Beckett was too embarrassed to press further.

Racking his brain for another excuse to press politely for an invitation to take *Morning* and pay for it when he could, Beckett asked Yeats if he could bring Maurice Sinclair, Cissie and Boss's son, to visit the studio the following Saturday afternoon. Again Yeats was noncommittal, and in a burst of emotion, Beckett blurted out how much he wanted *Morning* and asked Yeats to let him pay for it over time. Yeats quietly said of course, the picture was certainly Beckett's since he obviously liked it so much, and Beckett suddenly found himself in possession of a painting for which he saw no possibility of ever paying. Shamefacedly, he asked Frank for money and received several pounds, thus bringing the total Beckett owed his brother to more than ten pounds. May supplied the rest, and Beckett found himself owing her a total of thirty-six pounds. He has treasured the painting all his life and it has hung prominently in every place he has ever lived, but he acquired it at terrible cost, for his mother was once again at the center of command of his existence. Owing that much money made it incredibly difficult to oppose her. Now she talked constantly about coming to London to take a room in Gertrude Street where she could be close enough to look after him.[18]

Naturally this induced another outbreak of boils and nighttime tremors.[19] A sebaceous cyst formed on his neck, in the same spot as the "anthrax" which had plagued him for years. Another formed inside his anus, causing intolerable pain. He was forced into a humiliating consultation with Dr. Alan Thompson, who recommended hospitalization for immediate surgery. Beckett reluctantly agreed but was saved when the anal cyst ruptured that same day.

Sadly, he was forced to conclude that Bion was probably right: he was still unable to arrive at any understanding or acceptance of his relationship with his mother, nor could he tolerate living with her in the same house for longer than a week or two at a time. Still, he was determined to work at making this holiday end on a positive note.[20] He rented a car and, forcing himself to be good-humored, took his mother to visit cemeteries— first his father's grave, where she planted heather, oblivious to the bitter northeast wind and the boiling sea, and then the graves of grandparents and other relatives. Synge's *Deirdre of the Sorrows* was playing at the Abbey, and he suggested taking her, even though he detested the play, but she was shocked that he would suggest such entertainment when she was still, in her phrase, "alertly grieving."

Once again he found escape in the National Gallery or with the Sinclairs. They were in dire straits now, and Cissie turned to him with a sense of need he hadn't known since his father's terminal illness. With Peggy dead and Sallie in England, Boss and Cissie had Nancy, Deirdre and Maurice at home. Maurice had been in tenuous health since the family's flight from Germany, and in the hope that he would improve, Geoffrey Thompson prescribed a long stay in a more hospitable climate, so Maurice was about to leave for a village in Spain. Boss had tried to make a living at the antiques shop, and seemed on the verge of succeding when he discovered that he, too, had tuberculosis.

At first Cissie insisted on trying to care for him at home, but as his condition grew swiftly worse, she consented to having him enter a sanitarium in Newcastle, County Wicklow. Boss was possessed of an overactive sense of responsibility and his health was not improved by excessive worry about his family. Besides tuberculosis, he suffered from a heart murmur, palpitations and a severe case of nervousness.

The Sinclairs had no car, and so Beckett volunteered to use the rented car to take Cissie to see Boss at least twice each week. Cissie had not been well either and had been hospitalized several times recently for the crippling rheumatoid arthritis that eventually took her life. The strain was enormous, and several times she broke down, blaming her tears on grief for Peggy. But Beckett knew better; she was grieving for the living and not for the daughter dead in Germany.

This was the second time in his life that Beckett had been needed by someone, and as he had when his father died, he responded admirably. When he helped Cissie to adjust to Boss's hospitalization, his health improved, his mood brightened and he became imbued with a confidence that lasted as long as he had to console the Sinclair family. Once they had settled down into a routine that no longer required his almost constant attendance, his good spirits quickly dissipated and he was as depressed as he had ever been.

Murphy simply would not allow itself to be written, and he despaired of ever writing anything else. Rea Mooney, a popular actress at the Abbey Theatre, asked him for a poem to read during a radio broadcast and although he was so pleased that he wanted to write a new one for her, he could not even select one previously written. He was sure she felt he had affronted her and went out of his way to avoid her for the rest of his stay in Ireland.

Unable to write, he plunged into Italian literature and began to read a pile of books left in Cissie's house by a departing tenant. For a time he concentrated on Manzoni, Varchi, Giusti, and Machiavelli's plays, but he soon tired of reading Italian and turned to books on cinema which he borrowed from Niall Montgomery.[21]

He read books by and about Pudovkin, Arnheim and Eisenstein, and as many issues of the journal *Close-Up* as he could find. Suddenly he was filled with a new excitement and sense of mission: He would go to Moscow to study with Eisenstein! He had never been cut out to be a writer anyway, he rationalized in a long letter to McGreevy.[22] Perhaps work as a cameraman was what he had been intended for all along—certainly no harm could come of a year in Moscow learning the fine points of cinematic photography. He went to see a local expert, "father of Jelly Fitzgerald," who used a sixteen-millimeter camera and projector, but Beckett was disappointed to find that although the elder Fitzgerald was familiar with the methods of creating photographic montage and illusion, he had no interest in them and refused to teach them to Beckett. This convinced him that he needed to apprentice himself to a major studio to learn the latest techniques; but the time had come to leave Cooldrinagh and return to London and, like so many of his other ideas, this one was superseded by the activity or demand of the moment.

Yet he continued to talk about going to Moscow for more than a year, usually when he was casting around desperately for some direction to give his life. In the summer of 1936, when he was particularly depressed, he actually wrote to Eisenstein and suggested that he come to Moscow at his own expense and live there for a year as the master's unpaid apprentice, doing whatever Eisenstein wanted him to do. Eisenstein did not reply, and Beckett turned his attentions to Pudovkin. From him he hoped to learn how to edit film and perfect the zoom technique. He wrote a long letter, saying he wanted to revive the naturalistic,

two-dimensional silent film, which he felt had died unjustly before its time. Even though dramatic advances in color and sound
had been made in motion pictures by this time, Beckett had little
interest in them and preferred to concentrate on techniques of
the rudimentary silent film, unquestionably a major influence on
his own dramatic technique as well as on his one film script.

In spring, just as he was becoming convinced that he would
never be able to finish *Murphy*, something happened to release
whatever had been inhibiting his creative processes: Geoffrey
Thompson had come to England to begin a psychiatric residency at the Bethlehem Royal Hospital in Beckenham, on the
border of Kent and Surrey. Beckett had had no idea how to
move the novel beyond the early scenes in Murphy's boarding
house in the World's End. Now with Thompson close at hand to
provide documentation, Beckett conceived the central chapters,
in which Murphy takes a job in an institution loosely patterned
after the Bethlehem Royal Hospital.

"Lest an action for libel should lie," Beckett told John
Fletcher, "The Bethlehem Royal Hospital served only as a point
of departure of the Magdalen Mental Mercy Seat of *Murphy*."[23]

He went down to Beckenham several times that spring but
was unable to do more than snatch a brief visit with Thompson
in an occasional hour off duty. Beckett was anxious to be taken
on a tour of the wards so that he could examine the patients
firsthand, and Thompson promised to try to sneak him in sometime when no senior attendants were there. Just as it seemed this
might happen, all work on *Murphy* came to a halt when May
once again actively entered his life.

She had been out of sorts, she wrote, and thought a visit to
England would be just the thing to set her right again.[24]

In an almost insultingly insinuating tone, she said she knew
how busy he was with his writing and would not dream of
taking him away from it without some sort of compensation. In
return for his companionship for one month, she agreed to pay
him a large enough sum of money to make it well worth his
while. Nearly destitute, he agreed. In late July, she crossed to
England, and they began a month-long holiday that took them
from Devon on the south coast, to Gloucester, and north to her
brother's home in Newark, Nottinghamshire. He left her there

and returned to London via Litchfield, where he made a pilgrimage to Samuel Johnson's birthplace. The month passed
without incident because he had had the foresight to take along
large quantities of sleeping pills which knocked him out each
night and kept him dazed during the greater part of the day.
The rest of the time he spent swimming, sometimes as often as
three times daily.[25]

When he returned to Gertrude Street he was surprised to
find a letter from Simon and Schuster, the New York publishers,
asking him to send all his published writings because they were
interested in bringing them out in American editions. He asked
Chatto and Windus to send *Proust* and *More Pricks* and urged
Reavey to send *Echo's Bones* the minute the first copy was
bound. He was still rewriting "Malacoda" while waiting nervously for page proofs, even though he was convinced it could
never be a real poem but only an emotional response to the
repressed pain and anger he felt at his father's death.

He felt that Reavey was taking too long to bring out the
book and attributed this to Reavey's overextending himself in
too many enterprises. But as long as there was still time, he
decided to register several complaints. "I hope the *Bones* are not
covered in the canary of your prospectus," he wrote angrily. "If
this is your dastardly intention and the covers have not been put
in hand, be an angel and change it to *PUTTY* [Beckett's
emphasis]."[26]

One reason Reavey took so long was because he planned to
combine poetry with art in each Europa Press volume—thus
splitting the cost between writer and artist. For Beckett's book
he suggested that Stanley William Hayter submit engravings, but
Beckett was adamantly against it. He did not want the effect of
his poetry to be either diminished or enhanced by anyone else's
creation, and so he bore the entire cost of the volume himself.

He tried to write other poems during this time, poems
which he labeled "involuntarily trivial," and which have either
been incorporated into other works, abandoned or destroyed.[27]

The weather was so beautiful in London that fall that
Beckett spent long afternoons at Round Pond in Hyde Park,
where legions of elderly kite flyers gathered each day. He was
moved to declare that he wanted to live his entire life in a haze

of perpetual Septembers.[28] *Murphy* was still stalled. He tried to inspire himself by watching the shabby old men who arrived with their kites dismantled into separate pieces, each carefully wrapped. The old men lovingly assembled the kites in time for the first gust of wind to carry them so high above the rooftops of London that birds often were sighted flying far below them. Every so often the men tugged gently on the strings, as if to keep the kites from losing height, and when the afternoon light began to fade, they pulled them gently in, dismantled the kites and left the park as the guard called, "All out, all out."

The sight so moved Beckett that, no matter what happened within the pages of his novel, he knew it would end at Round Pond with one or several old men flying kites:

> My next old man, or old young man, not of the big world, but of the little world, must be a kite flyer. So absolutely disinterested, like a poem, or useful in the depths where demand and supply coincide, and the prayer is the god. Yes, prayer rather than poem, in order to be quite clear.[29]

He was steadily amassing characters for the novel. A neighbor on Gertrude Street became "The Old Boy." This was a man who lived in the opposite building who was reputed to have been in domestic service and was in the habit of looking out his window at the activity on the street, resting his shaving mug on the windowsill while he lathered his face. Sometimes, on sunny days, he drank his tea there, again resting his cup on the sill; often he left crusts of bread there for the birds. One day Beckett saw The Old Boy escorted from the house by several policemen, charged with an unspecified felony; he never returned to Gertrude Street, but his cup remained on the windowsill where he had left it and occasionally a bird flew down to pick at the moldering scraps of bread.

Now he had Murphy, Celia, The Old Boy and one or several kite flyers. He had scenes set in the World's End, Round Pond and a still-unnamed mental hospital. What faced him was to link them up within the framework of the narrative. The analysis was (in Beckett's opinion) still limping along, and he had almost reached the point where he felt strong enough to tell Bion that he wanted to end it after Christmas, 1935, since he felt the results were hardly in keeping with the expenditure of time and money.[30]

Bion must have sensed this, because one day in October, he astonished Beckett by proposing that they meet for dinner several nights later and then go on to the Tavistock Clinic to hear a lecture by Jung.

Jung, then sixty years old, gave five lectures in the Tavistock series, from September 5 to October 4, 1935.[31] Beckett attended the third lecture and it had a powerful impact on him. Jung spoke of association tests and their importance in the analysis of dreams. He said that unity of consciousness was an illusion, citing the tendency of a complex to "form a little personality of itself:"

> Because complexes have a certain will power, a sort of ego, we find that in a schizophrenic condition they emancipate themselves from conscious control to such an extent that they become visible and audible. They appear as visions, they speak in voices which are like the voices of definite people. (p. 80)

Since complexes could live their lives apart from the intentions of the person in whom they exist, Jung believed that the personal unconscious consisted of an unknown number of complexes, or what he termed fragmentary personalities. He used this idea to explain that a poet had the capacity to dramatize and personify his mental contents:

> When he creates a character on the stage, or in his poem or drama or novel, he thinks it is merely a product of his imagination; but that character in a certain secret way has made itself. Any novelist or writer will deny that these characters have a psychological meaning, but as a matter of fact you know as well as I do that they have one. Therefore, you can read a writer's mind when you study characters he creates. (p. 81)

Jung referred to a diagram he had drawn in an earlier lecture[32] which portrayed the different spheres of the mind in gradually darkening colors, in circles of decreasing circumference, until the personal and collective unconscious was reached, shown as a black circle at the very heart of the drawing. When the conscious autonomy gives way to a fascination with the unconscious, there is an increase of energy in the unconscious section of the mind which gradually grows strong enough until it overcomes the conscious. "Finally," Jung said,

> The patient sinks into the unconscious altogether and becomes completely victimized by it. He is the victim of a new autonomous activity that does not start from his ego but starts from the dark sphere. (p. 82)

At last Beckett had the catalyst he was looking for to move Murphy out of West Brompton and into his (Murphy's) mind. Jung, in combination with Geulincx, Descartes and Malraux, provided him with the necessary stimuli to shape the novel.

Beckett was bothered by Jung's contention that the characters an author creates are indicative of the state of his mind because Beckett himself likened the creative process to more than inspiration; it was tantamount to a seizure of his conscious faculties by an autonomous force which seemed to well up from someplace deep inside himself and to commit itself almost independently to paper. To hear Jung say much the same thing was indeed corroboration of the validity of such a process, but it was also somewhat frightening. There would be many times in the future when thoughts of this lecture contributed to mental blocks during which he was unable or unwilling to write.

However, if individual statements or aspects of this lecture can be ranked in importance, a casual comment Jung made in reply to a question during the discussion following his lecture had the most lasting effect on Beckett. In response to a question about the dreams of children, Jung mentioned a ten-year-old girl who had been brought to him with what he called amazing mythological dreams. He could not tell the child's father what the dreams signified because he sensed they contained an uncanny premonition of her early death. Indeed, she did die a year later. "She had never been born entirely" (p. 107) Jung concluded.

Beckett seized upon this remark as the keystone of his entire analysis. It was just the statement he needed to hear. He was able to furnish detailed examples of his own womb fixation, arguing forcefully that all his behavior, from the simple inclination to stay in bed to his deep-seated need to pay frequent visits to his mother, were all aspects of an improper birth.

His relationship with May was not really so unusual in a country where men tended "to make sweethearts of their mothers."[33] What was unusual was that such attentions were usually paid by middle-aged Catholic bachelors and not by members of the Anglo-Irish upper middle class. With Jung's words, Beckett finally found a reasonable explanation of his relationship with his mother. If he had not been entirely born, if he did indeed have prenatal memories and remembered birth as "painful,"[34] it seemed only logical to him that the aborted, flawed process had resulted in the improper and incomplete development of his own personality. It was an explanation that satisfied him and gave an enormous feeling of comfort. It strengthened his belief that he could justifiably end the analysis when the year ended, and it even gave him the strength to face the prospect that he could not hang on much longer in London and would soon have to consider going to live permanently in Ireland.

Beckett used Jung's remark in *All That Fall*, a radio play he wrote in 1956. Maddy Rooney speaks of hearing "a lecture by one of these new mind doctors."[35]

> I remember his telling us the story of a little girl, very strange and unhappy in her ways, and how he treated her unsuccessfully over a period of years and was finally obliged to give up the case. He could find nothing wrong with her, he said. The only thing wrong with her as far as he could see was that she was dying. And she did in fact die, shortly after he washed his hands of her. (p. 83).

Mr. Rooney cannot see what is so wonderful about that, and Mrs. Rooney replies:

> No, it was something he said and the way he said it, that have haunted me ever since . . . when he had done with the little girl he stood there motionless for some time, quite two minutes I should say, looking down at his table. Then he suddenly raised his head and exclaimed, as if he had had a revelation, the trouble with her was that she had never really been born! He spoke throughout without notes. (Pause) I left before the end. (p. 84)

When Beckett wrote *All That Fall*, his postwar reputation was in the ascendant. By this time he had formulated his final, mature approach to fiction; all his work was dominated by his obsession with the human condition. The long passages taken directly from his life are still there, but they are disguised, made impersonal, and for those without knowledge of Beckett's life, they are stripped of even the barest clues which might identify them with any recognizable human being. By then Beckett no longer found it necessary to undercut each serious statement with an archly flippant remark. He had mastered the technique of incorporating biographical statements into the texture of his work so that no such comment was needed. His certainty in his method required neither apology nor derision. He had thus effectively freed himself of the constraints of the fictional method which he had railed against in *Dream*. He had learned to give in to his unconscious creative instinct, to abandon himself to the creative voice inside him, and in so doing, had forged a style so impersonal that he has often been faulted for his clinical abstraction. Yet these same works are so intensely personal, so filled with his own life that it is painful for him to reread them: to discuss them is an unthinkable horror. From Joyce, he learned the folly and futility of explicating, apologizing for or even discussing his work. But when he created his postwar fiction there was another reason for his refusal as well: any such discussion might lead to personal revelation.

However, when he wrote *Murphy*, this technique was far in his future, so that Jung's lectures and Beckett's general interest in psychiatry were important to the novel in the same sense that his readings in philosophy and literature were—as an intellectual foil and as an appropriate extension of his own ideas and interests. *Murphy* was written within the form of the traditional novel; it is picaresque. What makes it unusual is that Beckett wrote it in a decade when social and political novels had so captured the public consciousness that to write anything as uncommitted as *Murphy* was automatically to invite rejection by most publishing houses. A novel about the inside of a man's mind, especially one who worked in a mental hospital, was either dismissed as a passé holdover from the experiments of the 1920's

or criticized as a useless exercise tantamount to unpatriotic activity. Nevertheless Beckett, who confided in no one except
McGreevy about the novel he was writing, continued to listen
to his inner voices. Intrigued by Jung's idea of the independent
personality of the creative impulse, he allowed his own creative
impulses free rein. Oblivious to external circumstances or
opinions, he continued to write.

At the beginning of October, 1935, Beckett had written
approximately twenty thousand words of *Murphy*—words
which seemed to lose their color and interest as soon as he wrote
them and which formed chapters that seemed so meaningless and
cold that he wanted to throw them away as soon as they were
written. By the end of the month, after he had heard Jung, this
feeling passed. He knew it was simply a matter of continuing to
put words upon paper until they formed a cohesive unity. He
still feared that his characters were lifeless, both unloving and
unlovable, but he did not let it worry him because he was finally
leaving London and he thought he could resolve his problems
with the novel once he had settled in Dublin.

After two years of intensive therapy undertaken in the
hope that he would be able to put his feelings about his mother
in perspective, Beckett said the most important reason he abandoned London and returned to Dublin was the fact that he
"owed" so much of himself to her.[36] "Owed" was a strange
word for him to use, and his tone was so tentative and apologetic
that he obviously meant to disguise the true reason from himself
as well as from others: his total, abject failure to succeed as a
writer.

"I hated London," he said years later, grasping for a facile
excuse to explain his uncustomary vehemence, adding "everyone
knew you were Irish—the taxi drivers called you 'Pat' or
'Mick.' "[37] He considered all the people in London as a collec-
tively hostile mass to be encountered as seldom as possible.
Ordering a meal in a restaurant, buying a newspaper or riding in
a taxi were ordeals. He shrank from more sophisticated contact
as well, and as time passed, he intensified his refusal to do anything to further his career by refusing to attend any social
gathering where literary persons might be.

If he ever found himself in the company of influential editors and writers, he invariably found them lacking in some way or another and would have nothing further to do with them. He offered all sorts of excuses, claiming they were not intellectually stimulating, they were beneath him socially. He usually made no attempt to conceal his contemptuous feeling that they were grubbers and plodders who labored in the mundane field of commercial journalism because they were untalented. His relationships with these men often became openly insulting, and no doubt were instrumental in keeping work away from him.

The real reason he was uncomfortable among them was his inability to relate to people. Strangers in groups frightened him, individuals he met for the first time made him tense and awkward; he imagined they all thought he was begging for a handout of a review or a commissioned article and it made him embarrassed and ashamed. As time passed, solitude seemed the only possibility, even though he knew that solitude did not lead to contacts that brought publication and, with it, income. The only person he liked who might have been able to help him was Charles Prentice, but Prentice was often away from London for extended periods of time and when he was there, Beckett was too shy to ask him.

One of the things Beckett claimed to have learned during analysis was that he could no longer afford to divorce himself from the life around him, that he needed to force himself to enter into the activity of the creative marketplace if he expected to support himself as a writer. Thus, his behavior towards people who might have helped him is especially puzzling, because he needed only to observe the surface civilities and be slightly more amenable. This was certainly the lesson instilled in him time and again in his sessions with Bion, yet his rigidity hardened into the attitude that success should come to him on his terms. When no recognition came and none seemed likely in his immediate future, he did what he had always done when society overwhelmed him: he returned to the confines of Cooldrinagh and the coldly disapproving gaze of his mother, whose arms, nevertheless, were open metaphorically to clasp him to her bosom. He had learned little about himself during the past two years.

He decided it was time to "pull the plug on London"[38] in

October, 1935, but delayed his return to Dublin until just before Christmas. May had written in October to tell him that her annual sojourn in the beach house had done her enormous good. Her cheerful letters spoke of how she had convinced herself to face the future with gusto and to put Bill's death and her "active mourning" [39] behind her. As if to persuade Beckett how much she had changed, she told of making Frank take her to visit Cissie, a move she knew would convince him of the miraculous reversal of her state of mind.

Letters such as these were the excuse Beckett was looking for to convince himself that he could maintain his equilibrium while living under his mother's roof. McGreevy had serious doubts about this; he urged Beckett to leave London if he wished, but to go anywhere except Dublin. This, he urged, was the time for Beckett to visit Spain. But Beckett was adamant; he insisted that he owed too much of himself to May, and said if he moved anywhere, it would be to Dublin. Actually, he had little choice in the matter, for his fixed income could no longer keep up with rampant inflation in London and would most certainly have been inadequate anywhere on the continent.

Beckett broke the news to Bion and officially ended the analysis shortly before Christmas.[40] Bion discreetly suggested that Beckett was not ready for such a move because he was still not free of the crippling neurosis engendered by his relationship with May. Bion told him that as soon as he was under her roof, May would abandon her cheerful optimism and return to her old complaints, chief among them her insistence that Beckett commit himself to what she considered proper behavior and a suitable life in Dublin.

Beckett was undeterred. As usual, once he announced the move to his mother, he vacillated. As if to hasten his decision, or to make it definite once and for all, he was struck early in December by the painful idiosyncratic pleurisy which usually felled him in times of crisis, and the cloacal cyst flared up as well.[41] He was barely able to make the journey to Ireland and, once there, collapsed into bed and the ministrations of his mother.

He was ill for the first few weeks of December and was surprised by the inundation of visitors. Cissie, Maurice and

Deirdre Sinclair, Susan Manning, Alan Thompson, Brian Coffey, even Rudmose-Brown—all came to Cooldrinagh for the first time in years and were received amiably by May in the parlor before being sent upstairs to Beckett's sickroom. Her gracious reception of people she disapproved of seemed a good sign that her change of mind was sincere and lasting.

But by mid-January, 1936, when he was weak but better, he had to admit sadly that Bion was right about the pattern May's behavior would follow. Her graciousness had given way to vituperation, and her steely silences were harder than ever. His nighttime tremors and anxieties returned, worse than they had ever been. To make matters worse, Frank, one of Dublin's most successful young businessmen, had become an eagerly sought, eligible bachelor. May used the difference between the two brothers as another weapon with which to taunt Beckett.

Once again he withdrew from society. He never went into Dublin, he saw no one, he wrote nothing. He spent his days sitting in his darkened study or taking his Kerry Blue bitch for short, desultory walks in the vicinity of the house. He knew he was reverting to the automatous state which first drove him to seek help, but he was powerless to stop himself. Independently of his mother's constant harping, he was forced to concede that his residence in London had been a waste of time and money. As he neared his thirtieth birthday, he found himself with a far from finished novel, living in his mother's house with no likely chance of escape, and with no significant income.

May refused to give him money, hoping to goad him into finding employment. This seemed an unreasonable demand to Beckett, who seriously believed he had the right to be supported by his family. He resurrected his old raincoat, sneaked his books out of the house in its pockets and took them to the second-hand stalls along the quays of the Liffey where he sold them for little more than the price of a drink.[42]

As winter dragged on, dissipating the promise of the new year in all-pervading fog and cold, Beckett's shabby figure was often seen shuffling along the quays in the darkening winter afternoon. He began to make restless forays through the countryside, walking from five to ten miles each day, which he tossed off as a way to save carfare and avoid masturbation, and which kept him from succumbing to the explosive urge to blow up himself, his mother and the house.[43]

May was aware of his pent-up rage and was wise enough to sheathe her barbs and treat him more kindly. They arrived at an uneasy truce and slowly he began to adjust to life at home and to contact old friends. He tutored Maurice Sinclair, then preparing for his university scholarship examination in French.[44] Ethna MacCarthy, substituting at Trinity for the ill Rudmose-Brown, asked Beckett to help her prepare the syllabus for a course in Provençal literature. He submerged himself in both these tasks.

Murphy seemed hopelessly stymied, and he wasn't encouraged much by the reception accorded *Echo's Bones* by his family and friends. Everyone treated it with what he called reserved silence, even his beloved Cissie. He had sent three copies to Cooldrinagh before he left London, and though he searched for them whenever he was alone in the house, he could not find a single one. He told McGreevy sarcastically that he was confident they would turn up on the bookshelf within the next year or two, for *More Pricks* had undergone similar banishment at May's hands, but now, with a bit of searching, could be found on one of the higher, out-of-reach shelves.[45]

He expected this sort of treatment from his family, but he was angry at the noncommittal reception of others. "Five lines of faint damn in *Dublin Mag*"[46] came from O'Sullivan, which Beckett considered worse than no notice at all. Ethna MacCarthy and Con Leventhal, whom he considered his best friends in Dublin, remarked only that they had read all the poems before they were printed and so had not bothered to buy the book, a particularly wounding blow.

"My friends here esquivent the *Bones* for the most part," he wrote to Reavey. "What shall they say, my not-even-enemies. May it stick in their anus!"[47]

Then he made the aggravating discovery that the few friends who did want to buy the book were unable to do so because there were none in Dublin. Blanaid Salkeld, poet and mother of Cecil Salkeld, made three special trips to all the bookstores in Dublin and couldn't find a single copy. Beckett was livid with anger when she told him, and fired off a series of caustic letters to Reavey demanding to know why the book had not been distributed. Reavey sent soothing but evasive replies, saying copies had been sent to all major stores in England and Ireland, and that all appropriate periodicals had been flooded with review copies as well. Nevertheless, Beckett was unmollified because he could not find a single person in Dublin who had received a book from Reavey. Time passed and *Echo's Bones* remained unsold and unreviewed.

Reavey, in London, was trying to interest prospective investors and contributors in another *European Caravan*, which he had taken over when Samuel Putnam returned to the United States and gave up his plans for subsequent editions. He had set up a literary agency, European Literary Bureau, was trying to acquire moneymaking clients for it and was working to keep alive his ties to Paris publications by placing his own writings and those of clients. He had just contracted to publish books of poetry by Denis Devlin and Brian Coffey and was preparing some of Paul Eluard's poetry for an English translation. In short, he was heavily overextended.

This infuriated Beckett; after all he had gone through to scrape up the money for *Echo's Bones*, he had no intention of having it end up in unsold piles on the floor of Reavey's office, but there was little he could do from Dublin except send increasingly angry letters.

Hoping to soothe him, Reavey wrote that Eugene Jolas had expressed great interest in having Beckett write a prose piece for a forthcoming issue of *transition*. Beckett immediately sent Reavey the still unpublished *Censorship in the Saorstat*. To bring it up to date, he added a paragraph about books most recently banned, including *More Pricks* and his own listing number (465).[48] The article is little more than an extended editorial decrying the act of July 16, 1929, which established a board of censors to determine what books should be allowed into the Republic of Ireland. Beckett dismissed the bill as "panic legislation" in a country which legislated "sterilization of the mind" while banning all forms of contraception.

Once again there was a misunderstanding: Reavey claimed he sent the article to Jolas, but Jolas said he did not receive it in time to use it. No matter, Jolas said, because he was more inter-

ested in reprinting some of the poems from *Echo's Bones* (free).
Beckett replied acerbically that Jolas was welcome to print as
many as he liked, provided he paid for them.[49]

These problems frustrated Beckett, but the flurry of literary exchange, more than he had experienced in his two years in
London, also made him feel that it might be possible to fashion a
writing career while living in Cooldrinagh. Edward Titus wrote
from Paris asking for a long essay similar to *Proust* on any philosopher he liked. Beckett turned again to Geulincx and girded
himself for forays into Trinity College, where he read in the
Long Room. He soon tired of the exercise and gave it up without ever writing the essay, saying the only thing he might have
written would have been a literary fantasia.[50] Actually, he was
reluctant to begin a new major work until he could bring
Murphy to some sort of conclusion—a pattern that would repeat itself and cause him serious problems for the next two years.

In the meantime, Reavey asked him to contribute new
translations of Eluard's poetry for *Thorns of Thunder*.[51]
Beckett refused as graciously as he could, saying he was too
busy with the final revisions of *Murphy* to get involved. He was
horrified a month later to receive the prospectus for the book
with his earlier translations included, and wrote a scathing letter
objecting to his inclusion, to the preface, to the sense conveyed
by the publicity blurb and most of all, to the fact that he had not
been consulted after his initial refusal to contribute. It was too
late to have all references to himself removed since the pages
were already printed, and he had to content himself with calling
the book an abomination, swearing to have nothing further to
do with it and to have no further dealings with Reavey, whom
he was convinced he had been mistaken ever to trust.[52] He
turned in fury to *Murphy*, his only hope for independence, and
determined to finish it.

CHAPTER TEN

Murphy:

"WHO IS THIS MURPHY,

. . . IS HE, HAS HE, ANYTHING AT ALL?"

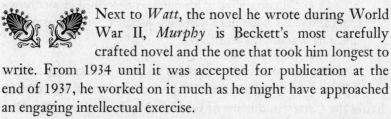 Next to *Watt*, the novel he wrote during World War II, *Murphy* is Beckett's most carefully crafted novel and the one that took him longest to write. From 1934 until it was accepted for publication at the end of 1937, he worked on it much as he might have approached an engaging intellectual exercise.

Most of his characters were based on people he had known, but his ultimate intention was to make *Murphy* an illustration of philosophic principles; thus, there was a certain amount of structure and form he needed to invent and then impose upon the characters. Once he had decided upon their number, sex and personality, all that remained was to invent a suitable framework for them to interact in order to bring his already determined plot to a successful conclusion.

The first step for Beckett was to get inside a mental hospital. Beckett never told Geoffrey Thompson that he was writing a novel which had a mental hospital for its setting. He didn't even say that he was writing a novel, but only admitted off-handedly when pressed, and then in tones of enormous agony and dissatisfaction, that he was "trying to write something."[1] He visited Thompson whenever he could, and as they walked along the grounds of the Bethlehem Royal Hospital, Beckett asked countless questions about every patient they encountered. When he finally got to walk through the wards, he found all that he had hoped for. The patients became the composite model for Mr. Endon, the quiet little man who plays chess; a "tab," i.e., a dangerously suicidal patient, "voted by one and all the most biddable little gaga in the entire institution."[2]

Murphy, whose name is the most common surname in Ireland, is, like all of Beckett's heroes, a man of some education and indeterminate origin. He is a Dubliner without family or occupation who lives in a condemned building in London's West Brompton and finds comfort only when he can strip off all his clothing, tie himself into a rocking chair with seven scarves[3] and rock himself into a trance:

> He sat in his chair in this way because it gave him pleasure! First it gave his body pleasure, it appeased his body. Then it set him free in his mind. For it was not until his body was appeased that he could come alive in his mind, as described in section six. And life in his mind gave him such pleasure, such pleasure that pleasure was not the word. (p. 2)

Beckett meant Murphy (heir to the line of antiheroes begun with Belacqua) to demonstrate the possibility of successfully living the Cartesian duality of mind and body without the necessity of integration. There are the same influences here as in Beckett's earlier writing: Descartes, Geulincx, Dante, and the game of chess, which until now he had played sporadically but which from this time became one of his abiding passions. He was also interested in astronomy and astrology, and so the heavenly sciences became the means of placing the action within time in the novel. All Murphy's seemingly random actions are set within a specific period, and every date is presented with information about the movements of heavenly bodies. Although the reader of *Murphy* may have to consult calendars and astronomical timetables, and although the plot does not proceed chronologically (Beckett uses techniques of flashback, narrative commentary and overview), the reader knows exactly what time and date it is throughout the novel.

Beckett uses chess to provide the denouement: Murphy and Mr. Endon play a game which could only be played by two madmen who give the impression of moving their pieces without actually doing so. It is a game based on the assumption that a piece should not be moved unless it can be returned safely to its original position. Beckett and Thompson spent long hours playing such a game, which they originally constructed as an intellectual problem. Beckett argued and then tried to demonstrate that once the pieces are set up on the board, any move from then on will only weaken one's position, that strength lies only in not moving at all. The ideal game for Beckett was one in which none of the pieces was moved, for from the very first move, failure and loss were inevitable.

Thus, the stars and the game of chess establish the principles of movement and stasis upon which the novel is built—the stars, whose movement is circular and repetitious, and which do not decay; and the pieces on a chess board, which cannot move in cycles (especially the pawns, which can only move forward), and for which, therefore, all movement is movement toward loss. It is, of course, clear that the fate of chessmen is, to Beckett, analogous to the fate of man.

The contrast between the perfection of heaven and the squalor of earth is drawn at the very beginning of the novel: "the poor old sun" is "in the virgin," (p. 2), but Murphy has been living with a streetwalker named Celia Kelly since she picked him up "the previous midsummer's night, the sun being then in the crab" (p. 12). Not content with fixing the meeting in time, Beckett specifies the place:

> She had turned out of Edith Grove into Cremorne Road, intending to refresh herself with a smell of the Reach and then return by Lot's Road, when chancing to glance at her right she saw, motionless in the mouth of Stadium Street . . . a man. Murphy. (pp. 12–13)

Throughout the novel, the narrator plods methodically through such descriptions, sometimes with humor, at others with sharp, black irony. The first-person narrator is unnamed in *Murphy*—there is no intrusive "Mr. Beckett," nor does he seek to impress the reader by insisting that he "was there," as in *More Pricks*. Beckett allows this narrator to be all-seeing and all-knowing, to comment anywhere in the novel as the action unfolds. Portions of the novel and all of chapter six are within Murphy's mind, but for the most part, the novel deals with externals, i.e., what happens to his body. Murphy's body is in conflict with his mind over Celia: "The part of him that he hated craved for Celia, the part that he loved shrivelled up at the thought of her." (p. 8)

All the kite flyers have been merged into Mr. Kelly, Celia's kite-flying grandfather:

> "Who is this Murphy," he cried, "for whom you have been neglecting your work, as I presume? What is he? Where does he come from? What is his family? What does he do? Has he any money? Has he any prospects? Has he any retrospects? Is he, has he, anything at all?" (p. 17)

Celia begins at the beginning:

> Murphy was Murphy. Continuing then in an orderly manner she revealed that he belonged to no profession or trade; came from Dublin . . . did nothing that she could discern; sometimes had the price of a concert; believed that the future held great things in store for him; and never ripped up old stories. (pp. 17–18)

Murphy sometimes receives money from an uncle in Holland, but not enough to keep both him and Celia unless she practices her profession, which he is unwilling to have her do. Celia has delivered an ultimatum: either Murphy finds work or she returns to streetwalking. Murphy, calling himself a "chronic emeritus" (p. 11), refuses to take such drastic action without first consulting his stars. He asks Celia to spend sixpence to have a swami "famous throughout the civilized world and the Irish Free State" (p. 32) cast his horoscope.

The horoscope yields the pleasant (for Murphy) knowledge that he should not seek work until all his lucky signs are in conjunction, which is not for another year, the first Sunday in October, 1936. Celia refuses to accept Murphy's dependence on his horoscope, and prepares to leave. An eyeball-to-eyeball confrontation ensues:

> He opened his eyes, cold and unwavering as a gull's, and with great magical ability sunk their shafts into hers, greener than he had ever seen them . . . (p. 39)

This does not sway Celia. Murphy asks for a clean shirt and prepares to go job-hunting. He becomes embroiled in the embarrassing process of finding a job, and in a humiliating incident applies to become a chandler's "smart boy," but " 'E ain't smart . . . . 'e aint a boy . . . 'E don't look rightly human to me" (pp. 76–77) and he is refused. He cheats a waitress of an extra cup of tea at lunch and goes off to a park to eat a packet of biscuits; except for the one he likes least, they are promptly devoured by a dachshund belonging to Miss Rosie Dew, a lady afflicted with Duck's disease.

In Dublin, meanwhile, Neary, his former teacher, has been beating his head against the buttocks of the statue of Cuchulain in front of the General Post Office; there he is encountered by his former pupil, Wylie. Neary is in love with Miss Counihan, who is in love with Murphy, who supposedly went to London in the first place to amass enough of a fortune to support Miss Counihan in the style to which she wished to become accustomed. In frustration, Neary abandons his school in Cork when Murphy fails to return after sufficient time, and with Cooper, his alcoholic man-of-all-work who can only stand or lie, but not sit down, sets out for London upon Wylie's advice to find Murphy himself. In the meantime, complexities mount: Wylie and Miss Counihan become lovers. When they fail to hear from Neary in reasonable time, Wylie, Miss Counihan and Cooper all go to London to seek Murphy, thus bringing the number of persons who want to find him to four. They are joined by a fifth, Celia, for by this time Murphy has found employment as a male nurse at the Magdalen Mental Mercy Seat and seems well on the way to overcoming the part of himself that he hates but that loves her.

The job has come about through Austin Ticklepenny, the "pot poet," whom Murphy encounters while eating lunch. Ticklepenny is anxious to quit his job at the hospital because he fears that contact with lunatics will drive him crazy, but he doesn't want to resign until the end of the month so that he will not have to forfeit his salary. Murphy as his substitute seems a good idea to them both. Murphy is struck by two of the statements in the swami's horoscope; that he should "inspire, lead, act as custodian," and that "the lunatic would easily succumb to him." At the MMM Murphy moves into a garret which is accessible only by a ladder which he pulls up after him; the garret is unheated, but has a skylight to the stars. He steals his rocker on a day when Celia is out of their old room and rigs an elaborate contraption to the water closet down below to provide gas heat for his attic: when the chain is pulled to flush the toilet, gas is turned on and Murphy lights it.

For several weeks he happily goes about his work in the wards, supervising inmates and being supervised in turn by two sadistic brothers named Bim and Bom.[4] He is delighted to find in the patients human beings who have successfully withdrawn from the real world into the madness of their minds. Their success in achieving a state whereby all their physical needs are satisfied while they contribute nothing to the world intrigues Murphy, and as he makes his rounds, he studies them, particularly Mr. Endon, who must be watched carefully to insure that he does not manage to commit suicide by apnoea, i.e., suspension of breathing.

In what must be the only chess game of its kind,[5] Murphy and Mr. Endon play forty-three moves of brilliant noncommunication during which Mr. Endon never once removes his concentration from the three ranks on his side of the board while Murphy struggles, first, to imitate Mr. Endon's moves, then to sacrifice wildly all his pieces.

Murphy plays white because Mr. Endon refuses to make the first move: "if presented with White he will fade, without the least trace of annoyance, away into a light stupor." (p. 244)

Murphy's first move is a perfectly respectable chess opening but the narrator cites it as the "primary cause of all White's subsequent difficulties." (p. 244)

By the ninth move, Murphy has managed, despite his strong opening, to duplicate most of Mr. Endon's moves. On the tenth move, Murphy moves another pawn, inviting Mr. Endon to attack him. Mr. Endon ignores it, but continues to move his pieces back and forth and from side to side within the three ranks closest to him. Now, because Murphy has moved so many pawns, he finds himself unable to duplicate Mr. Endon's moves turn by turn—often he must take two or even three moves to place his pieces in positions similar to Mr. Endon's. On the twenty-first move, Murphy has moved so many pawns that he is unable to continue to follow Mr. Endon at all, and he begins to move wildly. Mr. Endon, perfectly self-contained, continues to exchange the places of his pieces: the bishops move to the squares originally inhabited by the king and queen, and the king and queen to those of the bishops. The knights and rooks reverse places, and the pawns continue to guard the lot. The narrator notes that "high praise is due to White for the pertinacity with which he struggles to lose a piece" (p. 245), as Murphy continues to offer his queen and Mr. Endon refuses to take it. With the thirty-fourth move, Murphy is ostensibly in check, but Mr. Endon again takes no notice. The last nine moves find Murphy in a frenzy to communicate, wildly shoving his pawns, placing his queen and king in suicidal positions. Mr. Endon, who has never once in the entire game been aware of Murphy, ends with all his pieces arranged neatly on his side of the board in very much the manner in which he began.

What is interesting about this game is Murphy's unnecessary resignation following Mr. Endon's forty-third move. He could have moved his queen one more move, forcing Mr. Endon into either confrontation or retreat. Mr. Endon would have had to capture Murphy's queen or disturb the symmetry of his pieces. There is no way that Mr. Endon could have ignored such a move if Murphy had made it. Mr. Endon would have been forced to acknowledge Murphy's existence. The fact that Murphy chose instead to resign demonstrates that he accepted defeat in something more than a game of chess: he is defeated by Mr. Endon himself, forced to realize that there will be no communication between them.

Murphy drifts into a mental state beyond time in which his rounds, the inmates, the game, all give way to a state of nothingness. In this instance Murphy's mind leaves the world without benefit of rocking chair and scarves. Coming back to the reality of the MMM, he finds Mr. Endon switching the lights in the patients' cells off and on at random. He leads Mr. Endon gently to bed, tucks him in, then kneels down and takes his head into his hands and stares deeply into Mr. Endon's eyes:

> The relation between Mr. Murphy and Mr. Endon could not have been better summed up than by the former's sorrow at

seeing himself in the latter's immunity from seeing anything but himself. (p. 250)

Murphy's search for perfection is ended. He has at last found an impenetrable being, a sphere so perfectly contained that it will admit nothing into it. Mr. Endon's mind needs nothing, it wants for nothing. And in finding this perfect mental state, Murphy also realizes that he can never attain it himself. *Ubi nihil vales, ibi nihil velis*, Geulincx states—where I can do nothing I ought not to will anything—and this has been Murphy's failure: he has not been able to forgo wanting to do something, in this case, to reach Mr. Endon.

What sets Murphy apart from Mr. Endon, finally, is his sanity. Knowing that he is sane, realizing that he can never reach a mental state comparable to Mr. Endon's, he must admit failure. It is too much for Murphy. He is stubborn; in a sense, greedy. He wants both the mental states, of sanity and insanity, yet he is unwilling to give up his control over his own rational mind. He hesitates and in doing so, he realizes that he will always hereafter be lost to himself. There will be no perfection of the mind for Murphy.

Shortly thereafter, when Murphy is once again in the garret, tied to his chair, someone pulls the chain below in the water closet. Murphy, in a trance, cannot light the gas jet. Gas fumes seep in, exploding when ignited by Murphy's candle. The question of whether or not Murphy has committed suicide is neatly evaded because the date on the note he left behind has been burned off. Murphy lit the candle knowing that it was only a matter of time until someone below pulled the chain—but even this is not proof, for Murphy is notoriously absentminded.

Murphy has left instructions for the disposal of his body in a note addressed to Neary:

With regard to the disposal of these, my body, mind and soul, I desire that they be burnt and placed in a paper bag and brought to the Abbey Theatre, Lr. Abbey Street, Dublin, and without pause into what the great and good Lord Chesterfield calls the necessary house, where their happiest hours have been spent, on the right as one goes down into the pit, and I desire that the chain be there pulled upon them, if possible during the performance of a piece, the whole to be executed without ceremony or show of grief. (p. 269)

This request is never granted, as Cooper, who has been entrusted with the remains, throws the packet in anger at someone who offends him in a pub:

By closing time, the body, mind and soul of Murphy were freely distributed over the floor of the saloon: and before another dayspring greyened the earth had been swept away with the sand, the beer, the butts, the glass, the matches, the spits, the vomit. (p. 275)

Of all Beckett's novels, *Murphy* is the most controlled, the most polished. There are few of the arcane references, arch commentaries and narrative interjections which allowed Beckett to show off his considerable learning in *More Pricks* and *Dream*. Unlike the later fiction, which Beckett simplifies and strips of all the classic structures and strictures of the novel, *Murphy* moves within a complicated time scheme. Its structure allows Beckett to move easily from Murphy's physical circumstances to his mind, to the other characters and then back to Murphy.

Murphy, with his gull's eyes, spavined gait and ruined feet, is not exactly a pleasant hero, but he is capable of evoking sympathy. His death is poignant. Although the disposition of his ashes is mock-heroic, Beckett evokes a feeling of real sadness when Cooper's stiffened body gives way and he is able to sit down for the first time in more than twenty years. The final chapter is suffused with tender sadness. Celia, who has gone back to streetwalking, wheels her distraught grandfather home after he accidentally loses his kite in Kensington Gardens. It is closing time in the gardens of the Western World. "All out," (p. 282) the ranger cries.

The prose throughout is spare and precise. The baroque overstatement of the previous works has given way to an almost shocking understatement. Irony is undercut by wit; Beckett's humanity, which at first seems to be totally lacking, is shown upon closer reading to be there but in sympathetically discreet language. Beckett's characters have been accused of being one-dimensional, especially because of his concentration on their physical abnormalities and mental quirks, but the crises that occur in their emotions alleviate the reader's natural revulsion to their infirmities so that they become simply beings who suffer.

Beckett called all the characters in this novel hateful, including Celia, who was supposed to represent the idealization of the feminine principle.[6] (Her green eyes and several other characteristics indicate that she is a descendant of the line of heroines coming from the Smeraldina and the Alba, loosely based on Peggy Sinclair and Ethna MacCarthy, and to a lesser extent, the other women with whom his liaisons were more casual and fleeting.)

For the first six months of 1936, Beckett labored over the novel, reshaping it even as he was sending it to publishers. Finally, in July, he sent a typescript to McGreevy and hesitantly asked for his opinion. He was astonished and delighted when McGreevy pronounced all the characters who peopled the book to be lovable surprises.

McGreevy's only reservation concerned the amount of the book which remained to be read once Murphy had met his death. Beckett sent a long and thoughtful reply:

> The point you raise is one that I have given a good deal of thought to. Very early on, when the mortuary and Round Pond scenes were in my mind as the necessary end, I saw the difficulty and danger of so much following Murphy's own "end." There seemed two ways out. One was to let the death have its head in a frank climax and the rest be definitely epilogue (by some such means as you suggest. I thought for example of putting the game of chess there in a section by itself). And the other, which I chose, and tried to act on, was to keep the death subdued and go on as coolly and finish as briefly as possible. I chose this because it seemed to me to consist better with the treatment of Murphy throughout, with the mixture of compassion, patience, mockery and "tat twam asi" that I seem to have directed on him throughout, with the sympathy going so far and no further (then losing patience) as in the short statement of his mind's fantasy on itself. There seemed to me always the risk of taking him too seriously and separating him too sharply from the others. As it is I do not think the mistake (Aliosha mistake) has been altogether avoided. A rapturous recapitulation of his experience following its "end" would seem to me exactly the sort of promotion that I want to avoid: and an ironical one is I hope

superfluous. I find the mistake in the mortuary scene, which I meant to make more rapid but which got out of hand in the dialogue. Perhaps it is saved from anticlimax by presence of M. all through. I felt myself he was liable to recur in his grotesque person until he was literally one with the dust. And if the reader feels something similar it is what I want. The last section is just the length and speed I hoped, but the actual end doesn't satisfy me very well.[7]

Murphy, as John Fletcher has noted, is Beckett's "last citizen of the world."[8] Yet for all the work Beckett lavished on this novel, it seems to have little beyond sentimental meaning for him. His comment about the conclusion perhaps sums up his feeling toward the book—it just does not satisfy him very well. It represented a significant development over the sophomoric obliquities of his earlier fiction; by writing it he had demonstrated that he could conceive and write an entertaining work. Nevertheless, he found it a trifle too commercial, too willing to pander to public taste. When he wrote it, he could not say exactly what left him feeling vaguely dissatisfied. Not until he began to write the prose of his postwar years did he know what bothered him: Murphy was indeed a "citizen of the world," and Beckett's greatest satisfaction would come when he learned to free his characters from the world and let them roam free in the smaller world of their minds.

CHAPTER ELEVEN

1935–38:

"I AM DETERIORATING NOW VERY RAPIDLY"

 In late spring, 1936, Beckett felt he had revised *Murphy* enough that it could be shown to publishers. Chatto and Windus returned the manuscript within a week; in quick succession it was rejected by Constable, Lovat Dickson, Frere Reeves, and several others.[1]

He sent typescripts to Simon and Schuster and Houghton Mifflin,[2] both American firms, which kept him waiting inordinately long for their rejections. In the next three months, more than fifteen British firms rejected *Murphy*, and Beckett was growing tired of paying the postage to send out typescripts. His mother greeted the postman (the "consumptive" who whistled "The Roses are Blooming in Picardy" in *Watt*)[3] as he delivered the mail each day, and she stared in stony silence as Beckett shamefacedly rescued his manuscript.

At the end of August, when he owed thirty-six pounds to Frank and was depressed by a curt rejection from someone he was counting on heavily to take the novel, he decided to end his ban on commerce with Reavey and asked him to become his agent: he could no longer bear the "unavoidable degradation" of dealing directly with publishers and the continuing humiliation of rejection, and he did not know another agent.[4] He decided to force himself to leave *Murphy* and go on to other things.

He wrote an early version of the poem "Cascando,"[5] and

accepted an invitation by the German firm Rohwalt to translate the poems of Joachim Ringlenatz into an English miscellany for Faber and Faber. He spent little more than a week reading them before he decided that Ringlenatz was second rate and not worth his time, but he did not give up the commission just yet, in case nothing else came his way.

In July, the *Dublin Magazine* printed "An Imaginative Work!", Beckett's review of Jack B. Yeats's *The Amaranthers*, which Beckett sent to O'Sullivan unsolicited. He was surprised when it was accepted but disappointed that it was cut to five hundred words and printed with a title he thought effusive. The review prompted O'Sullivan to ask for poetry, and Beckett sent "Cascando."[6]

With the publication of the Yeats review, he found himself drawn increasingly into the society of literary Dublin. He had taken pains to avoid "the *Dublin Magazine* Crowd," (as he called them) claiming that since his return from London there were fewer nice people in Dublin and far more barbarians than he remembered.[7] Yet he visited Seumas O'Sullivan at home, claiming he was only accompanying Cissie when the visit had actually been his idea. He no longer seemed to think of himself as a down-at-the-heels, failed outsider, and he slid into company on a more comfortable, secure footing. He also fell into the Dublin habit of calling on people during their "evenings" or "at homes." At Constantine Curran's he saw Herbert Gorman, who was in Ireland to do research on his projected biography of Joyce. Several days later, he met Gorman at Jack B. Yeats's and garnered enough courage to introduce himself and talk about his own days in Paris. Gorman told him that Joyce's group had dwindled down to a handful of faithful followers who all banded together to damn "the rats who left the ship when the franc kaput."[8] He lunched with Brian Coffey and his family at their home, the residence of the president of University College, and actually enjoyed a discussion on ecclesiastical architecture. He met Denis Devlin for walks in St. Stephen's Green to while away the time until Devlin heard news of his posting with the Irish Diplomatic Corps.

He worried that McGreevy was not writing as frequently as usual, and he commented in what was to become a line of great symbolic importance in *Waiting for Godot:* "No sign of Tom. So no explain . . . remember one thief was saved."[9]

At Cissie's he reencountered Cecil Salkeld, who had just returned from Germany with his wife and daughter (Beatrice, later married to Brendan Behan). Beckett and Salkeld had always regarded each other warily, each unsure of the other's talent, both unwilling or unable to commit themselves to either open friendship or animosity. Beckett described their relationship as the "mutual jealousy of two drunks."[10] He was fond of Salkeld's mother, Blanaid, a great Dublin hostess and a poet in her own right, and this fondness might be why Beckett was more tolerant than usual of her son. In a town where legendary drinkers abounded, Cecil Salkeld was truly one of the great ones.[11] Drinking was one of the two bonds he and Beckett shared; the other was Kassel, where Salkeld had been the Sinclairs' neighbor.

Salkeld was a great friend of Austin Clarke, and it was inevitable that he and Beckett should meet. Clarke had never forgiven Beckett for classifying him among the "Antiquarians" in the *Bookman* article; now Beckett was slightly embarrassed when they met because he had named the "pot poet" in *Murphy* "Austin Ticklepenny" and he knew Clarke was sure to take umbrage if and when the book appeared.

Beckett described Clarke at this time as both pathetic and sympathetic, but said of himself that he was so desperate for any kind of literary contact that he was willing to embrace anyone with even the vaguest literary sensitivities.[12]

He also began to go around with his uncle Gerald, partly because Dr. Beckett reminded him so much of his father, with his penchant for a drink, a joke and a rousing bout of exercise, and partly because he was settling into the family once again and wanted to reestablish contacts with his Beckett relatives. (He had always identified more with the Becketts than the Roes, a fact which had not escaped his mother.) Beckett and his uncle swam and played piano duets and engaged in long philosophical conversations about coral reefs, Torquemada and how to coexist peacefully with Dublin society (by "looking the pisses in the eye inversely as the square of the distance").[13] May considered that sort of language disgusting.

As Beckett relaxed, his idiosyncratic ailments disappeared, he gained weight and it actually seemed as if living in Dublin would be possible for him after all. He had reckoned without his mother. May's demands that he find some work to support himself increased in direct proportion to his good health. When she began her usual entreaties for him to join the firm, he offered to lick stamps for Frank but threatened that his saliva would burn holes in the envelopes.[14]

As usual, May made sure all her friends knew how unhappy she was to have a thirty-year-old son lounging around the house all day long. Mary Manning Howe, the daughter of May's friend, Mrs. Susan Manning, had married the American lawyer and biographer, Mark de Wolfe Howe, and was living in Boston. She wrote to tell Beckett that a lecturer's position in English was open at Harvard, and she was sure that her father-in-law could secure it for him if he liked. He thought about it for a day or so, then declined when he learned that he would have to ask Joyce for a recommendation because Joyce's name carried enormous weight at Harvard. He passed the notice on to McGreevy, who was on better terms with Joyce than he. McGreevy pursued the lectureship, but lost out because his letter arrived too late to be considered.

Beckett's friends were worried about the strain his joblessness was causing and those who knew him well began to send him advertisements. Geoffrey Thompson sent one for a position as French translator in Geneva; Beckett applied, but forgot to sign the letter and enclose his address. He was too embarrassed to pursue it further.[15] Rudmose-Brown sent a notice for a lectureship in Italian at the University of Capetown, South Africa.[16] At first Beckett decided not to apply, but Rudmose-Brown was so insistent that he did. He asked Rudmose-Brown and Jack B. Yeats to give him recommendations, and went through the motions of collecting an academic dossier before he wrote a curt note withdrawing from the competition.

He had other ideas of what to do with his life: first, he wrote the formal letter to Eisenstein, who did not reply. Then, Beckett decided to become a commercial pilot. He had never flown.

"I think the next little bit of excitement is flying," he wrote to McGreevy. "I hope I am not too old to take it up seriously nor too stupid about machines to qualify as a commercial pilot. I do not feel like spending the rest of my life writing books that no one will read. It was not as though I wanted to write them."[17] This gloom was no doubt provoked by the royalty statement he had just received from Chatto and Windus: in the year just ended they had sold two copies of *More Pricks* and twenty of *Proust*.[18]

Seumas O'Sullivan sent a brief note asking Beckett for a formal meeting, which surprised him because he was used to running into O'Sullivan casually when he was in Dublin. A written request signaled something else, and he went with some curiosity. O'Sullivan did indeed have a surprise: he said he wanted to retire and offered the editorship of the *Dublin Magazine*, saying he would pay all printing costs for three years with Beckett to begin the purchase of the magazine after that.[19] Beckett thanked O'Sullivan as effusively as he could manage, pretending to be greatly honored while stalling for time, hoping to make a graceful escape. From then on, he managed to evade O'Sullivan or to deflect the conversation and it was not long until O'Sullivan stopped mentioning it. He was probably relieved by Beckett's refusal, for the two men had never really understood each other's approach to literature.

Meanwhile, *Murphy*, under Reavey's care, continued its peregrinations. In short order, it was returned by Covici-Friede, Simon and Schuster, Heinemann and a score of others. Beckett began, first in jest, then grimly, to keep a neat, handwritten list of publishers who had rejected the novel. It grew to contain forty-two names. The intensity of his anger and hurt at its continuous rejection was such that he could barely bring himself to talk about it as late as 1974. He keeps the list, he says, because it comforts him to know that so many people were wrong about his writing and that he was right all along.[20]

Beckett tried to go on to new writing, but nothing much seemed to excite him. He spent a lot of time reading, in his own word, "wildly": Goethe's *Iphigenie* ("and then Racine's, to remove the taste"); Chesterfield, Boccaccio, Fischart, Ariosto and Pope; Trigny's *Hello* ("very very bad"); Grillparzer ("not the best of him—*Hero and Leander*, only *Jason-Medea*, of which third part at least magnificent"); Cecil's *Life of Cowper* ("What a life! It depressed and terrified me. How did he ever manage to write such bad poetry?"); a memoir of D. H. Lawrence ("appalling"); Pastor Fido; Guarini; and finally, a single-minded concentration on the writings of Samuel Johnson and all the writings about him.[21]

He was beginning to think seriously of collecting information about Johnson in much the same manner as he had about Descartes. He was not yet sure of what he would do with it, but the fascination that had drawn him on a pilgrimage to Litchfield had intensified now to the point where he no longer wanted to contain his excitement, but to tell all his friends about it. Brian Coffey sent him the label of a bottle of Barclay's beer from London, which used Johnson's portrait as a trademark,[22] and from the United States, Mary Manning Howe brought several new critical studies which were not available in Ireland.[23]

Mrs. Howe was in Ireland because she had written a play called *Youth's the Season,* which Hilton Edwards and Michel MacLiammoir consented to produce at the Gate Theatre if she would rewrite parts of it. She asked Beckett to help her, and he was responsible for several major changes. He created a character named Ego Smith, a bartender and foil for all the other characters who tell him their troubles. Ego Smith is on stage throughout the play but says nothing in the final version of the script. Originally, Beckett wrote a speech for Ego Smith which was to be the focal point of the play, allowing him to give his vision of the world: "My conception of the universe is a huge head with pus-exuding scabs—entirely revolting." Edwards and MacLiammoir thought the speech accurate but disgusting and refused to keep it. Beckett also suggested that the hero should kill himself before the end of the play, but again the producers rejected his idea.

Finally, Beckett suggested that it would not be successful unless there was a character offstage who could be heard steadily flushing a toilet. Mrs. Howe and her producers were puzzled by Beckett's fixation with suicide, bartenders and flushing toilets, but he assured them their usefulness in furthering action would be readily apparent when they read his own novel, *Murphy*.

This brief experience in theater fascinated Beckett, and he

began to hang around on the fringes of various dramatic groups in Dublin.[24] The Dramiks, a group which gave performances in the Peacock Theatre at the Old Abbey, were especially interested in German Expressionism and performed plays by Toller, Werfel, Wedekind and others, sometimes mounting a production of a French play. The playwright Denis Johnston was a member of this group, and Beckett listened to his ideas about production and dramatic theory. He drifted to productions of the Drama League, run by Mrs. William Butler Yeats and Lennox Robinson, the real center of dramatic activity in Dublin, composed mostly of actors from the Abbey and Gate who gave Sunday night productions several times each year. Programs were innovative and often controversial, but they escaped censorship because it was a private club. The Drama League was known especially for productions of Pirandello's *Henry IV*, *Naked*, and *Right You Are if You Think You Are*. The group Beckett was most intimately involved with was the Dun Laoghaire Theatre Group, run by Deirdre McDonough, assisted by his friend, Arland Ussher. There was a high level of amateur enthusiasm and interest in contemporary theater among the members of this group, and their conversations were spirited and intelligent. Beckett took no active part in their productions, nor did he enter into their conversations, but he always seemed to be on the periphery, listening, watching rehearsals, frowning near-sightedly.

Perhaps it was his peripheral involvement with theater, coupled with his interest in film, that turned his thoughts to writing drama. At any rate, he began to think seriously of turning what he had come to call his "Johnson Fantasy" into a play. By early summer he felt he had it all in his head, ready to be written, and only needed privacy to commit it to paper.

He seemed to be inventing excuses to keep himself from writing: first Sheila and Donald Page were visiting, and he did not feel that he could do any serious work with them in the house.[25] He and Joseph Hone spent a brief holiday at Ussher's family home at Cappagh. Then he helped Mrs. Howe with her play. Reavey came for a day to see a football playoff,[26] and suddenly it was September and he still had not written a word.

Murphy by this time had been to the twenty-fifth publisher and was still not taken, and the uncertainty of what would become of it no doubt had much to do with his inability to settle down and write.

Life in Cooldrinagh was threatening to erupt because of Beckett's continued joblessness. Then as the summer went on, hostility consumed May because he was seriously interested in a woman and she knew nothing more about it than she could glean from Mrs. Susan Manning, who had little more than third-hand speculation to offer.

Two young women from Boston, both in their early twenties, friends of Mrs. Howe, were spending the summer in Dublin.[27] Betty Stockton was there with her family, and her friend Isabella Gardner was there to keep her company. Mrs. Howe asked Beckett to tea to meet her friends, and he went with greatest reluctance, because he detested social conversation and had a distinct aversion for polite feminine company.

Beckett was thirty years old and no stranger to women when he met Betty Stockton. He hinted discreetly in letters and conversations of sexual relationships[28] but these were usually with women he called euphemistically "ladies of the evening," for whom he found places in his fiction, probably melding a number of them into composites of Winnie, the Frica, Ruby Tough, Lucy and Thelma née bboggs. He had probably been genuinely in love with Peggy Sinclair. He had been wildly infatuated with Ethna MacCarthy, as had most of his generation of Trinity students, but their relationship was much like that of Belacqua and the Alba, whom he modeled after her: a sophisticated older woman who regrets kindness to a younger man because it only encourages his infatuation. The Frica was modeled upon a young woman of his own social class and background whose family had been friendly with his since they were both children. She made no secret of her infatuation for him but she was so obvious in the methods with which she tried to entrap him that he was always able to elude her. He rewarded her passion with a scathing portrayal in *More Pricks*.

He had known one other class of women, the intellectuals he knew in Paris and Germany. These were women who supported themselves and often their children on their own earnings and incomes. Their relationships with men were open and direct, a distinct contrast from the ritualistic courtship and subsequent marriage of the people he knew in Dublin. Several of these women became his lifelong friends, especially Kay Boyle, Nancy Cunard and Mary Reynolds, but he seemed to circle around the others with wariness, as if he was uncomfortable around women who were in command of their own lives. He had been chased for several years by an Irishwoman he first met in Paris at the Joyces' and who turned up in London or Dublin from time to time. He crowed gleefully when his noncommittal, desultory behavior towards her made her burst out that he was unable to say anything nice to or about anyone but the most abject failures and thus he was certainly incapable of any feeling or expression for normal women.[29]

His relationship with women, then, is probably best described as fleeting and therapeutic; unable to relate to anyone, he was most certainly unable to put aside thoughts of himself long enough to feel any emotion for another. For him, romantic love was something to snicker at, and he reserved his most sarcastic comments for it. The thought of himself romantically involved was, until now, unthinkable.

But Betty Stockton was a totally different kind of woman, a kind he had never met before. She was barely twenty and has been described by people who knew her then as charming, romantic and enchanting.[30] She had grown up in an atmosphere of refinement and cultivation which enhanced her natural sparkle and gave her a dimension of maturity beyond her years. She was a sophisticated debutante who knew her own value as a person; aware of her natural beauty, she used it as a charm and a gift to others and never as a means to a selfish end. She was generous, witty, gentle and amusing, and Samuel Beckett had never, in all his years, met anyone like her.

He began to invent excuses to call on her and to present her with poems he had written. She thought Beckett was an interesting, if slightly odd, older man of thirty. She was young and impetuous and liked someone else better. She threw the poems away as soon as she received them.

He never spoke seriously of his writing and she did not know that he had published anything. She assumed he was having a difficult time adjusting to the fact that he had to settle down and go into the family business, and thought the poems he wrote were only his version of a romantic fling. All he told her of himself was that he had been secretary to James Joyce in Paris, taking great pains to explain Joyce's commanding role in modern literature. She knew nothing of Joyce and was not interested in Beckett's careful description of *Ulysses* and *Work in Progress*. Beckett seemed chagrined that his precise, repetitive descriptions of Joyce's importance to his life meant nothing to her. The sight of Beckett, blinking incomprehensibly behind his round glasses, made her feel guilty that she had been unkind, and so she could not refuse his invitations. Often, he simply appeared at her hotel, uninvited and unannounced, and she, ever polite, invited him along on her outings.

One afternoon, driving back to Dublin from an afternoon in the country, Beckett, Betty and her friends stopped at a beach lined with sandy pebbles to watch the moon rise. While the others gloried in the whipping wind and the mist rising off the water, Beckett spasmodically picked up handfuls of pebbles and, like Molloy with his sixteen sucking stones, placed them first in one pocket, then another; finally, as if growing tired of the private game he played with himself, he threw them all into the surf. He stood there, gawky and angular, in emotional misery. Betty was suddenly ashamed of her insensitivity to his mood that afternoon, and asked if he was cold. "No," he replied, "not cold. I just shiver sometimes." At that moment she thought he was the most vulnerable human being she had ever seen.

Betty was uncomfortable with his unorthodox manner of courtship but she was unable to reject him outright until several days later, when he came again to her hotel inviting her to drive to the Valley of Pigs "to listen to the silence." She thought he was slightly crazy and made some excuse and declined. Several days later, when her family left Dublin for a house they had rented in the country, she asked her friends not to give Beckett her address. He found out, of course, but was bitter and hurt and did nothing to see her again.

As the summer drifted on, he grew silent and tight-lipped when friends mentioned Betty, but he never asked about her. He drifted into a sexual relationship instigated by the woman he called the Frica, but almost before it began it was ended by both their mothers, who realized the unsuitability of the liaison and saw to it that both their errant children were separated by great physical distance.[31]

The situation in Cooldrinagh had deteriorated to the point where it now made Frank ill. He was sick all summer, and doctors were unable to cure him.[32] The most serious malady, a neuritis of the right shoulder, made him unable to move his right arm without excruciating pain. Fortunately he was left-handed, so he was able to continue some of his work, but his business was so successful that he had more than he could have taken care of had he been entirely well.

Ever since Beckett's return from London, Frank had taken advantage of his brother's presence to escape from May and had taken short holidays every few weeks. These escapes no longer proved satisfactory, and he began to come down with the same sort of irritating, painful physical ailments as his brother. In his titular position as head of the household, Frank suddenly exploded and announced that the three of them could no longer go on living together. He told Beckett that the demands of business and family were impossible to bear any longer, that all life was being strangled out of him. Beckett had to conclude sadly that Frank's life was much worse for his presence. Seeing Beckett do nothing all day long and still be supported was a festering irritation. But it was worse for Frank when Beckett was away, because the entire burden of their mother rested on his shoulders then. Frank proposed selling Cooldrinagh, putting May in a smaller house and taking a flat in town. He suggested Beckett get a job and set himself up somewhere, too. Neither of them had any idea what would become of their mother if they went through with this plan, and so, of course, nothing much came of it as soon as calmer tempers prevailed.

Escape came for Beckett in September, when Mr. Sean Cagney's cohorts sent a substantial refund from the tax bureau. With a little more money he borrowed from Frank and his mother, the pittance from royalties, and what he had left of his annual income, he decided to go to Germany to look at paintings.

He had become interested in art history through McGreevy and wherever he lived, became thoroughly familiar with the museums and galleries. Since his return to Dublin, he looked upon the National Gallery as a place of solace and refuge, and spent many long afternoons there hiding from family, friends and prospective employers. He had almost decided that if he were to live in Dublin permanently, the only job he could take would be something connected with the gallery. This decision relieved him of much of the guilt he felt for not having a job, and for a time it silenced his mother's imprecations. It also paved the way for temporary escape, because he told her the trip to the continent was meant primarily to prepare himself for a job should the personnel shifts he expected in the gallery actually occur. This was the most promising gesture he had ever made toward gainful employment. May therefore loaned him money and promised to send more at specified intervals throughout his journey, but she warned that *Murphy* had better be in publication, with a substantial advance in hand, because she wanted all her money back as soon as he returned.[33]

From the moment of his return to Dublin, he had begun to talk about going away. For more than three years he had talked about Spain, but the Civil War made the trip impossible now. He thought briefly of Amsterdam and Copenhagen, but they were too expensive. For several years he had been reading Italian literature voraciously, yet he never had the desire to do more than make a brief stop in Florence to visit museums. Of Paris he spoke not at all; it was as if the city had vanished. The break with Joyce had deeply scarred him, and even to pass through was unthinkable. By a process of elimination, Germany became the only country left to him.

What was supposed to have been a pleasant holiday meant to rekindle happy associations turned out to be six miserable months in a Germany he no longer recognized, where he was usually lonely and sick, with most of his time spent worrying about *Murphy*. He had not been in Germany more than a week when he was forced to recognize that its claim on him was only a matter of associations which could not be recaptured. He admitted that once he had seen all the pictures and struggled to regain the language, he would be happy to leave.[34]

On September 29, he sailed from Cork to Hamburg, the sprawling port city celebrated in Ireland for its sexual, political and artistic freedoms. A large contingent of Irishmen had gone there in search of one or another of these, and Beckett had been among them during his visits to the Sinclairs. On this trip he stayed in a sleazy boarding house and spent most of his time in museums, coffee houses and beer gardens. He took short trips, one to Luneburg, which had haunted him since he first saw it with Peggy years before. He wrote of this fascination several years later in *L'Expulsé* (*The Expelled*):

> There were other heaths much closer, but a voice said to me it's the heath of Luneburg that you need. I didn't use the familiar form with myself very much. The element "lune" must have influenced me somehow. Well, the Luneburg Heath didn't please at all, but not at all. I came back disappointed, at the same time relieved.[35]

His original plan had been to walk across Luneburg Heath south to Hanover, but the weather was bad and he took trains. From Hanover he went to Brunswick and Hildesheim, then east to Magdeburg, Potsdam and Berlin, arriving in mid-December, 1936.

Reavey wrote to him in Hamburg, saying that Simon and Schuster had "regrettably" turned down *Murphy*, claiming it had a "brilliant 5% appeal" but was otherwise unsellable.[36] Stanley Nott, the "last resort," was interested, but informed Reavey that he would only take *Murphy* if an American publisher could be counted on to share the printing costs ("to share the shame," as Beckett called it).[37] Houghton Mifflin still had a manuscript, but they were unhappy about (of all things) the title and were not willing to make a decision.

Beckett had chosen *Murphy* as the title for several reasons; because it was the most common surname in Ireland, thus standing for the Irish "everyman," and because he had loved Fritz Lang's movie, *M*, and wanted to pay it homage in some way of his own. Houghton Mifflin's editors were afraid the title was too Irish and would limit the book's appeal. They asked for a catchy new title and a new name for the principal character. After so many rejections, this seemed silly. The usual complaint of everyone who read the manuscript was that it was too long. They suggested numerous cuts, especially chapter six, "Murphy's

Mind," which they thought either superfluous or confusing. Beckett wanted so much to get the novel published that he was willing to comply and wrote to Reavey, saying he was ready to cut the book down to its title if that would help. Now, he said, he was prepared to go even further and change the title—"Quigley, Tromhebereschleim, Eliot, or any other name the publishers fancy!"[38]

Still, he felt he must make a last attempt to save the book as he had written it. He wrote a long letter to Reavey trying to explain what his intention had been in writing such a seemingly obscure novel and why it needed to be left intact:

> Let me say at once that I do not see *how* [Beckett's emphasis] the book can be cut without being disorganized. Especially if the beginning is cut (and god knows the first half is plain sailing enough). The latter part will lose such resonance as it has. I can't imagine what they want me to take out. I refuse to touch the section entitled *Amor Intellectualis quo M. se ipsum amat*. And I refuse also to touch the game of chess. The horoscope chapter is also essential. But I am anxious for the book to be published and therefore cannot afford to reply with a blank refusal to anything.
>
> Will you therefore communicate . . . my extreme aversion to removing one-third of my work proceeding from my extreme inability to understand how this can be done and leave a remainder? But add that if they would indicate precisely what they have in mind, and the passages that cause them pain, I should be willing to suppress such passages as are not essential to the whole and adjust such others as seem to them a confusion of the issue. . . . Do they not understand that if the book is slightly obscure it is because it is a compression and that to compress it further can only result in making it more obscure? The wild and unreal dialogues, it seems to me, cannot be removed without darkening and dulling the whole thing. They are the comic exaggeration of what elsewhere is expressed in elegy, namely, if you like, the Hermeticism of the spirit. Is it here that they find the "skyrockets"? There is no time and no space in such a book for *mere* [Beckett's emphasis] relief. The relief has also to do work and reinforce that from which it relieves. And of course the narrative is hard to follow. And of course deliberately so.[39]

Because his mail was held for him at post offices along the way, Beckett was often out of touch with Reavey. Earlier in November, he saw a picture of two apes playing chess in a German rotogravure, with one saying in disgust to the other, "What! You are giving away your Queen? Sheer Madness!" This seemed the perfect cover for *Murphy*, and he sent the photo to Reavey with instructions that it should be sent with the manuscript to prospective publishers. Unknown to Beckett, Reavey had no intention of showing it to anyone until contracts had been signed. In a decade when social conscience and political activity dominated publishing, it was one thing to write a novel as apolitical as *Murphy*, but quite another to offer this proof of the lack of seriousness with which even its author beheld it.

Reavey warned Beckett that he should not count upon Houghton Mifflin because quibbling about the book's title was probably an excuse for more serious dissatisfaction. Beckett suggested Reavey begin to establish contacts with other publishers:

> I would prefer of course to be done by Dent or even the Hogarth Private Lunatic Asylum than by Stanley N. [Nott] . . . But if all else fails I would prefer to be done by Nott than not at all. The chief thing is to get the book *OUT* [Beckett's emphasis]. Better a bougie than a burst bladder.[40]

He concluded dispiritedly that all suggestions as to deletions and addenda would be "grovellingly received," and settled down in a boarding house beside the Berlin zoo and the Kurfurstendamm, where he spent a lonely Christmas in a cold room with a bottle of whiskey for company.[41]

His introduction to Berlin had not been pleasant: he had had to eliminate Hellenstadt and Guedinburg from his itinerary because he ran out of money and needed to go directly to Berlin to await the next check from his mother. He was forced to spend his first week there marking time until it arrived.

When he went to look at paintings he thought the collections "stupendous," but he was disappointed to find the modern wing of the museum closed and all the paintings removed. In the galleries it was the same: there was no modern art on display anywhere. This brief remark is one of the two or three oblique references Beckett made during his six-month trip to the Ger-

man political situation, and here he only comments on the fact
that the museum wing had been closed, without stating or questioning the reason why.

In all the letters he wrote during this time, he seems obsessed by two overwhelming concerns: *Murphy* and himself. It
is almost as though Beckett moved throughout a phantom country in which he was the only occupant, paintings were the only
objects and museums and galleries the only buildings. A natural
thought is to wonder if Beckett feared the possibility of political
interference or censorship, but in conversations many years later
he said this thought had not occurred to him and that he had
only vague recollections of the society around him.[42] The
feverish political situation, which dominated all activity in Germany, left him confused and withdrawn, and only exacerbated
his feeling of solitude and statelessness. Perhaps it was the
knowledge that Germany had become another place where he
could not reside permanently—making his return to Ireland an
actuality that could be postponed but not prevented—that
brought on another onslaught of idiosyncratic illnesses. He had a
bursitis or pleurisy (he couldn't decide which) that paralyzed
his shoulders and upper back. An anal cyst, the worst ever,
formed in mid-January. He had planned to leave Berlin for
Dresden just after the New Year, but the cyst prevented his
departure for more than ten days until it ruptured and sub-
sided.[43]

In spite of these disabilities, Beckett was surprisingly social
in Berlin in the early weeks of 1937. He had met an aging,
querulous Jewish art historian in Hamburg whose position at the
museum had been terminated by the government. She came to
Berlin for the holidays and introduced Beckett to Frau Sauerlandt, the widow of the late director of the Hamburg Museum.
At Frau Sauerlandt's home Beckett heard changing groups of
artists and writers rain curses on the government for curtailing
or even forbidding their activity. Frau Sauerlandt wanted to
take the diffident Beckett to see first-hand what was happening
to artists in Germany, inviting him to meet Nolde, Schmidt-
Rottluff and Heckel, but Beckett declined. He described these
people as "proud, angry, poor and put-upon," and had no interest in their very real problems. His health occupied his mind

entirely, and his only concern was to see if he couldn't manage to cope with it long enough to go on to Dresden, Munich and several other places before it forced him to return to Dublin.

"I am very tired and only want to go home and lie down, but I feel I shan't be in Germany again after this trip," he wrote. "Travelling as I do with the living wage of charity coming through regular every month and the aversion to human beings hardening with every outing, I shall never learn what to do with my tither of life."[44]

To while away the time he was confined to his room, he tried to write poetry, but the only thing he could manage was nineteen lines he called "Whiting," which, with several minor changes, became the poem "Ooftish," published a year later in *transition*.[45]

He was momentarily cheered to hear that McGreevy might join him in Dresden, but when he arrived there, a brief message informed him that McGreevy had been unable to raise the money.[46] Beckett actually enjoyed the journey from Berlin, perhaps because he thought he had something to look forward to in Dresden. On his way he was surprised to find a trove of modern paintings still on exhibit in Halle, many by Kirchner, whom he admired especially. Dresden he found disappointing: too ornate, overwhelmingly dominated by bad Italian painting, badly lit and hung, but there he met all sorts of interesting people. Cissie Sinclair and Cecil Salkeld had given him an introduction to Dr. Will Grohmann, who had been denounced and dismissed from his position as director of the Zwinger Gallery by the Hitler government in 1933. Grohmann took Beckett to visit the best private collections in Germany, ranging from Cézanne, Léger and Chagall to Archipenko, Munch, Nolde, and Kirchner. To his surprise, there was also a Kokoschka portrait of Nancy Cunard, painted in Paris in 1924.

Grohmann himself owned a formidable collection which included paintings by Picasso, Klee, Kandinsky and Mondrian, as well as the contemporary Germans. Grohmann, a Jew, was isolated from most artistic activity of non-Jewish colleagues, but he introduced Beckett to the few persons in Dresden who continued to associate with him. Beckett met Frau von Gersdorff, a Russian born into the princely Obolensky family, and her German husband, who supplemented his income by giving Russian lessons to German soldiers.[47] They took him to a lecture on the Russian novelist Andrei Biely (called "The Russian James Joyce") by Professor Fedor Stepun, a friend of the von Gersdorffs.

Stepun spoke at length about Biely's family situation: his wife, Assya Turgeneva, was a relative of the great Russian writer, and her sister (who had lived in Dresden for many years) was married to an Italian named Pozzo. It was probably the first time Beckett heard the name he later gave to one of the characters in *Waiting for Godot*.

This group was so isolated in Dresden that any congenial newcomer soon found himself swept into its collective bosom, and Beckett was no exception; he had intended to spend several days in Dresden, but they would not let him go for several weeks. He didn't mind the delay, for he had no strict itinerary, and as long as his health remained stable he was prepared to drift.

He dreaded the thought of going home with nothing definite to report about *Murphy*. In short order, he heard from Reavey that Dent, Faber and Faber, Secker and the Hogarth Press had all refused it.[48] Once again he turned to poetry to occupy himself, but he wrote two and a half lines in two weeks and tore them up in disgust.[49]

"Murphy does not serve me well," he wrote to Reavey, "to have written little or more would have been better."[50]

Despite the steady succession of refusals, Reavey was confident that sooner or later someone would publish *Murphy*. To soften the latest blows, Reavey sent J. W. Dent's letter of rejection, written by Richard Church, a man Beckett knew and respected.

> I have now read Samuel Beckett's novel and I think this man is a most remarkable and highly equipped writer. The humor, the sophistication, the sense of structure, and the clear originality make me agree with you that he is a man fully worthwhile fostering. I have been on the telephone with Harold Raymond of Chatto & Windus, and I said what I think about the book,

and also that I believe they are making a mistake if they let him go. Raymond has accordingly asked to see the mss. again and I am taking the liberty of sending it to him. But he does not want Beckett to know this in case he has to come to the same conclusion as the other directors and again disappoint the author. For our part, we can only take on a limited amount of immediately unremunerative work and our hands are already full with one or two authors of the better kind on whom we lose money at present, and as you know, this technique cannot be extended in an unlimited way. Otherwise I should not hesitate about urging my directors to accept Beckett's book. I much appreciate your thought in sending it to me.[51]

Church's letter was followed by another refusal, this time from Hamish Hamilton: "Alas, Beckett's book is as obscure as I feared. I don't feel that I can make an offer. Many thanks all the same."[52]

Like *Murphy*, Beckett continued his peregrinations. From Dresden he had intended to go to Florence, but at the last minute he abandoned this plan and elected to stay in Germany to keep in closer touch with Reavey. He stopped briefly in Bamburg and Nuremburg.

Arriving in Nuremburg late one evening, tired, dirty and disheveled, he badly wanted a bath and bed. He walked into the first hotel he saw and found that he had stumbled unwittingly into the general headquarters of high-ranking Nazi officials who were in the city for a party congress. Although the guards at the hotel door wanted to detain him, he was able to put his fluent German to good use and leave quietly without causing an incident. Nuremburg was too regimented in its military efficiency, and he hurried on next morning to Munich.

Nuremburg was regimented, but Munich was frightening. Most modern painting had been destroyed or hidden; there was only one private gallery which dared to exhibit Klee, Munch and Nolde.[53] There Beckett met an American graduate student who was writing a thesis on the influence of nineteenth-century German painters on American primitives. He found it incongruous that the man should be writing on such a subject under a Nazi regime dedicated to destroying all art not approved of by the state. There was another student, a German writing on

Proust, who knew Beckett's monograph. To submit a thesis on a writer who was both foreign and Jewish seemed the ultimate in audacity or stupidity—Beckett was not sure which—but he dwelt more on the fact that the man knew his book than on the circumstances of the thesis.[54]

Beckett arrived in Munich late on the first Friday afternoon in March, just in time to pick up his mail before the post office closed for the weekend. There was no word from Reavey, but he received pleasant, unexpected letters, from Jack B. Yeats and Mary Manning Howe, who was working to arrange an American commission for him with Houghton Mifflin. Still dragging its heels over *Murphy*, the American firm was interested in a volume of critical essays. They had turned down *Proust* earlier, saying it was too short for separate publication, but now were interested in using it as the cornerstone of a volume of essays to include Gide, Céline, and Malraux. If *Murphy* had been settled when this letter came, Beckett might have written the essays, but as things stood he was incapable of beginning anything. He was angry with himself for not being more enthusiastic, especially since he knew how terrible it would be to go home and face his mother with bad news about *Murphy*. He passed the letter along to McGreevy, suggesting he try to interest Houghton Mifflin in his essays on Aldington and Eliot.[55]

In the same post, he received a disturbing letter from his mother, writing at length about the cancerous growths in the beloved Kerry Blue bitch whom he included in *More Pricks*, but not saying what was being done with the dog. This was a sign of trouble which Beckett recognized immediately: May's letters on this trip had gone from chatty and cheerful to brief statements accompanying his checks. Her final ploy was one which had worked before: to write in detail of problems and illnesses she knew would infuse him with guilt, but to say nothing of the outcome or disposition of anything. As in the past, it seemed to be having the effect she desired.

His plan was to go on, to Augsburg, Ulm, Stuttgart, Karlsruhe, Freiburg, Colmar, Strassburg and Frankfurt, but he could not. The journey was over, mentally if not yet physically, and all he wanted was to get out of the country. The thought of trains and boats, with all the changes required, was too awful to consider, so he moved into a boarding house where he lived frugally for the rest of the month, saving his money for his first plane flight.

By flying he could get a much better rate of currency exchange and could make the journey in one short day. Early in April, 1937, he flew from Munich to Frankfurt and Amsterdam, then changed planes and flew to London, spending just seven hours in transit.[56]

He was supposed to be Geoffrey Thompson's house guest in London, but he was not in the mood to be social, so he paid for a room at Mrs. Frost's. Beckett was not surprised to learn that Bion was still hoping he would continue the analysis. Even if he had wanted to, Beckett could not have gone on with it; his mother controlled the purse strings, and she wanted him at home. He knew it was madness to go, but he felt he had no choice. All he wanted was to be quiet and alone in a room for which he did not have to pay. His correspondence shows that he was disoriented as well as exhausted. In the midst of a rambling letter to Ussher, full of incoherent comments about art, books he was reading and the futility of continuing his journey, he suddenly inserted the following paragraph: "My memories begin under the table, on the eve of my birth, when my father gave a dinner party and my mother presided."[57] With a sinister matter-of-factness, he decided there was only one course of action for him: to turn his mind back to 1925, and to begin all over again to kill himself.

He returned to Cooldrinagh the day before his thirty-first birthday and was greeted indifferently by his mother and brother, who were not surprised to hear that *Murphy* was still not placed and that he had done no work to speak of while he was away.[58]

As soon as Beckett returned, Frank told him that he had become engaged to Jean Violet Wright and expected to be married in August. This announcement was made matter-of-factly, without elaboration, and was followed by the equally terse statement that he would begin to look for a house as soon as possible. It was a sad fact for Beckett to admit, but he and Frank had been unable to communicate for years. Now, this attenuated statement was Frank's way of saying that Beckett would soon have total responsibility for their mother's care and companionship.

As Beckett was depressed, any announcement, no matter how serious, made little impression on him. Perhaps it was because he showed so little emotion and made no reaction to Frank's engagement that May fell into a pattern of behavior deliberately designed to provoke him. Her first act was to have the Kerry Blue bitch chloroformed without telling him.[59] She had done nothing about the dog when he was in Germany except to send letters hinting of the animal's imminent demise. When he came home, she brushed off his inquiries, saying nothing needed to be done just yet. But as soon as he went off to spend an afternoon with Jack B. Yeats, she had the dog put to sleep. When Beckett came home he found his mother prostrated in bed, so full of grief (feigned or real) that she was incoherent. For two days he was compelled to sit beside her, calming her hysteria, ministering to her every need, until she became quiet and reasonable. Her behavior thus kept him from being able to express his anger with her for killing the dog without telling him, prevented him also from expressing his own sorrow and served to bind him closer to her. For as long as she was ill, he could not think of leaving her side.

Throughout this episode Beckett's reactions were muted, which encouraged May to more openly aggressive behavior. "This morning Mother urged me to apply for the post of assistant librarian in the National Library, at £150 a year, assuring me that my ignorance of Gaelic was of no significance,"[60] he wrote to Mrs. Howe. May seemed under the delusion that, because he was William Beckett's son, he would automatically be given the position. She had taken to invoking her husband's name in almost every conversation, saying "Bill would have liked . . ." or "Bill would have approved," or most galling of all, "when in doubt as to behavior, simply ask oneself what Darling Bill would have done in similar circumstances."[61] At first he was able to ignore these remarks, but as part of his mind grew resigned to permanent attachment to his mother, another part began to smolder with shame and rage. His parents' marriage had never been the idyllic relationship May had conjured up since Bill's death, and the sound of his beloved father's name tripping off her tongue in such outlandish statements made him able to admit for the first time just how much he hated his mother. Open admission of his hatred for her was a purgative experience which released a flood of irrational behavior. For the next few months he was like a wild man, drunk, disorderly, harmful to himself and capable of frightening his mother with the possibility of physical violence toward others.

Still, she was undaunted in her determination to make him fit into the role she thought he should play. No sooner had he persuaded her that he could not apply for the library job than she came up with another, this time through one of Frank's friends, who knew that Lord Rathdowne was always absent from his estate in Carlow and needed a resident agent. This job would have kept Beckett in Ireland, close enough for his mother to visit frequently, but far enough away that he could maintain a sense of independence. It paid three hundred pounds a year, and a free house was one of the perquisites.[62] He was not about to rusticate himself, so he passed the information to Arland Ussher, who didn't want it either. Joseph Hone did, however, but by the time Beckett was able to send the particulars to him in Switzerland, the job had been filled.

Somehow May found out about the position as lecturer at Capetown, and she began to hound him to be more aggressive. Rudmose-Brown was also worried about Beckett's aimless drifting, and he, too, urged Beckett to complete the application he had begun months ago. Beckett asked Walter Starkie and Sir Robert Tate, his other professors at Trinity, to give him recommendations,[63] but did so only to silence his mother and Rudmose-Brown:

> Ruddy wants me to bury myself in Capetown as lecturer in Italian and wrote a long testimonial calling the kettle white as snow. Tate and Starkie also perjured themselves. Thus armed, I am in a position not to apply.[64]

In quick succession, he withdrew from the Capetown job and the Ringlenatz translation and refused to write a review of Denis Devlin's *Intercessions* for *Ireland Today*. He also refused even to apply for a job in the University of Buffalo's English Department, which had been arranged for him by Mary Manning Howe, who had been drawn long-distance into May's job hunting. Beckett would not even meet the chairman of the English Department when he came to Dublin that summer, but wrote sarcastically to Mrs. Howe in a parody of his mother's speech: "So you see, the man *won't* [Beckett's emphasis] work!"[65] He was taking perverse delight in thwarting his mother's efforts. He escaped from her nagging by cleaning up the little top-floor room at Clare Street, where he intended to force himself to write about Samuel Johnson, whom he called "The Great Cham" and "the Harmless Dandy."[66]

Beckett's original idea was to write a play in four acts, called *Human Wishes,* after Johnson's poem "The Vanity of Human Wishes."[67] He intended to explain Johnson's esteem for "the imbecile Mr. Thrale"[68] by concentrating on Mrs. Thrale's relationship to the mature Johnson, and his obsessive, unspoken love for her. At their first meeting in 1764, Johnson was fifty-five and Mrs. Thrale twenty-three, married and pregnant. Mr. Thrale, whom she respected but did not love, died in 1781, when she was forty and Johnson seventy-two. There followed a four-year-long flirtation between Mrs. Thrale and Dr. Johnson, which ended abruptly when she married Gabriel Piozzi. Johnson, in a thunderous rage, decreed that he would never hear Mrs. Thrale's name mentioned again, and died without forgiving her in December, 1784.

Beckett wished to fashion a play from these few biographical details, with one act devoted to each of the four years between Thrale's death and Mrs. Thrale's marriage to Piozzi. For the first time in quite a long time Beckett was caught up in the excitement of a new work, and he wanted to share it with his friends. His comments about Johnson shed as much light on Beckett as on his subject. To McGreevy, he wrote:

I have been working . . . on the Johnson thing to find my position . . . more strikingly confirmed than I had dared hope. It seems now quite certain that he was rather absurdly in love with her all the fifteen years he was at Streatham, though there is no text for the impotence. It becomes more interesting, the false rage to cover his retreat from her, than the real rage when he realizes that no retreat was necessary, and beneath all, the despair of the lover with nothing to love with, and much more difficult.[69]

To Reavey:

> My efforts to document my Johnson fantasy have not ceased. The evidence for it is overwhelming. It explains what has never been explained, i.e. his grotesque attitude toward his life and Mrs. Thrale. It is hard to put across . . . he being so old at the crisis, i.e.: she could hardly have expected much from him. We will make him younger and more virile than ever before.[70]

To Joseph Hone:

> Still there is a mass of material that would be useful. e.g. in the Annals, his recollection of the first time that the heaven-hell dichotomy was brought to his mind when he was in bed with his mother after 18 months. Heaven she described as the happy place where some people went, hell was the sad place where the rest went. She does not seem to have been high church. The following morning, so that she might impress the information on his mind, she required him to repeat to Farmer Jackson, her serving man. But he would not. All this would come in quite naturally in the last act, i.e. his fearing his death, when he was being reproached by his clerical friend, Taylor, for holding the opinion that an eternity of torment was preferable to annihilation. He must have had the vision of *positive* [Beckett's emphasis] annihilation. Of how many can as much be said.[71]

The ten pages of the extant manuscript begin with Act I, a room in Bolt Court, Wednesday, April 4, 1781.[72] Beckett lists the four characters who are on stage as the curtain rises, with stage directions in parentheses following their names:

> Mrs. Williams (meditating)
> Mrs. Desmoulins (knitting)
> Miss Carmichael (reading)
> The cat, Hodge (sleeping—if possible)

They are waiting for Dr. Johnson to return from Mr. Thrale's funeral. From comments about Hodge being a "very fine cat," Mrs. Williams turns the conversation to "knotting" (i.e., "knitting"), which leads in turn to an exchange of insults among the first five pages of typescript.

Then Levett enters, "slightly, respectably, even reluctantly drunk." He stands peering at the company but is ignored by the three women until he "emits a single hiccup of such force that he is almost thrown off his feet."

The three women, startled, "survey him with indignation," but Levett is absorbed only in himself. He leaves the room, not shutting the door behind him, and his footsteps are heard on the stairs. The three women make "gestures of disgust. Mouths opened and shut," and they returned to their occupations.

An exchange follows, curiously presaging Beckett's later dramatic writing, especially *Waiting for Godot:*

> *Mrs. W.* Words fail us.
> *Mrs. D.* Now this is where a writer for the stage would have us speak no doubt.
> *Mrs. W.* He would have us explain Levett.
> *Mrs. D.* To the public.
> *Mrs. W.* The ignorant public.
> *Mrs. D.* To the gallery.
> *Mrs. W.* To the pit.
> *Miss C.* To the boxes.
> *Mrs. W.* Mr. Murphy.
> *Mrs. D.* Mr. Kelly.
> *Miss C.* Mr. Goldsmith.
> *Mrs. D.* Let us not speak unkindly of the departed.

In the last four pages, the three women speak half aloud, half to themselves about death. The scene ends as Miss Car-michael reads a quotation about death, provoking Mrs. Williams to wager a guinea that the author is "Brown":

> *Mrs. W.* Turn to the title page, my child and tell me is it Brown.
> *Miss C.* (turning to the title page) Taylor.

What finally stopped Beckett from writing the entire play was the problem of language:

> It was a question of putting it into the Irish accent as well as the proper language of the period. It would not do to have Johnson speaking proper language, after the manner of Boswell, while all the other characters speak only the impossible jargon I put into their mouths.[73]

Since he wanted the play to be performed first in Ireland, he insisted that Irish inflections be incorporated into the speech patterns of his characters and spent hours consulting linguistic texts hoping to find a precedent. Then he decided to make Johnson speak only the words which were actually found in Boswell, but he could not extend this veracity to the speech of the other characters. Finally, he was unable to concentrate on eighteenth-century attitudes and conversations. He found it impossible to remove himself, with his twentieth-century sensitivities, from the manuscript. Too much irony, if not outright sarcasm, were in this play, and he did not want to impose his sensitivities on "The Great Cham."

Also, it was an ambitious production, and the full four acts would have required a large stage divided into several levels with a great deal of movement and interaction among the characters. There were to be numerous entrances and exits, many sound effects, and much theatricality requiring elaborate stage directions. In the ten extant pages, with the exception of one or two indications, such as the one to turn the pages of a book, Beckett's only stage direction is (silence). Almost every speech is followed by this single instruction. With hindsight, one can surmise that the man and his medium were not yet suitably matched; synthesis of the playwright with his material would not come for many years. By late summer he abandoned the play. "The Johnson thing has gone away to be died," he wrote to Reavey, "I mean the idea of it. For nothing has been degraded to paper. I have been too tired."[74]

Beckett abandoned the play, but not Johnson, whom he still reads. He finds much that appeals to him, particularly the melancholy moods and depressions which characterized Johnson's later life:

> . . . there can hardly have been many so completely at sea in their solitude as he was or so horribly aware of it. Read the Prayers and Meditations if you don't believe me . . . she [Mrs. Thrale] had none of that need to suffer or necessity of suffering that he had . . . he, in a sense was spiritually self-conscious, was a tragic figure, i.e., worth putting down as part of the whole of which oneself is part . . .[75]

Beckett takes perverse delight in listening to scholars place him squarely in the tradition of Fielding and Sterne. "They can put me wherever they want, but it's Johnson, always Johnson, who is with me. And if I follow any tradition, it is his,"[76] he replies. Johnson's life as well as his work has appealed to Beckett. Johnson had psychological problems of his own, and like Beckett, he was a late bloomer. Beckett may have identified his physical afflictions with Johnson's—i.e., his boils, with Johnson's scrofula. Most importantly, in both men there is a love of theory and abstraction, and an incredible erudition, leading at times to an astonishing similarity of style.

Beckett thought so little of this play that he did not mention it to his official bibliographers.[77] When he speaks of his plays, he always calls *Waiting for Godot* "my second play" and refers to *Éleuthéria* as "the first."[78] He grows impatient when someone wants to discuss the Johnson manuscript. Beckett first alluded to the fact that he had kept the incomplete manuscript in 1947 in a casual conversation with Reavey, who did not pursue the subject. In 1958, he talked about it to his American director, Alan Schneider, again expressing his inability to capture speech patterns to his satisfaction. When Schneider asked to read it, Beckett refused brusquely. The American scholar Ruby Cohn asked Beckett for the manuscript in the late 1960's, and he gave it to her, saying he was glad to be rid of it.[79]

As soon as he returned from Germany in the spring of 1937, his nightly anxiety attacks began, but this time he was philosophical about them. He had resigned himself to living in his mother's house, on handouts from her and his brother, for the rest of his life:

> I feel that I shall meet most of my days from now on here and in tolerable content, not feeling much guilt at making the most of what ease there is to be had and not bothering very much about effort. After all, there has been an effort. But perhaps I am wrong.[80]

He had a constant pain in his pelvic bone and was often overtaken by sudden bouts of panic which now invaded his daylight hours. He was afraid something terrible was going to happen:

I am quite convinced, with the barren nub conviction of birth
having sprung the trap, that at this rate it is only a matter of a
few years before a hideous crisis, compared to which the last
was a word to the wise and which I shall be as little fit to deal
with as a bull calf with its castrators. There are still physical
things that I dare not think of. I am doped and buttoned up in
sadness . . .[81]

Previously, he had managed to control his drinking so that his
mother may have been aware that he came home drunk but she
never actually saw him. He had been careful to frequent out-of-
the-way pubs where he was unlikely to meet anyone who knew
her, but now he was filled with reckless abandon and didn't care
who saw him. One night after a wild spree, he sailed into the
lobby of one of the best hotels in Dublin, commandeered stationery and wrote long drunken scrawls to his friends, among
them the following to Ussher:

I am deteriorating now very rapidly. An insensible mass of
alcohol, nicotine, and feminine intoxication. A heap of guts.
With no end for.[82]

He gave up even the pretense of writing, and no longer felt
compelled to walk around with a pensive air for his mother's
benefit.[83] When Seumas O'Sullivan asked him to review Louis
MacNeice's Out of the Picture, he refused and passed it on to
Blanaid Salkeld.[84]

He had so little regard for himself that he even insulted his
dear friend Nancy Cunard, who fortunately did not realize it.
She was soliciting opinions from 148 authors for a pamphlet
called Authors Take Sides on the Spanish Civil War, and she
asked Beckett to reply to two questions: "Are you for or against
the legal government and the people of Republican Spain?" and
"Are you for or against Franco and Fascism?" Beckett's reply
was a facetious Irish phrase: "Up the Republic!" Miss Cunard
wrote again, demanding some sort of amplification, for she was
deeply committed to Spain and the pamphlet. When Beckett did
not answer, she printed his original statement exactly as he
wrote it.[85]

Then, in a move he knew would create a serious rift with
his mother, he agreed to testify for Boss Sinclair's brother in a

libel case against Oliver St. John Gogarty. All dealings with the Sinclairs enraged his mother; testimony in a courtroom would be reported in the papers and would, in her opinion, show the world her shameful burden, as Beckett's disgraceful company would be known. Beckett's main reason for agreeing to testify was not, as May insisted, to punish her, but because Boss had been terribly hurt by Gogarty's book, *As I Was Walking Down Sackville Street*.[86]

Three weeks before his death on May 4, 1937, at the County Home in Rathdrum, Boss read Gogarty's scathing description of an old usurer, a Jew who had a predilection for little girls, whom he enticed into his antique shop for purposes of sexual molestation. In Gogarty's account, the old usurer had twin grandsons who inherited not only the shop but their grandfather's sexual preferences. Morris Harris, grandfather of the twins, Harry and Boss, had been a well-known figure in Dublin who bequeathed his antique shop to his twin grandsons when he died.[87]

Not content with the scurrilous passage about their grandfather, Gogarty quoted a long poem about two Jewish brothers, one "gaitered" and the other named "Willie." It was common knowledge in Dublin that Harry Sinclair always wore gaiters and Boss's given name was William. On his deathbed, Boss made Harry swear that he would take action against Gogarty, and he asked Beckett to appear as witness.

Beckett knew what he was in for when he agreed, but he didn't care. When his mother berated him, he told her flatly that Boss wanted it, and besides, it would amuse him.[88] He knew that gossip would be raked up, and that he was in for all sorts of innuendo because of his joblessness and his authorship of *More Pricks*. This was probably the only time he was happy that *Murphy* was not yet published: it would have been one more round of ammunition for his attackers.

In June, he and Robert Kahn drove down to Cappagh in Beckett's ailing automobile for several days to visit Arland Ussher.[89] (These friendships infuriated May, who had a pronounced streak of anti-Semitism.) When he returned, he went from one drunken debauch to another, not caring who saw him. At home, he was openly drunk, possibly hoping to provoke his mother to throw him out. His correspondence is riddled with repression and hostility. "More and more stupid and more and more listless,"[90] he described himself; "I would write to you seriously if I thought you were susceptible to unreason," he wrote to Ussher, then broke off abruptly to write two full verses of the German round song, "Ein Hund Kam in Die Kuche, Und Stall dem Koch im ei . . ."—the song he used so effectively in *Waiting for Godot*.[91]

His behavior had a serious effect on his mother and brother. First, May was felled by what doctors described as "flu and laryngitis,"[92] but which really seemed to be a lingering psychosomatic ailment. Just when she was beginning to recover, she and Beckett woke up one morning to find everything in the house covered with blood. One of her dogs had managed to sneak into the house after a fight in which an artery in his tail had been severed, and he had jumped on every piece of furniture, trying to find comfort. Once the dog had been delivered to the veterinarian (where he was treated and recovered), May, filled with self-pity, got out of bed and insisted on cleaning the house herself, even though she had two servants in residence and could have hired all the extra help she needed.

At the same time, Frank had a blister on his arm which developed into a serious case of blood poisoning. It was opened and stitched while he was under general anesthetic, but was very slow to heal. There was some fear that Frank would have to postpone his wedding, but he insisted he would be well enough for it to take place as planned on August 25. He was buried in work at the office, was house-hunting and was exhausted by all the prewedding festivities. Beckett tried to keep out of Frank's way because he felt guilty that he moped around doing nothing constructive while Frank seemed a prisoner of frenetic circumstances.

Then it was Beckett's turn to be ill. He had "gastric flu," probably psychosomatic, a reaction to all the illness and activity around him. In an effort to shut it all out, he tried to read and made a surprising discovery:

> When I was ill I found the one thing I could read was Schopenhauer. Everything else I tried only confirmed the feeling of sickness. It was very curious. Like suddenly a window opened

in a fog. Always knew that he was one of the ones that mattered most to me.[93]

He seemed almost sad when his symptoms disappeared and he
was no longer able to justify staying in bed.

He was badly in debt to Frank because of his excessive
drinking and also because he had been obliged to buy a number of
presents during the summer. He sent a gift when Mary Manning
Howe gave birth to a daughter in June; he sent a Meissen cup
from Harry Sinclair's shop when George Reavey married
Gwynned Vernon; and now he had to buy something special for
Frank as soon as he could bring himself to ask May for another
loan. "I borrow and go blind," he said taciturnly.[94]

Two nights before the wedding he went to a party in the
Glenora Valley just outside Dublin where friends had rented a
house for the express purpose of holding drunken brawls. He
became falling-down drunk, lost his favorite hat (one his father
had given him), watch and a bottle of Jameson's whiskey. He
cut his head badly when he went home in the early hours of the
morning and, discovering that he had lost his key, tried to use his
head to batter down the back door of Cooldrinagh.[95]

It was hard to believe that his fights with his mother could
reach a higher level of vituperation, but they did. When she saw
him with his head swollen and bandaged and realized that he
would have to be best man for Frank in his battered condition,
she screamed at him, saying it was time he left Ireland once and
for all.

"It isn't of course, to be taken very seriously," Beckett
commented; "it has happened so often before and will again, but
I suppose each time there is a little less to be bound."[96]

Frank and Jean went driving through Scotland for their
honeymoon, leaving Beckett unbearably tense with his mother
and a house full of Roe relatives. Jean and Frank had bought a
beautiful house in Killiney, called The Shottery, high on a cliff
with a splendid vista overlooking the ocean, but would live in
Cooldrinagh for several weeks after their honeymoon until they
could occupy it.

While they were away, May seemed determined not to
allow herself to become provoked by anything Beckett did. She

decided suddenly that Cooldrinagh was too large for two persons, went through enormous fuss to rent it on a long-term lease
and was girlishly flirtatious when she talked about the cozy cottage the two of them would take. Beckett hoped this would
happen, reasoning that once she was out of the big house with all
its memories, she would be forced to take an interest in her new
surroundings and live in the present. She had just about decided
to accept a tenant when she discovered that someone in his
family was tubercular and hurriedly called it off. Sadly, Beckett
realized that she would have found something wrong with every
prospective tenant, because she simply did not want to leave
Cooldrinagh.

Murphy, meanwhile, was still being passed from one publisher to another. He wrote a poem to Reavey to express his
contempt for the latest rejection:

> *Oh Doubleday Doran*
> *Less Oxy than moron*
> *You've a mind like a whore on*
> *The way to Bundoran.*[97]

Still, the very thought of attempting to adjust to life alone with
his mother was enough for the usual effect: he was bedridden
with another attack of "gastric flu" for ten days in September.[98]
On the first day he was able to leave his bed, he drove into
Dublin, collided with a truck and demolished the car. He
claimed it didn't matter, that he had wanted to replace it with a
bicycle anyway. He was prosecuted for dangerous driving, and
instead of quietly paying his fine, went to court and fought it.
The decision went against him—and sent his mother into her
most towering rage.[99]

Something happened between September 21 and October
15 that gave Beckett the courage and determination to make the
abrupt decision that he would stay no longer in Ireland, no
matter how his mother begged or threatened him, even though
Frank was upset that once again he was walking out and dump-
ing the whole burden onto his shoulders. Whatever the reason, it
was serious enough that Beckett did not even confide it to
McGreevy, nor has he ever spoken of it to others. Perhaps it was

simply the culmination of six months of self-destructive behavior that hardened his resolve to leave; perhaps May grew
weary of the endless fighting and asked him to go once too
often, so that his pride would not let him renege; perhaps he was
able at last to admit openly that he had been wrong to think
himself well enough to deal with her. Whatever the circumstances, he announced that he was going, and he went.

At first, he intended to go to London, not thinking much
beyond what he would do once there. To save money, he made
tentative arrangements to stay either with the Reaveys or
McGreevy; or else he would take a room with Mr. and Mrs.
Frost. Then he decided to become completely independent and
asked McGreevy to reserve a separate room in his boarding
house. He said he had had his fill of mothers and surrogate
mothers and planned to live without them for the rest of his
life.[100]

Then, evidently with no prior thought, he suddenly announced that he would bypass London and go directly to Paris.

When May heard this, she knew he was serious. There was
one last trick left to her: she ordered Frank not to tell Beckett
where she was going and left for a secret destination where she
intended to remain in seclusion until (she hoped) he changed his
mind about leaving. May sent word through Frank, who had
moved into The Shottery, that she would permit Beckett to lock
the door of his study and keep the key. This way, she said, all his
things would be in order when he came to his senses and returned.[101]

With Frank living in The Shottery and May gone away,
Beckett had several weeks alone in Cooldrinagh. He described
his feelings to McGreevy:

> Instead of creeping about with the *agenbite* as I suppose I
> ought, I am marvelling at the pleasantness of Cooldrinagh with-
> out her. And I could not wish her anything better than to feel
> the same when I am away. But I don't wish her anything at all,
> neither good nor ill. I am what her savage loving has made me,
> and it is good that one of us should accept that finally as it has
> been all this time . . . I simply don't want to see her or write
> to her or hear from her . . . and if a telegram came now to say
> she is dead I would not do the furies the favor of regarding

myself even as indirectly responsible, which I suppose all boils down to saying what a bad son I am, then amen. It is a title for me of as little honor as infamy.[102]

In mid-October, with as much of his income as he could collect, augmented with money borrowed from Frank, he took the boat for England on the first leg of his journey back to Paris, the place where he had been as happy as he believed himself capable. He still did not know where his mother was, and his brother did not see him off. He went alone, and he did not look back.

CHAPTER TWELVE

1938–39:

"NO MATTER HOW THINGS GO,
I SHALL STAY HERE"

Beckett arrived in Paris the last week in October, 1937, and looked for a place to live in Montparnasse. His finances were perilous, and he tramped the streets from one hotel to another until he took a room he could not afford in a small pension.[1] Several days later a room became vacant at the Hotel Liberia, and he took it, thinking he would be there for a week at most until he found an apartment.

However, the long-delayed libel action between Harry Sinclair and Gogarty was abruptly scheduled to begin early in November. This meant that Beckett had no sooner arrived in France than he had to spend his tiny hoard to return to Ireland. Harry Sinclair had promised to pay his expenses, but Beckett knew that Sinclair was even poorer than he, and bravely insisted that he would pay his own way, with Sinclair to reimburse him when and if money for damages was awarded.

He decided to return to Dublin by way of London to see for himself what Reavey was doing with *Murphy*. Fortunately, and at the same time unfortunately, McGreevy wrote to say that he had planned to take a holiday in Paris to be with Beckett and since he could not change his plans, Beckett was free to use his London room.

Where he would stay in Dublin was another matter. Frank had written that May ended her self-enforced exile and returned

to Cooldrinagh, saying that she was quite ill and had to have a
series of abdominal X rays. Under the circumstances, Frank
thought it best if Beckett did not stay at The Shottery, and
suggested that he either do something to alleviate their mother's
suffering or else avoid all communication with her entirely.[2]

A few weeks in Paris had done for Beckett what psychoanalysis and two years in London had failed to do: in the past
such information about his mother's health would have induced
so much guilt that he would have slunk unhappily back to her
bedside; now he was able to say that he was sorry for her
troubles and wished her well, but he arranged to stay with Sean
O'Sullivan.

The action began on November 23, in a courtroom filled
with curious spectators. Gogarty's biographer, Ulick O'Connor,
described the scene:

> The case created a sensation in Dublin. There is an illusion
> common among Dubliners that they are potential writers or
> barristers. The opportunity of seeing both professions simul-
> taneously was not to be missed. There were queues for seats
> in the gallery of the court.[3]

At the beginning of the trial, all Dublin was on Sinclair's side,
hoping that he could indeed "get Gogarty," who had many
enemies. Sinclair's testimony, however, in which he actually produced records of his grandfather's alleged indiscretions and
readily agreed to their veracity, created a quandary for Dublin's
citizens. How could they support Gogarty, whose vicious pen
had castigated them all at one time or another, who mocked
Dublin and all in it while still claiming to be more Irish than
anyone? But even more difficult, how could they rally to the
side of a man who would produce in a public court evidence of
his grandfather's guilt in a disgusting and disgraceful crime? It
was a relief when Beckett was ushered to the stand to give testimony, as he was more easily classified by the spectators as someone at whom they could laugh.

Shortly before he went to Paris, Beckett gave the following
affidavit:

> I purchased a copy of the book, *As I Was Going Down Sack-
> ville Street* from Green's Library, 16 Clare Street, Dublin. My

attention had been called to it by the many advertisements I had read and the notoriety of its author. On reading the paragraphs . . . I instantly inferred that the lines . . . referred to Mr. Henry Morris Sinclair and the late Mr. William Abraham Sinclair and that the words "old usurer" and "grandsons" referred to the late Mr. Morris Harris and his said two grandsons. I also considered that the words constituted a very grave charge against the said Henry Morris Sinclair and his late brother.[4]

Beckett was cross-examined by J. M. Fitzgerald, K.C., one of the most brilliant barristers in Ireland:

> *Fitzgerald:* You have made an affidavit in which you led the court to believe that you were an impartial, independent person, but you forgot to tell the Court that it was your uncle-in-law who suggested that you should buy the book?
>
> *Beckett:* I said in my affidavit that my attention was attracted by the book because of the notoriety of the author and the advertisement it had received.[5]

Fitzgerald asked Beckett where he lived, and Beckett replied innocently that he lived in Paris. Fitzgerald wanted the jury to hear this, knowing that Paris, to the average Dubliner, was synonymous with decadence and debauchery. Fitzgerald asked Beckett what he had written to justify calling himself an author. "I have written verse, fiction, and literary criticism," Beckett replied.

Next, he asked if Beckett were the author of *Marcel Prowst*, deliberately mispronouncing the name although he spoke perfect French. As Fitzgerald had hoped, Beckett icily corrected him, thus strengthening the jury's adverse reaction to his testimony.

Fitzgerald then read an extract, which supposedly was "a blasphemous caricature of Our Redeemer," but the passage he quoted as coming from *Proust* was actually taken from *More Pricks Than Kicks*. This time Beckett did not correct him, knowing that Fitzgerald was hoping he would, so that he could make scurrilous remarks about the title.

Fitzgerald continued:

> Q.—Was Proust a man who indulged in the psychology of sex?
> A.—I have not been aware of that.

Q.—But you have written about him. How long did it take before your book was banned by the censorship of Ireland?

A.—About six months.

Q.—I suggest it was banned because it was a blasphemous and obscene book.

A.—I have never discovered why it was banned.

Q.—Do you call yourself a Christian, Jew or Atheist?

A.—None of the three.

Somewhat later, Fitzgerald asked Beckett if he had written a book "By the title of Horoscope with the letter 'W' prefixed."

By the time he sat down, Fitzgerald was confident that he had irreparably damaged Beckett's credibility as a witness. He had made exactly the right impression on the Dublin jurymen, inclined to have a touch of pious simplicity in their attitude toward religion and literature.

In his summation the following day, Fitzgerald vilified Beckett further. According to the *Irish Times*, Fitzgerald

> . . . would pass away from Mr. Beckett, the "bawd and blasphemer from Paris." He might well have stayed in Paris, because they would like to know why, of all the respectable people he knew, Mr. Sinclair should select that "bawd and blasphemer" from Paris to make an affidavit in the case to lead to the belief that any ordinary reasonable man reading the book would have identified Mr. Sinclair. Could they imagine "that wretched creature" making representations to the High Court as an ordinary reasonable man?

Fitzgerald's fiery rhetoric may have impugned Beckett as witness, but it was not enough. The jury found Gogarty guilty of libel and fined him nine hundred pounds in damages, plus costs. Gogarty claimed the action cost him more than two thousand pounds and said it was the main reason he left Ireland to live in the United States.[6] Beckett took a gloomier view when several years went by and Harry Sinclair had not received a cent of the money; all the action had accomplished as far as he was concerned was to turn over "the family manure."[7]

Fitzgerald's vicious castigation left Beckett both angry and humiliated. With the newspapers gleefully reporting all his testimony, he knew it was pointless to call on his mother. He went to Clare Street to apologize to Frank away from home, hoping to spare him further embarrassment. Frank was noncommittal and suggested that it would be best if Beckett returned to Paris without trying to see May. So he left immediately for Paris, vowing never to return to Dublin. As soon as he got back, Beckett wrote a long letter to Frank, apologizing again for the distress he had caused, and repeating his readiness to write to May whenever Frank thought it best. He was hurt when Frank did not answer.[8] May Beckett was mortified by the newspaper accounts of the trial, but she found release for her fury by blaming it all on the Sinclairs, whom she avoided for the rest of her life.[9]

If Beckett had any lingering doubts about the wisdom of moving to Paris, the trial took care of them. Years later he gave a truncated account of how he came to live in Paris:

> I didn't like living in Ireland. You know the kind of thing—theocracy, censorship of books, that kind of thing. I preferred to live abroad. In 1936 [sic], I came back to Paris and lived in a hotel for a time and then decided to settle down and make my life here.[10]

Paris represented all that was good, pleasant and intelligent, and he desperately needed to be there to gain some semblance of control over his life, to give order and meaning to it so that he could be completely independent for the very first time. In Paris he could have the privacy to spend his days and nights as he pleased. Cafe sitting, unlike pub crawling, was an accepted way of life, not a shameful act to be hidden or explained away. He could find sexual freedom because relationships were open and honest; no one's reputation was irreparably damaged when a man and woman met in a cafe to share a brandy and cigarette. Granted, the publishing possibilities were more limited because of the difference in language, but this was something he hoped to circumvent with *Murphy*.

By December 3 he was once again in the Hotel Liberia, and there, on December 9, 1937, he received a telegram from Reavey with the joyous, almost unbelievable news that Routledge had accepted *Murphy* for publication the following spring. After two years and forty-two publishers, the book was finally sold.

Herbert Read liked it enormously, and had insisted that Routledge take the novel for the spring publishing list. Read met
with some initial opposition among the firm's directors, but his
reputation for choosing successful books was such that he
eventually persuaded them. Not only did Routledge take
Murphy, but they agreed to pay an advance against royalties of
twenty-five pounds—a veritable windfall.[11]

Beckett's only comment at the time was "no jubilation, but
bien content quand même."[12] Later, when Reavey sent the contract, Beckett returned it unsigned—purely an omission, but one
Beckett still felt had some significance. When Charles Prentice
wrote to say how delightful he found the book, Beckett replied
that he felt less about its being taken than he had when it was
being rejected. All along he had been sure that *Murphy* would
be published eventually, but it had been too long in coming, and
for the time being at least, he could feel little emotion about it.
Nevertheless it was a marvelous augury which gave him the
confidence and enthusiasm to settle down in earnest.

He had gone to Paris intending to break out of his self-
imposed isolation, and almost as soon as he dropped his bags, he
began to look up old friends. He had a wild, drunken reunion
with Brian Coffey and Alan and Belinda Duncan, and had a
surprise encounter with Richard Thoma, who divided his time
between Paris and Poitiers. He saw Alfred Péron and was delighted with the ease with which they resumed their friendship.[13]
He wanted to telephone Georges Pelorson but was reluctant
to do so because he knew that any contact with Pelorson would
be reported to Eugene and Maria Jolas and eventually to Joyce.
He wanted to meet Joyce again and realized it was only a question of time until Joyce heard of his return, but he was so
frightened that he would be snubbed and rejected that he could
not bring himself to make any move.

However, he had been welcomed so warmly and fit in with
such ease among his friends in Paris that he gathered his courage
and decided first to call Pelorson and, if that went well, to telephone Joyce. The trial had interfered with his intentions, but on
the night of his return, he did so. Coffey and the Duncans met
him at the station and took him to dinner, and fortified by a
great deal of wine, he placed the call.

Nora answered the telephone and asked him to chat with her while Joyce finished dinner. She spoke as if Beckett had been away for a matter of weeks rather than years, and was full of amiable chatter. When Joyce came on the line, he was distant but polite and said he hoped to see Beckett sometime soon; in fact, if Beckett were free, why didn't he come around immediately, as there was a small service that he could perform which would be of great help . . .[14]

Joyce wanted Beckett to help Giorgio read the galleys of parts one and three of *Work in Progress*. He suggested offhandedly that Beckett could expect to be paid, thus placing Beckett in an uncomfortable position. He feared Joyce would cast him in his old errand-boy role. He could not accept the role even if he wanted to; on his own financially, he simply could not afford to devote time to Joyce's whims. Nevertheless, it was unthinkable to refuse any request of Joyce's, no matter how absurd, during their first conversation in years.

So he and Giorgio spent the next three days in Villa Scheffer, Helen and Giorgio's home, poring over the galleys, a stupefying task that seemed to go on forever. Joyce produced 250 old francs which he gave to Beckett along with an old overcoat and five ties he no longer wanted. Beckett was humiliated, but he took them all because it was easier to be hurt than to hurt.[15]

As an extra fillip, Joyce invited Beckett to dine on Christmas night with him and Nora, Giorgio and Helen, Paul and Lucie Léon, and Eugene and Maria Jolas. Beckett accepted quietly, without the alacrity he would have previously shown, simply because he thought it might be a pleasant way to spend the holiday.

He was concerned about reviving close contact with the Jolases, and this was no doubt part of the reason he was so cautious about moving back into Joyce's orbit. He had never liked Maria, whose mother-hen concern for Joyce seemed to him more like hovering interference. He detested the evenings when she and Joyce would sing together, calling them "caterwauling" or "shrieking."[16] Eugene Jolas struck him as a flamboyant personality with grandiose ideas who lacked the intelligence and commitment to transmit them into coherent form.

Nevertheless, Beckett had barely returned to Paris when he was swept up into the whirlpool of *transition:* Jolas wanted to print his review of Devlin's *Intercessions*, written the previous spring and still unpublished.[17]

Joyce was concerned about the momentary oblivion of *Work in Progress* (which he hoped would be ready for publication in six months on the anniversary of his father's birthday, July 4, 1938), and with Jolas's cooperation, decided to commission a collection of essays similar to *Our Exagmination* to bring it back into the public's eye. Beckett's coming to Paris could not have been more fortuitous, for Joyce had just persuaded *La Nouvelle Revue Française* to print one of these essays, and he expected Beckett to write it.

Beckett accepted the assignment reluctantly, and for several weeks made halfhearted attempts to write it. Several days before Christmas he decided to drop the matter entirely and not to refer to it unless Joyce asked directly. He also made up his mind that he would write nothing further on command for Joyce.

"If that means a break, then let there be a break," he wrote McGreevy. "At least this time it won't be about the daughter."[18]

Still, it was difficult to stay clear of the Joyce household. Beckett and Giorgio had been like brothers during Beckett's first sojourn in Paris, and the two men resumed this close relationship as soon as Beckett returned.[19] Giorgio's marriage to Helen was disintegrating, and Beckett found himself in the midst of the Joyces' continuing family drama. Helen received word, shortly before Christmas, that her father was desperately ill in New York. Christmas was an ordeal, with Beckett used by all the Joyces as a buffer to pass ideas and avoid communication. Against his parents' wishes, Giorgio succumbed to Helen's persuasions and agreed to sail with her to America shortly after the New Year.

They had all planned to celebrate the New Year in a gala night out, but when Beckett arrived at the flat, he found Nora in a frightful state, refusing to go while the others refused to go without her. For more than two hours Beckett sat in a corner of the room, trying to remain inconspicuous while Joyce unsuccessfully pleaded with Nora to change her mind. Finally Joyce sent him to join Helen and Giorgio, and Beckett ushered in the New Year trying to dispel their gloom.[20]

For Christmas Beckett had received a blue necktie with a pattern of stars, sent anonymously from Dublin, which he was sure was from his mother. He wrote a long letter, suggesting they bury their old grudges and try to become friends, and was greatly relieved when she sent an affectionate reply saying she had toasted him with champagne on Christmas night and would be happy to meet him in London for holidays if he insisted on staying away from Ireland.[21] He wrote about the necktie after the war in *La Fin* (*The End*), the story about his departure from Ireland and settlement in Paris.[22]

So many people came and went over the holidays that Beckett had little opportunity to do any work or look for an apartment. A large contingent of the Dublin Irish passed through, and he saw them with confidence and pleasure on neutral ground. He had been with Joyce every evening since the disastrous New Year's Eve, and was becoming convinced that he could maintain both the friendship and his independence, though Joyce had not yet realized the change in him. He dangled tentative invitations for Beckett to accompany him to Zurich once *Work in Progress* was finished. He played the sly little game with Beckett with which he teased all his friends, forcing one and all to try to guess the real title of the book. Then he would sit for hours, deprecating his talent, waiting for Beckett to contradict and praise him. Beckett was good-natured about it all because he no longer felt any danger in the association. To him, Joyce was "just a very lovable human being."[23]

Joyce liked having Beckett "seated at his right hand,"[24] and so Beckett found his evenings suddenly filled with invitations to dinner parties to which the Joyces had been invited. The night after Christmas, he found himself seated opposite a woman who seemed to be studying him with more than a passing interest. He had met Peggy Guggenheim, the American heiress, during his earlier stay in Paris when he attended parties in the house on avenue Reille where she lived with John Holms. So many people had flitted in and out of these parties that their first meeting amounted to little. Now, with John Holms dead and the house rented, Guggenheim was crossing back and forth from London, where she had started an art gallery, to Paris, where many of her friends lived.

Guggenheim Jeune, her gallery, was located on Cork Street in the heart of London's art district. Initially, she had planned to feature paintings by old masters, but Herbert Read, who became her partner, persuaded her to share his interest in modern art. Guggenheim was living around the corner from Reavey (who was at 7 Great Ormond Street) on Lamb's Conduit, and their paths crossed often at parties and gallery openings. Reavey spoke of Beckett's new novel and she knew of Herbert Read's enthusiasm for *Murphy*, so that when she found herself in Beckett's company, she studied him. He squirmed under her direct gaze, hoping to divert it by concentrating obsequiously on Joyce, while she concentrated on Beckett more than on her dinner.

In *Out of This Century*, a thinly veiled account of her life, Guggenheim wrote about an Irishman she called "Liam" who was a friend of Beckett's. The best description of her at this time comes from him:

> Peggy was a Venus-like creature, charming, fluttering about from one thing to another. She didn't understand literary affairs but she was always picking up the bon mot, the good phrase. She was the rose between two thorns, as Sam and I called her then. She was sensual, taking—always interested in literature, but only in terms of what she could take from it or how it could be turned towards her. She recognized something in Sam, and I think she wanted to be a part of whatever good things were going to happen to him.[25]

In her book Guggenheim described Beckett as

> . . . a tall, lanky Irishman of about thirty with enormous green eyes that never looked at you. He wore spectacles, and always seemed to be far away solving some intellectual problem; he spoke very seldom and never said anything stupid. He was excessively polite, but rather awkward. He dressed badly in tight-fitting French clothes and had no vanity about his appearance. . . . He was a frustrated writer, a pure intellectual.[26]

After dinner, the entire group adjourned to Villa Scheffer for drinks and conversation. When the evening ended, Beckett, who had tried to seem oblivious to Guggenheim's frank and unabashed staring, surprised her by asking if he could walk her home. It was a long walk to the rue de Lille, where she was living in a borrowed apartment, but she gamely matched his long-legged stride. When they arrived, Beckett, according to Guggenheim, "did not make his intentions clear but in an awkward way asked me to lie down on the sofa next to him. We soon found ourselves in bed, where we remained until the next evening at dinner time."[27]

They talked for hours, she eager to listen to his ideas about art and literature, he drunk enough to expound at length. At one point, when she mentioned a liking for champagne, Beckett jumped out of bed, rushed out and bought several bottles. Later, as they sat in bed drinking and talking, he told her of his friend, the Dutch painter, Geer van Velde, whom he considered a great artist, and he asked her to give him a one-man show. She filed the information in her mental file of possibilities, reluctant to commit her gallery to an unknown. But he became wildly excited, saying there was a painter even greater than Geer van Velde who must be honored first—Jack B. Yeats. Long discourses on Irish painting followed, but her attention span lapsed and she remembers very little else of what he said.[28] He promised to bring her a copy of *More Pricks Than Kicks* and spoke excitedly of *Murphy*, which he was confident would be a major success when it appeared in the spring. He had finally read Céline, and told her that *Journey to the End of the Night* was the greatest novel in both French and English literature. She thought he seemed almost ashamed when he said this, as if the spirit of James Joyce were in the room with them. When Guggenheim asked him about Joyce, he replied brusquely that she didn't understand what he was trying to say: Joyce was the master, there was no one to equal him. He existed on one plane in literature, alone and incomparable. It was on the next lower plane, where everyone else existed, that Céline was the greatest. Beckett had also been reading *Mea Culpa*, Céline's pamphlet written after his return from Russia in 1936, denouncing the "proletariat paradise" he did not find there, and Guggenheim found it curious that he discussed it only in terms of the language and imagery, that the political content made no impression on him. Beckett told her he had no time for politics. He said he accepted life fatalistically, and political activity, even discussion, was a waste of time.

Late the next evening, when both were exhausted with words, emotion and experience, the idyll ended as Guggenheim left Beckett drowsing and went off to a dinner engagement with someone else.

"Thank you, it was nice while it lasted," Beckett said, according to Guggenheim, as she left.[29]

The affair became public when Joyce, "to whom he [Beckett] was a sort of slave,"[30] was unable to reach Beckett the next day. However, the affair seems to have ended almost before it began, as Beckett went back to the Hotel Liberia, to Joyce and to his haphazard reading and writing. The next day Guggenheim moved into the house of Beckett's friend, Mary Reynolds (whom she calls "Agnes" in her book) and busied herself with other things.

Shortly before the new year[31] they met by chance one night on a traffic island in the boulevard du Montparnasse, then went back to Mary Reynolds's house, where they stayed for almost two weeks.

> We were destined to be happy together only for this short period. Out of all the thirteen months I was in love with him, I remember this time with great emotion. To begin with he was in love with me as well.[32]

"Looking back on it now," Guggenheim recalled in later years, "I don't think he was in love with me for more than ten minutes. He couldn't make up his mind about anything. He wanted me around but he didn't want to have to do anything about it."[33] She called him Oblomov

> . . . from the book by Goncharov that Djuna [Barnes] had given me to read long before. . . . I made him read the book and of course he immediately saw a resemblance between himself and the strange inactive hero who finally did not even have the willpower to get out of bed.[34]

He seemed to take inordinate pride in the nickname, and gave
her the distinct impression that he was actively trying to emulate
the lackadaisical behavior of the Russian character. He urged
McGreevy to get hold of the book at once and shared his own
copy with Geer van Velde and Brian Coffey.[35]

Throughout their affair Beckett entertained her with his
sardonic sense of humor, and his "strange and morbid ideas
which were quite original."[36] She found him exciting because
he was so unpredictable:

> The thing I liked best about our life together was that I never
> knew at what hour of the night or day he might return to me.
> His comings and goings were completely unpredictable, and I
> found that exciting. He was drunk all the time, and seemed to
> wander around in a dream. I had a lot of work to do because
> of my gallery and often I had to get up in the afternoon to
> see Cocteau, who was to have the opening show. Oblomov ob-
> jected to this, he wanted me to remain in bed with him.[37]

At the end of the time in Mary Reynolds's house, Beckett,
according to Guggenheim, "allowed a friend from Dublin to
creep into his bed."[38] He explained his transgression by saying
that he had been unable to put the young woman out of his
room when she came there, implying that passivity and submis-
sion seemed to him the most sensible behavior at the time. He
told Guggenheim that "making love without being in love was
like taking coffee without brandy,"[39] from which she inferred
that she was the brandy in his life. Still, she was angry and
unforgiving and sent him away.

He went back to the Hotel Liberia, where an invitation was
waiting for him from Alan and Belinda Duncan to go to the
movies. In the early morning hours of January 7, when the three
were returning home after a long time in a cafe, they were
stopped on the avenue d'Orléans by a man Beckett recognized as
a pimp who operated in the quarter.[40]

The pimp, whose name ironically was Prudent, fell into
step beside Beckett, asking him for money. When Beckett said he
had none, Prudent persisted, offering to provide the services of
his best girl if Beckett would make a small loan. Again Beckett

refused, and quickened his step. Prudent grabbed him by the arm and grew more vociferous in his demands. Beckett, irritated, flung his arm away, pushing Prudent to the ground. The pimp jumped up, whipped out a clasp knife and shoved it into Beckett's chest.

Beckett fell to the ground bleeding profusely; the knife struck into the pleura on the left side of his chest and missed his heart only because the heavy overcoat he wore halted its penetration. The Duncans, in a state of shock, shouted to the deserted streets for someone to stop the assassin. A young woman happened by who gave them the calm direction they needed. Suzanne Deschevaux-Dumesnil, a piano student, was hurrying home after a late evening concert when she came upon the scene. Quickly she helped to wrap Beckett in Alan Duncan's overcoat and arranged a makeshift pillow before she called an ambulance.

Beckett was taken to the Hôpital Broussais. He had come very close to death—though how close was not known for a week because Beckett's room was on a different floor from the X ray equipment and the doctors considered him too weak to be moved.

Guggenheim, meanwhile, had had a change of heart, and wanted to apologize to Beckett. She telephoned all their friends to no avail, then set out unsuccessfully to look for him. The next morning she telephoned Nora Joyce, who told her what had happened. Joyce, unhappy that Guggenheim had taken Beckett away from him, was one of the first to find out about the stabbing because he wanted to see Beckett the night before and had telephoned the hotel repeatedly.

That afternoon Joyce went to Hôpital Broussais. Leaning heavily on Paul Léon's arm for guidance as his eyes were particularly bad at this time, he went from one ward to another seeking Beckett. When he finally found him, Joyce insisted that Beckett be moved into a private room at his expense.[41]

The stabbing threw all of Beckett's friends into an uproar, but especially the Joyces, whose flat was "like the stock exchange, telephone calls from everywhere."[42] Helen and Giorgio were supposed to sail to the United States the day after it happened, and consented to go only when Joyce promised faithfully to send bulletins of Beckett's progress. Nora insisted on making a special custard pudding, and even before Beckett was able to sit up in bed, Joyce donated his favorite reading lamp for Beckett to use as long as he was in the hospital.[43]

Beckett, meanwhile, was rather enjoying the excitement. Once his initial discomfort and worry were over, he noted with some delight that Hôpital Broussais was "Verlaine's hospital."[44] When Coffey and Joyce visited him at the same time and found themselves standing on either side of his bed, he introduced them "over my dead body."[45] He tried to persuade Guggenheim to hire McGreevy to work in the London gallery. He agreed to translate a preface written by Jean Cocteau for the catalog of Guggenheim's first show, Les Chevaliers de la table ronde, scheduled for May.[46] He was being assisted in correcting the proofs of Murphy by Alfred Péron, who wanted to collaborate on a French translation for La Nouvelle Revue Française. He even wrote a poem—four short lines, his only writing for months—which he said "dictated itself to me."[47]

The freeing of his creative processes from whatever had been blocking them was obviously a sign of great importance to him. "How lovely it is being here, even with a hole inside . . . brighter than the whole of Ireland in summer," he wrote to McGreevy.[48] The stabbing, a random incident, would have incapacitated him entirely if it had happened in Ireland, but in Paris it was only something to be borne as a matter of course. The stability and ease with which he accepted it is apparent in his attitude towards the many people who wrote or visited him. Instead of trying to withdraw from them all, as he would have done several months earlier, he welcomed their concern and relished their attention. He was almost miraculously friendly and sociable—even toward his mother and brother, who flew to Paris as soon as they heard of the incident.

The news had reached them through Dr. Gerald Beckett, who was on his way to the Gaiety Theatre in Dublin with his three children when he saw a crowd gathered around a newsboy hawking a paper with the provocative headline "Irish Poet Stabbed in Paris, Early Morning Attack."[49] Jokingly, Dr. Beckett suggested buying a paper to see if they knew the victim. It was he who had the unfortunate task of telling May about this latest public humiliation inflicted by her younger son. At the hospital, May spent her days sitting by his bedside, silent, worried, and unnerved by the constant flow of visitors, all so different from the people she knew in Dublin, all so far removed from her world. Nevertheless, her bedside vigil opened the lines of communication between them and healed the breach caused by his departure from Cooldrinagh. When she left, Beckett was surprised to discover that he had felt waves of affection, esteem and compassion for her. "What a relationship!" he concluded.[50]

On January 23, 1938, Beckett was discharged from the hospital. May and Frank saw him back to the Hotel Liberia, then, to his great relief, returned to Dublin. Peggy Guggenheim had also taken a room there to aid him during his convalescence and he was terrified that she and his mother would meet.[51] Her presence in the hotel was a complicating factor in his life, for he had become interested in Suzanne Deschevaux-Dumesnil when she had visited him in the hospital, and he preferred to see each woman without the other's knowing it.

Suzanne Deschevaux-Dumesnil came into Samuel Beckett's life as an organizing force of great strength and tranquillity. Peggy Guggenheim aptly described the difference between them: "She made curtains while I made scenes."[52] The very first act of their relationship—the manner in which Suzanne took charge at the scene of the stabbing—has been characteristic of their forty-year relationship. She herself was thirty-eight when they met, seven years older than Beckett. Tall, rawboned and plain, she was nevertheless handsome; sure of her own worth, she gave off an aura of poise and repose that made her attractive, interesting, and at the same time soothing.

She was a serious and talented pianist, both performer and teacher. There were colonial connections in her family, giving rise in later years to legends that she was a native Algerian, the daughter of a Berber chieftain, or (as Peggy Guggenheim called her) a "simple native girl." None is true. Her family had always lived in Troyes, France.

From the beginning of her relationship with Beckett, she preferred self-effacement and managed without fuss to erect a wall of privacy around herself even more impenetrable than his. She seemed to sense that Beckett, who claimed to have had his fill of surrogate mothers, really could not do without one. She has devoted her life to filling his every need, from providing food and doing laundry to acting as his literary agent and even, for a short time, financial provider. Like Peggy Guggenheim, she decided that she wanted him and then matter-of-factly, definitely, moved into his life. He allowed her to do so, exhibiting the passivity that has colored most of his relationships with women.

When he was released from the hospital, he still had a great deal of discomfort from the wound, and doctors warned that his lungs would be a barometer forecasting the approach of inclement weather for the rest of his life.[53] The doctors wanted to continue observing him as an outpatient, but since he never woke up before noon and his appointments were scheduled for 9:15 a.m. he never kept them. He did manage to correct proofs for *Murphy* and bemoan the fact that Reavey had never shown his beloved apes to Routledge. "I shall pass the rest of my life regretting the monkeys," he said sadly.[54]

One last complication remained before the printers locked the type for *Murphy*. Someone at Routledge had decided to insert a publicity blurb within the covers of the book itself. He wrote a scathing letter to Reavey, demanding that the blurb be removed, and then had to send mollifying letters when he discovered that not only had Reavey written it, but also that it had been his idea to have it appear within the book.[55] Routledge was determined to exaggerate the Irishness of the novel, even binding it in a green cloth cover. Thus, the offending blurb, which stressed the "Irish genius" and "Celtic waywardness" of "Sam" Beckett was an offense he would not tolerate. The merest suggestion that he was an "Irish" writer enraged him. Witness his remarks to McGreevy, who had just written an essay on Jack B. Yeats which Beckett felt dealt less with the man as a painter than as an Irishman:

> . . . your interest was passing from the man himself to the forces that formed him. . . . But perhaps that also is the fault of my mood and my chronic inability to understand . . . a phrase like "The Irish People" or to imagine that it ever gave a fart in its corduroys for any form of art whatsoever, whether before the union or after, or that it was ever capable of any

thought or act other than rudimentary thoughts and acts delved into by the priests and demagogues in service of the priests, or that it would ever care or know that there was once a painter in Ireland called Jack Butler Yeats. This is not a criticism of the criticism that allows as a sentient subject which I can only think of as a nameless and hideous mass whether in Ireland or in Finland, but only to say that I as a prod of prejudices prefer the first half of your work with its real and radiant individuals to the second with our national scene.[56]

Some years later a reporter asked Beckett how a small country like Ireland could have produced so many great writers since the last half of the nineteenth century. "It's the priests and the British," Beckett replied tersely. "They have buggered us into existence. After all, when you are in the last bloody ditch, there is nothing left but to sing."[57]

Even though Beckett was still supposed to be confined to the Liberia, Joyce insisted that Beckett attend his fifty-sixth birthday party on February 2. A dinner given by Maria Jolas, "Jolases-Molases, bawling her lungs out," was an event he would gladly have missed, but he wanted to give Joyce a bottle of the Neufchâtel wine he loved, and so he went, knowing that Joyce would be grateful for his presence. There were fifteen people present, and as he expected, Mrs. Jolas and Joyce's friend, John Sullivan, sang after dinner, and Joyce danced in his old style, as he had not since Lucia had been hospitalized.

There Beckett renewed contacts with persons who had been helpful to his writing previously and who offered to help again. Philippe Soupault wanted to see his newest poems (there were none) and Nino Frank wanted to introduce him to filmmakers and producers. A direct offer came from Jack Kahane, who asked Beckett to undertake the first English translation of the Marquis de Sade's Les Cent-vingt Jours de Sodom.

Beckett had been interested in Sade for some time, and he needed money badly, but he hesitated. When he met with Kahane later that month to discuss terms, he insisted that he should be allowed to write a translator's essay making clear his opinion that much of the book was indescribable obscenity but that the visions of love and physical ecstasy were as extraordinary as anything written by Dante.[58] Beckett finally rejected the offer because he was afraid that he would become known not as the author of *Murphy* but as the translator of filth, and blamed or muzzled for the rest of his writing career.

It was a difficult decision. He needed money and Kahane's terms were good. But as with every other decision affecting his career he had made thus far and would make in the future, he simply could not take the route of financial expediency but had to satisfy his artistic integrity before all else. He decided to wait for *Murphy* to make his reputation for him.

He was hard-pressed at this time for clothing as well as money. The police had taken everything he was wearing at the time of the stabbing and were holding it as material evidence. Fortunately spring came early and he had little need for his overcoat, but the rest of his wardrobe consisted of little besides the suit on his back. He was afraid to ask outright for his clothes because he was in the process of applying for a permanent alien residence visa and was afraid any untoward incident might hinder it. He still remembered his precipitous eviction from France after the Doumer incident in 1932.

By French law, Beckett was required to confront his assailant in the courtroom, and in mid-February, 1938, he went dutifully to the Palais de Justice, where he found Prudent sitting forlornly on a narrow wooden bench. Beckett was directed to sit down next to him to wait until the case was called, and so found himself in the incongruous position of exchanging pleasantries with the man who had stabbed him.[59] After some insignificant chitchat, Beckett asked Prudent what he had done to inspire such drastic behavior. Prudent drew his shoulders up and with a Gallic shrug replied indifferently, "I don't know."

Critics have often pointed to this incident as the basis for much of the futility, despair and meaninglessness they find in Beckett's writing. At the time, however, it amused Beckett enormously and became a story which he enjoyed telling his drinking companions for years to come.[60]

Beckett did not want to press charges against Prudent because that would have involved further attendance at a subsequent trial, but French officials took a serious view of the crime and required Beckett to do so. At the trial, Prudent (whom Beckett called "the desperado") was sentenced to only two months in the Prison de la Santé, even though it was his fifth conviction.[61] Several weeks later Beckett heard further of the escapades of Prudent:

> There is no more popular prisoner in the Santé. His mail is enormous. His poules shower gifts upon him. Next time he stabs someone they will promote him to the Legion of Honor. My presence in Paris has not been altogether fruitless.[62]

Beckett's clothes disappeared somewhere in the files of the French bureaucracy, never to be returned. He had stopped wanting them anyway; he was grateful to be spared the removal of two-month-old dried blood and the repair of torn fabric.

Beckett was feeling more and more at home in Paris, even though he still had not found an apartment. It seemed as if each time he set out to do some serious house-hunting, something happened to keep him from it.

Nancy Cunard had just come back from Spain. He was uninterested in her left-wing politics (or any politics), was disappointed in the poetry she published in her Reanville series and was bored with her endless, frenetic nightclubbing. But it was better than being alone so he allowed himself to be led into any engagement that she instigated.

The next distraction was the publication of *Murphy*. The novel was officially published on March 7, 1938, but not with the instantaneous success Beckett wanted. There were reviews in the most important English publications and though they were not effusive, they were positive, even though critics were hard-pressed to find an appropriate niche for such a novel. The *Times Literary Supplement* included it with several others under the catchall heading of "Political and Social Novels":

> Beneath the traffic roar of crudeness there can be heard the small voice of a genuine horror and disgust. This book may be sterile but it is not negligible.[63]

There were reviews also in the *Listener*, the *Spectator*, the *Sunday Times*, the *Observer*, and the *New Weekly*, by Edwin Muir, Kate O'Brien, Dylan Thomas, and others.[64] In general, all the reviewers recognized in *Murphy* something different from the usual fiction. Several were complimentary, but most couched their opinions in cautious but polite phrasings. Dylan Thomas wrote a thoughtful review calling the novel "difficult, serious, and wrong," saying that Beckett had "not yet thrown off the influence of those writers who have made *transition* their permanent resting place."[65] Thomas's review is full of phrases crying to be requoted: "Murphy is the individual ostrich in the mass-produced desert" . . . "a series of obscure events in lunatic asylums and lodging-houses that might have been created by P. G. Wodehouse, Dickens, and Eugene Jolas working in bewildered collaboration" . . . "Mr. Beckett's humour . . . is Freudian blarney: Sodom and Begorrah."

Beckett found Dilys Powell's review in the *Sunday Times* particularly irritating. "It is gratifying to have my *intentions* [Beckett's emphasis] revealed to me after all this time," he wrote to Reavey.[66] For Kate O'Brien's *Spectator* review he had kinder words: "I am very obliged to her."[67]

In general, the reviews did not please him. Brian Coffey, describing a visit to Paris, wrote to Reavey:

> Paris was very quiet except among the journalists who appear to be busy getting the headlines of the next war ready. Sam seems a little depressed, perhaps about the *Murphy* reviews, but that will be put right sooner or later.[68]

Beckett wrote to Arland Ussher, "The critics have all behaved with the same arrogance. Like the dog's hindquarters when the spine is touched in the right place."[69]

Beckett cashed the check for the second half of his advance for *Murphy* and spent it to pay his debts. Routledge was pleased with sales, but royalties, trickling in slowly but steadily, were not yet available to him. He found himself short of funds to pay his hotel bills, and so the search for an apartment finally took paramount importance in his affairs.

Geer and Lisl van Velde tried to persuade him to go to Holland with them to investigate the possibility of settling in Amsterdam, which they claimed had the reputation of offering all that Paris had while being cheaper. To save money until he could find an apartment, Beckett thought he might go to Brittany to stay with Alfred and Marie Péron, who had taken a job in a lycée there, but he changed his plans when he discovered they were returning to Paris to live as soon as the term ended. Even though he said *preferring* to live in Paris had changed to *having* to live in Paris, he stayed there because it was where he really wanted to be.[70]

Early in April he found what he was looking for at 6 rue des Favorites, in the working-class Vaugirard quarter of the 15th Arrondissement, far removed from the cafes of Montparnasse.

Beckett described it as "6 Rue des Favorites (formerly Impasse des Favorites, not far from the still existing Impasse de l'Enfant Jésus)."[71] He said it was "not a bad little place, studio, soupante, bedroom, bathroom, hall, the necessary house and kitchenette. On the 7th floor and well away from Gare Montparnasse."[72]

By his thirty-second birthday he was in the apartment, but still without conveniences: "Having taken it furnished and having no furniture. I am promised at the corner store a bed, but not for a week, so I expect to sleep in the bath until then."[73]

People were very good about giving him gifts for the apartment, especially Nora Joyce, who took the opportunity to get rid of several large pieces of furniture she no longer wanted.

The Joyces had returned from a month in Zurich. Beckett was disappointed when they went without him, for Joyce had dropped hints that he wanted Beckett to go with them, but when the time came for him and Nora to depart, Joyce suddenly stopped talking about it to Beckett and went off abruptly. Beckett was sure that Joyce's evasion had something to do with his earlier relationship with Lucia. It didn't seem to occur to him that Joyce might have been backing off from the strong filial intimacy his presence and Giorgio's absence (he was still in the United States) had caused.

Lucia was the one possible point of contention remaining between the two men, so Beckett was delighted upon Joyce's return to Paris when an opportunity arose for him to insert Lucia's name normally and naturally into a conversation. McGreevy had mentioned an English review of Joyce's *Storiella as she is syung*, where special mention was made of Lucia's drawings which accompanied the text. Beckett told Joyce about the review and was immediately commissioned to procure a copy.[74] With this incident the last barrier in their relationship was finally surmounted, and Lucia, instead of being an embarrassing topic which both men tried to avoid, became a subject commanding much conjecture and conversation.

Joyce was worried and confused about Lucia because she had suddenly begun to suffer from all sorts of strange maladies.[75] Her teeth were in terrible condition, but she was so weakened by infection that she was unable to sustain even the most routine dental care. Several doctors disagreed on the cause of the infection or the proper treatment, and Joyce suddenly decided that all Lucia's problems could be traced to a psychoneurosis which had festered dormantly until brought on by untreated infection in her teeth. He brought in specialists to examine her, and wanted to begin psychiatric treatment immediately. He was quite excited about his ideas, poor man, and willing to grasp at any straw where his daughter was concerned.

Joyce discussed all his ideas with Beckett as if Lucia had never been a barrier between them, and Beckett listened attentively, then suggested that Joyce contact Geoffrey Thompson. Beckett wrote to Thompson for Joyce, and Thompson sent a cautious reply saying that he would be glad to help but did not give any overt credence to Joyce's theories.

Joyce's excitement and belief that he had at last found the cause of his daughter's illness soon dissipated because of his own precarious health and his concern for *Work in Progress*. He was afraid that war would break out before the book was properly launched, and Lucia, like everything else in his life, took second place to his writing.

Despite all the help from his friends, it was an expensive proposition for Beckett to set up housekeeping, and he turned his attentions seriously to *Murphy*, hoping to sell it in other countries. He and Péron (who hoped to translate it) had given a copy of the book to Raymond Queneau, just appointed a reader by Gallimard, but Queneau rejected it several months later, saying the translation would be too difficult and costly because of Beckett's arcane use of English.[76]

Helen and Giorgio had given the book to Helen's cousin, Margaret Frohnknecht, who was a reader for Random House and Harcourt Brace, and Beckett had high hopes that she would be able to sell the book in the United States. Helen and Giorgio recommended it enthusiastically, but Joyce was more laconic with his praise. "I think he has talent," he told Giorgio.[77]

Péron suggested that he try to turn some of the poems in *Echo's Bones* into French in an effort to establish himself as a man of letters in France. As a first step, Péron translated *The Alba*, which was published that spring in Luc Decaunes' *Soutes*.[78] Beckett thought it was not one of Péron's best efforts, feeling that Péron had followed the English original so closely that an awkward and graceless French poem resulted.[79]

Beckett had begun to write short verses in French the previous year, partly because he was inspired by emotions and images of Paris, but mostly because he wanted to see if he could write poetry that was French from conception and not just English verse transferred to another language. At this time he had the feeling that he would probably write a great deal of poetry, and that it would quite naturally be in French.[80] It seemed to be the most accessible literary form for one who was writing in a foreign language.

From the last month of 1937 to the fall of 1939, he wrote twelve short, untitled poems which were not published until 1946 as a cycle in *Les Temps Modernes*.[81] In the mid-1960's, when Beckett discussed these poems with Lawrence Harvey, he said they had been written in "a period of lostness, drifting around, seeing a few friends—a period of apathy and lethargy."[82] Beckett's statement isn't completely true. They were written when he was very anxious for a French publication and was trying to amass enough material in the least possible time. He wrote an extremely conciliatory letter to Reavey suggesting that European Literary Bureau/Europa Press bring out a volume of his poetry in both French and English, and was disappointed when Reavey refused.[83]

These poems differ from the earlier English poems of *Echo's Bones* in several ways. There are no arcane references, no convoluted phrasings or verbal ingenuity. The language prefigures the quality for which Beckett would become best known in his postwar French writings—the directness and simplicity with which he presents and expresses deep emotion. The poems are hermetic in the sense that the narrator is usually enclosed, either within a room or within his memory and mind. However, they are filled with images of exile, the dichotomy of love and sex, the absence of love and the fatalistic acceptance of life. As in the earlier English poems, there are common ordinary incidents which are once again expanded and made to stand for the human condition.

However well they hold together as a cycle, it is best to remember that they were written individually over a period of several years, usually in moments of despair, quite possibly as attempts to allow his imagination to lead him into a longer work, or else as substitutes for the idea of the next work, which did not seem to come.

With publication by Reavey no longer possible, Beckett turned to the self-translation of *Murphy*. Alfred and Marie Péron were now reestablished in Paris, where Péron had taken a position at the Lycée Buffon. Beckett and Péron fell easily into the habit of meeting for a late-afternoon drink when Péron finished his classes; then they went to Beckett's apartment and worked for several hours to turn *Murphy* into a French novel. At one point, as Beckett voiced his misgivings that the task would be impossible, Péron suddenly said, "I can do that, it's easy." Then he recited the first sentence of *Murphy* in English, snapped his fingers and translated it into French. They looked at each other, delighted, and decided it would not be so difficult after all.[84] Unfortunately, the rest of the translation did not proceed as smoothly or as easily, and it was not really completed until after the war, when Beckett finished it alone.

Beckett was barely installed in the rue des Favorites when he had to go to London for the opening of Geer van Velde's exhibition at Guggenheim Jeune. The show was not the success that Beckett hoped it would be. The critics dismissed van Velde as an imitator of Picasso and the paintings did not sell. Peggy Guggenheim bought several, each time under a different name; Beckett, along with several others, bought paintings on "the stuttering system" (i.e., on installment), but public reaction was dim and dampened everyone's ardor. Even an open house, heavily advertised and to which everyone with any likelihood of buying a painting was invited, failed. Only the good friends were there, and they all drank heavily but silently. At the same time, Jack B. Yeats, whom Beckett had been boosting as the next likely candidate for exhibition in Guggenheim Jeune, voluntarily withdrew from further consideration, claiming that his paintings were totally unsuited to such a setting. Beckett was disappointed but Guggenheim was relieved.

To lighten the gloom and dispel the bitterness that encompassed the van Velde exhibition, Guggenheim invited a group for a weekend at her country house, Yew Tree Cottage in Petersfield, Sussex. Geer and Lisl van Velde, George and Gwynned Vernon Reavey accepted; Beckett, after much deliberation and indecision, decided to go along.

There, he told Guggenheim what she had suspected all along, that he had ended their affair because of someone else:

> Oblomov told me he had a mistress and asked me if I minded. Of course I said no. She sounded to me more like a mother than a mistress. She had found him a flat and made him curtains and looked after him generally. He was not in love with her and she did not make scenes, as I did. I had met her once in his room before she was his mistress, when I was, and I could not be jealous of her; she was not attractive enough. She was about my age and we were both older than Oblomov.[85]

At this point Guggenheim no longer cared what Beckett did with the physical aspects of his life because she had become engrossed in her gallery and other men. She accepted the news calmly, which was a surprise to Beckett—no doubt because he was expecting a scene that never materialized.

They spent the weekend at Yew Tree Cottage taking photographs and drinking wine in the garden, on long walks and brief excursions in the car. On Saturday afternoon, Guggenheim drove them all to the seacoast to walk along the beach. The weather was chilly and a heavy wind blew, making the walk more effort than pleasure. Suddenly, Beckett stripped off all his clothes and plunged into the water, swimming swiftly away from shore. He went out so far that the others were frightened and began to call him back. No one dared go into the water because they were not strong swimmers and it was rough. Finally, when he was ready, Beckett swam back to shore, toweled himself briefly with a sweater, dressed and walked to the car as if nothing had happened. Everyone was upset by the incident, especially since Beckett had only just begun to regain his strength since the stabbing. They all thought he had been foolish to risk his health since he was prone to chest colds and bursitis, but no one remonstrated because his attitude brooked no criticism or comment. The ride back to Yew Tree Cottage took place in constrained silence.[86]

The van Velde exhibition was the last obligation Beckett felt bound to honor, and he went back to Paris convinced that now at last he could settle down and get to work. He deliberately avoided Guggenheim and the van Veldes, the Joyces, and the Duncans. He even wanted to refuse invitations to parties given by Devlin and Coffey, but felt he had to accept as both men were leaving Paris shortly.[87]

His books arrived from Dublin in three large crates and he had to spend one miserable day in the Gare des Battignolles to pass them through customs. Once he got them into his seventh-floor apartment, he had to leave them lying in piles along the walls because he could not afford bookcases. Nevertheless, just having his books around him induced a feeling of permanence he savored, he wanted to start writing again, and he wanted to try to do something with the unfinished play about Samuel Johnson.[88]

As always, there was an interruption to the contentment of his life. Frank had been corresponding occasionally, each time with a new tale of an illness or affliction that had befallen May. May seemed to have adjusted to her loneliness, and had actually written letters to Beckett in which she relished having the house all to herself; but lately she had begun to read herself to sleep by candlelight, as she had done more than thirty years before when there was no electricity in Cooldrinagh. One night she fell asleep with a book in hand, and woke up to find that the candle had dripped and the sheets were on fire. She burned her hands badly putting it out, and instructed Frank to say nothing about it. Of course he did, with the result that Beckett was actually moved to tears. He commented that the involuntary evocation of feelings such as these were probably the part of his relationship with her that had not been, nor ever could be analyzed away.[89]

Then Frank became ill with an undiagnosed illness which was probably caused by overwork and tension, since Jean, who was due to deliver a child in June, had begun to have birth pains two months early. All this deepened May's melancholy and her letters to Beckett conveyed her depression. She was too fragile to attempt even to meet him in London, but she wanted to see him. He decided to go to Dublin in mid-July and stay for a month. He made a silent vow, swearing to spend one month each year with her in Ireland for as long as she lived. When he later told her, it seemed to calm her and made their relationship less strained.[90]

Once in Dublin, Beckett was chagrined to find that no review of *Murphy* had appeared in *Dublin Magazine*, where he had counted not only on an early notice, but a favorable one. McGreevy had the assignment at first, but withdrew because he feared his effusive praise would cause more skepticism than interest, since everyone in Dublin who might possibly buy the book knew of his close friendship with Beckett. Austin Clarke asked for and was given the assignment when McGreevy demurred, and now Beckett feared that when a review did appear it would be decidedly unfavorable.[91]

Beckett hoped to do a lot of reading in Dublin in preparation for writing once he returned to Paris. He was bored with Vigny's Journal, which he read in what he called a bawdlerized Larousse edition. From Brian Coffey he borrowed Jacques Maritain's *Humanisme Integral* (*True Humanism*), which led to interesting discussions between the Catholic Coffey and the nonbeliever Beckett, but he was not visibly persuaded by Maritain's philosophy. He was irritated by *Tristram Shandy* despite its great facility and decided then and there that he had little liking for Sterne. He was fond of Oliver Goldsmith, however, and was disappointed to learn that Seumas O'Sullivan was working with

Gogarty on his biography, for Beckett always thought of Goldsmith as "a very nice man." The thought of Gogarty, and to a lesser extent O'Sullivan, writing about him was dismaying.[92]

He found his mother much the same as when he had last seen her; now she was in a flurry of activity getting ready to move to Greystones because she had rented Cooldrinagh from September through December. If she found she did not miss the big house too much, she planned to sell it the coming spring. Beckett was lucky, in a sense, because she was so distracted with all the preparations for moving that she had less time to nag at him.

He was very sociable during this visit. Cissie and two of her daughters had just returned from a long stay in South Africa, and he was saddened to see Cissie ravaged by rheumatoid arthritis and the girls wan and forlorn, but was pleased to find Sonny (Maurice) Sinclair busily preparing for his "Little Go" (i.e., the intermediate) examination. Beckett spent the weekend in Donegal with Jean, Frank and their infant daughter Caroline, born June 26, the anniversary of William Beckett's death. At the conclusion of a visit to Jack B. Yeats, the two men left Yeats's studio together, a long-standing custom, so that Yeats could buy his evening paper. Yeats commented with evident feeling that it had been six or seven years since the first time they had gone out together to buy a newspaper. "Six or seven years should mean a lot to me, but they don't seem to and it doesn't matter," Beckett wrote to McGreevy.[93]

Most of Beckett's friends noticed a new calmness about him, a strength and maturity which they had not seen before.[94] Instead of the world-weary, affected intellectual who had come home from Paris after École Normale, they now saw a quiet man, sure of himself and his writing, who had no need for wild drinking sprees or shocking language. He seemed interested in what his friends were doing, he asked questions about the new Irish writers, and he seemed to enjoy conversations without exhibiting any of the sarcasm and superiority he had hitherto shown for Dublin literary society. Much of this new attitude was due, of course, to the fact that he no longer felt trapped within it. He could listen to the backbiting slander, the damn-with-faint-praise and the rare comment of genuine appreciation for his own work and the work of others, knowing full well that at the end of his holiday he would return to the sanctuary of his Paris apartment and the more amenable society of his friends there.

Now he could enjoy the beauty of the countryside, the overpowering lushness of the greenery, the meandering country lanes illuminated by gentle twilights. All the sights and sounds of full summer were there to entertain him, and when they ended, he would not be there for the cold dampness of winter's gray days and endless nights. Paris was his home now; that knowledge sustained him until he could get back to his books, his friends, his beloved apartment.

Beckett's original intention had been to take his bicycle back to Paris, but to go first to St. Malo to meet Alfred and Marie Péron for a short holiday in Brittany.[95] Instead, he returned directly to Paris in late August and then drove to Brittany with Suzanne Deschevaux-Dumesnil in Peggy Guggenheim's car, which she loaned him in exchange for his apartment. Neither seemed to care by then that the exchange was made to facilitate arrangements to be with someone else and not each other.[96]

Beckett spent most of his time writing in the little village of St. Breveyen L'Ausient. Péron was convinced that Beckett would be enormously successful as a writer of literary and artistic criticism in France, and at his urging, Beckett began to write an essay he called "Les Deux Besoins" (The Two Needs).[97]

The essay was a difficult chore, as he made his first groping attempt toward conceptual expression in a foreign language. "Les Deux Besoins" was based primarily on the content of the logic courses he had taken at Trinity College. It is filled with geometric diagrams, and reminded more than one of his friends of a take-off on Yeats's *Vision*, which also depended on geometric diagrams to illustrate its points. Only three typed (double-spaced) pages long, "Les Deux Besoins" continues the development of Beckett's idea that art results from the artist's quest to rid himself of extraneous knowledge in order to refine his perceptions into a clear, distilled vision of the fundamental inner being: art comes from the abandonment of the macrocosm for the pursuit of the microcosm. Man is doomed to failure, for he can never commit or abandon himself completely to his inner voice. The eternal struggle to do so—and the artist's constant turning inward—creates conflict, and in turn forces him to create art. This vision of the preordained failure of the artist gives rise in Beckett's noncritical writing to the figure of the quest-hero, doomed to follow the tortuously turning path of his inner self on an endless, timeless plane where there is no real definition, no end and no accomplishment. The goal is always tantalizingly beyond reach. On the one hand, it is a grim, joyless task, this pursuit of art. On the other, it is the true way to find satisfaction—peace lies only in pursuit.

Beckett wrote the essay upon Péron's insistence that he was capable of more sustained writing in French than short poems or translations of his own novels. Beckett worked hard at it, but was near desperation when he discussed it with Brian Coffey.[98] "I don't know where I'm going with it, this thing has petered out," he said ruefully.

However, Coffey noticed that the language of the essay seemed to be a positive attempt to think in French. All the phrases had a definite French cast to them, and were more than French equivalents of English phrases. He told this to Beckett, who was quite pleased, saying, "At least the exercise hasn't been a total loss."

Beckett finished what is now the only extant manuscript and showed it "to a sculptor who disappeared in the war,"[99] but did nothing further with it. To try to publish an essay on the needs of man seemed ludicrous with a war going on.

When the holiday with the Pérons ended, Beckett and Suzanne drove back to Paris on a zigzag path through Normandy. Guggenheim went back to London and Beckett took possession of his apartment amidst the ominous rumblings that came from Germany. His French friends were convinced that war was imminent, and Beckett was afraid they were right. It was a prospect he was not ready to face.

By mid-September, when Neville Chamberlain went to Berchtesgaden, all Paris was in a frenzy of anticipation. On

September 24, 1938, the French government called one million reservists to active duty. Several days later, in reply to an urgent letter from Reavey demanding to know how he fared and what, if anything, he had written, Beckett replied:

> I heard Adolph the peacemaker on the wireless last night and thought I heard the air escaping at slow puncture. But no matter how things go I shall stay here on the 7th floor with my own handful of sand. All I have to lose is legs, arms, balls, etc. and I owe them no particular debt of gratitude as far as I know. The streets are full of khaki-cum-civils debating angrily in requisition trade vans and at night curfew lighting. . . . I have promised Péron in the event of mobilization to evacuate in his car his children, his mother-in-law, his aunt-in-law. . . . Here there is great afflux of tenderness, even in the commerce of Vaugirard.[100]

Péron was only one of Beckett's friends whose life was thrown into confusion by the fear of impending war. Guggenheim, in England, was completely distraught and ran back and forth between her gallery in London and her cottage in Sussex trying to decide what to do about her children, her paintings and her lovers.

The Joyce family was more seriously troubled. Helen had had a nervous breakdown and was in deep depression in a private sanatorium in Montreux, Switzerland.[101] Lucia had been evacuated from Ivry, France, to La Baule, Switzerland, and on September 30, Joyce and Nora went there to be near her. When Chamberlain returned to England announcing "Peace in our time," the Joyces quietly returned to Paris, where Joyce seemed relieved that he would be able to finish the last few pages of *Work in Progress*. He had so little left to write, only the last pages of Book IV, Anna Livia Plurabelle's monologue.

Once again he asked Beckett's help, and errands and other tasks occupied him and Joyce's other dependable stalwarts for the greater part of the fall. By the end of November, when Beckett was on his way to Greystones to spend the holidays with his mother, the book was finished and Joyce gave him the final ten pages of text to read on his journey. Beckett was so excited to have them that he finished reading by the time the

Metro deposited him at the railway station and telephoned Joyce to express his enthusiasm.

Beckett did not really want to go back to Ireland so soon, but he was at loose ends now that his usefulness to Joyce had come to a temporary end. He was finished with Peggy Guggenheim; Suzanne was still living with her family and she would not be free during the holidays; and everyone else seemed to have dispersed to places outside Paris, so that he was all alone. When Arland Ussher expressed surprise that Beckett was so soon again in Ireland, he hurried to reassure him that the visit was only temporary and that he had no intention of taking up residence in what he called the land of his unsuccessful abortion.[102]

"My mother has been wintering on this cote de misere since September," Beckett wrote to Ussher. "What does not face north faces east. She is the worse for it. But from the window she can see the cemetery where my father is 'at rest.' "[103]

Relatives who came to call on Beckett during that holiday season found him quiet and sober. He kept to himself, took long walks along the rough and windy coast, and occasionally tapped the piano. He spent most of his time silent and brooding in one of the comfortable chairs before the fire, worrying that war would break out before he could return to Paris. When his holiday duties were ended, he hurried back, leaving his lonely mother in the tiny cold house with the roiling Irish sea on one side and desolate Redfern Cemetery on the other.

Samuel Beckett returned to Paris with a flat limestone pebble in his pocket that he had picked up on the banks of the River Liffey. He took it to Stanley William Hayter in his Atelier 17 and asked him to engrave a few lines from *Anna Livia Plurabelle* on it in time for presentation to Joyce on his birthday.[104] *Work in Progress* was now officially *Finnegans Wake*, printed at last, and scheduled to be delivered in time for the party. Beckett wanted to give Joyce a very special gift in honor of the double occasion, but also because he had a premonition there might not be another birthday celebration. It seems to have been his most pressing task for the next three months.

His only regularly scheduled activity was to lunch each

Tuesday with Péron and to play tennis afterwards when the weather permitted. The lunches were supposed to have been followed by an afternoon of translating *Murphy*, but the original reason had been superseded by tennis, and translation became the activity they saved for a rainy day.

Beckett's correspondence, which had been voluminous, suddenly slackened. There are few of the long letters recounting his daily activities or the long philosophical passages on printing, music or writing over which he used to spend more time than he did at his writing. He seems to have gotten over the need to "keep in touch." France was becoming home to him, and the obsessive need to know all that was happening in London and Dublin had gradually disappeared.

Once more he couldn't seem to settle down to his writing. He gave *Love and Lethe*, translated the previous year, to Jean-Paul Sartre, who in turn gave it to Jean Paulhan for *La Nouvelle Revue Française*, but could scarcely bring himself to inquire about it, and Paulhan was in no hurry to accept or reject it. In a frank confession, Beckett admitted that he was not doing anything in Paris that he could not do just as well in the Seven Bells or the Beggar's Bush, the two pubs he had frequented while living in Gertrude Street.[105]

Most of his time was spent going around to the Joyce flat or meeting friends who passed through Paris. Dinners with the painter Jankel Adler filled an occasional uneasy evening for Beckett, for Adler was preoccupied with the idea that war would come. Beckett, apolitical as always, chose to ignore such conversations by ordering more drinks. He had become friendly with John and Mary Buckland-Wright, whom he met at Hayter's Atelier 17. John Buckland-Wright, a native of New Zealand, was one of Hayter's leading engravers, and his wife, a Canadian by birth, was a translator. They lived in a cozy Left Bank apartment warm with domesticity and good feeling, and Beckett often visited them. Dinners and conversations in their apartment helped to make the long winter evenings pass and also to take his mind off the work he was not doing.

By the end of February, he had good reason to be grateful for the Buckland-Wrights' kindness: for more than two weeks he was confined to bed with a dismal bout of flu that left him so weak he was able only to toss and turn and ask for liquids whenever friends came to visit.[106] Everyone he knew seemed to be sick: Gwynned Vernon Reavey passed through Paris on her way to the van Veldes and the sun in Cagnes-sur-Mer, she, too, debilitated after the flu. The Joyces, finding their flat too large without Lucia, decided to take a small one, and the move left them both exhausted and depressed. It was not a happy time in Paris, as Hitler began to make his final menacing moves before declaring war.

On March 15, 1939, German forces occupied Czechoslovakia. Within weeks, Hitler began to extort concessions and seize lands throughout Europe. Joyce was certain it was a personal affront designed to keep the world from paying homage to *Finnegans Wake,* and he grew irritated and increasingly difficult to amuse. Beckett was still too weak to dance the constant attendance on Joyce that might have cheered the latter up, and it remained for the others in his coterie to do so.

By the end of April, Beckett still had not recovered completely. He lost more weight than someone as naturally thin as he could afford and was gaunt and haggard, more hawklike than ever. Now it was his turn to think that a week with the van Veldes in the hot southern sun might restore him to health, but he was beset with minor complications—someone passing through from Ireland who had to be seen, a lack of money, then the possibility of a reviewing assignment that never materialized and finally, a decided lack of interest. He stayed in Paris as spring flowed into full summer. Brian and Bridget Coffey, married since the previous fall, were living just outside Dampierre, and Beckett spent several Sunday afternoons taking long walks with them in the beautiful countryside surrounding the village.

His fortunes took a turn for the better in June, 1939, when Reavey sent him two hundred francs, his current royalties for *Murphy,* and in early July, an additional fifty francs. This sum would make his annual visit to Ireland much easier. He had planned tentatively to make the trip in August, and was relieved to know that he could do so with money earned from his writing. Since his return to Paris from Christmas in Dublin, only two short commissions had come his way, and these, translations for the *London Bulletin*, came via Peggy Guggenheim and paid only a pittance.[107]

By the end of July, he was on his way to Dublin via the long sea route from Le Havre to Cobh. He went directly to Greystones, where May was still in the little house overlooking the cemetery. As usual, there was an initial tension between Beckett and his mother, but the first visit of Frank and Jean with baby Caroline gave an air of genuine gaiety to the grim little house. Ann and John Beckett came to see him, and soon the Becketts fell into a routine of afternoon swims, long walks on the beach with the dogs and piano duets in the evenings. Mollie Roe came with Sheila Page and her two daughters to stay for several weeks, and the little house was filled with all the wet clothing, toys and treasures of a summer house on the beach.

It depressed Beckett utterly. He longed to get away from all the noise and confusion. With Hitler poised to strike at any moment, he feared for his friends in France. The conversations about the Dublin Horse Show and yacht clubs and the business success of his contemporaries (as told by his mother) jarred his nerves. Only Mollie and Sheila, who both lived in England, were apprehensive about the world situation, and they took pains to hide their feelings so they wouldn't spoil the holiday, since an earlier conversation about the possibility of war had greatly upset May. When Beckett calmly insisted that war was inevitable, she became furious, and others, sensing that a confrontation between them was brewing, were careful to steer the conversation away from the subject.

On September 1, Hitler's troops marched into eastern Europe, and the holiday atmosphere of Greystones turned as damp and gray as the weather. Sheila Page knew that it was only a matter of time before her husband was called into the British army and she left for London immediately. Frank sensed that Beckett would want to return to France, but he hoped it would only be to clear out his belongings. May veered between icy grimness, refusing to believe that Beckett would go back to Paris at all, and tender concern that she would lose him if he went.

For two days the tension mounted. September 3, 1939, dawned bright and clear, such a fine morning that Beckett and

Mollie Roe decided to take a long walk along the beach before lunch. When they came back, they turned on the radio and heard that minutes before, England had declared war on Germany. France was expected to follow before the day was out.

May managed to control her emotion, and asked him to stay in Ireland as calmly as if she were asking him to stay for tea. "I've promised so many friends I'd get back," was all he said, and he began to pack.[108] He went to Killiney to say good-bye to Jean and Caroline, then Frank drove him and Mollie Roe to the ferry for Holyhead. When they arrived in London hours later, everything was blacked out. Finding their way through the darkened city was difficult, but Beckett only knew the blackout for a matter of hours, long enough to say farewell to a few friends. He and Mollie Roe parted at Victoria Station, not to meet again until 1953 in Sweetwater, Surrey.

1939–42:

"ON THE TROT"

Beckett returned to Paris, to find his apartment an isle of calm in a sea of confusion. All around him people were fleeing for southern France, where they thought they would be safe from the German invasion, which was expected daily. Geer van Velde decided he and his wife, Lisl, were safer in France than in his native Holland, and passed through Paris just long enough to collect their belongings and move permanently to Cagnes-sur-Mer. Peggy Guggenheim, ostensibly on her way to Megève to make arrangements for her children, who were then living with Lawrence Vail and Kay Boyle, spent most of her time in the Dôme drinking Pernod, torn between the desire to stay in France as long as possible and what she felt was her duty—to evacuate the entire Vail household either to England or America. The Joyces were at La Baule in Switzerland, where they were desperate to see Lucia settled.

Mary Reynolds, an American citizen, stayed quietly in her little house behind the walled garden in Montparnasse; like Beckett, she was carefully appraising the situation before taking action. Meanwhile, Reynolds's friend Marcel Duchamp, whom Beckett had come to know well at her house, and with whom he played some of the most stimulating chess games of his life, was quietly planning to leave for the United States if the Germans invaded France. There was no news of Sartre, or Jean Giono, or any of the other French literary figures with whom Beckett had

had a peripheral acquaintance, or of Alberto Giacometti, with whom he had formed a friendship, mostly of amiable silences.[1] Alan and Belinda Duncan had gone to Brittany, Jankel Adler was arranging his affairs before going to England to join the British army and Djuna Barnes sat on her bed like a great brooding bird in a black feathered cape, her red hair flaming, biting her fingernails, drinking and smiling, refusing to move or be moved. Péron seemed to be the only one sure of his course. He knew his regiment would be mobilized, and he prepared to go. When the word finally came on September 20, he was sent to Lorient, where he fed the horses in a cavalry unit and worried about his wife and children back in Paris.

Amid all this frenzy, while all his friends urged him to "Come to his senses in time to get out,"[2] Beckett decided calmly to stay. Hitler seemed permanently occupied on the eastern front and there appeared to be no immediate danger to Paris. Beckett thought (correctly) that France was not about to attack Hitler from the west, and so he reasoned that Paris would be safe for an almost indefinite period.

In the face of adversity he set to work: he began to translate *Murphy* with seriousness and dispatch. When he learned that he could not stay in France without papers showing he was a neutral alien, he made the proper applications. Weeks passed with no results, so he went to Constantine Cremin at the Irish Legation, who was able to tell him only that governments functioned slowly in times of crisis, and that he must be patient.

By mid-October, the Joyces had returned to Paris. Lucia was as comfortably settled as they could make her under the circumstances, but now Helen was on the verge of another breakdown and Giorgio had moved out of their house. There was tension between the Léons, who were close to Helen, and Joyce, who, when he had to choose, was a father, not a father-in-law.[3] There was a serious breach in Joyce and Léon's long friendship at this time, causing Beckett a certain amount of difficulty, as he was the friend of Paul and Lucie Léon as well. Joyce found himself depending more and more on Beckett now that he did not have Léon. Eugene Jolas was in New York, and his wife was moving the students in her school from Neuilly to St. Gerand-le-puy, so there was simply no one else. Paris was an unbearable hazard for Joyce, whose bad eyesight made moving about at night under curfew conditions and bad lighting a nightmare. The duodenal ulcer which later claimed his life began to trouble him seriously. Worry about his children aggravated his discomfort: Lucia and Helen could not be responsible for their movements, and Giorgio faced conscription into the French army. As if to emphasize the severity of the situation, winter began early, with unseasonably bitter weather. Nora Joyce found herself unable to cope with housekeeping, and in December, when a fuel shortage shut down the heating unit of their building, the Joyces moved into the Hôtel Lutétia with Beckett's assistance.

On one occasion, when they went back to the flat to collect some books, Joyce, in a state of extreme agitation, played the piano and sang at the top of his voice for half an hour. "What is the use of this war?" he demanded of Beckett, who could not give an acceptable answer, as he felt there was a need to stop Hitler. Joyce was convinced there was never a reason for war, but what was worse, this one was distracting the world from reading *Finnegans Wake*, where he had clearly outlined its futility for all those who were too preoccupied with the current conflict to read it.[4]

In early December there was a brief diversion when Reavey took a room at the Lutétia as he passed through Paris on his way to Madrid to become a member of the British Legation. In an effort to cheer Joyce, Beckett suggested they all dine in one of his favorite Italian restaurants off the boulevard St. Germain, but the evening was unsuccessful. Joyce ate little and seemed preoccupied and edgy, turning constantly to Beckett who seemed to be the only one able to keep him calm.[5]

Joyce's family affairs continued to disintegrate. Helen was hospitalized in Suresnes, and Stephen, who had lived with his grandparents briefly in the Lutétia, was sent to Madame Jolas. Joyce promised her that he and Nora would spend Christmas at St. Gerand-le-puy, but before he left Paris, he went on wild sprees, drinking heavily and spending money with abandon. Beckett was with him on several of these wild debauches, and on one occasion Joyce noted with some satisfaction that they were "all going downhill fast."[6]

Yet, in spite of all the commotion associated with the Joyce family, Beckett found time to work. He still tried to write French verse, usually one or two lines left incomplete. By mid-December, only four chapters of *Murphy* remained to be translated. The apartment on the rue des Favorites still had heat and hot water, and Beckett stayed there, rarely going out.[7]

As Christmas week approached, he found himself becoming indispensable to Joyce, who seemed weak, tired and defeated as he boarded the train for the visit to St. Gerand-le-puy with unaccustomed docility. It was a sad parting for Beckett, and a prelude to a grim, lonely Christmas in a darkened city that waited for an invasion that did not come.

He did not see the Joyces again until February 15, when he and Giorgio went to St. Gerand-le-puy for Stephen's birthday.[8] There was much snow that winter, which added to Joyce's difficulties in getting about. Still, when Beckett arrived, they managed several walks, with Joyce in dark glasses, leaning heavily on his cane, his pockets full of stones to throw at the numerous neighborhood dogs who came to sniff at him out of curiosity and of whom he was terrified. The talk was of *Finnegans Wake*, and Joyce, bitter and angry, asked Beckett if anyone in Dublin had read it. With real sadness, Beckett had to tell him that except for certain Jewish intellectuals, no one was interested. Kafka had preempted him.

In April, Beckett returned to St. Gerand-le-puy for a few days at Easter, this time to face a barrage of questions from Joyce about Giorgio, who had been strangely uncommunicative since February. Beckett was unable to answer the questions, as his own existence had been solitary and dull. There was some comfort for both men in the news that Helen's brother, Robert Kastor, was on his way from America to take her home.[9]

From St. Gerand-le-puy, Beckett went to Brittany to see Alfred and Marie Péron. Péron had been transferred to a post as liaison officer with a British ambulance unit there and had a short furlough. The two men spent several days walking and talking about the inevitability of invasion, and what Beckett should do when it came. Péron asked Beckett once more to take care of the evacuation of his family, and told his wife to look upon Beckett as his brother, to go to him if trouble came.[10] Both men knew it was only a matter of time until Hitler turned west toward France. Péron felt firsthand the futility of it all: from a professorship in the Lycée Buffon to feeding cavalry horses only emphasized the absurdity of the situation.

On June 9, what the French have come to call *l'Exode* began. The roads leading out of Paris to the south were jammed with people carrying whatever they could in whatever vehicle they could find. There were cars with mattresses tied to the roofs to ward off bullets from low-flying German airplanes; bicycles, carts and carriages held poultry, livestock and treasured possessions.

On June 12, Beckett boarded one of the last trains to leave the Gare de Lyon for Vichy, where the Joyces were staying. His papers were not in order and he had no money, as no French bank would cash his check drawn on an Irish one. He knew he could not stay in Vichy, since government officials were pouring in to establish what would be the new government once Paris was occupied and France had officially fallen. Joyce found a friend to cash Beckett's check,[11] and with this small amount of money, Beckett headed south with no plan except to evade the Germans. He sent a postcard to Reavey in Madrid warning that he might turn up there if he could find a way out of France.[12]

On June 13, Beckett started south on foot, but soon found a train which was hopelessly delayed and moving very slowly. He squeezed on board and jammed himself into a corner, managing to get as far as Toulouse. He jumped off the train before it reached the city, and thus evaded a roundup of aliens who were being detained in a refugee camp. After several cold nights sleeping in alleys and on benches, and cadging food whenever it seemed safe, Beckett worked his way out of Toulouse and headed for Cahors on a bus. He found refuge with several others who had no papers in a shop selling Catholic religious articles. Famished, exhausted, soaked by a torrential downpour, he considered himself fortunate to have a small spot to sleep on on the bare floor.

Cahors was a repetition of Toulouse: very little food, wary officials on the lookout for strangers and aliens, and no place to hide; and Beckett, with his Irish-accented French, was likely to be spotted as soon as he spoke. From a chance encounter he learned that Mary Reynolds was in Arcachon, and he knew she would give him shelter and rest. He hid in the back of a truck and arrived there, bearded, filthy, and broke. It had taken him almost a month to make the circuitous journey.[13]

Mary Reynolds, ever generous, helped him to find a room in Arcachon at the Villa St. George, 135 boulevard de la Plage, and loaned him money until he could contact his family. However, he wrote a postcard to Reavey first, implying that he was without funds and wanted to return to Ireland.[14] Reavey was deeply concerned, but because he was a British subject—and Britain was now at war with France—he could do nothing immediate and direct. He went to the Irish Legation, which contacted Frank Beckett at once. Reavey waited for Beckett to come to Madrid, as his postcard hinted he would, but May and Frank told the Irish Legation that Beckett must return to Dublin via Portugal. Several weeks passed, and no one seemed to know what had become of Beckett when Reavey received the following letter from the Irish Legation in Madrid:

> You will be interested to learn that our department wired us as follows on 9th August: "Please wire position Samuel Beckett." We replied the same day as follows: "Mr. Beckett has written to a friend here Mr. George Reavey giving his address as Villa Saint Georges (sic) 135 Bd. de la Plage Arcachon Gironde. It would appear he is anxious to return to Ireland via Portugal and is in financial difficulties." The brother at Dublin apparently wasted no time in establishing contact with external affairs.[15]

Beckett did, in fact, try to make arrangements to travel via Portugal, but red tape delayed him repeatedly. Then, as time went on, he realized that there was no immediate danger in Paris, and like many others, he became part of a reverse migration back to the city.

He arrived at the rue des Favorites in October, to find Paris in the brilliant autumn weather as dull and deadened as the gray uniforms of the occupying Germans. Everywhere there were breadlines and blackouts, but his apartment and books were intact. He considered himself lucky.

He intended to live quietly as a neutral alien, to tend to his writing and to see if he could help any of his friends who were still in Paris. He wanted to stay in France as a visible symbol of sympathy for his French friends while observing the restraints which he felt his Irish citizenship imposed upon him. His Jewish friends had all disappeared, and so he was astonished one day to see Paul Léon walking openly down a street past German foot patrols and officers sitting in cafes. Léon assured the horrified Beckett that he intended to go into hiding the very next day, as soon as his son received his baccalaureate degree, but he gambled one day too long. He was arrested and interned near Paris, and killed as a Jew by the Nazis in 1942.[16]

All around Beckett senseless arrests and killings were commonplace. Even more devastating was the knowledge that numerous friends were either collaborating openly with the Germans or indirectly toadying to them. He found himself unable to remain neutral any longer. Now that the war touched his friends, it was no longer a philosophical exercise—it had become grimly personal. Léon's incarceration was just one of the events which led to Beckett's abandonment of neutrality: "I was so outraged by the Nazis, particularly by their treatment of the Jews, that I could not remain inactive,"[17] he said. Long after the war, when an interviewer asked Beckett why he had taken an active political stand, he replied, "I was fighting against the Germans, who were making life hell for my friends, and not for the French nation."[18] He was being consistent in his apolitical behavior.

By the end of October, 1940, Beckett was a member of the fledgling French Resistance. From the moment of German conquest, a spontaneous desire to organize and overthrow sprang up all over France—especially in Paris, where so many highly educated and articulate people congregated. Some arranged themselves in large, loose groups and divided up activities and responsibilities, becoming so preoccupied with organization that they often disbanded through internal squabbling before they accomplished anything. Other groups, small and tightly organized, worked well until eventual carelessness or betrayal led to their downfall. Accounts of Resistance activity are often in conflict, even though substantial effort has been made by the British and French governments, private individuals and scholars to write definitive histories. Each side claims different figures for casualties and successes, and often accounts conflict as to which side led a particular movement.

Beckett tends now to dismiss his role in the Resistance as "Boy Scout stuff."[19] In many ways, this could be a succinct commentary on all Resistance activity for 1940 and 1941. Most groups knew that in order to survive they should stay small in size, recruit persons with impeccable credentials, use only code names and move with the utmost discretion. But this was easier said than done. Friends and neighbors were burning to get involved; each person seemed to bring in someone else, until the various cells grew so large that code names, credentials and secrecy broke down. There were actually sections of the city where various Resistance groups met and compared notes quite openly, thus allowing the Germans to keep them under casual surveillance: the British groups frequented the Café Lorraine in Montmartre, while the cafes in Montparnasse became headquarters for the many French groups which had formed according to political party or literary or artistic clique.[20] These early efforts may, indeed, have been "Boy Scout stuff"; still, if it had not been for them, the foundations for the eventually successful Resistance activity would have taken much longer to be built.

Beckett was asked to join the Resistance by Péron, who had been detached from his military unit after the fall of France and was now back teaching in the Lycée Buffon. Péron had worked briefly on the fringes of a group which came to be called the *Groupe du Musée de l'Homme*, but his real work began when he founded a Resistance cell, or *réseau*, which at first was known casually and openly as the "group at the Lycée Buffon," and later by the code name *Étoile*.[21]

Péron's intention was to establish a cell to create and disseminate anti-German propaganda throughout the occupied zone, but his ideas were changed somewhat when Jeannine Picabia asked him to take a more active role in collecting information.[22] She was eighteen, the daughter of surrealist painter Francis Picabia and Gabrielle Buffet-Picabia, and an ambulance driver when France surrendered. She traveled widely with a medical group going to camps where French prisoners were interned and interrogated before they were released and told to return to their homes. In doing so, she saw a great deal of German troop and supply movements. No one seemed to pay much attention to her—just another young girl in uniform handing out food and medical supplies—and so she found it simple to get information that would be of great importance to the Allies. However, there was no one to whom she could tell it at this time.

After several months of exhausting work, she found herself in Toulouse, where she met a German general who was amused by her youth and activity and gave her permission to use his car to drive to Cannes to see her father, from whom she had had no word since the war began. Several days later, Picabia found herself in Marseilles early in the morning, waiting for gasoline across the street from the American consulate. On impulse, she walked in and told them what she had seen in the north. They listened carefully, then the American officials told her to go on to Cannes to see her father while they investigated. Several days later a man she now remembers as Colonel Paul Gimpel came to her father's house and asked her to return to Paris to collect information and pass it on to the British.

In October she returned to Paris and contacted Péron, who knew how important English speakers would be in their work. He suggested they recruit a friend of his, a young Irishman who spoke fluent French. Picabia was delighted when she found out he meant Beckett, for she had heard her mother speak of him. Gabrielle Buffet-Picabia had become fond of him in Mary Reynolds's house, where they had often met. Beckett and the others all thought themselves an agreeable group, and were quite pleased with their initial informal arrangement. Péron was to continue his work with *Étoile*, recruiting students, teachers, and trustworthy intellectuals whose major work would be propaganda, and he would also be a liaison with Picabia, who would head a *réseau de renseignement*, or information-gathering cell to be called *Gloria*, also her personal code name. As for the others, their real identities were known to each other, and they made no attempt to keep them secret. They were too new at espionage to realize that if a member of their *réseau* were captured and tortured, they would all be betrayed by a confession, for they all knew each other's names and addresses.

Beckett was known as "Sam," or *"l'Irlandais."* At first his job was to be a *bôite aux lettres,* or a dropping point for all the raw information collected on the intelligence missions. He was to translate all the information into concise English, and often had to decide on its value or importance. Usually he wrote it out on plain sheets of paper, to be collected by a man called Jimmy Reed,[23] who carried it to a collection point in an ordinary envelope hidden in one of his overcoat pockets. This procedure troubled Beckett, whose neighbors were beginning to wonder about the heavy foot traffic up and down the seven floors at the rue des Favorites. He was terrified that such casualness would lead to their arrest if they did not find a better way to carry the information. When he suggested microphotography, Picabia very quickly agreed. Soon Beckett was not only collecting, collating and typing the information at the big round table in his apartment, but also turning it into microfilm which the couriers carried hidden in the bottom of a box of matches. There was some shuddering among *Gloria*'s members when a young courier, more brave than intelligent, came back from an expedition bragging of how he had offered a light from a box of matches with film inside to a German soldier inspecting his papers.

Soon Beckett was doing more than collecting information. He took several trips into Brittany and Normandy, getting as close as he could to the cordoned-off areas around the seaports, where he received information from people who worked in the shipyards in and around Brest and the submarine pens in Dieppe. He also made occasional forays into the unoccupied zone at Châlons to pass and receive information.

All this time *Étoile* and *Gloria* were growing, at first only among trusted friends. Mary Reynolds's house was a favorite rendezvous; surrounded by a high wall, with a small garden, it was secluded and easy to enter unseen. Reynolds sheltered fugitives, allowed Resistance groups to hold clandestine meetings and several times uprooted some prize shrubs and bushes in order to bury tin boxes with vital information. One *réseau* member, a gifted thief, went out each night to cafes and restaurants where large numbers of Germans congregated, returning each time with an article of German clothing which was hidden in Reynolds's garden until needed. When he was apprehended by the Germans and taken into headquarters for questioning, he stole the stamp used for the official seal on registration papers. It, too, went under a bush in Miss Reynolds's garden, and was taken out when anyone needed forged identification papers.[24]

Gabrielle Buffet-Picabia, a frail, tiny woman then in her late fifties, wanted to help, and so her job was to cross back and forth from Châlons to Lyon, carrying information and acting as decoy or camouflage for persons on the run. One of her favorite resting places was an SNCF sleeping car on the edge of the railroad yard outside Lyon where displaced persons rested while making their way to the unoccupied zone. It was a great boon to tired Resistance workers, who were often dirty and cold as well, for the Germans had neglected to cut the heat and hot water lines and the railroad car was the only warm lodging in the area that they had not requisitioned. However, Buffet-Picabia had to forgo her comfortable night's sleep when some of the other regular users began to greet her cheerfully with "Bonjour, grand-mère."[25] It seemed a warning to all of *Gloria* that they should be more discreet.

In early January, 1941, Picabia was again summoned to Marseilles, where a man called "Jean" told her to go back to Paris and make contact with Jacques LeGrand, whose code name would be F-54. He would become her alter ego, or co-director of *Gloria*, and from this time on she would be known as F-52. Officially, when transmitting information by radio to England, the *réseau* would identify itself as *Gloria SMH* (His Majesty's Service backwards—another device to confuse the Germans).

LeGrand became one of the *Gloria*'s most valued and trusted members during the second phase of the Resistance, when activity was organized, secret and efficient. Neither

Picabia nor LeGrand knew at the time, however, that *Gloria* was also entering into its second phase, one that would eventually bring its downfall.

In mid-January, 1941, Beckett heard the sad news that Joyce had died in Zurich of a perforated duodenal ulcer. "Our group," as Lucie Léon called Joyce's friends,[26] was scattered everywhere. Nora, Giorgio and Stephen were in Zurich; Eugene and Maria Jolas and William Baird and his wife were in America; Stuart and Moune Gilbert in Dax, Free France; and Philippe Soupault in Algiers. Only the Léons, Beckett and Léon-Paul Fargue remained in occupied Paris.

These were the grim years, when the daily menu included rutabagas and bread that was black and tasteless. Coffee was ersatz, and meat was almost nonexistent.[27] Still, this did not deter Lucie Léon from inviting Beckett, Fargue and Madame Cheriane (who later became Madame Fargue), to dine together on February 2 in memory of Joyce's birthday. The evening passed in a sense of extraordinary spiritual communion. Lucie Léon wrote:

> It seemed to me that there was no war that night in Paris, no German occupation, and that Joyce's gentle spirit was there in the room where he had spent so many hours talking with Paul.[28]

They reminisced about Joyce until the realization of their loss made them so sad they could not go on. They played Joyce's two recordings of *Anna Livia Plurabelle*, but the sound of his voice was almost more than anyone could bear.

That evening enabled them for a brief moment to forget war. Paris was what it had been when Joyce was there, when life was always a party, when there was always someone to talk to and something exciting to do. When the evening ended, they all knew the pattern of their lives had been inexorably changed, and that more sadness and loss would lie ahead of them.

Beckett went back to the rue des Favorites, to his camera and his typewriter and the odd bits of information that came his way on the covers of matchbooks, scraps of menus, torn bits of newspapers and cigarette wrappers. *Gloria*, originally a handful of friends, now had more than forty members and the number seemed to be growing daily.

Suzanne Deschevaux-Dumesnil was now living with Beckett at his apartment and had become an active member of *Gloria,* carrying information, messages and miscellaneous equipment between the rue des Favorites and Mary Reynolds's house. On one occasion she was indirectly responsible for saving the entire *réseau.* Picabia had picked up a kitten with a broken leg on one of her reconnaissance missions, and she took it to her home on the rue Chateaubriand to nurse back to health. Shortly after, she was called to London for a briefing and had to be prepared to meet a pickup plane on a field outside Paris at a moment's notice. She asked Beckett to keep the cat while she was away, and he agreed. The cat was called *Victoire,* for luck, and the name appealed to him.[29]

In the meantime, Suzanne met Buffet-Picabia at Mary Reynolds's for last-minute instructions, and was given an assignment to carry a message to two elderly sisters who lived in an apartment not far from Beckett's. When she arrived, she found the two sisters sitting terrified in a room full of German soldiers who were hoping to catch unsuspecting agents who came to the apartment. The chief interrogator asked Suzanne what she wanted. She replied calmly that she had come to tell the women that her husband had set the cat's broken leg and it was recovering nicely. The interrogator did not believe her, and suggested she take them to see the cat. Suzanne agreed with trepidation, because Beckett occasionally left the camera lying on the big round table where anyone who came into the flat could see it. But she had no choice, and so, accompanied by two soldiers, led the way to the rue des Favorites.

Fortunately Beckett was out and the table was clear of incriminating material. Even more fortunate, Beckett had been studying *Mein Kampf* and making detailed notes to help Péron in his propaganda work. When the Germans saw the well-thumbed, heavily underlined book with Beckett's copious notes, they began to trust Suzanne.

She was afraid that Beckett would return before the Germans left and they would discover that he had no neutral alien papers. Also, she expected him to be carrying information about the boats that the Germans used for transport on the Seine.

"I'm sorry, I must go to the station to meet my mother," she told the Germans. "Her train arrives very shortly from Troyes and I must be there."[30]

When Madame Deschevaux-Dumesnil stepped off the train, she saw Suzanne waiting for her, surrounded by three burly German soldiers. At this point, since everything Suzanne told them had proved true, they clicked their heels and left.

It had been a terrifying experience and left everyone shaken. Had Picabia gone to see the sisters instead of Suzanne, and had the Germans gone to the Picabia flat, they would have found the names of all the *réseau* members, the codes and the radio equipment used to transmit information to London.

Life in 1941 was full of narrow escapes, but still the work went on. It was a "sort of Penelope's web, continually unpicked by the Gestapo, of which the bloody threads were obstinately reknotted night by night."[31]

One of Picabia's most trusted workers vouched for a man she brought into the group. His credentials were excellent—he was the cousin of a trustworthy agent and had information about shipping on the Seine that was important and accurate, and so they made him a member. What they did not know was that the man had already been arrested, tortured and then released—and told that he and his family would all be killed unless he infiltrated a *réseau* and brought back useful information. Each Sunday morning the Germans instructed him to visit a certain cafe on his way home from church where he was to file a detailed report of all the persons with whom he had come in contact during the week. No one could figure out who the informer was, as they saw members of their group being picked off one by one. For all the care she took to vouch for the informer's reliability, the woman who brought him into the group suffered four years in a German concentration camp and returned to Paris after the war in broken health. Still, for every person who was arrested, another stepped in to carry on.

In the spring of 1941, *Gloria*, *Étoile* and the other *réseaux* which had been working independently began to overlap, and confusion was rampant. Péron had been collecting information and disseminating propaganda for more than a year when he was recruited by another Resistance leader who knew nothing of his work and asked him *to begin* just such an operation.[32] Not only did circuits overlap, but they varied enormously in size. Most of the *réseaux* had subcircuits with groups, cells, sabotage teams, reception committees and propaganda disseminators.[33] Often there were more groups than agents to be in them. The smallest, *Tutor*, consisted of one man who spent less than a week in France, but who spread such an elaborate network on paper that others who came after him thought they were going to make contact with one of the largest and best-organized of all the *réseaux*.[34] The largest, *Prosper*, numbered its available forces in the tens of thousands.

Prosper was led by Francis Suttill, son of a French mother and British father, who usually passed as a Belgian because of his accent. His attitude toward recruiting agents was debonair, which may have accounted for the high rate of casualties among them. *Gloria* was indirectly allied with *Prosper*, and both fell at about the same time. Of the 80 to 120 actual members of the combined groups (neither the French nor the British agree on an accurate count) fewer than twenty survived.[35]

By June, 1942, *Prosper*, whose agents had always tended to see too much of each other socially and to gather too openly to exchange information, was being decimated by the Gestapo. Armel Guerne, the second-in-command, was arrested in a stupid incident. The Gestapo pounded on the door of his apartment demanding that he surrender, and his wife, who thought it was a joke, threw open the door to find them with guns poised, ready to fire. Guerne had no time to escape by the back door. Suttill was arrested next, as were many of the cell's subleaders. All was in disarray and confusion.

British records state that some of "Guerne's intellectuals" (as they had come to be called) had the good sense to lie low, and they list Beckett among them.[36] This is not true, for Beckett never worked with Guerne.[37] From the latter part of 1941 through the first six months of 1942, Beckett had been wisely restricting his activity so that he came in contact only with a handful of the most trusted survivors of *Gloria*. Throughout this time, his work was often mundane and of little importance. He had stopped making the occasional trip to Normandy, Brittany or Châlons, and only acted as a *bôite aux lettres* in extreme emergency.[38] His intuition told him there was danger ahead, and he wanted to stay clear of it.

Some months earlier, a Catholic priest from Luxembourg had joined *Gloria*. The Abbé Robert Alesch, formerly of St. Maur, claimed to be in Paris as a student, an administrator, and as a minor functionary in the hierarchy of the Catholic Church. He volunteered his services, saying that as a priest, he could travel freely throughout the occupied zone, and would be able to bring back valuable information about the eastern regions. Abbé Alesch soon became known as "the Bishop."[39] He received and carried information, but most importantly for many of the agents, he was their priest and confidant. He heard their confessions, elicited information about where they had been, who their contacts were and what their next assignment would be. Often they came to him in the middle of the night for confession before setting out on what proved to be their last mission. What these hapless agents had no way of knowing was that Abbé Alesch was the *former* abbot of St. Maur, a dissolute, untrustworthy man who had been defrocked by the Church and almost immediately recruited by the Germans as a V-man, or informer. He was responsible for the destruction of *Gloria* and death to all but a handful of agents.[40]

By mid-August, only the original members of *Gloria* and *Étoile* were still free. Picabia went to Lyon to meet Péron, collect his information and proceed south with it.[41] Several weeks earlier they had met in Brittany where they arranged the Lyon rendezvous. As they parted, Picabia dared Péron to "bring some fresh cream" to Lyon. "I will, I promise," he said, as he waved to her departing train. She never saw him again. Péron was arrested on August 16, 1942 in the Marne-et-Loire as he was making his way to Lyon to meet Picabia. Most of the others in their group were arrested or "on the trot."[42] When Marie Péron heard of her husband's arrest, she sent a telegram to Beckett, undisguised and uncoded, to warn him:

Alfred arreté par Gestapo. Prière faire
nécessaire pour corriger l'erreur.[43]

Suzanne Deschevaux-Dumesnil was on her way to visit
friends in *Gloria* that day. When she arrived at their apartment,
she found the Germans ransacking the place while her frightened friends stared blankly, pretending not to know her. The
quick-thinking Suzanne pretended to have rung the bell for the
wrong apartment and was able to convince the Germans that
her story was true. She rushed back to the rue des Favorites.

Both she and Beckett knew it was only a matter of time
until the Gestapo came for them. Mme. Péron's telegram
reached them at 11 a.m. and by 3 p.m. they were gone.[44] They
simply left the apartment as if they were going for a walk and
never went back.

For the next two months, together and apart, they moved
from one Paris hideout to another. At one point, Beckett hid for
ten days under the false floor of the attic in Nathalie Sarraute's
house with her aged and ill father. Madame Sarraute, part
Jewish, had trained her young children to refer to her as their
governess and to call her "Mademoiselle." At this time she was
determined to remain in Paris, but as the war went on, she, too,
fled.[45]

Another time, Beckett hid in a tall tree in the woods outside
Paris with another member of the *réseau* while below them
Germans made periodic patrols with dogs and guns. When they
were able to get away, they found temporary refuge in a safe
hotel, where Beckett's companion, his mind unhinged by the
ordeal, jumped from a window and killed himself.[46]

By October, 1942, Beckett and Suzanne had secured false
papers and contacted a *passeur*, i.e., someone adept at smuggling
wanted persons through German lines into the unoccupied
zone.[47]

He was supposed to take them across the line, but in the
end, they made the journey openly by train from Châlons to
Lyon, relying on their forged papers. There, they had an acci-
dental encounter with Picabia, still on the run, who gave them
some money. When they left Paris they had had only enough
for train fare and were now desperate and hungry. They told

Picabia they hoped to make their way to Toulon, where a man called Professor Lob, a friend of Suzanne's, was teaching in the university.[48] Picabia promised to send them money there in care of Professor Lob, which she later did, but they never received it.[49]

On their way to Toulon, they somehow got word that Professor and Madame Lob had left and gone into hiding in a small mountain village called Roussillon in the Vaucluse. Beckett and Suzanne made their way south on foot, sleeping by day in the woods, in haystacks, occasionally in barns and sheds; and walking by night until they came to Roussillon, where they lived in hiding for the next two and a half years.

There Beckett worked sporadically with local Resistance groups, but he had lost the impetus and determination that drove him in Paris. *Gloria* was a chaotic ruin, he and Suzanne were in hiding, Péron was in a concentration camp and many others were dead. Mary Reynolds had quietly disappeared and no one knew where she had gone. Jeannine Picabia began to work for British intelligence units and spent the rest of the war wandering around France. Only Gabrielle Buffet-Picabia stayed permanently in Paris, where she turned her atelier on the rue Chateaubriand into a hiding place for flyers shot down behind the lines who hoped to make their way back to England.

For his work with *Gloria*, Samuel Beckett was awarded the *Croix de Guerre* with a gold star on March 30, 1945. The citation was signed by General Charles de Gaulle, President of the Provisional Government of the French Republic, by order of General Juin, Chief of Staff for National Defense, and read as follows:

> BECKETT, Sam: A man of great courage, who over the course of two years, demonstrated his effectiveness as an information source in an important intelligence network. He continued this work well past the limit of personal security. Betrayed to the Germans, from 1943 he was forced to live clandestinely and with great difficulty.[50]

Beckett received the *Croix de Guerre* with politeness, deference and courtesy—the same qualities he exhibited after the war for any award or honor that came his way. He accepted it graciously and was quietly pleased to have it, but he told no one about it. Other than Suzanne, Picabia and her mother, none of his friends knew about it as late as 1975.[51]

Beckett also received the *Médaille de la Résistance*, an award given to a large number of persons whose work had been genuinely valuable. Picabia recommended Beckett for the award; she herself wrote the citation (since lost) which Beckett thought "too much. Effusive, flowery—not at all necessary."[52]

The war had turned Samuel Beckett's life upside down, and was probably one of the most important factors in his development as the writer who captured the imagination of postwar society, but he had no need to keep it in the forefront of his life. As in one of the old Dutch paintings he admired so much, the war was part of his background, the idealized landscape, the necessary contrast accentuating the main figure, whose brooding, introspective eyes seem to stare with alarming relevancy while still hinting of an unreal, private time and place.

One part of his life, the glamour and danger of occupied Paris, was over. As he walked away from it toward the dry red earth of Roussillon, boredom, frustration and breakdown lay ahead.

CHAPTER FOURTEEN

1942–45:

"NO SYMBOLS WHERE NONE INTENDED"

In early November, 1942, more than a month after they fled from Paris, Beckett and Suzanne trudged into the village of Roussillon, their faces windburned and their boots caked with the thick red dust of the region, for they had walked by night and hidden by day the greater part of the distance from Lyon, almost 150 miles. Roussillon, high in the isolated mountainous region of the Vaucluse in southeast France, was secluded and relatively free from German interference. Consequently, it was a favorite hiding place for refugees. No one took notice when Beckett and Suzanne arrived, for townspeople were used to strangers in their midst. Mostly they moved on, but those who stayed tried to fit into the pattern of village life as discreetly as possible.

Beckett and Suzanne agreed that the most sensible course of action was first to find a place to stay, then to register with he authorities in the *mairie*, or city hall. Accordingly, on November 6, 1942, Samuel Barclay Beckett filled out a card which incorrectly noted his birthplace as Dublin, England; his nationality as Irish; his profession, none; the place from which he had come, Paris; and his address as the Roussillon Hotel Escoffier.[1]

This was the only hotel in the village, and was run by the widow of the great chef.[2] It was already crowded with refugees, among them the painter Henri Hayden and his wife, Josette. Beckett and Suzanne arrived while the Haydens were out for their daily afternoon walk. When they returned to the hotel, they saw two disheveled travelers sitting in the bar drinking wine.

"Come in, come in," Madame Escoffier called, "here are two more who have come from Paris."[3]

Eager for news from the outside world, the Haydens pressed into the tiny room but were halted by Beckett's reserve. His eyes, hidden behind the small round lenses of his glasses, took care not to meet theirs directly. In a soft, polite voice, Beckett said he was sorry he had no current news to give them because he and his wife had left Paris some time ago.

Other refugees included Robert and Toni Clerkx (the pen name of Jacoba van Velde, sister of Bram and Geer), who also lived in the hotel briefly before moving to another part of the village. There was a large colony of displaced Parisian Jews who were very gossipy and social; among them was a stage designer married to the daughter of Madame Mathieu, widow of the former mayor of the town. Beckett was careful to keep his distance from this group simply because their lives were so enmeshed with intrigue and backbiting. It was a sociability of the worst kind, which he always avoided.[4]

As soon as they recovered from the fatigue and tension engendered by their desperate journey, Beckett and Suzanne appraised their surroundings dispassionately and came to the conclusion that, under the circumstances, Roussillon was not a bad place to stay undercover. Food seemed to be adequate if not plentiful, and the villagers were all too busy with their own affairs to pry into the lives of the strangers who quietly filled up the town. Best of all, the war seemed so far away from the Vaucluse, except for a rare and infrequent reference to the *Maquis* (the local Resistance) or an occasional rumor that the Germans were coming.

Too soon the thrill of being safe from danger was replaced by boredom and monotony. Day followed seemingly endless day, in which the only variety was the decision whether to walk north or south on the afternoon stroll. The afternoon stroll lengthened into morning and afternoon walks, and each walk gradually grew longer until most of the day was taken up with exercise in an often futile attempt to fall bone weary into bed.

At first Beckett and Suzanne tried to maintain their distance from the other refugees. They nodded and smiled as they passed the Haydens on one of their strolls, but each couple was careful not to rush into friendship. Each felt it necessary to go slowly, for one never knew how long the war would last, and a too-easy intimacy might prove deadly if forced to drag on for a long time.

Two events transpired which diminished their reserve and led to a friendship that lasted until Hayden's death many years later. First, Beckett discovered happily that Hayden was a keen student of chess and a good player. The second was Beckett's introduction to a Miss Beamish (whose first name was unknown to everyone). Hayden, a Polish Jew, wanted to take English lessons to be prepared "when the Allies arrive," and each day he trudged down the village road for a lesson with Miss Beamish, whom he called simply "Miss."[5]

All the villagers were a little afraid of Miss Beamish and secretly made fun of her. Defiantly British, elderly, she wore heavy boots and baggy tweeds, and in a voice thickened from years of chain-smoking, loudly proclaimed to everyone that she was a first cousin of Winston Churchill. She lived in a little house about a mile from the hotel with her companion of many years, also named Suzanne, and two cats and two large, ill-behaved Airedale dogs.

Miss Beamish professed to be a novelist, and her idea of teaching English was to read Shakespeare and loudly declaim the more famous passages without bothering to explain what the words meant. Hayden became a familiar sight in the village as he walked back to the hotel after his lessons, reciting passages from *Hamlet* in a loud, theatrical voice, sometimes replete with stage gestures. All Miss Beamish's animals loved Hayden and followed yapping and racing in circles as he went. Late at night he would sit up in bed, still reciting Shakespeare while Madame Hayden implored him to go to sleep.

"The Germans are coming and you learn English!" she scolded.

"But the Americans will get here first and I have to be ready," he replied, as he continued to read.[6]

The same conversation was repeated several times each

week, until it became as habitual as the daily walks, and it never failed to amuse Beckett, who did not share his friend's incorrigible optimism.

Hayden wanted his two English-speaking friends to meet, especially since both were writers. He took a reluctant Beckett to meet Miss Beamish, and the two soon discovered that they had more in common than language. Miss Beamish had been born in Dublin of parents who came from Connaught, and her origins were deep in Ireland. She had lived in France for many years and, like Beckett, was fluent in French. Also like Beckett, she had chosen to stay in France during the war as a symbol of loyalty to her adopted country. However, it was more risky for her since she carried a British passport.

Every evening, Miss Beamish's loud, clear voice could be heard throughout the village as she sang Irish songs in a strong Connaught accent.[7] Beckett investigated discreetly and discovered that much of her singing was induced by the local wine. Soon he was going with her to the farm of a man called Bonnelly, who let him have wine and food as well.

Bonnelly was a silent, truculent man who kept to himself and had little to do with the other villagers. He made good wine, enough for his large family, and usually had some left over, which he sold to everyone but Miss Beamish at inflated prices. He always had an extra dozen eggs or piece of cheese, and he always took care of Miss Beamish before all others. Less frequently did he have anything for Beckett.

Bonnelly thought Beckett a very strange person, uncommunicative to the point of rudeness, with one overriding fixation: mothers. "Mothers of anything," Bonnelly remembers, "dogs, cats, humans, anything!" When a neighboring laborer complained in Beckett's presence that he was loath to go to work since it meant leaving his old and ill mother alone, Beckett insisted on taking the man's place, declaring emphatically that "one *should be* with one's mother!"[8]

Some time after *Waiting for Godot* was produced in Paris, Bonnelly heard that he was a character in the play. Vladimir tells Estragon, "*Nous avons fait les vendanges, tiens, un nommé Bonnelly, à Roussillon.*"[9] "I don't know why he put me in that play," Bonnelly said, puzzled. "I didn't know him very well and seldom talked to him. After the war, when he went back to Paris, he wrote me one letter but no one here could read his writing, and that was the end of that."[10]

Bonnelly introduced Beckett to a neighboring peasant named Aude, who became his friend. Aude lived about a mile north of Roussillon with his wife and a large number of strong, handsome, hardworking children. Once or twice a week Beckett went to Aude's farm, at first to buy supplies, but as he came to know and respect Aude, these trips usually included drinking wine and sharing a meal with the family. Soon Beckett went routinely to the farm in the early afternoon, worked for several hours before sharing the meal and a cigarette, and then trudged back into town after dark with his supplies. Usually he chopped wood or worked with the family in the fields, but he was not exchanging his labor to stave off hunger. Rather, it was labor in friendship, done out of boredom, and was seldom payment in exchange for supplies. Early in his confinement in Roussillon, Beckett had contacted his family, and for the rest of the war his mother and brother sent him money through the regular mail at specified intervals.[11] The sums were not large, but compared to the standards under which most of the refugees lived, Beckett was extremely comfortable and never lacked for food. There are stories of Beckett selling the sheets off his bed for a few cigarettes, of Beckett begging farmers to allow him to search already harvested fields for food—but they are apocryphal. People in the Vaucluse were able to go on with their lives throughout the war with relatively little interference from either warring side because the area was out of the way in the unoccupied zone. They had adequate food, never lacked wine and seldom went without cigarettes.

Time went on, blurred in an unvarying pattern of long walks and chess games punctuated only by news broadcasts. The radio became the lifeline to the outside world, and all activity stopped several times each day as everyone in the hotel gathered around the squawking set, trying to catch each word, weighing each phrase for special, unstated significance.

But as months passed, each stopped trying to convince the others that they were happy in Roussillon, for they were not. Theirs was a prison, albeit without walls, and the endless monotony was destroying them in different ways. For Beckett especially, the endless round of walks and chess and radio news was having a serious effect. His health began to decay. At first he simply stayed in bed for several days. Then coughs and colds and boils, manifestations of the psychosomatic illnesses that had plagued him all his life, lingered long after they should have been cured. Finally, he could not ignore the familiar symptoms of anxiety and depression. He still had enough self-control to realize that giving way to these fears was senseless, but nevertheless sleeplessness led to hallucinations and he was unable to ward off the feeling of imminent collapse.[12] Even the panacea of physical work was withheld from him as he had nothing but the generosity of Aude to provide him with something to do. Roussillon was a farm community, and people went to bed early because they needed the daylight hours for work. The hotel was noisy and crowded, and most of the people who lived there kept the same schedule as the farmers. When Beckett wanted to stay up late at night and into the early morning hours, there was no one to keep him company and nowhere to go. He had to be still in his room because the least movement could be heard in the other rooms and disturbed not only the sleeping Suzanne but other guests as well. Yet he continued to live at the hotel, as if to take a more permanent residence would be an admission that the war would continue indefinitely, and because living there gave him the feeling that he was free to leave at a moment's notice. Finally, even this mental ruse no longer gave him any comfort; for his peace and well-being, he had to move.

There was a small vacant house on the edge of the village, and he and Suzanne moved into it in 1943. It had a kitchen and living room on the ground floor, with a bedroom—little more than a sleeping loft—above. Outside the bedroom window was a balcony scarcely big enough for the large geranium he kept there. It was a small house, but it was private, and he was free to live and work at his own schedule. In this little house he began to write once again, trying for the first time since he wrote *Murphy* to produce a long work of fiction. What emerged from this period of exile was the curious novel *Watt*, his third and last written in English.

"What an idiotic game it would be! To write when there's no one to read what you've written," says a character in Simone de Beauvoir's novel of Paris immediately after the end of the war, *The Mandarins*.

"When everything has gone to hell, there's nothing to do but to play idiotic games," replies another.[13]

In much the same tone, Beckett called *Watt* "only a game, a means of staying sane, a way to keep my hand in."[14]

Beckett suffered a very real breakdown in Roussillon— probably his most serious—one directly related to the schizophrenic form and content of much of *Watt*.[15] To Suzanne and his friends it seemed as if he had fallen victim to the general malaise that afflicts persons incarcerated against their will for long periods of time. He slept long hours and when he awoke was sometimes disoriented. He made only minimal attempts to be part of life in the village, but at the same time he was always on the fringes, peering nearsightedly with unconcealed clinical interest at whatever was happening. He was scathing in his denunciation of life in Roussillon and hated the circumstances that placed him there. He followed a bizarre schedule of strange ritualistic tramps through the countryside despite the ridicule of his fellow exiles and the taunts of the villagers.

To some who observed him during this time, he seemed to be two persons: a man desperate to fit in, to be part of every activity and movement, but also one who rebuffed the slightest gesture of friendship. He seemed bewildered and confused. He felt guilty that he wasn't with his mother every time a letter came from her, yet he hated her for writing at all. There was guilt as well for his friends in *Gloria* who had not escaped, guilt for the man whom he was powerless to keep from jumping out the window and especially guilt towards himself for having fallen into the comparative lap of comfort once again. Roussillon, at first a refuge, had become a prison, one in which Beckett suffered in virtual solitary confinement as various parts of himself fought for control with the others. Self-hatred and his instinctive reach toward self-preservation were at war within him, and they caused a split; a "center" failed to hold, so that fragments of himself seemed to fly off in so many directions that he was on the verge of total disintegration—hence extended sleep as a refuge.

Because he was without access to psychiatric help, Beckett was forced to muster astonishing reserves of self-control to disguise his real intentions and feelings and to force himself to act as if nothing untoward were happening, as if his inner being were not a raging battleground. He discovered that the most effective way to bring himself under control was to channel all his confusion through his writing.

Still, no matter how much he wanted to use fiction to create order from the chaos of his life, Beckett could only bring himself to do so through diversion and disguise. He set up a smokescreen of obscurity and complexity behind which he carefully hid tantalizing clues for his readers.[16] He wanted—craved actually—both personal and public understanding. Yet the most insignificant form of contact which even hinted that someone was trying to become close to him signaled an intrusion, an invasion of his privacy, and it terrified him. He had made his aloneness into a sanctified obsession which he protected behind impenetrable, labyrinthine defenses. He would not permit himself to reveal himself. For Beckett, sanity became analogous with secrecy and cunning. He had to work to stay sane; thus *Watt* became his daily therapy, the means with which he clung to the vestiges of his idea of sanity.

Filled with permutations and combinations, endless mathematical meanderings, a mélange of suppositions and mental games, *Watt* ends with the ambiguous statement, "No symbols where none intended."[17] It is the sort of novel a man might write who wanted relief, solace and intellectual release from his physical surroundings. Beckett wrote *Watt* in a desperate attempt to stave off complete mental breakdown and filled the book with dialogues and scenes from his own life.

At times it verges on autobiography. "My memories begin on the eve of my birth, under the table, when my father gave a dinner party and my mother presided," he wrote to one friend before the war and repeated to another before he finally used it in *Watt*.[18] There are descriptions of the countryside around

Foxrock, allusions to his boyhood and constant references to the seasonal cycles of the plants and animals of Ireland. At other times, *Watt* is only an academic exercise for a vital mind hemmed in by the accident of war, which restricted his residence, access to books, friends and family.

Beckett's age and the circumstances in which he wrote *Watt* make the book especially significant in his development as a writer, coming as it does in his middle age—he was between thirty-eight and forty—and at a turning point in his life. The literary career which had barely begun to gain momentum after his return to Paris in 1937 had once again ground to a halt, and this time, in the misery of war, there was a serious reason to doubt whether he would or could ever resume it. It was not his conscious farewell to his native language, as some scholars insist;[19] at the time he wrote it, he had not considered writing fiction in any language but English. His prewar attempts to write in French had been poetry or criticism because it seemed sensible to write these forms in the language of the most accessible publications. Fiction, especially anything that might evolve into a novel, was still something he felt constrained to deal with in English. Even after all his time in Paris and his years of serious study of French, Beckett still felt insecure about writing the language, and he was not about to expose himself to the ridicule and criticism awkward grammar and syntax might evoke.

Unconsciously at first, then with gradually dawning perception, he watched his own writing become less and less like Joyce's as he concentrated for a single meaning, explicit, immediately apparent, in the most ordinary language possible, and with profound implication for his own personal existence as well as for the universal audience.

"I meant what I said," Beckett has snapped over the years when pressed to explain his writing. It is a phrase he first uttered when referring to *Watt*.[20] Just as he also uses the final words of the novel to emphasize this statement, he asks his readers to accept the surface meaning of all his words without looking deeper. All the while, however, Beckett takes enormous pains to disguise what he really means beneath the surface.

Watt, the character who gives the novel its title, is one of a succession of persons who have been servants in the house of a

Mr. Knott. There is no reason why Watt should be singled out as protagonist, just as there is no reason why he should not. He is first encountered in a railroad station where he takes a train, gets off at a specific stop and walks along a road until he comes to Mr. Knott's house, where he is expected. He enters Mr. Knott's employ, stays for a specific period of time, leaves, and then travels to his final destination, an insane asylum. There, he recounts his adventures to Sam, a fellow inmate, but not in the order in which they occurred.[21] In the process of his peregrinations, Watt undergoes a specific mental deterioration. He is unable to distinguish reality from fantasy, and insists throughout on trying to impose rational meanings on irrational situations.

> For Watt's concern, deep as it appeared, was not after all with what the figure *was*, in reality, but with what the figure appeared to be in reality.[22]

Like Murphy, Watt clearly perceives the world around him. But unlike Murphy, who tries to perfect the hermeticism of his mind before he realizes that he is doomed to sanity and cannot surrender to his inner being, Watt is afraid even to recognize what lies in his mind. If he is to be at peace with his surroundings, he must go one step further and enter what Raymond Federman has called a "zone of creative consciousness where he would no longer be bound by temporal and spatial dimensions."[23]

It is his inability to allow himself to be transported into this zone that ultimately drives Watt to the asylum. He is too much of this world to surrender to the structured confusion of Mr. Knott's house, a haven of absurdity in the midst of a chaotic world. Watt cannot accept this immediate refuge, mad though it is, because he knows firsthand of the greater madness lurking beyond.

As an example of how Beckett disguises his ultimate meaning even while insisting on the reader's acceptance of his immediate meaning, he tacks on several pages of Addenda at the end of the novel, to which he adds the footnote:

> The following precious and illuminating material should be carefully studied. Only fatigue and disgust prevented its incorporation.[24]

His admonition should be heeded. The Addenda begin with a capsule description of his mother, speak of a thinly disguised Dublin character and bring his father's predilection for the Leopardstown racetrack into it. There are snatches of verse from poems he abandoned long ago and occasional snippets of some in progress. Beckett inserts himself:

> The maddened prizeman . . . never been properly born . . . for all the good that frequent departures out of Ireland had done him, he might just as well have stayed there.[25]

He expresses his yearning for the apartment on the rue des Favorites, carefully describing the working space: "a round wooden table, of generous diameter, resting on a single massive conical frustrum, filling the middle space." Towards the end of the Addenda, as if he has revealed too much, there is the abrupt notation to "change all the names," followed by Beckett's final warning: "No symbols where none intended." He has said too much, and now must confuse and baffle any determined reader who has persisted until the end of the book.

Immediate comparisons spring to mind between Beckett and Watt, Mr. Knott's house and World War II, the asylum and Roussillon. They are all valid and deserve critical elaboration. *Watt* is often cited as one of Beckett's most obscure and puzzling books, deliberately secret, tantalizing, revealing only to withdraw into qualification and denial. It is surely an autobiographical writing, albeit autobiography hidden and confused, as Beckett was himself while he wrote it. It is the first of the maddening fictions where Beckett deliberately steps in to undercut and belie any meaning or appreciation. Just as the reader is settling into a warm, cozy read, Beckett steps in to douse him with a cold shower of verbiage. He has no system, no easy answer for anything, and he won't allow the reader to find one either.

In his own life, Beckett was deeply afraid that lack of structure in his daily existence would have serious consequences for his mental stability, as it had in the past. He was adept in recognizing the symptoms of disintegration that beset him before a period of depression, and he knew that he would have to impose some sort of order onto his existence. He began to work on

Watt with regularity, a minimum of three hours each day. Twice, sometimes three times a week, he visited Aude to work, eat and buy provisions. Each evening he and Hayden played chess while Josette sketched or painted the two of them as they sat bent over the board.[26] He and Suzanne took long walks each day, and he and Miss Beamish met for wine and conversation with increasing frequency. The stage designer, whom he was beginning to know better, spoke of the theater in Paris with longing and frustration, and Beckett spoke to him of the Gaiety and the Gate, of Racine and German Existential drama.

With the Allied invasions of Europe, the war was drawing closer to Roussillon. Most of the people were involved with the *Maquis*, the local Resistance, in one way or another.[27] Allied planes flew over and either dropped supplies or landed to unload them, and the villagers went out to the fields to gather and hide them before the Germans and their French sympathizers found out. Peaceful Roussillon erupted into violence over these materials. In one instance, a shipment of tobacco was overlooked in the darkness and confusion, and the next morning the man on whose field it lay reported it to the police. Before long, he was found with a bullet in his head.[28]

The *Maquis* were a loose, disorganized collection of persons who came and went with great frequency and who were neither counted upon nor missed. Most of their work was haphazard: whoever was available or in the mood took part in whatever was happening. The poet René Char was the titular leader of the *Maquis* in the Vaucluse, but there were so many others who headed small bands and claimed supreme authority that, as with the Resistance in the Occupied Zone, no history currently exists which can be relied upon as definitive.

Other refugees who had taken part in political activity before coming to Roussillon joined the *Maquis*, but at first Beckett wanted no part of it. He had exhausted his physical and emotional resources when he fled from Paris. He was reluctant to jeopardize his precarious sanity or his ability to concentrate on writing. It was only a matter of time now until the Germans were defeated, and he planned to exist quietly until then. Suzanne agreed with him; one exodus was all that she wished to endure. But Beckett could not deny that he had been with the

Resistance in Paris, and the local people knew about it, so the peace he wanted was not to be his.

One evening Beckett allowed himself to be coaxed into joining a group that went out each night to sabotage anything that might be useful to the Germans. From then on he worked with the *Maquis*. Unlike his work in Paris, where he had been instrumental in establishing and organizing *réseau* activity, Beckett simply did what he was told by the local *Maquis* leaders. First, they only asked him to hide small quantities of dynamite in his house, and he agreed, but he was frightened at the thought of having it inside, and so he put it on the terrace next to his geranium, where it was clearly visible. Suzanne was alarmed and ran to the Haydens, saying Beckett was surely mad to have taken the dynamite in the first place, and was even more so for putting it in clear view. The Haydens persuaded Beckett to put it in the kitchen instead, under some loose floor boards. On a second occasion, he hid grenades for the *Maquis*, but this time insisted on keeping them on the terrace, no matter how Suzanne begged him to hide them. Several times he disappeared for several days at a stretch, returning in the middle of the night, dirty and tired. It was understood that he had been with the *Maquis*, but no one asked questions.

Encounters with the Germans became more frequent and more serious. One day, several German soldiers were gunned down on the outskirts of the village, where their bodies lay decomposing on the road because the local residents were terrified of German retaliation and would neither approach nor bury them. Miss Beamish heard about it and with her customary British bravado, set out with her shovel slung over shoulder to bury them. Cursing loudly, she roared through the village toward the bodies, berating those who had come to stare at her as she passed.[29] Hayden, who heard her coming, followed along in her wake, saying as sternly as he could, "Now look here, Miss . . ." but she was not dissuaded by his fussing. Finally, he shrugged his shoulders and joined her. They took turns shoveling until the bodies were buried.[30]

When the Allies landed on D Day, there was jubilation in Roussillon. Madame Escoffier brought out her second-best wine—she was saving the best for the first Americans who reached the village—and the villagers and refugees mingled freely, forgetting all their past hostilities and differences.

Beckett became increasingly nervous at the thought that his unwilling exile seemed to be ending. The news from his mother and brother throughout the war had not been good. Doctors had diagnosed May's condition as Parkinson's disease, which later became the cause of her death. It had been more than five years since Beckett had seen her, and he was both anxious to get to Ireland and worried about what he would find. Now more than ever, he hovered over the radio news broadcasts.

On August 24, 1944, the first American soldiers came to Roussillon. Overhead, parachutes filled the sky, and in the village, truck convoys roared to a screeching halt as happy villagers surrounded them and pulled the soldiers down for hugs and kisses. Madame Escoffier brought out her best wine, and the real celebration was under way. The Haydens, who were living in a house with a common wall to the hotel barroom, got used to the thumping which was Madame Escoffier's signal for Henri to come and translate. Hayden went around the village beaming, telling everyone how farsighted he had been to learn English, since he was now, in Beckett's absence, the official village translator.

Beckett had gone out several days previously with the *Maquis,* to make the roads leading into Roussillon secure for the advancing Americans. Now they returned, marching along the road in a file, singing the *Marseillaise* at the top of their lungs and brandishing their rifles. To the rear and on the outside of their phalanx, Beckett marched without a rifle, his head bowed, grimly serious and silent. The war was over, and he was grateful, but he had no time for wine and celebration. Two years was long enough, and he wanted to get back to living his own life on his own terms.

Almost immediately he began to withdraw from life in Roussillon and plot the quickest way to leave. One frustration piled upon another: the Allied soldiers warned that return to Paris would almost surely be forbidden, as occupied France was still dangerous territory and civilians were not allowed to pass freely from one zone to another. Beckett chafed under what seemed to him unnecessary delay as Christmas and the New Year came and went. Shortly thereafter, he, Suzanne and the Haydens decided they would take a chance and try to find places on the train from Avignon to Paris. Beckett was elected to inquire about arrangements, and so he trekked to Avignon, where he was told that rail service was sporadic and risky, as civilian papers were subject to rigorous examination before anyone was allowed on board. With his Irish passport, and the fact that he had been in hiding for two years, there was the possibility that trouble might arise.

When he returned to Roussillon, he discovered that it was all academic anyway, as Henri Hayden had become seriously ill and would be unable to travel for some time. Once again Beckett was forced to wait. Each day he hoped that the money he had urgently asked Frank to send would arrive from Ireland, but there were currency restrictions in effect, and Frank could not mail such a large amount out of the country.

Finally, in April, 1945, Beckett decided he could wait no longer. He made the difficult decision to leave the Haydens behind and forgo the long-planned celebration of their mutual first night back in Paris. Desperate for money, he visited Aude, who loaned him seven thousand old francs.[31] With this money, he and Suzanne set out by bus from Roussillon, then by train from Avignon. The journey to Paris took several days, with one major delay when the train in which they were riding sat on a siding for twenty-two hours, just south of Lyon, close to the place where they had abandoned trains to walk the last way into Roussillon two years before.[32] There were further irritating delays while their papers were checked repeatedly. Miraculously, Beckett's Irish passport was still in order, but he had to explain over and over again where he had been for the past two years and why he had been out of touch with the Irish Legation.

Finally, he decided to bypass Paris and go straight to the coast in the hope of crossing the Channel more quickly. He told Suzanne to wait for him at the rue des Favorites while he went on to Ireland to see his mother and brother, untangle his affairs and then return to Paris as fast as possible. He was in a terrible hurry to get everything taken care of so that he could go back to Paris and settle down. He had a new novel, *Watt*, that pleased him and he wanted it to be published as soon as possible. It was the only positive aspect of the years from 1939 to 1945, which he viewed as a tragic but unavoidable waste. He had no more time to fritter away, no matter what the circumstances.

Beckett soon discovered that the only way he could get to Ireland was through England, which was quite all right, as he wanted to see about publishing *Watt*. He also hoped to find some money due him for *Murphy*, for he had had no communication with Routledge since 1939 and had received no royalties.

To his dismay, he learned that of the 1,500 copies printed, 782 were unsold and had been remaindered in 1942. He was furious with Routledge, and demanded to know why they had not honored the clause in his contract which gave him the opportunity to buy unsold copies before they were disposed of cheaply.[33] Routledge's explanation—that no one had heard from him since 1940 and didn't know if he was alive or dead— meant nothing to Beckett. He recovered his equanimity to ask Herbert Read if he would be interested in sponsoring *Watt*, and Read, remembering *Murphy*, expressed keen interest. Beckett left it with him on condition that he make a decision within the month.

Beckett was in a hurry to get to Dublin, and spent little time in London. However, he did call on Gwynned Vernon Reavey to see if any other royalty checks had accrued. There was one, but it was for an inconsequential amount.[34]

He went shopping on Oxford Street to buy toys for Frank's children, Caroline and the infant Edward. There, he quite literally bumped into Jeannine Picabia.[35] It was a joyous reunion, for they had had no contact since *Gloria* was decimated in 1942, but their joy was tempered by the fact that neither knew whether Péron, his wife, and sons had survived the war.

Picabia had just come from a debriefing session at British intelligence headquarters where she had been reliving the last days of *Gloria*, and when she told Beckett about it she began to cry. Beckett swooped her tiny figure under his gangly arm and insisted that what she needed was an afternoon touring toy shops. He cheered her up as he bought Caroline a large doll and

Edward a bright, flashy train. With gifts in hand, he set out at last for Dublin.

He found his mother living quietly in her house on New Place, just around the corner from Cooldrinagh, which she had finally forced herself to sell. She still wore the same severe black tailored clothes as before the war, but her tall, angular figure seemed sadly shrunken within them. Her once regal carriage was now diminished and distorted by shaking and quivering—visible manifestations of the Parkinson's disease which had become so pronounced during the past year. He was both frightened and sad to see her so unable to command her own body—she who had always been so imperiously in command of everything within her orbit.

She had a new maid, a new gardener and a new dog. Instead of a Kerry Blue, she kept a spoiled Pomeranian whose sharp staccato bark gave everyone but herself severe headaches. She still kept a donkey and cart, but the daily afternoon rides were reduced to those she took during the infrequent visits of her grandchildren and their friends. Even these were becoming fewer, as the children, in their cruelty, were afraid of or made fun of her infirmity. Caroline, who was now seven years old, was embarrassed by her friends' teasing comments and invented reasons not to visit her grandmother.[36]

Frank had also changed greatly in the past six years. He had gained weight, settled down and become, in his brother's eyes, "middle-aged."[37] He was a prosperous businessman, overworked but thriving, repeating his life exactly as their father had lived his. Frank had his yacht club, golf club and rigorous walks through the hills in back of Killiney bay. He was a deacon in Tullow Parish of the Church of Ireland, a member of the building committee and an usher every Sunday at services. He seldom went to the theater, never read books, and he and Jean entertained other couples exactly like themselves. Frank smoked, drank and ate too much. He was as hearty as their father had been, and this worried Beckett, though he said nothing. The gulf that had kept them from communicating before the war seemed unbridgeable now.

Caroline was a tiny, doll-like version of Beckett, with the same piercing blue eyes and aquiline features, and Edward was a roly-poly, jovial little boy who was the image of his grand-father. Jean worked to present an image of tranquil domesticity, which was always destroyed when she and May were together, for they were two strong women who resented each other's authority. For Beckett, family life in Ireland was as foreign as life in Roussillon. More than ever, he wanted to get back to Paris to find the only stability he had ever known.

As soon as he arrived in Dublin, he tried to arrange his finances with his bank and learned that the wartime restrictions forbidding the removal of pounds sterling from Ireland and England were still in effect. This grim news meant that he would have to find other means of support for what looked like an indefinite period of time if he went back to France. He thought he would be able to circumvent this restriction, but Frank's solicitors convinced him it could not be done.

This was a minor setback, however, for when he presented himself to have his papers renewed, he was told that the French government no longer permitted resident aliens. There were severe shortages throughout the country in all aspects of life, and foreigners were forbidden to return until they had been alleviated. The thought of Suzanne alone in Paris without a job, and perhaps even without an apartment, terrified him. He had no idea if she had made it safely to the rue des Favorites or if she had found the apartment intact.[38] If they had been legally married, she could have claimed Irish citizenship and traveled to Dublin. As a French citizen, she was trapped within her own country. At home, he discreetly skirted the subject of Suzanne and their marital status, and May avoided all comment. She had absolutely no interest in the woman who now filled all the needs of his life. She never asked about Suzanne and they never met.[39]

Except for business trips into Dublin, Beckett was content to sit at home. All his cousins and aunts were anxious to see him, and there were interminable teas with enormous quantities of food. He seemed to abstain deliberately from eating, content with a single cup of tea and the thinnest slice of bread and butter. One of his cousins made a casual remark about a sumptuous tea table and was unprepared for Beckett's scathing reply. "My friends eat sawdust and turnips while all Ireland safely gorges . . ." His voice drifted off and he shook his head as if to rid his eyes of the sight of so much butter and cream.[40]

Most of Beckett's Irish friends had spent the war years in Dublin, and he met them reluctantly, usually by accident. He had come back from Roussillon even more silent and taciturn than when he left Dublin in 1937, and this was interpreted by his friends as an intensification of his unsociability. Actually, it was a state of mind induced by so much solitude and despair that it was difficult for him to overcome. He had been bored, depressed and frustrated for such a long time that it had become ingrained in him.

To Brian Coffey, he seemed a man in a terrible hurry when they met accidentally in the Gresham Hotel. Beckett would not even stop for a drink and brightened only long enough to say that he had brought a new novel out of France and was pleased with it and optimistic for its success.[41]

Denis Devlin, on leave from his diplomatic post in Washington, was bringing out a book of poems. Again, Beckett only relaxed long enough to say that he had a new novel, and he hoped Devlin's good fortune in finding a publisher would rub off on him.

His meeting with Tom McGreevy, however, was not at all what he had hoped for. McGreevy had taken a series of sycophantic positions, as amanuensis for an influential priest and, most recently, as a writer for a Catholic journal, the *Capuchin Annual*. He was firmly settled into a life that would soon lead to his appointment as the director of the National Gallery—arranged (even though he was extremely talented on his own merit) by powerful members of the Catholic priesthood. McGreevy lived a domesticated life in a comfortable apartment with his widowed sister and her daughters and spent his evenings regaling his pub companions with stories of the wickedness of life in London and Paris, which he claimed he was thankful to have escaped. On Sundays at Mass, he always sat in the same pew where he could be clearly observed as he walked with such pious devotion to the Communion rail that many Dublin matrons claimed they attended Mass more to watch him than to pray.[42] Seeing McGreevy like this was both a devastating blow and a liberation for Beckett. It was a blow because he no longer had the outlet— the safety valve—of pouring out his confidences to McGreevy. He had little in common with his old friend, and from this point on, their correspondence became the somewhat strained communication between two friends who are reluctant to give up an old intimacy and who still care too much to break off relations completely. It was a liberation for Beckett because it broke his last important link with Ireland.

Still, it was hard to break away. McGreevy had written a critical essay on Jack B. Yeats before the war, and it was finally about to be published. Naturally McGreevy wanted Beckett to write a favorable review for the *Irish Times*. Beckett didn't want to, because of their well-known friendship, and because McGreevy quoted his expression that Yeats's painting had grown "Watteauer and Watteauer," a remark they had painstakingly fussed over in order to make it seem spontaneous. Nevertheless, he would not refuse McGreevy any favor, and so he wrote it.[43]

While he was dealing with the *Irish Times*, Beckett submitted a five line poem, "Dieppe."[44] He wrote it originally in French, but translated it in response to an editor's suggestion that his short writings were welcomed for publication. When the poem appeared, his mother was, as usual, bewildered, but this time pleased instead of angry.

However, his hopes for more serious publication were shattered when Herbert Read wrote that Routledge had rejected *Watt*. He became depressed, but his responsibility to Suzanne and his drive to return to Paris exerted the necessary pull to bring him out of it. Beckett wrote to George Reavey in London and asked if he would once again act as his agent and try to place *Watt*. At the same time, he gave a copy of the typescript to Denis Devlin, who took it to America in the hopes of finding a publisher there. James Greene, Brian Coffey's brother-in-law, was a literary agent with Curtis Brown, and Beckett asked Coffey to give him a third typescript of the novel.[45]

Thus, with copies of *Watt* in interested hands in Ireland,

England and the United States, Beckett began to concentrate all his attention on a swift return to France.

Besides his feeling for Suzanne and concern for the Haydens, Beckett now felt an even more urgent desire to help Marie Péron. Alfred Péron had gone to war in 1939, telling his wife that she was to look upon Beckett as a brother if anything happened to him. In mid-June, 1945, Beckett received a letter from Marie Péron telling him, after almost three years of uncertainty, the circumstances of her husband's death.

Arrested by the Gestapo in August, 1942, Péron was shunted from one detention camp to another for the rest of the year. In early 1943, he was deported to Mauthausen, the camp used at first for "the final Jewish solution" under Adolf Eichmann's command and later as an extermination camp for Allied secret agents and Resistance leaders. Péron managed to survive until the liberation of Mauthausen at the end of April, 1945, even though he had been beaten, tortured and starved. By May 1, he had been shipped on a stretcher to a Red Cross camp in Switzerland, but his health had been so badly broken that he died there that day, and his body lay unidentified for several weeks. Madame Péron, who had seen Suzanne soon after she returned to Paris, knew that Beckett was in Ireland, and she sent a letter which reached him in June. Péron's death was the final event which firmly committed him to life in France. His feelings of guilt at leaving his mother were nothing compared to his overwhelming sense of responsibility to those with whom he had lived and suffered, and to the survivors of those who had not come through.

Beckett's own physical condition demanded medical attention. He was too thin, slept badly, and his teeth were rotten and decayed after more than four years without attention. Dr. Andrew Ganly, a classmate at Trinity, cleaned and filled as many as possible,[46] but had to pull a great many which were too far gone to be saved. Beckett's teeth have bothered him ever since. Alan Thompson gave him a thorough physical examination and discovered nothing wrong that rest and attention to

diet would not cure. Beckett had been dreading this examination, but it turned out to be the means of his quick return to
Paris. Dr. Thompson casually mentioned that he had volunteered to join a hospital unit sponsored by the Irish Red Cross
Society, which was sending a one-hundred-bed hospital unit to
the French Red Cross. The French Ministry of Reconstruction
had asked the Irish unit to set up camp in the bombed-out city
of St. Lô as soon as they could organize a staff.

Thompson told Beckett to hurry, because the staff was almost complete but there was still need for persons fluent in
French. Beckett went directly to the Red Cross offices to volunteer his services and was accepted as a storekeeper-interpreter.
His departure was scheduled for sometime in advance of the
regular staff, which was supposed to depart in early August.

Beckett planned to travel to London for a few days to
check on the whereabouts of *Watt* before returning to Paris,
but he did not leave Dublin until early August, and then went
directly by sea to Cherbourg, with 350 tons of supplies on the
Menapia.[47]

When the *Menapia* arrived in Cherbourg harbor, his first
assignment was to supervise the transfer of supplies to vehicles
which then had to navigate the rutted roads through land mines
and the abandoned machinery of war to St. Lô. Beckett, an aid
to Colonel T. J. McKinney, was of enormous help, as his fluency in French enabled both sides to cut through haggling,
negotiating and red tape. The countryside had been devastated
by Allied bombings and heavy fighting, and everything was reduced to rubble so small and fine that when they were able to
joke, they laughed that even the rubble was rubble.[48]

St. Lô was selected as the site for the hospital because of its
central location almost directly south of Utah and Omaha
beaches, and because it had been one of the hardest hit cities
during the fighting. By the time Beckett arrived, enterprising
photographers had prepared booklets of photos called *St. Lô,
Capitale des Ruines, 5 et 7 June, 1944*, showing before and after
scenes of the major streets and buildings.[49] Only a few shells of
bombed-out buildings were left standing. The cathedral had no
roof and most of the interior had suffered heavy damage.

The French government, through the Ministry of Reconstruction, had agreed to provide the necessary liaison services to the Irish Red Cross hospital, to transport all the goods and supplies from Cherbourg, to erect a number of huts on a vacant site outside the city to serve as the hospital and to guarantee essential services such as water, sewage, light and heat.

When Beckett and the advance party arrived in St. Lô, they found several large wooden sheds, unfinished inside, unlighted and unheated. The process of finding equipment and workmen to proceed with all due haste was time-consuming. He went back and forth to Paris, which only added to his frustration as he was unable to do more than snatch a brief nap in his apartment while waiting for decisions to be made in various bureaucracies. Even more galling, he discovered that the "storekeeper" part of his title was meant literally: he had to keep detailed records of staff, patients and supplies, so that he often found himself working seven days a week with no respite from the constant good cheer of the Irish staff, the recalcitrance of the German prisoners who constituted most of the work force and the abject misery and sickness of the patients. By the end of August, miraculously, things were very much in order, and a large contingent of doctors and nurses arrived from Ireland. In early September an outpatient department was established, and by the end of the year inpatients were being accepted.

By mid-October the need for Beckett to be constantly on call had dwindled and he was able to give up some of his responsibilities. As interpreter, he was more valuable to the Irish in Paris than in St. Lô, and he was finally able to return to the rue des Favorites on a semipermanent basis.

With his return to the rue des Favorites, which he thought would be more or less permanent, Beckett finished two poems which he had begun to write at St. Lô. The first, "Mort de A. D.,"[50] was in memory of Dr. Arthur Darley, one of the Irish doctors, who contracted tuberculosis and became the first patient in the tuberculosis unit of the hospital where he had come to be a member of the staff.[51] The second, "St. Lô," was published the following year in the *Irish Times*.[52]

As winter fell, the hospital functioned more routinely and fewer urgent messages went back and forth between St. Lô and Paris. Beckett was personally pleased because it meant that he need not feel guilty about abandoning his post before the work was completed. Now that he was sure he could stay in his apartment, he no longer needed an excuse to stay in Paris; and now that he was beginning to think that he could write once again, he did not want to be distracted.

He submitted his resignation, effective in January, 1946, but before it was accepted, he was called upon for one more service. Matron Mary Crowley, who had not been able to travel with the other Irish staff members the previous August, was due to arrive in Dieppe harbor in the early morning hours of Christmas Eve, aboard the *Isle of Thanet*, a converted coastal vessel now put into rescue service.[53] Beckett was asked to meet her.

The ship docked in the midst of a severe coastal storm that dropped many feet of snow on northern France. Beckett had driven through the storm from Paris in a Red Cross jeep, intent on driving Matron Crowley the two hundred miles to St. Lô before dawn on Christmas day. There was very little conversation because he had to concentrate on the driving, which was perilous. They drove through the snow, avoiding craters in the road and abandoned vehicles. Many bridges were blown up, necessitating frequent detours through minefields. Beckett drove on relentlessly, stopping only twice during the ten-hour drive. The first time was at a little cafe in a now forgotten village, where he disappeared briefly and reappeared carrying a steaming soup bowl filled with coffee laced with cognac. Matron Crowley, though famished and freezing, refused it, saying she "never took spirits." "Well you've got to now," Beckett insisted. "You can't get a thing to eat here—all the gold in the world wouldn't buy a piece of bread today in this area." She drank it without another word.

They arrived in St. Lô just as midnight Mass was starting. The snow, which had fallen inside the bombed-out, roofless cathedral, was frozen hard, glistening like white satin on the floor. The sky had cleared and was full of stars. On either side of the congregation, mines were piled up against the still-standing walls. Three very old men played violins while the congregation sang hymns with deep emotion. The only intact portion of the cathdral was the altar of the Virgin Mary, and enough candles had been gathered by the villagers to light it brightly.

On the fringe of the candlelight, the ruins gleamed in the ghostly shadows. Beckett stood stiffly while Matron Crowley knelt and prayed. She sensed his discomfort and spared him her verbal gratitude when the Mass was ended. Afterward he took her directly to her hospital quarters and then commandeered a bed for himself for a few hours' sleep. Early the next morning, when she tried to find him to thank him, Matron Crowley was told that he had gone back to Paris before dawn.

Beckett was not through with St. Lô yet. Matron Crowley was put in charge of all the nurses in all the wards. As the civilian populace returned in ever increasing numbers, the hospital began to fill up. There were wards for medical, surgical and ophthalmic patients. German prisoners who were well enough worked in the hospital, but the sick ones were patients until they recovered enough to help. Even the military sent patients. The French, British and Americans had all established hospitals of their own in the sectors under their control, but many of their patients were shunted off to the Irish. The greatest problem came from the maternity and children's wards, which were especially vulnerable to the rats and other vermin that roamed throughout the ruined town. It was virtually impossible to find chemical controls since none of the occupying armies had any to spare. Beckett was asked to do what he could: a hurried telephone call came to Paris asking him to find something to kill the rats. He went to friends at the Curie Hospital Department of Pathology—friends he had met through Péron—and they gave him a solution to put on bits of corncob which were scattered around the wards in strategic places where the rats ate them and then crawled away to die.

It was the last service he performed before his resignation took effect. Somehow it was a fitting one—the new year had begun with a triumph, new life over pestilence and death. He left the poison with Matron Crowley and hurried off to Paris for the last time, without waiting around to know the results. Killing rats was his last personal act of warfare.

CHAPTER FIFTEEN

1946–48:

"THE SIEGE IN THE ROOM"

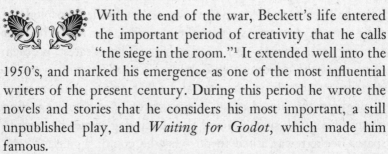 With the end of the war, Beckett's life entered the important period of creativity that he calls "the siege in the room."[1] It extended well into the 1950's, and marked his emergence as one of the most influential writers of the present century. During this period he wrote the novels and stories that he considers his most important, a still unpublished play, and *Waiting for Godot*, which made him famous.

Beckett was forty years old when he was able at last to take up permanent residence in Paris. For the previous fifteen years, the time of life during which most individuals establish themselves in their professions, Beckett had been living through what might well be called a period of arrested development. He had resisted all his mother's efforts to shunt him onto a track of propriety and boredom in Dublin, and chose instead to lead a "literary life," a convenient refuge, as it had been for many others of similar background and education who converged on Paris in the 1920's and 1930's.

Wanting to lead the life of a writer and having something to write about were quite different things, as he learned during the long stretches when nothing would come and he had nothing to say. He found he had no coherent literary purpose and no philosophical foundation for his commitment. At times he would lash out and say that, after all, it was not as if he wanted to spend his life sitting in a room staring at a blank piece of paper, or even worse, writing books that no one wanted to read. These were the periods when he had flirted with filmmaking, flying; they include the year-long period of indecision when he could not make up his mind to go back to teaching.

Then, at the age of thirty-three, when he finally faced reality and concluded that life in Dublin was impossible under any circumstance, the war came along to destroy his first real commitment to the literary life and his first real opportunity to see if he could make a living entirely from his writing.

It is interesting to speculate what sort of writer Beckett might have become if it hadn't been for the war; from his correspondence and conversation, it seems likely that he would have concentrated on criticism and reviewing as the most immediately remunerative, and might have turned to poetry and fiction in his spare time with the hope that these forms would eventually free him from the drudgery of the other.

His writing seemed likely to continue in this direction when he returned to France in 1945. While he was still at St. Lô, the editors of *Cahiers d'Art* asked him to write a critical essay on the painting of Bram and Geer van Velde. He called it *La Peinture des van Velde, ou: le mode et le pantalon*. The title comes from the joke he used later in *Fin de partie* (*Endgame*), of the tailor who unfavorably compares the world created by God in seven days to the pair of trousers he constructed flawlessly in several months. Like most of his critical writing, this article was solicited, and is, says Beckett, "best forgotten."[2] St. Lô was no place from which to renew old publishing contacts or seek new commissions, so he turned to fiction. Also dating from the last months of 1945 is an unfinished manuscript called *Les Bosquets de Bondy* (*The Groves of Bondy*)—in colloquial French, a den of thieves.[3] It seemed to lead him nowhere, so Beckett set the manuscript aside and tried to go on to something else. He made a number of brief attempts to create fiction, but left them unfinished, intending to work on them later.

These are what Beckett calls his "trunk" manuscripts; he does not want them to be published, yet he cannot bring himself to discard them.[4] He kept them, in various stages of completion or abandonment, until 1974, when he suddenly decided they

should be put in order and some of them published. He has
worked on them more or less steadily since then.

Beckett did follow one short work of fiction through to
completion. Originally called *Suite*, he changed the title to *La
Fin (The End)*. Unlike the others with which it is grouped in
the *Nouvelles et textes pour rien (Stories and Texts for Nothing)*,[5] *La Fin* is the mono-tonal account of an unnamed narrator
who relates memories of a town, the countryside, the sea, the
mountains, and the people he meets in these places. It ends with a
prefiguration of the writing to come:

> The memory came faint and cold of the story I might have
> told, a story in the likeness of my life, I mean without the
> courage to end or the strength to go on.[6]

By April, 1946, with no income from his writing, Beckett
found the money he had brought from Ireland was almost gone.
With funds there still impounded, he had no choice but to go to
Dublin to get more. Since his fortieth birthday was imminent, he
decided to spend it with his mother.

There had been no word about *Watt* from any of the persons who had manuscripts, and he spent much of his time in
Foxrock writing letters to find out what had become of it.
Devlin had had no luck in the United States, but was willing to
continue his efforts at his own convenience; Greene was weary
of trying to sell the unsellable and wanted to return it; and
Reavey, intent on reestablishing his own publishing endeavors,
had done very little to date, but was now willing to devote most
of his time to it.

In a very short time, Reavey reported that several publishers had rejected it for much the same reason: they claimed *Watt*
was not at all the sort of book people who had been through a
terrible war would want to read, and suggested that Beckett stop
trying to "disguise his wartime memoirs within the framework
of fiction" and write a "realistic account" instead![7] This interpretation astonished Beckett; it seemed a grim portent of a dupli-
cation of the protracted publishing history of *Murphy*.

Some years later Beckett's friend, Professor W. S. Maguinness, who had been with him at Trinity College, suggested
that like Xenophon, who had written of the return of the ten

thousand, Beckett should write the same sort of book, which would make his fortune as well as his reputation.

"I'm not interested in stories of success," Beckett snapped, "only failure."[8]

While Beckett was in Ireland, Leslie Daiken, the poet who had been his student at Trinity College, asked him to contribute poems for a projected anthology of Irish poetry to be published by the American firm of Devin-Adair. Beckett seemed to regard his poems in English as belonging to another life, and refused to allow Daiken to use them. He also refused to write new poems, saying the blame should be laid on Ireland because it made him restless, idle and incapable of creativity.[9] Without telling Beckett, Daiken asked Reavey to select poems from *Echo's Bones*, which he sent without Beckett's permission. Beckett was not surprised the following August to receive a rejection letter from Devin-Adair for poems that were "not sufficiently Irish."[10]

This trip to Ireland introduced Beckett to a group of refugees called the "White Stags" who had settled in Dublin to avoid the war.[11] They were mostly English artists and writers who found it difficult to continue their work in Dublin because they were Bohemian in their dress and conduct and because many of them were blatantly homosexual. Beckett seemed to gravitate naturally to this group, which he compared to a displaced version of Montparnasse. At the same time, he saw much of the group that surrounded Owen Sheehy-Skeffington and his French-born wife, Andrée, so that he found himself involved with persons at opposite ends of the social spectrum.

With the first group there were wild arguments about art, life and sex, and all-night drinking bouts that often led to fistfights and brawls. His mother was shocked when he came staggering home repeatedly in the same disastrous condition as during his monumental prewar bouts. With the other group, he attended elegantly refined dinner parties, conversed in French and Italian, and heard informal concerts of chamber music performed by members of the Sheehy-Skeffingtons' circle.

This fragmentation of his life contributed to the "sense of pain and urgency"[12] that drove him to recklessness and excess. He careened about the countryside with his cousin, William Heron, usually ending up in a pub called the Brazen Head, where drinks were served after closing time as long as there was someone to buy them. Often automobiles were wrecked, clothing lost or destroyed, and sometimes jewelry was removed from the body of a senseless drunk. Casual sexual encounters occurred in a haze of whiskey and were unremembered when the participants were sober.[13] Most of Beckett's friends were frightened by the wildness and savagery of his mien and shocked that he was part of this group. Others excused his behavior as due to his reaction against the horrors of war, which, not having been a part of, they could barely understand. Some of his erratic behavior was induced simply by his being in Ireland and the necessity to stay there for a prolonged period of time while he restored his finances; most of it was caused by the dilemma his writing had produced.

Since writing *Watt*, he had become aware that he tended to write only about himself. His fiction relied on persons or places (especially in Ireland) that had figured importantly in his life. He knew that his writing was autobiographical, realized the danger, but was helpless to change his style. If he continued, he seemed doomed to permanent unpublished oblivion—indeed, *Watt* seemed to prove this point—but he had no control over words that sprang unbidden from his unconscious and committed themselves to paper, so that he was often astonished to read them later and discover that he had little or no memory of what he had written.

The excessive drunkenness was not (as his mother feared) a repetition of his prewar behavior, but was instead a refuge from the reality of his writing. To relieve some of the tension these self-confrontations induced, he resumed his old habit of walking nonstop for miles. On one of his late-night prowls, when he had been drinking just enough to make his thought processes churn, he found himself out on the end of a jetty in Dublin harbor, buffeted by a winter storm. Suddenly the vision occurred which was to result in the voluminous production of the next few years, the kind of writing that has come to be defined as "Beckettian."

He inserted part of this revelation in the final text of

Krapp's Last Tape (*La Dernière Bande*), but an earlier version of the manuscript is more revealing:

> Intellectually a year of profound gloom and indigence until that memorable night in March, at the end of the pier, in the howling wind, never to be forgotten, when suddenly I saw the whole thing. The turning point at last. This I imagine is what I have chiefly to set down this evening against the day when my work will be done and perhaps no place left in my memory and no thankfulness for the miracle that—for the fire it set alight. What I saw then was that the assumption I had been going on all my life, namely . . . clear to me at last that the dark I have been fighting off all this time is in reality my most . . . unshatterable association till my dying day of story and night with the light of understanding and . . .[14]

Two comments which Beckett made long after this night further enhance its importance. To the poet John Montague, who was troubled one night in the late 1960's in Paris with a poem which would not allow itself to be written, Beckett described the thrill of elation which followed his recognition of the direction his writing should take, and suggested the solution that had worked so well for him: "Ah, Montague, what you need is monologue—*monologue!*" Beckett repeated, holding up one thin finger to emphasize his point. "That's the thing!"[15]

To Ludovic Janvier, Beckett stated that the "dark he had struggled to keep under" was ultimately to become the source of his creative inspiration.[16]

Thus, this revelation has two distinct aspects: first, Beckett's realization that all his writing would henceforth begin from within himself, with his memories and dreams, no matter how ugly or painful; second, that no clearly defined fictional character would be needed to tell these stories, as no distancing is necessary between the teller and the tale. The first person narrator speaks from this point on in Beckett's fiction. Gradually, as he sharpened the prose of the stories, discarded the novel *Mercier et Camier*, and moved on to the trilogy of novels, *Molloy, Malone meurt* (*Malone Dies*), and *L'Innommable* (*The Unnamable*), his first person monologue became stripped of the externalities of place, plot and time. He reduced life to a series of tales told first by one, then by the other, perhaps all by the same voice. All Beckett needed was speech to construct his fictions. He discovered he could make his life universal, to represent the lives of all men.

In a bitter moment during this time, he confessed that he "was doomed to spend the rest of my days digging up the detritus of my life and vomiting it out over and over again." He continued in a more positive mood, saying, "optimism is not my way. I shall always be depressed, but what comforts me is the realization that I can now accept this dark side as the commanding side of my personality. In accepting it, I will make it work for me."[17] This discovery gave him a strength of character and sense of purpose that he had never felt before. There would be times to come when his exterior self would be battered by circumstances, but this new resolve would never desert him. He would have serious difficulties in his future with writing blocks, depressions and near breakdowns, but a part of him would always be withdrawn and inviolate, untouched by anything.

In May, 1946, with money in his pocket and ideas filling his head, Beckett returned to Paris. For the first time he found that he was able to confront the blank paper without hesitation. Earlier he had been unable to sustain any sort of creative momentum, and had to augment short spells of writing with spurts of conviviality. Now he wrote steadily, stopping only when fatigue made it impossible to continue. He finished *Suite* quickly and submitted it at once to Jean-Paul Sartre at *Les Temps Modernes*.

Beckett had known Sartre since his time at the École Normale Supérieure; they had been introduced by Alfred Péron, who was a member of Sartre's class of 1924.[18] Theirs had always been a distant relationship; there was something wistful about the way Beckett studied Sartre from afar in much the same manner as he had stood on the fringes of other groups, from Joyce and his friends, to the peasants of Roussillon. He often marveled at the openness and directness with which Sartre formed relationships, dispensed literary advice, and carried on his own literary career with such unassuming equanimity. But Sartre's custom of sitting in the cafes on the boulevard St. Germain to conduct his business and do his writing made Beckett uneasy,[19] and Sartre moved in literary circles which made Beckett uncomfortable, so their relationship remained somewhat formal and stiff as the years passed. Still, it seemed to Beckett that Sartre would be one of the few persons in Paris with authority over a publication who would be willing to take a chance on his writing, and so he sent the story with high hopes for its acceptance.

Through a curious mix-up, only the first half of the story was printed. Beckett sent the first half of the typescript to Sartre, who accepted it after a cursory reading. Sartre passed it to Paule Allard, who was in charge of the magazine's editorial content, and—not aware that the story was incomplete—scheduled it for the July, 1946, issue. When Beckett sent the second half, the error was discovered, but it was too late; the first half had already been printed and could not be excised.

Simone de Beauvoir, Sartre's associate at the magazine, refused to believe that it was a mistake and not a deliberate act on Beckett's part. She would not accept the second half of the story. As far as Beckett was concerned, it was all very stupid; he was sorry for it, but he wanted his entire story to be printed. De Beauvoir insisted it had been an affront, and would not budge. The official version of the incident varies: Beckett calls it a misunderstanding based on an editorial mistake; de Beauvoir claims she refused the second half because it was not in keeping with the general tone of the magazine.[20] But Beckett remained on good terms with Paule Allard, who saw that his *Poems 38–39*, the twelve poems written in French before the war, were printed in the November issue.

In July, Beckett began to write *Mercier et Camier*, a second draft version of *Les Bosquets de Bondy*. It was his first attempt at a novel since *Watt*, and his first in French. Its genesis is in the terrible feeling of guilt engendered by his abrupt departure from Ireland in 1937 and his mother's angry seclusion. This novel captures much of the depression and indecision of Beckett's life during this period as it continues the line of vagabond heroes which began with Belacqua and developed with Murphy and Watt. Mercier and Camier are the first of his vaudevillian

couples, and in many ways, the precursors of Vladimir and
Estragon in *Waiting for Godot*. If there is a chronological linear
development to his writing, *Mercier et Camier* marks the first
tentative approach toward what Beckett calls the "mature" fiction of *Molloy*, *Malone Dies*, and *The Unnamable*. In the
trilogy, Beckett relentlessly reduces his characters from pitiful
creatures with few possessions—a hat, a pot, a stub of pencil--to
voices who have only the inner torments of their past life to
sustain their present existence, and are doomed to repeat themselves until finally, even the voice, their last vestige of humanity,
is stilled.

In *Mercier et Camier* the journey shapes the plot as the two
men parade on an endless quest. Despite its somberness, it is a
warm and funny book, occasionally tinged with stinging sarcasm. There are secondary characters, skillfully and swiftly
delineated, so bizarre that even the two oddities of the title are
struck by their madness. Mercier and Camier are otherworldly
figures themselves, but they need the trappings of the real world
in order to give their story coherence, and this is no doubt part
of the reason why Beckett chose to abandon them and go on to
the Molloys and Malones of his later fiction.

Mercier et Camier was written just before *Molloy*, or possibly during the same time, since Beckett himself is not sure
when the idea for *Molloy* came to him.[21] There are large
chunks of dialogue which he later transferred directly into
Waiting for Godot, but unlike the play, in *Mercier et Camier*,
simple speech is encumbered by a plot with progression and
movement, albeit circuitous and often contradictory. There is a
narrator, as in *Murphy* and *Watt*, one who announces at the
beginning of the story that he accompanied the characters
throughout their journey and can tell the story as he pleases.
Occasionally he injects an acerbic comment, and he thinks nothing of slowing down, speeding up or otherwise circumventing
the progress of the "pseudo-couple," as Beckett later describes
them in *The Unnamable*.

Mercier et Camier is about voluntary exile, much like
Beckett's own. While it can be read as the odyssey of Beckett
and the other young Irishmen who went to Paris in the 1930's
hoping to gain the same success as Joyce, it can also be read as

aspects of Beckett's personality. In Dublin, he had been easily recognizable in his shapeless, dirty raincoat. He had problems with bicycles. In a drunken moment, he lost his favorite hat, which he mourned long afterward. It is the raincoat, however, which best symbolizes the final division of the first thirty years from the rest of his life, as well as this novel's place in his canon: when he left Dublin, Beckett threw his away, just as Mercier and Camier, after throwing theirs away, walk off into their own uncertain future, looking back now and again at the heap on the ground—unwilling to go on with it, but hesitant to abandon it.

The same unwillingness to give up something once he has committed it to paper characterizes Beckett's subsequent relationships with this novel. He was dissatisfied with it: it was drawn too directly from his life, too thinly disguised; ultimately it just did not work as fiction. Although he was now writing directly in French, there was still too much "Englishness" about the plot.[22] The narrator, the vocabulary, the descriptions—all were too lush. He was unsure of his French and afraid he would be ridiculed by the critics if there were subtle mistakes in the grammar and syntax recognizable only to native French speakers. This thought haunted him, but he sent the novel to Éditions Bordas, the French publishers of *Murphy*, and turned relentlessly to the next idea.

In one week, from October 6 to 14, 1946, Beckett wrote "L'Expulsé" ("The Expelled"). This story seemed to write itself, as the initial momentum carried him until it was finished. It is a simple tale: the narrator is expelled from the house in which he grew up, then tells of his movements through his native city where no one knows him and people either scorn or mock him. He takes a carriage drawn by a horse and spends the rest of the story with the driver, the horse and/or the cab.

At the beginning, the narrator, who is trying to count the steps of the house he has left, talks about memories:

> Memories are killing. So you must not think of certain things, or those that are dear to you, or rather you must think of them, for if you don't there is the danger of finding them, in your mind, little by little. That is to say, you must think of them for a while, a good while, every day several times a day, until they sink forever in the mud. That's an order.[23]

This, in effect, was what he had discovered that night in Ireland. With increasing confidence, he confronted all the devils inside himself and used them in his writing.

Beckett's living habits during this period puzzled everyone who knew him well because he seemed to be writing in a trance, yet living the life of his characters. Since so much of his writing was about death (or so it seemed to Suzanne and the others), they were actually afraid he would die before he finished.[24]

He slept by day and wrote at night. When he had written all he could, he prowled the deserted streets looking for a late-night cafe where he would quickly drink enormous quantities of liquor. In the apartment, he was isolated and withdrawn, as if he were reliving what he had written, dredging so deep that he could not come back to the surface of his consciousness without much painful effort. As his characters spiraled deeper and deeper into their own miseries, so too did he. Not surprisingly, he became ill.

Ostensibly he had flu, cold and was generally run-down. But the doctor could find no reason for the lingering after-effects and Beckett silently concluded that they must be psychosomatic once again. In despair, he allowed Suzanne to arrange for sessions with a homeopathist.[25] Suzanne imposed a rigid diet of natural foods and tonics which their friends were convinced was either curing or killing Beckett.

The homeopathist recommended a change of scene to start, and so Suzanne arranged to rent a small cottage in Avondant, Eure-et-Loire, for October and November. Life in the country had its usual soothing effect on Beckett because he could take long walks; in effect, it was transporting all the best of Ireland to France without any of the pain engendered by relationships with people. He passed the time pleasantly, walking and writing. Instead of the enormous quantities he needed to sustain him in Paris, a single glass of wine with dinner satisfied him. It was the first time in his long relationship with Suzanne that they were in a situation where life was pleasant; they were content to be where they were and doing what made them happy.

It was a short happiness, for reality in the form of money intruded as soon as they returned to Paris. Beckett was earning little more than pocket money with his writing, and his Irish income was once again running out. Max-Pol Fouchet had agreed to publish "L'Expulsé" in the December issue of *Fontaine*[26] but Beckett would not receive enough money from it to last a week.

Suzanne was an excellent seamstress and she began to sew to augment their meager income.[27] She made exquisite baby clothes, but had a limited market for her handiwork because none of their friends had children. She disliked dressmaking, but did it because they needed the money. For a while, she was their sole support. It mattered little to Beckett where the money came from as long as he could continue to write. He resented his dependence on her at first, but she made no demands and seemed pleased to devote her life to meeting his needs, so he accepted.

Their relationship had become one in which she catered to all his comforts, seeing that he had food, clean laundry and linen, and he allowed her to live in his apartment and do all that she wanted for him.[28] It was a curiously asexual relationship but it suited them both. Because they were intensely private persons who confided in no one and allowed no questions, people soon accepted them as they were and stopped asking.

There was a brief problem when Beckett's friends began to invite him to parties. Mary Reynolds once gave a dinner party for Kay Boyle and her husband, and invited Beckett and Suzanne, Gabrielle Buffet-Picabia and several others from their "old group."[29] Suzanne was shy and quiet and seemed ill at ease. It was one of the last times she accompanied Beckett. She decided she would no longer accept invitations because she simply did not care for social evenings. Her purpose in life, as she saw it, was to insure that nothing interfered with his writing. She went to Troyes to see her mother and sister occasionally, but except for these visits and meetings with a few old and trusted friends, she stayed quietly at the rue des Favorites waiting to care for Beckett. She had her own friendships, fewer and more private than his. She was close to her family, liked the theater and enjoyed concerts. She was content to spend long periods of time alone, even more so than Beckett. She was secure in the strange life she defined for herself and was happiest when she could live it.

When the Haydens came back to Paris, she called on them and made sure they were taken care of, but it was they who issued invitations that she never accepted.[30]

This freed Beckett from every responsibility except to himself. None of the mundane clutter of life stood between him and his work anymore. He reacted matter-of-factly to her decision, and was pleased with the artistic and personal freedom it gave him.

At the same time, it was an embarrassment. At first he made excuses to explain her absence from all the invitations she had refused. Finally he told the truth, that Suzanne no longer wanted to join the parties. He gave friends the option of no longer extending invitations to him, but most were as embarrassed as he, and they told him he was always welcome. The awkwardness of the moment passed. Privately, many of his friends were concerned, but those who were persistent enough to talk to Suzanne discovered that she simply did not want to do more than take care of Beckett. She had no wish to be a part of his life outside the privacy of their home. To her, all the rest was the Public Beckett, and it did not interest or concern her.

One other story published in the *Nouvelles* dates from late 1946: "Premier Amour" ("First Love"), written between October 28 and November 12. At first it became another "trunk" manuscript and was not published until 1970 in French. One of the reasons Beckett withheld it was that it was too autobiographical, for he was still struggling to perfect the techniques of disguise and concealment that infuse his later writings. Another more important reason was his unwillingness to publish it "while the woman in question is still alive."[31] As a narrative, it has none of the stylistic experimentation that marked the earlier English and the first few French writings, but it is not yet stripped down to the barren obsessiveness of his subsequent first-person narrations. With "Premier Amour" he felt again the same inadequate control of the language and the same fear that he would be mercilessly criticized for faulty syntax and grammar if he submitted it for publication. However, he did not worry overlong about it, for another story was forming. He began "Le Cal-

mant" ("The Calmative") two days before Christmas and
finished it before the new year of 1947.

In 1955 Beckett told John Fletcher that each of the three
stories might be called by another name: "L'Expulsé," "Prime";
"La Fin," "Limbo"; and "Le Calmant," "Death." (Ruby Cohn
adds that "Premier Amour" might well be called "Pre-Prime.")[32]
"Le Calmant," the story of death, begins "I don't know when
I died,"[33] a portent perhaps of *Malone meurt* (*Malone Dies*).
Throughout, the narrator tells himself stories in an effort to
keep calm as he journeys from one place to another. It is probably the most polished of all the stories and the true predecessor
of *Molloy*.

In all the stories, the narrators live on the fringes of society
and know that they are scorned. They all remember their
fathers, who are usually associated with hats and bequests of
money.[34]

In May, 1947, Beckett summed up his activity since the end
of the war:

> *Murphy* in French is due this month from Bordas, my own
> translation and not a very good one. A novel, *Mercier et
> Camier*, short, has also been accepted by Bordas and should be
> out this autumn. A book of long short stories (*Quatre
> Nouvelles*) is ready but has not yet found a publisher. Two
> have appeared separately, in the *Temps Modernes* (*Suite*) and
> *Fontaine* (*L'Expulsé*). Thirteen poems, old, have appeared in
> the *Temps Modernes*, and shortly before leaving Paris, I fin-
> ished a play in three acts called *Éleuthéria* or *L'Éleuthéromane*,
> I'm not quite sure, and which Madame Clerkx is handling as
> she handles all my work in French with more or less success.[35]

In fact, *Mercier et Camier* was never published by Bordas.
The contract for *Murphy* gave Bordas first refusal of the author's next book (in this case *Mercier et Camier*), and they had
actually scheduled it for publication. Bordas planned to tout
Murphy as a comic novel, in the spirit of the Routledge blurb
that had so distressed Beckett ("What Spirit! What Gusto!"),
and *Mercier et Camier* was to be advertised as a French music
hall–vaudeville farce.[36] Though there was much in *Mercier et*

Camier that was incomprehensible, even sinister, to French readers, the publishers were sure that it would sell as an example of
the "new" writing in Paris. With the *Quatre Nouvelles*,[37] however, Bordas preferred a waiting game: if *Murphy* sold well, it
would have some effect on sales of *Mercier et Camier;* and if
Mercier et Camier did not disappoint the publishers, then they
would consider the *Quatre Nouvelles*. For Beckett, this plan had
nothing of immediate value. Suzanne was still sewing and he had
begun to translate articles from English into French for *Reader's
Digest* for two dollars a page.[38]

The humiliating sales of *Murphy*—only six books sold by
June, 1948—caused bad feelings which finally led to the cancellation of all the agreements between Bordas and Beckett. Bordas
blamed the poor sales on Beckett's refusal to do anything to promote the book. Bordas wanted Beckett to be nice to the critics,
to do what the French call *service de presse*, to give out complimentary copies and to be available for interviews. There is no
question that Beckett wanted *Murphy* to succeed in France, and
certainly no question that he needed the money such success
would bring, but he could not comply with Bordas's request.
His need for privacy was so obsessive that he could never allow
himself to be put into a situation where strangers would have the
right to invade it. Typically, when Bordas pressed him, he grew
stubborn and silent, choosing to escape as soon as possible from
the confrontation. The total inability of each to understand the
other's point of view or to find an effective compromise led to
the break-up. Bordas wanted nothing to do with *Mercier et
Camier* now that Beckett had proven so intractable with
Murphy. As far as he was concerned, Beckett was free to find
another publisher, when he would relinquish all his rights. In
spite of Beckett's recalcitrance, the critics were generally favorable to *Murphy*, but it still sold poorly. By the time Beckett
went under contract to Éditions de Minuit in 1951, only ninety-
five copies of an edition of three thousand had been sold.

In the hope of stimulating further new writing, Beckett
began to frequent galleries and museums for the first time since
before the war. He went to exhibits of Van Gogh and Bonnard
at the Orangerie des Tuileries and the Louvre, and was angry

when guards forbade him to examine the paintings with a magnifying glass.[39] His vision, never good, suddenly dimmed, and the little round glasses he had worn for years were no longer strong enough. Since he could not afford an examination by a doctor he simply went into a Prix Unique (the French equivalent of Woolworth's) and tried on glasses until he found a pair that gave him clear sight. To the horror of many of his friends, he continued the practice well after his writings had made him financially independent.[40]

His illnesses of the previous fall—bursitis, cold, headaches, insomnia—came and went with such frequency that pain and malaise seemed constant conditions of his everyday life. He consulted Suzanne's homeopathist again and the same prescription was suggested: time out of Paris in warmth and sun. Maurice Sinclair and his bride, Mimi, were in Menton and they invited Beckett and Suzanne to visit. He wanted to go, but he had promised his mother he'd come to Dublin in April, and so he spent most of a damp March in Paris closeted in his apartment writing a play.

"I turned to writing plays to relieve myself of the awful depression the prose led me into," Beckett commented in 1972. "Life at that time was too demanding, too terrible, and I thought theater would be a diversion."[41]

Éleuthéria (his first title, *Éleuthéromane*, proved unsatisfactory) marked the second time he turned to drama when prose failed him—the first, of course, the Johnson manuscript of 1936. Like the aborted *Human Wishes*, *Éleuthéria* uses a divided stage spotlighted according to where the action takes place. *Éleuthéria* is Beckett's longest dramatic work, a three-act play with seventeen characters and three sets. The title is from the Greek word for freedom, and the action concerns the efforts of young Victor Krap to free himself from the constrictions and restraints of his bourgeois family.[42] The family living room, overstuffed and cluttered, fills half the stage in the first two acts, while Victor's hotel room, with its Spartan bed and chair, fills the other half. The sets symbolize two ways of life: Victor's inactive, indecisive squalor, and the family's middle-class uprightness. Victor's room is near the impasse de l'Enfant Jésus—the dead-end street off the rue de Vaugirard whose name so caught

Beckett's fancy that he purposely distorted its nearness to the rue des Favorites in letters to friends.[43] The action, which takes place in Paris on three successive winter afternoons, is played during Act I in the Krap living room and in Act II in Victor's room. In the third act, Victor's room fills the entire stage.

In all his succeeding plays, Beckett's stage directions are so precise that directorial license is severely limited. By contrast, in introductory notes to *Éleuthéria*, Beckett writes only that the text concerns the principal action and that marginal action is the concern of the actor. Victor's father dies between Act I and Act II, but the audience is made aware that he understood and even sympathized with his son. A struggle follows during which other members of the family try to lure Victor back into its fold. In what is meant to be a serious traditional three-act play, Beckett gives his characters names like Krap, Piouk ("puke"), Skunk and Meck ("*mec*"—French for pimp).

Subsequent works have their genesis in *Éleuthéria*: Krap senior cannot urinate and he knocks the manservant around in intimations of *Waiting for Godot*; Victor speaks in Act II to a glazier in conversations similar to those found in *Mercier et Camier* and which lead ultimately to conversations between the boy and Vladimir in *Godot*. The boredom felt by the female characters and their conversations remind one of *Play*. The obsession with self typified by a man on a bed in a room, and the comment about the play being within a play are all found throughout the rest of the canon.

On January 18, 1947, Beckett opened the first of two *cahiers* (the school exercise books in which he wrote most of his works of this period) and in painstaking longhand, he wrote on the cover "Éleuthéria/Acte I/Samuel Beckett."[44] The work seems to have gone smoothly at the beginning. In his customary style, he wrote only on the right-hand pages, with an occasional word or phrase blacked out or written over. On the left-hand pages, a word or phrase appears here and there, sometimes accompanied by a tiny doodle. By the time he was one-third of the way through the first *cahier*, the ease with which he had proceeded changes to frustration: an entire left-hand page is covered with doodles, and at the top of the facing right-hand page, he stopped to list the characters on stage at that moment. A series of diagrams covers the rest of the page: the characters are shown sitting around a lamp and the door is clearly marked. Arrows point to and from the characters and the lamp. A large circle, apparently a table, is also indicated. Finally, in what must have been great frustration, everything is scratched out furiously with rough pencil markings. In the second notebook, containing Acts II and III, the writing seems trouble-free until the end of Act II, then another page of stage diagrams follows, all crossed out with a large "x" in ink. From this point on, there are as many doodles as there are pages of text: musical notes; funny men in bowler hats with large heads, no bodies and long skinny legs; and shapeless masses of ink lines.

Obviously, Beckett had trouble bringing *Éleuthéria* to a satisfactory conclusion. Towards the end of the play a spectator jumps onto the stage and demands to know who wrote the play: "Beckett (il dit Bequet), Samuel Bequet." Interestingly, Beckett returned to the Huguenot spelling of the name used by his first ancestors in Ireland.

One of the problems with the play stemmed from Beckett's inability to give Victor the proper dialogue to state his reasons for rebellion against his family and the society in which they live. In a play in which everything else is carefully stated, fully delineated, and logically explained, the failure of the central character to stand for something—anything—is a major failure. No doubt if it had been produced it would have been another of the many plays about a young man's revolt which may or may not have enjoyed a brief, successful and moderately lucrative run; but unquestionably it would have been forgotten within a year or two. It is simply not a memorable play. Its interest lies in its place in the canon and it is important primarily to scholars interested in tracing a line of development in Beckett's writing.

Although Beckett has relented with other manuscripts and permitted them to be published years after he wrote them, he remains adamant with *Éleuthéria*. Even though his French publisher, Jerome Lindon, accepted *Éleuthéria* for publication at the same time as *Waiting for Godot,* and even though he needed the money, Beckett withdrew it. *Éleuthéria* is so unlike the other plays and is so atypical of what Beckett has come to stand for in the theater that he will never allow it to be published simply to insure that it is never performed.

By the time Beckett left for Dublin in late March, he had given *Éleuthéria* to Toni Clerkx, who sent copies to likely producers. Some rejected it immediately because it was too cumbersome and thus too expensive to mount. Others read it later and decided it was not worth production. Madame Clerkx finally took it to Jean Vilar, who was in charge of the Théâtre Nationale Populaire. Vilar knew of Beckett's prewar writings and was interested, but in the best bureaucratic tradition, misplaced the manuscript. When he found it months later, Vilar again expressed interest, but said the play was too long. He asked Beckett to rewrite it into one long act. Beckett refused to make the change and withdrew it. It was another disappointment; in the meantime, Suzanne continued her sewing.

Beckett went to Dublin by way of London to check on the peregrinations of *Watt*. He was technically committed to have Richard Marsh act as his literary agent because Marsh had purchased the European Literary Bureau before the war from Reavey. But Beckett felt more comfortable working with someone he knew, and so he officially engaged Reavey as his agent.

Reavey asked Devlin for the extra copy of the typescript, then wrote to Beckett saying he "saw Denis and got *Murphy*."[45] Reavey's confusion of the two novels pleased Beckett, for he wanted readers to think of *Watt* as the continuation of a series. He asked Reavey to do what he could with the novel, but implored him not to devote all his time to it:

> It is an unsatisfactory book, written in dribs and drabs, first on the run, then of an evening after the clod-hopping, during the occupation, but it has its place in the series, as will perhaps appear in time.[46]

He warned Reavey not to expect him to make changes to suit possible publishers, and added that it had already almost been accepted but for his refusal to move the scene in the railway station to the beginning of the novel, and he would not allow a word to be changed elsewhere.

But a month in Ireland produced the usual malaise: "Don't bother about it [*Watt*] unless you feel like it," he wrote to Reavey. "He is a nice fellow but his word is certainly without importance."[47]

May Beckett's health was steadily deteriorating. On previous visits he took her to donkey races or dog shows, or even occasionally to the National Gallery, but now, far too shaky to appear in public, she was confined to the home. The tension underlying their conversations gradually built until every meeting became a chore. Mealtimes were agonizing, as May's impatience with herself carried over into sharp comments directed at Beckett. He, full of anguish at her condition, endured without rebuttal. Several members of his family, in speaking of this time, all feel sure that Beckett did not "hate Ireland, but hated instead his mother."[48] They seem to think he might have stayed more or less permanently in Ireland until May's death if she had not been so acerbic. In conversation, Beckett showed more genuine curiosity about local activities than ever before. He inquired about everything from politics to archeology, and seemed zestily invigorated by his long walks about the countryside. He recounted in painstaking detail his observations of trees, rocks, roads and animal life. Later, his relatives were surprised to find many of the same descriptions in the novels he wrote when he returned to France. Perhaps they mistook his literary curiosity for a sudden love of Ireland. Like Joyce before him, Beckett was probably committing to memory all that he wanted to use of Ireland so that he could leave the rest behind.

One pleasant experience was the exhibition of modern French painting at the National Gallery, where Geer van Velde sold three pictures—one for the then enormous sum of 150 pounds. The exhibition was worth several visits, and Beckett spent long afternoons happily gazing at the pictures.[49] He called on Alan Thompson and Andrew Ganly for medical as well as social reasons and was not noticeably cheered by their findings. Thompson still recommended rest and restoratives; Ganly was appalled by the condition of his teeth. Beckett left their offices convinced that homeopathism—or better yet, no medical attention at all—was the best he could do for himself. Suzanne's

homeopathist in Paris had given him a new experimental tonic
for Parkinson's disease, and Thompson agreed to administer it to
Mrs. Beckett.[50] For a time it seemed to give encouraging results,
and he urged Beckett to continue sending it; however, this, too,
soon proved useless, and May's moods continued to be morose.
When all else failed, Beckett took refuge in excursions to the
Brazen Head for bouts of drinking that brought blessed oblivion
well into the next day. At the end of June, he returned to
France.

Now he really needed a rest, and the money he had brought
from Dublin supported him and Suzanne for six weeks in Menton when they visited Maurice and Mimi Sinclair. They
"camped out" in a rented, semi-isolated villa at 56 avenue Aristide
Briant, where they cooked their food in the open air over a
charcoal brazier. The house was half-filled with barely service-
able, ramshackle period furniture. There was a brief spell of
rain, unexpected and therefore depressing, but the visit was exactly what Beckett needed, despite the primitive living conditions.[51]

He was cheered when Reavey wrote that Hamish Hamilton
was about to take *Watt*, and would send a representative to Paris
upon Beckett's return to discuss the contract. Beckett replied
drolly that all he wanted was money. Hamilton's interest in
Watt extended also to Beckett's current activity. "I don't know
what I can say . . . about future work," he wrote. "All I
would have to offer in English being translations from my own
French. Perhaps, to encourage him with *Watt*, I should say I
expect soon to resume writing in English, than which until now
few things are less likely."[52]

It was quite a dilemma: he finally seemed to have a publisher eager to commit himself to *Watt*, but he himself was becoming deeply committed to another novel in French. "I am
getting on with another book in French entitled probably
Molloy," he wrote offhandedly to Reavey.[53]

In the beginning *Molloy* seems to have moved more slowly
than his other postwar writing but this was because external
events prevented him from sustained writing. While at Menton,
he had an abscess in the jaw and more trouble with his teeth.

When he recovered, he was too tired and debilitated to write for a long time.

By mid-September, when they returned to Paris, Beckett heard from Toni Clerkx that Hussenot-Trenier was interested in *Éleuthéria* and almost published it. "But only almost," Beckett said.[54] Clerkx told Beckett she would no longer be able to represent him because she wanted to work at her own writing, so he decided for the time being to do nothing further with work already written, but to concentrate on the new novel instead. Suzanne was reluctant to see him closet himself away while nothing was being done to place finished work. He was adamant, however, and refused to do anything himself. He had admitted long ago that he hated to deal with publishers, and was only too happy to turn his affairs over to friends who enjoyed commercial interchange; as for himself, he preferred privacy.

Suzanne, even more private than he, decided that their financial situation was too serious to survive a publishing hiatus and she decided to act as his agent. In the fall she took *Éleuthéria* from Clerkx and followed it through the remainder of its peregrinations until Beckett withdrew it from consideration. It was Suzanne who tried to persuade Bordas to bring out *Mercier et Camier* that fall as they had originally intended. But with *Murphy*, in print since May, having sold almost no copies, she was unable to persuade them to exercise their option. Sadly, she brought *Mercier et Camier* back to the rue des Favorites while they tried to think of what to do next. On a more mundane level, it was Suzanne who called for and returned the translations upon which they depended for their sustenance to various now forgotten periodicals.

In November, Reavey and William MacAlpine went to Paris to see Beckett for what was supposed to be a holiday weekend, and Reavey broke the news that Hamish Hamilton had also refused *Watt*. There was nothing left for Beckett but to write, and he turned his attention seriously to *Molloy*.

In later years, Beckett said that he conceived "*Molloy* and what followed the day I became aware of my stupidity. Then I began to write the things I feel."[55]

Beckett said he wrote the three novels which comprise the

trilogy with difficulty, "but with elan, in a sort of enthusiasm . . . *Malone* came from *Molloy*, the *Unnamable* from *Malone*."[56]

"Strength was certainly needed to stay with Camier, as it was needed to stay with Mercier," Beckett said, "but less than was needed to fight the battle of the soliloquy."[57]

He began to write *Molloy* in September, 1947, and by January, 1948, he was finished.

The only person he saw during this time with any regularity was Marie Péron. He intended to send *Molloy* to a publisher as soon as he finished it, but he wanted to be absolutely sure that it was truly a French *roman*, and not simply an English novel translated into French. He decided that he needed help and asked Madame Péron to work with him. Each day they met to go over what he had written the night before. For several hours, word by word, they worked over the manuscript, occasionally changing a word or phrase, sometimes the structure of an entire sentence or paragraph, to make *Molloy* seem the writing of a native Frenchman.[58]

Molloy is a deceptively simple novel. It is divided into two sections:[59] in the first, Molloy tells his story in two paragraphs, the first of five hundred words, the second of about forty thousand; in the second part, Moran tells his story, and in keeping with the regularity of his character, his story is divided by normal paragraphs throughout.

Molloy is in his mother's room and has been there at least a year. He was brought there in some sort of vehicle and does not know what has happened to his mother. He writes a story for a man who comes once a week to collect the pages, and he begins the story for the reader by telling how his journey began. He was in the lee of a rock, crouched like Belacqua or Sordello—he forgets which—when he saw two men walking by, whom he calls A and C. (In the French version they are called A and B.) C has a cocked hat and carries a stick, which Molloy calls a club. In the second part of the narrative, C approaches Moran with the club, and so the initial apparition becomes of significant importance. Molloy dismisses them both from the story at this point, and tells of his journey to see his mother.

He fastens his crutches to the crossbar of his bicycle and

sets out, but he is arrested at the ramparts of the town and questioned by the police for the way he rides the bicycle. They release him in the late afternoon and he goes to the country. Sometime afterwards he finds himself in the town again, where he runs over a dog owned by a woman named Lousse. She protects him from irate bystanders and takes him into her home. Molloy is not sure how long he lives there because she drugs his food, but he does know that he has replaced the dog in her affections. When he leaves, he discovers that his bicycle is missing, so he goes without it, on crutches.

Molloy wanders, then thinks about settling more or less permanently in an alley, then contemplates suicide. Finally, he goes to the seaside to renew his sixteen sucking stones—one of the great comic passages in Beckett's fiction—and explains at length how he transfers sixteen small smooth stones from various pockets to his mouth and back again in an effort to suck all of them equally. The tone of the novel abruptly changes: the image of his mother haunts him, and so he begins to try to go to her once more. No longer able to hobble, he crawls. He hears a distant gong, then a voice tells him not to fret, for "they" are coming. Finally, at the edge of the forest, he sinks into a ditch from which he is rescued, taken to his mother's room and made to write his story. The plot is circular; it ends as it began.

The second part of *Molloy* introduces Moran, unusual among Beckett's characters because he has a first name, Jacques. Moran is a fastidious person, a practicing Catholic, a householder and proud of his property. He is employed by Youdi (a colloquial French word for Jew), who sends Gaber one Sunday morning to tell Moran to make a report on Molloy.

Gaber tells Moran and his son, also named Jacques, to leave at once to look for Molloy, whom Moran seems to know. Moran's disquiet grows: he is anxious, then confused, until he finally admits that he is losing his head and floundering. His rigid schedule has been disturbed and he can't cope with change. He misses the last Mass and receives private Communion which still does not calm him. He eats lunch later than usual, which upsets his stomach. In the process of getting ready to start out, he gives his son an enema and feels sharp pain strike his own knee while doing so.

Moran is a private detective of sorts, whose job is to track down people like Murphy, Mercier and Camier. He is bewildered because he won't know what to do with Molloy if he finds him, for Gaber left no specific instructions.

Soon after Moran and Jacques begin their journey, pain strikes and Moran's legs become paralyzed and he sends Jacques to buy a bicycle. In the meantime, as he lies in the woods, C approaches and asks him for bread, which he exchanges in return for C's club. The next day a different man approaches Moran and asks after the first. They exchange a few words and Moran clubs him to death. His stiff leg bends normally for a while, but soon he is paralyzed again.

Jacques returns with the bicycle, Moran rides on the carrier and his son pedals toward Molloy's region. They quarrel, and Jacques abandons Moran. Gaber appears with an order for Moran to return home. Moran wants to know if Youdi is angry with him for failing in his mission, but Gaber, who has been chuckling, says that Youdi told him, "Life is a thing of beauty . . . and a joy forever."

"Do you think he meant human life?" Moran asks, but Gaber has disappeared.[60]

Moran begins his return home, growing more decrepit as the journey progresses. When he arrives he finds his house deserted, his bees dead and his hens running wild. He arrives in the spring, and spends May and June in his garden. In August, he determines to leave again, as soon as he writes his report. He wants to be free, to live close to the earth. The second part ends with the report mentioned at the beginning, following the circularity of Molloy's story.

Molloy is Beckett's first novel with a hero who feels compelled to write down his experiences and thoughts. Whether this knowledge is correct is unimportant—what matters is that the effort to understand has been made and has had a purgative, tranquilizing effect. "It is midnight, the rain is beating on the windows," Moran, the second teller begins his tale. "It was not midnight. It was not raining," he ends. He has written his report, and is perhaps freer than before.

Beckett considers *Molloy* his first successful rendering of his own experience into fiction. Molloy's existence, his family

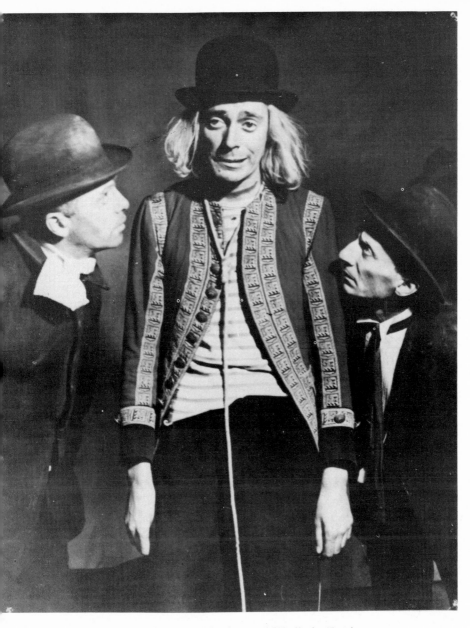

stragon (Pierre Latour), Lucky (Jean Martin), and Vladimir (Lucien
Raimbourg) in first production of *En Attendant Godot*, 1953 (Photo
Bernard)

Roger Blin as Hamm in fi
production of *Fin de Part*
1957 (Photo Pic)

Beckett in London for first British production
of *Waiting for Godot*, 1955 (photo supplied by
Reading University Library)

Hamm (Roger Blin, seated) and Clov (Jean Martin) in first production
of *Fin de Partie*, 1957 (J.-P. Mathevet)

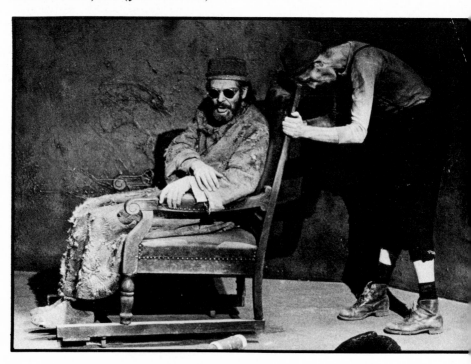

◄Winnie (Ruth White) in first production of *Happy Days*, New York 1961 (photograph supplied by Alan Schneider; © Alix Jeffry)

Patrick Magee, Jack MacGowran, and Roger Blin backstage during 1964 production of *Endgame* at The English Theatre in Paris (Camera Press, Ltd.)

◄Nell (Frances Cuka) and Nagg (Richard Goolden) in rehearsal for first English-language production of *Endgame*, 1958 (Keystone)

Billie Whitelaw in first production of *Play*, 1964 (Zoë Dominic)➤

Billie Whitelaw, Robert Stephens, and Rosemary Harris in first production of *Play*, London 1964 (Zoë Dominic)

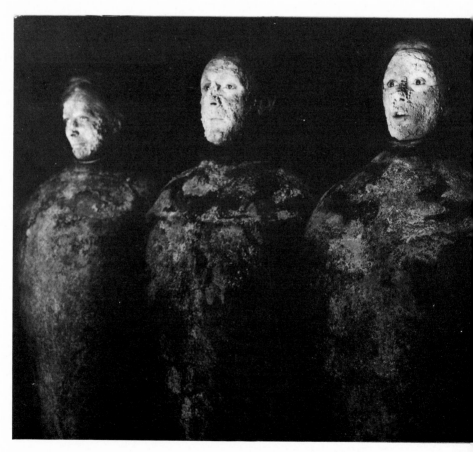

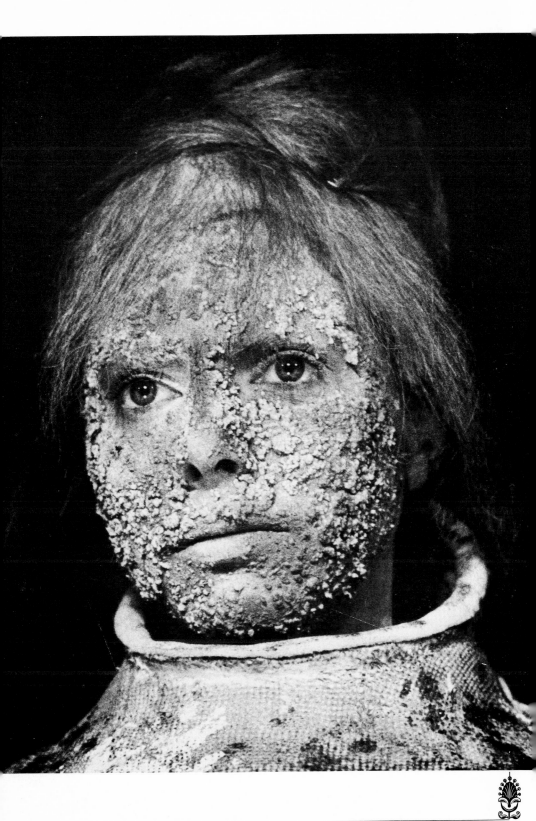

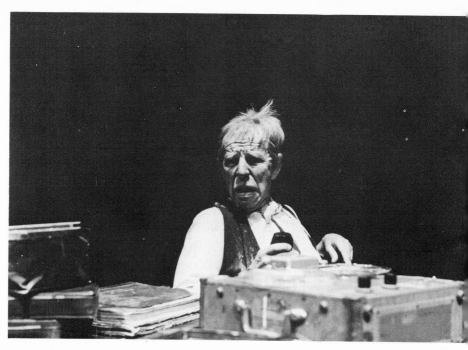

Hume Cronyn as Krapp in *Krapp's Last Tape*, directed by Alan
Schneider, 1972 (courtesy Hume Cronyn)

Beckett and Alan Schneider during the making of *Film*, 1964 (courtesy
Alan Schneider)

and friends—all are based on Beckett's life, but are successfully removed from it. The place names are vaguely Irish and slightly scatological: Bally, Turdy, Hole. The landscape is so much like Foxrock that his family and friends were astonished at how easily they recognized the descriptions. Molloy, Moran, Murphy, Yerk, Mercier and the others are names found routinely in the pages of *Thom's Dublin Directory*. Moran's neighbors, the Elsner sisters, recall Beckett's kindergarten teachers. Beckett's characters either have paralyzed legs or none at all. In his family, two uncles and a cousin each had one leg amputated due to what the Beckett family refers to jokingly as "the family circulatory problem."[61] A third uncle, Dr. James Beckett, a well-known and beloved figure in Dublin, lost both legs through diabetic complications, had severely restricted use of both his arms because of a debilitating muscular disease and became blind. He ended his life in much the same manner as Beckett's *Unnamable*, telling amusing stories to cheer up visitors who usually were horrified and depressed when they arrived to visit the once vital champion swimmer reduced to immobility, but went away in high spirits and good humor because of his infectious, indomitable optimism.[62]

Molloy is toothless, as Beckett feared he himself would be if his dental problems did not clear up. He wears dirty trousers and an overcoat similar to Beckett's beloved raincoat. His hat, a bowler, recalls Bill Beckett's penchant for that style of headgear. He sleeps during the day and his mental activity seems to take place at night. He is an intellectual, and says:

> Yes I once took an interest in astronomy, I don't deny it. Then it was geology that killed a few years for me. The next pain in the balls was anthropology and the other disciplines, such as psychiatry, that are connected with it, disconnected, then connected again, according to the latest discoveries.[63]

—a passage that evokes Beckett's mockery of his own love of pure knowledge. Molloy is utterly indifferent to major human concerns:

> As to his moral character, he combines nobility with sadistic violence (noble in general adversity, brutal when crossed by individuals); and he can often horrify the reader with his gross

indifference to major human preoccupations, such as the will to live and the impulse to procreate, both of which provoke his pithiest ironies. For he had no Camusian attitude of dignity in the face of "the only really serious philosophical problem," suicide, but is merely disappointed that he persistently fails to commit it.[64]

Molloy is one of the clearest statements of Beckett's on-going preoccupations: alienation, isolation, exile, and the separation of the body and mind, the last of which subsequently became more and more important in his writings.

"I am tired, of overwriting, probably. A book of short stories, two 'novels,' and a play in under two years. They go out into the usual void and I hear little more about them," Beckett wrote to McGreevy in his New Year's greeting of 1948.[65] He had finished *Molloy* just before Christmas and was badly in need of a rest. He wanted to get out of Paris and into the country, but could not. He continued to speak of his writings: "*Molloy* is a long book, the second last of the series begun with *Murphy*, if it can be said to be a series. The last is begun, and then I hope I'll hear no more of him. . . . Forgive all these details of my work, my life seems to be little else." He called his life "quiet and meager, with no friends, with only work to give it meaning."[66]

Since 1945 he had made periodic visits to Lucia Joyce at Ivry, but decided now to stop because they upset her too much. He was angry and depressed when Maria Jolas told him that Lucia's doctor said he had given up hope because Beckett no longer came to see Lucia. Beckett's visits had never been pleasant, but he made them dutifully, out of a sense of loyalty to Joyce. He personally felt that his brief meetings with Lucia were harmful because they gave her hope for a relationship that would never be realized; "bad" periods often followed his visits. Also, Lucia tended to speak of events that took place fifteen years ago as if they were current, and of people long dead as if they were still alive. In his own state of mind, so deeply involved with himself through his writing, it was more of a strain than he could endure.

Joyce's group had gradually filtered back to Paris: Sylvia Beach and Stuart Gilbert were there, but Beckett avoided them.

Nora and Giorgio sent Christmas greetings from Switzerland, where their situation was greatly improved now that American royalties poured in with regularity to pay off the debts Joyce had left. They invited him to visit, and he would have liked to, but he had no money.

Life in France was depressing. Beckett found it difficult to find any trace of the prewar France that had meant so much to him in the postwar maze of red tape, regulations and government struggles. What was worse, now that those who had left during the war were returning, old friendships were sometimes strained and unnatural. Overnight, some people suddenly declared themselves Resistance heroes, while collaborators tried to call as little attention to themselves as possible. People seemed to talk endlessly in an effort to explain their conduct during the war years, which Beckett found tiresome and irritating.

Materially, conditions were appalling. It was impossible for Beckett to live on his inheritance, which had been greatly devalued in postwar currency changes. To make matters worse, he was having problems explaining his sporadic residency in France to his Irish bank, and his Irish income to French tax officials.

He was humiliated when he applied formally for employment at UNESCO and was put on a waiting list. Paris was crawling with translators and he had no more to recommend him than any of the others. He and Suzanne were now totally dependent on her dressmaking.

In February and March, 1948, he began to give private English lessons to anyone willing to take them. It helped, but barely, and like his other earlier attempts to teach, ended in failure. His naturally silent demeanor was taken for dour disapproval by his frightened pupils, and one by one they drifted away.

Maria Jolas asked him to aid her in collecting and arranging her late husband's translations of René Char's poetry, but he was afraid her domineering manner would not allow him final control of the work and so he refused. Mrs. Jolas had sold *transition* to Georges Duthuit and it was now called *transition 48*. Beckett had three short French poems—previously written—which Duthuit accepted, and they were published in the June issue, with his own English translations on facing pages.[67]

At the same time *Derrière le Miroir* commissioned a critical article on the van Veldes, which led to a certain amount of distress in his life. Suddenly, everything seemed to happen at the same time: he received several other commissions for hackwork translations, so that with a few English pupils still hanging on, he found all his time engaged and none left for his own writing. In his frustration he wrote to McGreevy:

> I have a great desire to get on with my own work but can't get near it at the moment. I see a little clearly at last what my writing is about and fear I have about perhaps ten years courage and energy to get the job done. The feeling of getting oneself in perfection is a strange one, after so many years of expression in blindness.[68]

Even while writing *Molloy*, he knew that his next work would be a companion piece to it. He decided not to allow Suzanne to submit *Molloy* to publishers until he was sure of his progress with the new work. At that time, he thought only in terms of two, not three, novels. He expected that he would have said all he wanted with *Malone meurt* (*Malone Dies*) and further development of the theme would be redundant. In the French *Molloy*, Beckett wrote:

> Cette fois-ci, puis encore une je pense, puis c'en sera fini je pense, de ce monde-la aussi.[69]

whereas, in the English translation written several years later, the paragraph reads:

> This time, then once more I think, *then perhaps a last time* [emphasis mine], then I think it'll be over, with that world, too.[70]

Unlike *Molloy*, *Malone meurt* does not have a careful symmetrical structure. Rather, it is Malone, alone and dying in a room, writing his story. He offers no explanations, sets no scene: he simply begins to write and stops only at the moment of death. He is quite old, between eighty and one hundred. He lives in a room in a house, and a woman comes each day to bring him soup and a clean chamber pot. "Dish and pot, dish and pot, these are the poles," Malone says.[71] From his room he can see into the house opposite, where a couple lives, and he is not above watching their sexual activity. He has a long stick with which he rummages through his meager possessions and draws his table, on squeaky castors, close to his bed. He has his notebook and his pencil, and these are his most valued possessions. With them, he tells his stories. The first is of a boy named Saposcat called Sapo (Greek for "wisdom" and "dung"), who later becomes the old man, Macmann. Macmann lives in the House of St. John of God, where he engages in an affair with an old woman named Moll who wears earrings in the shape of long ivory crucifixes and has one tooth carved into the shape of "the celebrated sacrifice."[72] The keeper of this house, called Lemuel, takes his charges to an island for a picnic. Lemuel (a variant on the Old Testament "Samuel") is a violent man who slaughters two of the sailors with a hatchet, leaves someone else with a broken hip, and pushes off at night with the rest of his charges. Like *La Fin*, this novel ends with the hero in an open boat drifting out to sea.

If Molloy is the first of Beckett's characters who feels compelled to write down his experiences, Malone is the first who wants truly to know himself. Molloy gains a sort of purgation and peace with the knowledge that there are things he either cannot or will not accept. Malone writes to relieve his misery and boredom; above all, he writes to know himself. The pronoun "I" dominates this novel, as Malone constantly examines and reexamines his life:

> All I want now is to make a last effort to understand. . . . No, it is not a question of understanding. Of what then, I don't know. Here I go nonetheless mistakenly.
>
> I have no time to pick my words, I am in a hurry to be done. And yet no, I am in no hurry. Decidedly this evening I shall say nothing that is not false, I mean nothing that is not calculated to leave me in doubt as to my real intentions.
>
> I had plans not so long ago. Perhaps I have another ten years ahead of me . . . I shall try and go on all the same, a little longer, my thoughts elsewhere, I can't stay here. I shall hear myself talking, afar off, . . . talking of myself, my mind wandering, far from here, among its ruins.

This time I know where I am going, it is no longer the ancient night, the recent night. Now it is a game I am going to play. I never knew how to play until now.[73]

It is not surprising, in a book which owes its cohesion to the first person pronoun, that *Malone meurt* is the most autobiographical of all Beckett's fiction. The setting is much like Cooldrinagh, where the sounds, heard from the top story, of the elements and creatures outside are those the young Beckett must have heard. The lights gleaming off in the valley are those of the stone cutters who lived in the hills in ramshackle huts above Carrickmines. The Leopardstown racetrack, where Bill Beckett spent so many afternoons, and St. John of God's, the asylum where Beckett once played cricket, have figured in other works. The memories of the little boy seeing his first airplane and reminiscing about horse-drawn cabs on Dublin's streets must be Beckett's. Lambert is a thinly disguised rendering of Bonnelly and his family. The photograph of the donkey near the ocean no doubt refers to May and one of her animals.

Beckett has admitted that Sapo, with his "gull's eyes," bears an uncanny resemblance to himself. "He got a bit out of hand," Beckett told John Fletcher.[74] When Malone remarks that there is little difference between men and women, one is reminded that Beckett's mother, his wife and other women who have been important to him are all tall, gaunt, and androgynous, with a preference for mannishly tailored clothes.

With hindsight, this passage from Beckett's *Proust* suddenly takes on enormous importance:

> The only fertile research is excavatory, immersive, a contraction of the spirit, a descent. The artist is active, but negatively, shrinking from the nullity of extracircumferential phenomena, drawn into the core of the eddy.[75]

The completion of *Malone meurt* brought an astonishing change to Beckett's physical condition. While he was writing it, everyone close to him feared that he might quite literally die when it was finished.[76] As Malone's efforts to write grew more painful and exhausting, so did Beckett's. Suzanne was wild and begged him to stop; and when her imprecations went unheeded, she implored Maurice Sinclair to do something. They were both able only to stand by and watch helplessly as Beckett's relentless pursuit of himself through Malone continued.

But as soon as he had finished, he entered into a state of euphoria and became more gregarious than he had been for years.

This was a pattern which occurred repeatedly from that time on as he came to the end of a work: first there was euphoria, complete satisfaction with the writing, an eagerness for publication and a confidence that it would be well received; then, self-doubt would take hold of him until it grew into an obsession. He would be unable to face the work, for he had a positive horror of reading what he had written. It was too much of a shock to discover what he had dredged up from his unconscious. It was so self-destructive that he actually had to prepare himself, to gird up, to reread it. When he did force himself to read, he was always dissatisfied, and had it not been for his precarious financial condition and Suzanne's insistence that he allow her to send it out, he would most likely have held on to it so long that much of his writing might never have been published.

At any rate, when he finished *Malone meurt*, his mood and mental health were definitely on an upswing, and the rest of the year was filled with activity. He busied himself typing *Molloy* and *Malone meurt*. A happy interruption came when Tom McGreevy stopped in Paris for a few days in June and insisted on taking Beckett and Suzanne to see *Andromaque* at the Comédie Française. In mid-June his poems appeared in *transition 48*, and Duthuit suggested that Beckett work as a translator on a continuing basis for the magazine, an offer he eagerly accepted.

Beckett did not immediately commit himself to any work because he was too busy with a commission begun by Joyce's friends to have any spare time before his departure. A group had suggested to Nora and Giorgio that Joyce's body be moved from Switzerland to Ireland, as William Butler Yeats's had been from France. Since Beckett was going to Ireland for the summer, he was the logical person to investigate the possibilities, and they commissioned him to do it.[77]

He went to one of Dublin's leading undertakers, who was horrified at the thought of such a great sinner being transported

back to Ireland. When the man recovered his equanimity, he
told Beckett that it was a matter for the government. He was
next told that the Irish government could not consider the request for removal until the Swiss authorities had given their
consent. His efforts to gather information dragged on over the
summer as bureaucracies seemed to move like dominoes—the
problem for Beckett was to find one that would fall and set the
others in motion. At the end of August, he returned to Paris to
find the group of friends had become a semiofficial "committee."

When the Swiss members of the committee began discussions with the officials of the Canton of Zurich, they were told
abruptly that exhumation before twenty-five years after burial
was forbidden except under exceptional circumstances. The
canton officials said that the Joyce committee would have to
write a letter explaining the request, the "ideological" reasons
for it and what would take place once the body was removed
"in celebration" to Ireland. At this point Beckett washed his
hands of the entire affair. He was horrified at the thought of
Joyce's body being moved to Ireland in the first place, and he
wanted no part of the general fuss and commotion that seemed
likely to materialize if it were removed.

When the committee was finally convinced that the Swiss
officials took their law seriously and would not relax it without
extended effort and expense on their part, the plan was quietly
shelved and Joyce's remains were left in Zurich. When Joyce's
friends eventually decided he should have a monument,
Beckett's only part in the affair was an offer of financial contribution.

In Ireland, he found his mother in fairly good form, with a
new maid who was incompetent but so cheerful that May overlooked her failings. Her good humor made his visit easier.

Reavey wrote to him in Dublin suggesting that Cyril Connolly might be interested in something for *Horizon* of about
thirty thousand words. Beckett had nothing but the first half of
Molloy, still in French.[78] He thought it unlikely that he could
get the piece translated by the deadline, but was willing to try if
Connolly would accept it. Apparently Connolly would not, because Beckett made no attempt to do it.

He was still typing *Malone meurt* and wanted to finish before he returned to France:

> The last I hope of the series *Murphy*, *Watt*, *Mercier & Camier*, *Molloy*, not to mention the four nouvelles and *Éleuthéria*. A young publisher is interested, Editions K, I think, and I am preparing him for burial.[79]

The "young publisher" (his name forgotten by Beckett) toyed with *Molloy* for several months before rejecting it, and Suzanne began her solicitations once again. During the next two years she carried Beckett's novels to six different publishers, who all rejected everything he had written to date.

When he finished typing *Malone meurt* ("may he never come back," Beckett would say to friends[80]), he was still floating in a state of tranquil satisfaction. He liked what he had written, felt sure that publication would be forthcoming soon, and was pleased with the feeling of catharsis that the writing had induced in him.

Autumn in Paris was especially beautiful in 1948, with day after day of glorious warm weather, what Beckett and the friends who came from Ireland to see him called a real St. Martin's summer.[81] A younger generation of Becketts had gravitated to Paris; besides Maurice Sinclair, Hilary Heron and John Beckett were both there for a year on scholarship—she in art and he in music.

Beckett thoroughly enjoyed their company. It was one of the rare times in his life when he was not preoccupied with work, and the younger Becketts constantly amazed him, especially young Hilary and her Irish friends who wove their motor bikes with wild abandon through the merciless Paris traffic. Though the age difference between Beckett and his cousins was not more than ten or fifteen years, it seemed like a lifetime to him, and every so often they were disconcerted when they caught Beckett staring at them as if he hoped to fathom the difference between their joyous exuberance and zest for life and his own passive indifference.

He was of another generation and could not share the postwar euphoria of young lives still unblemished. While they were racing around Paris, hungry for every experience the city had to offer, he was content to stay at home and play Chopin on the piano. He practiced the symphonic *Études* with such fervor and dedication that his friends asked him jokingly if he were preparing for a recital. He parried their comments by replying that he was content because he was "happily doing nothing."[82]

Suzanne, who had been bearing the brunt of their efforts to stay financially solvent, was exhausted. One of her friends offered the use of a small chalet on the edge of the forest of Fontainebleau, and in late September she and Beckett went there for a brief rest.

When they returned, Beckett, habituated to the routine of daily writing, simply sat down as usual and waited for something to come. The euphoria that had filled him since the completion of *Malone meurt* had begun to dissolve in a restlessness and an urge to write again. By the time he returned from Fontainebleau, he was filled with doubt. This led to the need to try again with a new work, to grab for the now rapidly dissipating euphoria. It was as he thought: *Malone meurt* had indeed mined the depths of that particular trough and nothing more seemed forthcoming. The impetus to write was strong, but the memory of the enormous effort and frightening commitment required to write another such novel were more than he could subject himself to at this time. Unconsciously at first, then with increasing awareness and absorption, he found himself writing a play.

CHAPTER SIXTEEN

Waiting for Godot:

"A MARVELOUS, LIBERATING DIVERSION"

 En Attendant Godot (*Waiting for Godot*) sprang "full blown from Beckett's head" in a very brief time.[1] The first page of the French manuscript bears the date "9 Octobre 1948" and the last "29 Janvier 1949."[2] Beckett said he "began to write *Godot* as a relaxation, to get away from the awful prose I was writing at the time,"[3] and "from the wildness and rulelessness" of the novels.[4]

Beckett, who had had no experience with the actualities of theatrical production, considered writing for the stage "a marvelous, liberating diversion."[5] It was like a game for him to put speeches on paper, envision the way characters should move and speak—all within the confines of the printed page and his mind. It was much like chess: plotting moves, foreseeing changes and intellectualizing interactions. With *Éleuthéria*, it had gotten out of hand—too many characters and too much activity on the stage. This time he chose a simpler subject.

It is difficult to say which came first, the play or its title. Beckett has been careful to fend off the question and has chosen instead to give any number of reasons for the title, just as he does when asked about his decision to write the play in French. In a 1972 conversation he said, with evident pleasure, that he "wanted any number of stories to be circulated," both about himself and his work: "the more there are the better I like it." But then, as if he had revealed too much, he immediately qualified this remark by saying that "it really doesn't matter to me what people think. They can believe whatever they want, it's all the same to me."[6]

When Roger Blin asked him who or what Godot stood for, Beckett replied that it suggested itself to him by the slang word for boot in French, "godillot, godasse," because feet play such a prominent role in the play.[7] This is the explanation he has given most often. The second most repeated story is that Beckett encountered a large group of people standing on a street corner one afternoon during the annual Tour de France bicycle race, and he asked what they were doing. "Nous attendons Godot," they replied, adding that all the competitors had passed except the oldest, whose name was Godot.[8] It is quite likely both stories figure at least partially in the name of the title figure; however, Beckett will never discuss the implications of the title. His friends are fond of the apocryphal story that it came from the time Beckett, standing on the corner of the rue Godot de Mauroy, a Parisian street notorious for prostitutes, was waiting for a bus and was accosted by one of the ladies. When he refused, she supposedly demanded in a huff what special creature was he saving himself for—was he "waiting for Godot?" Beckett himself has not commented on this version, but like so many other seemingly spurious incidents in his life, this one should not be totally dismissed.[9]

The question hounds him—as it is asked repeatedly—and it and the entire play have given rise to more books, articles and opinions than any other drama of this century. Godot has been made to symbolize God (even though the original play was written in French, and "Dieu" hardly sounds like "God"), Christianity, rebirth, redemption, hope and despair. It has been construed as an allegory of French resistance to the Germans and of Ireland to the English, of the relationship of Beckett to Joyce, and of so many more things that a sizable catalog devoted to the possible meanings of the title could be compiled with very little effort.

When the play was initially being talked about at the time of the first production and Beckett was pressed hard for an answer, he would snap "If I knew who Godot was, I would have said so in the play,"[10] or, "If Godot were God, I would have called him that."[11] He is insistent that he did not read Balzac's *Le Faiseur* (performed as *Mercadet*), in which the characters wait for a "Monsieur Godeau" to come and save them from bankruptcy and ruin, until after he had written *Godot*. He is equally insistent that Strindberg's *Dream Play* and Yeats's *The Cat and the Moon*, with its two beggars, lame and blind, have little to do with *Waiting for Godot*.

His admonition, "I meant what I said,"[12] should be taken seriously. He sat down to write what he hoped would be an immediately performable play, entertaining, easily accessible, financially possible to stage. To this day he maintains that *Godot* is a "bad play"[13] and expresses continuing amazement that people find so much in it. In fact, at times, he actually becomes annoyed with people who want to talk about it, because it so greatly overshadows what he considers his important work, the novels.[14]

Briefly, it is the story of two men, Vladimir and Estragon, who amuse themselves with conversation that alternates between hope and despair while they wait for a person called Godot to keep his appointment. In each of two acts of uneven length, they encounter a man called Pozzo and his slave, Lucky. In each act a young boy tells them that Godot will not come today but will surely keep his appointment tomorrow. In the second act a tree which has been bare in the first act suddenly sprouts leaves. "Not," as Beckett insists, "to show hope or inspiration, but only to record the passage of time."[15]

Like *Watt*, *Waiting for Godot* was written during a time in which Beckett wanted something very much and wished for time to pass. With the novel, he wanted the end of the war and the resumption of his normal life in Paris. With the play, he was killing time until both publishers and the public would recognize the importance of his fiction. Of the young Irish writers who surrounded Joyce in the 1930's, Beckett was the one who most desperately wanted recognition and would have been most bitterly disappointed had it not come about in his lifetime.[16] When he wrote *Watt*, Beckett disguised his anguished waiting through the tortuous games he played with the novel's prose. When he came to *Godot*, having turned to drama to escape the impasse of self-confrontation and revelation into which his novels had led him, he chose to write about the abstract idea of waiting for time to pass and for something important to happen in every man's life, directly inserting snatches of conversation from his own life, bits of songs, references to his past readings and expressions he used frequently in his everyday speech.

He wrote the play quickly but hesitantly. On the manuscript there are few of the agonizing pages of doodles and scribbles that characterize the earlier play, *Éleuthéria*. His handwriting is lucid and flowing, attesting to the ease with which he transferred his ideas onto paper. He wrote so rapidly that he was unsure of what names to call the characters. Throughout the first act Estragon was called "Levy," and did not receive his name until Beckett wrote it emphatically in bold, sharp strokes on the back of the last page of Act I.

At one point in the manuscript there is an actual letter written by Godot, and at another there is dialogue to suggest that Pozzo himself is Godot, but fails to recognize the two he has come to meet. Pozzo is called "le grand" and Lucky "le petit" until Pozzo introduces himself several pages later with "je m'appelle Pozzo." When Beckett was asked why Lucky was so named, he replied, "I suppose he is Lucky to have no more expectations . . ."[17]

The original French manuscript (which, incidentally, is the only one of his manuscripts Beckett still possesses and adamantly refuses to sell) was refined throughout the time before it was first published in 1952. Several months after publication, when Roger Blin produced it for the first time, the play was once again cut and polished to make it more striking dramatically. The text of the play at that time owes much of its finished form to Blin's acute sense of the theatrical. Beckett, who was still searching for his own dramatic style, recognized the value of Blin's changes and incorporated them into his own English translation. Thus, by the time the definitive edition of 1965 appeared, the play had been through what amounts to a revision encompassing some sixteen or so years, on stage and in print.

From the beginning of *Waiting for Godot*, when Estragon momentarily gives up pulling off his boot and announces "Rien à faire (nothing to be done),"[18] Beckett had the idea of what he wanted to do with this play fairly well in mind. He wanted to recreate a circus-cum-vaudeville atmosphere in a dramatic experience of total simplicity on which he would superimpose a pastiche of his ordinary, everyday thought and conversation. Above all, he wanted it to be good commercial theater, traditional yet different and effective.

The play is a curious one, coming as it does in his canon at this time. While it is every bit as biographical as the novels, and is in places even less disguised than they, it somehow transcends his life and becomes the most separate entity of all his writings. It is unique because it is so deeply rooted in his life and experience, while at the same time the text stands by itself, having universal meaning for a worldwide audience.

Beckett and Suzanne had a relationship which many of their friends described as being like two Irish "butties," trading vaudeville one-liners in the best music hall tradition.[19] "You should have been a poet," Vladimir says. "I was. Isn't that obvious?" Estragon replies.[20] It would seem that Beckett took ordinary conversations between himself and Suzanne and incorporated them verbatim in *Godot*. Friends were astonished at how like their ordinary conversations the play's dialogue seemed. It was as if Beckett had transported wholesale the teasing, whining, loving, caring and sometimes bitter conversations his friends occasionally overheard.

To say, however, that Vladimir and Estragon are direct representations of Beckett and Suzanne would be misleading, as Beckett shifts aspects of the real persons from one to the other of his characters. Vladimir and Estragon may seem to have clear-cut characteristics: Vladimir the intellectual, Estragon the more sensual; Vladimir the esthetic, tall and thin; Estragon short, fat and sometimes effeminate. Yet when the play is read closely, it is obvious how wrong these labels are, for each character at times assumes the traits of the other, blurring these distinctions and making them relatively useless. Unlike the "straight" and "funny" men in the classic vaudeville sketch who are always the same, Vladimir and Estragon have something of each at different times throughout the play. Beckett himself has said that *Waiting for Godot* is a play that is striving all the time to avoid definition, and as always, attention should be given to his words.[21]

Much has been made of the parable of the two thieves

which Vladimir tells to Estragon: "Two thieves. One is sup-posed to have been saved and the other . . . damned."[22] The image first took on meaning for Beckett as early as 1935, when he read St. Augustine's *Confessions*, and began to use the expres-sion to define either/or situations. It appears repeatedly in his correspondence from that time onward[23] and seems, in the play, to be the perfect anecdote for just such a dramatic situation. Beckett has told a number of scholars how much he liked the symmetry of the expression,[24] stressing that the symmetry is the only important aspect of the line, and religious meanings or any other meanings which his audience and critics wish to super-impose on it are definitely not his. Christian interpretations of the play have always irritated Beckett: "Christianity is a mythol-ogy with which I am perfectly familiar, and so I use it. But not in this case!"[25]

Vladimir begins the second act by singing a German round song which also appeared in Beckett's correspondence as early as 1937.[26] It highlights the apparent aimlessness and circularity of the beginning of the second act, and, as it ends with the line "and dug the dog a tomb," beautifully emphasizes the agitation and distraction of Vladimir and sets the scene for the pathos of his initial meeting in this act with Estragon. Once again, random information that struck Beckett's fancy sometime during his earlier life was made to do powerful work in his writing. Prob-ably the most important of the materials transposed from his life into his art concerns the boots and hats which figure promi-nently throughout the play.

To persons who knew him well before and just after the war, *Waiting for Godot* is a metaphor for the long walk into Roussillon, when Beckett and Suzanne slept in haystacks (when they were lucky enough to find them) during the day and walked by night.

While he was writing *Godot*, Suzanne wrote a brief story called "F——," which Beckett translated.[27] It is the story of a woman who encounters a man on a road; they literally run into each other. They have a brief conversation, then the man leads the woman into a ditch by the side of the road before he con-tinues his journey to F——. After a time, she leaves the ditch and walks along the road until she sees the roofs of a town

which she knows is F——, even without ever having been there
before.

The text is spare, controlled and strangely touching. It is so
much like one of Beckett's that one wonders where the writing
ended and the translation began. What makes it interesting is
that it was written at the same time that Beckett was writing
Godot, and in an entirely different way it captures the same
haunting sense of loneliness, encounter, loss and satisfaction.
The wind is wild, the weather miserable. It is dark night, but "in
the end, the night must end, he said."[28] This, and the thought of
the cessation of the sound of the man's steps gives the woman
great satisfaction, for she reasons that he must have arrived at his
destination, and now need only return, presumably to her. In
Beckett's play, Estragon and Vladimir congratulate themselves
that they have kept their appointment, and derive satisfaction
from that. In Suzanne's story, the woman reaches the outskirts
of the town and is content: "there I was. Or nearly." The
story's ending is a variant of *Molloy*, in which Jacques Moran's
opening statement directly contradicts the closing one: "It was
not midnight. It was not raining."[29]

During their long walk into Roussillon, Beckett and Suzanne were often at the mercy of the elements. It was early
winter when they made their way through mountainous southeastern France, in constant biting wind and occasional icy rain.
From his childhood, Beckett had suffered from recurring problems with his feet. When he was very young, he was often the
butt of his playmates' jokes because he walked with a curious
lurching gait, legs stiff and feet turned out, very much like
Charlie Chaplin's Little Tramp.[30] As a young man, he suffered
from all the afflictions of the feet he bestowed upon his fictional
characters, and as an adult in France, the problems of his feet
were magnified by the ill-fitting French shoes he wore.

Beckett and Suzanne took turns cajoling and pleading with
each other on their trek into Roussillon, as first one and then the
other despaired of ever coming to the end of their walk. In
Waiting for Godot, Vladimir and Estragon do the same:

Vladimir: Come here till I embrace you.
Estragon: Don't touch me!

> *Vladimir:* Do you want me to go away? . . .
> *Estragon:* Don't touch me! Don't question me!
> Don't speak to me! Stay with me![31]

Hats figure in the comedic routine, as the two tramps make a great show of exchanging their headgear in a juggling routine suggested to Beckett by the Marx Brothers movie *Duck Soup*.[32] Interestingly, when Roger Blin began to costume the actors for the play, Beckett insisted that the characters wear bowler hats, similar to those his father had always worn. It is the one point on which he was absolutely adamant and would not budge, and so Blin agreed. Almost as an afterthought, Beckett suggested, then insisted, that they wear black coats also similar to those worn by his father.[33]

Ultimately, what is so striking about the play, and what must have been particularly arresting to the first French audience, is the language. Beckett was the first postwar playwright to write dialogue in everyday ordinary spoken French. It must have been a surprise for literate audiences to hear characters on stage saying *merde* and trading insults with each other, things which were never done in the Comédie-Française. The language Beckett used in *Godot* is the language any group of *clochards* sitting on a bench or in a cafe might say to each other. The simplicity of speech is what the French heard in their everyday lives, but never noticed.[34] It was a revolution in language as well as in dramatic form. Until Beckett, drama had been removed from ordinary language by the very act of what the French call *écriture*, the art of writing. In many cases, the result was a stilted, artificial use of the language, plays that seemed to be written with quills, not pens. In *Godot*, the speech and energy of colloquial French gives Beckett's characters a vitality astonishingly new to the French stage. *Godot* might be the play "where nothing happens twice,"[35] but it happens in a way that had never been heard before.

Of all his writings, *Waiting for Godot* has the most paradoxical relation to Beckett's life. He sincerely believes it is a "bad" play, interesting as a period piece perhaps, but certainly not what he would have chosen as the vehicle to make him famous or as his outstanding expression of theatrical ability. Yet he clings sentimentally to the manuscript, and over the years has shown it only to a handful of close associates and fewer scholars. He sold other manuscripts which he considered more important or gave them away as the urge or the need arose, but no matter how seriously distressed his finances were, he would never consider parting with *Godot*.

The play has taken on more than a sentimental meaning for him; there is more than just the idea of waiting involved in it for Beckett. It is a longing for a past life, swept away by war, never to return. He, too, kept his appointments. He stayed in France during the war and returned to Paris when it ended, eager to settle down to the life he had known before. But everyone was dead or gone or irrevocably changed in some way or another. The city itself, five years after the end of the war, was just beginning to come out of the gray cloud which had enveloped it for the past ten years. Paris would recover, but it would never be the same. The Paris he had known and loved in 1939 could never be resurrected. He accepted the change, but was saddened by it. He no longer waited for something that would never come; he had accepted its loss with equanimity and moved on. But for Parisians who had not given conscious thought to their own predicament—that the war was over, yet nothing important was really settled—the element of waiting must have had a strong, albeit unconscious, appeal.

In retrospect, it is almost too easy to offer endless opinions as to why *Waiting for Godot* so captured theatrical sensibilities. When it was produced, Europe was caught up in what have come to be political clichés: Iron Curtain, cold war, social unrest, political upheaval, the nuclear age. Existentialism held sway in France and had attracted followers throughout the rest of the world. The older, cultivated and mannered literature no longer satisfied. Drawing-room comedies seemed jaded, as did the literature of the other extreme, Surrealism. Readers and audiences were hungry for something new with which to express the condition into which humanity had tumbled. In the simplicity of *Waiting for Godot*, they found the complexity of the human condition.

Several years after the play had made him famous, Samuel Beckett was traveling to London by air, incognito. As he settled into his seat and hid behind a large magazine, he heard the pilot welcoming the passengers over the loudspeaker: "*Le capitaine Godot vous accorde des bienvenues.*" Beckett said it was all he could do to keep himself from bolting through the door and off the plane. He wondered about a world which would entrust itself to a Godot.[36]

CHAPTER SEVENTEEN

1949–50:

"ALL VERY FINE, BUT THE VOICE IS FAILING"

 While he was writing *Waiting for Godot*, economic circumstances forced Beckett to divide his time between the play and working for Georges Duthuit. From 1948 to 1953, Beckett translated something for almost every issue of *transition;* much was unsigned and Beckett does not remember most of it. Besides ordinary translation, he often assisted writers with self-translation, or with expressing themselves directly in English. Gabrielle Buffet-Picabia, his former Resistance colleague, was one of these. She had written an article about Guillaume Apollinaire, but was unable to bring it to a satisfactory conclusion. Beckett worked with her at length on the article, which she feels is as much his writing as hers.[1]

Under Duthuit, in his lair at 96 rue de l'Université, the magazine's character changed from what it had been under Eugene Jolas to a presentation of the "best of French art and thought"[2] in English translation. Within a short time, Duthuit surrounded himself with writers and editors fluent in both languages and at the center of the current literary and artistic movements in Paris.

Duthuit was accustomed to working until noon in his office, then crossing the street to a small restaurant-bar for a long lunch and conversation.[3] He was usually joined by (among others) the painters Nicholas deStaël, Jean-Paul Riopelle, and Bram van

Velde; and by Pierre Schneider, Jacques Putman, and usually Beckett. In an atmosphere of tobacco smoke and pinball machines, they talked about everything except work. If the conversation veered to professional topics, it was in an abstract, theoretical way. Instead, they competed on the pinball machines or made dates to play tennis or to watch a professional match. The pun reigned supreme as verbal jousts filled the air in two or more languages. In retrospect, it seemed as if Duthuit's personality had enveloped these disparate individuals and made them into a cohesive group of people who cared about what happened to each other and who shared a very special moment in time. None had yet attained the fame and respect that would come to them all within a period of years, but all were on the verge of developing the maturity and direction which guaranteed that they would soon achieve it. These men and others formed the nucleus of a group in which frequent meetings were a necessity. It seemed as if they needed the short daily burst of conviviality to sustain them in their own work. In conviviality lay strength for the relentless solitude each had to face—the blank page or the empty canvas.

Beckett met with Duthuit and the others more or less regularly. To the others, he seemed a little more serious than they, because (again) he was always just outside the group, watching intently on its fringe. While they played pinball machines, he only watched. When their conversations disintegrated into heated, animated characterizations of art dealers and editors as men whose natural baseness made them insensitive to the merits of creation, Beckett listened but said nothing. Most of the others knew that he had several plays floating around Paris from one producer's office to the next, but he never mentioned them. Only one or two of the group knew that he had a substantial body of unpublished prose. While others spoke enthusiastically of overcoming resistance to their work, Beckett's attitude verged from amusement to skepticism to indifference. He came and went quietly, taking a new translation or depositing one already done.

Duthuit had the knack of instigating conversations that developed into articles for his magazine. Often Beckett's occasional interjection into these conversations was so apt that it provided the exact capstone to complete it. One such conversation about art led to the gradual withdrawal of the other participants until it became a dialogue between Beckett and Duthuit, who urged Beckett to write it. This was usually Duthuit's way of ending these conversations; among themselves, his friends and followers joked that whatever one said to Duthuit, his reply would be "take notes, take notes."[4]

Beckett did write these conversations, which became *Three Dialogues*, published in the December issue.[5] The article consists of an exchange between D. (Duthuit), who acts more or less as prompter for B. (Beckett), who reacts to his comments and questions in a fashion his bibliographers call that of an "intellectual clown."[6] Although the article seems to be a collaboration between the two, and indeed bears both signatures, it is primarily the work of Beckett, based on his conversations with Duthuit.

The first dialogue deals with Pierre Tal-Coat; the second, André Masson; and the third, Beckett's longtime friend, Bram van Velde. Beckett's close friendship with Bram van Velde really had its beginnings during the years with Duthuit. Before the war, he had seen more of Geer van Velde because he moved in the same circles and Bram was often away from Paris. Neither brother had attained much financial success before the war, but Geer was more apt to take a direct role in trying to sell his work than Bram, who was content to paint in isolation and in abject poverty. As Geer continued to paint in a derivative Cubist style, Beckett grew increasingly disenchanted with his work and equally so with his stubborn insistence that one or two relatively minor shows had earned him the right to demand high prices for his canvases, which nevertheless, did not sell. Their friendship went through a period of strain, which was relieved when Geer went to live permanently in Cagnes. In the meantime, Bram, who had hitherto been inordinately reclusive, began to appear from time to time on the rue de l'Université in Beckett's company.

Bram's painting had been growing more and more abstract, leading Beckett, in the *Three Dialogues*, to describe it as "inexpressive."[7] When Duthuit expressed his incredulity at what he termed "the absurdity of what you advance,"[8] Beckett stated with certainty that Bram van Velde was "the first whose hands have not been tied by the certitude that expression is an impossible act."[9]

In van Velde, Beckett found a visual counterpart for the futility of expression he encountered in his own writing, and he became so fixated on this idea and spoke of it with such ferocity that battle lines were drawn in the Duthuit camp. There were those who believed that what Beckett said about Bram in the third dialogue was an accurate expression of the painter's work, and those who felt that Beckett had planted a malignant seed in the painter's mind which would ultimately lead to his destruction as a creative person.

Beckett grew disconcertingly talkative, as he eagerly codified van Velde's work in a "fidelity to failure."[10] Bram appeared to many in the *transition* office as an innocent martyr literally created by Beckett's theorizing. Duthuit was as concerned as the others, resulting in one of the several instances in which his relationship with Beckett was decidedly cool. Painting was difficult for van Velde, who often had no money for food, let alone paint. Now, to be told that painting was an impossible act anyway, amounting to nothing, was something his friends feared he might take literally and use as the reason not to continue the struggle. As for Beckett, he had a hard, steely core which allowed him to control his feelings about the absurdity of writing, and to overcome these feelings by his compulsion to write. He simply wrote, oblivious of the outcome.

In retrospect, they need not have worried, for Bram van Velde, the childlike innocent, was so deeply involved in his own inner drama that he continued to paint as if nothing were transpiring around him. If one examines the paintings of van Velde since 1950, it is obvious that Beckett had little influence upon him: he was attuned to his own inner vision.

While Beckett was working with Duthuit, Suzanne was making the rounds of theatrical offices, this time with *Waiting for Godot*. By the time Beckett was ready to make his annual visit to Dublin in the spring of 1949, the play had been rejected by three producers and was now with the fourth.

The change in his mother was shocking. She had deteriorated so drastically since his last visit that she was a fragile, palsied creature beset by uncontrollable shaking. Sensing that her death was imminent, Beckett spent much of his time methodically destroying what remained of his possessions in Ireland. He spent one afternoon burning boxes of correspondence. Letters from Joyce, McGreevy and other friends in France, Germany and England, all disappeared in the fire, unread. He wanted to be sure that no bundled and parceled part of him would remain in Foxrock once his mother was gone. He was preparing himself for a clean, unsentimental break with his past.[11] Just as he relentlessly pared his writing, honing it to extremes of minimalism, so too did he attack his life and destroy large portions of it. Letters had been his lifeline during his long confinements in Ireland. Now he was killing that part of himself. Though he cannot bring himself to part with anything he writes, turning every insignificant scrap into a "trunk" manuscript, he could destroy, without any outward qualm, letters that had sustained his human relationships. He had no further need of this aspect of himself; he was content to turn the impersonality of his writing into the highly emotional, intensely personal center of his existence. The change in his relationship with McGreevy several years earlier seems to have been the penultimate break in his link with humanity. From that time on, all his letters have been carefully guarded when they touch on personal matters. He makes all the appropriate comments, from grief to joy, when responding to the letters of others, but he takes great care to speak of himself in polite but impersonal language. A number of persons who have corresponded with Beckett during the years, both before and after this time, speak of his letters as being "vehicles with which he insures the image posterity will have of him."[12] This is not such a strong statement as it seems at first; Beckett's postwar persona has been dedicated to the systematic stripping of dependence on externals. He may have been unable, like Murphy, to cross over into the abstract reaches of his mind, but he was determined to do the next best thing. He would live in the world he had fought for so many years, but he had discovered the secret of doing so on his terms: if parts of himself stood in the way of the life within his mind, he would simply destroy them.

Beckett spent most of his visit to Ireland quietly at New Place with his mother, only going into Dublin for such things as dental appointments. Once again his troublesome teeth needed attention, and he consulted Dr. Ganly, who was now married to Beckett's friend, Bridget O'Brien, daughter of the president of the Royal Hibernian Academy, Dermod O'Brien. He had known Bridget Ganly since his Trinity days, and since the war, Beckett had made a point of stopping at the O'Brien house on Fitzwilliam Square whenever he visited Jack B. Yeats. They found him more subdued than usual this year. When they asked about his writing, he dismissed the subject politely but firmly, saying he had written "nothing special."[13] Everyone began to talk at once, as they all insisted that Beckett was surely not serious. As groups of friends are wont to do in such situations, they began to tease him, joking that he had surely gone beyond *More Pricks* and *Whoroscope*, emphasizing the scatological in his titles, and at the same time inventing further comic adventures for Murphy beyond the grave. As they laughed and talked, Beckett seemed to shrivel, and his eyes took on a hunted expression that made them embarrassed for their sustained kidding. He gave them the impression that his writing was something mysterious which he was afraid to speak of; he seemed terrified of it, frightened by the actuality it represented, yet fascinated, as if he were a helpless victim confronting the instrument of his destruction. It was such an awkward moment that everyone was relieved when Beckett recovered his equanimity and left. When he had gone, they could not even talk about him, but changed the subject.

Radio Eireann was interested in putting together a program of recent Irish poetry, and Beckett was asked to contribute his work and to assist in selecting poems by Coffey and Devlin. He went to a luncheon in the Shelbourne Hotel, where he discovered that a fellow Portoran, Norris Davidson, had also been invited. Davidson, a successful popular novelist, was a year behind Beckett at Portora and remembered him clearly. Beckett wanted no part of old memories, and refused to discuss anything but the business at hand. His silence verged on rudeness, and as the meal progressed, he grew bored with the discussion of poetry as well. Suddenly, Beckett announced in a loud voice that he had not attended the ceremonies for Yeats's reinterment in Ireland, but that he had gone looking for the grave in the south of France some years before and had been unable to find it.[14] It was his sole contribution to the conversation, and it struck the others as decidedly strange. When Beckett left, Davidson made excuses for his behavior, saying he knew Beckett was under a strain because of family illness.

Among the few persons he saw during this visit were Sylvia and Alan Thompson, with whom he spent hours playing chess. Both men played to a good club standard and liked to surprise each other with unusual and daring moves. Once, Beckett made an extremely subtle move, its manifestations not immediately apparent even to him. He sat concentrating on the full implication of it, saying softly to himself "Ah, yes, ah, yes . . . " over and over. He raised his head slowly and announced distinctly that chess and music "had the same intellectual beauty—the unfolding of one was much the same as the other."[15] He seemed very pleased with this pronouncement, and sat nodding and smiling throughout the remainder of the game.

For once, he was reluctant to see his time in Ireland come to an end, mainly because of his mother's steadily failing health. It was almost as if she grew weaker before his eyes, and he knew it was only a matter of time until her death. May Beckett, as mindful as ever of the facade of manners behind which she had lived her life, said good-bye to her son as if this were any ordinary visit. They made their farewells with the same controlled courtesy which had characterized their relationship in recent years. No hint of emotion penetrated their politeness.

He returned to Paris to find that two more producers had turned down *Godot*, calling it, among other things, incomprehensible, boring, too highbrow, or too deep.[16]

Suzanne had heard of another director who was said to have been a great friend of Artaud, whom Beckett had admired.

His name was Roger Blin, and he was currently directing a Strindberg play somewhere in Montparnasse. She thought he might be more receptive to Beckett's work than the commercial producers she had thus far consulted. When she asked Beckett if she should take the script to Blin, he shrugged noncommittally, saying it didn't matter at this point—one refusal was as good as another.[17] He told Suzanne he would try to stop at the theater some evening to see a performance because he was curious to see how Blin would incorporate Artaud's ideas in a Strindberg play, but as time went by, he forgot about it.

UNESCO stepped into his life, offering him a commission for an English translation of essays and poems for a book celebrating the two-hundredth anniversary of Goethe's birth.[18] He spent most of the summer revising works already translated by others and preparing his own translations as well. One of these texts was Gabriela Mistral's poem "Recado terrestre," in Spanish, a language of which he knew only a smattering. With the help of a dictionary, Beckett put together a fairly competent translation, which he refined with the assistance of several friends and scholars who knew Spanish well, among them Octavio Paz and Gerald Brenan.[19] He made some extra money when the poem, entitled in English "Message from the Earth," was published by Duthuit in the December issue of *transition*.[20]

By early fall, there was no promise of publication for any of his work. English publishers still rejected *Watt*, and each rejection found Beckett desultorily going over the manuscript to make small changes. Whenever he was asked for a short prose work by a magazine editor, he always suggested something from *Watt*. Finally, several pages were accepted by *Envoy*.[21] He hoped that this excerpt would be seen by someone who liked it enough to publish the entire novel, but this was not the case.

With nothing more positive happening, Beckett began to turn disturbingly inward. He fell into his old habit of sleeping all day and roaming through Paris at night. His life had been surprisingly normal, even ordered, for the past year, and now Suzanne was both worried and irritated at the disintegration of what passed for routine in his life. Visitors to the apartment grew accustomed to calling in the late afternoon or early evening. They found Beckett preparing his supper/breakfast of scrambled eggs while Suzanne sat sewing by the window, berating him for his idleness.[22]

The problem was that another book was forming inside him, and he was unconsciously resisting it. He didn't know if he could go through another such relentless assault on himself, or even if he wanted to try. Actually, the choice would not be his, for he had not yet developed to the point where he could consciously decide what he would write. Once a work formed in his mind, no other was possible until it had either been completed or else abandoned when a satisfactory ending failed to come.

In this way, he began to write *L'Innommable* (*The Unnamable*), the last of the trilogy. Originally, Beckett intended to call this novel *Mahood*,[23] a title which he kept throughout the first draft of the manuscript. Upon revision, however, he decided that Mahood would only be one of the names of the speaker, and the entire novel would be told by an unnamed being who sits in a jar with his hands on his knees, unable to move. His head is "a great smooth ball I carry on my shoulders, featureless, but for the eyes, of which only the sockets remain."[24] He has no nose, and no sex, for "why should I have a sex, who no longer have a nose?"[25] His clothing consists of "a few rags clinging to me here and there."[26]

This being relates a series of tales for more than one hundred pages—the first dozen or so in normal paragraphs, the last hundred gradually merging into one continuous sentence as periods are abandoned and only an occasional comma interrupts the spew of words.

The Unnamable has always been where he is, and if not, he does not remember where he was before. He has a certain amount of information about himself which he cannot help but interject from time to time—of God, his mother, and his birthplace, "Bally I forget what."[27] He thinks of the normally paragraphed section of the book as a preamble, and says:

> I hope this preamble will soon come to an end and the statement begin that will dispose of me. Unfortunately I am afraid, as always, of going on. For to go on means going from here, means finding me, losing me, vanishing and beginning again, a stranger first, then little by little the same as always . . .[28]

and later:

> All these Murphys, Molloys and Malones do not fool me. They have made me waste my time, suffer for nothing, speak of them when, in order to stop speaking, I should have spoken of me and me alone. But I just said I have spoken of me, am speaking of me. I don't care a curse what I just said. It is now I shall speak of me, for the first time. I thought I was right in enlisting these sufferers of my pains. I was wrong. . . . Let them be gone now, them and all the others, give me back the pains I lent them and vanish, from my life, my memory, my terrors and shames. There, now there is no one here by me . . .[29]

This novel is really about the obsessive-compulsive need for words, not about Mahood, Worm, Basil or any of the others who are named in its pages. "At the end of my work there's nothing but dust—the namable," Beckett has said. "In the last book, *L'Innommable*, there's complete disintegration. No 'I,' no 'have,' no 'being,' no nominative, no accusative, no verb. There's no way to go on."[30]

In eliminating narrators and saying that the unnamable voice who speaks is his, Beckett's prose dissolves into fragmentary snatches of terror and despair. The words gather horrendous momentum as they tumble out headlong, then stop abruptly as the speaker retreats from panic into wily caution. Gradually they begin again, perhaps with another tale, perhaps with the same, slowly at first, until the same compulsive need for expression overtakes caution and nothing will satisfy but more words; and these spill forth, half-realistic, half-incoherent, ominous undertones reflecting Jung's third Tavistock lecture, in which he stated:

> The fascination of unconscious contents gradually grows stronger and conscious control vanishes in proportion until finally the patient sinks into the unconscious altogether and becomes completely victimized by it.[31]

What is revealed ultimately is Beckett, no longer hiding behind the detritus of the previous heroes, not even enveloped in the rags, mouth and voice of a new one. It is a strangely disquieting novel. The pain felt by the Unnamable is passed on to the reader through the technically perfect construction of the monologue. Every word in this novel is simple and uncluttered. No one word or phrase calls attention to itself; no passage stands out as more lyrical, more emphatic, more vivid than any other; yet each word builds upon all the others until the total effect is that of one striking image after another.

> All my life, since we must call it so, there were three things, the inability to speak, the inability to be silent, and solitude, that's what I've had to make the best of.[32]

So the Unnamable says. This is what Beckett needs to confront in this novel, and finally, to resolve.

> Mahood . . . I invented him, him and so many others, and the places where they stayed, in order to speak, since I had to speak, without speaking of me, I couldn't speak of me, I was never told I had to speak of me, I invented my memories, not knowing what I was doing.[33]

Now he wants to kill these memories, these mythical inventions of his fertile mind:

> When I think of the time I've wasted with these bran-dips, beginning with Murphy, who wasn't even the first, when I had me, on the premises, within easy reach, tottering under my own skin and bones, real ones, rotting with solitude and neglect, till I doubted my own existence . . .[34]

But he still is not ready to face himself; someone else has to die first.

> I'm looking for my mother to kill her, I should have thought of that a bit earlier, before being born.[35]

When the pain and trauma of this relationship ends at last, only then will his compulsive need to dredge it up and write about it cease—or so he thought.

"Not having been born properly," a hint of the play to come, *All That Fall*, and an echo of Jung's Tavistock lecture, is a leitmotif in *The Unnamable*. There is something pathetic in the Unnamable's continuous insistence that he has not lived because he was never born, as if, were he able to return to his prebeginnings, he could right all the wrongs or settle the uncertainties of what has passed for a life.

Beckett sees *The Unnamable* as the logical continuation of *Molloy* and *Malone Dies,* and he is right to insist that the three be published as a trilogy. Yet, as Alfred Alvarez has noted, "However inexhaustible a mother lode for quarrying academics the book may be, for the ordinary, even devoted reader, *The Unnamable* gets perilously close to being the Unreadable."[36]

Beckett needed this work at this particular time in his life. It helped him to cope with his mother's impending death and the feelings of dependency, guilt and neglect that haunted his relationship with her. He needed to write this novel; the pain he suffered in doing so is obvious, even embarrassing. It is one of his two favorite works and like the other, *Endgame,* it is one which gives him enormous personal satisfaction. Unlike *Endgame,* which was written during a period of cerebral exteriorization, *The Unnamable* came from the depths of his being. Having written it, he felt purged, relieved; drained, but peaceful. However, having written it, he brought himself to the edge of the abyss he had flirted with throughout:

> All very fine, but the voice is failing, it's the first time, no, I've been through that, it has even stopped, many a time, that's how it will end again, I'll go silent, . . . then the voice will come back and I'll begin again.[37]

He had written himself into a corner from which there seemed to be no exit. For the first time in more than six years, he found himself unable to write. He was blocked.

In the early spring, *Waiting for Godot* was returned by another publisher, and Suzanne decided not to waste any more time, so she took it, along with *Éleuthéria,* to Roger Blin. Strindberg's *Ghost Sonata* was still playing at the Gaité-Montparnasse, so she left both plays there for Blin, who was so used to receiving hand-delivered, unplayable manuscripts that he usually glanced at the titles and a few pages and then left them at the box office to be claimed by their authors the same day. In this case he read the two plays more thoroughly because he had heard Beckett praised by Tristan Tzara and Max-Pol Fouchet, and he had great respect for the critical judgment of both men.[38] Tzara had mentioned Beckett several times as being a very good but unknown poet. Blin once heard Fouchet read several of Beckett's French poems on a radio broadcast and he remembers being struck by the complexity of thought expressed in the simplicity of the language.

He took the plays home with him, read them quickly and found himself surprised at how carefully he wanted to reread and study them. When he caught himself in the process of envisioning how they would look on stage, he knew that he wanted to produce them. He frankly did not understand *Waiting for Godot*, but he liked it. He decided he should probably begin with *Éleuthéria* because it was more traditional and, to his mind, easier to cope with. It reminded him of Pirandello, and he thought the staging would present interesting problems which, if resolved properly, would provide memorable theatrical impressions. "Besides," he remembers, "there were no parts for women in *Godot*, and at that time, I found this highly unusual, even unsatisfactory."[39] However, the more he thought about the two plays, the more he thought he should overcome his hesitation and concentrate on *Godot*:

> *Éleuthéria* had seventeen characters, a divided stage, elaborate props and complicated lighting. I was poor, I didn't have a penny. I couldn't think of anyone who owned a theater suitable for such a complicated production. I thought I'd be better off with the *Godot* because there were only four actors and they were bums. They could wear their own clothes if it came to that, and I wouldn't need anything but a spotlight and a bare branch for a tree.[40]

Thus, Blin's decision was made.

Suzanne returned to the theater several weeks later to meet Blin personally. He expressed cautious interest in the play, but warned her that his associates were not enthusiastic, and if it were ever produced, it would only be through his perseverance. This meant that she and Beckett would have to commit themselves to indefinite periods of waiting while Blin scoured Paris for money and a theater, with no guarantee of success.

Since this was the first positive reaction Suzanne had received since Jean Vilar's tentative appreciation of *Éleuthéria*, she was satisfied to leave both plays with Blin, even on such tenuous footing. Beckett, in the meantime, had gone to see *Ghost Sonata* several times and was impressed with the production. He agreed with Suzanne that Blin should keep both plays as long as he remained committed to them, because Blin had produced Strindberg in a manner faithful to the letter and the spirit of the playwright's intentions. He was sure that Blin would show his play the same respect. Also, the theater was half-empty each time he saw the *Ghost Sonata*, and according to Beckett, a theater empty of all but the most serious playgoers presented the ideal condition for a performance of his own work.

Beckett met Blin for the first time in the rue des Favorites in early summer, 1950, just before his annual visit to Dublin. Blin wanted to talk about *Godot* in detail because the run of *Ghost Sonata* was coming to an end, and he was anxious to produce *Godot* if he could find a theater.

Blin's first idea was to stage *Godot* as a circus, because his initial reading conjured up images of clowns. The dialogue, which he called "*oui-non,*" reminded him of circus one-liners, and he thought a circus would insure the necessary understanding his actors would need to bring to such a play. He told all this to Beckett, who although adamantly against such an idea, was unsure about how to say so tactfully. After so many years of trying to find someone interested in his work, and at last finding someone he respected, Beckett did not want to upset a still delicate relationship.

Gently, he steered the conversation away from circuses to the films of Charlie Chaplin and Buster Keaton. From circuses and silent films, the talk veered to Irish drama. Blin had appeared in a French production of *Playboy of the Western World* and the men discovered they shared a deep admiration for Synge's play. After several drinks, like two old cronies, they compared their digestive problems, which both agreed were the result of too much whiskey and bad eating habits. Then they talked about American music, which they decided was more bad than good, and finally, they returned to *Godot*.

At this point, it suddenly occurred to Blin that a circus

would not only cost more money than he could ever hope to scrape together, but would also distract from the pathos and humor of the action unfolding on the stage and what should be paramount in the audience's mind—the dialogue. He told Beckett he thought he would rather stage it with the utmost simplicity, and Beckett replied very quietly that he knew Blin was the man for *Godot*.

In talking of this initial meeting years later, both men agreed that they had ended it infused with a feeling of kinship very rare in their lives. For Blin, Beckett became "one of the two most important people in my life. He and Artaud divide my sentiments between them."[41] For Beckett it marked the beginning of one of his rare friendships.

With *Godot* seemingly off to production in the near future, Beckett went to Ireland in mid-June, 1950, taking the manuscript of *L'Innommable* with him to type. Letters from Frank and Jean since his last visit had not been encouraging, and there had been no change in his mother's steady deterioration. By the time he arrived in Foxrock, her condition was so serious that she had to be moved to the Merrion Nursing Home in Dublin. His days passed in an exhausting, crushing depression brought on by long hours at her bedside. His nights were spent walking and talking with Geoffrey Thompson, to whom he complained bitterly of the so-called God who would permit such suffering.[42] In the little free time remaining to him, he worked, in an effort to shut out the circumstances of his mother's imminent death, translating extracts from *Molloy* and *Malone meurt*.[43]

In the early evening of August 25, on Frank and Jean's eighteenth wedding anniversary, May Beckett died quietly. All day long Beckett had sat beside her bed, watching her labored breathing, until he could stand it no more. Then he went for a walk along the Grand Canal, and when he returned to the nursing home, sat outside for a while on a bench, shivering in the evening wind. When he looked up at her window, he saw the shade go down, the signal that she had died. He immortalized the scene in *Krapp's Last Tape*:

> . . . the house on the canal where mother lay a-dying, in the late autumn, after her long viduity. . . . There I sat, in the

biting wind, wishing she were gone. Hardly a soul, just a few regulars, nursemaids, infants, old men, dogs . . . the blind went down, one of those dirty brown roller affairs, . . . I happened to look up and there it was. All over and done with at last.[44]

There was a ceremony in Tullow Parish Church, which Beckett, his demeanor stony, sat through, seemingly oblivious. Then May Beckett was buried simply in Redfern Cemetery, Greystones, next to her husband, whom she had mourned for seventeen years.

Beckett remained in Dublin long enough to be sure that Frank would be able to settle their mother's affairs. Jean saw to the dismantling of the house, and Frank took care of the estate. Beckett went back to Paris with only the suitcase he had had with him on arrival. He had disposed of all his effects the year before, and he wanted nothing of his mother's. What Frank and Jean did not want was given away.[45] He was sure he would never set foot in Ireland again, and there was nothing from his past that he wanted to save. With this rejection of May's effects, he had finally, symbolically, managed to kill her.

With his return, Suzanne now had three novels to leave in publishers' offices. She heard that a young man who had been with de Gaulle's Free French in London had come back to Paris and bought the publishing house which had grown from a war-time clandestine press. Les Éditions de Minuit had been founded by Jean Bruller, who, as Vercors, inspired all France with his novel *Le Silence de la Mer*. Jerome Lindon, the new publisher, was rapidly becoming known as the guardian angel of the avant-garde. Minuit may have been the center of all the exciting new writing in France, but not enough excitement was being generated to sell books. By November, 1951, when Lindon first saw Beckett's manuscripts, Les Éditions de Minuit was flat broke, and Lindon was seriously concerned about how long he could keep the firm afloat.[46]

Beckett seems already to have had an underground reputation in France, for Lindon had heard of him through Robert Carlier, a mutual friend. Carlier thought it amusing that six other publishers had already refused the novels of the curious Irishman who wrote in French, and since Lindon's fortunes were at such a low ebb, he joked that someone as unusual as Beckett, whose novels were unsellable, might be just the person to save Minuit. His words were uncannily prophetic.

In late October, Suzanne deposited the manuscripts on Georges Lambrichs's desk at Minuit. He was then secretary to the reading committee, but he did nothing about the novels until Lindon, during a conversation, spied them. Remembering Carlier's words, Lindon picked up *Molloy* and took it home with him. That night he read through the entire novel, and was decidedly impressed. The next day he tried to telephone Beckett only to discover that the author had no phone. Lambrichs told him the manuscript had been left by a woman with a different surname, but he had misplaced the paper she gave him bearing her name and address. Lindon sent a message by *pneumatique* to Beckett's apartment asking him or "the young woman" to call on him the next day. Suzanne appeared at the appointed hour, expecting to be given all three manuscripts with a polite refusal, but instead she was met by Lindon himself, who wanted to talk about contracts. She was so flustered that she hardly heard a word he said, and requested another appointment after she had spoken to Beckett. She rushed back to the rue des Favorites, where the good news tumbled out incoherently, as she begged Beckett to go himself to Lindon's office the next day and make the formal arrangements.

Strangely, the word he had been waiting for all these years left him unable to respond, and he sat there dazed, immobile and emotionless as the news slowly penetrated.

Lindon's action forced Beckett to make a decision. As long as there had been no action, a multitude of possibilities existed. A decision symbolized commitment, and an end to possibility or intention.

Even with the writing of *The Unnamable*, Beckett had still not sorted out his true relationship to his writing. Just as he had reacted in pain and panic when his friends in Ireland innocently inquired about his writing and then teased him when he was unable to answer, so did he panic when Suzanne told him of Lindon's decision. Publication meant self-exposure, and he was not sure that he could stand up to it. He viewed publication as making him helpless, easy prey to all sorts of explications and false understandings. It rendered him at the mercy of others, when what he really wanted was to remain aloof and unknowable.

When Samuel Beckett refuses to discuss his writing, it is not a pose but a protection, a necessary self-defense that permits him to remain elusive. He can find mental stability and continued creativity only so long as he remains free of categorization and commitment. He needed publication for financial reasons, he wanted it for egotistical ones; but it induced problems as severe, albeit different, as his complicated relationship with his mother.

Much as he wanted publication, he was absolutely incapable of acting in his own interest, and he told Suzanne she would have to follow the negotiations through to the end. Unmoved by her pleas, he was steadfast in his refusal to see Lindon.

Suzanne was terrified of making any business arrangements without Beckett, but also, she was determined that this opportunity should not slip away because of his recalcitrance. She insisted that Toni Clerkx accompany her to Minuit the next day, when Lindon was to have the contracts ready. To put all the negotiations on his behalf out of his mind, Beckett, in the meantime, began to write again. These were the first of the short prose pieces he turned to during the next two years whenever he had spare time or when pressures in his life grew so intense that he needed a release and a respite. The sight of him calmly writing an occasional word or sentence drove the nervous Suzanne into a state of anxiety; nevertheless, she persevered in her meetings and negotiations with Lindon.

The delay in coming to terms was caused by Beckett's insistence that all three novels be published together or not at all. Lindon definitely wanted *Molloy*, and after some initial hesitation, agreed to take *Malone meurt*. Of *L'Innommable*, he was not quite sure; but finally, because he wanted the first two, he accepted the third. He agreed to publish all three with "all due speed, as soon as possible."[47]

On November 15, 1950, Suzanne returned the contracts which Beckett had signed, and the process of publication began at last. *Molloy* was scheduled for January, 1951, *Malone meurt* for several months later. However, there was not enough time for the printer to complete his work on such short notice; thus, *Molloy* appeared in March and *Malone meurt* the following October.

Suzanne finally persuaded Beckett to call upon Lindon in his tiny second-floor office above the boulevard St. Michel several weeks after printing was under way. Lindon remembers an extremely polite man, reserved and quiet, with none of the voluble gush of gratitude so many other writers poured upon him when he first agreed to take their work.

Afterward, Beckett went back to the rue des Favorites in deep misery. Suzanne feared he was upset by the terms of the contract she had negotiated, which only gave him twenty-five thousand old francs (about $36.80 or £16) in advance against royalties. Quite the contrary, Beckett assured her, Lindon was such a nice young man that he (Beckett) was sorry to be the instrument of his bankruptcy. He was convinced that *Molloy*, like all his other works, "would go out into the void and be heard from no more."[48]

All his affairs were improving: several days later, he heard from Roger Blin, who was almost certain *Godot* would go on in the Théâtre Noctambules as soon as the current run of Adamov's *Grande et Petite Manoeuvre* ended. At the same time, UNESCO, pleased with his work on the Goethe book, gave him more than one hundred poems written by thirty-five Mexican poets and compiled by Octavio Paz, who was then a young student in Paris, to translate for immediate publication. With May Beckett's estate still not settled, the money was a godsend, but the chore was almost insurmountable. His Spanish was little better than it had been before his translation of Mistral's poem, and since time was so pressing, he contacted "a friend fluent in Spanish,"[49] with whom he split the commission. The friend provided quick literal translations for him to work with, and Beckett spent the next month or so refining them and, as he managed to do with all his translations of poetry, making them uniquely his own. When he had finished, shortly after the beginning of the year, he took them to UNESCO officials, who insisted that someone fluent in Spanish other than Paz check them for accuracy. Beckett contacted Gerald Brenan, who with his wife, carefully read every word he had written. Brenan was astonished to find only one tiny, insignificant error in the entire manuscript.[50] Beckett kept silent and did not tell him he had been helped, but in gratitude dedicated the book to Brenan.

Beckett said later[51] that he "loathed" doing it and vowed to himself that he would do no more translations for the "inexhaustible cheese," as he called UNESCO, no matter how straitened his circumstances.[52]

The translations languished in various bureaucratic files until 1958, when Beckett had achieved considerable fame for his own work. Then they were published with Beckett's name featured prominently on the cover, even though Paz had compiled it and C. M. Bowra provided a foreword. Beckett was annoyed with what he considered a blatant attempt to cash in on his blossoming reputation, but typically, his strongest comment was to say that the affair was "disquieting."[53]

Still in all, as the year ended, his personal affairs looked promising. There were publications, commissions and the hope that Blin would find a theater for *Godot*. Beckett had a premonition that his fortunes were improving: "The Annis Terribilis begins well," was his terse New Year's message to his friends.[54]

CHAPTER EIGHTEEN

1951–53:

"NOW THAT WE ARE EMBARKED
ON A DIRTY BUSINESS . . ."

 "Now that we are embarked on a dirty business together, I think we can say 'tu' to each other," Beckett told Roger Blin as the plans for the production of *Waiting for Godot* ground slowly on.[1]

Negotiations for Théâtre Noctambule had fallen through. Blin turned to Jean-Marie Serreau, who planned to open Théâtre de Babylone a little later in the year and wanted either a masque or a political play for his first production. Blin admitted that *Godot* was neither, but assured Serreau that once he had read the play, he would not settle for another. At the same time, Blin sent a copy of the script to Georges Neveaux, the Minister for Arts and Letters, because he learned that the French government awarded playwrights small grants of 750,000 old francs (approximately $400) to help defray costs of the first production of new plays in the French language. By now three scripts of *Godot* were circulating. Serreau had one, Neveaux another, and the third was with Jerome Lindon, who told Beckett he would publish the play if he had not become bankrupt by the end of the year.[2]

Domestic concerns dominated much of the spring of 1951 for Beckett. Suzanne's mother was beginning to suffer the effects of age, and Suzanne spent much of her time going back and forth from Paris to Troyes. One of her sisters came to stay with them briefly, and though she was welcome, they were crowded in the tiny apartment. Beckett's cousins came back and forth from Dublin, and there was a vast, time-consuming amount of correspondence with Frank concerning their mother's affairs.[3]

The last vestiges of war seemed gone at last, and friends from Ireland and England, whom he had not seen since 1939, were in Paris on their holidays. With his advances, translation fees, some initial money from his mother's estate, and his own affairs in Ireland finally in order, he was in better financial shape than ever, but he was still not well enough situated to afford all the entertaining these visits engendered.

He was tired and befuddled by all the negotiations involved in bringing out a book and seeking to produce a play. Since the war, he had led a hermetic life, seeing few people, and then only when he chose to initiate meetings. To write, he needed a buffer between him and the everyday exigencies of life; from food to laundry to friendships, Suzanne protected him. When he had written, he needed someone to call attention to his work; Suzanne, overcoming her own reclusiveness, did it. Once the work had been accepted, however, he had no choice but to deal himself with production schedules, mechanical details and artistic considerations. He was even forced to sit for his photograph—Lindon insisted on having one for the jacket of *Malone meurt*—and in April, Beckett went to Giselle Freund, who had taken excellent photos of Joyce before the war. She posed him looking away from the camera, staring at the floor, because he was uncomfortable in any other position.[4] So many people coming into his life in such quick succession left him exhausted and confused. He needed a rest, and so did Suzanne.

Henri and Josette Hayden had just bought a charming old stone house an hour's drive to the east of Paris in the tiny village of Reuil-en-Brie. When Beckett and Suzanne visited, he knew he had found what he needed. The countryside in the department of Seine-et-Marne rolls gently down to the two rivers which give it its name, allowing the eye to see long vistas of seemingly flat spaces with only an occasional undulant hillock in the distance. It is lush with the grapes that become the fine wines lining the walls of hundreds of miles of underground caves just to the east at Epernay. It fulfilled all Beckett's wishes for land "green and flat, but not *too* green or *too* flat."[5] There were country lanes, so much like those he loved in Ireland, where he could once again take long, undisturbed walks. There was even an occasional *tabac* on the edge of the villages where he could pause in his walks to drink a solitary aperitif. Beckett and Suzanne managed to find a small house in Ussy-sur-Marne that could be rented on a year's lease. It was not really suitable, but it was available, they could afford it and they were desperate to have some place to flee from the pressures in Paris. They signed the lease in late spring, planning to use it as a base to look for something they liked better.

On June 7, 1951, Roger Blin received a letter from the Minister of Arts and Letters saying that *Waiting for Godot* had been brought to his attention and he would have a decision on the outcome of the request for funds sometime in the near future.[6] This seemed encouraging, and Beckett trudged over to the Théâtre de l'Odéon, where Blin was rehearsing another play and waiting to tell him the news. In a desultory way, they thrashed through the "ifs" and "buts" of the situation. It did not comfort either man, but each felt it helped to ward off the feeling of hopelessness it would have been so easy to lapse into without such conversations.[7]

For a few weeks Beckett agonized over continuing to leave the production entirely in Blin's hands. Blin was absolutely committed to the play and was working to convince others that it was indeed very good, but he had his own needs to meet and was constantly busy with other commitments. His interest in *Godot* depended on how much free time he had left from his paying work. Suzanne thought they should continue to support Blin's efforts, but try to do something on their own as well. For the rest of 1951, she took extra typescripts to more than thirty theater directors in and around Paris without success.[8] The play, a metaphor on waiting, now became a metaphor for Beckett's life.

The novels were having better luck. From the start, both *Molloy* and *Malone meurt* sold, if not brilliantly, with regularity.[9] In September, in advance of publication, *Les Temps*

Modernes printed a segment of *Malone meurt*, entitled "Quel Malheur . . ."[10] The novel itself appeared on October 8, in an edition of three thousand copies. The printer, a Catholic from Alsace, prudently omitted his name because he thought it was a pornographic book and did not want to be prosecuted.[11]

Both novels attracted considerable attention. In 1951, the year of publication, there were at least twenty-six reviews,[12] nearly all of them favorable. Some of the titles were prescient examples of how his writing would be tagged from the very beginning: *une épopée du non-sens," "une Chronique de la décomposition," "en avant vers nulle part,"* and (one of the earliest in this vein) *"héritier de Joyce, l'Irlandais Samuel Beckett a choisi la langue française."* Four long articles about the novels also appeared; once again the titles were indicative of criticism to come: *"Le Silence de Molloy," or "Samuel Beckett, l'humour et le néant";* again, the stress on the obvious influence of Joyce.

Beckett had been free of Joyce's shadow since 1939, but now their names would begin to be linked irrevocably. At first Beckett was pleased by the association, but as time passed, the constant, facile comparisons became a source of irritation. The nagging fear that he would never quite escape Joyce became more and more a reality as comparisons increased in number.

Lindon was delighted with the success of the two novels, and agreed to publish *Waiting for Godot* and *L'Innommable* as soon as possible. He also committed himself, sight unseen, to "all future work"[13] and expressed his desire to publish *Watt* as soon as it could be translated. This pleased Beckett enormously, who felt vindicated to know that "the old misery,"[14] as he had come to call *Watt,* had at last found a publisher.

In 1946, a disillusioned Routledge had sold world rights to *Murphy* to Bordas, Beckett's first French publisher. In late November, 1951, Bordas decided to relinquish the popular line in favor of textbook and business and professional publishing, and to sell the world rights to *Murphy,* as well as the unsold stock—all for the price of the paper on which the remaining copies were printed. Lindon bought the rights and thus became Beckett's only publisher, with control of the world rights to all of Beckett's publications. (Curiously, in 1956, when *Waiting for Godot* had made Beckett world-famous, Lindon received a letter from Routledge, the original publisher of *Murphy*, saying that since he published all Beckett's other work, Routledge assumed he would like to purchase the world rights from them. Routledge evidently had forgotten that they had sold those rights to Bordas in 1946. This was typical of the confused state of affairs surrounding the sudden publication of so much of Beckett's work; even his publishers were unsure of who controlled the rights to it.)[15]

So much activity required Beckett's attention that he wrote nothing during 1951 and had no new work in mind. His only concern was *Godot*. He veered between the suspicion that perhaps it had not found a theater because it was indeed the bad play he thought it all along, and the dogged determination that it was as good as anything else on the Paris stage. He decided to step in and take a more active role in bringing the play before an audience. It was one of the most important decisions of his life. In effect, it signaled the end of his career as a writer of prose and the beginning of his long involvement with drama. The interesting pastime he had turned to when his muse was slow in coming was about to move from avocation to vocation. The private Samuel Beckett was about to become public—but on his terms.

On January 29, 1952, the first real encouragement that *Godot* would ever be performed came in a letter to Blin from Georges Neveaux:

Dear Roger:
You are indeed right to want to play *En Attendant Godot*. It's an astonishing play.
Not necessary to tell you that I am strongly for you.[16]

Through Neveaux's support, Blin received the 750,000-franc grant. They needed little more. In jubilation, Blin and Beckett began to look for actors. Blin wanted to play Vladimir but Beckett wouldn't let him because he had envisioned Blin as Pozzo from the first. The other actors who were the first selected have long been forgotten. Throughout most of 1952, the production was scheduled for the Théâtre de Poche in

Montparnasse as soon as Chekhov's long-running *Uncle Vanya* ended, but when more than six months elapsed since their selection, all three actors quit and went on to other roles.[17] Blin began to search for replacements and contacted several actors with prominent reputations. The refusal of one was more or less consistent with all the others:

> I can't possibly play in this piece by Beckett. . . . It's amusing to imagine, but how can I possibly do it? Situations are hard and I must look for something that will certainly play longer. I know of absolutely no one who would want to play in such a farce. You won't make any money—the public won't come to see it.[18]

In February, 1952, in an effort to stir up interest in a production, part of the play was broadcast on French radio,[19] and it attracted a surprising amount of interest for a relatively unpublicized venture. The tiny studio was jammed with people who wanted to see the author as much as to hear the play. Beckett, as an Irishman who wrote in French, had become something of a curiosity in Paris. However, Beckett disappointed his audience by staying at home to hear it. Many in the studio left before the broadcast ended.[20]

There was no question that interest in Beckett's work was growing. About this time, for example, a friend of Henri Hayden's wanted to put together a small book with paintings by well-known artists and texts by important writers; when Hayden suggested Beckett, the friend was delighted because his name was being mentioned as "a new, important writer."[21] But however well he was being received in France, English-language publication eluded him. The American firm Devin-Adair compiled a book called *One Thousand Years of Irish Prose* and refused an excerpt of *Murphy* because Beckett was "not well enough known."[22]

Beckett still found himself unable to write more than an occasional paragraph, most of which were later collected in the thirteen *Textes pour rien* (*Texts for Nothing.*)[23] There were too many intrusions vying for his time in Paris. Suzanne's sister came from Tunis and stayed with them for a month; then Suzanne brought her mother to the flat for another month. There

were endless meetings with Blin and Lindon, he was still translating for Duthuit and suddenly there was another translation
for UNESCO. Although he had sworn never to take another, he
took this one, which he called "stupid, ill paid, and typically
rushed,"[24] because he thought he would need all the money he
could muster when and if *Godot* ever came off the page and
onto the stage.

He began to play tennis again in an effort to dissipate some
of the frustration and pressure of life in Paris. He met Pierre
Schneider for several sets but soon discovered that he was no
match for the younger man. Years of heavy smoking had cut his
lung capacity and his vision had worsened. He had to be content
with watching professional matches, getting his own exercise in
long walks around the city streets.[25] He began to drink heavily
in the Dôme, the Coupole, the Rotonde, and the Closerie des
Lilas, all places where he had met his friends before the war. He
was still able to drink without being recognized, but he felt the
need for more privacy, so he went to the Rosebud and the
Falstaff, two lesser-known bars off the boulevard du Montparnasse that stayed open through the night. When he was with
friends, he liked to dine at Les Îles Marquises, where he ate small
amounts of simple fish dishes and drank large quantities of the
house white wine. Bobino, the music hall on the rue de la Gaité,
was one of his favorite haunts. He would go alone when he
could not persuade anyone to accompany him, and he always
took visitors from Ireland there for what he considered a special
treat.[26] He still had a passion for movies, which Suzanne shared;
it was one of the few things they did together.

More and more, he depended on trips to the country to
provide him with the solitude he needed for serious work. He
and Suzanne had been going to Ussy as often as they could. For
a time, he even talked of moving there permanently and keeping
the flat on the rue des Favorites for the times when he would
have to stay overnight in Paris. He thought he would be able to
manage his affairs from the country very well, but Suzanne was
not so sure. She and other friends pointed out how much he
liked to sit in cafes until the early morning hours and the extreme difficulty of doing so in a tiny farming village. He recon-
sidered, and decided to keep Paris as his base, but to spend as

much time in the country as possible. He had found a plot of land that he liked, and with some of his share of the money from his mother's estate, he bought it. Ussy became a refuge whose sanctity no one dared violate. An invitation to Ussy became the test by which his friends determined who was closest to Beckett, for it seemed that only those with whom he could truly relax were invited to spend the day, but, with rare exceptions, never the night. Later, he used the income from *Godot* to pay for the property, and told everyone that it was "the house that *Godot* built."[27]

With a local contractor, he built a small house, which he described as "two rooms on a remote elevated field beyond Meaux, about thirty miles from Paris," and said he "hoped to live there in the future, watching the grass try to grow among the stones and pulverizing the pretty charlocks with weedone."[28]

Of all the plans he could have chosen for the house, Beckett deliberately picked the simplest and the ugliest. It looked like little more than a customs shed, with one large kitchen–living area and a smaller bedroom. When friends teased Beckett about the simplicity of his dwelling and asked why he had not erected a more bourgeois structure in keeping with his new affluence, he smiled and said "it suits me fine."[29]

Frank and Jean and their children were among the first to be invited to Ussy. When they came to Paris for a holiday, Beckett took them to see the house being built. Both Jean and Frank were avid gardeners, and they had many suggestions for plantings. Together Beckett and Frank cleared the land of rocks and put in a lawn. It was one of the most satisfying afternoons they had shared for years.[30] It was the first time Suzanne had met Jean and Frank, and though she spoke no English and they very little French, there was a spontaneous affection generated by the hard work. It was one of the last happy times Beckett spent with his brother.

When he returned to Paris in late September, 1952, Beckett found a letter from McGreevy asking him as a favor to look after one of the porters from the National Gallery and his friend, who were coming to Paris "to see the sights."[31] They were two simple Irish workingmen who had never been outside

Ireland before and were awestruck by the sophistication of Paris. They wanted to see burlesque shows and girlie reviews, to visit Pigalle and all the seamy places they had heard about in Ireland. Beckett dutifully led them from place to place, even including a Paris bordello in their itinerary. Their admiration for Beckett was unbounded when he shyly admitted that the madam was a good friend who kept several spare bedrooms for friends who had trouble finding suitable hotel accommodations, and that one was always available for his friends. When it came time for the two men to fly back to Ireland, Beckett earned their everlasting gratitude by suggesting that, because they seemed so uneasy about flying, they might like to visit an English-speaking priest who would hear their confession. The holiday was such a success that the porter and a series of his friends made a trip to Paris and a visit with Beckett an annual event. He always had time for them, and seemed to enjoy it as much as they. These men knew nothing of Samuel Beckett, author and playwright; to them he was simply "Sam," who matched them drink for drink and topped their stories with his own, which were usually more ribald. He liked them for their simplicity, for accepting him simply as a man, a companion, a "butty." They put their trust in him to take care of them, and he did so with what was probably the nearest thing to genuine affection he had shown for years. He allowed them to see a part of himself few others were permitted to see: his unguarded, spontaneous behavior, which left him somewhat bewildered and puzzled with himself once they had departed and he had resumed his literary habits and friendships.

Toward the end of November, it seemed as if *Godot* would be produced at last. The audience for *Uncle Vanya* was slowly dwindling, and Blin and his actors were invited to begin rehearsals in the Théâtre de Poche. Beckett wrote the news to Blin, who had gone to Brittany on holiday, telling him to "swim, talk, void yourself—what waits for you is terrible."[32]

The actor who was supposed to play Vladimir had no idea what to do with his role, and he kept asking Beckett who Vladimir was, what he meant, how he had been conceived. Beckett only shrugged his shoulders and said nothing, and the infuriated actor quit. He was followed in short order by the others, who were also bewildered. A third set of actors had to be found. Soon a larger problem confronted them: the Théâtre de Poche would not be available until well after the middle of 1953 because the director had changed his plans and could not fit *Godot* into the new schedule until then. Once more they searched for a theater, and found a manager willing to schedule *Godot* immediately in the small Théâtre de Port Chasseur. Unfortunately, the stage was very small, too small, in fact, for a tree. The voluble manager saw no reason why they had to have a tree and thought they were silly to insist on it. "After all, she was offering me a theater, she said, and I should be glad to get it, but I kept insisting I had to have a tree and she threw me out." Thus Blin recalled being literally tossed out on the street with the few props he had brought into the theater.[33]

Beckett was disappointed but philosophical. Lindon was planning to publish *Godot* in an edition of two thousand five hundred copies on November 17, a date originally chosen to coincide with the performance,[34] and Beckett thought publication would do much to insure production. No matter how many setbacks the play suffered, Beckett always found a reason to believe that the situation would improve. In this case, he was right. Jean-Marie Serreau, who had wanted to mount the play a year before, now offered the tiny Théâtre de Babylone. On November 2, with ceremonious flourish by Blin and Serreau and dispassionate agreement by Beckett, contracts were signed and the production was officially scheduled for the following January.

Roger Blin directed, and finally agreed reluctantly to play Pozzo. There was serious disagreement between Beckett and Blin over this, because Blin, who was slender and graceful, did not want to play the part of the gross, fat Pozzo. Blin had a strange and disturbing dream one night of how Lucky should look and speak, and in his dream it was his own face that stared madly back at him. He took this as a symbolic portent and argued as persuasively as he knew how, but Beckett was his most rigid and insistent and made Blin abandon his vision.[35]

Since they had little money, they were limited to approaching actors who did not command high salaries, or who were friends of Blin's. They were fortunate to secure Lucien Raimbourg for Vladimir and Pierre Latour for Estragon. Raimbourg was almost sixty, older than the other actors, and had had a hard life and a difficult time securing acting jobs. He kept very much to himself, usually bringing his meager dinner to the theater because he could not even afford to buy coffee in a cafe. He had a wonderful sunny disposition, however, and was beloved by everyone associated with the production. Latour was there only as a favor to Blin. He had the misinformation that the French government paid all actors' salaries for thirty performances in any new play, and so he signed a contract for only that number. When the play was successful, he stayed on, but to the end he swore that he never understood a word of it and only did what Blin told him to do.[36] Serge Lecointe was cast as the small boy. Several actors now forgotten formed a succession of Luckys before Jean Martin took the part.

From the first cast meeting until the dress rehearsal, Beckett played as important a role as his director. Every aspect came under his intense scrutiny, sometimes leading to serious clashes of will; but most of the time, aware of Blin's far superior knowledge of the mechanics of theater, Beckett deferred to him. Originally the play was to be staged in the round, so that Pozzo could make circles as he walked and talked, to enhance the idea of circularity in the play, i.e., that the end was the same as the beginning, and the repetition of the waiting would go on indefinitely. However, this seemed to express too concrete an idea for Beckett, and he insisted that circularity be suggested but not clearly apparent.

Blin saw Vladimir as a professor, wearing a morning coat and stiff collar, to complement Beckett's idea that he wear a top hat instead of a bowler. Beckett thought that the professorship should be suggested, not stated, so Vladimir was costumed in a long dark coat but his trousers were ordinary daytime apparel and had nothing to do with his jacket. Estragon was depicted as one who was always cold and he was instructed to huddle, hugging himself in his own arms, while wearing a short, nondescript black jacket.

Beckett envisioned Lucky as a porter, with the short gray jacket and black cap worn by workers in Paris railway stations.

For several weeks, this was how he was supposed to appear, until Blin's dream, in which Lucky was a surrealistic personage garbed in nineteenth-century valet livery. He saw Lucky as "functional yet ceremonious, all red and green with brass buttons and gold braid, with boots and baggy pants, heavily made-up, with exaggerated white face, red lips and harsh black lines around his eyes—like a clown in a way, but not exactly—more disturbing."[37]

With Pozzo, both men were in agreement from the beginning. They saw him as an English gentleman farmer, carrying a case of wine bottles, wearing a MacFarlane jacket, a beautiful necktie, bowler hat and gleaming leather riding boots.

The setting was determined by money—the lack of it. Again, Blin turned to his friends, and he asked Sergio Gerstein to be the stage designer. It was a fine title, but when Gerstein asked how much money he could spend, Blin replied, *"Pas un sous de merde."*[38] What Gerstein could not scrounge, Blin added, he was to steal.

"Every day became apocalypse"[39] in the Théâtre de Babylone. Avant-garde in the French sense, the Babylone originally had been a large shop, then was converted to hold 230 folding chairs in front of a small, difficultly angled stage. Gerstein set up his shop in the basement. Beckett walked in once, looked at the tin cans, bits of cloth and wires that were the makings of the set, and walked out, never to return. It was the stage itself that presented the most difficulty. To keep the audience from seeing everything backstage, it was necessary to construct a backdrop of heavy cloth, but the only material they had was needed for other things, so the entire backdrop was hand-sewn from left-over scraps of material.

The tree consisted of long coat-hanger wires covered with dark crepe paper; in the second act, bits of bright green paper were added to represent the leaves. The base was hidden in a discarded piece of foam rubber someone found on the street. With three large oil cans with light bulbs inside, hand "projectors" were created: two for the back of the theater and one at the rear of the stage to give the effect of the sun and the moon. Originally they were meant to be moved by a string tied to a piece of wood, which was supposed to make a sweeping arc, constant in space and angle of movement, but this technique made the projected sun and moon differ in size as the arc changed. They had to recruit three people to move the cans manually, and though the movements were often jerky, at least they made the projection consistent in size. The first critics and scholars who saw the play and wrote about it were quick to assume the three projectors symbolized the Trinity, but in actuality, they represented the greatest amount of light that could be generated with such primitive equipment. The first act was done almost completely in semiobscurity, with lighting techniques of the most rudimentary kind reserved for the second.

When the technical aspects of the production seemed under control, rehearsals began. From the beginning there were problems of attitude, interpretation and understanding. Blin liked to rehearse with people coming and going around him. He was used to open sets, where friends could walk in or out as they pleased. Beckett wanted a closed set and gave orders that no one was to be allowed into the theater unless connected with the production. Blin persuaded him that it would be good publicity to have journalists drop in from time to time, and before long there were always visitors.

Blin never had a definite schedule in mind, but would come into the theater ready to rehearse whatever lines interested him most at that particular moment. Then he would spend several hours making the actors move their bodies and voices until he brought them to the point where they naturally conveyed the expression and movement he wanted. He seemed to be distracted and vague, to drift off into mental reaches known only to himself, but this was the only method which worked for him.

Beckett, on the other hand, wanted a rigid rehearsal schedule to be written out, from which there would be no deviation. When he finally accepted the fact that he could not force Blin to set one up, he took to chain-smoking and pacing at the back of the theater, alarmed as Blin spent whole days drilling on four or five lines. He was genuinely anguished as Latour and Raimbourg frequently moved from a scene in the first act to one in the second because the dialogue was so similar that it confused them. Beckett was wild, especially when the actor who was to play Lucky was so hopelessly befuddled by his part that he had to be dismissed three weeks before the opening when it became apparent he would never memorize his lines in time.

Blin turned to his good friend, Jean Martin, who took the part only because he was between engagements and did not expect *Godot* to last long enough to interfere with his next commitment. Beckett took Martin aside and demonstrated how he wanted Lucky to be played, complete with stammering and stuttering. Martin went to a physician friend and described the movements Beckett wanted. The doctor immediately told Martin that someone who spoke and acted as Lucky did would probably be a victim of Parkinson's disease. That evening in the theater, Martin told Beckett, who said "yes, of course." He mentioned briefly that his mother had had Parkinson's, but quickly moved on to another subject.[40] For Martin, Beckett during rehearsals was "demanding, always demanding." For an actor such as Martin, for whom intellectual understanding of the role was absolutely necessary, working with Beckett presented almost insurmountable problems. "Beckett does not want his actors to act," Martin said. "He wants them to do only what he tells them. When they try to act, he becomes very angry."

Lucien Raimbourg was exactly the opposite of Martin, and for this reason, he was the actor with whom Beckett was most comfortable. Because he didn't understand the play, he agreeably did everything Beckett wanted him to do, down to the last gesture. Raimbourg often tried to cheer up Martin by telling him not to bother searching for "any deeper meaning."

"Look Jean," he implored, "this play is simple! So simple a child could read every word of it. How can you not understand such language!"[41]

Raimbourg's brief statement is a succinct dramatization of what Beckett found so attractive about his approach to acting: he was an actor who simply did what the director (in this case, the author) told him to do, whereas Blin or Martin, who were always thinking, trying to bring their own interpretation to the character, to develop and grow with it, were a constant threat for Beckett because he could not control them.

Beckett's presence at every rehearsal gradually made everyone very nervous. Each day upon his arrival in the theater, they greeted him as a solid phalanx of doubts and questions. All eyes were on him, but he looked in panic toward the distant stage, as if he were trying to remove himself from the actors and their problems.

Blin, too, proved difficult to work with, for he began with perceptions so fine and subtle they were often difficult for the actors to fathom. As time went on, it became a matter of blind trust—the actors toward Blin, and Blin toward Beckett. Often, rehearsals proceeded through trial and error. For example, Blin wanted the play to open with Vladimir and Estragon huddled together and trembling. He had seen two monkeys in the zoo outside Paris one afternoon in just such a position and something about their attitude reminded him of *Godot*. They seemed to him to convey an atmosphere of expectation, hesitation and nameless fear. When he told this to Beckett, he expected either agreement or correction of an unwarranted assumption. Instead Beckett only smiled and said nothing. As rehearsals limped along, Blin gradually perceived that his idea was not what Beckett wanted, and was forced to come to another interpretation on his own; even then, he had to decipher Beckett's opinion from surreptitious glances and guarded comments.

Part of Beckett's unwillingness to correct, criticize or concur was courtesy, an unwillingness to malign sincere effort; but mostly, it was his awareness of his lack of knowledge of theater. He was hesitant to question something which he was afraid might have been done because of dramatic necessity, but from the very first there were signs of the dogmatic inflexibility and rigid insistence on his own vision which characterized his later productions.

Ultimately, it was the text which concerned him and which caused the most comment and dissension. There is an old saying in France that "each Frenchman thinks he is sole arbiter of his language." Every line of the play inspired conflict, as each actor insisted that Beckett—after all, still a foreigner—could not possibly have written such dialogue in correct French. Beckett insisted on the accuracy of what he had written and, sure enough, when experts were consulted, he was proven right. It amazed everyone.[42]

Throughout the shaping of the final version, Beckett was

concerned to move away from concrete realities into abstraction. For example, in the original text the young boy was supposed to bring a letter from Godot to Vladimir and Estragon. Even before rehearsals began, Beckett removed these passages because they presented not the idea of Godot, but Godot himself, which he felt localized the play into concrete exactitude. Well into rehearsals, Vladimir and Estragon rehearsed an exchange which included:

Estragon: *avec Bim*
Vladimir: *avec Bom, les comiques staliniens.*[43]

The passage was one Beckett liked, as it kept the dialogue moving between them like a skillful juggler's balls. He kept it in the text until quite far along in rehearsal, and it was in the first printing of the book, but was subsequently removed. He finally decided that remarks about Stalin destroyed the timelessness of the rest of the dialogue.

In another instance, a passage which worked beautifully in the original production was later omitted from the definitive French version but retained in the English. Vladimir and Estragon, who have been trading insults,[44] can find no word worse than Estragon's accusation, "Crritic!"[45] In the script, Beckett had written the curt phrase *échange d'injures* (they trade insults). Blin and the actors were startled by Beckett's shorthand in this instance, since all his other stage directions had been methodical and meticulous.

"We needed strong swear words, and so I wrote them down," Blin recalls. "We came up with *ordure* (fertilizer), *fumier* (shit), *curé* (priest)—they were all good, but the one which worked best to make Vladimir shut up was *architecte*. It seemed to us the worst insult that one could ever say."[46]

Jean Martin heard the ultimate insult in Brussels, where one of two taxi drivers swearing at each other, used "architecte" to win the verbal battle. When Martin told this anecdote at rehearsal, there were a number of people watching, friends of Beckett as well as of the actors. Someone (now forgotten) said architect was perfect—it conveyed the meaning of the entire play as well as of this particular scene, it was the anarchistic swearword par excellence, because the play was a tract against architecture, cities, organization of any kind. Martin interrupted the man's effusions to insist that the word meant nothing more than a well-known curse in Brussels, where tenements had been torn down more than sixty years previously to make way for a new Palais de Justice, causing the slum-dwellers to riot and, in their frustration, to blame the architects for the loss of their homes.

Throughout the exchange, Beckett sat in quiet horror, his eyes growing larger behind his round-rimmed glasess, nervously puffing on a cigarette as if this were the first time he was aware of the multiplicity of meanings his simple words would hence-forth inspire. To Blin, he confided quietly that they would try "*architecte*," but he did not think it would work. The lines were left in for the duration of the run, but when he rewrote the play, Beckett removed them. In the English version, the exchange was not deleted, but the word "architect" would have been meaning-less, so it was changed to "crritic!"—one of Beckett's favorite curses.

The problem of people coming into rehearsals became acute as they drew nearer to opening night, for word had gotten around Paris of the strange new play. At dress rehearsals, not only were journalists and friends there, but some "cafe society," or "beautiful people" had come by as well, bringing several fash-ion designers in their entourage. In the final scene, when Estragon's pants fell down, one of the designers began to giggle. As Latour proceeded with touching dignity to the end of the play, her giggles turned to shrill, high-pitched laughter. When the curtain fell, Latour rushed to Blin, furious, and swore he would not allow his pants to fall again. It had been a point of contention throughout rehearsals because Latour thought it made him seem ridiculous and he didn't want to do it. He was secretly ashamed to be taking part in the play in the first place, and he thought it was insulting to be required to drop his trou-sers on the stage. It was only through the patient persistence of Beckett and Blin that he had finally agreed to do it, but after the woman's outburst, he swore he would not let it happen again. Blin tried to talk to him, but grew angry and had to leave before he completely lost his temper. Then Beckett stepped in and spoke quietly for a long while. Finally Blin returned and he and

Beckett together persuaded Latour that it was absolutely necessary, and Latour reluctantly agreed to let his trousers fall all the way to the floor.

Pleased that the last troublesome incident had been resolved, Beckett left Paris for Ussy. He had waited for this moment for four years, but now that it had arrived, he could not face it. As with his novels, he could not bear to regard with objectivity what he had produced in a burst of unconscious creativity. He preferred to face his opening night jitters in the privacy of Ussy. Suzanne would attend the performance and tell him about it in every detail. Her sharp eye and excellent memory would record every nuance of the production, and that would be enough for him.

"Don't hold it against me for having stayed away," he wrote to Blin. "I couldn't take any more."[47]

From that moment on, avoiding first nights has become a custom he scrupulously observes. Although he has wandered in from time to time during the run of a play, sometimes sitting in the back of the theater unnoticed throughout the entire performance, he has never seen a first night.

He was horrified to learn from Suzanne the day after the first performance that Latour had only dropped his trousers as far as his hips, thus undercutting the effectiveness of Vladimir's admonition that he should raise them. From Ussy, he wrote hurriedly to Blin:

> One thing troubles me, the pants of Estragon. I naturally asked Suzanne if it fell well, and she told me that he keeps them half on. He mustn't. He absolutely mustn't. It doesn't suit the circumstances. He really doesn't have the mind for that then. He doesn't even realize that they're fallen. As for the laughter, which could greet their complete fall, there is nothing to object to in the great gift of this touching final tableau; it would be of the same order as the preceding scenes. The spirit of the play, to the extent to which it has one, is that nothing is more grotesque than the tragic. One must express it up to the end, and especially at the end. I have a lot of other reasons why this action should not be tampered with but I will spare you them. Just be good enough to reestablish it as it is in the text and as we always foresaw it during rehearsals. And that the pants fall

completely around the ankles. That might seem stupid to you but for me it's capital.[48]

Latour complied, and from the second performance his pants fell to his ankles exactly as Beckett intended.

On opening night the little Théâtre de Babylone was surprisingly full. Word had spread through the Left Bank literati that it was "an experience not to be missed"—this usually said in an attitude of conveying great knowledge while actually masking bewilderment as to what exactly the "experience" represented. Before the theater opened, people were lined up outside waiting to get in, and everyone, from the director to the technicians and ushers, was pressed into service, running to the cafe next door to get extra chairs.[49]

The critics who were there recognized that they had just seen something new and exciting in theater. Sylvain Zegel, in the first review of the play[50] said: "They [the audience] understood at least this much: Paris had just recognized in Samuel Beckett one of today's best playwrights." Jean Anouilh called it "Pascal's *Pensées* as played by the Fratellini Clowns."[51] Armand Salacrou said: "We were waiting for this play of our time. . . . An author has appeared who has taken us by the hand to lead us into his universe."[52]

Martin Esslin wrote succinctly of the attitude toward *Godot* that most Parisians held after the first production:

> Beckett first aroused attention by a *succès de scandale*. Whenever *Waiting for Godot* opened after its first night in Paris . . . it became the topic of conversation. Was it not an outrage that people could be asked to come and see a play that could not be anything but a hoax, a play in which nothing whatever happened! People went to see the play just to be able to see that scandalous impertinence with their own eyes and to be in a position to say at the next party that they had actually been the victims of that outrage.[53]

Suddenly, at the age of forty-seven, Samuel Beckett found himself famous. The critical acclaim which had eluded him all those years was now his, but most of it was puzzled, questioning, sometimes sarcastic. Like many who receive something eagerly sought and hitherto elusive, he found the sudden fame almost frightening. He chose to secrete himself in Ussy, hiding from his well-wishers. Suzanne coped with the congratulations, requests for interviews and demands for the author. He ignored the pleas of Roger Blin, who was besieged by a public demanding to know, "What does it mean!" There was no affectation in his seclusion, no truculence in his unwillingness once again to do the *service de presse*. He knew that he was not abiding by all the tenets governing the expected behavior of successful writers, and he worried about it, but he simply could not allow this invasion of his privacy. He had spent all his life hiding from revelation. The closest he had come to self-revelation had been in his novels, and it had brought him to a complete creative dead end. His friends and associates pleaded with him to give interviews to at least a few sympathetic journalists, and to come back to Paris and allow himself to be seen at the theater, but he could not. He stayed in Ussy and contented himself with Suzanne's detailed reports and did not return to Paris until January 19, two weeks after the first performance.

He had decided that the press and the public would simply have to take him as he was, on his terms. From the first performance of *Godot*, his life was no longer totally under his control, but he was determined to surrender only those parts of it which did not matter to him. From then on, Joyce's three-pronged weapon of "silence, exile and cunning" took on a new and important meaning for his life.

CHAPTER NINETEEN

1953–54:

"I CAN'T GO ON AND I CAN'T GET BACK"

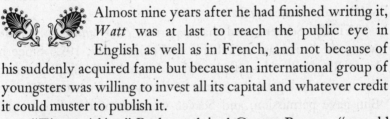 Almost nine years after he had finished writing it, *Watt* was at last to reach the public eye in English as well as in French, and not because of his suddenly acquired fame but because an international group of youngsters was willing to invest all its capital and whatever credit it could muster to publish it.

"*Tiens toi bien*," Beckett advised George Reavey, "our old misery, *Watt* [is due out] with the Merlin Juveniles here in Paris who are beginning a publishing business."[1]

Like so many other events in Beckett's life, the publication of *Watt* occurred in a roundabout way. In the winter of 1951, a young American named Richard Seaver saw a copy of *Molloy* in the window of Éditions de Minuit and bought it. He read it quickly and was "overwhelmed."[2] Seaver was an editor of the small literary quarterly *Merlin*, which had been founded the previous year by Jane Lougee, an American banker's daughter, and Alexander Trocchi, an Italian-Scots-Englishman, ostensibly for writing in English but also as a vehicle for their own writings. Besides Seaver, Trocchi and Lougee, the staff consisted of the English poets Christopher Logue and Austryn Wainhouse, and the South African writer Patrick Bowles. From time to time, they were joined by others, among them the American novelist Iris Owens, then writing under the name of Harriet Daimler. The group had more enthusiasm than money and operated

Merlin with a youthful zeal and sense of mission unmatched by any other comparable literary venture before or after the war.

As soon as Seaver read *Molloy*, he wanted to know something about the author, listed on the jacket cover as "an Irishman who writes in French." He went back to Minuit, bought *Malone meurt*, and read it with the same enthusiasm. He wanted very much to publish Beckett in *Merlin*.

The first step in acquiring a manuscript was to get in touch with Beckett, but Seaver discovered that although Beckett had quite an underground reputation, very few people knew more about him than the name of his publisher and that he lived "somewhere on the southern outskirts of Paris." Seaver sent several letters to Beckett in care of Lindon, but they were never answered. Beckett was apparently wary of such requests because he had received several shady proposals in this manner after the publication of the novels.

Finally Seaver heard that a portion of *Waiting for Godot* was to be broadcast on ORTF on February 17, 1952. Since he knew Roger Blin, he telephoned and asked if he might come to the studio during the broadcast in the hope of meeting Beckett. Blin gave permission, and Seaver was one of the disappointed few who stayed the entire evening, waiting for Beckett.

Several weeks later, Seaver was in his room when someone knocked at the door. He opened it to find a very tall man peering myopically at him through round-rimmed glasses. A bundle of manuscript bound up in a makeshift hopsacking cover was thrust into his arms, as the man, without a word, turned abruptly and plunged down the stairs through the gloom and clutter of the antiques-cum-junk in the shop below. When Seaver removed the hopsacking, he found the entire manuscript of *Watt*.

He read through it in the next few days and liked it as much as he had the other novels. Now, instead of wanting a short work for the magazine, he wanted the magazine to commit itself to publishing the entire novel. This decision was made at a time when the magazine was in serious financial difficulty, and was also under the scrutiny of the French government, which was threatening to make *Merlin* cease publication because foreigners were required to have a French partner, and *Merlin* had none, someone supposedly responsible should the foreigners abscond with unpaid debts. Austryn Wainhouse came to their rescue by introducing the *Merlin* group to Maurice Girodias, who published novels under the imprint of Olympia Press. Girodias, whose father, Jack Kahane, had asked Beckett to translate the Marquis de Sade in 1938, agreed to take the legal responsibility for *Merlin* in exchange for the editors' agreement to write books of light and serious pornography for his press, and to accept other translating commissions. The agreement was mutually satisfactory and the deal was concluded. Thus *Watt* was sold "by mistake to someone who thought he had bought another dirty book and did not bother to read it."[3]

The *Merlin* editors arranged for Beckett to meet Girodias to discuss the venture. With the exception of Trocchi, they were all much shorter than Beckett and at least twenty years younger. They surrounded him, bouncy and exuberant, while he loomed above them like a short-haired Elizabethan cavalier in a fur-collared windbreaker that framed his angular face like a ruff. As they walked, he turned from side to side as if bewildered by the chattering and confusion below his shoulders.[4]

When they arrived at the room Girodias used for a warehouse behind the bookstore at 13 rue Jacob, where Olympia Press had its offices, Beckett became withdrawn in the face of the enthusiasm of his youthful admirers.

"It was one of those absurd meetings," Girodias recalled, "where there was nothing you could say or do to get Beckett to enter into any conversation, to utter an opinion or to make any statement. We went ahead with the book because of the *Merlin* enthusiasm. By then I had read it, and I knew we had no hope of selling the book to tourists—they were only interested in porno. We printed two thousand copies and sold most of them over a five-year period, but it never failed to amaze Beckett whenever I told him one had been sold."[5]

Beckett's initial reluctance to contribute anything to the discussion probably stemmed from his reluctance to commit the book to Girodias. He had refused the commission from Girodias's father at a time when he was desperate for money because he did not want his name associated with any publishing venture the least bit immoral or unsavory. Now, after all the years of waiting for *Watt* to find a publisher and the unwavering belief he had had in it during that time, he was concerned to have it finally appear under the imprint of a publishing firm that commissioned young writers to produce pornography on demand and which was now beginning to publish Terry Southern and William Burroughs, American writers whose initial reputations were based on Paris-born pornography.

Watt was to appear under the joint imprint of Collection Merlin–Olympia Press, and he hoped this would mitigate the circumstances of publication. Also, to have *Watt* come out in English meant that American and English publishers would quite likely be interested enough to buy the rights from Girodias and print it in those two countries under respectable imprints. In their few meetings, Beckett made it very clear that this was his ambition, with what Girodias characterized as "that great vague blue stare and long silence."[6] For Girodias, with his other writers, it was a case of defending every publication to the censors; with Beckett it was simply putting the book in print in English so that another publisher could buy it.

The actual process of printing *Watt* was quick because Beckett would not discuss any change, nor did his editors venture to suggest one. Girodias found the song of the frogs disturbing because it called for painstaking, exact layout, as well as the song Watt sings at the end of the novel. Beckett insisted on retaining them even though it cost a significant sum for extra printing charges. Special blocks had to be made for both pages, and these caused the only "editorial problem" Girodias ever had with *Watt*. Shortly after the book was printed, the offices of Olympia Press were raided by a French vice squad in search of incriminating evidence for a pornography suit. They discovered the printing blocks and with enormous consternation and confusion, held them up to mirrors, trying to decipher what they were convinced was a pornographic code. They seized the plates as evidence for the prosecution.

In Ireland the novel was banned as soon as it appeared.[7] Beckett wondered if the publisher's imprint was sufficient to invoke this judgment from the Irish censors, or if they had actually managed to read the novel. He was neither surprised nor disappointed by their action.[8]

Little was written about *Watt*, probably because *Waiting for Godot* consumed the interest of writers and reviewers and overshadowed all his other works. Seaver himself wrote a review,[9] and the only other mention came in a *Spectator* review by Anthony Hartley that dealt with all his novels, from *Murphy* to the trilogy.[10] But it was *out*, and that was all that mattered to Beckett.

Unfortunately, when he tried to go on to other things, nothing much came but the snatches of prose he called the *Textes pour rien* when they were collected and published in 1955. He was in the midst of the "celebrated impasse"[11] which, in prose, lasted until he wrote *Comment c'est* (*How It Is*) in 1960. *L'Innommable* had brought him temporarily to the end of the kind of expression that required the probing of his inner torments. He no longer felt his mother's dour disapproval lurking in his unconscious, affecting his life and relationships, and with this powerful invisible obstacle removed, the need to continue to write such prose was not as overwhelming.

He was worried about his inability to write, and told McGreevy, in one of the rare letters written with the old unguardedness, "I feel very tired and stupid, more and more so, in spite of my often resting in the country, and I feel more and more that I shall perhaps never be able to write anything else . . . I can't go on and I can't get back. Perhaps another play someday."[12]

Perhaps if he had had the time to concentrate, an entirely new sort of writing might have emerged, something moving from *Godot* back to a more humane recording of the human condition, but in actual fact, his life was so busy that he simply had no time to write.

His teeth had become so painful that he reluctantly consented to have most of them pulled and replaced by false ones. As soon as he had finished his treatments, Suzanne discovered that she too required massive dental care, and they were quite occupied ministering to each other's physical needs.

Waiting for Godot had been scheduled for simultaneous performances in eight German cities in the fall, and he found himself busy with German actors, directors and producers who felt that a meeting with the author would insure that their performance became the definitive German one. He told them all to "go easy on the symbols—and the clowning."[13] A performance was also scheduled for Geneva, and Beckett was invited to be a guest, with all expenses paid—an honor he refused because acceptance would have put him at their disposal and meant that he would have to attend parties and performances and give interviews, which he could not abide.

All of the German companies had invited Beckett to be their guest, but none had suggested paying his way, which miffed him. However, the thought of seeing Germany once again intrigued him and he was tentatively planning to go with Blin for a tour of several productions, but "under my own steam, and . . . free to hide . . . vague dreams which will probably come to nothing through indolence and dread of society and discussion."[14]

Blin was in the south of France with Jean Martin to prepare for a tour of the provinces with *Godot,* and Beckett stayed on in Paris surrounded by the admirers the play had generated and by his boosters at *Merlin.*

The author of the curious play which sparked fistfights in the bistros and verbal repartee in the drawing rooms was now in great demand. Invitations to dinners and parties poured in, but he accepted few of them. He saw old friends, like Philippe Soupault, and went to the homes of new ones, such as Madeleine Renaud and Jean-Louis Barrault,[15] but for the most part, he refused everything discreetly. Like all newsworthy occurrences, the success of *Godot* and the fame it brought stirred old friends, some of whom he had not seen or written to for years, to write to offer congratulations. He has always been diligent about his correspondence, refusing secretarial help and replying promptly to letters;[16] now his burgeoning professional and personal correspondence took up a great part of each day. Lindon begged Beckett to allow someone at Minuit to assist him, but Beckett seemed horrified at the thought of a stranger peering into his life and continued to reply himself.[17] Also, increasing numbers of friends from England and Ireland came through Paris on holiday, and though he wanted to see most of them, their visits made inordinate demands on his time.

There were daily requests for manuscripts from other

countries; several American periodicals and one or two publishing firms wrote polite letters asking for an option to buy any new work in English, but he was suspicious of their sudden interest and piqued by their previous disdain. "Don't feel like trusting the Americans with anything," he wrote to Reavey, who was living in New York and anxious to resume his old role as Beckett's agent.[18]

Botteghe Oscure wanted a short piece, but he had once had an unpleasant contretemps with the editor, Princess Marguerite Caetani, and he refused sharply. It was difficult for him to control his churlishness when publishers contacted him. The sting of repeated rejections had wounded, deeper than even he had thought, and his response to their polite, sometimes obsequious requests, was to lash back and refuse them all. This probably was why he selected publishers in the United States and England whose firms were new, to whom he had never submitted anything, and who had therefore never been in a position to reject him.[19]

Barney Rosset wanted to introduce Americans to the newest and most exciting writings in Europe. Beckett was one of the first authors he signed for Grove Press. Ionesco and Genêt soon followed, and before long, most of the new French novelists published by Lindon in France were under contract to Rosset in America. Beckett took an instant liking to Rosset, partly because of his fervent commitment to publish unusual and difficult manuscripts, and partly because Rosset shared Beckett's penchant for late night rambles from one Montparnasse bar to another. One of their first meetings, ostensibly for a brief drink and business chat, was a nonstop talk and drink session that went on through the night.

"A strange man, indeed," Rosset wrote to his editors in New York after his first few meetings with Beckett.[20] Here was an author unlike any Rosset had ever met before, one who cared nothing for personal publicity or sycophantic gestures, but who was rigidly insistent on scrupulous attention to and admiration for his writing. "Beckett will be the death of us all, mark my word,"[21] Rosset wrote, when he first witnessed this side of Beckett.

Beckett had spent the summer translating *Godot* himself.

He was not satisfied with it and wanted to spend at least six months to a year on revisions before it was printed in English. Rosset wanted to publish it as soon as possible and had commissioned someone from his own firm to prepare a tentative translation in the hopes of persuading Beckett to allow Grove Press to move swiftly. Beckett quietly insisted that he would get on with the translation in his own good time. Promises of large sales and immediate American production did not sway him. He wanted to control the manuscript.

In the meantime, he had been meeting with Patrick Bowles and Richard Seaver, who both volunteered to help translate if Beckett wanted to use the time to write something new. Seaver had begun to work on *La Fin* (*The End*) shortly before Bowles agreed to do *Molloy*.

In what he considers the understatement of his professional career, Seaver called translating *La Fin* "hard."[22] Beckett's French is deceptive because it appears so simple, and the difficulty arises in translation because it is at the same time so personal that it is hard to convey in English. Each day, Beckett and Seaver would meet around noon at La Coupole to go over the translation. They had worked at least five hours daily for a week, when to Seaver's astonishment, he discovered they had only gone through four or five pages:

> Every word, every phrase, was gone over with meticulous care. Sam is the most polite as well as the nicest of men, so that whenever a word had to be changed, he prefaced it with how much he liked what I had done, "but . . . " or else he would say of his own French, "That's impossible, it can't be translated," as if what he had written wasn't any good, as if he were "putting down" his own original. What we ended up with was not a translation but a complete redoing of the original. And yet, even though it was completely different, he was totally faithful to the French. It was a completely new creation. I could not have taken the liberties that he did. I had originally approached translating for him as a service, and the only real benefit was that I hurried him up. Otherwise he would have agonized over it.[23]

With *Molloy*, the procedure was somewhat different. Beckett asked Bowles to complete an entire draft before showing it to him. Then he planned to check what Bowles had done, and to incorporate his own emendations. Bowles wrote of the work some years later:

> From the outset he stressed that it shouldn't be merely "translated"; we should write a new book in the new language. For with the transposition of speech occurs a transposition of thought, and even at times, of action. "You wouldn't say that in English, you'd say something else."[24]

When Bowles had finished his text, Beckett worried that it would be too un-American for Rosset because of the "rhythm and atmosphere" of the text. There was some question by both men as to whether Beckett should change the expressions most incomprehensible. ("Skivvy" and "cutty" were two he particularly worried about and finally eliminated in the English edition.)[25] When Rosset said he found some of Beckett's suggested changes to more American phrasing "curiously unenlightening," Beckett decided not to pander to public taste but to retain all the "English-isms" or more appropriately, the "Irish-isms."[26]

In his translation of *Waiting for Godot*, Beckett struggled to retain the French atmosphere as much as possible, so that he delegated all the English names and place names to Lucky, whose own name, he thought, suggested such a correlation.[27]

Beckett, in working with translators, even those as dedicated as Seaver and Bowles, soon realized that it created as much work as if he had done the translation himself. He also discovered that working with a translator diminished the amount of control he could exert, since his unfailing courtesy made it difficult for him to disagree with his translators' work. However, his hovering over and obsession with the text overcame his politeness; he would lunge suddenly into a convulsed babble of explanations and apologies as he corrected it to conform with his wishes. In the end, he decided the extra agony of this confrontation with another creative ego was something he could spare himself, and from that point on, he did his own translation.[28]

In September, 1953, Roger Blin mounted a second production of *Waiting for Godot* with the original cast (except for Lucien Raimbourg), again at the Théâtre de Babylone, to satisfy curious Parisians who had missed the much-talked-about first engagement. It was a brief run, which then went on to tour through France, Switzerland, Italy and Germany.

Beckett was tired and jumpy from daily rehearsals which began in the early afternoon, lasted till well after midnight and continued until the opening performance. He was more sure of himself with what he called "*Godot*—second series," and relied less on Blin's advice and trusted his own notions of what was best for the play. At the same time, he was meeting Bowles each morning for long sessions on the English *Molloy*, and was soon to begin meetings with the German translator of *Godot*.

"This will go on for years," he wrote to McGreevy,[29] "until 1955 anyway. An indigestion of old work with all the adventure gone. I tell me, take art easy, but nothing will come anymore. All contracted and unhappy about it."

Once again, Beckett was not in the theater for the opening performance of the second series, but once again, many of his friends had come to see it and it engendered another round of entertaining. He escaped from most of it by going off to Berlin for a few days to see the performance there. On his way back to Paris he stopped for several days in Strassburg and Lunewald, but the Germany he had known before the war was gone, and he had little desire to resume his rambles in art galleries and museums. He and Blin came back sooner than they had planned.[30]

There was a Dutch production of *Godot* in the offing, and he was concerned about it. "Can't bear to think what that was like," he wrote to Reavey.[31] Although he was gratified by the eager reception of the play, he was not happy to have it done away from his scrutiny. He winced when well-meaning individuals related details of such productions, even when they were enthusiastic. To Beckett, any production not under his piercing eye was a mess of excess, no matter how carefully the directors tried to follow his stage directions. In the end, to spare himself unnecessary agony, he turned over all requests for production to dramatic agencies and confined his concern only to those he could most directly influence. Over the years, this has come to mean all productions in Paris; a few in Germany, particularly at the Schiller Theater in Berlin; and those at the Royal Court in

England. There have been directors in other countries whose work he respects, especially Alan Schneider in the United States, but that has been the extent of his interest in American theater and others.

An offshoot of the requests for publication and production of his work was the increasing interest of critics and scholars who wanted to meet him before writing about him. Most of the Americans, who have been among his most skillful and successful exegetes, date their meetings and subsequent friendship with Beckett to this time. Many were curious to know more about the man who had created the astonishingly different works which were so eagerly taken up by their students. At the same time, they were completely ignorant of Beckett's prewar writings, his residence in France and his friendship with Joyce. He managed to tell those with whom he became friendly only the superficial details of his life, while at the same time making them believe he had told them everything. He grew adept at parrying their questions, and extracted from them, without ever asking, their complete and utter fidelity to his desire for privacy. Beckett managed to convince each person that he or she enjoyed his deepest friendship, and that it would be a mark of treason to divulge anything, no matter how inconsequential, of their relationship. He had boxes full of ordinary copies of *Echo's Bones* and *Whoroscope* which he presented to each person, usually with modest deference, and the gift of such precious rarities was usually enough to seal loyalty and friendship for life.[32] His habit of compartmentalizing his friendships grew more pronounced. Beckett's friends before the war moved in small enough circles so that each knew most of the others; but although they often saw each other, they were well aware that they rarely saw each other with Beckett—their meetings with him were almost always solitary. After the war, this compartmentalization became as pronounced as it is today. For example, when he was with the *Merlin* group, either singly or together, he never introduced them to any of his French friends they encountered, and vice versa, even when it might have been mutually beneficial. He still met the old friends from before the war, but usually it was they who arranged the meetings and he who attended. Although he saw that those who were in Paris during the run of a play received tickets—a large block of good tickets was always in his name—he never invited these people to join him afterward. Gradually, he came to relax his vigilance and stopped keeping all parts of his life separate from each other to the extent that he introduced a number of writers to Jerome Lindon, but that was a purely professional move on his part, for he recognized their potential as important writers and he wanted Lindon to benefit from publishing their books. Amazingly, while many of the people in the various phases of his life have known about persons in others, each has been reluctant to meet others for fear of seeming presumptuous and thus offending Beckett. When they have met, as has often been the case because of mutual professional concerns, each has been shy and hesitant about intruding on the other. When separate friendships developed, they were often reluctant to tell Beckett.

When they have been asked to discuss Beckett's curious propensity to maintain this almost frightening domination and manipulation of their friendship, many seem embarrassed. Several have offered the explanation that his life is to him an extension of his work, and as such, he must be allowed to set the ground rules. Since all this concerns a relationship with a gentleman noted for his Old World courtesy and charm and his unselfish concern for the person he is with at the time, what are viewed as "minor eccentricities" are overlooked by all.

"When you are with Samuel Beckett, he makes you feel you are the only person in the world, that no one else has even a fragment of his attention." This remark, made repeatedly in one form or another by his friends, perhaps indicates how Beckett has managed to cloak himself in secrecy while becoming one of this century's most celebrated writers.

"I have nearly finished revising my English version," Beckett wrote of *Godot*. "Just the second act to type. I don't think it can do any good in London, but then I didn't think it could do any good here."[33]

He had signed a contract to provide a finished script for a projected West End production by Peter Glenville and Donald

Albery within the first six months of 1954. He was longing to get to Ussy to finish it, but one thing and another kept him in Paris throughout December. Ethna MacCarthy had left Dublin to take a position as a staff doctor with UNESCO in Geneva. When she arrived to take up her duties, there were problems with her medical examination, and she was in Paris trying to persuade doctors there, on the basis of a second examination, to reinstate her. She turned to Beckett for help, and he took her to Constantine Cremin in the hope that something might be done quickly, but weeks dragged on with nothing settled. He had missed seeing McGreevy, who passed through Paris on his way from Germany, because of a conflict in several scheduled meetings. Suzanne's mother had been with them, and Suzanne was exhausted by the extra work her long visit entailed. Suzanne had further problems with her teeth, and her eyes were troubling her as well. Finally, Jean wrote that Frank had been ill throughout the fall with attacks of dizziness, fatigue, and low blood pressure. Beckett was relieved to hear that Frank had taken a business partner to ease the strain of the office.[34]

He longed for the quiet and seclusion of Ussy, where the little house was now quite habitable. From the main room he had a magnificent view of the broad sweep down to the banks of the Marne, but he wanted more privacy, so he built a high wall to surround the house, thus cutting off the view. At the top of the wall, he had the workman embed shards of glass so that no one could climb up or over.[35] He was glad he did when curious well-wishers found out who lived there and took to knocking at the gate unannounced. Once an energetic American scholar succeeded in pounding so hard that Beckett answered just to still the knocking.

"Does Samuel Beckett live here?" the intrepid researcher asked. "He's not here, I'm his brother," Beckett said quickly as he slammed the gate and bolted it. It was the only time he found humor in the situation, and repeated the story to many of his friends.[36]

At the same time, Ussy was a burden requiring hard physical labor on his part. He wrote long, detailed letters about the gardening and landscaping to Jean and Frank because they both loved those activities, and also to cheer Frank during his slow recovery. Caroline was in Paris with a school group, and Beckett and Suzanne entertained her at Bobino and took her to the movies and dinner. He clutched at her replies to his questions about her father's health, even though he knew she was very young and most likely not informed of his condition. He was relieved to hear Caroline say the doctors thought Frank was just overdoing and needed further rest.[37]

He was busy throughout the spring with other people from Dublin as well. In March, 1954, Jack B. Yeats had an exhibition of paintings at Wildenstein's Galerie Beaux-Arts, and Beckett was instrumental in placing an article in *Les Lettres Nouvelles* entitled *Hommage à Jack B. Yeats*.[38] He had thought of writing a long article himself, but discovered that he was so depressed by his lack of success with his own work that he could manage nothing more than a brief statement. He felt guilty about this, and so he wrote to McGreevy, knowing he would share the letter with Yeats and thus spare Beckett the necessity to make apologies. It was torture for him to try to prove or defend an achievement like Yeats's. He wanted to make obeisance, and he hoped that would be enough for Yeats. "Tell Jack Yeats he has lit a fire that will spread," Beckett concluded.[39]

It was more difficult to avoid Richard Ellmann, who had the cooperation of Joyce's family and his literary executors for the writing of a definitive biography. Suzanne had been in Zurich for the Blin production of *Godot*, and had seen Nora and Giorgio, who both expressed the wish that Beckett talk to Ellmann. Beckett met Ellmann several times but was guarded and elusive in his answers. He abhorred the idea of the projected book and resented what he construed as pressure from the heirs and friends to talk to a stranger about a friendship which was too deeply personal for him even to be able to think about clearly. When the book appeared, he claimed there were attributions made to him which were actually the suppositions of others. It resulted in strained relationships for Beckett with several of the persons who had been close to Joyce from 1930 to the end of his life; these strains have not been mitigated in the years since Ellmann's biography has appeared. To those who have pointed out the thorough, painstaking research and the scholarly value of Ellmann's book, Beckett says only that "he did not need to pry, to publish all those letters."[40]

Almost six months had passed since he had signed the contract for the English production of *Godot*, and it appeared now there would be a protracted battle before the play appeared in London. The Lord Chamberlain took offense at much of the language and insisted on significant changes before he would approve it. Beckett agreed to make some of the changes—"Fartov" became "Popov" and Mrs. Gozzo had "warts" instead of "clap"—but there were several deletions, especially of the hanging-erection and the dropped pants, which were quite unacceptable to him.[41] The producers would have to fight it out with the censors, for he would not budge.

In late April the news he dreaded came from Dublin, that Frank had lung cancer and was in the last stages of the illness. Beckett left immediately for Killiney and moved into The Shottery.

Frank had not been told he was dying, and accepted their explanations for his deteriorating health with the equanimity with which he had faced every other decision that had been made for him in his life. Beckett railed at the unfairness of it all, and berated himself as being somehow responsible for the sacrifices Frank had made.[42]

What hurt Beckett most of all was Frank's unfailing patience and good will. Frank felt constrained to cheer up those around him, and that only depressed them more. When Beckett could endure the strain no longer, he escaped late at night to Dublin, where he met old friends such as Geoffrey Thompson, and walked for miles back and forth across the Trinity College courtyards, lashing with frenzied invective at the ugliness and injustice of the world and the stupidity of God and man alike.

During the long summer days, Beckett tried to invent tasks that Frank could perform or supervise to keep his mind off his illness. Frank had always wanted a small lily pond in his garden, and Beckett set out to build one. Frank sat under a tree, tapping the cane without which he could not walk, his eyes shaded by the rumpled tennis cap he wore in those days.

Finally, in mid-August, 1954, they could no longer maintain their lies, and Beckett faced the heartbreaking task of telling his brother that he was dying.

Toward the end, when Frank was bedridden, the manifestations of the disease permeated the entire house, and the stench of the sickroom was so overpowering that Jean could no longer enter. As Frank lay in delirium, it was Beckett who ministered to him and sat with him until the end. Frank died on September 13, and was buried several days later in Dean's Grange Cemetery.

Once again there were details of an estate to be settled. Jean had no experience with finances, and it fell to Beckett to sort through Frank's affairs and insure that she and the children would have their needs met. Her immediate reaction was to sell The Shottery and move into a smaller house, but Beckett assured her it would not be necessary. He promised her that even if Frank's estate were not sufficient, he was in a position to make up the difference. He offered to take on the responsibility of educating Caroline and Edward as well.

His writings were now beginning to earn a considerable sustained income, and he prudently invested most of it, plus his share of his mother's estate. He and Suzanne were living as simply as they always had, and they were well-off.

When he felt fairly certain that Jean would be all right, Beckett returned to Paris to find the first copies of the Grove Press *Waiting for Godot*. He paid them little attention, and hurried off to Ussy to be alone. His brother's death, bringing with it intimations of his own mortality, was something he had to ponder and assimilate in the solitary refuge of the little house.

He also wanted to get away from the mess on the rue des Favorites, where he and Suzanne had engaged in an orgy of cleaning and redecorating. They had lived there for almost eight years; now, almost as if to wipe out all the afflictions that had beset them and their families, they painted the entire apartment, hired a carpenter to remodel and build bookshelves, and shopped for furniture and fabrics.[43]

In spite of their best efforts to cheer themselves, Beckett remained depressed. He blamed it on Paris, which he felt no longer agreed with him. He learned that Serreau's Théâtre de

Babylone had gone bankrupt, and even though he was hardly responsible, he felt guilty. Intimations of passing time were made vividly clear to him as another generation claimed Paris for its own in the presence of Stephen Joyce, who had left Harvard and come to live there. Stephen had no job and seemed to have no interest in finding one, which concerned Beckett as he saw his own youthful self in Stephen. It was also unnerving to see Sindbad Vail, Peggy Guggenheim's son, now a grown man and living in Paris.

He forgot about himself only when he plugged away doggedly at self-translation; he finished his revision of Bowles's *Molloy* and was now starting *Malone meurt* by himself. He wanted to write something new to occupy the time when he could not concentrate on self-translation, but the block that kept him from creativity seemed stronger than ever.

Ever since *Godot*, Roger Blin and Jean Martin had been asking Beckett to write a new play expressly for them, and the idea intrigued Beckett as a possible way to overcome whatever it was that kept him from new prose. As in the past, when faced with a creative impasse, he turned to drama, only this time the situation was different. He began to write this play as an intellectual exercise, and as the writing progressed, he found himself putting the new knowledge of theater he had gained from his experience with *Godot* to good advantage. Instead of putting himself in the position (or allowing himself to be put into the position) of being the involuntary vehicle from which the writing spewed forth, he concentrated all his mental faculties on calculated refinements as he plotted the moves of the two characters in the play he called *Fin de partie* (*Endgame*). For the next two years, until 1956, when it satisfied him, Beckett wrote two successive full-length, two-act versions before he finally pared it down to its present one long act.[44]

He told Blin that he was writing a play for him and Martin "avec complicité et amitié,"[45] and he went off to Ussy to seclude himself, in better spirits than he had been in for several years.

CHAPTER TWENTY

1955–57:

"NOTHING IS FUNNIER THAN UNHAPPINESS"

In the fall of 1954, Beckett received a letter from the warden of Luttringhausen Penitentiary in Germany, telling him that a convict had done a German translation of *Waiting for Godot* and was in the process of casting and performing the play.[1] The warden said the play had changed one of the most troublesome prisoners into a cooperative, scholarly individual, and he asked if Beckett would be willing to correspond with the prisoner to answer some questions raised by the translation. Beckett agreed immediately. Several letters passed between them, and Beckett was impressed with the convict's intelligence and sensitivity. When the play was performed, both the warden and the convict wrote detailed accounts to Beckett, telling him how it had affected all the prisoners, and how it stirred much discussion and comment, as each man found a personal meaning in the play. They invited Beckett to visit, and he wrote a sincere letter in reply, stating that he would if ever he were in Germany again, but he thought the possibility an unlikely one. In his reply, he returned the courtesy and invited them to Paris, should they ever have the opportunity. Little did he dream anything would come of it.

In January, 1955, when Paris was in the grip of extremely cold weather, Roger Blin received a message at the theater where he was working that a "half-frozen fellow" in light summer clothing was asking for Beckett.

It was the convict, who had violated his parole to come to Paris on the strength of Beckett's invitation. He was penniless and had traveled most of the way in freight cars or walking and hitchhiking. He had not eaten for several days and had caught a bad cold. Blin took him backstage while he tried to contact Beckett by calling several bars in Montparnasse, as there was still no telephone at the rue des Favorites. When he failed to reach Beckett, he borrowed a heavy jacket and took the convict out for dinner. He wanted to give him money for a hotel room, but the man had no identity papers and was afraid to try to register without them, so Blin took him to his apartment.

The next day it snowed, and the convict was afraid to go outside. Blin, who always bought his clothes in the flea market, told the man to help himself to something warm. While the convict was occupied in choosing his new wardrobe, Blin set out to find Beckett. He succeeded in reaching Suzanne first, who was terrified, convinced they would be killed in their beds, and who begged Beckett not to meet the convict.

When Beckett learned that a meeting with the convict could take place, he, too, was terrified—not because he feared for his life, but because he could not face the physical presence of the man. As long as the expression of friendship was abstract and removed, Beckett was willing to continue his share, but when it became real, it required a commitment he was unable to give.

Beckett urged Blin to send the convict away by saying that he was not in Paris, nor was he expected back for a long time. He gave Blin a substantial sum of money and asked him to pass it on. Blin was embarrassed, but did as Beckett wished. However, the convict was quite taken by life in Paris and had no intention of returning to Germany. He told Blin he would be happy to stay until Beckett returned, for there was nothing ahead but further imprisonment if he went back. For several days Blin was wild with alarm when he learned that the convict, a forger and counterfeiter, had gone to prison for losing his temper in a barroom brawl and slashing several men with a knife. Several days later, when he finally gathered his courage to evict the unwelcome tenant, Blin returned to his apartment to find a note from the convict saying he could not stand the cold in Paris anymore and was heading south. He thanked Blin graciously for his hospitality but made no mention of Beckett.

One of Beckett's more troublesome concerns during this time was the London production of *Godot*, originally contracted for in May, 1953, to be presented within the following six months. There were continuing problems with the Lord Chamberlain over the propriety of the language, but Beckett's reluctant agreement to change most of the offending passages smoothed the way for production sometime during 1954. However, he insisted on retaining the speeches in which Vladimir and Estragon express glee at the possibility that by hanging themselves they will produce an erection; also, that Estragon's pants must drop in the final tableau. There was a continuous flurry of correspondence and conversation, with little chance of compromise in sight. Beckett toyed with the idea of going to London to advise and assist the director, Peter Hall, but deferred his decision until he was quite sure the play would go on as scheduled in late summer.

Hall had approached most of the leading actors in the English theater to take part in the play, but was turned down by all of them, including Sir Ralph Richardson, Sir Laurence Olivier, and Sir Alec Guinness. As in France, the actors who took the parts were extremely able performers whose reputations were not of the first magnitude. Paul Daneman was signed to play Vladimir, and Peter Woodthorpe, Estragon. Peter Bull played Pozzo, Timothy Bateson was Lucky and Michael Walker was the boy.

As British negotiations moved ponderously on, an American producer, Michael Myerberg, wrote for permission to stage *Godot* in the United States, and Alan Simpson, an Irish producer, wanted to stage it in Dublin. The crush of agents, publishers and lawyers coming at Beckett all at once from so many different directions made him yearn for the tranquillity of Ussy, but it was difficult to get away because there were too many old friends from Dublin to entertain, among them, Ernie and Carmel O'Malley, Desmond and Mary Ryan, and Basil Rakoszi.

He managed ten days at Ussy, then returned to be best man at the wedding of Stephen Joyce to Solange Raytchine on April 15, 1955. He was reluctant to be on display in a semipublic gathering such as this, but he could not refuse Stephen.[2] It was one of the few occasions when he and Suzanne were seen together at a social gathering.

In May, H. O. White, professor emeritus at Trinity College, came to Paris with A. J. Leventhal. Beckett took them to dine at Chez Marius and Les Îles Marquises, to Bobino, to all the Montparnasse cafes and for miles of walking throughout Paris. As soon as they left, Beckett was free to go to Ussy, where he spent the greater part of the summer, content to garden and enjoy the sun.

Lindon had been asking repeatedly for another work, so Beckett decided to collect the thirteen short pieces he called *Textes pour rien* because he was convinced that he could do no more with them.[3] He chose the title from the musical term, *mesure pour rien*, a bar's rest. Beckett's ability and interest in music have been noted by many of his commentators, and in this work the structure is carefully moderated to permit the title to give an added dimension of musicality to the work, as the shifting themes and cadences are much like a musical score. These short prose pieces are shifting images, some extremely beautiful; others retain the harshness and grief of the trilogy, while still others are poignant yearnings for a happier, more protected time. For the most part, however, the violence of the trilogy is on the wane and the tone here is one of resignation.

In the serenity of his summer, Beckett alternated between writing *Fin de partie* and prose, which had begun to flow as he hoped it would when he turned to drama. This time he wrote in English, as if he thought it might lead to a way out of the dead end of *The Unnamable*.

He began a prose narrative about three days in the life of a person now old and weak, who had been young when the story began. The mother of the unnamed person used to hang out of her window to wave good-bye to him each morning. On the particular day the story begins, he meets a white horse. On the second day he is attacked by a tribe of stoats, and on the third, he meets a roadman called Balfe and wanders off into the country where he tramps through great clumps of ferns. There are echoes of the trilogy, as the hero says, "All I regret is having been born, dying is such a long tiresome business I always found," and "I was mad of course, and still am, but harmless . . ."[4] The hero has a mother who figures prominently in the story and dies in the end: "no tenacity of purpose, that was another thing I didn't like in her . . . always changing." There are memories of his father, who ". . . died when I was a boy, otherwise I might have been a professor, he had his heart set on it. A very fair scholar, I was too, no thought, but a great memory."

While the same basic themes that preoccupy him in the trilogy are found in this fragment, there is an enormous difference between it and the three earlier works. The raw, frightening, emotional revelation is missing. Instead there is a poignant nostalgia for a happier time. This work, like the others, begins with fleeting impressions from Beckett's life and memory, but unlike the others, consists of an intellectual attempt to shape his major preoccupations into a more public fiction. There is a sense of lightness and eagerness in this work that the others do not have. It begins briskly: "Up bright and early that day, I was young then . . . nice fresh morning, bright too early as so often." Even the shock of the next remark, "Feeling really awful, very violent," is mitigated by the briskness of the prose. As the narrator continues his tale, one senses how well Beckett has learned to use language. Perhaps the care required to write in French, or the difficulty of translating from French to English, taught him an exactitude and precision of expression that was missing from his earlier writing in English. Unfortunately, he quickly reached a point beyond which he could go no further. He gave the fragment the self-explanatory title of *From an Abandoned Work* and went on to other things.

The only blot on his otherwise blissful summer was the continuing vexation of the London *Godot*. Peter Glenville withdrew from the production, leaving everything in the hands of Donald Albery, who decided to go ahead with it at the Arts Theatre Club. So much time and money had been sunk into negotiations that the assorted producers, agents and lawyers for the London production all converged on Beckett to convince him to make the changes the Lord Chamberlain wanted. Beckett finally agreed, rather than place the production in jeopardy. He knew that he needed a London success if he were to be known as something more than the curious Irishman who wrote in French. American appreciation was welcome for the dollars it brought, but English acceptance had deep meaning for him. To protest the censorship, he decided to stay in France and not go to England at all.

The play opened on August 3, 1955. Peter Bull described the first night:

> Waves of hostility came whirling over the footlights, and the mass exodus, which was to form such a feature of the run of the piece, started quite soon after the curtain had risen. . . . The curtain fell to mild applause, we took a scant three calls and a depression and sense of anticlimax descended on us all. Very few people came round, most of those who did were in a high state of intoxication and made even less sense than the play.[5]

Without exception, the popular press dismissed it as rubbish. Milton Shulman called it "another of those plays that tried to lift superficiality to significance through obscurity . . . his symbols are seldom more demanding than a nursery version of Pilgrim's Progress."[6] *Punch* called it "a bewildering curiosity."[7] W. A. Darlington called it "admirable as a serious highbrow frolic, but would not do for the serious play-going public."[8]

Beckett, in Ussy, received the first notices the day after they appeared. "The shopkeepers seem to be making mincemeat of London," he wrote to McGreevy. "But I really do not know much about it at all. I did not get over for the opening and dare not during the run. I am tired of the whole thing and the endless misunderstandings. Why do people have to complicate a thing so simple I can't make out!"[9]

It remained for Harold Hobson and Kenneth Tynan, the two leading English theater critics, to reverse public opinion and start audiences streaming into the theater. Tynan struck at the heart of fashionable Mayfair and Belgravia when he wrote in *The Observer*, "It will be conversational necessity for many years to have seen *Waiting for Godot*."[10] Hobson's piece compared trying to capture the essence of the play with "trying to catch Leviathan in a butterfly net," but he urged everyone to see it:

> Go and see *Waiting for Godot*. At the worst you will discover a curiosity, a four-leaved clover, a black tulip; at the best something that will securely lodge in a corner of your mind for as long as you live.[11]

Beckett called Hobson's review touching and courageous, and said he read it with emotion.[12]

On September 12, *Godot* moved to the Criterion Theatre, where it played to capacity audiences until May, 1956. Now that success was assured, Beckett's curiosity triumphed, and he agreed to visit the play sometime later that winter.

In the meantime, two years of negotiations for the play to appear in Dublin were coming to a successful conclusion. Alan Simpson had hoped to stage the first English-language production of Godot. Beckett wrote to him:

> I think you had better read the play before we go any further. I have translated it myself into English, as literally as I could and am now revising this translation for American publication in the Spring. Frankly, I cannot see how an integral performance would be possible in Dublin, even in such a theatre as yours, because of certain crudities of language, if for no better reason; and I would not consent to their being changed or removed . . . if finally you feel you can undertake to put on the play as it stands, there should be no difficulty about permission.[13]

He added casually that Simpson was welcome to stage *Godot* whenever he wanted, but asked him as a matter of courtesy to check with the London representatives first. When the London producers learned that a Dublin production might precede theirs, they considered abandoning it altogether. At this point, Beckett hurriedly stepped in and asked Simpson to delay his production until the London opening.

When the Dublin production did open, the reviews were generally more favorable than they had been in London, partly because the reviews of Hobson and Tynan had been available for several months, and the initial shock of the English audiences had simmered down to a curiosity eagerly shared by the Irish theatergoing audience. Since Ireland was not bound by the censorship of the Lord Chamberlain, all the offending passages were retained, just as Beckett had written them, causing the critic of the Irish *Evening Herald* to comment that "Some of the grosser crudities, which were omitted or glossed over in London, were included here. They add nothing to the atmosphere, and are merely an attempt to out-Joyce the Joyce of *Ulysses*."[14]

With all the current productions well-launched and successful, Beckett decided to take a brief holiday in Zurich with Giorgio Joyce. He spent a week there at the end of October, visited Joyce's last haunts and saw his grave.[15] He returned to Paris and began a collaboration with his cousin John Beckett on a theatrical skit for the dancer Deryk Mendel. Beckett wrote it because he had just reduced *Fin de partie* to one act and needed a companion piece for a full evening of theater. He knew Mendel and admired his dancing, and he wanted to work with John Beckett, whose music he liked. The result was *Act Without Words I*, which Deryk Mendel directed and danced.

John Beckett returned to Dublin in mid-November, and Beckett found a disturbing hiatus in his life. With all productions of *Godot* running smoothly and all his publishing concerns under control, he had a great deal of free time. Michael Myerberg wanted him to come to Miami for the opening of *Godot* in January, and he was tempted by the offer, but decided that the enthusiastic relentlessness of the American press might be more than he could survive. He decided it would be a mistake to accept and went to London instead in early December.

The producers were doing very well financially with *Godot*, and they insisted on paying all Beckett's expenses. They booked rooms for him at the Regent Palace Hotel and tried to get him to attend parties and receptions, but he kept to his old friends as much as possible.

He did see every performance for five nights in a row, because the American director, Alan Schneider, wanted to study it for the coming Miami production. Schneider wrote:

> My fondest memories are of Sam's clutching my arm from time to time and in a clearly-heard stage whisper saying: "It's ahl wrahng! He's doing it ahl wrahng!" about a particular bit of stage business or the interpretation of a certain line. Every

night after the performance, we would compare what we had seen to what he had intended, try to analyze why or how certain points were being lost, speak with the actors about their difficulties. Every night, also, we would carefully watch the audience, a portion of which always left during the show. I always felt that Sam would have been disappointed if at least a few hadn't.[16]

Beckett thought the London production had too much clutter to it.[17] He wanted a harsher simplicity, and thought perhaps the rudimentary qualities of the primitive Babylone production were better suited than the charm and comfort of the Arts Club Theatre. The production reminded him of the plush overstuffed quality of English life that seemed to permeate the theater with all that he considered the worst of English society. He admitted, however, that this was only a personal impression and not an actuality on stage.

This was a curious time in his life—as his fame increased and more and more successful public figures sought him out, he retreated whenever possible to the comfort and security of old friendships. It was as if he had to confirm the solidity of the private foundation of his personality before he could allow any further public image to be constructed. His cousin, William Heron, living in Earl's Court in a small bed-sitter, was astonished when he opened his door one evening to a timid knock to find the by now quite famous author standing there holding a bottle of gin. "I heard you were here," Beckett said matter-of-factly, as he opened the gin,[18] offering no explanations about the years that had passed since they saw each other last. Heron had already seen *Godot,* and he told Beckett he liked it, calling it "the greatest English drama since *Hamlet* or some such."

"I'm glad you think so highly of it," Beckett replied, "I wrote it almost eight years ago and I never expected it to be played." He gave Heron a box office pass so that he could see the play whenever he liked.

Several nights later, Beckett telephoned and invited Heron to the Regent Palace for dinner. When Heron arrived, he was astonished by the grandeur of the hotel. "Are you staying *here?*" he asked.

"Yes," Beckett replied, "my agent booked me in." He said it sheepishly, but seemed secretly quite proud, and admitted it after several bottles of expensive, good wine.

Geoffrey Thompson was now associated with the Tavistock Clinic and living in Hampstead. Beckett visited, and they began a series of conversations as each sat in a large, comfortable chair beside the fire in Thompson's study and talked long into the night.[19] Beckett wanted to talk about his writing, and to ask Thompson about the curious manner in which his works seemed to write themselves. In their conversations they explored the process of creativity, never as an impersonal subject, but always as it related to Beckett.[20] He seemed eager to assign accepted symbols and motives to all that he had created, but when Thompson offered possible explanations that were not to his liking, he would leap from his chair, poke the fire and inquire about his godson (Thompson's eldest son). As these conversations continued over the years, Thompson found he was unable to see Beckett's plays as anything other than manifestations of severe depression and possible psychosis, and so he tried to avoid discussing them. Beckett sensed his reluctance to comment and was offended, especially when Thompson said he did not like *Endgame*. Beckett then ceased all discussion of his writing, but continued to send signed first editions and tickets for all productions.

He telephoned another Trinity classmate, Stuart Maguinness, a professor at London University, and invited him and his wife to dinner at a restaurant on the Strand. It was the first time they had met since university days, but the initial awkwardness of the meeting dissolved as Beckett went out of his way to be a charming host. His geniality was so unlike his previous behavior that Mrs. Maguinness told him repeatedly what a delightful companion he was. He seemed puzzled by her comment, and kept insisting that he hadn't changed at all.[21]

As Beckett became famous, his old friends noticed a change for the better in his attitude toward society. He seemed to have overcome his inability to engage in polite discourse and bowed to the necessity of doing so. His neighbors in Montparnasse often saw him in the more fashionable cafes, seemingly engaged in pleasant conversation with foreign editors, publishers and scholars. They marveled that he was able to overcome the old anxieties and take part in all sorts of negotiations with such apparent ease. Most of his conduct, however was a facade behind which his reclusiveness still lurked.

"Things are now very grand with me," he wrote to McGreevy. "It is time now I made big changes in my way of living, but I doubt if I have the energy."[22]

Two days after Christmas, 1955, he wrote to Alan Schneider, "If I don't get away by myself now and try to work, I'll explode, or implode. So I have retreated to my hole in the Marne mud and am struggling with a play."[23]

The strain of enforced conviviality was taking its toll. Once again he was plagued by idiosyncratic cysts and had to make the tortuous journey to Montmartre where his doctor, a radiologist, had offices. In treating the cysts, the doctor discovered a large lump in his lung which was diagnosed as possibly cancerous. He warned that an operation might be necessary, but decided first to treat it for several weeks with radiation. At the end of that time, it dwindled to practically nothing, and the threat of an operation was ended. Beckett was naturally relieved to know that he did not have cancer, but his attitude throughout this uncertain period was strangely unruffled. He accepted it fatalistically. While he railed against fatal illness in others, he was resigned to what he considered his own imminent, inevitable demise. This indifferent attitude extended into the professional aspects of his life as well, an indication of the seriousness of his depression.

On January 3, *Godot* opened in Miami to a hostile press and an audience that walked out with such regularity that it created a standing joke: the only place in Miami to be sure of finding a taxi was just after the first act curtain at the Coconut Grove Playhouse.[24]

Michael Myerberg, the American producer, had asked for the option to produce the play following the success of the first production in Paris and shortly after Beckett signed the contract for publication by Grove Press. In the United States, Beckett was then known only to a devoted band of intellectuals and academics. Myerberg, however, was a shrewd investor, who recognized the value of a theatrical property which had had such an unsettling impact on French theater, traditionally unshakable except for major innovations. When the London production gathered momentum, he flew over to see it and confirmed his initial impression that this was a play which could hold an audience and thus had great commercial potential.

Myerberg had a reputation for daring and innovation in the theater, but with *Godot*, these talents worked against him. He made two important decisions which affected the initial presentation of the play: he cast Bert Lahr as Estragon, and he opted for Broadway instead of the then noncommercial off-Broadway, where the play should most logically have gone.

He originally wanted Garson Kanin to direct the play, but at the last minute, Kanin decided not to do it. Myerberg then chose Alan Schneider on the recommendation of Thornton Wilder. Wilder was pleased that Myerberg wanted to produce *Godot* because he had read the play as well as several of Beckett's prose works, and thought Beckett was a major talent who could bring a new excitement to the theater.[25] He gave Schneider the highest recommendation, based on Schneider's direction of the revival of *The Skin of Our Teeth*, and Wilder's word was enough to make Myerberg back the young director, who had only two other Broadway credits thus far.[26]

Instead of the traditional tryout towns of New Haven and Philadelphia, Myerberg elected to open the play in Miami at the height of the tourist season, where audiences were more in tune with Catskills humor and show-girl extravaganzas. As Bert Lahr said, "Playing *Waiting for Godot* in Miami was like doing *Giselle* at Roseland."[27] In the best ballyhoo tradition, Myerberg sold out the two-week tryout engagement more than a month in advance by advertising the play as "the laugh sensation of two continents." Everything about the production was slick: he approved a highly stylized set consisting of a large mound that confronted the audience like a huge parabola, blocking their vision and constricting the actors' movements.

The glittering opening-night audience included Tennessee Williams and Walter Winchell, but by the end of the first act, two-thirds had left. The next day, the line formed early at the box office, not to buy tickets, but to demand refunds. The

Miami *Herald* was surprisingly understated, with a headline that read "Mink clad audience disappointed in *Waiting for Godot*." The audience, openly hostile to the play, was, as one local critic reported, "more in the mood for *Guys and Dolls*." There was none of the "laugh riot" the advertisements had promised. The actors began to receive hate mail, especially Bert Lahr, of whom one angry fan demanded,

> How can a man, who has charmed the youth of America as the lion in *The Wizard of Oz*, appear in a play which is communistic, atheistic, and existential?[28]

After two weeks there seemed no reason to continue the debacle, and Myerberg canceled the show. As John Lahr has written, Myerberg was largely responsible:

> He had billed the production falsely, mounted it outrageously, and brought it to a town with no sympathetic audience to sustain an experimental play.[29]

In retrospect, Myerberg said of the Miami production:

> I went too far in my effort to give the play a base of popular acceptance. I accented the wrong things in trying to illuminate corners of the text I felt were left in shadow in the London production. For instance, I cast the play too close to type. In casting Bert Lahr and Tom Ewell I created the wrong impression about the play. Both actors were too well known in specific types of performance. The audience thought they were going to see Lahr and Ewell cut loose in a lot of capers. They expected a farcical comedy, which *Waiting for Godot*, of course, is not.[30]

But Myerberg was not ready to give up on *Godot*. He learned from his mistakes, and this had been one of his most costly, to his ego as well as his purse. He still planned to bring the production to Broadway, but not without first making changes. He fired Schneider. Then he allowed Ewell to quit. He was determined, however, to keep Bert Lahr, and in doing so, to emphasize the comedy without stressing it in his advertising.

Beckett, in France, heard very little about the Miami production, except that Miami had not been the most successful choice of a tryout town, and that the production, with significant changes, would move to Broadway in the spring. He was strangely apathetic to it all, and his only personal reaction was to comment to friends that "he could do with some dollars."

He replied movingly to a letter from Schneider, who had been so distraught by the fiasco that he had only been able to write a few brief, blame-taking lines.

"Success and failure on the public level never mattered much to me," Beckett wrote; "in fact I feel much more at home with the latter, having breathed deep of its vivifying air all my writing life up to the last couple of years. . . . For the moment all I can say and all I want to say is that this Miami fiasco does not distress me in the smallest degree, or only in so far as it distresses you."[31]

With the move to New York, Myerberg sought an entirely different audience. He bought advertising space in *The New York Times* appealing for seven thousand intellectuals to support the play, warning casual theatergoers to stay away:

> This is a play for the thoughtful and discriminating theatre-goer. We are, therefore, offering it for a limited engagement of only four weeks. I respectfully suggest that those who come to the theatre for casual entertainment do not buy a ticket to this attraction.[32]

The play ran for more than one hundred performances, to audiences who stayed after it ended for panel discussions of the play's meaning. The Grove Press text went through several printings, as the audience snapped up copies each night as they left the theater.[33]

Herbert Berghof directed this production, managing to induce an element of cerebration significant enough to counteract Lahr's clowning. E. G. Marshall provided intellectual foil as Vladimir, Kurt Kasznar played Pozzo, Alvin Epstein was Lucky and Luchino Solito de Solis was the boy. This production, like those in London and Paris, made Beckett's name more than an academic password. It also made him financially independent for the first time, for the Americans had come through with the "dollars" he wanted.

The American production had been through more upheavals than either of its European counterparts and was probably the most original of the three because Beckett had no direct connection with it. However, every one of the major participants, except Lahr, made a special effort to see and study the London production. Myerberg, Schneider and Marshall all saw more than one performance and based what they did and didn't do on what they had seen. Thus, while their basic approach to the play was new, much of it represented a reaction to the British production.

Beckett, in France, was naturally more interested in how the New York production fared than he had been in any other except the first one in Paris. When Myerberg saw that *Godot* would have a long run, and when the cast began to hold panel discussions after each performance, he saw another chance for advantageous publicity and asked Beckett to come to see one performance. He planned to ask Beckett to make himself available for interviews or meetings with the audience, but shrewdly said nothing about it. He also said nothing about paying Beckett's expenses, which was the real reason Beckett finally refused the invitation.

"They want me to go to New York, but they won't pay my fare, so there is no question of that," he wrote to McGreevy. "*Godot* has been playing on Broadway for the past week in what seems to be a dreadfully wrong and vulgar production. On the whole, the criticisms I have seen have not been too bad, but they don't tell me how the play is going and I am quite in the dark as to that."[34]

It was still an unsettled time for Beckett, and he continued to careen back and forth between Ussy and Paris. Faber and Faber had published a British edition of *Godot* on February 10, 1956, and he was slightly buoyed by the decent initial sales. He kept busy by translating *Malone meurt* for Grove Press. He was temporarily stymied on the play which became *Fin de partie*, and could not bring himself to work on anything else. But by April 12, 1956, Beckett had finished the first stage of *Fin de partie* (*Endgame*), a long, two-act, handwritten manuscript in French with four characters, referred to variously as A (or Guillaume), B (or James), P (Pépé or Walther) and M (or Mémé).[35] This manuscript contains a great deal of stage activity and much busywork. There is a frenzied to-do with ladders, alarm clocks, telescopes, pain-killers, bug-killers, and other paraphernalia. The actors seem to be in constant motion, and action takes precedence over language and ideas. B (later to be Clov) becomes other characters through costume changes, leaving one in doubt as to whether Beckett meant to have a total of six characters or only four, with one assuming two disguises—it is never really made clear. B (Clov) becomes a woman—wears a wig, false breasts, a skirt, and speaks in a woman's voice—all because A (later Hamm) has ordered him to procure one. It is also B (Clov) in this version who sees a boy outside, leaves the stage, then reenters in child's clothing and learns how to run errands for A (Hamm). This version is more diffuse in characterization. There is variety in the color of the clothing, and the faces of the two main characters change from red to white between the acts. There is also much Biblical allusion, all removed in later versions. Clov reads the story of Noah and the flood and tells of the families who are descended from Shem in great detail.

John and Beryl Fletcher, tracing the evolution of this manuscript, which they call "packed with incident and variety . . . more diffuse," note that "the dramatic line is much clearer in the final version and the point pushed home more forcibly."[36]

Three typescripts followed the manuscript.[37] The first is little more than a clean typed copy of the manuscript version, but the second is a redaction that is close to the final printed French text. When he finished typing the second one, Beckett wrote the names Nagg, Nell and Clov at the beginning, as if he had just decided on them. In the third typescript, all four characters are called by their final names from the very beginning.

These revisions proceeded slowly, and an indication of the problems they posed for Beckett can be seen in the final disposition of the *Fin de partie* papers. The manuscript and three typescripts are in Ohio State University Library, a further manuscript version of the early Act Two is in Dublin in Trinity College Library; Beckett has notebooks in his possession that contain other rewritten sections of the play, and still other parts have become "trunk" manuscripts that Beckett still hoped to revise for publication and production twenty years after he had finished the play.

What finally evolved is a play that Beckett called "rather difficult and elliptic."[38] *Fin de partie* is about two men, Hamm and Clov, in a room—perhaps a living room—but also the room in which Hamm sleeps. To one side, there is a kitchen, the province of Clov. Hamm is blind and crippled. He is confined to a wheelchair. Clov is sighted, but cannot sit down. He is perhaps younger than Hamm, and although he assumes attitudes of a servant, he maintains his independence and distance. To one side, there are two galvanized trash cans, in which live Nagg and Nell, who are the parents of Hamm.

Begun as a conscious intellectual exercise, Beckett managed to shape the play as he desired, into a deliberate exercise for the theater that drew heavily on techniques he had learned through his involvement with the various productions of *Godot*. There is much attention to theatrical detail in *Fin de partie*. Stage directions are clearly spelled out. Instructions on how to speak lines are abundant: actors are told variously to heed adverbial admonitions such as "irritatingly," "admiringly," "exasperatingly," on almost every printed page. Beckett tells his actors how to sit, stand, move chairs, walk, be wheeled, raise and lower lids. This play marks the beginning of his preoccupation with dramatic exactitude, his need to specify every nuance and gesture that may take place on his stage.

Fin de partie also incorporates snatches of his life, but they are far fewer and more impersonal than in *Godot*. Cissie Sinclair had recently died, felled by crippling rheumatoid arthritis that had stiffened her entire body, so that as she sat in her wheelchair, she often instructed those who pushed her to "straighten up the statue, will you?"[39] In postwar years, Beckett discreetly called upon Cissie whenever he visited his mother in Dublin. Cissie lived with some of her children in a small house on the coast at Raheny. Often Beckett took her for walks, pushing her chair along the road that climbed up from the sea, bent in much the same position as Clov is when pushing Hamm. His visits to her marked some of the happiest times of the last years of her rather sad life. Even though crippled, Cissie still befriended the outcasts, characters and Bohemians of Dublin. One of her prize possessions was a telescope given to her by one such character, Old Tom Casement, and she used it to watch the ships in Dublin

Bay or the antics of the birds as the tides changed along the beach. Cissie died in a dreary county home, a source of great anguish for Beckett; the Beckett relatives find much in the lines spoken by the characters in *Fin de partie* to remind them of the circumstances of Cissie's last home.

There are snatches of Beckett's readings: Eubulides of Miletus, whom he calls "that old Greek" because he forgot his name; Shakespeare, with paraphrases of *Hamlet, The Tempest* and *Richard III*, and allusions to *King Lear*; and others as well, from the Bible to Baudelaire.

But the most important aspect is the game of chess in this, the one play of Beckett's that is always governed by exterior intellectual concerns. An Irish writer of Beckett's generation, a friend for many years who has had innumerable theoretical and philosophical discussions with him, feels certain that any interpretation of *Fin de partie* must begin with the influence of Marcel Duchamp, the artist, who "wrote little and spoke less,"[40] and was also a formidable chess expert.

Beckett knew Duchamp throughout the 1930's in Paris, having met him at Mary Reynolds's house. Beckett frequented the same cafes where the best chess players congregated, as did Duchamp, and he followed the chess column that Duchamp occasionally wrote for the Paris daily newspaper, *Ce Soir*.[41]

In a study of Duchamp, Arturo Schwarz stated that chess "provides the perfect metaphorical model for Duchamp's life and works."[42] Duchamp himself said

> Chess is a sport. A violent sport . . . that does imply artistic connotations in the actual geometric patterns and variations of the actual setup of the pieces and in the combinative, tactical, strategical, and positional sense. It's a sad expression though— somewhat like religious art—it is not very gay. If it is anything, it is a struggle.[43]

In 1932, Duchamp coauthored a book that Beckett knew well, *Opposition and Sister Squares Are Reconciled*,[44] a book that is still considered a major contribution to chess literature. It deals with the endgame, or the third division of a chess game.

Generally speaking, a chess game has three parts: first is the opening, in which pieces are brought out and strategies instigated. In the next section, or middle game, the two opponents organize their moves. In the last part, the endgame, there is either a conversion of the advantage into a win, or else an attempt to nullify the disadvantage incurred in the middle game— also in search of the win. Usually in the endgame, there are no longer enough pieces left on the board to initiate an attack upon the king. This is when both kings are free to come to the center of the board, to confront each other, seemingly uncaring, as they execute the few limited moves still possible.

There are two analyses of Duchamp's book that are particularly apt in light of Beckett's play. Pierre de Massot, one of the first to review Duchamp's book, wrote:

> This work is concerned with that very special point of the endgame in chess when all the pieces have been lost, and only the Kings and a few pawns remain on the board. And this special "lone-pawns" situation is treated only for the even more particular situation in which the pawns have been blocked and only the Kings can play . . . only certain moves and in limited number are possible . . . the authors [Duchamp and Halberstadt] are the first to have noticed the synchronization of the moves of the Black King and the White King.[45]

Henri-Pierre Roché described it this way:

> There comes a time toward the end of the game when there is almost nothing left on the board, and when the outcome depends on the fact that the King can or cannot occupy a certain square opposite to, and at a given distance from, the opposing King. Only sometimes the King has a choice between two moves and may act in such a way as to suggest he has completely lost interest in winning the game. Then the other King, if he too is a true sovereign, can give the appearance of being even less interested, and so on. Thus the two monarchs can waltz carelessly one by one across the board as though they weren't at all engaged in mortal combat. However, there are rules governing each step they take and the slightest mistake is instantly fatal. One must provoke the other to commit that blunder and keep his head at all times. These are the rules that Duchamp brought to light (the free and forbidden squares) all to amplify this haughty junket of the Kings.[46]

The American scholar Ruby Cohn observed Beckett in Berlin, where he has gone throughout the 1970's to direct various productions of his plays. In a 1967 production of *Fin de partie*, Cohn says Beckett made the following statement to the actor who played Hamm, which seems to support Roché and Massot's interpretation of Duchamp's book:

> Hamm is a king in this chess game lost from the start. From the start he knows he is making loud senseless moves. That he will make no progress at all with the gaff. Now at the last he makes a few senseless moves as only a bad player would. A good one would have given up long ago. He is only trying to delay the inevitable end. Each of his gestures is one of the last useless moves which put off the end. He's a bad player.[47]

Much has been speculated about the meaning of *Fin de partie*, or *Endgame*, but one thing is certain: when Beckett told some English-speaking friends that he had written a play called *Fin de partie*, they translated it as "End of the game." "No," Beckett replied emphatically. "It is *Endgame*, as in chess."[48]

In keeping with the chess analogy, everything in this play is balanced, and each movement, action or speech depends on another. "There are no accidents in *Fin de partie*," Beckett has stated. "Everything is based on analogy and repetition."[49] A line of tragedy is often followed by one of comedy. There is pathos, undercut by bathos. It is a play within a play: Hamm and Clov realize they are actors, that dialogue keeps them upon the stage; at times they fear the introduction of subplots, at others they speak of asides. For every story that is told, there is an appropriate response. Clov draws back the curtains, first on one window, then on the other, in an identical repetition of the action. The list of moves, countermoves and responsive moves does not need to end here, but these are enough to demonstrate the point.

A critical exegesis can be fashioned to carry chess as the dominating motif throughout the play, but others are possible. Much has been found in *Fin de partie:* King Lear, Hamlet, Noah in his ark; even Beckett and Suzanne in Roussillon, or Beckett in Ireland. The stage, with its windows high up on the back wall, has been interpreted as the interior of a human skull, also as a bomb shelter containing the last remaining human beings on earth. Hamm has been called Joyce and Beckett's father; Clov, Beckett the disciple and Beckett the son. The possibilities have been explored by critics and scholars who find in *Fin de partie* endless opportunities for the brilliant workings of their own minds.

Fin de partie has been performed in a child's playpen, a boxing ring, a chicken-wire cage and an approximation of the interior of a human skull. It has been made into an opera, a slapstick comedy replete with American slang, and a modern dance. The many imaginative adaptations of the play can only be hinted at here.

Some of Beckett's comments may (or may not—depending on one's turn of mind) illuminate what he intended the play to represent and what meaning it should convey. Several times, in rare unguarded moments, Beckett has said that Hamm and Clov are Vladimir and Estragon at the end of their lives. Once he qualified this remark, stating that Hamm and Clov were actually himself and Suzanne as they were in the 1950's—when they found it difficult to stay together but impossible to leave each other.[50]

Beckett told Patrick Magee, who played Hamm in a London production, that he had no idea what went on in Hamm's mind. "You're on your own to figure that one out, Pat," he said. When Magee asked Beckett to tell him how he envisioned Hamm, Beckett replied without pausing, "Oh, he's a monster, not a human being. Only the monster remains." But this remark seemed to frighten Beckett, and he softened it by saying "No, no, he looks like you, Pat. Just like you."[51]

Beckett characterized the general tenor of this play as one of "extreme anxiety."[52] Hamm is afraid Clov might leave him. At the same time, he must be afraid that Clov will be able to find a life for himself outside the room, and also that Clov might find nothing but a terrible void.

In a German production, Beckett told the actors that "Hamm says no to nothingness."[53] Later he hold the actors who played Hamm and Clov, "Your war is the heart of the play. Clov has only one wish, to return to his kitchen. That must always be evident, as is Hamm's effort to detain him."[54]

In this production, Beckett admitted that he had a favorite line in the play: Hamm's response to Clov's observation that

Nagg is crying: "Then he's living."[55] But he stressed that the most important sentence in this particular production should be "nothing is funnier than unhappiness."[56]

In a French production, Beckett was asked why Nagg and Nell were in trash cans. What was this to represent? Did it mean that Beckett had no respect for old age and thought people should be discarded like garbage? No, that had nothing to do with it, Beckett said. He confined Nagg and Nell because technically it was the only feasible way to have them make their abrupt but unobtrusive entrances and exits. Originally, he had planned to have them in wheelchairs, but it was evident even before rehearsals began that their chairs would detract from Hamm's mood of magnificent isolation that was to dominate the stage. More important, they were to be aged and infirm, incapable of pushing themselves on or off the stage. Who, then, was to push them, and how were they to be pushed without colliding with Hamm or forcing him to move or be moved? "It was simply a question of logistics," Beckett said. "I put them there so they can pop their heads up or down as needed and nothing else is called for."[57]

Fin de partie has been read variously as a play about hope: there is after all, a flea; a rat is still in the kitchen; and what looks like a small boy, a potential procreator, is sighted outside. It has also been read as a play of despair: a dying couple and two men who make meaningless moves against the nullity of being that will soon relentlessly overtake them.

This play, fertile exegetical excavation that it is, caused Harold Hobson, one of Beckett's most perceptive commentators, to write in 1973:

> In recent years there has been some danger of Mr. Beckett being sentimentalized. Self-defensively we are driven to persuade ourselves that his plays are not really filled with terror and horror, but are, at bottom, jolly good fun. Well, they are not jolly good fun. They are amongst the most frightening prophecies of, and longing for, doom ever written.[58]

Perhaps Beckett himself should have the last word. In a letter to Alan Schneider, Beckett addressed himself to the rash of commentary the play had engendered shortly after the first French performance:

But when it comes to journalists, I feel the only line is to refuse to be involved in exegesis of any kind. And to insist on the extreme simplicity of dramatic situation and issue. If that's not enough for them, and it obviously isn't, it's plenty for us, and we have no elucidations to offer of mysteries that are all of their making. My work is a matter of fundamental sounds (no joke intended) made as fully as possible, and I accept responsibility for nothing else. If people want to have headaches among the overtones, let them. And provide their own aspirin. Hamm as stated, and Clov as stated, nec tecum nec sine te, in such a place, and in such a world, that's all I can manage, more than I could.[59]

Beckett wrote most of *Fin de partie* in Ussy, with periodic interruptions of varying duration when he needed to return to Paris to take care of the accumulation of things connected with his work and to answer his personal letters.

Nancy Cunard, whom he had not seen since before the war, wrote to tell him how much she enjoyed the London *Godot*. He thanked her for her sentiments, but told her "the French production was more like I wanted, nastier . . ."[60]

Cunard passed through Paris on her way to her home in the Lot, and she invited Beckett to lunch with her. He found her "very wraithy."[61] He was surprised to notice how nervous and fidgety she was, and wondered if this was something new or if he had simply not noticed it before. He wondered if it might not have something to do with his own current mood and disposition.

In general, the luncheon seemed to have cheered him up. Cunard told him about Aldington, who had settled near Montpelier and was very happy there. The thought of one as sociable and garrulous as Aldington living quietly in a remote village and liking it appealed to his own sense of himself and his feeling for Ussy. Cunard had kept in touch with Walter Lowenfels, and Beckett was happy to hear that he was prospering. They spoke little of Henry Crowder, who had died sometime previously, because she was still too deeply affected by his loss.

Beckett touched Cunard when he told her he still had *Negro* "snug on my shelves, unlike most of what I once had, and even a few *Whoroscopes* . . ."[62] He had gotten into the habit of giving away books to anyone who expressed even the slightest interest in them, so his having kept this one was significant. Possessions, always unimportant to him, now seemed to have even less value. In a mood of self-deprecation, he told Nancy Cunard, "The dog is duller than ever but its friends know it doesn't mind if they get up and go away . . ."[63]

Unlike Joyce, who seized anyone recently come from Ireland to demand avidly all the gossip, literary and otherwise, that a visitor could recall, Beckett's interest was dispassionate and detached. When Vivian Mercier called on him, he listened with respect to all of the latest happenings in the Irish theater and to news of the latest publications.[64] He asked polite questions about persons he knew, or about the fate of a particular work, but the impression he gave was one of intellectual interest without emotional involvement. The Ireland that affected his senses was the landscape he wrote about in his books—the familiar countryside through which he had so often walked with his dog, his father and brother, and the quiet lanes where he pedaled his bicycle.

During the course of the visit with Mercier, Beckett confided to him that his inability to write anything for such a long time had considerably depressed him. He felt "all dried up, with nothing left but self-translation."[65]

Beckett entered into a continuing correspondence at this time with a London bookseller, Dr. Jacob Schwartz, who asked for manuscripts, typescripts or first editions of his earlier writings. Schwartz cautioned that nothing would command a very high price, but felt the material would bring a respectable amount and would also serve as an incentive to increase the value of subsequent sales. At first, Beckett was amused that his scribbles could have any value to anyone, but as he thought about it, it seemed a good idea. *Godot* had been his chief money-maker thus far, and though it brought more money than he had had in all his adult life, he was still not as independently wealthy as he would like to be. He had had so many health scares during the past few years that he was convinced of his imminent mortality, and selling manuscripts seemed a good way to guard against the poverty he feared a sudden eclipse of public approval might bring. Also, he was worried about the exorbitant amount of money Suzanne had begun to spend. Most of what he had earned from his postwar writings was invested by "his man"[66] almost immediately to keep Suzanne from spending it. Years of deprivation had released a flood of desire, and she began to dress with an elegant simplicity that screamed of money. She bought so much furniture and so many accessories for the apartment that its Spartan simplicity was soon overwhelmed by bourgeois clutter. Beckett worried and complained about Suzanne's carelessness with money but to little avail, for she continued to dress and behave in the manner she thought befitted her status as consort of a world-famous playwright.[67]

Beckett corresponded cautiously with Schwartz at first, but by the end of the year, after several brief meetings, he decided to accept the offer. For the next few years, Schwartz was responsible for all the Beckett manuscripts sold, most of which were purchased by American universities.[68]

In May, he went to Ussy, determined not to emerge until he had done some significant work on *Fin de partie*. At the beginning of the year, he had still been working within the two-act framework. In April he apologized to Schneider for not having any new plays, saying he had finished *Fin de partie* but didn't like it: "It has turned out a three-legged giraffe, not to mention only the architectonics, and leaves me in doubt whether to take a leg off or add one on."[69] He was determined to reshape this unsatisfactory two-act version before leaving Ussy, and worked steadily throughout the month. "Up to my navel in sudden work," he wrote to Vivian Mercier on May 15, 1956.[70] By June 4, he had sunk even further in the morass of writing: "Up to my eyes and in rather a panic," he wrote to McGreevy.[71]

He had been invited to propose a program for the Marseilles Festival the coming autumn, and he hoped to finish *Fin de partie* in time for rehearsals and subsequent presentation. At the same time he was working on the final version of *Act Without Words I*, as well as what later became *Act Without Words II*, and in the midst of all this new work, he still felt compelled to go back to Paris, where Blin and the original company were presenting a revival of *Godot* at the Théâtre Hebertot. He attended all the rehearsals, commenting more freely and making more suggestions than he had done with the first production, and in general, taking a more commanding role in it.

Then, there were the usual social commitments that he felt he could not refuse: a piano recital by Monique Haas, the pianist and wife of Marcel Mihalovici; a holiday visit from Mimi and Maurice Sinclair and their children; a visit from Nancy Sinclair Cusack and her husband, Ralph; and the annual visit of Barney Rosset, who brought a splendid radio-phonograph with microphones and all the latest attachments as a gift. Beckett and Suzanne took it to Ussy, where they spent quiet evenings over a cup of tea listening to Dietrich Fischer-Dieskau's recording of *Die Winterreise*.[72] The interruptions, pleasant though they were, went on and on. Nancy Cunard sent him her book about Norman Douglas, prompting Beckett to surmise that he and Douglas "would not have got on."[73] Cyril Cusack wrote that Liam O'Brian was translating *Godot* into Irish, and Beckett was "unexpectedly pleased about this."[74]

His correspondence mounted. "I am overwhelmed with silly requests and letters, most of which I feel I have to answer, till I hate the sight of pen and paper."[75]

In spite of all, he kept on, working whenever he could find a few spare moments. He knew that meeting the deadline for the Marseilles production would be difficult, if not impossible, and he dreaded the effort involved; nevertheless, he plodded toward completion because he knew that his mental stability was growing more precarious with each passing day, and without the work to occupy him, he would soon give way to "a kind of hollering inertia."[76]

Writing was the catalyst which held him together and kept him from flying apart in every direction at once. For the first three weeks of June, he worked nonstop on *Fin de partie*, until he reduced it to a long, cohesive single act. He wrote to Schneider that it was "longish, hour and a quarter I fancy. Rather difficult and elliptic, mostly depending on the power of the text to claw, more inhuman than *Godot*. My feeling, strong, at the moment, is to leave it in French for a year at least . . . I'm in a ditch somewhere near the last stretch and would like to crawl up on it."[77]

Unfortunately, he did not meet the Marseilles Festival deadline, but rationalized his disappointment by saying that a Paris premiere was better after all, and so the search for a suitable theater got under way once again.

In June, Trinity College published *From an Abandoned Work* in the student newspaper,[78] prompting an outraged Beckett to write to H. O. White that the editors, in their undergraduate enthusiasm, had made a mess of it by trying to correct his punctuation and divide the text into paragraphs. He had asked them either to print it as he sent it or not at all, and they simply ignored him. He tried to contain his anger by saying that he should probably be accustomed to being improved behind his back, or be used to the good intentions of "well-brought-up young blue pencils," but he was livid with rage because they had interfered with his text, something he had not permitted since before the war when he announced his willingness to change anything offensive in *Murphy*, even the title. After *Godot* he was in a position to present his publishers with a work they were instructed to print exactly as he himself had typed it (for he trusted no one to type for him); they were not to change a comma without first consulting him. In fact, at Grove Press, there was a standing joke that they had both a "house" style and a "Beckett" style, and they scrupulously followed the latter no matter how it might deviate from the former.[79]

In early July, officials of the BBC wrote that Sir John Gielgud wanted to know if Beckett had a script suitable for radio, and if not, would he consider writing one. "Never thought about a radio play technique," he wrote to Nancy Cunard,[80] "but in the dead of t'other night got a nice gruesome idea full of cartwheels and dragging feet and puffing and panting which may or may not lead to something." It was the genesis of *All That Fall*, and he worked sporadically on it during the summer, finishing the first draft in a burst of energy in September, 1956.

It served as an excuse for evading the work he had scheduled for himself. He was supposed to have spent the summer translating *L'Innommable* for Grove Press, but could not bring himself to do it without first making extensive psychic preparation. His correspondence and his comments to friends all show the same sort of statement: "I should be translating *L'Innommable* but it's an impossible job,"[81] or "it requires much courage."[82] Facing this novel meant returning once more to plumb the depths of the relationship with his mother; even so long after her death, it was terrible to contemplate.

To avoid it, he began again to read the classics which had given him so much pleasure in the past. He had been rereading Milton since he wrote *From an Abandoned Work*, which contains the memory of an afternoon he spent with his father, when he described Milton's cosmography. Milton's verse "Insuperable height of loftiest shade," ran through his mind constantly, leading him to all sorts of reflections,[83] and lately he had begun to reread *Paradise Lost*. He turned briefly to Elizabethan drama, but it did not satisfy him. For the first time in years, he turned to Racine, and read rapidly through *Andromaque*, *Phèdre*, and *Bérénice*. He particularly admired *Andromaque*, because he felt that it gave him more understanding of the changes in current theater. Of *Bérénice*, he commented dryly, "That's another one where nothing happens."[84]

His reading was a further reflection of the need he felt to reexamine his roots and to arrive at some understanding of the fame that had suddenly engulfed him. At a time when he was literally inundated with manuscripts and books by new and aspiring authors, when his own publisher sent works of possible interest to him, and when his friends were all anxious for him to comment on their latest work, Beckett chose to return to the works which had had the greatest meaning for him in the past. When conversations with friends turned to the latest novel that was sweeping Paris, or the play that was the latest rage, they found Beckett uninformed and uninterested.

Even the few writers who have become his friends sometimes feel that he is unfamiliar with their work. "I send him all my work as it appears, and he always writes a lovely note to thank me, but I know when we meet and begin to talk that he hasn't read one word I've written. I don't mention it because it embarrasses him." It is a comment repeated by more than one of the young writers whom Beckett has befriended.[85] Many of his friends find Beckett's knowledge of poetry and his ability to quote vast passages superb—until the era of the 1930's. His understanding and appreciation seem to have ended with the Surrealists who were his friends and contemporaries.

By October, negotiations with Hebertot had broken off, and now the same weary process of finding a theater for *Fin de partie* was about to begin in earnest. Beckett was despondent at the thought of it: "Future directors expect you to arrive with your text under one arm and millions of franc notes under the other and this now seems to be the established practice. With *Godot* after all, we had a state grant of 750,000 and now nothing but a gloomy graceless act, a complicated mime, and no Beaux Yeaux."[86]

Attempts to house the play came to nothing. It was rejected by the Théâtre des Champs Élysées, Petite Marigny, Théâtre des Oeuvres and all the nameless others who had refused *Godot*. Beckett grew depressed as the rejections came in.

> I feel sullen, silent, sot, always brooding and never thinking, of the somebodies REVENGE (by Marston, is it?), and wonder how even old friends can put up with it. It is not easy to get through the ages with self so estranged.[87]

The weather was miserable, a cold and rainy fall, and he could not even release his tension with long walks through the countryside, but was forced to pace up and down in the small house at Ussy without relief. "Everything is drenched and dripping here, and without definite work on the stocks there does not seem much point in this deep silence and emptiness."[88] When he heard that *Godot* was reopening in New York in November, he wrote to Nancy Cunard, "*Godot* reopening Broadway November with an ALL NEGRO CAST! That's my best news."[89]

But *Fin de partie* was uppermost in his mind, and he saw the year drawing to a close without any hope of a production. "I am panting to see the realization and know if I am on some kind of road, and can stumble on, or in a swamp," he wrote to Schneider.[90]

Six months of bickering, haggling and entreating were consumed before Beckett finally conceded that production in France would be impossible in the near future. Only two theater directors had expressed minimal interest; one actually allowed Blin and his company to begin rehearsals, then summarily evicted them. Everyone was puzzled by the difficulty. Even though *Godot* had been the show of the season just a few years ago and Beckett was now hailed as one of the leading dramatists of the day, no theater director wanted to take a chance on the new play. It was too easy to fasten on Serreau's bankruptcy at the Babylone, even though it had happened well after *Godot*, and so see the same fate in store for anyone foolhardy enough to take a play where two old people crouched in garbage cans, a third could not stand up, and a fourth could not sit down.

It seemed almost unbelievable, but after several years of the most exhilarating, heady success, Samuel Beckett had suffered another total, humiliating rejection. No one wanted this play, his favorite. Had the rejection come from Ireland or England, it would have meant little, but coming from France, it was tragedy and catastrophe combined.

On January 13, 1957, Beckett, in Ussy brooding over *Fin de partie*, strained to capture the sound of the elusive BBC Third Programme so that he could hear the first broadcast of *All That Fall*, but the reception was so poor that he had to give up. He had found the BBC pleasant to work with, and the problems presented by radio technique interesting, and he fully intended to write further scripts as soon as the opportunity presented itself. In *All That Fall*, he instructed the studio to use Schubert's *Death and the Maiden*, his favorite music, because he knew of no other music so heavily imbued with such sorrow.[91] But he was especially anxious to work with John Beckett, and was already considering how he could incorporate music into any future radio plays. He wanted to collaborate with his cousin so that the music would be written especially for the play and would have no meaning or overtone except for the work at hand.

With negotiations for *Fin de partie* at a standstill in Paris, he was working furiously to perfect the English translation for George Devine and the Royal Court Theatre, with whom he had signed a contract the previous fall. Devine wanted to present *Endgame* before *Fin de partie*, but Beckett agreed to give him the translation only because he thought there would be no question that the first production would take place in Paris. Now, with events so different from what he had envisioned, he turned to translation with a purpose, hoping to whip through it in a month, allow two months for rehearsal and schedule the first performance in English for late April.

At the same time, he was busy checking the Italian transla-tion for *Molloy* because Italian was a language he knew well, so he had no intention of allowing publication until every word read to his satisfaction.[92]

Minuit published *Fin de partie* and *Acte sans paroles I* on February 1, 1957, and even though he did no *service de presse* to celebrate the occasion, there was still an afternoon of signing books and other negotiations that called for several days in Paris.

Caroline Beckett came to live with a French family and learn the language, which meant several more days in Paris while he assured himself that she would be well cared for.[93] Since Suzanne had cut herself off so effectively from all their mutual friends, she had further removed herself from aspects of Beckett's life unrelated to his work by cutting herself off from the Irish relations. Claiming that she knew no English and was a bore and a hindrance to their relaxation and affability, she would appear only long enough for a handshake and a brief greeting. Beckett was embarrassed by her refusal to entertain his family, but made polite excuses, saying she was shy about not knowing English.[94] Fortunately, Henri and Josette Hayden were now spending the greater part of their time in Reuil-en-Brie, and their apartment on the rue Montparnasse was at his disposal. He used it to lodge his family, and became a good customer of several small Montparnasse hotels, where he quietly insisted on paying all the expenses of visiting friends.[95]

Suzanne had even stopped coming to Ussy now, and Beckett found himself alone there for great stretches of time, content to sit outside his front door in the sun, to putter lack-adaisically about the garden. Silence and solitude mitigated his withdrawal from unpleasantness, in this case the Paris theater, which he believed had treated the new play with deliberate malice.[96]

But the English translation was faltering, and the April date for promised delivery to Devine was almost upon him. "I find it loses power in English," he complained to McGreevy, "all the sharpness gone, and the rhythms. If I were not bound by contract to the Royal Court Theatre, I wouldn't allow it in English at all."[97] There was a raw, sharp ugliness to the French text that he could not approximate in English. The spare French prose seemed to become twisted into an effusive English that he was unable to control.

This was especially crushing because, of all his writing, *Fin de partie* was the work which gave him great hope that at long last he was in command of what he chose to write. With *Murphy* and *Watt*, he believed that he had tried to write successful fiction and failed, that both books were derivative, trivial and without major import. He was deeply satisfied but unnerved with the trilogy. *Godot* was a sentimental favorite, but he sheepishly considered it a facile attempt to make quick money.

But with *Fin de partie*, he had consciously set out to write a play that would not only set forth a cogent representation of his view of humanity and life, but one that would be a careful, artfully constructed theatrical vehicle. To him this play represented the pinnacle of his writing to date. The affection and tenderness he felt for this script was unlike anything he had ever felt before. There was no sense of the wonder of its creation, only a feeling of enormous satisfaction in his own craftsmanship. He dedicated *Fin de partie* to Roger Blin, who, with Jean Martin, had inspired it, and sent him a copy of the finished typescript with the following note appended:

> For you, if you really want it, but only if you really want it. Because it really has meaning, the others are only everyday.[98]

Thus, the rejection in France was especially devastating; it was as if his favorite child had been reviled and rejected. Typically, he chose to withdraw from the society which had rejected him, and in doing so, temporarily crippled his effectiveness to cope with other aspects of his life.

When Brian Coffey sent him a poem he had recently written and a long letter reflecting on their prewar Paris days, Beckett replied first in anger, then with resignation, that there were no "good old days," there were no "good new days," there

were simply "no good days" at all. To yearn for anything in
life, past or future, was unrealistic and a waste of time.[99]

In early March, Robert Pinget's translation of *All That Fall*
(*Toux ceux qui tombent*) appeared in *Les Lettres Nouvelles*,[100]
signifying the completion of a successful collaboration instigated
by Jerome Lindon, who was concerned about Beckett's periodic, brooding introspection, and even more disturbed by the
time he insisted on lavishing on self-translation. Lindon felt that
Beckett should content himself with a brief inspection of the
translation someone else had made so that he could devote all his
time to writing. Beckett admired Pinget's writing and was receptive to Lindon's idea that he just might be the collaborator and
translator Beckett had despaired of ever finding. He found
Pinget's translation quite good, and with a few suggestions on
his part, accepted it as definitive.

Pinget was one of the few persons who was first Beckett's
friend, and then became Suzanne's. For the first time in many
years, Suzanne was leading a life not dominated by Beckett's
work. She had always maintained her ties with one or two
women friends whom she knew before meeting Beckett, but they
were the only ones now who were a part of her life without
having been first a part of his.[101] She was growing more positive
about venturing out alone—she had gone to Toulouse, Geneva
and Zurich for Blin's touring productions of *Godot*, and she was
forming new friendships of her own. She and Madeleine Renaud
and Marthe Gauthier had gone on brief holidays to Switzerland
and Germany; she and Jean Martin became friends, and now,
she and Pinget formed a friendship independent of Beckett.

There was no problem for anyone in maintaining dual
friendships, for it was clearly understood that Beckett and Suzanne lived separate but parallel lives; they had long ago agreed
that their interests were too diverse and their friendships too disparate for any other arrangement. They conveyed their apparent ease in such an unusual situation to the friends involved,
so that it soon became a matter unquestioned and accepted. It
helped to alleviate the situation their friends found themselves
in when Beckett began to be seen discreetly in the company of
other women.

In the 1930's, Beckett's physical attractiveness and dark, brooding silences had prompted Wyn Henderson to tell Peggy Guggenheim that Beckett had the same forbidden quality of a monk or priest that made him irresistibly attractive to women.[102] Now, it amused his friends to see how women clustered around the still handsome and now successful author, and how politely he avoided all their advances. However, when he began to be seen regularly with a younger woman, it was a surprise to everyone. In all his years in Paris, he had lived a Spartan life. The only women he saw at all were those who were on the periphery of his life, with whom he had to associate because of their relationships with men who were his friends or colleagues. He seemed uncomfortable around unattached women, and like Joyce, was especially uncomfortable around creative women, whose intelligence he found prickly and abrasive. It was a common belief among his friends that he had not yet written a play which had a part for a woman because he could not bear the thought of working with one. His attitude toward women ranged from careless indifference to basic distrust and irritated dislike. He gave the impression that women were necessary inconveniences, and in an attitude that his French friends found "very Irish" professed to find true happiness only in the company of good male companionship late at night in a pub.

In fact, on one such occasion, an old friend teased him about a night twenty years earlier, when Beckett escorted a prostitute through the Westland Row railway station and ducked behind a pillar hoping to avoid being seen.[103] Beckett turned to a young poet who was with them to explain his relationship to women in general. He concluded, "This thing called love, there's none of it, you know, it's only fucking. That's all there is—just fucking."[104]

"Oh, come now Sam, you can't mean this," they cried in unison, in disbelief.

"I do indeed," he repeated, "there's only fucking."

Thus, it was especially surprising to see Beckett obviously enthralled by a woman who was not only highly intelligent—she supported herself and her children through creative work—but also one who was sharply talkative and fiercely independent. His relationship with her gave rise some years later to *Play*, the brief work in which husband, wife and mistress are trapped forever, side by side in urns, condemned to repeat the details of the affair over and over when a bright light shines upon them, to cease when the light moves on to another of the unholy trio, and to stop when the light stops.[105]

By mid-March, Beckett had to admit to Devine that the translation of *Fin de partie* would not be finished on time, and he was unsure when or if it would ever be ready. Devine wanted to produce the play, and since he could not have *Endgame*, he invited the French company to bring *Fin de partie* to London for the world premiere.

Blin and Martin had rehearsed it sporadically for the past four months, and were at the peak of readiness, and they urged Beckett to accept Devine's unorthodox offer. Blin and Martin left in mid-March and moved into a small pension on Ebury Street, where Beckett joined them. They hoped to have more privacy and a more homelike atmosphere than a hotel would provide; but after three days Beckett could not stand the enforced conviviality and moved into the Royal Court Hotel.[106]

For four weeks he worked with the cast, the designer, Blin and Devine. Then, just as rehearsals moved into the critical stage, he received a wire from McGreevy saying that Jack B. Yeats was dying. Six months earlier Yeats had written his annual Christmas letter to Beckett, saying that he knew he would die soon and wanted to make his farewells to his friends in his own good time and in his own way.[107] The letter was deeply moving, and Beckett vowed then that he would go to Dublin at any cost if he were warned beforehand. When the message came, he spent a frantic day trying to make arrangements. There were no seats on any of the flights to Dublin, which meant that he would have had to travel by train and boat; even so, there was no assurance that he could get a flight back. He was about to make the trip anyway when the telegram came to tell him that Yeats had died on March 28, in the Portobello Nursing Home. Beckett would have gone to the funeral, but the same problems with transportation remained and so he reluctantly stayed in London for rehearsals. He asked McGreevy to send flowers in his name, and to apologize to their mutual friends for his unseemly absence.[108] "The light of Jack Yeats will always come with me," Beckett wrote sadly to H. O. White.[109]

He threw himself into the last rehearsals of *Fin de partie* so that he could leave for Paris before opening night and duck all the journalists whom he had thus far successfully eluded. What particularly troubled him was the movement and rhythm of the play. He timed the pauses between speeches down to the split second, and insisted that Martin count to himself as he moved about the stage, timing his steps.

Martin wanted Beckett to realize that no matter how well he spoke the language, he was still a foreigner who writes in French. The first word of the play caused endless conflict, with Beckett insisting that Martin pronounce it "Finnnnnni," dragging it out slowly, as long as possible, as one would say in English "finnnnnnish." Martin insisted that this technique might work very well in English but not in French, where the speaker would still observe the rules of grammar and speak it in the clipped, abrupt accents of proper French speech. When Blin agreed with Martin, Beckett grew furious and insisted shrilly that they must follow his instructions.

A little later, when he was somewhat calmer, Beckett said, "You must realize that Hamm and Clov are Didi and Gogo at a later date, at the end of their lives." Then he turned abruptly and said, "Actually, they are Suzanne and me," and walked out of the theater.[110]

Finally, there was the problem of the music at the end. Each beat counted, but it was played in such a way that it was in direct contrast to how the actors, who were also counting, were supposed to move. Tempers frayed and nerves were taut when Beckett finally gave up and decided it was all right. Martin was exhausted and still unsure of what Beckett wanted. Relations between Blin and Beckett were tense, as Blin, the titular director of the play, had been replaced by the author as the real director.

The Royal Court Theatre, though small, was magnificently appointed compared to the small studios where they had performed in Paris, and the settings and costumes were grander than Beckett had originally envisioned. Hamm appeared on a golden throne with splendid robes edged in fur. He wore a red handkerchief over his face as the play began, and his makeup was brick-ruddy. When he was writing the play, Beckett read a book about the effects of long-term incarceration on prisoners, which claimed that the complexions of prisoners who were denied access to life outside their cells often turned a deep, brick red.[111] Beckett liked the idea and incorporated it into Hamm's and Clov's makeup, but in subsequent productions he decided it was an affectation of reality that intruded upon the timelessness he hoped to evoke. On one point Beckett was absolutely certain: there was to be no intimation of comedy in this production at all. He wanted no aura of laughter, no possibility of humor. It was to be stark, grim, deadening, hopeless—these were all words he used to describe what was taking place on the stage.[112] This was as far as he would go in interpreting the play, saying it was the only "level" necessary for understanding or acting.

He left London in dejection several days before the opening, and spent the afternoon before his flight in the Heathrow Airport cocktail lounge with A. J. Leventhal, who had come to review it for the *Dublin Magazine*. They were waiting for Suzanne's plane to arrive from Paris, when Leventhal was to escort her into London while Beckett boarded the same plane for the return flight to Paris.[113]

He was disappointed in the production, which he thought was entirely too commercial. He thought it was a slick attempt to pander to public taste, and was unhappy because in spite of all, the actors were acting, and not simply following his instructions.[114] "Things in London were very difficult and exhausting," Beckett wrote to McGreevy.[115] To Alan Schneider, he wrote "The creation in French in the Royal Court was rather grim, like playing to mahogany, or rather teak."[116]

The London critics were baffled and negative except for Hobson, and even he admitted puzzlement. The French press reacted with patriotic indignity at the imagined slight of the premiere of a French play before an English audience. Attracted by the commotion, the management of the Studio Champs Élysées agreed to stage it, beginning on April 27.

"Here," Beckett wrote to Alan Schneider, "the hooks went in . . ."[117] Hamm had been divested of his velvet robe and wore a simple tattered coat. The chair he sat on was a simple wooden armchair on wheels, and the makeup had been toned down a shade, though it was still reddish in hue. In the simplicity of the smaller French theater, Beckett found the play had the power to evoke the response from the audience that he wanted.

On top of the usual infestation of summer visitors to Paris, he found himself once more plagued with cysts. This time a large one lodged just above his palate, making speech difficult and swallowing virtually impossible. He was forced to have an operation on the upper jaw to correct the problem, and discovered that he needed further surgery on his teeth. In spite of the tremendous effort to save them, he came to the reluctant conclusion that the only way to rid himself of pain was to have all his remaining teeth pulled and be fitted for dentures.

He and Suzanne managed to spend a few days with Lindon and his family at Étretat, but even that brief holiday was blighted by unseasonable cold and rain. In spite of that, he liked the place, for it reminded him of Joyce, who had made several visits there.

To McGreevy, he listed his activities of the previous six months:

> Translation of *All that Fall* into French and German, of *Fin de Partie* into German and English, of *L'Innommable* into English, of *Malone Meurt* into German, of *Echo's Bones* and other odd poems into German, and sick and tired I am of translation and what a losing battle it is always. Wish I had the courage to wash my hands of it all. I mean to leave it to others and try and get on with some work.[118]

He was under pressure to finish the translation of *Endgame* promised to Barney Rosset for publication that winter. The previous April, he had written to Schneider:

> I have not even begun the translation. I have until August to finish it and keep putting off the dreaded day . . . it seems funny to be making plans for a text which does not yet exist and which, when it does, will inevitably be a poor substitute for the original (The loss will be much greater than from the French to the English *Godot*) . . . I have nothing but wastes

and wilds of self-translation before me for many miserable months to come.[119]

True to his word, Beckett finished the translation on August 12, 1957.

At the end of September, Alan Schneider came to Paris to see *Fin de partie* and to discuss techniques for the American production scheduled for the coming January. Once again the two men attended performances and compared texts, with Schneider following the play, English translation in hand, reading by the light of a small flashlight until the usher told him politely that he was distracting the actors.[120] For four nights in a row they saw the play, talked to the actors, checked technical aspects and then went off to talk further.

No matter how many questions Schneider asked or how trivial they seemed, Beckett answered each one with painstaking precision, until Schneider asked why Hamm and Clov's faces were red. "Why was Werther's coat blue?" Beckett countered, gently leading Schneider to the realization that it was not the director's function to explain the author's meaning to the actors in a play, but to lead them to an expression of whatever can best convey that meaning to the audience. Beckett wanted Schneider to believe that Hamm and Clov were not representative of a universal situation, but were two personalities operating within the framework of a specific, localized incident.[121] It is interesting that Beckett was willing to speak to Schneider in such detail, while Blin had to be content with shrugs and disclaimers.

The French *Fin de partie* seemed likely to run forever, but Blin and Martin were tired of it. They had been with the play for well over fifteen months and wanted to get away. They were incredibly depressed, had begun to doubt their sanity as well as their ability, and were relieved when, after ninety-seven performances, the run finally ended.[122]

The German production began, a disappointment to Beckett, who hoped that the English version would be better. However, Devine, who had had no problem with the French version, could not get the English translation approved by Beckett's old nemesis, the Lord Chamberlain, who wanted the line, "that Bastard, he doesn't exist," changed to "that swine, he doesn't exist." It was all right for British audiences to hear God called a swine, but bastard was too much. Only in French could the deity be thus vilified. Beckett had already agreed to many more irritating minor changes than he liked, and once again, grew stubborn in the face of opposition. After much discussion, the Lord Chamberlain was persuaded that since the word had been allowed to burn English ears in the original French production, it was silly to insist on the change now. He withdrew his objection, but the stalemate had dragged on for almost a year, and *Endgame* was not performed at the Royal Court Theatre until October 28, 1958.

By the end of November, 1957, Beckett canceled his appointments and retreated to Ussy to put the pieces of himself back together. He was exhausted from ". . . a tiring time in Paris with people from London and New York to see and entertain and be entertained by."[123] Suzanne was not well, and she, too, had gone to Ussy for the first time that year.

He wanted very much to hear the broadcast of a passage from *Molloy* with music by John Beckett which the BBC Third Programme aired in December along with *From an Abandoned Work*, but once again, the reception was bad. Briefly Beckett was tempted to go to London to listen to it, but the impulse passed almost before it came. The isolation and silence of Ussy suited his mood better.

"I couldn't have managed it in the old days, or indeed five years ago," he wrote to McGreevy. "What I find more and more difficult to cope with is Paris and people and speech. I can't do it without a drink, and alone I am quite content with a few glasses of wine at dinner."[124]

He had always been a heavy drinker, especially of Irish whiskey, and was responsible for introducing it into several out-of-the-way bistros in the 15th Arrondissement where he liked to go when he wished to avoid the more public cafes of Montparnasse.[125] Now, for the first time, he was concerned about the way he could not face appointments and people without first fortifying himself with whiskey. His meetings tended to last much longer than he would normally have permitted because of the loosening effect of the liquor.

He had become fond of the American painter Joan Mitchell, who had been married to Barney Rosset. To Beckett, Mitchell was a younger version of Bram van Velde, and to him she expressed the same relentless quest for the void that he found in the older man's painting.[126]

Mitchell was a soft-spoken woman who expressed her thought clearly in visual concepts with a minimal amount of verbiage. Beckett, always more at home with painters than writers, found this an appealing quality, especially in a young American woman so unlike any he had ever met before. Her large, sprawling canvases drew him in, and he would pore for hours over the intricacies of the paint and the patterns. He liked her refusal to explain or justify her art, since it reflected his own inability and unwillingness to discuss his writings. And, as an added attraction, Mitchell was a prodigious drinker, whose conversation became more rarefied and intriguing the more she drank. She and Beckett became companions at this time, and it was to Mitchell that he turned when life in Paris became too hectic. She was the one person with whom he could drink, relax and talk, and her friendship became a crutch he leaned on heavily.

After almost a half-century of obscure starvation Bram van Velde began to appear in Paris, so that Beckett came to be seen more and more with him, Mitchell, Jean-Paul Riopelle, and Alberto Giacometti. Night after night they gathered in the Dôme; Beckett and Mitchell to talk and drink, van Velde and Giacometti to watch them and each other and to drink in wary silence several steps back from the bar. Riopelle, a vibrant personality, often became angry with conversations he found deliberately depressing and stormed out through the revolving door into the Paris night. On one occasion Mitchell tried to stop him. Beckett followed Mitchell into the door but was too drunk to extricate himself. Round and round he whirled, while Giacometti, like a giant, brooding toad with hooded eyes, sat and watched and said nothing, and while tourists pointed at the poet of nothingness and despair.

1958–60:

"PERHAPS MY BEST YEARS ARE GONE. . . .
BUT I WOULDN'T WANT THEM BACK.
NOT WITH THE FIRE IN ME NOW"

 Beckett spent the first two months of 1958 in Paris, laid up with a series of minor ailments probably brought on by his depression at not being able to write prose. The operation on his jaw had been successful but was slow to heal. Headaches and insomnia plagued him. He was irritable and jumpy, bothered by the flood of people and mail that poured down upon him. His publishers kept asking when they could expect another novel, and he finally convinced them that he doubted he could produce one.[1]

He was writing, however, in moments between visits from old friends and from scholars and critics who tramped through Paris on pilgrimage to the rue des Favorites and the Montparnasse cafes.

The previous year, when *All That Fall* was broadcast by the BBC, Beckett had met several of the actors, among them Patrick Magee, an Irishman fond of whiskey and a good story, with a boisterous personality and mellifluous voice that enthralled him. Magee's vibrant energy swept Beckett along without allowing him time to consider his own listlessness.

When he heard Magee reading what he had written, Beckett thought of writing another radio play specifically for him, but what he actually wrote became the stage play *Krapp's*

Last Tape. Ever since he had seen *Acte sans parole I* played on the same bill as *Fin de partie*, Beckett had been dissatisfied with the combination and wanted a different short piece to conclude the program. Although he liked *Acte sans parole I*, the mime somehow detracted from the despair with which he wanted his audience to leave the theater. As he wrote *Krapp's Last Tape*, he became convinced that it would be a good companion piece to the Royal Court production of *Endgame*, and began to think of it for the stage rather than radio.

Beckett claims he had never seen a tape recorder before writing *Krapp*,[2] and had no idea how one operated. It seemed a novel way, but still the best, to portray a man trying to recapture his memories.

For the subject matter of *Krapp*, Beckett turned away from the arid intellectualism of *Fin de partie* and returned to his own life. It is one of the most openly autobiographical of his writings, and one which he worked over with painstaking precision in an attempt to disguise these traces.[3] "Miss McGlone" began as "Miss Beamish," but by the third typescript the name was changed; her dog, now simply called "bitch," was originally a Kerry Blue. A long passage quoting "Johnson's Dictionary on 'viduity' " is excised in the first draft. And the abrupt beginning of the earliest typescripts, depicting a brusque, confident thirty-seven-year-old Krapp at the peak of his power, was gradually abandoned for the shuffling old man who bumbles around the stage eating bananas, fussing with his possessions and glorying in the sound of the word "spoooool!"

This play marks a new step in Beckett's writing: once again he confronts himself, but this time without the searing, wrenching pain and exhaustion which his previous writings contain. For the first time, he wrote about his mother's death, and also wrote openly of Peggy Sinclair, with overtones of *Effi Briest* and the bleak Baltic landscape. Even Cissie Sinclair appears, here called by her other nickname, "Fanny." There is the humiliation of the French *Murphy*, with only seventeen copies sold; there is the moment of revelation of his own artistic style; there are walks on the heath with his dogs. He transposed the frustration brought on by Miss Beamish's singing night after boring night in Roussillon into a gentle soothing sound from his Irish past. Almost every sentence recalls some parts of his life, yet reality never intrudes upon the artistic integrity of the play.

Alec Reid describes *Krapp* as "total theatre":

> It is not the words, the movements, the sights severally which produce the impact; it is the new experience, evoked through their combination on stage. This process involving eye, ear, intellect, emotion, all at once, we shall call total theatre.[4]

Krapp's Last Tape is Beckett's first postwar writing in English. Beckett told Magee that he was astonished when he first heard him speak because Magee's voice was the one which he heard inside his mind. Thus it seems likely that the return to English was a matter of expedience because of the English-speaking actor. If so, the choice nevertheless had important consequences. It seems to have brought on a surge of self-awareness that resulted in the autobiographical subject matter. It may also have affected the tone: comparing *Krapp* with the trilogy, which it resembles most in theme, one sees that the English play is a much gentler work; it has none of the harshness of the novels, and the despair is tinged more with sadness than with hostility. After the catharsis of the trilogy, he could return to the memories of his earlier life with enough emotional security to recollect meaningful moments, to present them movingly but without pain. With *Krapp*, there is an overwhelming sense of emotion, but it is an emotion recollected in tranquillity. Beckett ends the play on a note of self-realization, as an old, exhausted Krapp sits in his darkened room coming to the end of another reel of tape. He reflects:

> Perhaps my best years are gone. When there was a chance of happiness. But I wouldn't want them back. Not with the fire in me now. No, I wouldn't want them back.[5]

It is a poignant reflection of Beckett himself.

Midway through the writing of *Krapp*, Beckett flew to London for ten days in mid-February to consult with George Devine about his latest battle with British censorship. By now his refusal to comply with the Lord Chamberlain's directives had reached the newspapers, an event which Beckett deplored, though his producers were pleased because they hoped the publicity would help lift the ban. But the idea of being involved in something so silly in the first place, and having it become public, was distasteful to Beckett. Whether or not newspaper publicity and private lobbying were effective is not known, but the ban was removed quietly a short time later, paving the way at last for a London production.

A similar crisis, brewing since the previous autumn, had come to a head while he was in London. The *Tóstal*, an annual festival of plays and music held each spring in Dublin, had scheduled works by Sean O'Casey and James Joyce. Its council asked Beckett to contribute something to round out the program. He had planned to give them three mimes, *Act Without Words I* and *II*, and a third, unfinished text he subsequently decided to jettison, and for which he substituted *Krapp's Last Tape*.

The archbishop of Dublin refused to offer the votive Mass which traditionally opened the *Tóstal* if the O'Casey and Joyce offerings were performed as submitted. The council was unwilling to override the archbishop's veto. As a result, a dramatized version of *Ulysses*, called *Bloomsday*, was quickly banned, and O'Casey's play, *The Drums of Father Ned; or, A Mickrocosm of Ireland*, would be accepted only if O'Casey agreed to "certain structural alterations."[6] O'Casey refused. When Beckett learned the story, he withdrew permission for his plays. He was so enraged that as a further protest he refused to allow his plays to be performed anywhere in the Republic of Ireland. As far as Beckett was concerned, the entire episode was one more example of all that he found wrong with Ireland. Of all the disappointments and frustrations connected with the presentation of his work, it was the one which caused the most lasting rancor. He was unusually vituperative when he talked about the incident, and he used it to illustrate his theory that the Catholic Church, toward which he had long been hostile, and the British government were responsible for the surprising number of great writers who had appeared in Ireland in the short time since the nineteenth century.[7] Several years later, in a late evening conversation in Paris at the Falstaff Bar, Beckett recalled his fury at what he characterized as the Irish inability to overcome fear of the Catholic Church, and gave a short, bitter lecture on the subject.

"When you are in the last ditch, only one thing is left—to sing," Beckett began, by way of illustrating his point. When his audience looked puzzled, he continued: "*Il nous ailes en culer a la gloire*," which he translated immediately as "They have buggered us into glory!"[8]

Beckett stayed quietly in the home of his English publisher, John Calder, when he was in London, seeing no one who was not directly connected with his professional activities. He met briefly with Donald McWhinnie, the director of *Krapp's Last Tape*, and with Magee, and was pleased by the reaction to it. It was the one positive aspect of his trip. He returned to France in time to see Tom McGreevy, who was on his way to Brussels for an art convention.

Jake Schwartz came to Paris in March, and Beckett made plans to transcribe *From an Abandoned Work* so it could be sold. Schwartz had already sold the typescripts of *L'Innommable, Act Without Words I* and *II*, and *All That Fall*. He wanted the manuscript of *Fin de partie* but Beckett could not bring himself to part with it yet and planned to offer *From an Abandoned Work* instead, but could not find enough time to transcribe it because of all the appointments and interruptions. Besides, he was in the midst of what he called "a sharp spell of work,"[9] pursuing what became a dead end in French. It was a fragment of a manuscript, which grew to several pages before he consigned it, still untitled, to the pile of "trunk" manuscripts.

He was developing a real friendship with Jake Schwartz. A chance remark sometime earlier about the difficulty of finding his favorite Lapsang souchong tea in Paris led Schwartz to send several large packets, and the spontaneous gesture was immensely pleasing to Beckett.

When he dined with Schwartz, Beckett mentioned his innate passion for knowledge, which demanded periodic satisfaction, leading him to confide shyly that he secretly dreamed of reading through an entire multivolume set of an encyclopedia. Several weeks later, when Schwartz had returned to London, Beckett received a notice from French customs officials that his parcels from England had been cleared. Upon checking, he discovered five large boxes filled with a complete set of the *Encyclopaedia Britannica*, an unexpected gift from Schwartz. Beckett was delighted, and wrote a thank-you letter saying he hoped to gain both pleasure and instruction in the years to come—provided they came.[10] Beckett took the encyclopedia to Ussy, since that was the only place where he could find sufficient time to read and study at his leisure.

Schwartz also sent an autograph of Charles Stewart Parnell, which he had picked up at auction in London, and Beckett tucked it between pages of "Ivy Day in the Committee Room" in his copy of Joyce's *Dubliners*. A final gift was a copy of Stanislaus Joyce's book, *My Brother's Keeper*, which Beckett was not able to bring himself to read for some time after he received it. His attitude toward it was the same as his attitude toward the memoirs and biographies of people he had known in Paris before the war, which were suddenly coming out in profusion: they had every right to publish whatever they pleased, or to allow whatever they liked to be written about them, but for him to read any of these books was something akin to voyeurism. Eventually he relented and read any that came his way, expressing his disapproval of them all.[11]

To repay Schwartz for the many kindnesses he dispatched regularly from London, Beckett sent every scrap of material connected with his writing, from actual manuscripts and typescripts to autographed copies of radio transcriptions and each new printing of his published work. When Schwartz received the four typescripts of *Krapp*, he wrote an appreciative letter, telling Beckett how much the play reminded him of Ireland. This made Beckett angry, and he corrected Schwartz icily, saying the play had nothing at all to do with Ireland and had only been written as a vehicle for Pat Magee.[12] Schwartz's comment was too close to the truth, which he did not want to confront.

Devine was hoping to complete negotiations so that *Krapp* and *Endgame* would go on at the very end of the theatrical season in May, and Beckett was determined to be there to "make a nuisance" of himself at rehearsals.[13] Working with Blin on something as complex as *Fin de partie* had given him the confidence to feel totally secure in directing something so much easier to stage. He was both relieved and saddened to hear from Devine that the production could not be mounted in time and had been postponed until October.

He had greatly overextended himself that spring. He had promised Bram van Velde to go to Berne, where more than one hundred of the artist's paintings—almost his entire life's production—had been assembled for an exhibition at the Kunsthalle. He was far behind in the translation of *L'Innommable*, promised to Barney Rosset by early June. Marcel Mihalovici had asked him to write a libretto for a half-hour opera which had been commissioned by a German opera house, and Beckett had accepted. He was once again pursuing what seemed more and more likely to be another elusive, abortive French text, and felt that something would come of it if only he did not have to interrupt it to travel.

In the face of these obligations, Beckett told Bram he could not get away to Switzerland. Bram was insistent, however, and Beckett finally relented. For once the idea of evading work by doing something that might be pleasurable was more attractive than continued plodding at the dreary task of translation and the frustration of the new work which would not come. He, Bram and two others, drove to Berne at the end of April, 1958, and stayed there for four days of festivity.

One of the paintings in the private Mueller collection particularly impressed him—Cézanne's self-portrait, painted near the end of his life. Beckett thought it "overwhelmingly sad, a blind, old, broken man."[14]

Ida Chagall Meyer, the daughter of the painter and wife of the director of the Kunsthalle, was Beckett's hostess, and he was awed by her graciousness and hospitality. She introduced him to Frau Carola Giedion-Welcker, Joyce's friend from his days in Zurich, and to the doctor in whose arms Joyce had died, who railed on and on that Joyce would have been saved had it not been for the original misdiagnosis of his condition. Beckett was relieved when the doctor was persuaded to leave and he no longer had to listen to the details of Joyce's death.

"The exhibition very fine and my reception very magnificent," he told McGreevy. "Too many more or less forced visits to private collections, too many plays . . . too many receptions and convivialities and people for me. Never a moment alone. I was glad to get back."[15]

The enforced conviviality affected Beckett as it usually did, and he retreated to Ussy, leaving Suzanne in Paris. He worked relentlessly on the translation of *L'Innommable*. Despite his holiday, he managed to complete it by the first of June, but he was exhausted by the effort and dissatisfied with the result.[16]

In search of release and relief, he turned to Dante for the first time in years, and reread his old, well-thumbed copy of the *Paradiso*, which included the Botticelli drawings he so loved. He turned next to the *Purgatorio* where he studied the Botticelli drawing of Belacqua, which he thought captured exactly the pose he envisioned in Dante's exceptionally admirable lines:

> *E un di lor, che mi sembiava lasso,*
> *sedeva e abbracciava le ginocchia,*
> *tenendo il viso giù tra esse basso.*[17]

An art dealer he had met in Paris had told him that Ussy had a long history as the place where wandering Irishmen roamed, and when Beckett was tired of reading he went to investigate the seventh-century Merovingian crypt of Agilbert, who had spent years in Ireland, and also that of an unknown Irish princess called Ste. Ozanne. Columbanus had passed through Ussy, and the Blessed Adon, who founded the little town of Jouarre. Beckett was suffused with even deeper kinship with his property now that he knew so much about the other Irish wanderers, and when he returned to Paris, it became a favorite topic of conversation.[18]

Roger Blin and the original cast of *Fin de partie* had been invited to the Venice Biennale, and Beckett was also invited with all expenses paid, but again he refused because he interpreted this as an obligation to appear and be present upon command of the Biennale sponsors. Blin asked him to come along privately, at his own expense, but Beckett decided he had had enough meetings, exhibitions and all organized presentations for the time being. He stayed in Paris at the end of June to meet Pat Magee and Donald McWhinnie, who had come to discuss *Krapp*. Beckett was at ease because both men felt as he did about the play; nevertheless, he still intended to go to London in October for rehearsals to make sure the first production would be exactly as he wanted.

In the meantime, he discovered that *Godot* and *Molloy* had been very successful in Yugoslavia, earning a large amount of dinars that could not be brought out of the country. At Jerome Lindon's urging, Beckett and Suzanne decided to spend the month of July there. Suzanne had begun to take short trips with her friends and for some time she had been asking Beckett to go away with her, but there never seemed to be a long enough period of time free from obligations to make the trip worth-while. Now, with the dinars accumulating, Beckett thought it might be a way to find out if he could travel unrecognized and enjoy a private respite from life in Paris.

To his surprise, he was almost unrecognized in Yugoslavia, where they spent the entire month in Belgrade, Zagreb, and small towns on the Gulf of Fiume. The bright sun and warmth, the sparkling water and the tranquillity of the slower pace of life, were relaxing and restorative. Yet he still felt the need to go directly to Ussy when they returned to France, and spent most of the first week after his return sleeping.[19]

When he finally went to Paris, he discovered a family crisis brewing. His nephew Edward Beckett, who had begun to play the flute only six months previously at St. Columba's, had won the school's coveted senior music cup. Jean was delighted with his success, but her pleasure changed to alarm when Edward announced that he intended to pursue a career in music and refused to continue his preparation for the School of Engineering at Trinity College. She asked Beckett to use his influence to deter Edward from what she considered a course of madness. When Jean asked him to intercede, Beckett suddenly found himself a surrogate parent, trying halfheartedly to talk Edward out of a musical career. It was ironic that he who had gone against the family wishes to pursue his own writing career should do this, and he had little taste for the role. He telephoned Edward and found the young man insistent that he would not register at Trinity in anything but music.

Edward had been studying with André Prieur, a French citizen who lived in Dublin and played with the Radio Éireann orchestra, and who had been a student at the Paris Conservatoire with Jean-Pierre Rampal. Prieur was one of the finest teachers in all Ireland, and his success with Edward's instruction impressed Beckett, who felt that Edward's talent must be considerable to produce such rapid results. He wrote to Prieur, who replied that Edward's was a major talent, and he should not only be encouraged, but actively pushed toward a musical career. Beckett knew he could not tell this to Jean; as far as she was concerned, Edward had been brought up to become the third generation of Becketts to run the family firm, and music should only be his hobby.

Beckett had always trod warily where Jean was concerned, finding in her too much of his mother's determination; thus, he tried to take the most diplomatic course of action. Since there was still time before the decision had to be made about Trinity, Beckett urged Edward to continue his flute lessons, but also, in the interest of family peace, to continue to prepare for the engineering entrance examinations. There was always the possibility that his playing was nothing more than beginner's fluke, no matter what Prieur thought, and he wanted to give Edward all the time possible before having to make what would become an irrevocable decision. He cautioned Edward to keep his musical ambitions to himself for the time being, and the crisis abated.

September and October passed in the usual flurry of people to see. McGreevy passed through Paris on his way from Lucerne to Dublin. Beckett was anxious to see him, for McGreevy had had a heart attack the previous spring and Beckett had worried a great deal on his friend's behalf, but he almost missed McGreevy because of so many other appointments. After much frenetic juggling, he arranged one brief evening for a dinner that ended all too soon. The same thing happened when H. O. White came to Paris: Beckett was committed to an evening with Donald McWhinnie and Patrick Magee on White's only free evening. Stephen Joyce called unexpectedly at the rue des Favorites, detaining Beckett just as he was about to leave for an appointment. He sat nervously while Stephen, serious and anxious, asked if he knew of any job possibilities. Beckett asked a few questions about Stephen's preferences and capabilities, but he was vague and Beckett in a hurry, and so nothing much came of the meeting. The young man was quiet and earnest, and wanted very much to find some position where he could succeed on his own initiative and not as James Joyce's grandson.

The constant press of British and American visitors exhausted Beckett, and he had not really recovered from the persistent insomnia that had plagued him since the beginning of the year. He looked forward to going to London, where the last week of rehearsals of *Krapp's Last Tape* and *Endgame* were in progress. He longed for a quiet week in Ussy before departing, but there was no time, and he rushed to Orly airport from a business meeting just in time to board the departing aircraft.[20] He checked quietly into the Royal Court Hotel, which he found dreary and inhabited by English county families, but it was handy to the theater.[21] He went to every rehearsal, where he sat hunched over, clutching at the seat in front of him, staring intently at the action on the stage.[22] Occasionally he walked to the rear of the theater and paced rapidly back and forth while he dragged deeply on a cigarette, as if puffing intensely would assuage his worry and alleviate whatever troubled him. George Devine was quiet, patient and sensitive enough to realize Beckett's anxiety for both plays. He was careful to consult Beckett at every step in the development of rehearsals, and to listen intently to his suggestions. He was able to probe without offending, and his soft-spoken queries brought forth from Beckett detailed replies that even seemed to soothe him as he spoke.

Beckett was fascinated with the old-fashioned box tape recorder with its large spools. Under McWhinnie's meticulous direction, Magee moved in and out of the single spotlight, exactly as Beckett had envisioned it.

The setting of *Endgame* was as ornate as the original *Fin de partie* had been, but Devine, who was also playing Hamm, directed the production to incorporate the majesty of the costumes and scenery into the lofty delivery of his lines, so that Jack MacGowran, as Clov, skittered around the fringes of his chair as the perfect foil. It was not what Beckett has envisioned, but he realized that he had been basing his conception on the

French version of the play, and agreed that Devine had managed to remain faithful to his basic intentions while still creating a production entirely in keeping with the English translation.

Directing in England was an exhausting business. He had thought he was well equipped to deal with any problem that arose, but finally concluded that he had been wrong not to conceive of the difference in the two countries and to be better prepared to deal with it. Then, too, there was the difference in the personalities of his two directors: Blin was stubborn in a more visible way; Devine was equally insistent on his directional authority, but he was able to win his way softly, with none of the Gallic determination that sometimes threatened to disrupt the French rehearsals. Devine was as hesitant and mannerly as Beckett was himself, and Beckett was not accustomed to having his demands, issued in the form of polite requests, heard with equal courtesy while they remained unmet. It was an unnerving experience, but nevertheless one in which both men wanted to please and were determined to succeed.

Beckett was driven into frantic seclusion throughout rehearsals by the occasional reporter or photographer who penetrated the security of the theater. The sight of a tape recorder other than the one on stage terrified him. He would run backstage and hide until the offending journalist was evicted. He crept back and forth between the hotel and the theater, and except for telephone calls to his cousin Sheila Page in Surrey and to a few old friends, he could not be persuaded to go anywhere.

Only John Calder succeeded in persuading Beckett to dine at his home. When Beckett arrived, he discovered that several other guests had been invited. He was so nervous about meeting new people that he sat down at the piano and spent the entire evening playing to himself. If anyone tried to engage him in conversation, he pretended to concentrate on his playing and did not answer. He seemed ready to bolt at the slightest provocation, and so everyone politely ignored him.

He was anxious to get back to Paris to continue working on the French translation of *Krapp*, but he did not feel ready to leave yet. As the days drew closer to the opening performance, he kept changing his departure date one day at a time. Suzanne,

Blin, Lucien Raimbourg and his wife, and Jean Martin, had all planned to come to London in a group for the opening night, and all begged Beckett to stay, too. He insisted that he would make his usual departure just after the dress rehearsal, and said he would meet them at Heathrow just after they landed and before his plane took off. Finally, when he realized that he could not tear himself away even after the dress rehearsal, he telephoned Suzanne and told her that he would stay on to see the play with her and the others. He sent a note to several friends, among them Nancy Cunard, writing "in haste and stupor,"[23] to ask them to join the party in the Queens Restaurant after the performance. Guests that night found Beckett in surprisingly good form, carefully seeing that glasses remained filled and food was passed, urging them all to be festive, as if to distract from the tension of the coming reviews.

Both plays received generally poor notices. Hobson, Beckett's strongest defender, was unusually quiet and restrained. Tynan was vitriolic and wrote a parody called "Slamm's Last Knock!"

> Foreground figure a blind and lordly cripple with superficial mannerisms . . . Sawn-off parents in bins, stage right, and shuffling servant all over the stage . . .
>
> . . . .
>
> Slamm: Is that all the review he's getting?
> Seck: That's all the play he's written.
> Slamm: But a genius. Could you do as much?
> Seck: Not as much. But as little.[24]

By the time the review appeared, Beckett had gone to Ussy. All the excitement and tension of the production, his insomnia and irregular habits had taken their toll, and he was run-down and sick. He had cold and flu and was depressed. Sleep and solitude seemed the only cure.

At the end of November, he felt recovered enough to chuckle over Jean's letter about Edward's latest crisis: his flute leaked and needed to be replaced. Several days later, he received two urgent pleas which caused him to take the first plane to

Dublin. Jean was increasingly concerned about her finances and unable to decipher any of the statements her bank managers and accountants provided, and Edward was now openly insisting he would not go to Trinity. His grades were slipping, and The Shottery was filled with the same sort of tension that Beckett had known as a child at Cooldrinagh. The second plea came from Ethna MacCarthy, who was dying of cancer and wanted to see Beckett. Ethna MacCarthy was one of the few women with whom he could feel totally at ease. Intensely feminine, she still had a hard intelligence and total unconcern for her appearance that made her enormously appealing to him. He could have loved her deeply had she given him the chance; instead she gave him lifelong friendship. At this point he was convinced it had been the better of the two emotions.

He spent the first ten days of December, 1958, at The Shottery, and saw no one except those he had come to see. There seemed no easy answer to the situation between Edward and Jean, and Beckett despaired, as mother and son, both intractable, acted out the roles he and his mother had played in the previous generation. The rest of his time was spent with lawyers and financial managers, and it saddened him to realize that life was reduced to the papers one accumulated in passing through it. On Beckett's last day in Dublin, Tom McGreevy was determined to have closer contact than a telephone conversation and he made the (for him) difficult journey by train to Killiney. Now even long walks were forbidden, as McGreevy's exercise was restricted. Unable to be his usual ebullient self, he could do little to cheer Beckett. The specter of ill health and death was too much with them; it was Beckett's first visit to The Shottery since Frank's death, and that memory was still vivid. He had to face the knowledge that from now on, he would probably come back to Ireland only for family crises, illnesses and funerals. At that time it was a painful thought, and it was not until many years later that he and his cousins could joke openly that "Sam only comes to Dublin for funerals."[25]

Fortunately, he was able to elude publicity, and flew back to Paris as unrecognized as he had come. He spent two days with Suzanne, then went alone to Ussy for the rest of the month.

Suzanne was busy with her own friends and family, and there were holiday parties and festivities that she wanted to attend. Beckett stayed in the country. He welcomed the new year with silence, solitude and sleep.

Throughout January, 1959, he forced himself to write prose. He communicated his misery and sense of failure to Jake Schwartz, saying he was leaving theater and radio for the time being and trying without success to write serious prose. He was terrified that he had come to the end of what he called his career as a writer proper.[26]

Several days earlier, he had received one of the most meaningful honors in his entire life, but even it could not relieve the gloom that engulfed him. H. O. White wrote on behalf of Trinity College to ask Beckett if he would consent to receive an honorary doctorate of letters at the next commencement. Beckett was genuinely surprised by Trinity's offer, and replied that he felt he had no right to it, saying White was well aware of his need for personal obscurity and dread of public notice. However, he added that there was no question of his declining such an honor from his own university, and that he would accept it with emotion and gratitude.

Yet in the letter, full of warmth for the honor he was to receive, Beckett could not keep his pessimism from creeping in: writing was becoming increasingly difficult for him, he said, but nevertheless, he kept trying. He concluded sadly that he had never felt "less doctorial or literary" in his entire life.[27]

Characteristically, he told no one except Suzanne about the honor. He wrote to McGreevy and said only that he planned to be in Dublin for a week or ten days in June and hoped to see him—no mention of the degree to the only person in his entire life with whom he had ever been open and honest. "I am a very dull dog," Beckett has been known to say of himself disparagingly. "My life is dull and without interest. It is best left to the professors, who know more about it than I do."[28] He seems to be unable to share any news of himself, or to envision that anyone, even his closest friends, might want to share the joys or sorrows that come his way. His friends and associates soon grew used to finding out about Samuel Beckett's honors and awards from the newspapers. They seldom heard of anything directly from him.[29]

Beckett finally told McGreevy about the degree on May 17, when the information was made public. "TCD have taken the strange notion to give me a Litt. D."—it was his only comment.

The degree was officially awarded on February 25, 1959, but Beckett actually received it at commencement ceremonies that year on July 2, in Dublin. The following citation was presented along with his degree:

> A graduate in modern literature of this University, for a while one of our lecturers in French, then a friend and helper of James Joyce in Paris, and now celebrated throughout the literary world as playwright, novelist, poet, satirist, critic and translator, Mr. Samuel Beckett has established his right to be named among the outstanding men of letters educated in Trinity College—Congreve, Farquhar, Swift, Goldsmith, Wilde, and Synge, to mention only some of them. Perhaps it is not an unjustifiable comparison to recall how in ancient Greece the philosopher Diogenes (who, like two of the characters in Beckett's *Fin de partie*, lived for awhile in a tub) exercised his mordant wit and vivid symbolism against the follies and vices of the age. But this our modern Diogenes shows a greater compassion and humanity when he brings out weaknesses into the light of truth: indeed his famous *Waiting for Godot* is in a sense a modern equivalent of the Psalmist's *Expectans expectavi*. It is well known that Mr. Beckett cares little for the outward emblems of fame: he does us all the more honour in coming to receive our honours today.[30]

In March, Beckett's translation of *Krapp's Last Tape*, *La Dernière Bande*, appeared in *Les Lettres Nouvelles*.[31] He abandoned the libretto for Marcel Mihalovici's opera commissioned by the Bielefeld Company: "All commissions paralyze me, I simply cannot write on command," Beckett has stated repeatedly.[32] Instead, he persuaded Mihalovici to write music for *Tous ceux qui tombent*, *La Dernière Bande* or a third work which had not yet been given a title. Mihalovici chose *La Dernière Bande* because of the new musical possibilities involved in a character who must sing as both a young and an old man, and whose voice on tape must be accompanied by a live orchestra.[33]

Mihalovici asked Beckett to explain the text to him, and Beckett agreed to go through it line by line while Roger Blin acted it and Mihalovici took careful notes on the cadence of the text, its rhythm and length. During the next fourteen months, Mihalovici reworked the ten pages of Beckett's text into a musical score of two hundred sixty pages, yet in spite of the expansion, the time it took to present the opera was only fifteen minutes longer than that needed for the original play.

To differentiate from the stage play, Mihalovici called his opera simply *Krapp*, or *The Last Band;* in German, *Das letzte Band*. Elmar Tophoven translated the play into German. Beckett's command of German was excellent, but he still felt more secure entrusting the official translation to Tophoven, with whom he had had previous successful dealings. As they spoke the translation aloud, Mihalovici listened carefully, asking them to change words or inflections to make the words more suitable to the music; when that was impossible, he changed the score. Despite the inherent difficulties in such a painstaking operation, the collaboration proceeded with enormous good grace. When the work was finished, Beckett thought it very good,[34] and Mihalovici was pleased that none of the original poetry of the play had been lost in the transposition to music.[35]

Just as Beckett was working hardest with Mihalovici and Blin, he received a letter from Alan Simpson telling him that the Dublin University Players planned to present the Irish premiere of *Endgame* and *Krapp's Last Tape* at the end of March. He was shocked by the news, first because he had never rescinded the ban on his work in Ireland, and second, because he felt morally obligated to give Simpson and his Pike Theatre the first refusal for any Irish productions.

Hasty telephone calls to Curtis Brown, his London agent, informed him that blanket permission had indeed been given to the Players, as prior consultation with the author was not part of his contract with them. Beckett was upset and distressed by the affair, but since it was only several days until the March 30 opening he decided not to stop it. He was somewhat consoled when the critics called it a spectacular flop, even though the bad reviews were directed more at his play than at the acting.

There was talk in Paris of a revival of *Waiting for Godot*. Jean-Louis Barrault was about to take over the Odéon Branch theater and wanted to revive an important play in the 1960 season. Beckett was willing to allow the production if Roger Blin agreed, for he felt morally obligated to consult Blin in all negotiations for *Godot* within France. Barrault had not officially taken over the theater and was therefore unable to announce his plans, so the agreement was made *en principe*. Beckett was interested in keeping *Godot* alive in the public's mind in France and was willing to set aside his reservations about this production. He liked Barrault, but was not convinced of his ability as a theatrical entrepreneur, and he confided to friends that he felt no great confidence in Barrault and was not too sanguine about the project.[36] Beckett wanted a production on a large scale, particularly on the big stage of the Théâtre Odéon, where Blin and Martin would have the audience and publicity he thought they and his play deserved. He lobbied quietly for such a production throughout the summer whenever he met Barrault, and in September, Barrault announced publicly that *Godot* would be presented at the Odéon the following February. No contracts had been signed and nothing was legally binding, leading Beckett to comment wryly that he would believe it when the curtain rose for the first performance.[37]

Brendan Behan had come to Paris to see two of his plays which were playing in two different theaters. As always, he sought Beckett, asking for him around Montparnasse, and starting out several times for the rue des Favorites. Each time he stopped at the first cafe, where he proceeded to get roaring drunk, and so, to Beckett's relief, the two men never met during this visit. Behan had gotten into the habit of looking for Beckett in 1952, when he would show up in the early morning hours and pound on the door until Beckett or Suzanne admitted him. He was always drunk, and talked for hours, until Beckett managed to move him on his way. On one particularly bad morning, Beckett, who had slept very little, was awakened by a drunken, shouting Behan well before 6 a.m. For three hours he listened to Behan's ravings, until it was time for rehearsal of *Godot*. He persuaded Behan that a good friend wanted to hear all about his latest work, and steered him to the *Merlin* office, where a lonely and hungover Christopher Logue was drinking solitary early morning coffee. Mumbling something that passed for an introduction, Beckett pointed the blowsy Behan in the direction of the nearest ramshackle chair and hastily departed, leaving the startled Logue to cope with his querulous visitor.[38]

Behan soon discovered that Beckett was an easy touch, and whenever he was in trouble, Beckett was the first person he contacted. One night after a serious barroom fight, Behan was arrested by the French police and spent the night in jail. He telephoned Beckett, who came around early the next morning, paid the fine and gave Behan a lecture on the evils of drink, plus a substantial amount of money to tide him over until he left France. Behan bragged about it when he got back to Dublin, saying Beckett knew exactly in what order to take care of a man's needs.[39]

Behan was a tiresome bore for Beckett, but his extreme courtesy kept him from showing it. They were a curious contrast: the lean, ascetic Beckett, product of lawn tennis and yacht clubs, public school and good manners; Behan, the scruffy exborstal boy from a tenement off the North Circular Road. But these differences did not bother Beckett as much as Behan's irrepressible Irishness and his insistence that an accident of birthplace must always result in an intimate bond of friendship. It was the raucous, barroom, "we-are-all-Irishmen" state of mind that Beckett had fled, and so it was especially galling to find that it had caught up with him in Paris.

There was much Irish theater in Paris that spring: Siobhan McKenna was starring in the Dublin Gate Theatre production of Shaw's *Saint Joan* at the Théâtre des Nations. Beckett and Suzanne had been invited to a performance by resident Irish friends, and he accepted because he was interested in appraising McKenna, who had been suggested as the Irish actress most suitable for any play he might write. However, he was not to see her in this play, for Suzanne became ill and was too weak to be left alone. All winter long she had had what she called "*la grippe*," and her health seemed to Beckett to become more precarious each day. She had been ill before, but never for so long. He wondered if the circumstances of their life might not be partially responsible for her malaise. They had always been crowded in the small apartment, but now that his work was appearing all over the world, each day the postman strained under the burden of heavy packages of duplicate copies of his books printed in a babel of languages, and the sacks of letters were truly overwhelming. Being without a telephone had long ceased to be a matter of stubborn pride or smugness; it was a terrible inconvenience. With Suzanne's compulsive shopping, there was not a spare inch of space.

Both had agreed several years before that they would have to change their way of living, and now they could no longer postpone the decision. They found a new cooperative building still under construction on the boulevard St. Jacques, with a large apartment on an upper floor. It had two large bedrooms, a study, a large bath, a kitchen and dining space. Even though a Metro station was directly in front of the building to the south, it seemed to be suitable because all their rooms faced north, with a view of Notre Dame, and, in the far distance, Montmartre. Unfortunately, Beckett's study looked down on the exercise yard of the Santé prison, where Monsieur Prudent had been jailed and the Abbé Aleche hanged. He learned to keep his eyes raised and to look directly into the distance at the inspiring sight of the cathedral, but was unable to drown out the moans and shrieks of the prisoners that disturbed his sleep in summer when all the windows were open.

The apartment has two separate doors at the entrance, which prompted several inquisitive scholars to assume that he and Suzanne lived in different apartments. Now that he was able to give an occasional interview, he grew skilled at parrying the question of his marital status until exasperated questioners contented themselves with writing that he "may or may not be married."

The plan of the apartment was such that, upon entrance, one could go either directly into Beckett's study and then into his bedroom, or else through the second door into the living room. Now that he and Suzanne were leading such separate lives, it seemed the ideal floor plan. The apartment was promised for early 1960, but was not available until the end of that year, leaving Beckett and Suzanne to chafe at the interminable construction delays that kept them on the rue des Favorites for another twenty-one months.

Beckett equated Paris with a nightmare from which he was trying to escape,[40] and wanted to be able to stay in Ussy because he was finally getting started on prose. He envisioned a work divided into three parts and had written the first. He expected it to be short, and more difficult and impersonal than anything he had written thus far. With each word he felt he crawled an inch nearer to something many miles away.[41] The work became *Comment C'est* (*How It Is*), the perplexing prose work his critics have called a novel for want of a better word.

Just as he was hitting his stride and the writing began to go well, he received word from Dublin that Joseph Hone had died. There seemed to be too much illness and death among his friends, and the news of Hone's death affected him so that he could not work. To take his mind off his unhappiness and frustration, he began to read steadily for the first time in almost a year. He was utterly absorbed in Roger Casement's *Black Diaries*, which he thought were both authentic and fascinating.[42] He had known old Tom Casement, Cissie's good friend, in Dublin, but knew of Roger only by reputation. When he finished, he went on to Freud's biography, sympathizing in the third volume with the thirty-three operations for cancer of the jaw which Freud endured. In perspective, his own problems with teeth seemed insignificant.[43] A friend sent him an Aldous Huxley novel, but Beckett could not read it. "Can't take him any more. I never could. No use. Unremittingly smart."[44]

On June 22, Beckett flew to Dublin for the Trinity College awards ceremony. He was caught by reporters at the airport, but managed to express his feelings of honor while gracefully avoiding questions about his personal life and affairs, such as the self-imposed ban on his plays in Ireland, why he wrote in French and whether he would ever return to live in Ireland. He had flown alone, so that no photographs could be taken of him with Suzanne, nor any questions asked about their relationship. Jean and Caroline met him at the airport, and he went directly to The Shottery, where he stayed until July 2, the day of the award.

Caroline celebrated her twenty-first birthday on June 26 with a large party.[45] In the midst of the festivity, in a house filled with young people, music and confusion, a taxi pulled up to the door and Suzanne and a friend alighted unannounced. They had flown from Paris to be there for Beckett's degree, but had not told anyone they were coming. Beckett was not at The Shottery that evening, having fled to the sanctuary of McGreevy's quarters while the party was in progress, and so Jean and Caroline had to put aside their hostess duties long enough to see that the two women were made comfortable. Jean's French was minimal, and Caroline's that of a schoolgirl; Suzanne and her friend spoke no English, and so the situation was confused and hectic until all the guests departed and Beckett returned.

Suzanne was present at the award ceremonies, but she sat quietly and anonymously, and departed without anyone noticing her. When Beckett received the degree he was so pleased that he allowed a most uncharacteristic, smiling photograph to be taken. It was one of the few public occasions when he appeared to be thoroughly enjoying himself.

It was probably the happiest time he had spent in Ireland in years, but he wanted to get out before the happiness faded. The next day he flew to London, then went to Surrey, where he stayed with his cousin Sheila and her husband, Donald Page.[46] He had been to their home several times in the postwar years, usually managing at least an overnight visit when he was in London for a play or other business. Sheila was as close to him as if she were his sister, and he liked her husband, a large, handsome businessman who loved the quiet of his country home and was a boon companion on long walks. The Pages were great bridge players, and Beckett often played with them.

Several of Henri Hayden's paintings hung in their living room, a gift of the painter in return for staples and medical supplies Sheila had sent to Paris at Beckett's request just after the war. Over the years, Beckett gave her several other paintings, statues and mementos or works of art which were given to him and for which he had no use.

"They'll put me in the monastery yet," he explained sheepishly to McGreevy when he had gone "back into the quiet now with great relief."[47] From Surrey he went directly to Ussy, where he spent the rest of the summer working on *Comment C'est* with a slight feeling of satisfaction. His only disturbance came with the death of still another Irish friend, Ernie O'Malley, late in the summer, and shortly after that, the sudden death of Denis Devlin. He avoided the usual rush of summer visitors from New York and London by conveying his sentiments on the telephone (by now he had one installed at Ussy) or with occasional day trips into Paris.

In early September the BBC nominated the radio play *Embers* that he had written for Jack MacGowran and Patrick Magee for the Prix Italia. To his great surprise, it won.[48] The award ceremonies were to take place in Sorrento, and Beckett, feeling rested and in a better frame of mind than usual, allowed Suzanne to persuade him to attend. They were forced to participate in organized excursions to Capri and the surrounding areas, and Beckett was both angered and exhausted by his enforced attendance. When it was over, he headed straight for Ussy, as usual.[49]

In October, he decided that the walk to his little house from the railroad station was too long and he was too old for it. Since he could not depend on taxis, he decided to buy a little car, a small Citroën which at first he intended to keep for use only between the station and his house. However, he found himself wanting to travel between Ussy and Paris at times when there were no trains, and with so many parcels and so much luggage that he needed more private transportation. He loved the little car, and was soon roaring through the streets as if he had been driving in France all his life. His technique had not changed since his days in Dublin, and so he found himself quite at ease in the daredevil racing that passed for driving in Paris.

McGreevy was one of Beckett's first passengers, as he passed through Paris on his way to a holiday in the south of

France. When he returned, he told Beckett that he had seen Richard Aldington for the first time in many years, and that Aldington's financial circumstances were strained. Aldington had helped Beckett many times when he was a successful and celebrated novelist and Beckett only a poor graduate student at the École Normale Supérieure, so he sent twenty-seven thousand old francs as a gesture of friendship and in gratitude for the many favors Aldington had done for him.[50]

In Paris, Beckett met Bram van Velde for the first time since the previous year in Berne, just long enough to agree to loan his two pictures for the forthcoming exhibition. Van Velde wanted Beckett to go with him in a repeat of the Berne experience, but Beckett begged off, saying he was too tired and too mired in his latest work. He was still working on *Comment C'est*, but could not bring himself to write more than two or three hours a day, so it advanced very slowly and he thought it was very bad writing.[51] He admitted that he had "always written fast, too fast," and rationalized that this was perhaps a fault. He convinced himself that writing slowly was perhaps not so bad after all, for it gave him greater opportunity to be aware of what he wrote each day, and to play a greater, more conscious part in shaping the final manuscript than he had in his earlier writing.

He envisioned at least six more months of work before he would be satisfied with the manuscript, and called it a "horribly difficult new work in French. The hole I have got myself into now is as 'dumb of all light' as the fifth canto of Hell and by god no love . . ."[52] One thing he knew without doubt, was that as long as life lasted for him, writing was a necessity. The young man who wailed, "God knows it isn't as if I ever wanted to spend my life writing,"[53] had been lost somewhere in Roussillon and a dedicated, compulsive writer had taken his place.

Postponement and delay characterized the beginning of the new decade, as one disappointment followed another. The new apartment, promised for occupancy in January, 1960, would not be ready until April. Blin and Barrault had serious differences of opinion concerning responsibility for the Odéon *Godot*, and what appeared to be an unreconcilable divergence of views on the staging of the play led Barrault to cancel it. Beckett was exasperated at Blin's stubbornness but hesitant to approve Barrault's ideas, which were quite different from his own, so he was torn in two directions. He detested squabbles concerning vision and authority. He believed that, as the author, he knew best what should take place on the stage, and he resented being shunted aside when production began.

For Beckett, the perfect stage vehicle is one in which there are no actors or directors, only the play itself.[54] When asked how such theater could be made viable, Beckett replied that the author had the duty to search for the perfect actor, that is, one who would comply fully with his instructions, having the ability to annihilate himself totally.

"Not for me these Grotowskis and Methods," Beckett storms. "The best possible play is one in which there are no actors, only the text. I'm trying to find a way to write one."[55]

This is a very important statement about his work by a man not given to commentary or explanation, one which explains much about the direction and evolution of his writing for the theater during the last fifteen years. The reverence in which he held Stanislavski's ideas when he was a young prose writer had changed radically now that he was a mature playwright.

Beckett had two productions at the same time in two different countries, but the news of both was at best guarded. In London, *Act Without Words II* opened at the Institute of Contemporary Arts on January 25, with reviews ranging from puzzled to disapproving. In New York, *Krapp's Last Tape* opened at the Provincetown Playhouse on January 14. There, the initial notices were bad, which did not surprise Beckett at all. He expected misunderstanding and misinterpretation from American critics and audiences. At the same time, he was enormously pleased with the scant news of the production that reached him at Ussy after the play opened. As usual, he and Alan Schneider had pored over the script in long and detailed study sessions. When Schneider returned to New York, letters flew back and forth as rehearsals progressed. Once Beckett read the reviews Schneider sent, as well as the director's own analysis of the production, he became convinced that it had been done exactly as he wanted it:

> For me, I never had such good notices, even though the Atkinsons and Kerrs are furious. The action or staging sounds very remarkable, and the director seems to have done all I asked him to do.[56]

Still, the critical reception rankled. Schneider describes the reaction to Beckett's plays in terms of a domino theory:

> First they [the critics] say *Godot* was terrible, then when I do *Endgame*, they say, Well, *Godot* was not so bad but *Endgame* was awful. So I direct *Krapp*, and the critics say *Godot* was really good—terrific—but what happened to *Endgame?* And *Krapp* was really lousy. As each new play comes along, the previous ones get better while the current one is awful. Critics can't seem to comment on what's before them without dragging in the other ones and rationalizing their previous reactions.[57]

As articles and books about his writing proliferated, Beckett found that everything written seemed to be extreme. He was the new darling of the universities, where endless seminars debated his symbolism, mythology and meaning. Publications with pretensions to seriousness printed articles that usually began puzzled and ended with the grudging admission that he was an original thinker, and quite possibly one of the most important writers of the twentieth century. Yet, the most public, accessible commentary came from the newspapers and magazines which reviewed his novels and plays, and these brief statements all too often contained only superficial summation and opinion, tending to be highly negative because of it. Ever since *Godot*, Beckett had read everything that had been written about him or his work. Now he decided that it was too frustrating, and determined not to do so any longer.[58]

The past eight years had wrought great changes in his personality: meeting people and conversing with them amicably had required enormous fortitude and strength. He had learned to overcome his aversion to strangers, to answer their questions, to make them go away feeling pleased about the meeting. He had suddenly been thrust into a position where he was called upon to exhibit tact, courtesy and even friendship. For the first time in his life, he could not live as he wanted, but was dominated in all that he did by the responsibilities his writing had engendered. His every action seemed a reaction to demands initiated by others. He sometimes wondered if the result was worth the effort, especially just after the opening of a play, with more of the same carping reviews and public antipathy. At times it seemed there was no pleasure involved in creation: writing itself was often difficult and tortured, production usually a clash of personalities and a matter of catering to fragile egos, and publication only brought forth another plague of symbol-hunting scholars wanting to know "What does it all mean?"

Increasingly, as the years since *Godot* passed, he wondered himself about his life as well as his art. The silence and solitude of Ussy sustained him through a difficult period in his life. At the same time, the press of business in Paris kept him from complete withdrawal, so that the two places balanced each other and his life. Now that Suzanne no longer came with him to the country, he found himself for the first time in his fifty-four years entirely responsible for his own needs and wants. This was an enormously strengthening experience, which made reentry into Paris and the immediate barrage of others' demands less harrowing.

For Beckett the important decision during this time of introspection was to continue to write and to ignore the external world as much as possible while doing so. This decision was made slightly easier when Schneider sent the next batch of reviews, which included Tom Driver's statement that *Krapp* was "the best theatre now visible in New York,"[59] and Robert Brustein's view of *Krapp* as the "perfect realization of Beckett's idea of human isolation."[60] He had amended his decision not to read anything about him or his work: he could at least glance at whatever came his way, but would not consciously seek out anything that had not been sent.[61]

He was deeply involved in *Comment C'est*, and it was as personally disturbing as the trilogy had been. He sensed that the direction in which the work was evolving was all wrong, but he felt powerless to change it.[62] He thought perhaps it might dis-

516 ♣ SAMUEL BECKETT

integrate in the same manner as *From an Abandoned Work*, and so he gave parts of it for publication and production to test himself, to determine if he really was free of it and could truly write no more.

The quarterly review X had published a fragment called "L'Image" the previous November;[63] he sent another fragment, which he called "translation of opening of French Work in Progress" to John Calder for Pat Magee to read at a *Music Today* concert in April.[64] These convinced him there had to be more to this work than two brief fragments, and he continued to write, thinking he had at least another year before it would be suitable for publication. Even then, he felt sure he would want to "sit on it" for another year.[65]

At the same time, he wanted to write again in English, and hoped to do it concurrently with the French prose. He had no idea what it would be about, but knew that the form would be drama.[66] Herbert Blau, codirector of the San Francisco Actors' Workshop, asked Beckett about his use of two languages:

> What enlivened and disturbed him most was my remark about the language of his dramas. I said that by writing in French he was evading some part of himself. (pause). He said yes, there were a few things about himself he didn't like, that French had the right "weakening" effect.[67]

Blau was not the only one to comment on Beckett's evasion of self; Pierre Schneider suggested that writing in French was not so much evasion as an attempt to state his deepest thoughts without actually confronting the inner sphere in which these thoughts were located. Schneider made this remark in connection with *Endgame*, when he tried to explain to Beckett what exactly he had found so disturbing about the play. It engendered Beckett's enmity and caused a rift which was not mitigated for several years until Schneider told Beckett that he found *Happy Days* an entirely different experience.[68]

There were others, of course, who hesitantly voiced the same opinions, but they were always careful to state their reactions tentatively for fear of offending Beckett. He had grown increasingly sensitive to criticism of any sort, so those who wanted to remain in his good graces were careful to find something positive to say about his writing, no matter how vague they had to make their remarks.

Thus, it was no accident that he chose to write *Happy Days* in English. It was a deliberate attempt to accomplish several things at once. First, he was sensitive that none of his plays had been an instant commercial success, popular from the first performance, and he wanted public acclaim. Second, there were many things he wanted to comment upon, and since they were mostly things Irish and English, his native tongue was most suitable. He didn't think it made sense to incur derision by castigating the Catholic Church and the British government in French.

The original manuscript, called "Willie-Winnie Notes," contains long scathing passages attacking the Catholic Church, its priests and religious observance in Ireland; denouncing the effect of church domination on the Irish people; and finally, describing the evils, both of omission and commission, for which British government in Ireland was responsible.[69]

These preliminary notes were not written, however, until the autumn of the year, for commitments and responsibilities interfered with writing. The continuing problem of Edward Beckett's education required his intervention again. In March, 1960, he managed to persuade his nephew to continue to prepare for entrance to Trinity, and was relieved when Edward began to study docilely for the engineering examination.[70]

On March 22, *La Dernière Bande* opened at the Théâtre National Populaire's Théâtre Recamier in Paris, with Roger Blin directing and R. J. Chauffard as Krapp. It was part of a double bill, with Pinget's *La Manivelle* (published in the next *Evergreen Review* in Beckett's translation as *The Old Tune*).[71]

Originally Beckett had offered the part to Blin, but Blin was "too tired, tired of Beckett, in need of something different,"[72] and he turned down the role in favor of directing it. But the old fire was missing. Beckett attended every rehearsal and did as much, if not more, of the directing than Blin. It was an extremely competent production, yet not the success that he wanted, and the reviews ranged from moderate to positive. Beckett was angry about this, and the friendship that had endured severe stress in the past was finally broken. Beckett vowed that he would never again entrust Blin with a play. For several years the two men took care not to meet, and when they did so inadvertently, engaged only in guarded courtesies.[73]

In the midst of rehearsals, Beckett received a letter from Connolly Cole, literary editor of the *Irish Times*, asking him to contribute an article for a special tribute on March 30, 1960, Sean O'Casey's eightieth birthday. Beckett declined the honor, using rehearsals of *Dernière Bande* as an excuse, but agreed to participate in the tribute. He sent a brief statement:

> To my great compatriot, Sean O'Casey, from France where he is honored, I send my enduring gratitude and homage.[74]

Cole asked Beckett to enlarge his tribute, but Beckett wrote again, stating it was impossible for him to do so.[75] He was embarrassed to write more than a respectful phrase in tribute to other men, beginning with his homage to Jack B. Yeats, and continuing through his life in later tributes to such diverse figures as Richard Aldington and Avigdor Arikha. He considered his relationships too private to allow for public comment.

Beckett and O'Casey had never met. When the ill-fated *Tóstal* banned O'Casey's play, Beckett sent a brief note, to which O'Casey replied equally briefly, thanking him for his withdrawal. Other than that, the two men contented themselves with respecting each other from afar. Beckett admired O'Casey's work, but preferred the plays of Synge and the later Yeats. O'Casey, for his part, thought Beckett too pessimistic, too immersed in the sorrow and ugliness of life, and at times, too amoral.[76]

Though he did not know O'Casey, Beckett knew his wife, Eileen, and was very fond of his daughter, Shivaun, whom he had met at the home of Amy and John Gibson.[77] Gibson, a radio producer for the BBC, was an Irishman married to a Frenchwoman, and Beckett took an instant liking to them both. John Gibson was an affectionate, witty Irishman, fond of drink and talk, and Amy was a superb cook who prepared fish, Beckett's favorite food, in marvelous ways. One evening, after a performance of one of the radio plays, Beckett allowed himself to be persuaded to dine with the Gibsons, even though John had collected a large number of people on his way from the studio to his home and Beckett usually avoided such gatherings. There, Beckett sat across from a thin, shy young woman, Shivaun, who was then sixteen. Shivaun, an aspiring actress, was ill at ease in his company, and Beckett devoted himself to making her feel comfortable.[78]

When the dinner was ended, he escorted her back to her lodgings in a taxi, and asked her to call on him when she was in Paris. From that time on, whenever Shivaun was in Paris or Beckett in London, they met. Beckett fussed about her health, claiming young women ruined their health with diets, and insisted on taking her into restaurants, where he hovered anxiously while she obligingly stuffed herself with creams and cakes and he peered with myopic intensity as she ate, as though watching for an immediate bloom of good health in her cheeks. Shivaun introduced her mother to Beckett several years later when Eileen went to Paris for an O'Casey play. Again, he was impeccably courteous, taking her to dinner, showing her the best shops, and sending small gifts to her hotel before her departure.[79] He had become adept at making gracious social gestures and was no longer irritated by feeling compelled to do so.

In April, there was still another delay with the new apartment, and the moving date was officially put off until August. This left Beckett to make elaborate arrangements to house and entertain his aunt Peggy (Mrs. Gerald Beckett), and his cousins, Ann and Peter, since Suzanne, unhappy at the newest delay, had gone in a huff to Troyes to be with her mother.

He was grateful to have his little car, and took the three Becketts out to Ussy, where he proudly displayed his cottage and garden, pointing with pride to the lawn he and Frank had put in on Frank's last visit before his death.[80] He took them all over Paris, and they walked so much that Mrs. Beckett complained she would have him to blame for the arthritis she was sure to get from all the unaccustomed exercise. Ann Beckett and her mother lagged behind while Beckett and Peter raced on ahead, engrossed in conversation. Dr. Peter Beckett was a psychiatrist who had completed part of his training in America, leading Beckett to ask probing questions about the differences in theory and practice in England and America, especially in Kleinian as opposed to Freudian analysis. He was particularly interested in the British theory of rematriation, and asked detailed questions and surprised Peter Beckett with his facility with psychiatric vocabulary and familiarity with technical terminology.

It had been a long time since Beckett was able to talk about these things with Geoffrey Thompson, and since then he had continued to read psychiatric literature. His own writings provoked a stream of questions which Peter Beckett thought must have been personal; but both men conducted these conversations behind a polite and impersonal facade, as if both agreed it was best to be mutually protective of the cause of Beckett's interest.[81]

They took long drives to the country as well, and stopped for lunch one day at Châlons. When they paused in the busy town square to search for a restaurant, Ann Beckett was upset by Beckett's unaccustomed emotion. He shook tears from his eyes and said, "You should have seen this place the last time I was here—there were bodies in the square, shot by the Germans in retaliation . . ." His voice drifted off, and he could say no more. It was the only time his family had heard him mention the war since it had ended, and they were embarrassed by not knowing how to change the mood. Lunch was a series of awkward silences punctuated by too much chatter, and the afternoon seemed cloudy and sad from that point on.[82]

By mid-August, the delay with the new apartment had been extended to late fall. Now Beckett encouraged Suzanne to make long visits to her family and friends, and in an effort to take her mind off the interminable delays, he took her to concerts and art galleries, and to dine with the Mihalovicis and the few friends they had in common. Tom McGreevy came to Paris to see the Poussin exhibition, but because of a large number of commitments, Beckett managed only a few excursions to the gallery, leaving Suzanne to entertain him instead.

The apartment was far enough along toward completion that Beckett went there every day to work. In spite of all the delays and interruptions, he finished *Comment C'est* in late

August, though he could not decide whether it was finished or whether he had simply abandoned it. Lindon wanted the manuscript immediately, and Beckett gave it to him with reluctance, feeling strangely uneasy about letting it go.

"I hope you can sell fifty copies," Beckett told him glumly.

"But I shall sell at least two hundred and fifty to three hundred the first week," Lindon replied optimistically. The remark cheered Beckett, especially when Lindon added that the book had had the same effect on him as his first reading of *Molloy*.[83] Lindon planned a quick publication, hoping to have the book on sale by November, in time for holiday book buyers.

Comment C'est continues Beckett's chief preoccupations: the problem of identity, the obsession with words, the nameless teller of tales. Beckett originally intended the entire book to be printed as one long paragraph, unbroken by punctuation, capitalization or typographical marks of any sort, and the extract in X was printed in this manner. He changed his mind and divided the printed extract in *Evergreen Review* into short verses of varying length, usually no more than ten lines separated from each other by a gap of white space; he retained this division in the book. The only stops throughout are the natural pauses for breath. This technique is an integral adjunct of the text, for the voice can only speak when he has stopped panting, and the spaces between verses are meant to indicate labored breathing.

The book has three parts of equal length; the first, before Pim, has the speaker recounting descriptions of his life. The second tells of his dealings with Pim. In this section he gives himself the name Bom, and tells of the methods he employs to communicate with Pim. The third section seems to be the precursor of some of Beckett's later writings, especially *Le Dépeupleur* (*The Lost Ones*). In *Comment C'est*, the speaker extends the relationship between Pim and Bom to infinity, employing mathematical calculations to define the unity and separation of the innumerable couples, only to destroy by refutation the entire concept of the book in the closing pages. What remains is mud, slime and darkness, through which the speaker crawls, dragging his meager possessions with him in the pitiful sack he holds against his naked belly.

There are occasional references to his family: his mother,

in a large hat on a veranda, with her young child kneeling on a pillow, clad in white nightshirt; his father, who makes his living in the building trade; a grandfather who did the same; even Beckett and Suzanne on the rue des Favorites:

> image a woman raises her head from her needlework and looks at me the images are all at the beginning part one I say it as I hear it I see them in the mud soon they will cease

> She is ten yards from me fifteen yards she says at last to herself all is well he is working

> my head lies on the table my hand trembles high wind the little clouds move fast the table slips from light to shadow shadow to light.

> it isn't over she stoops blindly to her work again the needle falters in the cloth and stays she draws herself up and looks at me again she has only to call me by my name come and feel me but no

> my stillness she more and more uneasy suddenly leaves the house and goes to friends.[84]

Beckett spent eighteen months writing *Comment C'est*—tortured months of false starts and stops, of dogged persistence, and at the end, uneasiness that it might not have been worth the effort. It seems to be a curious addendum to *The Unnamable*, and so it is perhaps unfortunate to insist on calling it a novel. Instead, more attention should be paid to the language, and some consideration should be given to calling it a prose poem, after the manner of the French Symbolists—so familiar to Beckett—who often disregarded conventional poetic devices in an attempt to capture a particular image. *Comment C'est* is a work which requires careful, slow reading, one which almost demands to be spoken, in order to savor the full flavor of the language. It is surely Beckett's attempt to create a new form in writing, an attempt to distill and synthesize the raw emotion of *The Unnamable* into an intellectual expression. He has gone one step beyond the trilogy with *Comment C'est:* he has organized his private chaos into a universal expression of the human condition.

A year later, in a conversation with Tom Driver, Beckett said that art had previously struggled with the tension between "mess" (i.e., the confusion of existence) and "form." Until now, he posited, art had struggled to withhold mess and to impose form. "How," Beckett asked, "could the mess be admitted, because it appears to be the very opposite of form and therefore destructive of the very thing that art holds itself to be?"[85]

He answered his own question, saying the mess could no longer be kept out "because we have come into a time when 'it invades our experience at every moment. It is there and it must be allowed in.' "[86]

Beckett elaborated on this idea, in what is probably the best explanation of what he tried to do in *Comment C'est:*

> What I am saying does not mean that there will henceforth be no form in art. It only means that there will be new form, and that this form will be of such a type that it admits the chaos and does not try to say that the chaos is really something else. The form and the chaos remain separate. The latter is not reduced to the former. That is why the form itself becomes a preoccupation, because it exists as a problem separate from the material it accommodates. To find a form that accommodates the mess, that is the task of the artist now.[87]

When he had given the manuscript of *Comment C'est* to Lindon, Beckett wanted nothing more than a lonely month at Ussy, but throughout the fall, he was preoccupied with continuing problems. The apartment was supposed to be ready in late November, and for the first time it seemed a realistic date. Suzanne had quite given up hope, and the rue des Favorites was littered with packing cases, boxes of books and piles of possessions that she had grown weary of moving from one corner to another. She was listless and bored, and they were getting on each other's nerves. He was grateful for her visits to friends such as Marthe Gauthier, who lived in Cluny, or her mother and sister in Troyes.

Edward Beckett wrote to say that after a miserable summer cramming for "grinds," he had passed his engineering entrance examinations for Trinity on the second attempt. That situation seemed settled at last, except that Edward added somewhat belligerently that he was continuing flute lessons more intensely than before, and was following his uncle's example, as he had learned to drive and was now having great sport on the roads at Malahide. Beckett was worried about the other things in which Edward might be "following his example."[88]

There was a continuing influx of people to see and problems with forthcoming editions of his work. The recalcitrant printer of *Comment C'est* claimed first that it ruined his eyes, then that it was pornography, and he would not set the type. Publication was delayed until the following January, thus spoiling Lindon's plans for holiday sales. Limes Verlag, Beckett's German publisher, was planning a trilingual edition of his poems, and Calder and Boyars was compiling a bilingual French and English edition. Jerome Lindon, who had been asking Beckett to collect his poems for several years, was understandably upset that such volumes were appearing in other countries but not in France. Beckett felt he had no recourse but to let the planned German edition stand because he had committed himself to his German translator, Elmar Tophoven, and to the publisher as well. He asked Calder, in England, to understand that he could not allow the French poems to appear in English translation at that time because he did not want his English poems to be translated into French, and the only way he could insure this would be for Calder to content himself with publishing only the poems written in English and those which had already been published in Beckett's own translation from the French.[89]

In early November, when things were as quiet as he thought they would ever be, he dashed to Ussy for one week; then he had to return to Paris to attend to the last details of Mihalovici's opera before its German premiere. The revival of *Godot* was once more in the works, and there were more self-translation, proofs and other details of simultaneous publishing in several countries that generated endless meetings and appointments.

The apartment, miraculously, was almost ready for occupancy. The carpets had been installed, there were a few bits of furniture, and every day he carried several boxes of books to his new study.

He was so pleased to have a study, a private room in Paris where he could shut the door and write undisturbed, that he moved into the apartment well before it was legally ready for occupancy. The previous month, he had begun to work steadily on the new play in English, writing on the cover of a notebook, "Willie-Winnie notes, Ussy, October 8, 1960."[90] He was burning to get on with it, with "the excitement . . . when one knows there is something there and that it is merely a question of time servicing it."[91] He sat in the steady, cold northern light, enjoying the silence of the still empty building, writing the first version of *Happy Days*.

After twenty-three years, he left the rue des Favorites without a backward glance, relishing the space, tranquillity and privacy of his new home.

1961–62:

"BACK TO THE BATTLE, LIGHTS
AND VOICES"

 For Beckett, the year 1961 began with great mis-
giving. He could see nothing ahead but un-
planned activity and interference to keep him
from his work, and there seemed little likelihood that he would
be able to impose any structure upon his life. His holidays were
disrupted by the usual stream of visitors—from A. J. Leventhal,
who had been commissioned by an English publisher to write a
book about him, to his cousin Sally Sinclair Armstrong, on her
way from her home in England to visit her brother Maurice in
Geneva.[1]

Suzanne had not yet moved into the boulevard St. Jacques,
but Beckett announced emphatically that he was definitely installed, with all the dust of the rue des Favorites shaken off, and
he considered the move to have been worth the long wait.[2] Still,
the unfamiliar noises disturbed him, and he had not been able to
rest well. He continued to work on the new play, but with the
same sensation he had felt when writing *Comment C'est:* "Same
strange feeling of wrongness, but necessary wrongness."[3]

He fell into the habit of concentrated reading to fill the
periods when he could not write. He usually read through the
entire canon of a particular author, and at this time, he was absorbed in W. B. Yeats's *Collected Poems*. In the past, he had
deliberately shunned Yeats's poetry and knew only his most

famous poems—those which no Irishman living in Dublin could avoid—and had concentrated on the plays, for which he had great respect and admiration. There were lines in *The Countess Cathleen* that he knew by heart, and passages from *At the Hawk's Well* that never failed to move him.[4]

A curious change had taken place in his relationships with other writers: now that he was an established, celebrated playwright, other dramatists who studied his plays wanted to share their ideas, and—in most cases—to pay him homage. Audiberti, Adamov, and Arrabal all came to meet him. Ionesco, who lived across the street from the Café du Dôme, sometimes stopped him there for conversations, but usually the two men regarded each other warily. The previous year, Beckett had received a letter from Harold Pinter, who was beginning to be written about as his disciple and successor, much the same as he had been written about in relation to Joyce. Pinter told Beckett that he had had the greatest respect for his writing ever since 1949, when he chanced across a fragment of *Watt* in an Irish journal. He told Beckett how he had returned to London, looked for his other writings and eventually bought and read every postwar publication.[5] Beckett was touched by Pinter's admiration; he wrote a charming letter in reply, and the matter seemed to end there.

Roger Blin was directing the Paris production of Pinter's play *The Caretaker* (*Le Gardien*), and Pinter was attending rehearsals. Blin thought the rift between himself and Beckett had gone on for too long,[6] and when Pinter said he wanted to meet Beckett, Blin offered to introduce him and a meeting was arranged. Precisely at the appointed hour, Beckett strode into Pinter's hotel, shook hands vigorously and began to talk nervously. Pinter was surprised to find him so vibrant, and especially so talkative, for he had been warned to expect long, listless silences. They chatted for a time, and then Beckett suggested they take his little car to a run-through of Pinget's *La Manivelle*. Originally, Beckett had told Pinter he could only spare one hour, and now Pinter found himself being invited for the entire evening. At 8 p.m., they went out for a "quick" drink, which lasted until 3 a.m. Pinter wishes now that he had had a tape recorder or had at least taken notes, for the conversation encompassed "all the drama of the Western World and then some, with large smatterings of philosophy, politics, and our mutual passion, cricket."[7]

Pinter got the distinct impression that Beckett was so involved with his own vision that he had little time and little desire to read contemporary literature. Beckett preferred to talk of classical drama, particularly Racine, for whom he expressed his never-ending admiration and continuing amazement at being able to find some new interpretation relevant to his own writing each time he read the plays. When they talked about Beckett's own work, he insisted repeatedly that none of his writing possessed any form, as if he wanted Pinter to challenge the statement. Pinter disagreed, saying that Beckett's writing seemed to him a constantly courageous attempt to impose order and form upon the wretched mess mankind had made of the world.

"If you insist on finding form, I'll describe it for you," Beckett replied. "I was in hospital once. There was a man in another ward, dying of throat cancer. In the silence, I could hear his screams continually. That's the only kind of form my work has."[8]

At 3 a.m. Beckett suggested they go to Les Halles for onion soup. To Pinter's embarrassment, it gave him horrendous indigestion:

> so bad I thought I was dying. Suddenly Beckett disappeared, leaving me alone for such a long time that I thought he had abandoned me. More than half an hour later he returned, bearing a bicarbonate of soda, which he had gone halfway around Paris to find. I swear it saved my life.[9]

Beckett deposited Pinter at his hotel at dawn, but returned to drive him to the airport that afternoon. When Pinter returned to London, he began the custom of sending Beckett manuscript copies of his plays. Each time, he received a brief reply, directly to the point and usually exactly right. Pinter explained:

> For example, with *Silence*, he wrote a brief note saying he liked it, but suggested that I reconsider speech one, page five. I read it, and thought there was nothing wrong with the speech,

and I kept it in. I felt I understood the dangers Beckett was referring to, but I thought he was wrong and I was right. I wrote back and said thanks, I'd listen to it in rehearsal, and let him know what I decided. After about two weeks, Peter Hall, who was directing, called me and said everything was going just fine except for one speech, which was giving him a great bother. I said I knew which one—speech one, page five—and to go ahead and cut it. Beckett was right after all.

Another time, in *Landscape*, Beckett wrote, saying the last lines were very worrying, and that I should explain carefully to the actress how I wanted them to be said. I told him I couldn't do that because I had an idea what I wanted, but perhaps the actress wanted to do something different. I said I was certain that Peggy Ashcroft would understand how I wanted it to be done. Beckett was terribly concerned about this attitude of mine, saying I must tell the actress what to do, that I just couldn't leave things open this way. I said I preferred to leave things open, and he accepted this, but I don't think he understood it because it's not his way.[10]

Pinter always sends Beckett advance copies of his plays, but Beckett never consults Pinter before his are performed. He listens respectfully to Pinter's opinions of the productions, and usually sends a signed copy of the texts when they are published, but he never solicits advice or opinion while he is in the process of writing.

In February, Beckett went to Bielefeld for the premiere theater performance of Mihalovici's *La Dernière Bande*. A few weeks earlier, a concert version had been given at the Théâtre National Populaire in Paris to a lukewarm audience and unimpressed critics, but in Germany, with William Dooley singing the role of Krapp, the opera was both a critical and popular success. Mihalovici was enormously pleased and Beckett was, too. He saw the opera as something entirely different from his play, a separate entity, and the warmth with which he expressed his elation was for a work he admired but for which he felt no responsibility at all. Beckett flew to Bielefeld, but drove back to Paris via Amsterdam.

The side trip was carefully planned so that no one would wonder where he was during the next few weeks. For the past few years, Beckett had been uneasy with the responsibilities of his estate, increased by the financial success of his writing. His own health fluctuated between idiosyncratic illness and perfect fitness, but the steadily increasing number of friends who had died convinced him that his own demise was imminent. Suzanne had been in poor health for several years, and now she had a constant cough and had lost an alarming amount of weight. Beckett knew that he would have to legalize their relationship so that Suzanne would become his heir and executor if anything happened to him, but doing so was bound to bring the publicity he detested. He knew there would be endless commentary comparing him to Joyce, who married Nora late in their lives for the same reason. As an Irish citizen whose financial affairs were concentrated in England,[11] he had to be married there to insure the legality of the ceremony and Suzanne's right to inherit his estate.

Early in March, Beckett packed a few clothes, threw a large box of unanswered mail and the manuscript of *Happy Days* into his Citroën and drove to Calais.[12] He took the ferry to Dover, then drove to Folkestone, where he booked rooms under an assumed name in the Bristol Hotel. The next day, he contacted the registrar of marriages, and explained who he was and why he wanted to avoid the notoriety any announcement of his presence and impending marriage would surely bring. The registrar, D. A. P. Cullen, was sympathetic and promised to process the papers as secretly as possible when the time came. However, Beckett was required by English law to maintain continuous residence for at least two weeks before the marriage ceremony, and so he had somehow to conceal his presence during that time. He was there alone because there was no minimum residence for Suzanne; she was only required to be present at the actual ceremony.

For the next two weeks, Beckett spent most of his time in an uncomfortable hotel room answering letters and working on *Happy Days*. He was afraid even to walk outside for fear someone would recognize him. Then he discovered that he could travel about England as long as he had a fixed abode, so he spent a weekend with Sheila and Donald Page, took an excursion to Brighton and spent several days with other friends who lived near Dover.[13] The marriage was scheduled for March 25, and as the day approached, all seemed to be without incident. Suddenly, Beckett received a telegram from Gerald Beckett telling him that John had been in a serious automobile accident and was in the hospital in critical condition. He telephoned immediately, thinking he would have to break his English residence and go to Ireland, but Ann Beckett persuaded him to stay in Folkestone, as even she and her mother were only allowed into the hospital to see John once or twice each week.[14]

On March 22, Suzanne arrived, and on March 25, the marriage ceremony was conducted in the presence of two employees of the registrar's office who had never heard of Samuel Beckett and wondered why there was so much secrecy. Samuel Barclay Beckett stated that he was the son of William Frank Beckett, a deceased quantity surveyor; he gave his occupation as writer, his residence the Bristol Hotel, and his status as bachelor. Suzanne Georgette Anna Deschevaux-Dumesnil gave no occupation and listed herself as the spinster daughter of Paul Victor Deschevaux-Dumesnil, a deceased sales representative. At the time of their marriage, she was sixty-one years old and he was several weeks short of fifty-five.[15]

Of all their friends, he told only McGreevy and Leventhal, and she told no one. There was no ceremony to mark the occasion, and no congratulations were offered to the bride. She wanted no flowers or champagne, no telegrams, no recognition of the event. The first time she even mentioned her wedding day was in a casual conversation with Jean (Mrs. George) Reavey the following summer, when Reavey said the only liquor she had ever drunk had been a ritual glass of champagne on her wedding day.

"I didn't even do that. A wedding day was nothing to celebrate," Suzanne said disparagingly.[16] For Mr. and Mrs. Beckett, the marriage had taken place only for purposes of legality; otherwise it was meaningless.

The couple drove back to Paris and told anyone who asked that they had been away at Ussy. Quietly, they resumed their usual pursuits; together they went off to Étretat for a weekend with Lindon and his family; then Beckett resumed his usual frantic schedule and Suzanne disappeared behind the veil of privacy that separated her life from his.

The long-postponed revival of *Waiting for Godot* was in rehearsal at the Théâtre Odéon, exactly where Beckett hoped it would be staged. He became a definite presence at every rehearsal, a brooding force of which the director and the actors were always aware, smoking endless cigarettes, hunched into a third-row aisle seat or peering over the shoulders of the technicians backstage. He demonstrated movements to the actors, told them how to sit, to walk, to fall. As usual, he ignored their probing, puzzled questions and directed their attention to the exterior movement and speech. More than once he repeated his dictum that his work was a matter of simple, fundamental sounds, and that the actors should not look for meaning but should concentrate on what he intended them to do. The play opened to a full house, and as the run continued, so did the crowds and the good press. It had been scheduled to close at the end of June, but as public acclamation continued unabated, hasty plans were made to extend it through July.

In May, Beckett received word that he had been named to share the annual *Prix International des Éditeurs* with Jorge Luis Borges. It was his first major recognition, one especially meaningful because it was awarded by literary figures from all over the world and not just Europe. It was the sort of recognition that he wanted; increasingly, reviews of his work had stressed the morbid and the negative to the exclusion of other facets, and his reticence and unavailability for interviews contributed to the pervading tone of sarcasm. Thus, this award was especially meaningful because it recognized his contribution to the art of writing, which had come to be the only thing of meaning in his life.

Characteristically, he made no reference to it in his correspondence, and dismissed it as quickly as possible when any of his friends mentioned it.[17] One of the reasons for his reluctance to discuss the award was because it led so many people to speculate publicly that he was now a serious contender for the

Nobel Prize. Even the newspaper accounts of the *Prix des Éditeurs* made the connection between the two prizes. *"Un Nouveau Nobel?"* questioned *L'Express* in its headline.[18]

However grateful he was for the prize, it still was a source of unhappiness, as it exacerbated his already strained situation with Suzanne.[19] The greater his success and acclamation had become, the greater her discontent had grown. In the past few years, she had spent money wildly on personal adornment, and she had decorated her part of the new apartment lavishly. In fact, the discrepancy between her part of the apartment and his was so shocking that Beckett stopped inviting friends to visit because he could not bear their undisguised expressions of surprise. He had a sitting room, with a plain, angular sofa, a chair, a wooden table and bookcases stacked against stark white walls on which he hung his paintings by Jack B. Yeats and Bram van Velde. In his bedroom were only a thin cot covered by an undistinguished spread and an ordinary chest of drawers. By contrast, Suzanne's section of the apartment was crammed with large French furniture; every bit of wall and floor space was hung or filled with an assortment of heavy, baroque objects.

The gulf between her ornamentation and his simplicity was indicative of more than their decorating tastes: it represented a chasm in their relationship which they no longer cared to bridge. She resented his fame and felt that he should have made a more public acknowledgment of her important role in bringing it about. She wanted to be known as the helpmate who had made his success possible. He wanted nothing at all known about himself, least of all details which he considered of no more than domestic import. He felt he had demonstrated his gratitude to her by marrying her when both considered the ceremony a mockery.

Thus, when public speculation about Beckett as a candidate for the Nobel Prize began, Suzanne was filled with envy and hostility. When the telephone rang, she would say, "You answer it—it's the Nobel Committee for you." When he asked if the mail had come, she would say, "Yes, your Nobel Citation arrived today." When he asked if there were messages, she would say, "Only from Stockholm." She was not discreet with these remarks, and thought nothing of making them when other people were present.

They had nothing in common anymore, but neither thought of parting. Beckett began to envision their relationship as one of ineluctable bondage, and from then on, veiled references to their situation began to appear in his writing.

By the end of May, he had finished *Happy Days*[20] and spent a few days away from Suzanne at Ussy. The news from Ireland was not cheering, for John Beckett had not made normal gains in his recovery. A recent operation to pin the bones in his arm had failed, and he was still in the hospital. Beckett planned to go to Dublin in mid-June to see what he could do for his cousin; then he planned to go to London to take care of business, and to Surrey to visit Sheila Page and Mollie Roe.

Before he could leave, he had proofs to correct and the somewhat disheartening business of organizing his remaining original manuscripts. He had broken with Jacob Schwartz when he discovered that his manuscripts had fetched higher prices than Schwartz had told him.[21] He discovered this accidentally, when an American bookseller, Henry Wenning, told Beckett he had had to forgo buying the manuscript of *Comment C'est* because it was so expensive. When Wenning told Beckett how much his manuscripts now commanded, Beckett shook his head sadly and said, "It's not important, but I was paid only a tiny fraction of those sums."[22]

Originally Beckett had begun to copy out his writings by hand for Schwartz because he needed the money. Then he continued to do it out of a sense of obligation to the man who had so thoughtfully sent a gift with each small check. Besides manuscripts, Beckett sent Schwartz his galleys and page proofs (to which he affixed his autograph) and anything else that might possibly have monetary value because it bore his signature. Now, to find out that he had received only a pittance from Schwartz was bitterly disappointing—more because of the breach of friendship than the money. From that time on, Beckett referred to Schwartz as "the Great Extractor,"[23] and Henry Wenning became his official agent for such matters. Throughout their conversations, Wenning had been appalled by Beckett's naïveté in his dealings with booksellers and bibliophiles, but gradually he realized that the relics and artifacts of his profession meant very little to Beckett; only the writing itself was of value. Beckett gave Wenning a sack full of signed first editions as a gift, including a copy of the rare *Henry-Music*. He admitted they were his personal copies, but refused to take money for them. For a time, however, Wenning received nothing to sell, because all that Beckett still owned were the manuscripts of *Molloy* and *Waiting for Godot*; the former because it was one of his personal favorites and the latter for purely sentimental reasons.

When Wenning did sell something, he rarely sent the check to Beckett, for there was always "a friend," someone "down and out on his luck temporarily,"[24] to whom Beckett asked Wenning to send the money directly. Beckett's needs were few and easily satisfied; he had spent most of his life on the fringes of genteel poverty, and now that he had wealth, his habits had changed very little. He didn't need all the money that came to him and so he gave some of it away to those who did; the rest he cautiously invested.

At times this resulted in some unpleasantness. Lucia Joyce, after a silence of many years, began to write to him again because of such an act of generosity. There had been a reunion at Sylvia Beach's flat the previous January to discuss republication of *Our Exagmination*. Among the guests were Stuart and Moune Gilbert, Marcel Brion, Robert Sage, Maria Jolas and Beckett. Both Faber and Faber in England and New Directions in the United States had allowed the book to go out of print; the rights had reverted, and now the book was free to be taken on by someone else.[25] As Beckett left, he told Sylvia Beach quietly that he wanted his share of the proceeds to be sent to Lucia, to help pay for the costs of her confinement at St. Andrew's Hospital, Northampton, England.[26] As a result, he began to receive depressing letters from Lucia, talking of events that had happened thirty years before as if they were current, and of people who were long dead. He dutifully answered all her letters, and this in turn caused her to send birthday and Christmas gifts to him.[27] Naturally, he reciprocated. Lucia's periods of lucidity alternated with those of total withdrawal, and it was impossible to predict how long each would last. He soon grew accustomed to the erratic nature of her correspondence, but he never ceased to feel pained and distressed by it.

By early June, Beckett realized—not without some relief—that he would have to postpone his trip to Dublin because of pressing commitments in Paris and London. He sent the script of *Happy Days* to Alan Schneider, who was moving ahead rapidly with plans for an autumn production in New York. George Devine also had a copy of the script for the London production, which was originally scheduled to take place before the first New York performance.

Devine wanted Joan Plowright to play Winnie. She was the most illustrious star who had thus far been interested in appearing in one of Beckett's plays, and he was pleased by the glamour her name would lend to the production. On a very brief trip to England, Beckett met Devine during the intermission of John Osborne's *Luther* (which he thought "unspeakable"),[28] but their few moments of conversation settled nothing; the world premiere seemed destined for New York, as Plowright had another commitment which would delay the English production. In New York Schneider moved ahead his plans, signing Ruth White for Winnie and John C. Becher for Willie. *Happy Days* was officially scheduled to open at the Cherry Lane Theatre on September 17, on a triple bill with Edward Albee's *The Death of Bessie Smith* and *The American Dream*.

Since Schneider's other commitments kept him from traveling to Paris, and since Beckett was unwilling to go to New York, the two men began an extensive correspondence to smooth the way for the production as Beckett would have wanted it had he been there to direct. Beckett's letters could easily become a textbook for *Happy Days* should he ever decide to publish them.[29] They are long and painstaking, filled with minute directions for action and how it should correspond to speech; detailed descriptions of lighting, even to the physical properties, brand name and positioning of each individual bulb; and a series of drawings in pen and ink done by Beckett to show exactly how he wanted Winnie and her mound to appear, and what the position of Willie should be at all times in relation to her.

There was so much correspondence that Beckett had little time for anything else that summer except correcting proof and entertaining visitors. The Bielefeld production of *Krapp* gave two performances at the Théâtre des Nations in early July, and it was a gala event, as McGreevy and others came from Ireland and other friends came from Holland and Germany. *Godot* was still playing at the Odéon, so that Paris seemed to be one grand Beckett festival to the celebrating friends who descended in even greater numbers than usual.

Harold Hobson was one of the British contingent who came to hear *Krapp* and see *Godot*. The critic and the playwright had become friends when both discovered a mutual passion for cricket. During Beckett's brief trip in June, he and Hobson had a relaxed lunch at the home of John and Bettina Calder[30] and then went on to a match at Lords. Beckett was disconcerted several days later to see an article in the *Times* in which Hobson had related most of their luncheon conversation. Even though it dealt almost entirely with cricket, Beckett was still unhappy because it was about his personal life, not about his work. With Hobson in Paris, the opportunity seemed ripe to speak of this matter, even though the situation was delicate because Hobson was no ordinary journalist and friendship was involved.

Everything seemed suddenly to happen at once: McGreevy, whose health had been deteriorating for several years, had made a special effort to be in Paris for the *Krapp* evening. Now, as he was about to depart for Ireland after what Beckett feared might be one of their last meetings, complications arose which prevented them from personally saying farewell.

Hobson had driven to Paris in his own car, and on the morning of McGreevy's departure, it broke down completely. Hobson's French was inadequate for the emergency, and he telephoned Beckett to come at once to help him. Beckett spent the entire day telephoning garages and going from one to the other until he found one who guaranteed that the car would be repaired by the following morning. Hobson seemed so helpless and frail in the face of the catastrophe that Beckett spent the entire day ministering to his needs. During lunch, he found the opportunity to ask Hobson for more discretion in writing about personal matters, to which Hobson readily agreed, expressing regret that he had unknowingly violated Beckett's confidence. Beckett assured Hobson that his integrity as a journalist had never been in question, but a personal idiosyncrasy compelled him to avoid the spotlight whenever possible.[31]

In mid-July, Beckett succeeded in getting away to Ussy for what he hoped would be at least ten days of undisturbed rest and his first opportunity to begin the English translation of *Comment C'est*.

The first thing he saw when he entered the gates at Ussy was the iron shutters of his little house hanging bent and awry.[32] The windows were broken, the door ajar, and everything strewn from one end of the house to the other. He had been burgled. There was much of value to a bibliophile in the house: books, papers, letters, manuscripts and a small painting by Henri Hayden—all of which were disdained by the intruders. Instead they ate all the food in the larder, drank the wine and left the empty bottles, and then packed up most of the household goods and all of Beckett's underwear. He reported it to the police, who were not interested, since they had approximately twelve such burglaries a week in the summer homes near Beckett's which dotted the banks of the Marne. And so, he squandered most of his precious ten days cleaning the mess and organizing his papers.

He returned to Paris to work with Elmar Tophoven on the German translation of *Happy Days*, which was scheduled to open on September 30 at the Schiller Theater Werkstatt in Berlin.

It was now highly unlikely that a British production could be mounted before the year ended, and by September, Beckett had to give up all plans to go to Ireland because he was too busy in Paris. He was relieved to have good news from John Beckett. The surgery to correct the problems caused by the accident had been successful, and he was due to be released from the hospital within the month. The idea for a radio play had come to Beckett that summer, and he asked John to collaborate on the music. It was an idea which did much to impel John's swift recovery, and it gave Beckett something to look forward to besides endless self-translation. He wrote *Words and Music* in late summer and early autumn, and completed it by November 20, the date he affixed at the end of the manuscript.

Another reason he decided to postpone a trip to Dublin was the imminent arrival of Edward and Jean Beckett. After a year at Trinity, Edward finally convinced his mother that he was going to become a professional musician and would not return to the engineering school.[33] He made arrangements through Prieur in Dublin, and with Beckett's assistance in Paris, applied for and was accepted at the Paris Conservatoire. Jean seemed resigned to the decision, and soon Edward was settled into the same pension on the rue D'Assas where Strindberg had lived, and was caught up in the excitement of his studies and life on the Left Bank. Within a few weeks, Beckett was proudly telling friends that his nephew was "an old Montparnassian."[34]

Edward spent much of his time in the boulevard St. Jacques, where Suzanne fussed over him as if he were her own child, making sure that he had enough to eat and that his laundry was done. Beckett was proud of him, accompanying him to concerts and taking him to the cafes and bistros of the quarter, introducing the young man to all the bartenders and regular customers. They grew to be a close little family, with Edward's presence having a decidedly domestic effect on Beckett and Suzanne's relationship.[35]

Once Edward was settled, Beckett returned to his translations. He was struggling intermittently with *Comment C'est* and had finished the first draft of the second part. He decided to call it *How It Is*, the last three words of the book, which could just as well be the first, imitating the circularity of *Ulysses* and *Finnegans Wake*. Also, he deliberately used the impersonal pronoun because he wanted to give his speakers a more emphatic dehumanization by removing their sexuality. He wanted to keep the English as faithful to the French as possible, then—forgetting the French—to write an English version that would satisfy him. After that, he had to render *Textes pour rien* into English and *Happy Days* into French.

"I've a good year of labour and hard and dull and no possibility of new work," he told McGreevy, "very tired and periodically disturbed and interrupted."[36]

From New York and Berlin, he heard simultaneously that *Happy Days* "came in for a lot of abuse, but appears to be reviving fairly cheerfully in both places. Can't ask fairer than that."[37]

In New York, the play became the highlight of the 1961 season, running for one hundred performances and bringing an Obie to Ruth White. *Happy Days* was nonetheless subject to the same turns of fortune that dogged the rest of Beckett's plays. Walter Kerr, who still loathed them, disassociated himself from the Obie judging committee in protest over the inclusion of both the play and Miss White among the nominees. *Time* was to have printed a major review praising the play, which the producers were depending on to increase the audiences and ultimately the run, but it was crowded out by news of movies and sports.[38] Thus, the initial negative reviews had nothing to counter them, and it remained for public acceptance by New York theatergoers to induce other critics to review the play in a more positive manner. It was a slow, frustrating process, but in the end both Beckett and Schneider agreed that they considered it a positive experience.

Beckett had been away from the art world since he ended his association with Duthuit and the *transition* group, but suddenly found himself caught up in a whirl of gallery openings, parties and celebrations, beginning with a Bram van Velde retrospective at the Knoedler gallery in Paris. He bought a gouache by Avigdor Arikha, a young Israeli artist living in Paris who had become a good friend. Arikha—short, wiry and nervous—was a veteran of the 1948 war in Israel, and in Beckett's opinion, painted the vision at the void.[39] A young Spanish painter, a friend of Jean Martin's, had been given a job at Galleries Maeght with the promise of a group show, and this called for celebration at Lindon's. Other parties followed the Arikha and van Velde shows, until Beckett yearned for Ussy, where he had spent only forty-eight hours the entire past month.[40]

When he finally escaped to the tranquillity of the country,

he was unable to plunge directly into his own work, and gradually eased himself into it by reading and tending to his correspondence. He was saddened to hear from Sylvia Beach that Harriet Shaw Weaver had died in England. Even though he had only met Miss Weaver on two brief occasions, he felt the same kinship and respect that all Joyce's friends directed toward this selfless woman who had been so important in Joyce's life. "I bow again to what she did and shall think of her when I think of goodness,"[41] he wrote to Miss Beach. He replied to Kay Boyle, trying to remain noncommittal in response to her impassioned demand for his opinion of the Adolf Eichmann trial. As far as Beckett was concerned, he had made his last political statement when he killed rats at St. Lô.

When he finally finished all his correspondence, there was nothing left to do but settle down to the chore of translation, and he began to work on both *How It Is* and *Oh les beaux jours* simultaneously. In mid-December he took a break to correct the proof of the Calder and Boyars edition of *Poems in English*. He returned them with a brief note to the editor that he was very pleased with the quality of the book and wished he could say as much for the poems.[42]

"Lucky you," he complained late one night in a bar to John Montague, "with all your work still ahead of you while I have nothing left but to translate my own poor miseries."[43]

Beckett spent the first two months of 1962 at Ussy, working on translations, writing one new radio play and polishing the manuscript of *Words and Music*.[44] He had written *Words and Music* the previous fall in English, in response to a continuing plea from Donald McWhinnie and the BBC for as many radio plays as he could write, and also for John Beckett, as a means to speed his recovery from the automobile accident. The new radio play was *Cascando*, written in French at the request of Marcel Mihalovici and the ORTF. This play was originally called *Calando*, a musical term meaning diminishing in tone (equivalent to *diminuendo* or *decrescendo*), but Beckett changed it when ORTF officials pointed out that *calendos* was the slang word for cheese in French.[45]

The only other appropriate title seemed to be *Cascando*, even though Beckett had already written a poem with this title in 1936. From the Italian, it means stumbling, falling, tumbling, and is usually associated with rubble or jumbled ruins, which is exactly the situation of the play, with one speaker, the Opener (l'Ouvreur), who directs another, the Voice (la Voix).

Beckett told Alec Reid this play was "about the character Woburn, who never appears."[46] It concerns the efforts of the Voice to tell a story about a man named Woburn that will satisfy the Opener, thus allowing the Voice to remain silent from then on forever. When the Voice falters or the Opener grows tired of hearing him speak, music is heard.

Beckett's usual preoccupations comprise the activity of this play: the Opener is afraid to begin, perhaps because he fears the same repetition of themes which can never be resolved to his satisfaction, thus necessitating still another opening. Also (perhaps because of the adversity of the reviews and criticisms of Beckett's other writings), the Opener expresses his increasingly overwhelming need for withdrawal and isolation, and his steadfast refusal to offer any comment in return. The Opener comments:

> What do I open?
> They say, He opens nothing, he has nothing to open, it's in his head.
> They don't see me, they don't see what I do, they don't see what I have, and they say, He opens nothing.
> He has nothing to open, it's in his head.
> I don't protest any more, I don't say any more, There is nothing in my head.
> I don't answer any more.
> I open and close.[47]

Words and Music makes music a more integral part of the text, giving it the status of a character. Croak is similar to the Opener, in that he directs the two others: Words, also called Joe, and Music, who is called Bob. Each night, Croak forces Words and Music, who seem to be in his bondage, to talk about themes which might bring him some semblance of peace, such as "love," "age," and "the face"; but Words becomes confused and substitutes "sloth" for love. Words and Music clash throughout, as the poetry and music are seldom synchronized. Finally, in despair, Croak shuffles away with a deep sigh. This is probably the most straightforward of Beckett's radio plays, and in some sense, the least satisfying. There is no brooding presence of a Woburn to give the play a universal symbolism and raise it above an ordinary exchange of Beckett's pervasive preoccupations—the impossibility of love, the inability to conquer language and the resulting overindulgence of prose, which is once again unsatisfactory and therefore abandoned until the next time.

John Beckett, excited by the project, had already completed the music by March, when Beckett was satisfied with *Words and Music* and saw no need to rewrite further. The BBC accepted the script for broadcast on the Third Programme sometime that fall; Felix Felton was signed to play Croak, and Patrick Magee took the part of Words. Mihalovici postponed writing his music for *Cascando* because of other commitments, and it was not broadcast until October 13, 1963. Roger Blin directed and played l'Ouvreur, Jean Martin was la Voix.

The weather that spring was as leaden and gray as the political situation. As the date approached for the signing of the Algerian cease-fire at Evian-les-Bains, the situation in Paris grew increasingly grim. Police patrolled conspicuously, and persons with Algerian connections were uncomfortable and uneasy. For Suzanne, whose family had colonial associations and whose sister lived in Algeria, this was an especially trying time. She had been in bed for weeks with the same chronic pain and cough and showed no sign of improvement. Lindon, whose sympathies for Algerian liberation had made him a prime target for surveillance and repression, was suffering serious financial losses as well as the threat of the loss of publishing permits without which he could not remain in business. Beckett quietly loaned him large amounts of money needed to keep Éditions de Minuit afloat. In the years since, Lindon has expressed his gratitude for Beckett's generosity on this and several other occasions when Lindon's political views made publishing difficult.[48] Sartre asked Beckett to add his signature to the letter written by 121 other writers and artists protesting the Algerian war, but he declined. He refused to take any active part in the struggle which split France into two hostile camps—those who wanted independence and those who fought against it. As with World War II, his official attitude was that of a guest in a foreign country, and he would not openly offend the hospitality that allowed him to live there.[49]

One of the happier events in Paris that spring was the announcement that Thomas McGreevy had been named an Officer of the Legion of Honor by the French Government, which earlier had given him the Cross of Chevalier in 1948. There was a gala reception at the Irish embassy in honor of all the Irishmen who had been honored by the French government, and Beckett was invited. He declined the invitation and all others of an official nature. There was also a constant stream of invitations for premieres, openings, and parties. He replied to every one courteously and promptly, but rejected them unless he felt bound by some obligation to attend. An Irish couple, resident in Paris and famed for the very grand party they gave every year, sent their annual invitation; for the first time he breached his own personal etiquette and made no reply. He had never attended their parties and resented being asked. He thought it was time that people such as they, who supposedly knew him well, realized he could not abide large gatherings and stopped inviting him. His rudeness troubled him, but he had been telling himself for years that he needed to simplify his life, and this was one way to begin.[50]

He did accept one invitation, even though it, too, was a gala event—the opening in Paris of Mary Manning Howe's play, *The Voice of Shem*, an adaptation of *Finnegans Wake*. A large contingent of Dublin Irish was there, as well as the Paris Irish, and there was a festive reception after the performance at the Irish embassy. During the intermission, the wife of a prominent Dublin cultural figure whom Beckett had known slightly began to harangue him for writing what she called "mud and slime and filthy creatures." Why, she demanded, did he "waste his obvious abilities on the lowest forms of humanity?" Why was he "obsessed with all that is wrong with life?" Beckett stood grimly silent, eyes cast down at the floor, while the woman continued vehemently. The moment came to an embarrassing end when the woman finished her diatribe and went away, obviously satisfied with her little speech.[51] When it was over, Beckett made no reference to it.

He was rescued by Roger Blin, whose presence provided an excuse to leave. Blin was on his way to Zurich and Geneva, where he had been invited to direct a Swiss production of *Endgame*.[52] He told Beckett that requests for interviews had taken a new form: journalists no longer wanted to discuss the implications of the play, but wanted instead to know something personal about the author. Unfortunately, the invisibility that Beckett clung to was almost gone. He could no longer sit with friends in the Dôme or the Coupole without being stared at, having his picture taken, and even (to his horror) being asked for his autograph by tourists. On several occasions he was recognized by American scholars who thought it their right to sit at his table and engage him in long conversations about his writing. Usually they were polite and so was he. But on one occasion, a thoroughly obnoxious person ignored Beckett's stubborn silence and demanded repeatedly to know the meaning of one of his novels. Beckett endured the situation far longer than any of his friends thought he should, and finally, in one of his few public outbursts of anger turned on the intruder and said, "Oh for god's sake, shut up and go away!" Afterward, he apologized for his outburst to his friends, then shook his head sadly and invited them to go with him to a workingmen's bar on a little-known side street where they were sure to be unrecognized.[53]

The time had come when he thought he must allow something to be written about him, and he chose Lawrence Harvey to do it.[54] Harvey was a young professor at Dartmouth College whom Beckett had met the previous fall when Harvey came to live in Paris for a year. Beckett had avoided all scholars whose interest was the least bit biographical, but he took a liking to the quiet, earnest Harvey, who was studying seventeenth-century French literature. As he came to know Beckett, Harvey suggested that he would like to write a detailed study which, for clarification and accessibility, would include biographical details.

In the winter of 1961, Beckett gave permission in a curious manner for Harvey to write a semibiographical study. Harvey was living in a tiny house in a Parisian suburb. One night, in the midst of a storm, came a knock on the door. When Harvey opened it, Beckett was standing there, soaked by the rain, holding a bundle of papers. "I thought you might be interested in these," he said. He went inside just long enough to exchange pleasantries, then went back to Paris.[55] When Harvey examined the papers, he discovered that Beckett had given him the only extant manuscript of *Dream of Fair to Middling Women*, the still unpublished short story entitled *Echo's Bones*, all of his critical texts to that date, a typescript of *Éleuthéria* and several important short manuscripts.[56]

Early in their meetings, Harvey decided to limit his study to Beckett's poems and his critical writings.[57] This was a deliberate decision, made because Harvey's academic specialty did not include contemporary literature, and he felt unqualified to criticize the novels and plays. Also, there was a question of magnitude: a critical-biographical study of Beckett's entire canon seemed likely to become a multivolume project.

In the months that followed, Harvey wrote a study of *Whoroscope*[58] and Beckett was pleased with it: "His huge study of *Whoroscope* is most done, and of course, as I have told him, out of all proportion to its occasion. It was rather pleasant to be reminded of all I had once known, and old Baillet, and quite forgotten."[59] Beckett directed Harvey to only one of his friends—McGreevy; he told him to be sure to speak to his enemies, but said he would have to find his way to them unaided.[60] As Harvey continued, Beckett seemed reconciled to telling more than his curriculum vitae and Harvey continued to probe ever deeper. McGreevy was upset by Harvey's persistent questioning, and wrote hurriedly to ask Beckett if he was sure he knew what he was doing. Beckett replied, "My feeling about the whole thing is that it will be done in any case, and the more accurate the better."[61]

True to his promise, Harvey submitted the entire manuscript to Beckett in 1969, before it was published, but Beckett discovered that he was unable to bring himself to read it. The experience was too unnerving; he simply could not deal with it. He was shocked by his inability to control himself, but he recoiled from the manuscript in horror, as if he were Dorian Grey, looking in the mirror at his own imperfect self.[62] He insisted that all but the barest details of his father's death and his mother's illness be excised completely. He removed all the names of persons who had been important to him.[63] Then he gave the typescript to A. J. Leventhal and asked him to read it carefully and remove all further biographical references.[64] The book thus became the excellent critical study that it is, with only fleeting biographical references. It had been a painful experience for both men, especially for Beckett, who discovered that he still could not relax the control over his privacy that seemed, even to him, to veer from silly affectation to desperate need.

In May, after several weeks of indecision, Beckett decided not to accompany McGreevy to the Venice Biennale, where the Irish section had mounted an important exhibition of the paintings of Jack B. Yeats. He gave the excuse that he was too busy with events in Paris and might possibly have to go to London; then he admitted the real reason—"too frightened of the press"[65] —and sent his two paintings instead.

He felt an overwhelming need to sequester himself in Ussy. Nevertheless, invitations continued to pour in which he felt he could not ignore. He had met Igor Stravinsky the previous year in Amsterdam, and now he was invited to lunch with him, his wife and Robert Craft in their rooms at the Plaza Athénée. He drove in from Ussy for the day in his "sardine can," as he had christened his little Citroën. Craft described him then as having ". . . a furrowed forehead, a wrinkled and aggrieved face, long fingers, a good deal of silver mining in his teeth. His startlingly blue, deep-set eyes, along with the way his hair stands up, suggest a bluejay . . ."[66] He was able to control the hysteria which lurked beneath the surface of his demeanor, except for his eyes which most of his acquaintances interpreted as having a "hunted" or "startled" appearance. It took enormous amounts of inner reserve to sustain his equanimity on such occasions, and he was always relieved when they ended, no matter how much he liked the persons involved. Stravinsky was in the midst of a quarrel with a critic, prompting his wife to proclaim that all critics should be ignored. Beckett disagreed, reminding her wryly that "critics live such a long time." He quizzed Stravinsky on the possibility of notating the tempo of the performance of his plays, and was especially interested in timing the pauses in *Godot*. Stravinsky liked the idea but thought the circumstances of dramatic production were too variable to make such directions enforceable.

After several solitary weeks at Ussy Beckett dashed into Paris again on May 30 to meet Suzanne at Orly airport, where she had flown from Geneva. Roger Blin was touring with a French company of *Waiting for Godot* and Suzanne had celebrated her improved health by going to Switzerland for a holiday. She discovered that mountain air made her breathing much easier, and urged Beckett to plan a real vacation with her anywhere he liked in the Alps. He was too busy to agree at that time; the following morning he drove Suzanne to her mother in Troyes, and headed back immediately for another concentrated work session at Ussy.

He was "on edge with life in Paris,"[67] and tried to stay away for as long as he could. *Happy Days* was just out in the Faber and Faber edition, and he was determined to forge ahead with the French translation, which he had definitely named *Oh les beaux jours*. He was translating *Words and Music* (*Paroles et musique*) into French and *Cascando* into English. At the same time, he was writing a new play, which he called simply *Play*, and which was not an easy task.

"I have been here for the past week struggling with a new short play I can't get right," he wrote to McGreevy. "Back to the battle, lights, and voices."[68]

He immersed a man and two women up to their necks in tall urns, with their faces made up to resemble the material of the jars in which they are confined, so that their humanity seems to have disappeared and they have become one with the objects that enclose them. He gave them no names; they are "Man," "Woman 1" and "Woman 2." None of the three knows that the others are present; each speaks only when a light is directed upon him and stops when the light either goes out or moves on to another.

The play is about adultery:

W1: I said to him, Give her up. I swore by all I held most sacred—

> *W2:* One morning as I was sitting stitching by the open win-
> dow she burst in and flew at me. Give him up, she
> screamed, he's mine . . .

> *M:* We were not long together when she smelled the rat.
> Give up that whore, she said, or I'll cut my throat—[69]

The characters speak in flat voices, unaware of each other
and of where they are. As the play unfolds, the audience is made
aware that it knows more than the characters about what is
happening on the stage, and it is a disconcerting experience. W2
asks, "Are you listening to me? Is anyone listening to me? Is
anyone looking at me? Is anyone bothering about me at all?"
and the feeling engendered is one of happening upon an embarrassing moment with no means of graceful exit. The experience
is almost as if the audience becomes the fifth character (if the
light is the fourth), wandering accidentally onstage during a
performance, to be greeted with the snickers and hisses of still
another audience, actually the audience's own subconscious observing its reaction. *Play* is a totally theatrical experience, probably the most perfect example of Beckett's considerable dramatic skill, but it was hard to write and took a long time. He
wrote each part separately, then interspersed them, working
over the proper breaks in the speeches for a long time before he
was satisfied.

One of the major problems with bringing it to successful
realization was the manner in which his own life was divided
into segments, so that his concentration was fragmented and
time to work on it not nearly as available as he would have liked.
There were more letters from Lucia, on holiday in Wales, suggesting that he contribute to the nurses' fund at the sanatorium,
and he did so, to please her.[70] Henri and Josette Hayden insisted
that he interrupt his work to lunch with them at Reuil-en-Brie.[71]
Edward Beckett came to spend a weekend at Ussy, resting before going to Dublin for the summer. But Beckett refused to go
through papers belonging to Joyce's estate when Maria Jolas
asked him by telephone to help her, saying he wanted no part of
Joyce's literary remains, especially now that Ellmann's biography had appeared.[72]

Now that he had a car, Beckett felt obligated to meet

friends when they arrived at Orly airport, and to drive them back again when they departed. The little "sardine can" made so many trips back and forth that Beckett boasted he could make it in his sleep.[73] Usually he made the trip unannounced, surprising friends who had no idea he would be there to greet them when they emerged from customs.[74]

Thus he surprised George and Jean Reavey. On the trip into Paris, he told Jean Reavey that he could not comment on several plays she had written because he had decided sometime earlier not to allow himself to be put into a position where he would have to do so. Instead, he launched into a self-conscious discussion of the process of writing a play, using himself as an example. He described it as a three-fold process: first, putting himself inside the characters; then, as their creator, trying to keep a certain objective distance, while at the same time, visualizing every word and movement from the audience's viewpoint. He had to envision everything. He felt the need to hear the play and see it, and employing an overview of the total stage business forced him to simplify his writing in order to keep it all in his mind, thus making it more dramatic and more stageable.

Beckett said that he had not visualized *Godot*, but had simply written lines, one after the other, that looked good on paper. "I was lucky," he said, "that the dialogue when spoken sounded as good as it read."[75] When he wrote *Fin de partie*, he tried to visualize the entire concept of the play, but it required too much concentration and he found himself reverting to the technique that worked in *Godot*—writing dialogue until he was satisfied with the way it looked on paper, occasionally saying a line or two aloud. From then on, it was not enough for Beckett to write the lines, occasionally "hearing" them as he did so; instead he "spoke" every line out loud before committing even a word to paper. His maxim—that every playwright should plumb the depths of his own mind, in control of everything that happens on stage, envisioning it as if he were the audience—became difficult to follow, so that his plays became increasingly unconventional. He felt that it made his work simpler, but more playable. It was the only way in which he could gain the stark, controlled effect he sought.

Beckett cautioned Jean Reavey to be aware of every movement she wanted the actors to make before she wrote a word. He said he even knew what direction his actors would face before they spoke because what he made them say depended on it. He needed to know for himself where the aspirations and pauses fell, and whether or not his words would be comprehensible as well as believable to the audience. He said that he not only spoke his lines, but sometimes shouted them, and sometimes even said one character's lines while making the movements of another.

For Beckett, the director was the least important person during the writing of a play, in part because he always visualized himself as the director, and also because his most important consideration was the audience. He compared his role as playwright and his relationship within the play's audience as similar to an artist who hangs his painting on exhibit for the first time.

Beckett defined a play in terms of unity of stage time, stage space and stage situation. In his utilization of stage space, he found himself tending more and more toward restriction of movement, because for him, "each actor has his own home on the stage. He finds it and he keeps to it."[76] Beckett believes that this tendency to restrict space makes an actor comfortable and gives him the power to project himself into the role.

As a possible illustration of his statement, Reavey offered *Happy Days*, where Ruth White had created a world in miniature while trapped in her little mound, with her parasol, her purse and its pitiful contents. Yes, Beckett agreed, the play could not have worked if Willie had had more movement or if the people Winnie mentions had been dramatized physically. The play depended on tightness in space and time to be effective. He said that when *Godot*, which was first performed on a small stage, was moved to a larger theater, what had formerly taken the characters only one or two steps now took many. They were farther away from each other, and the stage business became complicated, as much more had to be accomplished physically while the lines were still spoken at the pace perfected in the smaller theater. Beckett said he thought his work was best performed in small theaters. He spoke with distaste of theater-in-the-round, saying it imposed an often insurmountable burden on the writer, who might not have visualized his play in such an arena while he was writing it.

He urged Jean Reavey to pay attention to modern music, because he believed it was the strongest influence on modern drama. He likened the stripped-down simplicity of many contemporary scores to a willingness to take greater risks in the search for new forms, and it was this willingness to confront failure that made it so exciting. Pinget's *La Manivelle* was just about to open; Beckett had been attending rehearsals regularly and insisted that the Reaveys attend a performance. He used this play as an illustration of how important the proper use of music could be to a playwright, especially one who was cognizant of the importance of uniting the two disciplines. He himself had become fascinated with Bartok's music. Alan Schneider always brought a record when he came to Paris, usually Handel or Schubert, but on his last visit, Beckett quietly implied that he would be interested in studying Bartok's music to see if it might be useful to his own writing.[77]

For the brief time that the Reaveys were in Paris, Beckett put himself entirely at their disposal. From the first luncheon at Orly to the last dinner at the Closerie des Lilas, he saw that all their needs were met, even taking them to his bank when they needed to cash a check. When they expressed surprise that he still transacted his business in a branch office near the rue des Favorites, now decidedly out of the way since his move, Beckett said it was much simpler for him to go where they had known him for years than to subject himself to the scrutiny of the staff in a more convenient office.[78] When the Reaveys were ready to depart for London, Beckett insisted on driving them back to Orly, even though it meant arriving at their hotel at 7:30 a.m. Punctual as always, he found Jean Reavey helplessly trying to convey the alarming news in English to the French concierge that the elevator had stuck between floors with her husband and all the luggage inside. Beckett dashed up the four flights and peered through the opening in the roof at the hapless Reavey.

"Ah, Godot has arrived at last," Reavey exclaimed in greeting, but Beckett was not amused.[79] He set to work with businesslike authority to instruct the concierge in the intricacies of elevator operation, and soon they were speeding to the airport. In rather strained silence, they arrived just in time to board the flight after the briefest farewell.[80]

The next day, he and Suzanne were at Orly again, this time on their way to a much needed holiday of their own. Suzanne was suffering again from debilitating cough and was losing weight. Her doctor insisted that she needed a complete rest, preferably in a high altitude, and so they were on their way to Kitzbühel, Austria. They stayed in a small hotel on the side of a mountain, where Beckett alternated periods of working on *Play* with long walks and frequent rests on a sunny terrace. Suzanne's health improved quickly and on August 27 they returned to Paris. But within days, the cough was back. He fell into the same maelstrom of people to see, things to be seen to, and work not working out.[81] The vacation had been little more than an interruption for him.

Musical events which he felt obligated to attend also infringed on his time. Edward Beckett, just back from a three-week master course in Cologne, was playing with a small quintet; Beckett went to hear him, and went with him to hear others.

He was surprised when he encountered Stravinsky and his wife at a concert on the eve of their departure for Russia and the great musician came over before the performance and spontaneously embraced him. Stravinsky repeated his embrace as he left the theater, and Beckett was deeply moved by the demonstration of respect.[82]

There were problems with the London production of *Happy Days* and he decided to go over for rehearsals before the November 1 opening. When Beckett wrote the play, he assured Donald McWhinnie that he would be the director, since McWhinnie's direction of *Krapp's Last Tape* had pleased him, but now George Devine decided that he wanted to direct it himself, and Beckett was in a quandary, since his contracts with the Royal Court gave Devine authority in such matters as direction and casting. Devine wanted Joan Plowright to play Winnie and had delayed the production once on her behalf, then agreed to wait until after her marriage to Sir Laurence Olivier. Plowright had become pregnant soon after her marriage and was forbidden by her doctor to act until the child had been delivered. When her son was born, Plowright wanted to rest and asked Devine to postpone the production a few months longer. By this time,

McWhinnie had gone on to other commitments of his own, effectively freeing Beckett to concede to Devine's direction. All seemed well until Plowright became pregnant again, thus postponing production for another year if they waited for her. By this time, she was no longer sure if she wanted the part, because attractive opportunities to work with her husband had been offered. Beckett was bitter about the excessive delay and the loss of a name star, and he urged Devine not to wait any longer.

Still looking for a well-known actress, Devine asked Vanessa Redgrave, who wanted no part of anything written by Beckett. Peggy Ashcroft also refused, and Ruth White, who had been superb in New York, was not free. Devine finally signed Brenda Bruce, of whom Beckett knew only that she had a superb reputation. At that point, he would have accepted anyone, just to get the play on, but Bruce proved to be all that her reputation said, and when the play finally opened, she gave a commanding performance as Winnie.

Beckett had also been working off and on during the past year with Jack MacGowran, preparing a one-man show called *End of Day* for a first performance at the Gaiety Theatre in Dublin on October 5, 1962, as part of the *Tóstal*. MacGowran and Beckett had first met in 1957, during the BBC broadcast of *All That Fall*.[83] In the years since, MacGowran had become one of Beckett's leading interpreters and one of his favorite companions. MacGowran—tiny, fragile, highly charged—lived to act and really only came alive when he was on stage. Beset by problems in his later life, MacGowran turned to pills and liquor in an effort to stave off the deep depressions that plagued him. Beckett understood MacGowran's moods and did much to keep him from giving way to the darkness and terror. He wrote *Embers* and *Eh, Joe* especially for him, and recommended casting MacGowran to all his directors. When Donald McWhinnie conceived the idea of a one-man show with MacGowran reading from Beckett's works, Beckett encouraged the project. MacGowran directed all his energies toward the show, and became so engrossed in it that he seemed to have overcome his own anxieties. At first MacGowran intended to do straight readings, but as he thought about it, he developed a different idea:

I knew that readings would not appeal. So I developed a composite character of the intellectual tramp, and this became my central figure. I began with Molloy: "I shall soon be quite dead at last"—well, what he is saying is "I am going to be, in spite of all," and then he goes on to his reminiscences of his father, his mother, his youth, his experience, how he finds no answers, the moments of happiness, the humor, the double vision of tragedy and comedy, because these after all are closely allied and Beckett saw them at one and the same time. This is why it is so hard to determine if the lines are funny or tragic. Despair is the wrong word here. Generally it is human distress. No one ever despairs for long in Beckett. Their predicaments are so much worse than life but they have to be to make them apparent.

The key word in my show is one I think is the key word in all Beckett's writings: "perhaps." He is sure of only two things: he was born and he will die. Perhaps the world will be better— perhaps God will be there—this may happen and Beckett will be pleased. There is more hope than despair in Beckett and I felt I had to correct the seriousness with which he is taken. I was upset by what people leave out of their interpretations of him, and I was upset when I put my show together by all that I had to leave out. I had to settle for shape and form and development—to find a line of thought and continue on with it.[84]

MacGowran was entirely responsible for the script, which he did not show to Beckett for his prior approval. Subsequently Beckett worked with MacGowran on the script and made substantial changes because he approved generally of the content but not the shape, and so the text was much refined in the succeeding versions.[85] Beckett was responsible for the costume MacGowran wore: a very old, too-large overcoat, ragged at the bottom, dirty and black, held together with a large pin. He also wore a grimy scarf, a tattered brown handkerchief, a pair of old beat-up work shoes several sizes too large, trousers too short and no socks. Ming Cho Lee designed the setting, a large gray rock with a backdrop suggesting an overcast sky. Beckett approved of it primarily because it gave the impression of a small, womblike space.[86] Simplicity was the keynote of the setting and the interpretation as well:

Beckett told me that when I came to a passage with several meanings, the obvious one is the right one. He told me he did not create symbols where they did not exist, only where they are apparent. He kept repeating that line from *Watt*—"no symbols where none intended." At that time he was very annoyed with the symbol-hunting scholars who seemed to be breathing down his neck all the time.[87]

MacGowran's show played in Dublin for one week, then opened in London at the New Arts Theatre on October 16. Beckett was in the audience for the opening—a rare event—but MacGowran needed the reassurance of his presence and he could deny MacGowran nothing. MacGowran was another friend for whom Beckett felt obligated to appear at Orly. It was, however, more than obligation which found him waiting at the exit from customs each time MacGowran came to Paris: it was a feeling of responsibility for the wispy man who had become one of the best interpreters of his work and whose mental condition so closely paralleled his own.

Unlike Beckett, who took great pains to compartmentalize his friends, MacGowran wanted everyone he was fond of to meet, and thus insisted that Beckett drive with him to Orly to meet José Ferrer, his then wife Rosemary Clooney, and her musical director, Bob Thompson. MacGowran had warned Ferrer and Clooney of Beckett's reluctance to meet strangers and of his aversion to adulation, and so they maintained a respectful distance in their conversation. Thompson, however, was so surprised to meet Beckett that he lavished praise on him and then fired questions about his writing. As always, the subject turned to the question of Beckett's indebtedness to Joyce.

"Yes, I did a great deal of work for Mr. Joyce," Beckett replied. "I believe him to be one of the greatest writers and he is a man for whom I hold enormous respect." Then, as if he wanted to be sure that Thompson understood what he was saying, enunciating carefully, Beckett replied at length to the question of his indebtedness: "I am sure that every letter, every syllable, every word, every sentence, every paragraph, every page, every chapter of every book, had meaning, because that is the way Joyce committed his thoughts to paper. In my case, I write because I have to—I don't mean for money—but for my

own needs. I don't know where the writing come
am often quite surprised when I see what I have ⟨
paper. Writing, for me, is an entirely different pɪ
was for Joyce."

He continued, still choosing his words with caɪ₎. ₌ₜ ₌₌
be fatuous of me to pretend that I am not aware of the meanings
attached to the word 'Godot,' and the opinion of many that it
means 'God.' But you must remember—I wrote that play in
French, and if I did have that meaning in my mind, it was somewhere in my unconscious and I was not overtly aware of it."

For the first time during this long speech, Beckett broke
into a wry grin. "And besides, there is a rue Godot, a cycling
racer named Godot, so you see, the possibilities are rather endless. . . ."

Thompson asked another question, but Beckett had talked
enough for one session. "I can't possibly comment further upon
my work," he said abruptly, signifying an end to his graciousness. "To enlarge upon it, to explain it, would imply that I felt
superior to it. I've said all I can about the writing itself. Further
comment upon my part would be sheer arrogance."[88]

During the month he was in London, Beckett lived quietly
at John Calder's flat, going to rehearsals of *Happy Days* and
spending weekends with his cousins in Surrey.

"What brings you to England this time, Sam?" Mollie Roe
asked him.

"I've written another misery," he replied; then, as if pleading with her to accept it, he reached out and grabbed her hand
and said, "But I had to do it! I had to do it!"[89]

John Beckett was in London for *Words and Music*, which
was broadcast for the first time on the BBC Third Programme,
November 13. John was a good friend of Brendan Behan, now
confined to a private London nursing home where he was in the
midst of an "aversion" treatment to cure him of his alcoholism.
John wanted to visit Behan, and Beckett went along. It was the
first time he had actually seen Behan since 1952, and the change
was shocking. From his bed, Behan told long, rambling, incoherent stories about drugged greyhounds. Beckett had to admit
that he had never before seen Behan when he was sober, and the

sight of his hulking carcass lumped under the wrinkled bed-clothes signified a terrible waste of spirit and talent.[90]

Beckett flew back to Paris the day *Happy Days* opened at the Royal Court and immediately set out for Ussy to work on *Oh les beaux jours*. The weather was clear and cold, with brilliant sun, and he basked in it just outside his front door, huddled from the wind, correcting his typescript.[91] By December 17, 1962, he had finished it and sent a copy to Roger Blin with a note reminiscent of the one he had sent with *Fin de partie:* "Here it is if you really want it, but you had better truly want it."[92] At the same time, he sent another copy to Adam Tarn for Polish publication in the theater journal Tarn edited in Warsaw. He and Tarn had been friends since Maria Jolas introduced them in 1956, and Tarn had had a number of Beckett's plays translated, printed and performed in Poland. Tarn had been extending invitations for Beckett to visit Warsaw since the first Polish production of *Godot* in 1957.[93]

"Can you guarantee that I can come to Warsaw without any public notice? That I can walk down the streets without anyone knowing me, and I will not have to attend large parties?" Beckett demanded.

"It's a small town," Tarn replied, "it's not like Paris. Everyone will know you are there; I can do nothing to keep you isolated."

"Then I can't come," Beckett stated flatly. When *Godot* was performed, he asked for photographs of the production and copies of the reviews (which Tarn translated before sending) and for detailed critiques by Tarn and others whose opinions he respected, such as the translator Julian Rogozinski. He wrote to Tarn, saying it seemed to be exactly the sort of performance he wanted, "very Chaplinesque," and that only perhaps in Israel had it been done more to his satisfaction.

Now, with *Oh les beaux jours*, he was about to begin the task of mounting his first major production in France in six years, and he was eagerly looking forward to it. This production, he would insist, would carry the mark of his own personal direction. He was determined.

1963–65:

"I SHALL HAVE TO GO TO NEW YORK . . ."

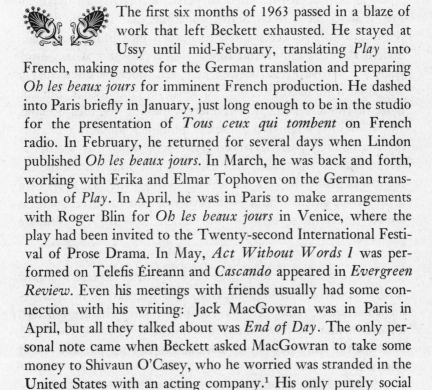 The first six months of 1963 passed in a blaze of work that left Beckett exhausted. He stayed at Ussy until mid-February, translating *Play* into French, making notes for the German translation and preparing *Oh les beaux jours* for imminent French production. He dashed into Paris briefly in January, just long enough to be in the studio for the presentation of *Tous ceux qui tombent* on French radio. In February, he returned for several days when Lindon published *Oh les beaux jours*. In March, he was back and forth, working with Erika and Elmar Tophoven on the German translation of *Play*. In April, he was in Paris to make arrangements with Roger Blin for *Oh les beaux jours* in Venice, where the play had been invited to the Twenty-second International Festival of Prose Drama. In May, *Act Without Words 1* was performed on Telefís Éireann and *Cascando* appeared in *Evergreen Review*. Even his meetings with friends usually had some connection with his writing: Jack MacGowran was in Paris in April, but all they talked about was *End of Day*. The only personal note came when Beckett asked MacGowran to take some money to Shivaun O'Casey, who he worried was stranded in the United States with an acting company.[1] His only purely social event took place in May, when on the same day he attended new exhibitions by Henri Hayden and Bram van Velde. For more

than four solid hours he was bombarded by well-wishers, old friends and strangers, and he felt as if he were on exhibit as much as the paintings.[2] He fled to Ussy, where he had more proofs to correct and a new translation. And, as always, there was the crushing weight of correspondence which he persisted in answering without assistance. The queries from American scholars were inundating him, and he learned to reply as briefly as possible. He told them all that he could be as deep in unconscious meaning as they cared to make him. An example of how he fended specific queries can be seen in his reply to William York Tindall, who asked if he had read Werner Heisenberg's *Uncertainty Principle*. If so, Beckett replied, he had "succeeded in repressing it."[3]

Another series of letters flew back and forth across the Atlantic as Barney Rosset tried to persuade Beckett to make his first visit to the United States sometime that year to film an original script. Rosset wanted to branch into filmmaking, and invited Beckett, Pinter and Ionesco to create new works especially for Grove Press. Beckett hesitated, since he knew that it was almost impossible for him to write on commission. But the more he thought about it, the more appealing the idea became, and in March he allowed Rosset to announce publicly that during the coming year he would write something that would be filmed shortly thereafter. Actually, by the time the announcement was made, Beckett had already written the first draft of a script about a man who is both perceiver and perceived, who is always under the scrutiny of the camera, which is the ultimate perceiver.

For the next few years, Beckett's life centered almost totally upon his writing, directing and translating for performance—theater, radio, television and now film. His life fell into a pattern: first to Ussy for solitude and time to work, then into Paris for the endless meetings with actors, agents, publishers and scholars.

In late May, he went to Ulm-Donau for the last few rehearsals of *Play* (*Spiel*), which was to have its world premiere on June 16. He expected to be there only until the dress rehearsal, when he and Suzanne planned to go to Innsbruck for several weeks' holiday. However, he became so caught up in technical difficulties with the lights and urns that he stayed on until the premiere. The lighting was of particular concern, as it has continued to be in every production of the play with which Beckett has been associated. In the first production, the light was meant to come from a single source, preferably one mobile spot, swiveling at maximum speed from one face to the other and situated at the center of the footlights, thus lighting the three faces from a very short distance and from below. When one spot was used, great dexterity was required on the part of the technician to insure that the light went on and off rapidly on each face, with no blur as it passed from one to the other. At first, three separate spotlights were used, but Beckett found this unsatisfactory because they were so obviously three lights and did not give the impression of emanating from a single, inquisitorial source.

As he worked with the technicians, Beckett discovered a curious difference between theater in Germany and that in France and England.[4] The German technicians seemed infinitely more patient, more willing to respond to his most insignificant remark and to strain for a perfection that had only been approximated in his other productions. The German director seemed more interested in perfecting the play according to what the author intended than in terms of his own directorial vision. As for the German actors, they were so docile and so willing that it seemed Beckett had discovered at last what he had previously only dreamed about—actors who were willing to efface all aspects of themselves. He was fascinated as minor contretemps between the director, the actors and the technicians were all resolved without temper for the good of the play as determined by the author. Beckett watched, astonished, as one of the actors failed on the first attempt to perform a bit of stage business exactly as he [Beckett] wanted it, and was castigated unmercifully by the director in front of the entire company and an assemblage of visitors and journalists. If this had happened in England or France he would have expected the actor to walk off the set. At Ulm-Donau the unwitting offender stood in docile silence, straining to capture the director's every word so that the next attempt would be perfect.

When Beckett finally left Germany, it was with the intention of returning soon as the official director of any play of his that was to be produced there. It marked the beginning of a continuing and satisfying relationship with modern German theater.

As for new work, he had written his last play for the theater—or so he told himself and others.[5] It seems incongruous that even as he found himself completely involved in things theatrical, he was making public statements to the effect that he was through with it. Theater had served a very important need in his life; it gave him financial security, allowed him to break the block that had overpowered his creative faculties and, perhaps most importantly, it provided the mental stability to adjust to a life-style that previously would have destroyed his emotional equilibrium. It is curious that he could insist that he would have nothing more to do with theater even while he was planning to take a more active part in directing his plays; nevertheless, for nearly two decades, each production for Beckett has been "the absolute last one." It is always "The finish—the end. Now it's time to return to the important writing." And for him, the "important writing" always means prose.[6]

His critics have argued whether he is a playwright who happened to write novels or a novelist who also wrote plays. One can only speculate on Beckett's reasons for insisting on this distinction, but there are several known factors which might have some bearing on it. First of all, there is the question of health. Both he and Suzanne had been plagued for years with all sorts of never-ending, troublesome afflictions; both were convinced they could not continue a life as active and involved as they had been accustomed to living. Beckett insisted that if he were lucky, he had only a few good years left to live, and he wanted to concentrate on a major work. Each repeated attempt to produce prose had either drifted off in abandoned failure or else became transmogrified into some form of drama. He was convinced that with time and freedom from interruption, he could channel his efforts into some successful prose. Thus, retreat from all things worldly, especially the enforced convivial-

Roger Blin (Photo Pic)

Thomas McGreevy in the early 1960s, shortly before his death (courtesy Elizabeth Ryan and Margaret Farrington)

Beckett in Paris, 1965 (Jerry Bauer)

Beckett receiving an honorary degree from Trinity Colleg
Dublin 1960 (courtesy Jean and George Reavey)

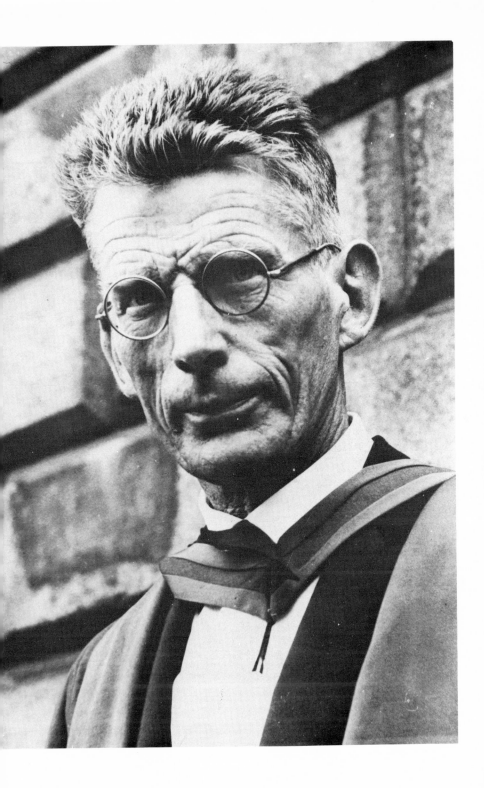

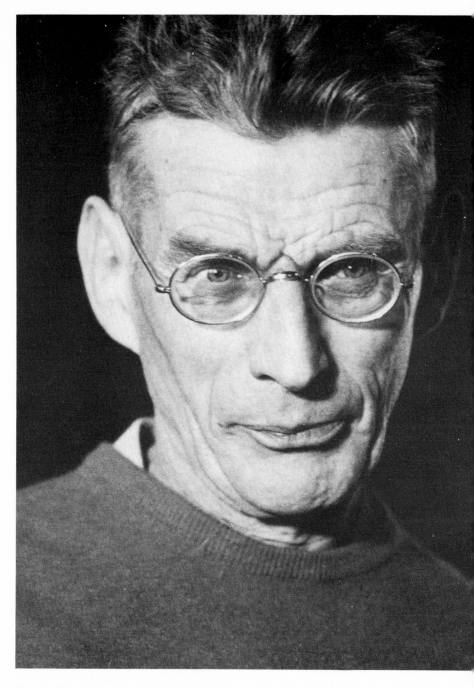

Beckett in London, 1964 (Zoë Dominic)

Beckett in Paris, 1964 (Giselle Freund, Magnu

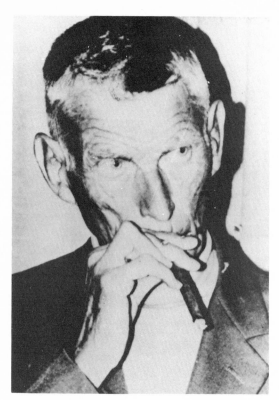

Beckett in Tunisia just after winning the 1969 Nobel Prize for Literature (Wide World Photos)

Portrait of Beckett by Louis leBrocquy, 1965 (courtesy
Louis leBrocquy)

◄Beckett in 1971 at the studio of Stanley William Hayter
(courtesy George Reavey)

Beckett in London, 1973 (Jerry Bauer)

ity of the theater, into an austere, self-imposed monastic life seemed to be his only course.

Also, there was the simple feeling that now, when he had enough money to live as he pleased, he should be able to do so. There was a part of him that was unable to accept the fact that he was no longer a private person. He was still innocent enough to believe that he could tell all the interviewers, publishers, producers, scholars, and even the merely curious, that he no longer wished to be involved with them, and that they would all disappear from his life, as if by magic.

Even the little bars off the main boulevards were no longer sanctuaries because he was recognized and sought after there as well. All that seemed left to him were dinners in private homes, which he disliked because he could not control his comings and goings without appearing rude, or the back tables at the Closerie des Lilas, where tourists seldom congregated. It was sad to see him insisting with childlike authority that he would no longer live this way, while at the same time he continued to make himself available to almost everyone who wanted to see him.

Because he stayed in Ulm-Donau longer than expected, there was no time for a holiday; he had promised Blin to be in Paris by the third week of June to start rehearsals of *Oh les beaux jours*. The previous winter, when Blin first read the script, he had told Beckett he was puzzled by Winnie and was unable to think of an actress who could portray her. He asked Beckett to describe Winnie as he envisioned her, so that he could look for an actress similar to Beckett's description. Beckett described Winnie as "a little heavy, actually a little bit fat, about fifty, well-preserved. A virile woman, perhaps, with expressive eyes and a large bosom."[7]

This posed a problem for Blin, because the actresses who fit Beckett's description all verged on the comedic:

> I couldn't think of anyone who could have all the characteristics and not look merely ridiculous five minutes after the play started. That physique, in the situation where she was buried in the sand, constituted a kind of caricature. But the role necessitated an actress who had dramatic and comedic

possibilities at the same time, someone who could suggest a whole range of possibilities.[8]

Blin thought of Madeleine Renaud, who was totally unlike Beckett's description:

> Although she didn't correspond to the physical character, she could project the total image of Winnie, and the role would be spoken by a voice which could bring the utmost to the text, which in this play was more important than the acting. There were two things of paramount importance in this play, Winnie's voice and the music—they constituted dramatic effect. If they were right, then the acting would be right, everything else would be right.[9]

Blin told Beckett that he wanted Renaud, and reluctantly Beckett agreed: "When you have the greatest voice in the French theatre, you do not insist on other, less important qualities."[10]

Beckett worked steadily with Renaud and Jean-Louis Barrault, who played Willie, from June until August. Because of Beckett's overpowering presence, Blin did not call himself the director, but instead billed it as a *"présentation de Roger Blin,"* which caused confusion among the critics, who thought he planned to make a speech before the play.[11] He did this on purpose, in an unsuccessful effort to give himself more authority, for he knew that Beckett would insist on a commanding role in the production and he wanted to protect his own part in it.

The first performances were given in the Odéon Petite Salle, a small theater inside the larger Odéon Théâtre de France, but almost immediately the play was moved into the larger theater. In order to keep a feeling of intimacy and confinement, Barrault limited the seating to the orchestra and the first balcony and moved the stage forward over the orchestra pit. Matias designed the setting, creating a bright orange sky for the background. In the New York production, the sky had been blue, but Matias wanted to stress heat more than pleasure. He wanted the audience to be discomfited by the intense glare brought on by a sky in gradations of a single color; the top was bright orange, and the very bottom was pale, which Blin remembers as so pale that it sometimes seemed to be gray. Renaud, as Winnie, was dressed in rose, and the strip of sky directly behind her also had a rosy glow. The platform which comprised her mound was all of orange shaded toward brown. Because the audience's eye was constantly disconcerted by all the orange, it was always drawn back to the actress, whose rosy glow was the only comforting area on the stage. As the play proceeded and Winnie's situation became more grim, the lights gradually faded until only one remained, casting a gray shadow on her, until even that was extinguished. Beckett was delighted with this setting, and was ecstatic with the lighting, about which he had acquired a phenomenal expertise from the German production of *Play*.

No matter how much his cast urged him, Beckett would not go to Venice with them for the opening. He chose instead to steal away to Ussy, where he returned to the grind of translation, correspondence and proofs. While Blin was in Venice, where *Oh les beaux jours* was garnering impressive reviews, *Happy Days* opened in Dublin at the Eblana Theatre, with Marie Kean giving a performance as Winnie that won universal raves. To have a play so well received in Ireland was an astonishing piece of news, and it cheered Beckett for the coming opening in Paris.

As was his custom, he reserved a large block of seats for his Irish visitors, and was pleased to hear that H. O. White planned to attend. White, retired from Trinity for several years, was in poor health and afraid to make the journey alone, so he invited R.B.D. French to go with him.[12] When they arrived at Orly on the morning of the first performance, they found Beckett waiting to drive them to Paris to take them to lunch. Beckett sat nervously throughout the meal, toying with a cigarette, then patiently assisted the fragile old man up the stairs to his hotel room before going off to take care of the last-minute details of the performance.

That night, White insisted on attending the play, even though he had to be led into the theater by someone on either side of him. Afterwards, Beckett hosted a party at the Falstaff, and against French's advice, White went. The party was festive because the play had gone well and everyone knew it. In fact, it was the biggest and happiest opening night celebration for any of Beckett's plays in Paris, and he was an unusually convivial host.[13]

At 2 a.m., French returned to his hotel, leaving White, who insisted on staying until the very end. At 4 a.m., exhausted but exhilarated, White's long day ended when Beckett brought him back to his hotel. For the next few days, in spite of all the demands on his time now that the play had opened, Beckett entertained White.

White returned to Dublin in pouring rain, was led from the airplane directly into a wheelchair and then taken to his bed, from which he emerged only briefly until his death a short time later. His few days in Paris had been one of the happiest events of his life, and he told everyone who came to see him that Samuel Beckett was one of the truly good persons he had been privileged to know.[14]

At the end of 1964, Beckett discovered that he had worked on six productions, spending more than half the year in the theater. Besides those with which he was personally involved, there were others over which he brooded and fussed at a distance.

Play opened in New York on January 4, directed by Alan Schneider, following an exchange of correspondence that had consumed much of Beckett's time the previous winter. He sent drawings to accompany his directions, asking Schneider to make the urns taller and thinner than they had been in the German production. Also, he cautioned Schneider to make sure that the actors were either standing or kneeling, but not sitting inside them, as if some degree of actual physical discomfort had to accompany the sense of disorientation he wanted the actors to convey.[15]

In February Roger Blin took a touring company of *Fin de partie* throughout France. Beckett felt compelled to go over the entire production before Blin's departure, even though Blin probably knew more about how he wanted it performed than anyone.[16] Beckett was present during the entire week of casting and first rehearsals of Barrault's revival of *Fin de partie* in Paris, and since *Play* (*Comédie*) was being cast at the same time for a June opening, he found himself running between two theaters. He went to London in March for rehearsals of the first English production of *Play*, filled with ideas based on his observation of the Ulm-Donau *Spiel*. Also, it occurred to him in Paris, while watching the first run-throughs of *Comédie,* that the second reading of the script might work just as well if it were not a strict repetition of the first act. He likened it to "the light growing tired,"[17] and wrote to Devine to describe it:

> According to the text it is rigorously identical with the first statement. We now think it would be dramatically more effective to have it express a slight weakening, both of question and of response, by means of less and perhaps slower light and correspondingly less volume and speed of voice. . . . The impression of falling off which this would give, with suggestion of conceivable dark and silence in the end, or of an indefinite approximating towards it, would be reinforced if we obtained also, in the repeat, a quality of hesitance, of both question and answer, perhaps not so much in a slowing down of actual debit as in a less confident movement of spot from one face to another and less immediate reaction of the voices. The whole idea involves a spot mechanism of greater flexibility than has seemed necessary so far. The inquirer (light) beginning to emerge as no less a victim of his inquiry than they and as needing to be free, within narrow limits, literally to act the part, i.e. to vary if only slightly his speeds and intensities.[18]

The problem of this interpretation lay, of course, in the lighting. Mechanical spotlights were almost impossible to manipulate to Beckett's satisfaction, but he wanted Devine to use manually operated lights.

Other details of staging gave almost no trouble because the cast was intent on performing exactly as Beckett wanted. Rosemary Harris, Billie Whitelaw, and Robert Stephens all brought a passion and dedication to rehearsals which he had hitherto seen only in Germany. Whitelaw's deep brooding voice caught so many inflections that Beckett found himself at times listening to her instead of rehearsing the play. Whitelaw's voice had the same effect on him as Pat Magee's had had earlier, when he wrote *Krapp,* and he knew that he wanted to work with her again, perhaps even to write a play for her.[19]

His curiosity had the beneficial side effect of making him feel more comfortable at opening night performances, and he stayed in London for the opening of *Play,* which he assumed would be enthusiastically received. However, the critical reaction was mixed. Beckett's theater was moving towards minimalism, and the critics were unsure of how to deal with it. Ticket sales, however, were good.

After the performance, Jocelyn Herbert gave a party in her tiny mews house for the company and their friends. Beckett was relaxed and sat quietly in a corner conversing with several people, eating a small plate of fish and drinking white wine. Later, he played the piano to accompany Bettina Jonic as she sang Schubert lieder.[20] For some of the company, it was a startling sight, for they only knew him as the tyrant who dominated rehearsals. He had become a grim, exacting director who now had as much knowledge as anyone connected with his plays and he felt confident to speak on all aspects of the production, often with a severity and rigidity that he had not shown before. He worked well with Devine, he admired Herbert's settings and he respected the actors in the company—all of which should have made for happy working experiences, but often didn't. He wanted his own production and nothing less would satisfy him.

When he left London, he returned to Paris for rehearsals of *Comédie*. Once again there was the same tense situation: the official director, Jean-Marie Serreau, suffered the author's presence and allowed him to dictate his wishes throughout the production. But Serreau was involved with other theatrical ventures at the same time and used Beckett's continued drive to impose his views on the production as an excuse to neglect *Comédie* in favor of the others. Beckett thus became the director in everything but name. One week before *Comédie* was to open, the stage had not been built, the light did not work and the actors were unsure of themselves in the face of one lackadaisical director (Serreau) who left them to their own devices and another, a rigid perfectionist (Beckett) who was determined to control them. Beckett called the rehearsals as impossible as ever and said he was sick and tired of the whole thing.[21]

Fortunately for Beckett, his first directors became his friends, and their desire to retain his friendship took precedence over their desire to control productions. Alan Simpson described Beckett's single-minded determination to control his productions by comparing him with Brendan Behan: "Both men do what they want, when they want, how they want. . . . Beckett conceals it under charm."[22] Philippe Staib, who produced the Paris *Fin de partie*, described this feeling:

> The strength of the man is that he imposes his will without it ever being felt and without ever needing to insist. From the outside one can only have a profound desire to penetrate this closed universe, mingled with the certainty that such an ambition is impossible.[23]

Problems mounted with *Comédie*. Beckett delayed the opening for a week because Serreau had not acquired the proper lighting equipment. Tempers flared and the situation was tense, but Beckett would not permit the play to open in Paris until all was exactly as he wanted. Last-minute efforts to pacify him succeeded, and the play opened on June 14. He wrote petulantly to McGreevy that the production was not as good as it had been in London, even though he had done it "practically single-handed and long to get away from it all to Ussy."[24]

He only managed a few days at Ussy because he was committed to being in London on June 29 for rehearsals of *Endgame* with Jack MacGowran and Patrick Magee. He liked to work with the two Irishmen, and as usual, they managed to perform as he wanted with a minimum of friction on all parts. Rehearsals proceeded smoothly, as MacGowran was quiet, probing and questing, while Magee's confidence and ease were apparent even at the first reading.

"Sam, how would I say to Hamm, 'If I knew the combination of the safe, I'd kill you'?" MacGowran asked.

Beckett answered quietly, "Just think that if you knew the combination of the safe you would kill him."[25]

MacGowran paused, then spoke the line perfectly. It was this way throughout rehearsals during Beckett's short time there, and it was a peaceful hiatus before the hard work that was to come.

"I shall have to go to New York for a fortnight or three weeks in July or August and am not looking forward to it," Beckett wrote casually to McGreevy of his first trip to the United States.[26]

Beckett did not want to go to New York, but in this production his presence was essential. He was afraid of New York without ever having been there: to him it was one large, loud cocktail party, peopled with shouting journalists demanding interviews, and leering crowds of inquisitive onlookers. He had a deeply ingrained distrust of New York and the American literary establishment, going back to the days when he so desperately wanted to sell *Murphy*. But making a film was something he had never done, and as his ideas about theater evolved, it seemed that film was likely to provide him the ultimate control that he had been searching for since *Godot* was first staged. Lately, he had begun to posit the idea that the perfect play was one in which there were no actors, only the author's words and the audience to receive them. How he would present these words was still unsolved, but he was giving most serious thought to it.[27] In a film, he reasoned, the author would have perfect control over his material; once the actor perfected speech and movement, he would appear exactly as the author wanted. A film was a dramatic moment frozen forever, a sculpture of words and movement lovingly cut and shaped into the exact image of the author's creation. Or so he thought.

First of all, there was the question of casting O (or the object).[28] Alan Schneider wanted Charlie Chaplin, but Chaplin did not answer the repeated barrage of letters sent to him by Grove Press. Zero Mostel had other commitments, so Schneider turned to Jack MacGowran, who had suddenly become a salable commodity because of his role as the Highwayman in *Tom Jones*. MacGowran had a string of commitments lasting until the end of the year, which meant that shooting for the Beckett film had to adhere to his brief periods of availability if he were to take the part.

Suddenly the coproducers backed out, the cameraman quit; and the budget escalated at a dizzy pace even before shooting started. With all these delays, MacGowran's free time frittered away, and he was forced to back out and go on to other commitments. While Schneider, Rosset and the others involved in the project veered from depression to panic, Beckett calmly suggested that Buster Keaton would be wonderful if he were alive and well and willing. That was questionable, since Keaton had been offered the role of Lucky in the first American *Godot* and rejected it flatly because he couldn't understand it and considered it a waste of his time. Schneider feared that, with Keaton as O, it might turn out to be his film and not Beckett's, thus causing insurmountable conflict, but at this point that was Beckett's least concern.

Schneider flew to Hollywood, "to woo Buster,"[29] and stumbled into a bizarre remnant of the heyday of Hollywood. Keaton lived in a remote section of Los Angeles in a dilapidated house where nothing had been changed since 1927, not even the four-handed poker game in the living room, which Schneider apologized for interrupting. Keaton assured him that the game was imaginary, that Irving Thalberg, Nicholas Schenk and a forgotten fourth had long since departed. Thalberg owed him two million dollars, Keaton harrumphed, and Schneider mentally hoped that, too, was imaginary.[30]

Keaton had already read the script, flown to him earlier from New York, and his first impression was that it needed "fixing up:"

> Here he suggested some special business with his walk, or perhaps that bit where he could keep sharpening a pencil and it would get smaller and smaller. I said that we didn't normally pad Beckett's material.[31]

Schneider, usually exuberantly volatile, talked quietly and patiently until he convinced Keaton that the script was final, there would be no changes, that he would have to forgo all his comic trademarks and subjugate himself to the domination and discipline of the script as it stood:

> His general attitude was that we were all, Beckett included, nuts. But he needed the money, a handsome sum for three weeks work, and would do it. Yes, he remembered the *Godot* business, but he didn't understand that one either.[32]

With relief, Schneider flew back to New York, worrying all the way that signing Keaton was a mistake, but "like Everest he was there, and with Sam's encouragement, we had to have him."[33]

Once Keaton had been signed, Beckett flew to New York at last. Boris Kaufman had been persuaded to overcome his fears about a movie in which the camera would be rigidly confined throughout and agreed to direct the photography; Joe Coffey operated the camera and Sidney Meyers agreed to edit the film. Everything was ready to begin.

Beckett was in London with *Endgame* rehearsals when word reached him, and he made immediate arrangements to fly to New York. On July 10, he arrived at Idlewild Airport, where a small private plane whisked him to Barney Rosset's East Hampton estate. For the next three days, tennis and swimming punctuated long discussions, as Beckett explained the intricacies of his directions. The others tried to change his mind about the rigidity of the camera's movements, but Beckett refused to listen to their arguments.

On Monday morning, with an exact shooting script in hand, Beckett and the others ventured into lower Manhattan to begin filming. Beckett was terrified of the city at first; the July humidity was brutal for a lifelong European. The heavy trousers and jackets he brought with him were oppressively hot, but he never complained. The noise of trucks roaring over the cobblestones and the raucous sights and sounds of the streets were shocks to one accustomed to the leafy boulevards and cool gray buildings of Montparnasse.

Beckett stayed with Christine and Barney Rosset in their Houston Street home; with the Rossets and the rest of the group sheltering him from the curious crowd of writers and reporters who had come to get their first glimpse of him, Beckett grew less wary but still not relaxed as time passed. He liked Greenwich Village and explored there, even making a pilgrimage to the Cherry Lane Theatre, where so many of his plays had been performed. He liked to walk, and with handwritten directions from Rosset, patiently made his way around Manhattan.[34] Beckett enjoyed hunting for locations, and was childishly delighted when he found the red brick wall of an about-to-be-demolished building just under the Brooklyn Bridge, perfect for the opening scene.

Joe Coffey, the friendly, bearded, bearlike cameraman, drove an ancient Morgan which captivated Beckett, who loved tooting around New York in it. Coffey was a drinker, a storyteller, a warm and engaging man, and he and Beckett became instant friends. Coffey was entirely willing to do whatever the script required and, in spite of the heat, moved his heavy camera equipment uncomplainingly according to Beckett's directions, over and over, for hours on end.

Finally, with locations selected and the other actors ready to begin, all was in readiness for Keaton, who was staying in a midtown hotel. With trepidation, Schneider took Beckett to meet him. Beckett had admired Keaton for years; Keaton knew vaguely of Beckett's reputation as a playwright, but was puzzled as to what kind of man he must be. Schneider described their first meeting as "one of those occasions which seem inevitable before they take place, impossible when they do, and unbelievable afterwards."[35] Keaton was sitting in his darkened hotel room, drinking beer and watching a baseball game. Beckett was his most gracious and charming, and what little conversation there was originated with him. Keaton sat morosely with his famous deadpan countenance. Beckett faltered, grew hesitant, then awkward. Time dragged and Schneider was mortified:

> "Did you have any questions about anything in the script, Buster?"
> "No."
> (Pause.)
> "What did you think about the film when you first read it?"
> "Well . . ."
> (Long pause.)
> And so on. It was harrowing. And hopeless. The silence became an interminable seventh-inning stretch.[36]

The only interest Keaton showed came just as Beckett and Schneider were about to slink out. Keaton had brought along several of his old flattened-down Stetson hats, his trademark, and he asked Beckett if he could wear them. Schneider, "between Scylla and Charybdis,"[37] was relieved when Beckett said he thought it might be a good idea, and then demonstrated how Keaton could fix the handkerchief inside it that O wore to hide his face from E (the camera).

Making the film was difficult for Schneider, who had been a director only of stage plays until then.[38] Heat, delay and unfamiliarity with the vagaries of the medium sorely tried everyone's patience, but in spite of all, they finished in just under a month. During that time, Beckett and the others worked from early morning to late at night in one of the hottest and most humid Julys on record. At night they went to a small Italian restaurant in Greenwich Village to savor both the air conditioning and the beer after an exhausting day's work. Beckett, Coffey, Schneider—whoever was there—sat at one table, Keaton usually sat alone at another. Throughout the evenings, Beckett stole surreptitious glances in Keaton's direction while Keaton only had eyes for the checkered tablecloth and his bottle of beer.[39]

All through the filming, Keaton insisted he did not know "what the hell was going on,"[40] but he did everything he was asked to do with endless patience. He was well over seventy, overweight and wheezing, but he performed the film's opening scene countless times, skittering past trash cans and garbage piled high along a brick wall, which he was supposed to cling to as he ran. The summer heat was relentless, but Keaton navigated the obstacle course uncomplainingly and did not protest when the scene was jettisoned in the final cutting because of an unfortunate waving effect caused by the heat that had distorted the film. He ran up and down the narrow stifling stairwell and rocked patiently while the searing hot lights bore down as the camera focused hour after hour on his open, unwavering eye.

When the shooting ended, Beckett wanted nothing more than to have Joe Coffey point the Morgan toward the airport and the first plane to Paris, but there were too many good people in New York who had repeatedly visited him in Paris, and he could not risk offending them, so he stayed on for several days in the third floor room at the top of Rosset's house.[41] He dined one night with Kay Boyle at her daughter's Chelsea apartment, then walked home alone with Rosset's meticulously printed directions to guide him. Another night he dined with Horace Gregory and his wife, old friends from Dublin. Jean Reavey planned a special dinner to include all the foods mentioned in his writing, ending with a grand finale of *Banane à la Krapp*. George Reavey took him to the nearest approximation of a Dublin pub, Martell's, where Beckett perched precariously on the high wobbly stool at the end of the bar and struck up a garrulous conversation with the Irish bartender.[42]

There were many reporters on the set of *Film* who wrote stories about Beckett, but there were only a few to whom he actually gave interviews, among them John Kobler, then writing for the *Saturday Evening Post*. Kobler spoke French, had been in Paris, was cultivated and witty and became one of the most successful interviewers ever to approach Beckett. He wrote a long profile, in which Beckett discussed his 1938 stabbing, the rocky road to *Godot*'s first production, and some of his and Suzanne's activity during the war.[43]

His only foray beyond Manhattan and East Hampton came midway through the shooting when he took the train to Hastings-on-Hudson to dine with Jean and Alan Schneider. He was the first guest in their new home, and he commemorated the occasion by giving them a small Giacometti drawing that he had brought from Paris.[44]

At last his social responsibilities were ended, and he made a reservation on the early morning flight to Paris. Beckett and the Rossets retired early, to rise before 5 a.m. in order to catch the plane. At 8:15, the Rossets woke up, horrified to discover they had overslept. Rosset bounded out of the bedroom into the small dressing room that gave onto the hallway, to find Beckett sprawled in a chair, his bags beside him, sound asleep. He had been too polite to wake them, but hoped they might hear him rustling newspapers and wake up. Instead, he fell asleep. They were able to book space on the night flight, but that left the entire day to while away. Beckett dryly suggested they spend it at the airport, which gave Rosset the idea to go to the World's Fair in Flushing Meadows, which was on the way. With Beckett in tow, the Rossets made their way unnoticed through the throngs of tourists, sampling foods, going through exhibits, walking miles through heat and haze. Late-afternoon sun made them all groggy, and each withdrew into a private stupor as they plodded doggedly on. Suddenly, Christine Rosset realized that Beckett was nowhere in sight. After a frenzied half-hour, they spotted him sound asleep on a park bench, carefully cradling the two woven Greek shoulder bags he had purchased for himself and Suzanne.[45]

When he arrived in Paris, he found the weather cold and Suzanne sick. She had gone to Turin earlier in the summer, with

Marthe Gauthier and Madeleine Renaud, then proceeded leisurely through Italy until they came to Rome, where Renaud
gave several performances of *Oh les beaux jours*. When Suzanne
returned to Paris, the worrisome bronchial cold set in, and she
had been ill on and off for the rest of the summer. In September,
Beckett also became ill when a tumor formed on his jaw. He
was relieved when a biopsy proved it benign, but it still required
surgery. The thought of surgery depressed him, and in the midst
of his gloom, he read that Sean O'Casey had died. In times of
deep emotion, words were difficult, but he sent three words,
"All my sympathy," to Shivaun.[46]

He also heard that Adam Tarn, whose drama journal
carried news of Western theater to Poland, was being forced
by the Communist government to leave Warsaw.[47] Because
Tarn, like most other Poles, was a registered Communist, the
United States would not admit him; advanced in years and in
ill health, he was forced to settle on the frigid, windswept prai-
ries of Western Canada. Tarn stopped in Paris briefly, where he
and Beckett met as they had done annually during Tarn's trips
on behalf of the UNESCO International Drama Committee.
They sat glumly in a cafe for several hours, comparing their
afflictions. When time came to part, Beckett implored Tarn to
take money, introductions, manuscripts—whatever he needed.
Tarn had no need for physical assistance, but Beckett's generosity buoyed him on the long journey. When he arrived, he found
that Beckett had been busy, sending letters to a Canadian mil-
lionaire and patron of the arts whom he had met briefly that
year, urging him to "please look out for Adam Tarn, who was
one of the world's special people." Not content with that,
Beckett wrote repeatedly to Tarn, until he was quite convinced
that all was well.

The upcoming broadcast of *Cascando* on the BBC kept him
busy for several weeks, but by early November he realized there
was no sense in delaying the operation any longer and the tumor
on his jaw was removed. However, the incision did not heal
properly and further surgery was scheduled after the first of the
year. He finally got away to Ussy for a few days in December,
but then went to London for the first unexpurgated version of
Godot in England, which opened at the Royal Court on De-

cember 30, 1964, with Anthony Page directing. Nine years had
passed since he and the Lord Chamberlain had first clashed in a
battle of wills. Triumph was sweet, no matter how late it came,
and he wanted to be there.

"I intend to make this year a quieter one, with as much
Ussy as possible, and try and find out if there is any more work
in me," Beckett wrote to McGreevy on January 30, 1965. The
year had not begun quietly, and as January progressed, it
showed no sign of changing. While he was in London for
Godot, he met Dr. Colin Duckworth, who was about to write a
critical study of the play.[48] Beckett told Duckworth he was
using the unexpurgated Grove Press text for the London production and made the startling statement that he preferred it to
the French. It is perhaps the only time he has ever admitted a
preference for a translation over the original work. To the obvious questions—whether *Godot* is based on his relationship
with Joyce, whether Godot comes in the intermission and
whether Beckett's biography has a bearing on the interpretation
of the play—he gave the obvious facile answers, all "no." One of
Beckett's surprising answers came when Duckworth asked,
"What do you think the theatre is for?" Beckett replied,

> I don't know. *I'm not interested in the theatre.* [Duckworth's
> italics] I very rarely go to see other people's plays—only to
> see friends acting in fact.[49]

Duckworth points out that Beckett likes to see his own plays,
but only in the semiprivate situation of rehearsal, not in public
performance. "I'm not interested in the effect my plays have on
the audience. I simply produce an object. What people think of
it is not my concern."[50]

This observation is important to understand in order to
assess the kind of writing Beckett began after he had written
Play. He was no longer concerned with a peripatetic being compelled to wander on a relentless search for the self. From this
point on, the hero (or being, or voice—all are applicable terms)
is usually fixed, concentrating at various times on a past world
(usually fluid), a present world (usually confined) and a future
world (usually horrible to contemplate because of its infinite

fixed horror). Conventional theater had long been uninteresting for Beckett, but now the dramatic forms which emerged from his pen grew increasingly rarefied, as he searched for ways to eliminate the actor and to stamp his own presence upon his creations.

As an example of this tendency, Beckett suggested the following method of dramatizing *From an Abandoned Work* to Shivaun O'Casey, who was touring in the United States. O'Casey wanted to present the work in much the same manner as *Play*, with an actor's face spotlighted as he recited the text in monologue. Beckett wrote:

> This is not at all the kind of dramatic writing I had in mind when we talked in Paris, and I think the spotlight face presentation would be wrong here. The face is irrelevant. I feel also that no form of monologue technique will work for this text and that it should somehow be presented as a document for which the speaker is not responsible. At the same time, a completely straight undramatised reading is hard to manage in an evening of theatre with Shaw and O'Casey. What would you think of the following set up?
>
> Moonlight, Ashcan a little left of centre. Enter man left, limping, with stick, shadowing in paint general lighting along. Advances to can, raises lid, pushes about inside with crook of stick, inspects and rejects (puts back in can) an unidentifiable refuse, fishes out finally tattered ms. or copy of FAAW, reads aloud standing "Up bright and early that day, I was young then, feeling awful, and out—" and a little further in silence, lowers text, stands motionless, finally closes ashcan, sits down on it, hooks stick round neck, and reads text through from beginning, i.e. including what he had read standing. Finishes, sits a moment motionless, gets up, replaces text in ashcan and limps off right. Breathes with maximum authenticity, only effect to be sought in slight hesitation now and then in places where most effective, due to strangeness of text and imperfect light and state of ms. If you like this idea, you'll be able to improve on it. But keep it cool.[51]

Beckett enclosed a check with the letter, for O'Casey's company had little support, financial or otherwise, from the theatergoing public in the American hinterlands.

The check was an unexpected, unasked-for blessing, and was a gesture typical of Beckett. Unasked, he had donated a year's American royalties to Trinity College's fund for the new library, then gave several important short manuscripts because he "knew they have just spent all their money buying Synge's papers and don't have anything left."[52] He gave a short jettisoned manuscript to an Irish poet and authorized him to sell it because he was in need of money. He offered several of his new short writings to help Adam Tarn launch a new drama journal in Canada. When Tarn protested that Beckett was likely to encounter opposition from his English-language publishers, who had not yet printed them, Beckett replied, "I will tell them simply that Adam Tarn needs it, and they will comply with my wishes."[53]

Actors, writers, old friends, casual acquaintances—all were recipients of Beckett's generosity. Few had to ask for help, for he offered it if he even sensed the slightest need. Each gesture was performed with the exquisite courtesy and tact that governed all Beckett's personal actions; no one was made to feel even a hint embarrassed, and if any did and expressed these feelings to Beckett, it was he who was most embarrassed.[54]

As soon as he had caught up with business in Paris, Beckett headed for Ussy to gather his energies for the coming months. "She [Suzanne] does not like the country any more so I am always here alone," Beckett wrote to McGreevy. "The place is indispensable to me as a hideout. Paris becomes more and more difficult with interruptions and demands, difficult to evade and impossible to satisfy."[55]

Suzanne had worked out a new life for herself, partly from preference and partly from necessity. She discovered that she liked life in the theater, and especially the adulation that came to her on opening nights as the wife of the playwright. She traveled around Europe with Marthe Gauthier, and increasingly with Madeleine Renaud, and always sat in an aisle seat to receive the bouquet that theater managers always presented to her during curtain calls on opening night.[56] With Beckett so busy flitting from one country and one production to another, he was glad that she was able to fill her days with something that gave her pleasure. Increasingly, the subtle, insidious hostility between them had become overt and vicious.

Suzanne resented Beckett's relationships with other women, but this was minor compared to the resentment which festered because of his increasing ability to take care of himself. She was no longer needed to take messages, transport manuscripts, arrange meetings and negotiate contracts. He did everything, so that she, who had fulfilled his every need for years, now found herself in the position of legal wife but unnecessary appendage. Also, Suzanne, the professional musician, had always fancied herself a writer as well; in 1949, Duthuit had published a short story she had written and which Beckett translated,[57] and she really thought this was the beginning of her own career. Perhaps she might have succeeded if she had written more, but because of Beckett's unwillingness to market his own writing, she voluntarily put her own career aside to further his. In the years since, her pleasure in his success gradually eroded into recriminations for the cruelty of fate which gave her official status, wealth and public respect, but which took away the privacy, affection, and feeling of being needed. No doubt the close quarters of Ussy exaggerated the strain of their relationship; so as not to exacerbate it further, she chose to remain in Paris when he was in the country. In Paris, he had taken to living almost entirely in his study, bedroom and bath, leaving the rest of the apartment to her. Visitors to his quarters were sometimes astonished to discover that in the apartment they communicated by telephone—each with a different listing.[58]

At Ussy, he had time to finish *Eh Joe*, a short piece for television written for Jack MacGowran, and *Come and Go*, his own translation of *Va et vient*. Then he received an urgent request from the Schiller Theatre in Berlin: would he consent to come immediately to assist them with a production of *Godot?* He went, spending three weeks there in what he called an attempt to salvage the production,[59] but interrupted his stay for forty-eight hours to fly quietly to London for the Jack B. Yeats exhibition. When he arrived, he discovered that all galleries were closed on Saturday afternoon and he had made the journey for nothing. He managed to buy a catalog, but had to fly back to Berlin without having seen the show. This frustration lasted throughout the rest of his stay in Berlin, as the play lumbered to a grim conclusion. He left there depressed, and went straight to Ussy. His life seemed to become a continuing procession of bad news. There were family problems with his father's brothers in Dublin: his Uncle Howard was gravely ill in the Adelaide Hospital, and his Uncle Jim, devastated with side effects of diabetes, had had his first operation to check the disease, removal of a leg. His eyes were deteriorating rapidly, and his arms had been affected by a muscular disease, so that he could not even hobble around on crutches. He left the hospital threatened with amputation of the second leg. This re-creation of *The Unnamable*, life imitating art, especially in his own family, sunk Beckett into a deepening, horrified gloom. Edward was coming to the end of his studies at the Conservatoire, and his nervousness at the thought of impending examinations transferred itself to his uncle, especially since Jean Beckett had taken to bewailing the Trinity degree Edward would have had by now had he not insisted on a musical career. Suzanne was worse than ever with bronchial infections and colds, but was still determined to go first to Turin for a Blin production, then to Prague for Renaud's *Oh les beaux jours*.

As for himself, the long-expected second operation on his jaw was upon him, since the opening in his palate simply would not heal. In April he underwent surgery to insert a small plate at the back of his throat to close the opening in the palate. At the time, it seemed to be successful, but within a few weeks he realized that it had not healed properly. A third operation took place in late May, when finally, the situation seemed to be corrected.

Interspersed among his personal problems were the usual distractions of his work: he had a number of meetings with Madeleine Renaud, who was taking *Oh les beaux jours* on tour, first to London, then throughout France, Switzerland, to Vienna and Prague and finally to New York in September. There were all sorts of arrangements which required decisions by him, and it led to a hectic time in Paris. As a special favor, he attended one of Renaud's performances, and then joined her afterwards at the Méditerranée restaurant, opposite the theater. It was a fairly large affair in a restaurant that attracted crowds, just the sort of public gathering he usually took pains to avoid. But he went, despite the pain in his jaw, and no one even suspected that he was ill.[60]

Colin Duckworth came to Paris to take advantage of Beckett's offer to let him see the original manuscript of *Godot*, and Beckett received him at the boulevard St. Jacques with his unfailing courtesy, even serving tea at the end of the session. He apologized for the large can of condensed milk sitting unceremoniously atop a cream pitcher, saying he never had milk delivered because it was too difficult to arrange.[61]

In spite of everything, he was "working quite hard clearing up bits and pieces,"[62] when he received word that McGreevy had suffered a second heart attack and would be severely restricted for the rest of his life. McGreevy was frustrated during his recovery because he wanted to work on his memoirs, but became exhausted after the slightest exertion and could neither type nor write. Beckett found out about this from Brian Coffey, who had been in Dublin, and wrote immediately, asking if he might make a present of a tape recorder, but McGreevy was unwilling to accept it. He had difficulty talking into a void, and chose instead to struggle on with pen and paper.[63]

Just as word reached him of McGreevy's attack, news came of Mihalovici's sudden hospitalization for a fulminating appendix, emergency surgery and an extraordinary series of complications before his recovery.

In the midst of all this illness, there was one brief period of happiness for Beckett: Edward successfully completed his studies at the Conservatoire, and the family gathered to celebrate his success. John Beckett and his wife came from Dublin, along with Jean and Caroline, and Maurice and Mimi Sinclair came from Geneva. After the reunion, Edward went off for a month of study with Jean-Pierre Rampal, and Beckett flew to Courmayeur, Italy, to join Suzanne for an Alpine holiday. It was probably the best thing he could have done for himself at that time, and it was such a resounding success that they left all their holiday clothing in the little hotel there because they intended to go back very soon.[64] Suzanne's cold cleared up, as it always did in the mountains, but unfortunately his tooth and jaw trouble did not. His next bout of surgery was scheduled for early fall.

In the meantime, he returned to Paris and the usual round of meetings, negotiations and problems. Shivaun O'Casey had left her troupe somewhere in the midst of Kentucky because of a disagreement of purpose, and she wrote to tell Beckett; he replied immediately, asking if she wanted him to withdraw permission for *From an Abandoned Work*, and then worried like an anxious father about whether she had enough money. "Tell me if you need dollars," he pleaded, "I can get them to you."[65]

Increasingly in the past few years, he had found himself in the position of entertaining the daughters or nieces of his friends when they came to Paris. He had taken Fanny Howe, Mary Manning Howe's daughter, to stay with him and Suzanne while they still lived on the rue des Favorites.[66] He took Juliet Maguinness, Olive and Stuart's daughter, to Ussy, where he played records, cooked lunch and talked about chess and literature.[67] Rosemary Montgomery, daughter of his Dublin friend, Niall, went to dinner with him at Closerie des Lilas,[68] and he fed Melanie Carvill, Jack MacGowran's stepdaughter, regularly during the year she was a student in Paris.[69] When Elizabeth Ryan, McGreevy's niece, passed through Paris on a school tour, he insisted on meeting her at Invalides when she arrived and swept her and her bewildered traveling companions off to a hotel in a taxi.[70] For Caroline, his own niece, he stopped whatever he was doing and devoted himself to entertaining her whenever she was in Paris. He would spend weeks going to music halls, circuses, movies, the theater, to dinner and shopping. For all of these young women, none of whom was more than eighteen, he seemed a fussy older relative who amused them as he searched for interesting things to do. Later, as they reflected from a more mature viewpoint, they found it astonishing that he not only put aside his concerns but that he should have made them feel so important, interesting and welcome.

Alan Schneider stopped briefly on his way to Israel to tell Beckett that his and Barney Rosset's attempts to market *Film* had not been as successful as they had hoped. Even with Keaton, even though it had won the New York Film Festival award, they had had no luck persuading major distributors to take it. Now Schneider was proposing to enter *Film* in as many festivals as possible, beginning with the one in Venice in August, and Beckett agreed that this was the best approach. *Film* won the *Diploma de Merito* in Venice, and later was named the Outstanding Film of the Year at the London Film Festival. The following year, *Film* received the Oberhausen Film Festival *Preis der Kurzfilmtage*, the *Prix Special* at Tours and awards at the film festivals of Sidney and Krakow. Still, it was never a commercial success. Beckett was naturally pleased with the critical esteem, but he was secretly unhappy at his failure to reach the vast filmgoing population of the world who did not have access to his plays and thus never had the opportunity to see his work.[71]

In mid-June, Beckett was about to scurry off to hide in Ussy, as he did each year, to avoid the onslaught of Joyce devotees who flocked to Paris for Bloomsday on June 16, when he received a letter from two Americans who interested him. Patric Farrell, director of the Museum of Irish Art in New York, and Elsa de Brun, who paints as Nuala, asked to meet him briefly. He had an engagement to keep before he could reply to their letter but as he was crossing the rue Montparnasse, he was stopped by a couple—he, short, jouncy and voluble; she, tiny, blond and self-contained.

"You are Patric and Elsa," Beckett said to the astonished pair before they had a chance to introduce themselves.

Beckett consented to guide them on a brief tour of Joyce's favorite haunts, but all they managed was a stop at Fouquet's later that same night.[72]

Beckett spent most of the summer in Ussy, finishing *Eh Joe* and the French translations, *Dis Joe* and *Paroles et musique*. He was determined to write another novel, and did indeed amass a great number of prose pages. From this point on in his life, it is difficult to ascertain the order in which the published prose was written, for parts of one piece sometimes became parts of others, and those which were meant to be chapters of longer works often ended as separate entities. Beckett himself is not exactly sure of the order in which he wrote them, even though he tried carefully to date each notebook or typescript. What is definitely known about this period is that he was determined to break away from theater, and worked diligently at prose with results that he usually found unsatisfactory.

In August, more bad news from Dublin interrupted his concentration. A week before Caroline's wedding, Jean was rushed to Monkstown Hospital. She had been feeling poorly for most of the summer, but attributed the stomach pains and loss of weight first to chronic indigestion, then nerves, then perhaps ulcers. When the pain became so severe that she could no longer stand it, she consented to be hospitalized. Caroline was persuaded to go on with the wedding ceremony, and reluctantly went off afterward to a honeymoon on the Isle of Jersey. Edward went home as soon as his summer with Rampal ended, and it was he who kept in touch with Beckett by phone. As they feared, the diagnosis was bad: Jean had a large malignant tumor in her stomach. The prognosis was not entirely pessimistic; surgery was indicated, and the doctors were hopeful that subsequent treatment would result in at least a remission, if not a total cure.[73]

With this slim glimmer of encouragement, Beckett decided not to go to Ireland. It was harvest time at Ussy, a period he particularly enjoyed. Josette and Henri Hayden now lived in the country year round, and Beckett often walked across the fields to their little house to share a bottle of wine in the warm fall sunlight. Hayden was eighty-three years old, and doing some of his best painting. To see his friend in such lusty good health was enormously cheering to Beckett and it encouraged him to ignore his own maladies. Unfortunately, he could no longer ignore one which was becoming alarmingly serious.

"I would stay here [in Ussy] willingly for the duration," he wrote to McGreevy, "or rather, so long as I can see for myself."[74]

Something was wrong with his eyes, but since he had not had an examination for years, he had no idea what it was. It was a different sort of blurring, unlike the familiar distortion of his lifelong myopia. Everything was gradually becoming darker and dimmer, as if there were a gray haze between him and the rest of the world. He feared he was going blind, and wondered whether to consult a doctor or simply to grow resigned to the condition. For the time being he said nothing about it, not even to Suzanne. She was in Berlin, where Mihalovici's *Krapp* was being revived in September, but the condition of his eyes was frightening enough that he stayed at Ussy, working feverishly at old translations and new writing. The *Krapp* revival went badly, even though the same singer repeated the role; the critics were hostile and Mihalovici was deeply hurt by their reaction; he returned to Paris so unhappy that Beckett interrupted his stay at Ussy to go into Paris to dine with him, his wife and Suzanne.

Harold Pinter's plays *The Collection* and *The Lover* were on in Paris, and he went to a performance. Afterwards, he joined Pinter, Barbara Bray, and a number of other visitors from London in a long night of drinking at the Rosebud Bar. His nerves were on edge—the news of Jean was depressingly bad, his eyes were worse each day—and he grew angry over an ordinary conversation between Pinter and Bray. He swept up his drink and moved to a table in the far corner where a half-drunk workingman looked up long enough to register Beckett's presence, then slunk back down over his wine glass. Beckett spent the rest of the evening peering intently at the man, occasionally trying to engage him in a conversation. His friends tried to carry on as if nothing unusual had happened, but they were surprised and hurt by Beckett's unaccustomed quick temper.[75]

He decided to spend the remainder of the year at Ussy, concentrating on translation. There, he received a letter from McGreevy that touched him so deeply he was unable to concentrate. Despite his weak health, McGreevy went to see Jean in Monkstown Hospital, bringing flowers, fruit and books. Theirs had always been a relationship of friendly adversaries; now that both were in poor health they became friends.

In November, Beckett received a letter from Giorgio Joyce, who had been silent for several years. His pleasure in the letter gradually faded as he read the reason for it: Giorgio had consented to spearhead another drive to exhume his parents' bodies, this one led by a group of concerned American scholars.

The casual life-style of Joyce and Nora persisted even into death, for their bodies were in the same cemetery but separated by some fifty feet and several other graves; now, instead of moving Joyce's body to Ireland, this group wanted to move both bodies into a common plot of ground where they would be reunited beneath a commissioned statue. Giorgio had agreed to the project and asked Maria Jolas to organize all the Joyce group in Paris to contribute both money and services. Giorgio wanted Beckett to appear at the graveside ceremonies when the statue was unveiled, and to deliver a short oration written especially for the occasion. Beckett wrote to Patric Farrell, "Giorgio wrote asking me to unveil reunited dusts. Can't do a thing like that but I shall try and be there that day."[76]

To McGreevy, he was more blunt: "Giorgio wrote, asking me to perform. I said no, but will try to be there."[77] Actually he had no intention of going, nor did he intend to go to the party Maria Jolas was planning the following February at the American Center for the twenty-fifth anniversary of Joyce's death. Such memorials horrified him, and he tried never to be part of them.

On Christmas Eve, he returned to Paris for a quiet holiday with Suzanne, but even then he worked. He felt an urgent need to finish anything that required the use of his eyes, and he could not stand to let any paperwork accumulate, even the most insignificant correspondence. Christmas day—warm that year for Paris—found him in his study writing letters, apologizing for delays, and explaining sadly that he had spent the entire year on mechanical matters of little import, while the work that might have mattered had not gotten done.[78]

Through an open window he could hear the prisoners howling in the Santé, like wounded beasts. He raised his eyes to the Val de Grâce, and the Panthéon beyond, illuminated and shining brightly on this holiest of nights. He wondered fearfully how much longer he would be able to see it.[79]

1966–69:

"QUEL CATASTROPHE!"

 Ever since Sartre had rejected the Nobel Prize in 1964, a group of professors had become Beckett's avid boosters, nominating him year after year. "Thank you for your letter and for the great honor you do me," Beckett wrote to one. "If there is any justice I shall be spurned again and for good. What counts is the thought of the few such as you."[1]

"I don't want it, oh, I don't want it," Beckett would insist, rocking back and forth as he "hoisted a jar" with his Irish friends in the Falstaff. In the next breath, he would smile shyly and say, "Ah, but I'd have to accept if they gave it to me. It would not be polite to refuse the honor."[2]

Beckett had become the center of a hub of Irish writers who lived in Paris, as Joyce had been before. However, his relationship with the new generation was different: while Joyce encouraged adulation and accepted favors as if they were his natural due, Beckett went out of his way to do favors rather than receive them. When he joined his Irish cronies for long nights of drinking, they found it difficult to pay for a round, because Beckett insisted it was his right to do so. He introduced several of them to Lindon, who subsequently published their books. If he thought he could be helpful in promoting a magazine, an anthology or a collection of poetry, Beckett would delve into his "trunk" and give a manuscript without charge.

"Keep my share of the swag," he would say of royalties, "give it to some poor deserving person."[3]

He enjoyed this particular group of Irishmen, especially the puckish Con Leventhal, whose droll sense of humor was a perfect foil for his own. In the past few years, Beckett had had little opportunity for uninhibited conversation, and Leventhal, now retired and living in Paris, provided a sorely needed outlet for banter and fellowship. This was someone from home, who had been with him in the old days, before the fame and notoriety made privacy impossible; someone who remembered him when—even if "when" was not exactly his shining hour—and liked him in spite of (or because of) it.

Leventhal teased Beckett out of his gloom with memories of their own rousing drunks, of famous Dublin scandals or local characters. They gossiped like two old crones in a sleazy shebeen. The amount of Irish whiskey they consumed was prodigious, and more than once they followed a waning procession of lights, moving, as one bar closed, farther down the avenue to the next, until the small hours of the morning when the last one lowered its iron shutters. Usually they outlasted their younger companions, but on several occasions were glad to have one with staying power equal to their own. Beckett dispatched a note to John Montague after one of the more momentous occasions in thanks for "your invaluable help up that blazing boulevard."[4]

For Beckett, there was only one thing wrong with these occasions—they were not frequent enough. Although he kept insisting he had earned the right to privacy, he was unable to refuse any commitment in the theater, and moved from one to the other with little respite. In January, 1966, he began "fourteen weeks nonstop theatre, cinema and TV."[5] Claddagh Records, the Irish firm recently founded by Gareth Browne, was about to record MacGowran's *End of Day* under Beckett's supervision, with musical accompaniment by Edward Beckett on flute, John Beckett on the harmonium, and Beckett himself, who clanged a gong. Beckett proudly watched his nephew taking the first steps of his professional life and was delighted by John's growing success as a composer and performer.

He was also in the BBC studios to supervise MacGowran in a recording of *Imagination Dead Imagine*, and later was present when MacGowran and Denys Hawthorne recorded some of his poems. *Poems I*, the program that resulted from this reading, was compiled and narrated by John Fletcher. During the recording, Beckett mentioned casually to Fletcher that he himself would have chosen different poems. When Martin Esslin, the producer, heard this, he suggested a second series comprised of Beckett's favorites, which was broadcast later that same year.[6]

He returned to Paris in time to be present for the filming of *Play*, but not in time for the celebration of the twenty-fifth anniversary of Joyce's death at the American Center. A distinguished group had gathered to pay their respects, among them Lucie Léon, Stuart and Moune Gilbert, Jean Jacques Mayoux, Michel Butor and Giselle Freund. Beckett was asked by Mrs. Jolas, who had organized the event, to participate in some way, perhaps to give a short speech or to write something special for the occasion. He told Mrs. Jolas and everyone else who asked that he could not participate in any way but through his presence, and he convinced them that he would be in the audience, sitting insignificantly somewhere in "the back of the class."[7] He knew very well that he would not be there, since he had committed himself to being in London, and excused his absence by saying that he was unavoidably detained.

Giorgio pressed somewhat harder than Mrs. Jolas, because he felt that only Beckett could serve as the graveside speaker when Nora's grave was moved alongside Joyce's in late February in Geneva. Beckett tried to avoid refusing Giorgio as long as possible, hoping to elude him by saying that his time in London was indefinite and he had no idea when he would be free. Finally, when Giorgio said he would be willing to wait until the last minute, Beckett sent a letter saying that he simply could not perform at graveside ceremonies, but that he would try to be present on the occasion, again knowing full well that he would not be. When the time came, he wrote regretfully to say that pressing commitments kept him in Paris.

He was telling the truth somewhat: *Va et vient* was to open on February 28 in the Petite Salle of the Odéon Théâtre de France, along with Serreau's production of *Comédie*. They were part of a larger production entitled *Spectacle Beckett, Pinget, Ionesco*, along with Pinget's *L'Hypothèse* and two short plays by

Ionesco. Besides overseeing his own plays, Beckett also assisted Pierre Chabert with the production of Pinget's.

There was a noticeable difference in Beckett's attitude toward productions of his plays, depending on the country of performance.[8] In England, he always seemed tense, as if under siege, and gave the impression that he would bolt from the theater at the least provocation. He tried to keep rehearsals closed and sometimes grew so irritated with outsiders that he would call for abrupt recesses in the hope that they would tire of waiting and go away. Most of the time he seemed gloomy and depressed, eager to get done with it. In Germany, he was meticulous to the point of obsession. He rehearsed tirelessly, striving for the slightest nuance that would make the difference in his eye between perfect characterization and abysmal failure, a difference usually impossible for others to discern. Nothing escaped his scrutiny, even the work of the lowliest stagehand. He wrote detailed notes to himself on the working script, interpreting each movement with mathematical precision, explaining for his own benefit and the benefit of others, how he wanted each word to be spoken and what technical procedures should accompany the actors' movements.

In France, however, he was entirely different. He greeted Renaud and the others with deferential courtesy. After he had explained what he wanted the actors to do, he sat somewhere in the theater chain-smoking elegantly slim brown cigarettes while they performed large sections of the play virtually uninterrupted. During breaks, he explained with great patience—almost apologetically—what changes he wanted them to make, and then returned quietly to his seat while they began again. In other countries, he acted with the authority that came from total knowledge of the medium in which he worked, but in France he still behaved as an outsider who had somehow managed to penetrate the barrier between theater and the rest of the world, and was still somewhat shy in the face of the talent and authority of others.

Just as his writing seemed different in English from his writing in French, so, too, was his personality in the theater. One wonders, if he had written for publication in German, what sort of plays he might have produced in the language that seemed to bring out all that was compulsive, regimented, and methodical in his personality. In recent years he has remarked on several occasions that he has thought about writing a play in German, or that he has part of a poem or a bit of prose in that language; but when pressed, he passes it off as nothing, and says that he has never tried to write seriously in any language other than French or English. The feeling persists that this is one of the tantalizing hints he sometimes gives out about what he is really interested in or is trying to do at a particular time. There is no question that he has a large number of manuscripts that he may or may not allow to be published; yet, at the same time, he becomes angry at the thought that any of them might be published posthumously.

Beckett's feelings about posthumous publication were the subject of a conversation with Frederich Dürrenmatt, to whom he was introduced by Adam Tarn.[9] This was exactly the kind of meeting that Beckett tried to avoid, but he felt he had to consent to it because of his friendship with Tarn. They began by speaking French, which Dürrenmatt spoke poorly, with a heavy German accent. Dürrenmatt, normally a charming man, became increasingly frustrated at his inability to communicate with Beckett, and began to tell what were most likely humorous stories, but which were almost incomprehensible because of his faulty French. Frau Dürrenmatt seemed bored and Beckett stared glumly at the floor.

"Why don't you speak German?" Tarn demanded. "Mr. Beckett speaks very good German."

And so Dürrenmatt began to speak German, but Beckett continued to make his replies in French. The conversation turned to Brecht, specifically to the posthumously published texts, and then to Joyce, whose letters had just been published. Beckett grew angry and insisted that neither should have been published. "It's these widows who are responsible," Beckett raged. "When a writer dies, his widow should be burned on his funeral pyre. These 'literary widows' who claim they allow posthumous publication for 'scholarship' are guilty of a serious crime, and they should be burned alive for it!"

Tarn disagreed. "Look here, Sam," he countered, "for years you have been saying you will never allow your first play to be published and you won't let anyone read it. Yet you al-

ways tell me it's hidden away somewhere with all your other
failures. Why don't you burn them if you don't want anyone to
see them? Don't blame a widow for the writer's inability to
destroy something that is surely a part of himself." Beckett had
no answer.

As soon as *Va et vient* and *Comédie* were under way in
Paris, Beckett hoped to go with Suzanne for a holiday to the
Ligurian coast of Italy, but he had to abandon the idea because
there was too little time before he was to direct the Stuttgart
television production of *Eh Joe*.[10] Once again he used a theater
commitment as a convenient excuse for an engagement he had
no intention of keeping—the Scholars' Dinner at Trinity College. Leventhal wanted Beckett to go with him, and it was
harder to say no to someone who lived in Paris than to write an
impersonal letter of refusal to Dublin.

By the end of April, he was finally able to get to Ussy for
the first time since Christmas, and he began the tiresome task of
correspondence, hoping to get it finished quickly before turning
to translation and writing. Among other things, he sent a check
to the editors of *Hermathena*, the literary magazine of Trinity
College, to renew his subscription.[11] Unlike Joyce, who seized
upon every scrap of writing by and about Irishmen with indis-
criminate relish, Beckett chose to keep in touch selectively,
through the distinguished periodical which is probably the oldest extant learned journal connected with an Irish university.

He spent most of his time in Ussy until the end of June,
with only an occasional dash to Paris; then he went to London
to direct Jack MacGowran and Siân Phillips in the BBC production of *Eh Joe*.[12] From London, he returned to Ussy, and for
the rest of the month, worked at the translations of *From an
Abandoned Work* and *Watt*, which Agnes and Ludovic Janvier
were preparing for Lindon. Beckett had finally reached the
point where he simply could not take such an active role in the
production of his works, continue to write and still find time to
translate. Lindon had at last persuaded him that he needed help,
because the delay between the different language editions of his
writings was far too long. Janvier was a young man of good
looks and quick wit whose verbal patter appealed to Beckett.

Agnes Janvier was more retiring, but her far-reaching command of English, especially the peculiarity of Irish idioms and slang, were of one native-born. Hers was the steady hand which formed the translation into a careful work entirely in keeping with Beckett's own style.

The Janviers received surprisingly little criticism from Beckett, and he accepted their translation of *Watt* with only minor changes. This has puzzled some of Beckett's critics, who believe that the translation is not up to Beckett's own exacting standards. But Ludovic Janvier was used to getting his own way in such matters, and the quick strength with which he defended his translation might have intimidated the normally demanding Beckett; also, Beckett was anxious to get on with new writing and he simply wanted this translation done with as little fuss as possible.

Another reason he may have agreed so readily to the Janvier translation was the news from Dublin of Jean Beckett's rapidly deteriorating health. He knew it was only a question of time until he would have to make the sad journey to Ireland for another funeral. He was there when she died on August 21, 1966, after a year of hope that her stomach cancer would be checked, and then despair that it would not. She was buried next to her husband in Dean's Grange Cemetery on their twenty-ninth wedding anniversary. Beckett stayed at The Shottery long enough to make sure that Caroline and Edward were able to cope with the details of the estate. Caroline and her husband planned to move into The Shottery, so the gracious home overlooking Killiney Bay remained in the family, while Edward continued to maintain London as the base of his musical career.

Beckett avoided contact with everyone but McGreevy, who was in a permanently weakened condition but still working gallantly at his memoirs. They had become an obsession with him, as he struggled to remember every detail of his life. Now, as if sensing that he would soon die, he wanted to see his several hundred laboriously typed pages in print before he continued to write. Beckett read them but was saddened to see that they consisted of a hopeless mass of reminiscences of McGreevy's boyhood in Limerick—of little potential interest to publishers. He suggested that McGreevy allow him to speak to Lindon about a private edition of the memoirs, and went back to Paris prepared to finance the cost of the printing.[13] When he returned to Paris, it was one of his first matters of business, but McGreevy had lost interest in the project.

Beckett had been depressed by his stay in Dublin and returned to Paris hoping he had seen his homeland for the last time.[14] In Paris, he encountered further illness: Suzanne's mother was chronically ill, and there would soon be another funeral to deal with; Suzanne herself was weak and run-down from all the running back and forth to Troyes, and one of her sisters was also seriously ill.

Beckett had little time to help because rehearsals of *Comédie* were under way for an October third opening at the Odéon, and he began immediately to spend nearly all of his time in the theater. It had become a convenient refuge from personal problems and a means of circumventing deepening depression as well as taking his mind off his prose.

Several weeks after his return from Dublin, Minuit published his second prose text that year, *Ping* (*Assez* was published the previous January), and he signed a copy for John Fletcher, who was in Paris to question him about the bibliography on which he and Raymond Federman were collaborating. Beckett was flattered that two such able scholars wanted to undertake what he called "a thankless procedure,"[15] but was eager to have it done for another reason: it forced him to go through all his papers—published and unpublished—and put them in order. With Leventhal's assistance, he found most of his writings and arranged them (to the best of his recollecton) chronologically. But he had done such an enormous amount of hack writing that he simply could not remember whether unsigned articles were his or not. His eyes were becoming increasingly clouded over, and going through so much printed material was a strain; but he kept at it with unfailing patience, answering every question Fletcher asked him, responding immediately to every letter and spending hours going through voluminous files in the hope of discovering a missing paper.[16]

By December, the strain of so much hard work in the theater and so much illness and death in both families had ex-

hausted both Beckett and Suzanne. She began to search for someplace warm and sunny where they could go to escape the annual
madness of Paris in the holiday season. But Beckett quibbled,
saying Italy was too cold and too crowded, and Greece, too
risky. Finally he agreed to go to Cascais, Portugal, where they
were sure of sun and warmth. He was feeling "written out" with
all the short prose texts that had been or were in the process of
being published, and was disappointed that nothing had resulted
in a longer, more sustained work. He wanted a good long session
of sitting in the sun without any work at all, hoping that new
ideas would come to him. An idea for another play was forming,
and the thought of it made him unhappy. He wanted to sever
his connection with the theater, he told himself, and here he
was about to embark on another play. But if a play were all that
he could write, then it would have to do, for the only certainty
in his life was the compulsion to keep on writing.

With equal parts of relief and despair, Beckett discovered
that the idea for a new play had disintegrated into two unsuccessful attempts to write it. From February, 1967, to April,
1968, writing in French, he filled the greater part of a notebook
with a substantial portion of a play dealing first with two female
characters, then with one male and one female.[17] He constructed a general plan of the play and made detailed notes on its
timing, envisioning four separate sections divided into periods of
ten, twenty, five and ten minutes respectively; for each section,
he posed rhetorical questions, followed by comments concerning the projected characters. The central section, in which the
woman is left alone, seems to have been the core of the play, and
he wrote a considerable part of a monologue before he abandoned it. Part of this passage deals with an "explanation of the
methods, calculations, and handling of syringes and pharma-
cists's bottles."[18] At the end of the text, there is a series of
detailed calculations of regular dosages to be administered by the
syringe. This play occupied much of his time for well over a
year, and was the "new work" he spoke of when his friends
asked what he was doing.[19]

While he was writing it, he seemed pleased with his progress, or rather, as pleased as he would ever admit to being. His

correspondence and his remarks spoke of the difficulty of realizing it and the inability to bring the concentration to bear that creativity required of him; but at the same time these remarks were definitely lacking in the force that characterized those he had made while writing either *Endgame* or the trilogy. The intensity of the drive that compelled him to churn out something, no matter what, seems to have abated during this time, so that this time in his life could be interpreted either as a period of satisfaction or resignation. The short texts appeared with regularity, usually in periodicals, then in slim separate editions featuring pages of type of the size usually found in a child's primer and enormous margins on all four sides which only emphasized the works' brevity. His previous plays were staged with regularity all over the world and required constant supervision through correspondence. Then, too, he was tired, and the recent spate of death and illness among persons he cared for had contributed to an attitude in which he cared little for the urgency of creation. He probably decided it was time to relax a little—what he had told everyone he intended to do for many years previously. Cascais had been wonderful, and he wrote glowing cards and letters to friends telling them how much good the vacation had done him, and wishing them "all the best in the current recirculation."[20]

He went back to Paris in such good spirits that he actually attended the opening night of Serreau's film of *Comédie*—a Hollywoodlike affair complete with printed invitations, admiring fans and press photographers.[21]

Early in March he had an alarming accident which dampened his euphoria. He was standing in the garage next to his apartment building waiting for his car to be repaired when he fell into the mechanic's pit, breaking several ribs and suffering painful bruises. For the first time he was forced to realize how seriously his vision had deteriorated; he simply had not seen the gaping hole in the floor and had walked right into it, dropping six terrifying feet to the bottom.

For the first few weeks of his convalescence, he remained in Paris, apologizing to visitors for not being able to greet them at Orly and watching their reactions as he mentioned casually that he thought he might drive the little car to Ussy to use between the railroad station and his house.[22] He seemed to seek their concurrence that driving in Paris was a hazard he should forgo, but at the same time he gave the impression that he wanted reassurance that his eye condition would soon clear up and he would be able to drive through the streets of Paris once again with his usual reckless abandon.

He consented to see a doctor, who told him that he had glaucoma in both eyes. The right eye was the worse of the two and would eventually require surgery. It was still too early to tell if the condition in his left eye would advance to the point where it, too, would require surgery.

He wanted very much to keep his visual condition private, but it was virtually impossible to hide. He tried to restrict his meetings whenever possible to persons he already knew and trusted and tried to forestall situations where comparisons might be made between himself and other writers who had gone blind. Nevertheless, comparisons were soon made, of exactly the sort that he despised. Why, he was asked, did he think blindness was an affliction suffered by major Irish writers? Had not Joyce suffered horribly for years, and O'Casey as well? Was Beckett to be the third of a great triumvirate of Irishmen to be stricken with blindness? These questions made him cringe, but he usually controlled himself long enough to reply civilly that he was an individual who happened to be plagued by a condition most likely correctible and could not speak for others: "I am simply a man who is going blind. Any comparison with others is meaningless, ridiculous, absurd," he said vehemently, over and over again.[23]

As soon as he was well enough, he drove the little car, despite Suzanne's protests, to Ussy, where he intended to "hole up"[24] for the rest of the spring and all of the summer. There, he received word that Thomas McGreevy, after one final heart attack, had died in his sleep on the eve of St. Patrick's Day. With McGreevy's death, he lost the one person in the world in whom he had ever really confided. It was tantamount to losing a part of himself, and though McGreevy's death was not entirely unexpected, it was still a blow of tragic proportion. The only way he could cope with it was to go off by himself for a while and try to adjust to a world where McGreevy was no longer at the other end of a letter.

He played chess alone, following the games of the great masters, or else against computers, using game sheets and books purchased in Paris. He visited the local bistro, where he played billiards by the hour. He sat in the sun in his garden and basked in the silence and warmth. And, with enormous difficulty and at great cost, he had his piano moved from the Paris apartment to Ussy.[25]

He was settled quite comfortably for what he thought would be a good long time when a letter came from *Esquire* magazine, inviting him (and also Ionesco and Genêt) to Chicago for the 1968 Democratic political convention, each to write an article about the vagaries of the American political system. He was amused by the invitation at first because it had been years since anyone had had the audacity to suggest that he write anything other than his own. Then he became angry, and fired off a curt refusal, saying only that it would not be possible for him to attend.[26]

He made one of his first direct political statements since the war that fall, when he joined a number of prominent French writers who sent letters of protest to the Spanish authorities at Madrid in protest of the imprisonment of Fernando Arrabal, jailed for supposed blasphemy and treason to the Franco government. The letter was reprinted in French newspapers,[27] which caused him momentary uneasiness as a foreigner residing in France. But he was so incensed by the treatment of the young writer whom he had come to know and like—for his personality as well as his writing—that he felt compelled to add his voice and signature to the other protests. When Arrabal was subsequently acquitted, he felt he could justifiably take a certain amount of the credit for his release.[28]

Throughout the winter of 1967–68, Beckett suffered from a series of illnesses which he complained had laid him up in Paris and left him irritated because he could not get well enough to go to Ussy to write, or even to go away somewhere warm and sunny.[29] These illnesses began with a cold, bursitis and an unnamed virus that seemed to come and go with increasing regularity as time passed. What worried him particularly was the persistent hacking cough and pain in his chest. He gave up smoking for a short time, hoping that it would clear his lungs, but to no avail. Suzanne suggested a holiday in the mountains, since high altitude had helped her, but he had become enamored of the seashore and was beginning to look for the perfect resort— one handy to a major airport, with a secluded beach where he could take long walks, an excellent hotel and few tourists, none of whom would recognize him. This time he settled on Porto Santo, Madeira, and went there as soon as he had finished all the current business in Paris.

Michel Mitrani was directing *Dis Joe* for French television on February 2, and wanted some assistance from Beckett. They had "one or two conversations before shooting, nothing more,"[30] then Beckett met with Sir Laurence Olivier and Joan Plowright, who wanted to make a film of *All That Fall*.

Plowright and Olivier had written to him several times that winter, hoping to persuade him to allow the radio play to be filmed, and he always answered promptly and politely, telling them (and all others who had similar requests) that he could not permit any of his work to be performed in any medium other than that for which it had been written. He would bend only far enough to permit straight readings from the prose. Plowright and Olivier refused to accept his written refusals and made the trip to Paris and Ussy anyway. There, he greeted them with politeness and offered limited hospitality, but remained steadfast in his decision.[31]

In July, Edmund Blunden, in ill health, resigned the chair of poetry at Oxford, and several days later, Beckett received a letter from Enid Starkie, asking if she might nominate him for the position. He replied by the next post: "I am greatly touched and grateful that you should take such trouble in your thought for me and think me worth it. And it is such a sorry acknowledgement to have to reply, as I must, no, to everything. To you I need not try to explain and that it is enough briefly to say that such honours are not for me."[32]

He made another sad visit to Ireland in August, when word came that Mrs. Gerald Beckett, his dear Aunt Peggy, had died.

Reporters had been forewarned of his arrival and were waiting when the plane touched down at Dublin Airport, but he was tight-lipped and silent as he walked through them without making a statement.[33]

He went immediately to Greystones, where Ann Beckett was living in the family home, and stayed there until the funeral was over, dodging reporters who found out where he was and insisted on trying to interview him. He saw no one but family in the few days he was there and returned to Paris at the first opportunity. Since 1950 and his mother's death, he had been saying he was finished with Ireland and would not go there again. Now, at last, he hoped fervently that his words were true, and he has not returned to Ireland since.[34]

A visit to his doctor upon his return to Paris confirmed that his lung, which had ached off and on ever since he had been stabbed, was now inflamed in the area where the knife had penetrated the pleura many years before. The doctor prescribed rest and medication, and so Beckett and Suzanne planned to return to Madeira at the first opportunity.

They were in Paris for the holidays, and in a rare burst of gaiety, Beckett went to a New Year's Eve party at the Closerie des Lilas.[35] Shortly after, they went to Madeira and spent a month catering to their various maladies.

One of his first visitors when he returned to Paris in March was Adam Tarn, who had undergone surgery for lung cancer the previous November. Beckett greeted him with relief that he had come through the ordeal so well, and immediately the two old friends fell into the pattern of comparing illnesses. Beckett told Tarn he was not recovered from the lung inflammation and still experienced a great deal of discomfort in certain kinds of weather. He confessed that he still harbored secret fears that it was more than an abscess, and worried that he would suffer the same fate as his brother. Yet he was smoking again as heavily as ever, and had a laissez-faire attitude about cigarettes, claiming any damage would already have been done long ago.[36]

Tarn asked Beckett to meet another playwright, the Polish dramatist Slawomir Mrozek, who was known in Poland as Beckett's disciple. Mrozek admired Beckett enormously and didn't mind the comparisons at all, but he had never read *Wait-*

ing for Godot. He begged Tarn to find a copy so that he might read it before meeting Beckett; but when they met, he blurted out his guilty secret, then fell silent. Beckett was amused by the younger man's discomfort, and exerted considerable charm to make him relax. By the end of the afternoon, the conversation flowed as if they were two old friends enjoying one of their frequent meetings.[37]

This was a period of tranquillity for Beckett; his calm had developed gradually during the past two years until now it seemed to characterize his every action. No matter that the long play had dissipated, or that only short texts had evolved from the painful attempts to write prose; he seemed to have a sense of security, an acceptance of himself and even an enjoyment of his status and reputation. He had finally found the contentment he had sought during the past decade as he extended the periods of time he spent in Ussy. He had even found a sort of tranquillity in Paris: he still maintained a round of engagements, meetings and correspondence that would have felled many younger men, but he no longer seemed frantic and harried by all that he had agreed to do.

He had attained an equilibrium that gave him the stability and self-control he had worried about all his life, and there is no question that theater was responsible for it. He had been forced to become a semipublic figure through the production of his plays, and as the years went by and he became more secure in his directorial ability, he gained a control which carried over into his personal life as well. Now there was very little, if anything, that he could not cope with, no matter how distasteful.

In June, this composure was somewhat shaken when he saw the reviews of the New York production of *Oh! Calcutta!* Kenneth Tynan had asked him sometime the previous year to write a brief skit for an erotic review, and Beckett agreed when he heard that Edna O'Brien, Jules Feiffer, Leonard Melfi, John Lennon and Tynan himself were planning to contribute. All the contributions were to be listed anonymously on the program so that none of the contributors would be identified with his writing.

Beckett wrote "Breath," a 120-word skit consisting of light and breathing, lasting thirty-five seconds, and gave it to Tynan, assuming that it would be staged exactly as he had written it. He was furious when he discovered that of all the contributors, only he was identified, and not only that—his script had been changed. Where he had written:

> 1. Faint light on stage littered with miscellaneous rubbish. Hold about five seconds.

was printed:

> 1. Faint light on stage, littered with miscellaneous rubbish, *including naked people*. Hold about five seconds.[38]

In the book the text was opposite a photograph of naked bodies lying on stage among the rubbish, which further infuriated him.

Beckett contacted all his representatives in various countries and discovered that his contracts were written in such a way that he could do nothing in the United States, but could stop all other productions that did not adhere to the text as he had written it.[39] In one of his few displays of public anger, Beckett called Tynan a "liar" and a "cheat,"[40] prompting Tynan to send formal notice through his lawyers that he was not responsible for the travesty, which he claimed was due to others.[41] Through his lawyers, he told Beckett that further disparaging comments would force him to bring a libel suit, at which point Beckett decided the incident wasn't worth the argument and the attendant publicity and dropped it.[42] Instead of agonizing over it, as he would have done in the past had someone tampered with his material, he simply went off to enjoy himself at Ussy.

He planned to go to Berlin in September to rehearse Martin Held in a Schiller Theatre production of *Krapp's Last Tape*, and he wanted to be in good health for the coming hard work. He was anticipating the return to the theater with a certain amount of pleasure, but he had to cancel the trip when the lung condition suddenly flared, causing extraordinary pain. Doctors diagnosed it tentatively as an abscess located in the general area of the stabbing and prescribed antibiotics and rest, urging him to curtail all unnecessary activity. He was truly quite ill, and for once was not entirely displeased by an illness, for this one served as the perfect excuse to abandon his responsibilities and take a holiday.

This time he and Suzanne decided not to go to Portugal, which was too public and too accessible for their tastes. They went instead to Nabeul, Tunisia, a small village deep in the interior, where the weather was usually warm and sunny throughout October and November—the length of time they planned to stay. However, their visit was spent in torrential rainfall which caused severe floods that isolated the village from the surrounding countryside and from civilization at large—hardly ideal weather for one suffering from a lung condition. As the rain poured down, there was little Beckett could do but concentrate on his correspondence.

The telephone rang sharply on October 23, 1969, disturbing Suzanne, who answered it because Beckett was busy writing a letter. She listened quietly for a moment, said a few words to the caller and hung up. She turned to face Beckett, a stricken look on her face and whispered "*Quel catastrophe!*"[43] She had just been told that the Swedish Academy had awarded the 1969 Nobel Prize for Literature to Samuel Beckett. He was surprised at first, then agitated. Almost immediately he sat down to continue the letter, then got up at once to pace back and forth across the room in long loping strides, not knowing whether to be thrilled or frightened.[44]

1969–73:

"UN INCONNU CÉLÈBRE"

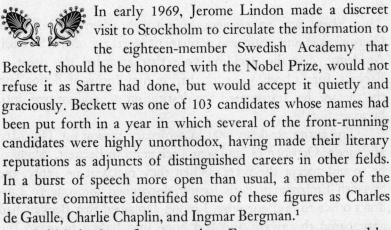In early 1969, Jerome Lindon made a discreet visit to Stockholm to circulate the information to the eighteen-member Swedish Academy that Beckett, should he be honored with the Nobel Prize, would not refuse it as Sartre had done, but would accept it quietly and graciously. Beckett was one of 103 candidates whose names had been put forth in a year in which several of the front-running candidates were highly unorthodox, having made their literary reputations as adjuncts of distinguished careers in other fields. In a burst of speech more open than usual, a member of the literature committee identified some of these figures as Charles de Gaulle, Charlie Chaplin, and Ingmar Bergman.[1]

It had also been five years since France was represented by the selection of Jean-Paul Sartre, and the time seemed propitious for another French author. In 1969, however, André Malraux seemed to be the favored candidate, especially since he no longer had any governmental ties and could be considered simply as a literary figure.

When Maurice Nadeau first suggested Beckett in 1957 and a sudden surge of recommendations by Americans followed, the Swedish Academy began a thorough study of Beckett's qualifications. Beckett seemed effectively out of the running when Erik Wahlund, the highly esteemed drama critic of *Svenska*

Dagbladet, wrote a long article comparing Beckett with Ionesco, Genêt and Witold Gombrowicz, and proclaimed Ionesco the most important dramatist. Wahlund called *Waiting for Godot* Beckett's "single first-rank work," and said that none of his subsequent writings had ever approached its depth of thought or structure:

> A single work—even if it be a masterpiece that could survive beyond the time and circumstances of its conception—seemed to this wary critic too tenuous a ground for the elevation of an author to the highest literary award that the whole world could confer. Wahlund himself preferred Ionesco, for the originality of his viewpoints and the variety of his subjects, his incisive dialogue, and his rich flow of black humor; these qualities . . . seemed more likely to bring fertility to the theatre of the future . . .[2]

Thus, there was an element of surprise when Karl Ragnar Gierow, poet and critic and permanent secretary of the Swedish Academy, cast the deciding vote that awarded the prize to Beckett, for "a body of work that, in new forms of fiction and the theatre, has transmuted the destitution of modern man into his exaltation."[3]

The entire academy met in a plenary session on Thursday afternoon, October 23, and sent a telegram to Beckett, asking if he would accept the prize. When they received no reply, the Swedish Embassy in Paris hastily dispatched someone to Lindon's office to find out why. Lindon explained that Beckett had anticipated the award and had gone into hiding to avoid the swarm of reporters that would have descended upon him in Paris. His choice of an isolated village in Tunisia was no accident, and had been timed to coincide with the Nobel announcement, and the lung ailment served as valuable camouflage for the real reason for the holiday.

Suzanne's exclamation was therefore not one of displeasure, but only the exclamation of a concerned wife who saw first that her husband's much needed rest was being ruined by inclement weather, and then that peace would be impossible because of the publicity the award would bring. They had a brief respite, however, before intrepid reporters found them, as only a handful of people knew where they were. Lindon delayed releasing the information to the public until he had made sure that Beckett was prepared to cope with the situation.

Despite Beckett's fame of the past decade, the Nobel Prize revealed how much of his privacy he had been able to guard. In Dublin, several hours after the announcement, the office of the *Irish Times* received a telephone call from the frantic editor of a Norwegian newspaper.[4] Facing deadline, he had no information about the prizewinner other than the press release issued by the Swedish Academy. The telephone rang often that night in the *Irish Times* office for the same reason, as newspapers from all over Europe phoned to find out something about the elusive man who had just won the prestigious award. Many were unaware that he had not lived in Dublin for years, but was a resident of Paris. Others who did know could not even find the address of his apartment there. It seemed appropriate that, as newsmen the world over scrambled to find him, Samuel Beckett was on the edge of a desert, cut off from civilization by threatening floods. The French press threw up its collective hands in Gallic despair and dubbed him *"un inconnu célèbre."*[5]

When Beckett was finally located, a group of determined reporters and photographers braved the rains and flooded roads to find him sequestered in his hotel room, unable to face this newest onslaught upon his privacy. He consented to meet with them briefly only after reporters agreed not to ask him any questions, nor to expect answers if they did.

He stood in the center of the hotel lounge, his great head hanging down in his characteristic angle of embarrassment. His fair hair was cropped short in an unbecoming crew cut, reminding more than one photographer of a recently released inmate of a concentration camp, but his face was tanned from the few days of sunshine before the rains began. Always thin, he was now painfully angular because the debilitating bout with the abscess had killed his appetite. When the photos were finally published, Beckett's pale blue eyes peered at the camera with an expression somewhere between hostility and fear.[6]

Only the sound of clicking cameras punctuated the deep

silence in the room as reporters kept their end of the bargain. One photographer, perhaps more sensitive than the rest, apologized softly to Beckett for this intrusion upon his privacy.

"That's all right," Beckett replied. "I understand."[7] These were the only words he spoke before he returned to his room.

The personal stability and mental equilibrium, arrived at after more than a decade of intense personal struggle, was shattered.[8] Nabeul was overrun with photographers and journalists; the number of congratulatory messages he received was staggering, and he labored diligently to answer them. Letters he received prior to the award were answered without mention of it, for he thought it would be unseemingly arrogant to do so.[9] He did not think many people would be interested to hear from him that he had just won the world's most prestigious literary prize. To those letters he received after the announcement, he made only a passing remark in reference to it. To Lucie Léon, he wrote that Joyce, not he, should have received the prize, for Joyce "would have known what to do with it."[10] To Adam Tarn he wrote that he had escaped and was continuing to escape the worst (i.e. the press), but dreaded to think what would happen when he returned to Paris in January, His only regret was that he could not properly celebrate because "alas, no Irish [whiskey] here—only Vat 69, or still lousier Donats."[11]

The feverish activity that surrounded him caused Beckett's health to disintegrate alarmingly. He confined himself to his room, a virtual prisoner, unable to take advantage of the sun, which had returned. His eyes grew steadily worse—when he left Paris, his doctor had told him his physical condition had to improve because the more seriously impaired eye might be ready for surgery upon his expected return in early January. He was frustrated that there was no chance to follow the doctor's instructions. Suddenly the muscles of his right hand began to contract, causing serious pain whenever he tried to hold a pencil, and handshaking was torture. He was afraid it was another idiosyncratic illness, especially as he was now virtually unable to eat or talk because another round of cysts had formed inside his mouth. His emotions were mixed when he returned to Paris and the doctor told him he was suffering from Dupuytren's contracture, a condition that would gradually cause his hand to curl in a ball as the muscles contracted and would not release to a normal state.

The literary community of the world celebrated the award, with the exception of Ireland, which characteristically refused to recognize a native son who had turned his back on his country and his language. The Irish were also incensed at the manner in which the prize was to be awarded. Beckett would not be present at the festivities; the laureate in literature traditionally addressed the academy and he had no intention of putting himself on public display. Also traditionally, when a winner is not present at the award ceremonies, his country's ambassador receives it in his stead. In this instance, Beckett sent word that he did not wish to be represented by the Irish ambassador, Tadgh Seosamh O'Hodhrain, but wanted Lindon to receive it instead. On December 10, 1969, King Gustaf Adolf handed Lindon the diploma, the gold medal and the check for seventy-three thousand dollars, while the audience applauded politely. But O'Hodhrain did not take the snub lightly; at the banquet that followed, he insisted on representing Beckett at the King's table, and was seated next to Lindon. Early the next morning, Lindon flew back to Paris with the diploma and the medal, but not the check, which was delivered to Beckett by private arrangement at a later date.

Meanwhile, as Nabeul grew intolerable, Beckett was faced with a dilemma: to stay on or to return to Paris for more of the same hounding torment, or to try to escape to another sunny, warm place where no one could find him for long enough that the trip would be beneficial. Suzanne made the arrangements, and on December 5, they flew to Cascais, Portugal. There they found a modicum of peace, but Beckett did not like the Hotel Cidadela, which he thought too grand and too public, even though Suzanne had gone to great lengths to find a place she considered secluded and private. By mid-January, 1970, he was weary from the strain of living in hotels and the long absence from the comfort and security of his things in France. It did not matter that his health was more precarious than it had been in Berlin where he had begun his odyssey five months earlier. He had been traveling since September, and he wanted to go home.

As soon as he arrived in Paris, the bombardment began.

He tried to forestall conversations about the prize, and when he could not, covered his embarrassment by telling an apocryphal story popular in the pubs of Dublin about William Butler Yeats, who was the last Irishman to receive the prize, in 1924. According to legend, the lord mayor of Dublin was the first person to receive the news, telephoned from Stockholm. He dressed in his ceremonial robes and carried the badges of his office through the streets in a horse-drawn carriage to Yeats's house. When he arrived, he stood on the steps and in ringing tones proclaimed Yeats to the curious crowd that had followed his carriage. Beckett's version of the story had Yeats hopping anxiously from one foot to the other, until, unable to contain himself any longer, he interrupted the long and boring speech to demand, "Yes, yes, just tell me what it's worth! How much will I get?"[12]

When Beckett finally received the money, he treated it with the same mixture of respect and unconcern he showed toward most of his income. In large sums and small, he gave much of it away during the next few years. He subsidized a number of artists, printers, painters and scholars. He poured money into new experimental productions. Old friends who wrote to tell him they were coming to Paris found he had arranged and paid for a hotel suite. He had wanted the prize badly, yet now that he had it, he seemed to feel almost guilty that so much honor should come to him who just twenty years before had feverishly written a play that no one wanted to produce. The time span from down-and-out Irish drifter to world-famous writer had been all too brief and would take some getting used to.

His publishers clamored immediately for some new work which they might issue with appropriate ballyhoo, but he had nothing to give them—at least nothing of book length that satisfied him. At Grove Press, Richard Seaver circumvented his protests and began to make plans for a Samuel Beckett reader, which would include all the short texts of the 1960's already published in England and France but still unpublished in the United States. The book was to include *Imagination Dead Imagine*, *Lessness*, *Assez*, *Ping* and several critical pieces by and about Beckett. When Seaver sent a proposed table of contents, Beckett's replies were vague, and Seaver was unable to determine how Beckett felt about the inclusion of the critical writings. After more than a year of indecision, Beckett finally wrote on April 11, 1971 (in reply to Seaver's letter of January 30, 1970), to say that he thought the *Three Dialogues* the "least tedious" of his critical pieces, but Seaver was free to do as he wished. As to the critical articles by others, Beckett was so scathing in his indictment of two of his most prominent American explicators and so lukewarm about the others that Seaver abandoned all ideas for any writings except Beckett's own.[13]

Lindon, in Paris, pressed hardest for a new text, and in gratitude for his efforts with the Nobel Prize, Beckett reluctantly offered *Premier Amour*, one of the four stories he had written in 1946 and withheld from publication for twenty-four years.[14] He told Patrick Magee that he only agreed to release it because "the woman in question was dead at last," and thus "could no longer be pained by it." Beyond that he would not comment.[15] Rosset and Calder pressed Beckett for an English translation, but not surprisingly, he was more reticent than usual to confront this text and delayed completion until 1973, even then grousing that he was not satisfied and wanted very little to do with it before publication and nothing afterward; saying had it not been for the pressure of the Nobel Prize, it would never have appeared in print.[16]

With the crumb he had tossed his publishers, Beckett hoped to be free to attend to his health, but another honor came his way, one which had been planned to capture some of the glow of the Nobel Prize and one with which he wanted to cooperate fully. A group of people connected with Oxford University, headed by Francis Warner, had been running a theatrical company since 1967, mounting productions aimed at raising enough funds to build a theater named for Beckett in Oxford. The chief donations came from Sam and Ayala Zacks of Toronto (170,000 Canadian dollars) and from the actor Richard Burton (250,000

American dollars, with the stipulation that it be called the Beckett-Burton Trust). Over the years, other friends and professional associates of Beckett and the company gave amounts ranging from several thousand British pounds to a handful of American dollars.[17] The early winter of 1970 seemed a propitious time to schedule a fund-raising evening, to garner the necessary amount of money before construction could begin. The gala took place on March 8, entitled *A Beckett Evening*, produced by Warner, and featured Siobhan McKenna, Richard Harris, Laurance Harvey, Patrick Magee, Huw Weldon and Wolf Mankowitz.

R. Buckminster Fuller was present as an honored guest, for he had accepted an appointment to be the architect of the Samuel Beckett Theatre, and had sent a splendid telegram saying he would donate his personal design and supervision in expression of his honor at the appointment. Sorel Etrog donated a sculpture to the theater and designed lithographs for a limited edition of *Imagination Dead Imagine*, with all proceeds to go to the theater building fund.[18] Avigdor Arikha donated two portraits of Beckett which were printed in a special limited edition souvenir brochure, and congratulatory messages poured in from publishers and producers all over the world.

The evening was indeed gala; a glittering affair which raised a considerable sum of money, but one which fell disappointingly short of the goal. Fund raising languished for several years until inflation made building on the original site impossible and Fuller's original design seemed doomed to be abandoned. Finally, in late 1975, another site was found—this one small and modest, beside the Oxford Playhouse—and definite plans to construct a theater of approximately seven hundred seats were made. The Samuel Beckett Theatre is supposed to be a geodesic structure designed by Fuller, planned to share the key facilities of the Oxford Playhouse, thus cutting construction costs and future operating expenses. As of the winter of 1977, nothing beyond the selection of the site has been done. The venture is not without its critics: widespread misgivings exist in Oxford among persons connected with the project as well as the general public, who feel that Oxford is not a large enough community to support such a grand theater. Warner insists that the funds are there, that ground breaking can begin on a moment's notice, but he is too involved with other ventures at present to make the commitment such a complicated project requires. What began as an altruistic project seems to have become mired in dissension engendered by strong personalities and the groups which have formed around them.

All the while parties and celebrations were being held in his honor, Beckett was at home in Paris, ill and making plans to escape "sunward," as he called his increasingly frequent trips to Mediterranean areas.[19] His doctor had refused to perform the eye surgery until Beckett rested and stabilized himself. This time he and Suzanne planned to go to Sardinia, hoping to find solitude there. He had not slept well since returning from Cascais. He had lost so much weight that his clothes hung from his body. Reading was out of the question and writing required too much effort. Like Joyce, who had had to write with thick crayon on oversized sheets of paper, Beckett could only scrawl brief notes with a thick black felt marking pen.[20]

He wanted the first operation as soon as possible, and his doctor told him that if he improved after the month in Sardinia, the operation could take place shortly after he returned to Paris. He was bitterly disappointed in June when he was told it could not possibly take place for at least a month; in late July it was postponed once again until the fall. In the meantime, he was supposed to rest, eat and sleep properly, and to take enough exercise to be able to withstand the strain of surgery.

Beckett spent most of the late summer and early fall confined to the apartment, stumbling irritably from bedroom to study as the days passed in agonizing boredom. He saw only a few intimate friends on extremely rare occasions and turned off the telephone so that no one could reach him. He isolated himself in his study—when the windows and door were closed it was almost soundproof—and the only sight came from the blurred, hard, gray-white northern light that penetrated on bright, clear days. One wonders if the dimness and isolation of this time might have been the inspiration for the harsh and sterile writings which were published in the years following.

By late September, he was well enough to satisfy the doctor, and the first operation was scheduled for October 15 in "the little clinic just around the corner from boulevard St.

Jacques."[21] All his friends were horrified by his cavalier attitude and worried that the doctor was not qualified, the clinic not properly equipped and Beckett's condition not yet stable enough to withstand surgery. But when the appointed time came, he simply walked into the clinic and checked himself in. That afternoon Suzanne sent a four-word telegram to Barney Rosset at Grove Press—"Operation successful, love Sam." A few days later, Beckett went back to his apartment to wait for the eye to heal. By November 5, he was once again hard at work at his correspondence, even though his vision was not much improved.[22] He was in good spirits, however, for the surgeon assured him that his prospects for recovery were excellent, and he was comforted by the knowledge that even if the operation on the other eye failed, he would at least have partial vision. By Christmas, still toiling with responses to the flood of good wishes from his friends, Beckett found that reading and writing were still "tricky,"[23] but he had abandoned the felt marker and was once more writing with his usual spidery-thin fountain pen.

Beckett's doctor was so pleased that the operation on the other eye was scheduled for mid-February, and in an uncustomary burst of confidence and enthusiasm, Beckett was already making plans to direct a new production of *Happy Days* at the Schiller Theatre the following August and September.

He stayed in Paris throughout the winter, cheerful enough to suggest meetings with friends for quiet dinners and conversation-filled evenings. He dined with Barney Rosset and spent a long night in congenial conversation that left Rosset exhilarated; he dined first with Bettina, then with John Calder (for they were ending their marriage); and in a burst of good feeling, attended the official opening of Bram van Velde's retrospective at the Musée d'Art Moderne, going afterwards to supper at Maxim's. He even went to see a show of van Velde's more recent painting at the Knoedler Gallery—something he had not done for years.[24] He maintained his health until early February, when he checked into the clinic once again and the second operation was performed without incident. By the first of March, he was able to joke that although his eyesight was still dim, his prospects were bright.[25] By mid-April, he was telling friends that his "castrated" eyes were doing as well as could be expected;

he could now read the time on the palace clock in the Luxembourg Gardens whenever he walked there and "God knows," he said, "one should be thankful for that."[26]

It was some time, however, until his eyesight returned to normal, and for more than a year he had problems with focusing his vision. He had grown so used to seeing through a thick gray film that the sudden onslaught of normal light was staggering. There was so much of it and it was so intense that for two months after the surgery, he only ventured outside the apartment for brief walks around the block, hugging the walls. Beckett literally ran into Desirée Moorehead Hayter, the young Irish wife of his friend, Stanley William Hayter, one day as he felt his way along the edges of buildings. He grabbed her arm as he shielded his eyes behind the thick dark glasses his doctor had prescribed and exclaimed in a bewildered voice, "The light—the light. I had forgotten there could be such light!"[27]

In mid-March, 1971, just as he was beginning to adjust to the strangeness of his distorted vision, he received the sad news from Ireland that his uncle Jim was dying. Bedridden for many years, blind, diabetic, with both legs amputated and movement in both arms impaired, Dr. James Beckett's death was nevertheless sad, as he had been one of the most charming and beloved men in Ireland. There was no question of Beckett's attending the funeral, for his doctor simply would not permit him to travel. He was relieved to have the decision made for him because his intense family loyalty, love for his uncle and respect and affection for his aunt Peggy would have caused him to fly to Dublin without thinking twice had he been able.[28]

Dr. Beckett's death marked the start of another round of continuing bouts of illness—some troublesome, some seemingly serious—that plagued Beckett off and on for the next two years. Once again there were spots on his lungs and intense pain in the area where he had been stabbed thirty-three years before. A series of hard, blind cysts broke out on his face and neck. In May, Suzanne arranged a holiday in Santa Margherita Ligure, a village near Rapallo on the Ligurian Coast, in the hope that it would reverse the deterioration in his attitude and health. But the weather was uncooperative, and several weeks after their arrival, Beckett wrote despondently to George Reavey that he was ill, and had gone there "in hope—so far deferred—of a little warmth and sun."[29] June brought improvement in the weather, and so they stayed on until July.

When he returned to Paris, he met Jean and George Reavey, who were there from New York, and dined with them glumly at Hayter's studio, suffering through a snapshot session while staring morosely at his wineglass.[30] He was tanned and rested, but constant interruptions and irritations beset him and shattered what calm he had brought back with him.

He had been in correspondence with Jack MacGowran in New York for some time concerning *Beginning to End*, the one-man show MacGowran had mounted with his assistance, using a pastiche of writings to create a dramatic unity. The show had been acclaimed in the United States, and MacGowran wanted to bring it to Europe. Beckett approved, and told MacGowran to get in touch at once with Albert Bessler, the dramaturg of the Schiller Theatre in Berlin.[31] As long as he was going to be there to direct *Happy Days* for the Berlin Festival, he thought MacGowran's show would contribute much to the program.

MacGowran had also been approached by an American company who wanted to make a ninety-minute film of *Beginning to End*, and this disturbed Beckett greatly. He saw the show as a unity which could not be expanded to fill that amount of time without suffering in the process. To him, it was an artistic unit, arrived at after much painstaking consultation and consideration, and he could not envision enlarging it unless he and MacGowran were free to spend a long time inserting new material, which he was too ill to even consider. He asked Mac-Gowran to negotiate for a film with the script as it was already written and as gently as possible let MacGowran know that he would not consent to the expansion unless he could control it.[32] When MacGowran acquiesced, there was another flurry of correspondence among them and Grove Press regarding rights for the film, and then with Bessler, who was delighted at the prospect of MacGowran's participation in the Berlin Festival. These negotiations with MacGowran took place between February and August, 1971. Concurrently, Beckett was trying to arrange for the release of American dollars from his royalties in the United States to help MacGowran through a bad financial period.[33] The negotiations were complicated because Beckett did not keep a bank account in the United States and so all monetary transactions had to be handled through Grove Press. There was any number of mix-ups, as money did not move fast enough and MacGowran was forced to borrow from others, then to make a series of financial maneuvers to return all the sums to their rightful owners.

Beckett was inordinately fond of MacGowran, so much so that when MacGowran made a number of obvious hints that his consuming passion was to own something by Jack B. Yeats, Beckett—to the astonishment of his close friends—gave away his beloved painting, purchased with such difficulty many years before. Why, his friends asked, had Beckett so easily given up one of the few possessions that had any real meaning for him?

"He asked me for it. He wanted it. I gave it to him." This was the sum total of Beckett's comment. His friends knew better than to question him further and the matter was dropped.[34]

Now, even as he sent money, he asked MacGowran gently and touchingly to try to hang onto the Yeats if at all possible without even hinting how much he wanted it back if MacGowran could not keep it.

Meanwhile, Beckett continued to make plans for Berlin. All his associates in the French, English and American theater were astonished that he would go to a country where he did not feel secure in the language to direct a play he had not translated. "I had to," he said matter-of-factly. "It was the only way I could get a play of mine put on exactly as I wanted it."[35]

On August 9, he flew to Berlin, in a mood which he described as "too tired, stupid, pushed and aching to write," and hoped that work in the theater would prove providential, even though he had premonitions which were not of the brightest.[36]

From the beginning, the production was beset by seemingly insurmountable problems. He rehearsed three different actresses for the part of Winnie before he found one who would stay with the show, and even then had to settle for rushed rehearsal periods wedged in during her free time from other commitments. The man who played Willie was bewildered by the part and so slow to follow Beckett's instructions that every moment spent with him was sheer drudgery. "Difficult rehearsals," Beckett called them, "tiring but not tiresome."[37] There were technical problems as well, and to top it all, MacGowran thrust Beckett into the thankless position of having to placate the Berlin Festival officials and harangue government agents in several countries, all at the same time.

MacGowran had depended for a number of years on a combination of pills and liquor to function, but they had seriously affected his health. On stage, he was carefully controlled, forcing his fragile body through sheer will to perform as he wanted it, but off the stage he spent most of his waking hours in a zombielike state. It was only through the dutiful ministrations of his wife, Gloria, and a devoted handful of friends that he was able to meet his commitments.[38]

MacGowran had sent word to Beckett of his expected arrival in Berlin, and Beckett went to the airport to meet him. MacGowran was not on the plane, and Beckett spent two frantic days trying to locate him. A lot of money had gone into preparation and publicity for MacGowran's performance, and Beckett was terrified that he simply would not show up.

MacGowran finally contacted Beckett, claiming that he had been unable to leave New York because he was in the midst of renouncing his Irish passport and seeking United States citizenship, and he had no valid papers with which to travel. Beckett and the Schiller Theatre officials intervened on his behalf with letters to officials on both sides of the Atlantic Ocean, and several days later MacGowran arrived, coping with the excitement by sedating himself so heavily that Beckett feared he would not recover in time to perform. However, MacGowran was always able to effect an almost miraculous change in himself whenever it was time to act, and he did so, to everyone's astonishment, performing so brilliantly that *Beginning to End* was sold out for most of the festival.

This continuing series of crises caused what Beckett passed off as "the usual aches and pains."[39] He was staying in his usual hideout at the Akademie der Kunste, but was still hounded by celebrity seekers, among them a number of nubile women who knocked on his door at night, sometimes bearing bottles of the Irish whiskey he loved. Beckett tried to joke about the resulting lack of sleep, calling it "highly undesirable, as Freud said of his cancer."[40]

He had planned to return to Paris when his Berlin engagement was over, to try to settle down to writing and translating for the first time in almost two years, but his health was so fragile that he knew he had to get away if he were to survive the constant drain on his physical resources. He returned to Paris at the end of September just long enough to pack for a holiday, and then he and Suzanne flew to Selmun, Malta. Despite the several thousand English residents, Beckett described Selmun as "the nearest antidote to Paris" that he had found in all his wanderings of the past few years.[41] The reverence for privacy on the part of the English, who carefully averted their eyes from him, was exactly what he had been searching for on all of his previous journeys. The weather was disappointing at first, but the quiet and emptiness of that part of the island were all the tonic that Beckett needed. When the sun appeared at last, he swam each day. As his general health improved, so too did his eyes, and for the first time in more than a year, he drove an automobile.

He was quite pleased with himself, and actually looked forward to returning to Paris in mid-November. Sadly, he discovered that Paris was exactly as he had left it: there were American journalists and scholars and he was too polite to refuse them an audience, so he trekked all over Paris trying to guard what little privacy remained to him by meeting them in out-of-the-way bars and hotel lobbies. There were persons involved in various aspects of production or publication of his work in other countries whom he felt obliged to see; and there were as always friends from "the old days—before the great fame"[42] who invited him to dine or have drinks in the hope of giving him a respite from the clamor that beset him. However good their intentions, the truth of the matter was simply that all conviviality had become unwelcome. It kept him from his desk, even though he felt that all he could do there was to answer correspondence. More importantly, it kept him from Ussy, where he had not been for more than a year, and Ussy was the only place where he could find the necessary solitude and contemplation that might lead to writing. In early December, he managed to get away, and discovered that his little cottage was "dilapidated, damp and gloomy, barely habitable, but worth the discomfort for the quiet."[43] However, the bitter mist from the Marne River that penetrated the walls and could not be dispelled induced all the old aches and pains, and for the first time, he was forced to withdraw back to Paris.

There, the pressure of life was exacerbated by another round of financial transactions with MacGowran. Beckett wrote to Seaver in response to MacGowran's plea for two thousand dollars from Beckett's royalties. Seaver passed the letter on to Rosset, necessitating further correspondence with Beckett, who was writing all this while to assure MacGowran that the money would be forthcoming. Finally, after the transactions seemed to have gone on for an inordinately long time, Beckett arranged with his bankers at Lloyds to transfer the money to Gloria MacGowran's account. In the meantime, Rosset sent a check for American dollars directly to MacGowran, who returned it to Beckett, saying he preferred to have the money paid directly in British sterling.[44]

At the same time, there were new publications of some of Beckett's previous writings. In June, Liam Miller of Dublin's Dolman Press, who was most anxious to have a Beckett publication appear under his imprint,[45] published Beckett's translation of Apollinaire's Zone, first published unsigned in *transition* in 1950. *Le Dépeupleur* (*The Lost Ones*), a short prose piece written in 1966, had been published by Éditions de Minuit early in 1971 and the translation had been promised to Rosset ever since. Beckett had worked sporadically on it, and finally, through great effort, was able to tell Rosset as the year ended that the translation would be his by the new year, 1972,[46] and not entitled "The Depopulator," as some had been calling it.[47] It appeared first in England, from Calder and Boyars, with two glaring mathematical errors which were quickly pointed out to Beckett. He wrote at once to Fred Jordan at Grove Press, asking him to change (from page 7 of the British edition) "eighteen high" to "sixteen high" and "eighty thousand" to "twelve million," but it was too late and the errors were not corrected until the text was reprinted.[48] *The Lost Ones* first appeared in the United States in *Fiction* because Donald Barthelme and

Marianne Frisch asked Beckett for an original text for the periodical. Beckett agreed, but Rosset and Jordan balked, saying they had already contracted to publish the complete work in *Evergreen Review* and did not want *Fiction* to print it beforehand. Barthelme and Frisch were adamant that they would not accept it unless they could have it first, and so Beckett wrote one of his gentle but firm notes to Jordan saying that he would be obliged if the text appeared first in *Fiction*.[49] In this, as in all other demands upon his publisher, he was given his way.

Beckett was fairly well convinced that works such as these—written in the 1960's or earlier—were all that he would publish from this point on. It was not that he had stopped writing—quite the contrary—it was simply that nothing seemed to allow itself to amount to more than a brief text, a few paragraphs abandoned almost before they were begun in the hope that the next inspiration would result in a longer, more sustained work. "Happy mortal, whose voice has not abandoned you,"[50] was his bittersweet pronouncement when a friend showed him a poem; "glad to hear work looking up for you—mine banal as usual,"[51] he wrote to another. He thought he would spend his time negotiating for productions of his plays or assisting in their presentation, and now and again issuing a brief "formerly aborted"[52] text to placate his publishers.

All this changed when he and Suzanne finally made their escape from Paris in February, 1972, for five weeks in Morocco. Inclement weather was becoming an unpleasant but established part of their escapes to the south ever since the stay in Nabeul. As usual, there was continuing cold, mist, wind and rain for the first three weeks of their stay, until the sun finally came out and rewarded them for their perseverance. While they were in Morocco, Beckett observed something that triggered a response to something he had seen on Malta, and it gave him the inspiration for two of the new plays he has written since then, *Not I* (1972) and *That Time* (1974).

He wrote *Not I* hurriedly, in twelve days, upon his return to Paris—from March 20 to April 1.[53] There had been hints for a number of years that Beckett would eventually write a play in which the actor was little more than a vocal conveyance for his artistic vision. Even before the first performance of *Waiting for Godot,* Beckett had said that all he wanted on the stage was "a pair of blubbering lips."[54]

In Malta he had seen Caravaggio's painting of the beheading of St. Jerome, and said he was struck by it as "a voice crying in the wilderness."[55] Caravaggio's painting, preponderantly black and solemn, violent and macabre, was an image that stayed with him after he left Malta. Then, in Morocco, he was sitting in a sunny cafe one afternoon quietly observing the human traffic on the street in front of him when he saw the second part of the inspiration for *Not I.* An Arab woman shrouded in a jellaba was hunkered down on the edge of the sidewalk—in Beckett's words, "crouched in an attitude of intense waiting." [56] Every so often, she would straighten and peer intently into the distance. Then she would flap her arms aimlessly against her sides and hunker down once again. Beckett was puzzled by the woman's anxiety and tension. Finally, a vehicle best described as a Moroccan school bus drove up and desposited a child, whom the woman swept into her arms and showered with endearments before disappearing into the throng. Beckett combined the darkness and drama of the Caravaggio painting with the Arab woman's intensity of waiting and created a mouth, a vivid red gash, the only visible object at the center of an altogether dark stage. Off to one side he placed a figure described as everything from "a huge, silent Druidic figure,"[57] to "a grotesquely tall, monk-like figure."[58] The mouth belongs to the speaker, an Irish woman of about seventy years of age, who recalls a life of premature birth, mechanical survival, and the avoidance of herself. Five times her voice erupts, denying the tortured screaming "SHE!" as she tries to cling desperately to the third person pronoun. The auditor, as the male figure is called in Beckett's text, responds a varying number of times in ever diminishing degrees by flapping his arms helplessly at his sides in what the stage directions call an attitude of "helpless compassion."

"I knew that woman in Ireland," Beckett said, "I knew who she was—not 'she' specifically, one single woman, but there were so many of those old crones, stumbling down the lanes, in the ditches, beside the hedgerows. Ireland is full of them. And I heard 'her' saying what I wrote in *Not I.* I actually heard it."[59] He wrote *Not I* in English, explaining almost apologetically "I don't know, I never know in advance what language I will write in,"[60] but in this case, it seemed only logical that he convey the anguish of an Irish woman in English rather than in French.

The monologue, the logorrhea that tumbles out of the crimson slash of a mouth so swiftly as to be unintelligible at times to the audience, should be performed in fifteen to seventeen minutes. When it ends, the audience is usually breathless from the aural assault and limp from an experience that seems to have encompassed them in the very long lifetime of the seventy-year-old speaker. (To Beckett's horror, the play was performed in Germany in a version expanded to more than forty-five minutes. He felt, as did many who saw it, that it had become a simple, boring tirade, with none of the magic of the abbreviated performance time he had specified in the stage directions.)

The writing of this play produced an almost miraculous change in Beckett. He was inspired to put the finishing touches to a brief manuscript he called *Still*, which he had promised for a long time to Hayter, who made etchings to accompany it.[61] In good spirits, he "disimproved some hours doggerelizing Chamfort's *Maximes*," and was quite pleased when he wrote

> Live and clean forget from day to day,
> Mop up life as fast as it dribbles away.[62]

Convinced that he would now do more serious writing and anxious to protect his health and his newfound tranquillity, Beckett left with Suzanne for Malta on September 1 for a stay of at least six weeks. He wanted to gird himself for a planned trip to England in November to assist with rehearsals of *Not I*.

There was enormous interest in *Not I* as soon as he announced that he had written it, and Alan Schneider and the Royal Court company vied to give the world premiere. Beckett wanted it to be performed first in England because he wanted to be in the theater during rehearsals and there was no question of his going to the United States. Finally, it was agreed that production would be almost simultaneous, with the English premiere a few days before the American. Alan Schneider arranged with Jules Irving, who was then director of the Repertory Theatre of Lincoln Center, to hold a two-part Beckett festival in November in the Forum: *Not I* was to be played on the same bill as *Krapp's Last Tape* and would be followed on successive evenings by *Happy Days* and *Act Without Words I*. Hume Cronyn and Jessica Tandy, with whom the idea for the Beckett Festival had originated, were to appear in all four plays, and the stellar Henderson Forsythe appeared as the auditor in *Not I*.

However, there were unspecified delays at the Royal Court, and when all the schedules were meshed, it was discovered that rehearsals could not begin until just about the time of the first American performance.

Schneider flew to Paris in August, continuing his custom of discussing the production with Beckett before beginning rehearsals. Barney Rosset, who was eager to publish the text, flew with him and so did Jessica Tandy, who was somewhat disconcerted at the thought of creating a role in a play by Beckett. Beckett met them at a restaurant for dinner.[63] As soon as they were seated, he took out five single-spaced typed pages and passed them around the table; and they read them in order as he passed them. When they finished, there was a puzzled but positive emotional reaction, although no one was able to respond to the play intellectually. Beckett seemed pleased by this, especially when all agreed they could not understand it. Nevertheless, they were happy to have a new work and agreed that they wanted it. As they were leaving, Tandy turned to Beckett and asked, "What happened to her in that field? Was she raped?" Beckett seemed shocked. "How could you think of such a thing!" he said. "No, no, not at all—it wasn't that at all."

Beckett asked Tandy if she had any questions before the evening ended. She had only one, about *Happy Days* (for she was too tired by the plane flight and too flustered by her initial reading of *Not I* to think of any others): How, she wondered, could Winnie be up to her neck in her mound, unable to move, and still speak her lines with such impassioned resonance. Tandy showed Beckett how difficult it would be to project a variety of mood and inflection with her neck elongated into the unnatural position the mound demanded. Beckett was brusque: this was a mere technicality. It had not occurred to him. He told Tandy to find a way to do it as he wanted, but he was unwilling to suggest what that might be.

Thirty-six hours after they had arrived in Paris, the trio

flew back to New York; shortly after, rehearsals began. Cronyn was troubled that the audience would not be able to understand what *Not I* was about if Tandy spoke the lines as fast as Beckett wanted. He sent a cable to Beckett, who replied, "I am not unduly concerned with intelligibility. I hope the piece would work on the necessary emotions of the audience rather than appealing to their intellect."

Beckett instructed Schneider that he wanted Tandy to be strapped against a backdrop so there would be no movement on stage except her mouth. He did not want the actress to move her head or hands, or to make any gesture that might possibly induce her to attempt to contribute something more to the part than he had indicated in the script. Tandy was arranged so that microphones amplified her voice and only her mouth showed. She was "black all over—black gloves, black hat, I felt like an old English hangman."[64] At first her face was blackened, but a cloth shroud produced a more effective image of blackness. She was enclosed in "a sort of black box" in which a man sat who kept the light focused on her mouth in case she moved even a fraction of an inch. There was what she called "an iron thing" fixed at the back of her head to lock it into place. Originally, there was also a forehead strap, but she could not speak with it and asked Schneider to remove it. Tandy played the role in a standing position, clinging to two iron bars at her sides for stability. A small inside light at the top of the box illuminated five oversized cards on which the script was printed in large block letters, but eventually she memorized it. Beckett had volunteered one piece of information during their meeting in Paris: he told Tandy to consider the mouth "an organ of emission, without intellect." The play was meant to touch the audience's wellspring, but she performed it as he instructed—as rote exercise.

The play was staged in the round, and this was responsible for the most difficult part of Tandy's performance—being wheeled on and off the stage. Beckett's directions called for the actress to be speaking her own made-up gibberish until she was in place, then to slide automatically into the script. At the end of the play, she was to drift off into gibberish again so that her voice could be heard even after the light focused on her mouth went out. It made Tandy feel isolated and disjointed as the box was wheeled on and off the stage. She had to adjust to an atmosphere "claustrophobic, horrible!" and to adjust her timing and delivery as well. The first few times she could not breathe or speak above a whisper, and could not attain the pace of speech. Her body was in a cold sweat. She longed for some advice or consolation from the author.

Diligently and patiently, Tandy worked to follow Schneider's understanding direction. Cronyn, a cerebral actor who approaches his roles with the intensity of a mechanical engineer studying a blueprint, wanted to know the reasons for every action, the writer's intention as well as the director's instruction, before he could fit comfortably into his parts. And an author who would not reveal his intention was, to Cronyn, "incredibly selfish and arrogant."

An icy contretemps happened between Beckett and Cronyn during rehearsals of *Krapp's Last Tape*. In the script, Beckett instructed that Krapp "curses." Further on, Krapp "curses louder," but Beckett did not specify what Krapp is actually to say. Cronyn told Schneider he thought the line should be "oh balls, rubbish . . . balls." Schneider agreed. There were four weeks of preview performances followed by an eight-week run of the plays. In the last preview, Harold Pinter was in the audience, and he was shocked by what he called Cronyn's ad-libbing. He sent a cable to Beckett, who was disturbed by Pinter's adverse reaction. Beckett cabled Schneider and asked him to delete the lines. This made Cronyn angry, and he wrote a tart letter to Beckett saying, "We know what you don't want us to say. What *DO* you want us to say? This minuscule point is balls and rubbish, especially at this time."[65]

Beckett replied immediately—a curt postcard—stating that if he had anything to communicate to the American actors, he would convey it through his director, Mr. Schneider. Cronyn framed it and gave it to Schneider as a good luck token on opening night.

Critical reception was generally favorable for all four plays, with both Tandy and Cronyn regarded as having given some of the finest performances of their distinguished careers. But Beckett, by now returned from Malta, was not convinced. "Alan wrote about rehearsals. Not encouraging—especially she.

Taking on too much," he wrote.[66] To another, "*Krapp* sounds a mess from all accounts. *Not I* not too bad."[67] But when the reviews were in and Schneider and others had written to praise the performances, Beckett softened his judgment:

> Thanks for your reactions to *Not I*. Encouraging to my hope that it may be theatre after all in spite of all. I don't think I'd agree about Cronyn from what I have heard.[68]

"Rehearsals in London December. Hope to find out then if it's theatre or not," was his judgment.[69]

He alternated time in Paris with time in Ussy from mid-November to mid-December, 1972, but the exhilarating effects of Malta were dissipated because of a reoccurrence of dental "adjustments"—extensive, painful, and supposed to be spread over a number of weeks. He was concerned that he would not be able to go to London and so persuaded the dentist to pull all his teeth at once because he was determined not to miss rehearsals. He left for London on December 19, and by Christmas he was beginning to chew again.[70]

Beckett had worked with Billie Whitelaw in the Royal Court premiere production of *Play*.[71] Whitelaw, tiny and fragile, has a voice that roams octaves, from deepest brooding to highest passion, and just as Beckett said that Patrick Magee's voice was the one he heard inside his mind when writing a man's part, so was Whitelaw's the female voice that he had listened to when he wrote *Not I*. Since 1964, Beckett had known that someday he would write a play for Whitelaw, and he was deeply disappointed that circumstances contrived to prevent her from giving the definitive premiere performance of *Not I*.

As soon as he arrived at the Royal Court Theatre, there were problems. Beckett walked into the first rehearsal and immediately inspired a barely veiled animosity in almost everyone connected with the production because he knew every line and had definite ideas about vocal shading, nuance, gesture and all technical aspects of the production. Anthony Page was the nominal director of the play, but there was no doubt that Beckett was really in charge.

This presented a situation so rife with conflict for Whitelaw that she was close to the breaking point all through rehearsals. On the one hand, there was Page, a director with whom she had worked before and whom she trusted to guide her to another brilliant performance. On the other, there was Beckett, prodding, probing, urging her to try a line "just once more," quietly contradicting Page with voluminous instructions. Whitelaw's script reflected the conflict, for by the time she had learned the lines and put it aside, it was a veritable rainbow of ink, with words circled and instructions and memoranda noted in different colors to denote whose they were—Page's or Beckett's.

Until now, Beckett had only been able to convince actors and actresses in Germany to give up their own identities and interpretations and to do exactly what he wanted them to do, but he was fortunate in London that Whitelaw was able to bring an extraordinary intelligence and sensitivity to her part, to manage to placate Page while still putting herself totally in Beckett's directorial hands, performing *Not I* exactly as he wanted.

Her most immediate problem was learning the script. Whitelaw could not have it printed in front of her, as Tandy had tried to do, because she could not synchronize her vision and speech. She tried to use a hearing aid, but it, too, interfered with her concentration and caused so much confusion that she gave it up. Finally, she forced herself to memorize the script. Beckett spent long hours with her in the living room of her spacious, sunlit Georgian house in Camden Town, sunk in a leather chair while Whitelaw sat on the rug at his feet, patiently saying the lines over and over in her native North-country accent. When Beckett heard her speak this dialect, he decided against making her try to approximate an Irish brogue—his one concession to Whitelaw.

After Beckett had gone back to his hotel, Whitelaw would sit with her family watching sporting events on television, practicing speed-speaking: when the time clock flashed onto the screen, she would count to ten clearly and succinctly for each second of time that elapsed. Her jaws ached but she developed muscular control and verbal clarity, so that she was able to deliver each line in a voice that could not only be heard but understood in the farthest row of the theater.

Still Beckett continued his demand for excellence, and rehearsals went relentlessly on in preparation for the January 16 opening. Whitelaw was rehearsing all day and spending all night walking the floors with her seriously ill son—and trying to keep this information from Beckett, for she realized he would not have been able to cope with the knowledge that she had other things on her mind and was not bringing her entire concentration to his play.

The strain took its toll when Beckett insisted on drilling her repeatedly on one brief phrase which he felt she had not got quite right. Whitelaw collapsed into hysterical tears, shaking and screaming. While the other members of the company tried to calm her, Beckett stood apart, white-faced and terrified. When she was in her dressing room, Beckett followed with a glass of brandy, intoning softly as a litany the phrase, "My God, Billie, what have I done to you . . . my God, Billie, what have I done to you . . ." while he gently stroked her hands.

Whitelaw, always the professional, was calm within a matter of minutes, and as she sat sniffing her brandy, Beckett switched immediately to an all-business demeanor and asked, "Are you better now? Do you think we can get on with rehearsal?" They never discussed the incident again. Whitelaw did not tell Beckett about her child and he never asked the reason for her momentary breakdown. He simply accepted it as something that had happened and was now over. He wanted to get back to work.

There was another problem, now that they were well into dress-rehearsal stage: Beckett wanted Whitelaw to be strapped to a backdrop just as Tandy had been, but Whitelaw found that she directed so much energy and tension into the upper reaches of her body—particularly into her arms and shoulders—that she often fell over flat on her face from the strain that resulted. She implored Beckett to give her something to hold on to, and finally he decided to have her seated in an armchair. This still did not work, for Whitelaw was tiny and the chair large, and gripping the arms far at the sides of the chair only misdirected her concentration. At last someone suggested placing an iron bar across the arms of the chair, and it worked. Whitelaw gave her performance strapped against the chair's high back, clutching onto the bar in front of her, so hard that she rubbed the skin off the palms of her hands.

People bought tickets for the production because it was featured on a double bill with Albert Finney playing in *Krapp's Last Tape*. Beckett had had little to do with Finney during rehearsals, leaving him entirely to Page, for early on he discovered that Finney would not take any direction from him. Rather than collide with what he considered a massive ego, Beckett simply bowed out of the picture. Speaking of these productions, he described Jocelyn Herbert's sets as her "great job as always," Whitelaw as "quite marvelous" and Finney as "hopelessly miscast."

The reaction to *Not I* was curious indeed. People had bought tickets primarily to see Finney, who received poor critical notices, but they left the theater puzzled and thrilled by *Not I*. There was a current of excitement in the first-night audience that kept seats filled for the run of the production.

Beckett stayed quietly in the Hyde Park Hotel until the night of the dress rehearsal. He had been in London for a month, with little time for anything but rehearsals and a brief visit to Hyde Park's Round Pond, where he found "Mr. Kelly without his kite," a sentimental reference to *Murphy* he wrote to George Reavey, to whom he was still grateful for his efforts to get the book published more than thirty years before.

Not I opened on January 16, 1973, but Beckett was not in the audience. He was still in London, however, because Whitelaw insisted that even though he would not come to the theater, she had to see him when the performance ended. He joined her and the others in the company afterwards at a quiet party at Jocelyn Herbert's.

He flew back to Paris on January 18, went to Ussy for two weeks, then "sunward" to Morocco.

He was thrilled by the events in London and pleased with the entire year. Despite the demands on his person and his time, he had written what he considered another major dramatic work and it had been generally well received in the English-speaking world. He knew that he would have to face the dreaded translation into French, but he was confident that he could do it in between sessions of new writing. For the first time since the Nobel Prize, he was unshakably confident that he had put his personal circumstances in order, and there would be nothing in his future that he could not handle.

1973–:

"A STAIN UPON THE SILENCE"

 "Work standing still prior to lying down," Beckett said when he finished *Not I*.[1] Since January, 1973, when he wrote to George Reavey that he had "finished nothing begun," had "begun nothing worthwhile," and suffered once again from "agonies of galloping speechlessness," he has assisted in productions of his plays several times each year in London, Berlin and Paris.

Limited editions of his works have appeared, among them the six-thousand-dollar edition of *Fizzles* with etchings by Jasper Johns,[2] *All Strange Away*, with illustrations by Edward Gorey[3] and *The Drunken Boat*, his 1932 translation of Rimbaud's poem.[4]

He has published two books of new prose and drama, several self-translations and a collection of writings that spans his entire canon. He has also written at least two new plays and has attempted to return to poetry.

Besides all that, when not on "The Paris-Ussy Shuttle," he has spent from two to four months each year in a Mediterranean clime—ostensibly to rest—usually Tangier or Morocco.

He has been elected to membership in the German Academy of Art and has been the subject of an entire edition of *Cahiers de l'Herne*, the prestigious French literary periodical, which as a review in the *Guardian* notes, "is one of the highest accolades a contemporary author can hope for."[5] A journal devoted entirely to his writing, *The Journal of Beckett Studies* (dubbed *JOBS* by the scholars and critics who devote themselves to his writings) is now being published in England,[6] and interest in Beckett studies is so great in the United States that informal plans are under way as of 1978 to found a Beckett Society of America.[7] And, in the winter of 1977, the Comédie-Française, the bastion of the French theatrical establishment, announced that *Waiting for Godot* would enter its repertoire the following summer under Roger Blin's direction.

Requests to adapt and perform his work have poured in from leading members of the theatrical profession throughout the world. Zero Mostel wanted to make a film of *Waiting for Godot*, but Beckett declined the offer with a terse note saying it "was not for filming."[8] Estelle Parsons and Shelley Winters wanted to mount a commercial production of *Godot* with themselves in the starring roles, but Beckett scrawled two words across Parsons's letter to Barney Rosset: "Definitely *NO*."[9] Beckett later told Rosset that it was important always to maintain the masculinity of the characters, that allowing women to play the parts made it something other than what he had written. For him, theater sex was not interchangeable, and an all-women *Godot* would be as spurious as if *Happy Days* or *Not I* were played by men. He added that an all-black production had been done sometime earlier in the United States, and even though the parts had been played by men, it was nevertheless not in keeping with his intention and detracted from the audience's concentration on the play itself.[10] Worse still, to his mind, was the unauthorized all-female *Godot* he called a disaster, mounted several years earlier in Israel, in which he was powerless to intervene.[11]

Patrick Magee asked for permission to mount a production similar to MacGowran's *Beginning to End*, and to this Beckett gave his consent, working with Magee on the program.

Nicol Williamson used parts of *How It Is* in a one-man show without first getting Beckett's approval, but Beckett decided not to intervene because he considered Williamson a friend after having worked with him in London.[12]

He became more directly involved, however, when Andre Gregory staged a full-scale production of *Endgame* featuring a set consisting of a chicken-wire cage and adding all sorts of additional dialogue to the script. Because of the bastardization of the script, Rosset wanted to stop the production entirely, even though Gregory had taken the proper steps to secure the appropriate permissions. A flurry of telegrams and letters flew to Ussy, and on February 13, 1973, Beckett wrote a long, thoughtful letter to Rosset outlining the possible courses of action open to him. He agreed that the Gregory production was unacceptable, but felt unable to stop it from his great distance without having seen it first. He was saddened by what he called the "omnipresent massacre and abuse of directorial function," and expressed his gratitude to Alan Schneider for having acted as a watchman and for sparing him from much of it in New York. However, he realized that an enormous amount of time, money and work had gone into Gregory's production—"no matter how misguided"—and so he decided to let it run for the period specified in Gregory's contract; then he would insure that the contract would never be renewed.

In the meantime, Gregory was in Paris trying to arrange with Madeleine Renaud for his version of *Endgame* to appear in the Bordeaux theater festival. Renaud, anxious to satisfy Beckett's feelings in the matter, asked what he wanted her to do. As always, he told Renaud that she was free to do whatever she pleased, but he left her with the impression that he would not be happy, and so she rejected Gregory's proposal. Gregory wrote to Beckett several times, once even sending a twenty-page letter of explanation, and Beckett replied with five brief sentences, stating that he had only passed on to Renaud what his friends had told him about the New York production, leaving the final decision up to her. He also told Gregory that he would not interfere if the production were brought to Paris, but Beckett's influence was such that Gregory's *Endgame* was never performed there.

Lee Breuer and the Mabou Mines Company secured permission through Jean and George Reavey for what was supposed to be a straight reading of *The Lost Ones*. Instead it became a dramatic monologue featuring David Warrilow on a gray cocoonlike set made primarily of foam rubber. In the course of the production, Warrilow disrobed and performed the remainder of the play in total nudity, while a young woman representing one of the lost bodies who inhabit the sphere sat naked at his feet. Usually Beckett would have been infuriated by a violation of the agreement, but because the Reaveys were involved, he did nothing to stop it. Instead, he satisfied himself with the laconic comment, "Sounds a crooked straight reading to me."[13]

Finally, Beckett sent a covering letter to Rosset, stating simply that he would not interfere with productions of his plays on aesthetic grounds even if he had the right to do so, because once started, there would be no end. To date, it is a policy he has stringently followed: whenever possible, he tries to maintain absolute control over all productions; when not possible, he ignores them.

His attempts at new writing, which had seemed such an exciting possibility after the success of *Not I*, amounted to very little. He turned to poetry in an attempt to start some creative impulse, but had to admit sadly that he could only produce twelve lines in French and "a rather dimmer companion in English."[14] From January, 1973, when he was in London for *Not I*, to February, 1974, he did very little that was not connected with previous writings. He tried to translate *Not I* into French for Madeleine Renaud, and was "bogged down through loathing of the original" in his attempts to translate *Mercier et Camier* into English.[15] He complained that he felt a persistent sense of deterioration and was too slack and stupid to write anymore.[16]

He became introspective again, but instead of brooding over his inability to write—and by extension, over his own mortality—he brooded sadly over the recent spate of deaths among his friends. In one brief sentence he conveyed his grief over the loss of good friends and his disgust toward a still-living contemporary writer whom he considered facile and second-rate: "MacGowran is gone, Raimbourg gone, Serreau very ill, and —— Academie Française!!!"[17]

He began to write long, depressing letters urging friends to "come and see me before the light goes out for us all,"[18] or "before the waters wash over us all";[19] and when he wrote his annual New Year's greetings, he wished them well for "the current excruciation."[20]

With the death of so many of his contemporaries, he began to dread the continuation of life as an old man in a younger society. Life suddenly became too terrible to continue, but he was unable to bring himself to end it through suicide. Instead, he began to consider ways in which he might disappear from society while still remaining alive and isolated. He actually went to his lawyer, hoping to be able to arrange his affairs in such a way that monetary transactions might continue to come to his beneficiaries without his involvement, but this produced such a flurry of anxiety among his legal representatives and his family, that he had to abandon the idea. Nevertheless, he still spoke of it to a few trusted cronies in late-night drinking sessions, hoping that their joint efforts might lead to a possibility he had not investigated.[21]

Over and over, he announced that each foray into the theater would be his last. "Here since late December [1975] directing *Godot* for the Schiller theatre (and for my sins)," he wrote to George Reavey. "Then back to Paris and more theatre with French *Not I* and yet another *Krapp*."[22]

A short time later he wrote again, saying that he was actually in rehearsal with Renaud, ". . . then farewell to theatre,"[23] and, "vast relief at thought of no more theatre," he wrote in his next letter.[24]

From April, when *Pas Moi* (*Not I*) got "off to a goodish start,"[25] through the end of 1975, Beckett remained free of all theatrical commitments. His output for the year consisted of "nothing much of interest, scraps of self translation and two short pieces for the theatre."[26] And, as always when he was not satisfied with his writing, he grew depressed.

"More and more withdrawn which I deplore but can't help,"[27] he told George Reavey. Soon after, he wisely accepted invitations to participate in directing his work in Berlin and London, for he realized that he could not be away from theater very long without sliding back into a depression and losing the mental equilibrium that had become so necessary if he were to continue writing. Much as he complained of it, the constant press of well-wishers, reporters, and genuine good friends brought him out of his melancholy moroseness and forced him into an almost jolly compatibility. Quite simply, being involved in the theater made his disposition as cheerful as it would ever be, and he knew it and was thankful for it.

He spent most of the summer of 1974 "holed up at Ussy" forcing himself to write. By September, he had completed *That Time* which he called of the *"Not I* family."[28] He returned to his own life to write this play, presenting a man's face, ghastly white and framed by an aureole of white hair, centered on an all-black stage. From the back and the two sides, tape recorded voices of the man as a child, a young man and an old man are heard alternately. Voice A evokes memories of a ruin where he had hid and played as a child (possibly the abandoned lead mines in the hills above Carrickmines). Voices B and C recall the dismal years during the 1930's when, huddled in the wretched green raincoat, he sought solace and warmth in the empty echoing halls of the National Portrait Gallery, and they evoke a long-ended love affair.

Writing *That Time* seemed to release an autobiographical swell that he had kept under control for many years, and shortly thereafter, he wrote *Footfalls*, another brief text, which seems to dwell on his mother's terminal illness. A woman named May (his mother's name) asks her mother (who is never seen, but is heard from behind a shaft of light supposed to represent a door ajar and a lighted room beyond) if she would like an injection or other ministrations performed. The mother speaks offstage, telling how May, as a child, was not content to pace back and forth on a strip of rug, but wanted it removed so that she might feel her feet fall on the bare floor. Later there is a curious story of a girl named Amy (an anagram of May?), but the play seems to be primarily one version of May Beckett's insomnia.

He wrote *That Time*, hoping that Patrick Magee would play the role, but he wrote *Footfalls* specifically for Billie Whitelaw, for whom he has a professional respect bordering on passion. After all his years in the theater, he had finally found an actress who possessed all the qualities he sought and was willing to sacrifice her autonomy to his control. It was a working relationship which thrilled him, and he could not wait to begin rehearsals with her. The Royal Court company mounted a two-part Beckett Festival in honor of his seventieth birthday in the spring of 1976. *Endgame* was performed one evening and the Schiller Theatre Company presented ten performances of the definitive *Waiting for Godot* as Beckett had directed it, in the German language. This production produced highly polarized reactions in all Beckett's friends and theater associates: one group thought it a superbly orchestrated production, with every movement exquisitely choreographed; the other group found it a graceless performance in which all the ebb and flow of vitality and movement had been rigidly and arbitrarily stilled so that the actors moved through the lines like automatons.[29]

The two new scripts became part of a triple bill with *Play*, and comprised the program of the second evening.

Harold Hobson, writing in the *Times*, entitled his review of the triple bill "The Heart of Darkness," and said that unlike *Waiting for Godot*, which was "really rather Rabelaisian," the two new plays give the "unmistakable suggestion . . . that Samuel Beckett has abandoned the park grounds of Rabelais' Abbey of Thélème for the bleak walls of the Port Royal. . . . In other words," Hobson continues, "he has become a Jansenist. He now believes in utter damnation. No soul can be saved by good works."[30] Hobson concludes a surprisingly subdued review (for one of Beckett's strongest supporters) with the almost obligatory remark that, "They may have to be fought for as 'Waiting for Godot' . . . had to be fought for," and calls the plays "poems of a strange and terrible beauty."

But Robert Cushman, writing in the *Observer*, was not so kind. Of *Play*, written some thirteen years earlier, Cushman says it ". . . now looks like a masterpiece. But not . . . *That Time*. Not this time."[31] Cushman admits a decided aversion to Magee's voice, but calls *That Time* "only a re-run of *Krapp's Last Tape* without the props; a process of refinement but not necessarily of enrichment." He is curiously evasive about *Footfalls*, concentrating his remarks on Billie Whitelaw, "who is extraordinary." Cushman states that Beckett directed the play and "he is a gentleman and a showman," but says little about the play itself. In general, the reviewers seemed unwilling to be unkind to Beckett but unable to praise his work.

The triple bill was repeated in Washington, D.C., in December, 1976, at the Arena Theatre under Alan Schneider's direction, with Donald Davis, Dianne Wiest, and Sloane Shelton. Mel Gussow, writing in *The New York Times*, called these plays "an authentic recapitulation of the original [Royal Court production]."[32] The American critic was more positive in his reaction, describing them as "strange, hypnotic and exquisite."

Reaction to the new writings has been as varied as one has come to expect any explication of Beckett's work to be. While the critics remain for the most part faintly positive, they are unmistakably puzzled by the quasi-effrontery of being asked to praise little more than brief exercises in which voices talk, heads breathe, arms flap and monologue spills out; or they are reluctant to praise the entire work for the few brief lines that continue the rapier-sharp commentary on the human condition of which Beckett is the acknowledged master.

"What in God's name is Sam trying to do?" asked one of his staunchest admirers in anguish after the first performance of *Not I*. "How much can he expect us to swallow and still come back for more?"[33]

"This is *not* theater!" cried another indignantly after seeing *Footfalls* and *That Time*. "This is an exercise in vanity, egotism and exorcism of some private demon. If we still had literary salons, these would be marvelous examples of closet drama, and frankly, that's where they belong."

On the other hand, scholars—and there are many, for Beckett has become the most written-about author of the twentieth century—have leaped to the defense of these plays, calling *Not I* "a second masterpiece comparable to *Oedipus Rex*."[34] In general, there was agreement that these plays signified a new movement and direction, still undefined, in Beckett's writing. J. D. O'Hara, writing in the *Nation*, suggests Beckett's recent brevity has evolved through a concern "with situations, not with the problems and resolutions that constitute plot. As a result his fictions have come to resemble prose poems and his plays approach tableaux vivants."[35]

These three plays were published in 1976 with a fourth, *Ghost Trio*, as "Ends," along with "Odds," four pieces called by the author "Roughs for Theatre and Radio," in a book entitled *Ends and Odds*.[36] Simultaneously, Beckett allowed publication of a collection of prose pieces, dating mostly from the late 1960's and the early 1970's, which he called *Foirades* (*Fizzles*). Some of these brief exercises were written specifically for Jerome Lindon's literary periodical, *Minuit;* others, such as *Still,* appeared in limited-edition publications and later in John Calder's *Signature Anthology.* Others were simply passages that he could not expand further.

Beckett defined *Fizzles,* which he claimed were "farted out,"[37] according to the definition in the *Oxford English Dictionary:* "1. The action of breaking wind quietly; the action of hissing or sputtering. 2. A failure or a fiasco. Exactly the sense of *foirade.*"[38]

O'Hara speculates: "Since they really are what they claim to be, the publication of the fizzles is puzzling."[39] Paul Grey, in *Time* said, "Coming from almost any author but Samuel Beckett, 70, these two collections might seem slight to the point of frippery."[40]

Nevertheless, scholars continue to find in these increasingly brief works the same themes which have dominated Beckett's canon, each successive one stripped more painfully bare, each grating more harshly on the rituals and relationships of life in the present century.

There is some speculation that Beckett intends, like his narrator in *Malone Dies,* to arrange his writing so that it ends at the same moment as his life. Jules Reynard, after all, was one of his earliest literary role models, and Reynard managed to write until the very end.

Perhaps there is another reason for the diminution of the writing. In the Tavistock lecture that had such lasting impact on Beckett, Jung spoke of the complexes that form personalities of themselves, appear as visions and speak in voices which are as the voices of real, definite people. Beckett has often called his prose writing a series, with each character supposedly evolving from all the preceding ones. His characters speak with different voices, sometimes assume different names and identities, tell their own stories and sometimes tell the stories of each other. But when the creation of these characters became too upsetting for Beckett, too terrifying because of the exploration and confrontation of himself, he turned to theater as release and salvation. Theater, with its enforced conviviality, required him to live an entirely different kind of life; his plays forced him to take an active role in society. It may not be too strong a statement to say that theater made him whole. When he tried to return to prose in the same self-exploratory manner with the fiction written after 1960, the characterizations became universal—but more important—depersonalized. There were no longer any "little complexes" waiting to form independent personalities, or if there were, they were not as pronounced. Beckett had less need to create them. There was not the same urgent wordiness. They came in short little gasps. Thus, the work diminished.

In all of this century, it would be difficult to come upon another writer who has so lived through his art that it has become the substance of his life. Beckett himself insists that his life is "dull and without interest. The professors know more about it than I do."[41] He abhors the interest in his person and insists with intense sincerity that "nothing matters but the writing. There has been nothing else worthwhile."[42]

Over and over again, he has said, "I couldn't have done it otherwise. Gone on, I mean. I could not have gone through the awful wretched mess of life without having left a stain upon the silence."[43]

Notes:

CHAPTER ONE 1906–23:

1. Samuel Beckett, *Waiting for Godot*. (New York: Grove Press, Evergreen Editions, 1954), p. 58. Samuel Beckett to DB and others.

2. Ann Beckett, August 5, 1972, Dublin; Caroline Beckett Murphy, August 9, 1972, Dublin; Mrs. James (Peggy) Beckett, August 10, 1972, Dublin; Dr. Peter Beckett, August 7, 1972, Dublin; Edward Beckett, January 25, 1974, London; and other members of the Beckett family and their friends.

3. Samuel Beckett, April 13, 1972, Paris.

4. Samuel Beckett, April 13, 1972, Paris.

5. Samuel Beckett to George Reavey; Reavey to DB, January 27, 1972, New York.

6. The Beckett family did not keep a family history, Bible or any other record in which important dates and events were entered. Few letters and photographs are extant since a recent burglary in the home of Beckett's niece, Caroline Beckett Murphy, when most were stolen from her dining room closet. There are one or two references to the name "Becquet" in genealogical documents in the National Library and the Royal Irish Academy Library, but none which can be directly connected with Samuel Beckett's family. Information cited here is commonly believed by Samuel Beckett and other members of his immediate family.

7. Ann Beckett.

8. Ann Beckett, Samuel Beckett, Edward Beckett, Caroline

Beckett Murphy. Frank Beckett became the sole owner of the firm after his father's death in 1933; in 1954, when his own death was imminent, he sold it to Ian MacMillan, who retained the Medcalf name for the same reasons. (Ian MacMillan to DB, January 16, 1974, Dublin.)

9. The following information is from Mary Manning Howe, Doreen Hogan, Dr. Andrew Ganly, all October 30, 1974, Dublin. (Mrs. Hogan is the daughter of the woman William Beckett could not marry.)

10. Information about the Roe family is from Mariah "Mollie" Roe and Sheila Roe Page, January 28, 1974, Guildford, Surrey, England; Caroline Beckett Murphy, Mary Manning Howe and John Manning, November 1, 1974, Dublin; and from records in the Customs House, Dublin.

11. Marriage license of William and Mary Roe Beckett, on file in the Customs House, Dublin.

12. Sean and Seumas Mandy, August 10, 1972, Dublin; also Ann Beckett, Caroline Beckett Murphy.

13. Marriage license of William and Mary Roe Beckett.

14. Anon. "Cooldrinagh, Foxrock," *Supplement to the Irish Builder*, February 26, 1903.

15. Mollie Roe and Sheila Roe Page.

16. Information about Cooldrinagh is from Mollie Roe, Sheila Page, Mary Manning Howe, John Manning, Sean and Seumas Mandy, Ann Beckett, A. J. Leventhal, April 14, 1972, Paris; Brian Coffey, August 12, 1972, London; and others.

17. This is the order in which May Beckett described her priorities to her niece, Mollie Roe.

18. Mollie Roe, Sheila Page, Mary Manning Howe.

19. Mollie Roe. The quotation is from *Footfalls* in *Ends and Odds* (New York: Grove Press, 1976), pp. 45–46.

20. Caroline Beckett Murphy.

21. Mollie Roe.

22. Photographs in possession of Caroline Beckett Murphy.

23. Among them, the late Mrs. Susan Manning and Mrs. William Elvery, mother of Lady Beatrice Glenavy. Lady Glenavy wrote of this in *Today We Will Only Gossip* (London: Constable and Co., Ltd., 1964), p. 48.

24. Alec Reid, "The Reluctant Prizeman," *The Arts*, November 1969, p. 63.

25. Mary Manning Howe, John Manning, Sean and Seumas Mandy.

26. Sean and Seumas Mandy, Mollie Roe.

27. Mollie Roe, Sheila Page.

28. In 1905, as members of the Dublin University Swimming Club, and as members of the Trinity Club Water Polo Team, Gerald and James Beckett captured most of the swimming championships in Ireland and England. Anthony Bailey, *A History of Trinity College, Dublin, 1892–1945* (Dublin: The University Press, Trinity College, 1947).

29. John Manning.

30. Mrs. Dorothy Elvery Kay's photograph is reproduced here following p. 114.

31. Samuel Beckett, *How It Is* (New York: Grove Press, 1964), pp. 15–16.

32. Ann Beckett, Caroline Beckett Murphy.

33. Mrs. Harriet Chance, August 9, 1972, Dublin; Caroline Beckett Murphy; Edward Beckett.

34. Ian MacMillan, present owner of Beckett and Medcalf.

35. Caroline Beckett Murphy, Edward Beckett.

36. Reid, "Reluctant Prizeman," p. 64.

37. Tom Driver, "Beckett by the Madeleine," *Columbia Forum*, Vol. 4, No. 3 (Summer) 1961, 21–25.

38. Reid, "Reluctant Prizeman," p. 64.

39. Jan Kott, October 2, 1971, New Haven; also stated in "King Lear or Endgame," *Shakespeare Our Contemporary* (New York: Anchor Book Editions, 1966), p. 159.

40. Samuel Beckett, November 17, 1961, Paris.

41. Mollie Roe, Mary Manning Howe.

42. Mollie Roe.

43. Samuel Beckett, "Serena I," in *Poems in English* (New York: Grove Press, Evergreen Editions, 1961), p. 35.

44. Sheila, now Mrs. Donald Page, lives in England. Mollie Roe, for many years a librarian at Princeton University, is now retired and lives near Mr. and Mrs. Page. Jack Roe is dead.

45. John Manning. Neither Manning nor Beckett's cousins remember the books he read at home, but in 1922, when he was junior prefect of Portora Royal School, Beckett was also a member of the library committee in charge of "care and maintenance of books and acquisition of new works." He is listed as having given one of the following books to the library during Michaelmas term, though which is not specified: Stevenson's *Dr. Jekyll and Mr. Hyde*, Kipling's *Plain Tales from the Hills*, Poe's *Tales of Mystery and Imagination*, Dowden's edition of Wordsworth's poems, Hannay's

Navy and Sea Power, and Simpkin's *Plot. (Portora,* Michaelmas Term, Vol. XVI, No. 1, 1921, p. 13.)

46. The information on the following pages comes from Mollie Roe and Sheila Page.

47. Mary Manning Howe, August 14, 1974, Woodbridge, Connecticut.

48. Mary Manning Howe.

49. The following information is from interviews with Mollie Roe, Sheila Page, Mary Manning Howe, Ann Beckett, Mrs. Peggy Beckett and other members of the Beckett family. Samuel Beckett wrote of it also in the unpublished *Dream of Fair to Middling Women.* A copy of the typescript of this novel is now in the Baker Library, Dartmouth College, Hanover, New Hampshire.

50. This description of William Beckett is a composite of a description made by Samuel Beckett to Thomas McGreevy, Brian Coffey, Mary Manning Howe, John Manning and others at various times.

51. ". . . the Elsner sisters, were they still living?" *Molloy,* in *Three Novels by Samuel Beckett* (New York: Grove Press, 1965), p. 168.

52. Earlsfort Place is now part of the Adelaide Road, just over the Leeson Street Bridge, and Numbers 3 and 4, where Samuel and Frank Beckett had their classes, are now Number 63, Adelaide Road. Le Peton was headmaster until 1922, when he was succeeded by W. E. Exshaw, who served until the school closed permanently in 1942.

53. Enid Starkie, in her autobiography, *A Lady's Child,* London, Faber & Faber, 1941, gives an impressive portrait of her own French governess and her parents' attitude toward French as a necessary part of their children's education.

54. This account comes from Norris Davidson, November 2, 1974, Dublin; and Andrew Ganly, October 31, 1974, Blackrock, County Dublin. Both were classmates of Samuel Beckett at Earlsfort House School.

55. The Dublin Southeastern Railroad no longer runs trains through Harcourt Street to Bray through Dundrum, Stillorgan, Foxrock and Carrickmines. The railway tracks have been torn up and the Foxrock station is now a private home.

56. Starkie, *Lady's Child,* p. 83.

57. Brian Inglis, *West Briton* (London: Faber & Faber, 1962), pp. 30–32.

58. John Manning; Vivian Mercier, December 28, 1977, New York.

59. Inglis, *West Briton*, pp. 30–32.

60. Thomas Garrett, Headmaster, Portora Royal School, January 18, 1974, Enniskillen.

61. Information about Samuel Beckett's career at Portora comes from Portora Royal School files and from Headmaster Garrett.

62. General Sir Charles Jones, November 11, 1974, London; Dr. A. G. Thompson, January 27, 1974, London; Dr. Alan Thompson, January 22, 1974, Dublin.

63. *Portora*, the student publication of Portora Royal School. This and all subsequent quotes about his achievements and activities are from *Portora* and are in the Samuel Beckett file at Portora Royal School, Enniskillen, Northern Ireland.

64. Alec Reid, November 12, 1971.

65. Brian Coffey, August 12, 1972, London.

66. I am grateful to Michael Davie for this information. Beckett is listed as S. V. Beckett, and toured England with Trinity College, Dublin, playing against an English county, Northants.

67. For information about Samuel Beckett's grades, I am indebted to the late Dr. J. A. Wallace, former Dublin physician and alumnus of Portora, who showed me the grade books for Northern Ireland public schools and explained the coding system. Four hundred was the maximum grade except for arithmetic, which was two hundred. Students were listed by number, not name. In 1922 Beckett was number 625; in 1923, number 159.

68. General Sir Charles Jones; Dr. J. A. Wallace.

69. In the 1922 edition of *Portora*. Information from the Samuel Beckett file at Portora. General Jones and Dr. Wallace are almost certain that Beckett was "Bat," but in a letter of October 17, 1975, to Vivian Mercier, Beckett denies having written this piece. Since there have been other incidences of selective denial in Samuel Beckett's memory of events at Portora, I chose to trust the recollections of Jones and Wallace.

70. Information about Murfet is from Vivian Mercier, April 29, 1974, Boulder, Colorado.

71. General Sir Charles Jones.

72. Letter from Miss Zella Morrow to Mrs. Val (Mary) Rogers, May 7, 1970. In Samuel Beckett file at Portora.

73. General Sir Charles Jones.

74. Dr. A. G. Thompson.

75. *transition*, 19–20, Spring–Summer, June 1930, pp. 342–343. Reprinted in Lawrence Harvey, *Samuel Beckett, Poet and Critic* (Princeton: Princeton University Press, 1970), pp. 299–301.

76. Dr. A. G. Thompson.

77. *Portora*, "School Notes," Vol. 2, Trinity term, 1923.

78. *Portora* notes in Samuel Beckett file, also Dr. J. A. Wallace, Dr. A. G. Thompson.

79. Samuel Beckett to DB, letter, March 27, 1977, Paris.

80. Harvey, *Samuel Beckett: Poet and Critic*, p. 301.

81. Mrs. Val (Mary) Rogers. 1969 letter with information prepared when Samuel Beckett won the Nobel Prize; Portora Royal School, Enniskillen, Northern Ireland.

CHAPTER TWO 1923–28:

1. Inglis, *West Briton*, pp. 122–123.

2. News clipping in *Trinity College Dublin—An Informal Record*, a ledger with handwritten notes and occasional newsclips kept by the Most Reverend J. H. Bernard, D.D., Archbishop of Dublin, Provost of Trinity College. Now in the Trinity College Library. The first entry in this journal is dated June 12, 1919, and the last June 16, 1926.

3. Dr. Arthur Aston Luce, August 8, 1972, Dublin.

4. Dr. Arthur Aston Luce and Professor W. S. Maguinness, January 24, 1974, London.

5. Dr. Arthur Aston Luce.

6. *Ibid.*

7. Information on card in Dr. Arthur Aston Luce's files.

8. Seumas Mandy.

9. Miss Aileen Conan, August, 1973, Dublin. Also in Padraic and Mary Colum, *Our Friend James Joyce*. (New York: Doubleday & Co., 1958), p. 12.

10. Bailey, *History of TCD*, p. 200. In the booklet *Facilities for Research and Advanced Study in University of Dublin (Trinity College)*, p. 11, the following entry is given for "T. D. Rudmose-Brown, M. A., Docteur d'Université (Grenoble): Author of 'Étude comparée de la versification française et de la versification anglaise' (Grenoble, 1915); 'French Literary Studies' (Dublin and London, 1917; New York, 1918); an 'Intermediate Text Book of French Composition' (Dublin, 1920). Papers, mainly on Metric, in *Modern Language Review*, etc. Specialist on French and English metric, and the first half of seventeenth century in France and Italy."

11. Bailey, *History of TCD*, p. 210.

12. Mary Manning Howe.

13. Sean and Seumas Mandy, Professor W. S. Maguinness, Dr. A. G. Thompson.

14. *Dublin University Calendar*, 1928–1929 (Dublin: Dublin University Press), pp. 156–57.

15. *Irish Times*, June 1, 1926. Oliver McCutcheon, a classmate who had vied with Beckett since their days at Portora, far surpassed him in accumulating prizes in their first three years at Trinity, thus gaining an edge on the moderatorships. McCutcheon was followed by two non–Foundation Scholars: Ethna MacCarthy, who was one of Beckett's closest friends at Trinity and became a well-known pediatrician and the wife of another friend, Dr. A. J. Leventhal; and Theresa Christina Mary Dargan who, as Ena Dargan, later wrote several popular books about her travels.

16. Samuel Beckett, June 19, 1973, Paris.

17. Ann Beckett.

18. *Irish Times*, June 1, 1926.

19. *T.C.D.: A College Miscellany*, November 13, 1924, p. 29.

20. *Ibid.*, June 3, 1926, p. 168.

21. Information about Beckett's motorcycles is from John Manning. Beckett is mentioned in *The Irish Cyclist and Motorcyclist*, March 11, 1925, p. 18.

22. Mary Manning married the American lawyer and writer Mark DeWolfe Howe. Christabel Manning married Robert Childers. John Manning lives in Dublin.

23. Mary Manning Howe.

24. Starkie, *Lady's Child*, p. 176.

25. Samuel Beckett, April 13, 1972, Paris.

26. Mary Manning Howe.

27. Caroline Beckett Murphy.

28. R.B.D. French, August 3, 1972, Newton Verney, Kilternan, Ireland.

29. Dr. Arthur Aston Luce.

30. Mary Manning Howe.

31. Mercedes Keating, November 12, 1971, Dublin.

32. Mollie Roe.

33. Dr. A. G. Thompson. Also, Georges Belmont, July 10, 1973, Paris.

34. Mollie Roe.

35. Dr. A. J. Leventhal.

36. Recently an Italian television company gathered a group of Irish writers at the Bailey, a Dublin pub, in an effort to film a show depicting the particular ambience of pub life in literary Dublin. A. J. Leventhal, Beckett's friend since 1927, was asked to recount some tales of Beckett. Leventhal, at a loss for something appropriate, invented the story that he and Beckett had been in the Bailey many years earlier at closing time, when the young and very drunk Beckett was refused another pint by the barman. Beckett turned to Leventhal and with mock heroic braggadocio, said, "Come into the arms, my beamish boy," punning on an old song as well as indicating they would take their thirst on to another pub called the Arms. Leventhal said the humor was lost in translation and the Italians cut this segment from the program.

37. Professor W. S. Maguinness.

38. *More Pricks Than Kicks.* (London: Chatto and Windus, 1934).

39. William Orpen, *Stories of Old Ireland and Myself* (London: Williams and Norgate, Ltd. 1924), pp. 43–44.

40. O'Casey's plays which had their first performances during Beckett's undergraduate years at Trinity include *The Shadow of a Gunman* (1923), *Cathleen Listens In* (1923), *Juno and the Paycock* (1924) and *The Plough and the Stars* (1926).

41. Inglis, *West Briton*, p. 99.

42. *Watt.* (New York and London: Grove Press, Evergreen Editions, 1959), pp. 252–253. All page references are to this edition.

43. Dr. A. G. Thompson, Professor W. S. Maguinness, Dr. A. J. Leventhal, Dr. Alan Thompson, Sean Mandy.

44. Harvey, *Poet and Critic*, mentions Charles C. Clark as the friend whom Beckett met in Tours. Harvey, in an interview (May 27, 1972, Hanover, New Hampshire) said Clark was a graduate of Yale University and was on holiday before entering graduate school in preparation for a career as a professor of French. Yale alumni

records show no listing for Charles Clark in the classes of 1923 through 1930. However, Charles C. Clarke, class of 1926, was the son of a professor of French and himself taught French for several years in the 1930's at Yale. This information is from Miss Marjory Jones, former Director of Alumni Records, and Emeritus Professor of French, Henri Peyre, who knew both Professor Clarke and Charles Clarke, Jr. However, efforts to locate Clarke, Jr., for an interview were not successful.

45. Harvey, *Poet and Critic*, p. 308.

46. Professor W. S. Maguinness.

47. He insisted that Maguinness take all the volumes of Proust but Maguinness demurred, saying he preferred to use the copies in the main library.

48. R.B.D. French.

49. In "A Wet Night," p. 49ff.

50. Dr. A. J. Leventhal, R.B.D. French, Professor W. S. Maguinness.

51. Ulick O'Connor, August 7, 1972, Dublin.

52. Mollie Roe, Mary Manning Howe.

53. These are Beckett's exact words for his family's attitude at this time. —Mary Manning Howe.

54. These notebooks are now in the possession of Ruby Cohn; April 20, 1973, San Francisco.

55. Roger Blin, July 8, 1973, Paris.

56. Dante, *Inferno*, trans. John Ciardi. (New York: New American Library, Mentor Classics, 1954), p. 59.

57. Dr. A. J. Leventhal, Professor W. S. Maguinness, R.B.D. French, Mary Manning Howe, Dr. A. G. Thompson, Andrew Ganly, Georges Belmont, and Ena Dargan, October 31, 1974, Dun Laoghaire, Ireland.

58. Much of the material concerning the Alba in *Dream* was rewritten and became "A Wet Night" in *More Pricks Than Kicks*. Also, in his copy of *Echo's Bones*, now in the Humanities Research Center (hereafter HRC), Austin, Texas, Beckett wrote on the page on which the poem "Alba" appears, "39 T.C.D." This was the number of his rooms.

59. Published as *Drunken Boat*, ed. James Knowlson and Felix Leakey (Reading, England: Whiteknights Press, 1976).

60. Dr. A. G. Thompson.

61. Mollie Roe, Caroline Beckett Murphy, January 17, 1974, Killiney, Ireland; Mary Manning Howe.

62. Samuel Beckett, November 17, 1971, Paris.

63. Headmaster Thomas Garrett.

64. Isabel McConnell, letter to DB, May 21, 1974. Her father was one such student.

65. Patrick Magee, March 25, 1976, Woodbridge, Connecticut.

66. Maurice Sinclair, letter to DB. August 17, 1973.

67. Starkie, *Lady's Child*, p. 55.

68. Estella Solomons was the sister of the prominent Dublin gynecologist, Dr. Bethel Solomons. She later became the wife of James Sullivan Starkey (Seumas O'Sullivan), founder of the *Dublin Magazine*.

69. Glenavy, *Gossip*, p. 36.

70. *Ibid.*

71. Orpen, *Stories*, p. 42.

72. Glenavy, *Gossip*, p. 36.

73. Orpen, *Stories*, pp. 42–43.

74. This marriage has been the source of innumerable rumors of Samuel Beckett's "Jewish ancestry." His ancestry, however, is entirely Protestant.

75. Glenavy, *Gossip*, p. 73.

76. Peggy Sinclair died of tuberculosis in Germany in May, 1933. Nancy Sinclair married Ralph Cusak and is now dead. Deirdre Sinclair Hamilton lives in Dublin. Sallie Sinclair Hammond lives in England. Maurice, the youngest child and only son, lives in Geneva, Switzerland. Information about the Sinclair family, unless otherwise noted, is from interviews and correspondence with Maurice Sinclair.

77. Mollie Roe and Sheila Page.

CHAPTER THREE 1928–29:

1. The following portrait of McGreevy, unless cited otherwise, comes from a series of interviews, conversations and correspondence with Elizabeth Ryan and Margaret Farrington, his nieces and literary executors; and with Samuel Beckett, Brian Coffey, George Reavey, Niall Montgomery, Thomas Wall, Liam O'Brien, A. J. Leventhal, Mervyn Wall, James Stern, Kay Boyle, Maria Jolas, and others.

2. Richard Aldington, *Life for Life's Sake*. (New York: The Viking Press, 1941) p. 351.

3. *Ibid.*, p. 350.

4. *Ibid.*, p. 351.

5. James Joyce, *Finnegans Wake*. (New York: The Viking Press, 1960), p. 556.23–24.

6. Aldington, *Life*, p. 352.

7. Both studies were published by Chatto and Windus in the Dolphin Series: *T. S. Eliot* in 1930, *Richard Aldington* in 1931.

8. Aldington, *Life*, p. 350.

9. Dr. A. G. Thompson, Professor W. S. Maguinness, Georges Belmont.

10. Brian Coffey, George Reavey, Georges Belmont.

11. Elizabeth Ryan, January 21, 1974, Dublin.

12. *Anglicists* are students who specialize in English language and literature, and *promotion* is the title for each yearly class. Simone Weil was a member of this distinguished class, but Beckett did not know her then or later.

13. Georges Belmont, July 10, 1974, Paris.

14. Colum, *Our Friend James Joyce*, p. 89.

15. Descriptions of Joyce from Georges Belmont, Maria Jolas, Kay Boyle, Brian Coffey, George Reavey, Walter Lowenfels, James Stern, Tania Stern.

16. Rayner Heppenstall, *The Four-Fold Tradition*. (London: Barrie and Rockliff, 1961), p. 148. In a letter to Thomas McGreevy, Beckett expressed irritation at Heppenstall for asking this question.

17. Joyce, *Finnegans Wake*, p. 112.

18. *Ibid.*, p. 467.

19. Richard Ellmann. *James Joyce* (New York: Oxford University Press, 1959), p. 411.

20. Giselle Freund, *James Joyce in Paris* (New York: Harcourt, Brace and World, Inc., 1965), p. 56.

21. Aldington, p. 350.

22. Israel Shenker, "Moody Man of Letters," *The New York Times*, May 6, 1956, section 2, p. x, i, 3. In a letter to DB, Shenker said that he had been careful not to say anywhere in the article that he had actually interviewed Beckett, but had used an obvious literary device in order to write it as one long quotation of Beckett's speech and thought. It is regrettable that Mr. Shenker was unwilling to be more precise, as this article has been quoted often by scholars who wish to interpret Beckett's work in terms of his life. Thus, whether or not Beckett actually said what Shenker states cannot be verified.

23. Georges Belmont, Brian Coffey, George Reavey.

24. Georges Belmont.

25. Throughout his life these numbers have had special significance for him. His brother died on September 13, his father on June 26. His brother's children were born on March 13 and June 26. Most of his characters' names begin with M, the thirteenth letter of the alphabet.

26. Georges Belmont; Maria Jolas, July 9, 1973, Paris; Kay Boyle, April 15, 1973, San Francisco.

27. Ellmann, *James Joyce,* p. 502.

28. Ruby Cohn, *Back to Beckett* (Princeton: Princeton University Press, 1973), p. 14.

29. These remarks stud Beckett's correspondence and have been the basis for long, thoughtful conversations between Beckett and (among others) Belmont, Coffey, Reavey, A. G. Thompson, Alan Thompson, Barney Rosset, Alan Schneider, Jerome Lindon, and Adam Tarn.

30. Ellmann, *James Joyce,* p. 616.

31. *Ibid.*

32. Georges Belmont.

33. Mollie Roe.

34. Maurice Sinclair, July 21, 1973, Paris. Beckett also called her "The Smeraldina" ("Little Emerald") in *Dream of Fair to Middling Women* and *More Pricks Than Kicks.*

35. Professor W. S. Maguinness, Dr. A. J. Leventhal.

36. Dr. A. J. Leventhal; John Montague, July 19, 1974, Paris.

37. The only known extant typescript is in Baker Library of Dartmouth College. Beckett gave it to Lawrence Harvey, who presented it to Dartmouth.

38. *Letters of James Joyce* (New York: The Viking Press), Vol. I, ed. Stuart Gilbert, 1957; Vols. II and III, ed. Richard Ellmann, 1966. (Hereafter referred to as *JJ Letters.*)

39. In a letter to John Fletcher, Ellmann wrote that it was quite unlikely that Joyce projected twelve essays without assigning them until later, thus supporting the idea that Beckett was a replacement for someone else. Quoted in *Samuel Beckett, His Works and His Critics,* eds. Raymond Federman and John Fletcher (Berkeley: University of California Press, 1970). (Hereafter referred to as *F & F.*)

40. *F & F,* p. 4.

41. Samuel Beckett, "Dante . . . Bruno . Vico . . Joyce," *Our Exagmination Round His Factification for Incamination of Work in*

Progress (London: Faber and Faber, 1972.) All references to this edition. (Entire book referred to hereafter as *Our Exagmination*.)

42. Samuel Beckett, June 19, 1973, Paris.

43. *Our Exagmination*, p. 3.

44. Frank O'Connor, "Joyce—the Third Period," *Irish Statesman* (12 April 1930), pp. 114–16.

45. *transition*, 16–17, June, 1929.

46. *JJ Letters*, Vol. III, p. 6.

47. Mrs. William (Jennie) Bradley, January 9, 1974, Paris.

48. Jennie Bradley, Maria Jolas, Kay Boyle, George Reavey.

49. Kay Boyle.

50. Michael Fraenkel, *Werther's Younger Brother* (Paris: Carrefour, 1930).

51. Lowenfels returned to America in 1934. Walter Lowenfels, July 12, 1974, Beacon, New York.

52. "Assumption," *transition*, 16–17, June, 1929, pp. 268–271. Quotations are from this issue.

53. Information about Beckett's relationship with Lucia Joyce, unless specifically noted, is based on interviews with Georges Belmont, Maria Jolas, Jennie Bradley, A. J. Leventhal, George Reavey, Tania and James Stern, Kay Boyle, Robert Kastor, Peggy Guggenheim, Mary Manning Howe, Gabrielle Buffet-Picabia, Adeline Glasheen and others who do not wish to be mentioned by name. I had hoped to write this entire book citing by name every single source, but in several cases, when interviews were granted only on the provision that the information be recorded anonymously, I have reluctantly complied.

54. Ellmann, *James Joyce*, p. 624.

55. *Ibid.*, p. 625.

56. Kay Boyle.

57. Ellmann, *James Joyce*, p. 661.

58. *Our Exagmination*, p. 3.

59. Kay Boyle.

60. Ellmann, *James Joyce*, p. 624.

61. Hugh Kenner, *The Pound Era* (Berkeley: University of California Press, 1971), p. 396.

62. Samuel Beckett, letter to Patricia Hutchins, December 18, 1953, in Trinity College, Dublin.

63. Ellmann, *James Joyce*, pp. 628–29.

64. From the printed menu in the papers of Thomas McGreevy.

65. Beckett does not appear in the souvenir photograph among Thomas McGreevy's papers. He was supposedly too drunk to pose, and hiding in the lavatory.

66. *JJ Letters*, Vol. I, p. 283.

67. Samuel Beckett, *Krapp's Last Tape and Other Dramatic Pieces* (New York: Grove Press, 1960), p. 25. Fanny was Cissie Beckett Sinclair's other nickname. There is evidence to suggest that the lines following the name refer to Cissie, as the same sort of language usually appears in *Dream of Fair to Middling Women*. References to the Smeraldina (Peggy) are usually followed by scathing references to "Fanny" who seems to be in a sentry position, on the lookout for misbehavior between the Smeraldina and Belacqua.

68. *Ibid.*, p. 27. One of the most striking images in *Effi Briest* occurs in the opening scene, when mother and daughter are sewing in the garden: "skeins of woolen yarn of various colors and an equal variety of silk thread lay in confusion upon the large round table, upon which were still standing the luncheon dessert plates and a majolica dish filled with fine large gooseberries." *Effi Briest*, trans. William A. Cooper. (New York: Frederick Ungar Publishing Co., Inc., 1966), p. 2.

69. Information about Beckett's visit to his family is from Mollie Roe, Sheila Page, Mary Manning Howe, John Manning, A. G. Thompson, Alan Thompson, Ann Beckett, Caroline Beckett Murphy.

70. Ann Beckett.

CHAPTER FOUR 1929–30:

1. Ellmann, p. 661.

2. In Beckett's copy of *Echo's Bones*, now in HRC, Austin, Texas, he has written "École Normale Supérieure, Paris 1929" under this poem.

3. Dr. Leventhal, and anonymous source.

4. Walter Lowenfels, "Extracts from *My Many Lives:* The

Paris Years, 1926–34," *The Expatriate Review*, Winter/Spring, 1972, p. 10 ff.

5. In a letter to DB, October 24, 1974, Beckett stressed that he did not study philosophy in TCD, "let alone Wittgenstein." He felt compelled to add this information because of the many comparisons between his writings and the philosophy of Ludwig Wittgenstein, which he abhors.

6. Quoted in *Murphy* (New York: Grove Press, 1957), p. 178.

7. Harvey, *Poet and Critic*, p. 305.

8. *T.C.D.: A College Miscellany*, XXXVI, November 17, 1929.

9. *T.C.D.*, XXXVI, March 6, 1930, p. 42.

10. Ellmann, *James Joyce*, p. 661.

11. *Our Exagmination*, p. 14.

12. This phrase or a variant thereof appears repeatedly in his correspondence with Thomas McGreevy, Arland Ussher, George Reavey, and others, and is one he used in his conversations with George Reavey and Brian Coffey during the next decade.

13. Information in this paragraph is from Ellmann, *James Joyce*, p. 662.

14. Georges Belmont.

15. Brian Coffey.

16. Georges Belmont, George Reavey.

17. Mme. Marie Péron, January 9, 1974, Paris.

18. Information about cafes on the following pages is from interviews with Samuel Beckett, Brian Coffey, Pierre Schneider, A. J. Leventhal, Barney Rosset, Maurice Sinclair, George Reavey, Alan Schneider, W. S. Maguinness, and others.

19. Brian Coffey; Samuel Beckett, June 19, 1973; James Stern, August 16, 1975, Tisbury, Wiltshire, England.

20. Originally published in *Echo's Bones*. (London: Europa Press, 1935), and reprinted in *Poems in English*, p. 33 ff.

21. Brian Coffey.

22. Professor W. S. Maguinness.

23. Pierre Schneider, January 14, 1974, Paris.

24. Professor W. S. Maguinness.

25. *This Quarter* was edited from Paris by Edward Titus, whose wife, Helena Rubinstein, lived in the United States to manage her cosmetics empire but was largely responsible for the magazine's finances.

26. *European Caravan,* compiled and edited by Samuel Putnam, Madia Castelhun Darnton, George Reavey and Jacob Bronowski. Part I (France, Spain, England and Ireland), (New York: Brewer, Warren, and Putnam, 1931).

27. *This Quarter II* (April-May-June, 1930), pp. 630, 672, 675–83, respectively.

28. Samuel Putnam, *Paris Was Our Mistress* (New York: The Viking Press, 1947), p. 97.

29. George Reavey.

30. Information about Samuel Beckett and Lucia Joyce comes from Maria Jolas, Kay Boyle, James and Tania Stern, George Reavey, Georges Belmont, Robert Kastor and from others who wish to remain anonymous.

31. Anonymous source.

32. Kay Boyle.

33. Georges Belmont, Maria Jolas.

34. Elizabeth Ryan.

35. These remarks to Reavey, McGreevy, Belmont. This notebook was lost sometime before or during World War II. Beckett does not remember the circumstances.

36. Samuel Beckett, letter to Nancy Cunard, January 26, 1959, HRC, Austin, Texas.

37. On the manuscript of *Whoroscope*, now among the papers of Nancy Cunard, HRC, Austin, Texas.

38. Published by Chatto and Windus, London, 1931.

39. Adrien Baillet, *La Vie de Monsieur Descartes.* 2 Vols. (Paris: Daniel Horthemels, 1691).

40. Georges Belmont.

41. For an excellent discussion of the background of Beckett's poetry, see John Fletcher's *Samuel Beckett's Art*, especially Chapter 3, "The Art of the Poet" (London: Chatto and Windus, 1971).

42. *These Were the Hours* (Carbondale: Southern Illinois Press, 1969), p. 111. Cunard is mistaken about Aldington and Beckett, for by this time they knew each other fairly well though they were not yet friends.

43. *F & F*, p. 6, note 5.

44. From the papers of Thomas McGreevy.

45. Georges Belmont.

46. Mollie Roe.

47. *Proust* was published in the series called Dolphin Books.

Following the text of each book was this excerpt from a review in *Time and Tide*: "The Dolphin Books, well printed and charmingly covered, are signs of the times. Messrs. Chatto and Windus are demonstrating their faith in the new discovery that there are more lengths in literature than were dreamt of in the publisher's catalogues of the previous generation." A publisher's blurb follows: "The series are uniform . . . in format, though the colour of the binding varies with each author. It includes and will include short original works of every kind—indeed its range is limited by size of volume alone." I am indebted to George Reavey for showing me his copy.

48. *Proust*, foreword. All quotes from *Proust and Three Dialogues with Georges Duthuit* (London: Faber and Faber, 1970).

49. Mollie Roe, the papers of Thomas McGreevy.

50. John Fletcher, *Samuel Beckett's Art* (London: Chatto and Windus, 1971), p. 19.

51. "The Thirties," A. J. Leventhal, in *Beckett at Sixty* (London: Calder and Boyars Ltd., 1967), p. 7.

52. As quoted in the blurb on the jackets of McGreevy's two books, *Richard Aldington* and *T. S. Eliot*, in the Dolphin series.

53. Samuel Beckett to DB, August 17, 1972, Paris.

54. Mollie Roe.

55. The other is Joyce, of course. This information from Jerome Lindon, June 19, 1973, Paris.

56. Thomas Wall, in an essay in tribute to Thomas McGreevy, *Capuchin Annual*, Dublin, 1967, p. 293. The book is in his possession.

57. Walter Lowenfels, "The Paris Years, 1926–34," Part 2, *The Expatriate Review*, Vol. 2, p. 10.

58. Samuel Beckett to Anne Chisholm Davie, April, 1975. Paris.

59. Sir Harold Acton to Anne Chisholm Davie, 1973. I am grateful to Davie, Nancy Cunard's biographer, for relating this incident to me.

60. Hugh Ford, *Published in Paris*. (New York: Macmillan, 1975), p. 282.

61. Number 18 in the Hours Press Series, Nancy Cunard, Publisher.

62. *F & F*, p. 7.

63. Ford, p. 282.

64. Sonnabel Records.

65. Marie Péron, January 9, 1974. All information regarding *ALP* from her.

66. Adrienne Monnier (see *F & F*, p. 312, note 3063).

67. It finally appeared in Vol. XIX, May, pp. 633–46.
68. *F & F*, p. 92.
69. *F & F*, p. 92.

CHAPTER FIVE 1930–31:

1. Beckett received his M.A. degree on December 8, 1931. Alec Reid and Vivian Mercier brought the circumstances of Beckett's M.A. degree to my attention.

2. Dr. Bernard's diary includes this clipping about Beckett from the Manchester *Guardian*, July 1, 1930. The distinction in Beckett's initial appointment was brought to my attention by Dr. A. J. Leventhal and Alec Reid.

3. All information concerning Beckett's rooms at Trinity is from Georges Belmont, R.B.D. French, A. G. Thompson, W. S. Maguinness, and Samuel Beckett.

4. Anonymous source.

5. Anonymous source.

6. The picture hung in Cooldrinagh until May Beckett's death, when it was given to Mollie Roe. Reproduced here following p. 114. The first drawing has disappeared.

7. The following information is from Mervyn Wall, A. J. Leventhal, Georges Belmont, John Manning, the papers of Thomas McGreevy, and sources who wish to remain anonymous.

8. Anonymous source.

9. Anonymous source.

10. Anonymous source.

11. Mollie Roe.

12. Georges Belmont.

13. *The Journals of Jules Renard*, ed. and trans. Louise Bogan and Elizabeth Roget. (New York: George Braziller, 1964), p. 248.

14. Georges Belmont.

15. Thomas McGreevy, letter to Jack B. Yeats, December 22, 1930.

16. Wall, *The Lace Curtain*, No. 4, Summer, 1971, p. 81. The incident took place in County Mayo.

17. The last remaining nude in the Dublin Municipal Gallery had just been removed on the grounds that it was "somewhat indecent." "Michael Smith asks Mervyn Wall some questions about the Thirties." *The Lace Curtain*, No. 4, Summer, 1971, p. 81.

18. "Jack B. Yeats: 1871–1957," *Dublin Magazine*, Vol. 32, July-Sept., 1957, pp. 55–57.

19. The papers of Thomas McGreevy.

20. Dr. A. J. Leventhal, John Montague, John Kobler, the papers of Thomas McGreevy, and an anonymous source.

21. Samuel Beckett, letter to H. O. White, April 15, 1957, in TCD, Dublin.

22. Letter from Alan Denson to Anthony Piper following an interview with Jack B. Yeats, September 30, 1954, as quoted in Hilary Pyle, *Jack B. Yeats: A Biography*. (London: Routledge and Kegan Paul, 1970), p. 146.

23. Aileen Conan, August 8, 1972, Dublin.

24. Samuel Beckett, June 19, 1973, Paris.

25. Georges Belmont, Dr. A. J. Leventhal.

26. Class notes of Aileen Conan, graciously loaned by her.

27. Class notes of Rachel Dobbins Burrows. I am grateful to Prof. Vivian Mercier for bringing them to my attention.

28. Mary Manning Howe, Georges Belmont, the papers of Thomas McGreevy.

29. Mollie Roe, Sheila Page.

30. In Beckett's correspondence to McGreevy, and in *More Pricks Than Kicks*, p. 70.

31. Georges Belmont.

32. R.B.D. French, Georges Belmont, Aileen Conan, Norris Davidson, November 2, 1974, Dublin.

33. Georges Belmont.

34. *T.C.D.*, XXXVII, February 26, 1931, p. 116.

35. Mary Manning Howe, John Manning.

36. George Reavey.

37. Jane Lidderdale and Mary Nicholson, *Dear Miss Weaver* (New York: The Viking Press, 1970), p. 303.

38. George Reavey.

39. *European Caravan*, pp. 475–480.

40. *Ibid.*, p. 475.

41. George Morevy Acklom, "A European Anthology," *The Saturday Review*, Vol. VIII, No. 29, Feb. 6, 1932, p. 505.

42. Jacob Bronowski, May 15, 1974, New York.

43. Letter to Beckett from Walter Lowenfels, April 8, 1931, advising him to take care of himself, in Walter Lowenfels's possession.

44. I am grateful to George Reavey for this clipping.

45. *New Review*, Winter, 1931–32, pp. 338–339.

46. *New Review*, Aug.-Sept.-Oct., 1931, pp. 98–99.

47. *F & F*, p. 9, n. 8. Beckett has acknowledged authorship of this piece.

48. The report of the editorial subcommittee for Hilary term, 1931, *T.C.D.*, XXXVII, June 4, 1931, p. 185.

49. Anonymous source; Mervyn Wall, January 16, 1974, Dublin.

50. Lawrence Harvey, May 27, 1972, Hanover, New Hampshire.

51. From the papers of Thomas McGreevy.

52. A. J. Leventhal, "Seumas O'Sullivan," *Retrospect*, ed. Liam Miller (Dublin: The Dolman Press, 1974), p. 12.

53. *Ibid.*, p. 13.

54. Mary Manning Howe.

55. From the papers of Thomas McGreevy.

56. Georges Belmont.

57. *T.C.D.: A College Miscellany*, February 12, 1931, pp. 86–87.

58. "Eneug II," *Poems in English*, p. 26.

59. Dr. A. J. Leventhal, Mary Manning Howe, Mollie Roe, the papers of Thomas McGreevy.

60. R.B.D. French.

61. The late Owen Sheehy-Skeffington then held the position until his retirement. In an essay celebrating Beckett's sixtieth birthday, Leventhal wrote that "Academism was not to Beckett's liking and after a few terms he fled. The College wits murmured that he wrote his resignation on a scroll of bumph but those in authority wailed because with him went the college master key." In conversation, January 19, 1974, Dublin, Leventhal admitted that he had "made up" this incident "to add a little humor" to his essay and said that "there was absolutely no truth to it."

62. Jack MacGowran, July 9, 1971, Lennox, Massachusetts; W. F. Pyle, August 7, 1972, Dublin; Alec Reid, November 11, 1971, Dublin; Lawrence Harvey; R.B.D. French; Dr. A. J. Leventhal.

63. Ann Beckett, Mollie Roe, Mary Manning Howe.

64. *T.C.D.: A College Miscellany*, February 4, 1932.
65. Harvey, *Poet and Critic*, p. 78.
66. *Ibid.*, p. 222.

CHAPTER SIX 1931–32:

1. Maurice Sinclair.
2. George Reavey, the papers of Thomas McGreevy.
3. Ellmann, *James Joyce*, p. 659; Lidderdale and Nicholson, *Dear Miss Weaver*, p. 310; and Maria Jolas, July 12, 1973, Paris.
4. Maria Jolas, July 19, 1973, Paris.
5. *transition*, 21 (March, 1932), pp. 148–149.
6. Maria Jolas, July 12, 1974. Mme. Jolas is sure that *Poetry Is Vertical* was written by all the signers together, although *F & F*, p. 92, n. 487, say that it "bears the stamp of Eugene Jolas's style."
7. Maria Jolas, July 12, 1974, Paris.
8. *F & F*, n. 487, p. 92.
9. Samuel Beckett, April 13, 1972.
10. *transition*, An International Workship for Orphic Creation, edited by Eugene Jolas (Servire Press, The Hague, Holland), 21 (March, 1932), pp. 13–20.
11. *F & F*, p. 12, n. 12.
12. *New Review*, II (April, 1932), p. 57.
13. *This Quarter*, V, Surrealist Number, guest editor André Breton, September, 1932.
14. Mollie Roe.
15. From the papers of Thomas McGreevy.
16. Beckett sent notes to George Reavey and Thomas McGreevy announcing his new address; also, Harvey, *Poet and Critic*, p. 257.
17. George Reavey, January 5, 1972.
18. *F & F*, in n. 14.2, page 12, explain how they arrived at the accurate date of this poem. Ellmann, p. 714, incorrectly dates the poem 1937. See also Harvey, *Poet and Critic*, p. 296.
19. Georges Belmont, George Reavey, Maria Jolas.

20. The Beckett-McGreevy correspondence is filled with references to Beckett's afflictions.

21. Walter Lowenfels, July 12, 1974, Beacon, N.Y. Miller, in a letter to DB, July 24, 1974, states he does not remember this occasion.

22. Walter Lowenfels, "The Paris Years," p. 13.

23. Walter Lowenfels, July 12, 1974.

24. Walter Lowenfels, "The Paris Years," p. 13.

25. *Ibid.*

26. In 1964 Beckett gave what appears to be the only extant typescript to Lawrence Harvey, who in turn gave it to Baker Library, Dartmouth College. Professor Harvey appended the following information to the typescript: "Unpublished, 214 pages, an earlier version of the ending (replaced by pp. 213, 214 and 214 verso in Beckett's handwriting in the final version) is appended and numbered pp. 197, 198 and 199. Corrections in Beckett's handwriting on a considerable number of pages. [*Dream* is] . . . the only extant record of Beckett's earliest substantial prose work. It is valuable for the insights it provides into the temperament, intellect, talent and interests of the young Beckett and constitutes the necessary point of departure in assessing his development as a writer."

27. Samuel Beckett, April 13, 1972, Paris.

28. Mollie Roe, Mary Manning Howe.

29. Mary Manning Howe.

30. From the papers of Thomas McGreevy.

31. Ellmann, *James Joyce*, p. 520.

32. George Reavey, the papers of Thomas McGreevy, Dr. Leventhal.

33. *Dream*, pp. 11–12.

34. *Ibid.*, p. 123.

35. *Ibid.*, p. 42.

36. Niklaus Gessner, *Die Unzulänglichkeit der Sprache: Eine Untersuchung über Formzerfall und Beziehunglosigkeit bei Samuel Beckett* (Zurich: Juris, 1957), p. 53.

37. He retained this description of Belacqua in "Yellow," *More Pricks Than Kicks* (New York: Grove Press, Evergreen Editions, 1972), p. 172. All subsequent references to this edition.

38. *Dream*, p. 101.

39. *Ibid.*

40. Beckett told James Knowlson the amount was seven hundred francs. *Drunken Boat*, p. 8.

41. See *Drunken Boat*, pp. 9–10.

42. Professor W. S. Maguinness, Dr. A. G. Thompson, Arthur Ellis, January 26, 1974, London.

43. Walter Lowenfels, George Reavey, Brian Coffey.

44. Samuel Beckett, letter to George Reavey, October 8, 1932.

45. Samuel Beckett, letter to Thomas McGreevy, June 22, 1933.

46. Samuel Beckett, letter to George Reavey, October 8, 1932.

47. *Ibid.*

CHAPTER SEVEN 1933:

1. Mary Manning Howe, Mollie Roe, Ann Beckett, Dr. A. G. Thompson, the papers of Thomas McGreevy.

2. Mary Manning Howe was one of the students.

3. Alec Reid, Brian Coffey, anonymous source.

4. Dr. Alan Thompson, January 22, 1974, Dublin.

5. It would have been impossible for me to have written a detailed and factual account of Beckett's life, work, thoughts and ideas without his letters to McGreevy. I am deeply grateful to Elizabeth Ryan and Margaret Farrington, McGreevy's literary executors, for allowing me to use them.

6. Samuel Beckett, undated letter to Thomas McGreevy; also letters of May 3 and 13, 1933.

7. Brian Coffey.

8. "Ding-Dong," *More Pricks*, p. 45.

9. Samuel Beckett, undated letter to Thomas McGreevy (the letter carried only the notation "23rd," but internal evidence suggests it was written in April, 1933).

10. Samuel Beckett, letter to Thomas McGreevy, "23rd."

11. Beckett gave the only extant typescript of the story *Echo's Bones* (not to be confused with the 1935 collection of poems) to Lawrence Harvey, who gave it to the Baker Library of Dartmouth College. On December 6, 1933, Beckett wrote to McGreevy that Charles Prentice's "fouting à la porte of 'Echo's Bones,' the last

story, into which I had put all I knew and plenty that I was still better aware of, discouraged me profoundly." It provoked him, he continued, to write the 5-line poem with which he ended the 1935 book of poetry, *Echo's Bones*. An early version of the poem is appended to the 1933 letter.

12. Samuel Beckett, letter to Thomas McGreevy, May 13 (envelope is postmarked 1933).

13. "Fingal," *More Pricks*, p. 24.

14. All quotes from "Ding-Dong," *More Pricks*, are found on pages 36–38.

15. Samuel Beckett, letter to Thomas McGreevy, "23rd," (internal evidence suggests April 1933). Beckett did not actually read Céline's book until 1938, when he was living permanently in Paris.

16. Samuel Beckett, letter to Thomas McGreevy, May 13, 1933.

17. "Ding-Dong," *More Pricks*, p. 38.

18. Samuel Beckett, letter to Thomas McGreevy, May 13, 1933.

19. Samuel Beckett, letter to Thomas McGreevy, June 22, 1933.

20. Samuel Beckett, letter to Thomas McGreevy, May 13, 1933.

21. *Ibid.*

22. Samuel Beckett, letter to Thomas McGreevy, July 2, 1933; also death certificate of William Beckett, the Customs House, Dublin.

23. Samuel Beckett, letter to Thomas McGreevy, July 2, 1933.

24. Mollie Roe.

25. Samuel Beckett, letter to Thomas McGreevy, July 25, 1933.

26. Samuel Beckett, letter to Thomas McGreevy, September 7, 1933.

27. Dr. A. G. Thompson.

28. Samuel Beckett, *Murphy*, p. 97.

29. The last will and testament of William Beckett, filed in the Principal Probate Registry, The Four Courts, Dublin, dated March 5, 1923.

30. Mollie Roe.

31. Legal documents dated September 12, 1933, on file in The Four Courts, Dublin.

32. Ann Beckett.

33. Samuel Beckett, letter to Thomas McGreevy, November 1, 1933.

34. Samuel Beckett, letter to Thomas McGreevy, October 9, 1933.

35. *Ibid.*

CHAPTER EIGHT 1934:

1. Information about Beckett's health is from the letters to Thomas McGreevy and interviews with Dr. A. G. Thompson and Dr. Alan Thompson.

2. Mrs. Hester Travers-Smith Dowden (1868–1949), was an automatist who never called herself a spiritualist, but instead, a psychic investigator. She was associated with Sir William Barrett and the Society for Psychic Research. For further information see *The Steinerbooks Dictionary of the Psychic, Mystic, Occult* (Blauvelt, New York: Rudolph Steiner Publications, 1973), p. 64.

3. Thomas McGreevy, as quoted in George Reavey's diary, January 17, 1936.

4. The following information is from Samuel Beckett to Thomas McGreevy, January 8, 1934, and Dr. A. G. Thompson.

5. Some of Bion's publications include *Experience in Groups and Other Papers.* (New York: Basic Books, 1961); *Second Thoughts: Selected Papers on Psychoanalysis* (London: Heinemann Medical, 1967); *Attention and Interpretation: A Scientific Approach to Insight in Psychoanalysis and Groups.* (New York: Basic Books, 1970).

6. Mary deRachewiltz, April 5, 1976, New Haven, Conn.

7. I base this interpretation on Beckett's own remarks in his letters to McGreevy, and on interviews with Dr. A. G. Thompson, Dr. Alan Thompson, Mary Manning Howe, John Manning, Ann Beckett, Caroline Beckett Murphy and the late Dr. Peter Beckett.

8. *Negro Anthology Made by Nancy Cunard*, 1931–33. Published by Nancy Cunard at Wishart & Co., 9 John Street, London, W.C.2, 1934. For Beckett's translations, see *F & F*, pp. 94–95.

9. *Contempo*, II, No. 13, February 15, 1934, p. 3.

10. *Dublin Magazine*, IX, July-September, 1934, pp. 84–85. All subsequent quotes from this edition.

11. *More Pricks Than Kicks* was banned from March 31, 1935, until January 1, 1952. It was listed in the Annual Reports of the Censorship of Publications Board and the Censorship of Publications Appeals Board for the years ending 31 December 1950 to 31 December 1951. It was listed in the category "Particulars of books the subjects of applications with which the board has been unable to deal up to the present by inability to obtain the requisite copies." In other words, someone applied to have the ban lifted, but no one could find a copy to read.

12. *JJ Letters*, Vol. III, p. 316. To Helen Joyce, August 9, 1934.

13. *F & F*, p. 14, n. to No. 16.

14. *Dublin Magazine*, IX, n.s. (July-September, 1934), p. 8.

15. *Criterion*, XIII (July, 1934), 705–707.

16. "Schwabenstreich," *Spectator*, No. 5, 517 (March 23, 1934), p. 472; "Proust in Pieces," *Spectator*, No. 5, 530 (June 23, 1934), 975–76. Neither of these reviews is included in *F & F*.

17. *Bookman*, LXXVII (August, 1934), 241–242. All subsequent quotations are from this publication. Reprinted in *Lace Curtain* (Summer, 1971), Dublin, pp. 58–64.

18. *Bookman*, LXXXVII (Christmas, 1934), pp. 10, 14, 111. This was the last issue of the publication and was a supplement to the December issue.

19. *Dublin Magazine*, IX, n.s. (July-September, 1934), p. 8.

20. *F & F*, pp. 14–15, n. 17.

21. Samuel Beckett, letter to George Reavey, June 23, 1934.

22. Harvey, *Poet and Critic*, p. 155.

23. Now in the Samuel Beckett Collection, HRC, Austin, Texas.

24. Dr. Schwartz, a London book dealer, was instrumental in putting together the collection of manuscripts now at HRC, Austin, Texas.

25. Mary Manning Howe.

26. Harvey, *Poet and Critic*, p. 273.

27. Hugh Kenner, *A Reader's Guide to Samuel Beckett* (New York: Farrar, Straus & Giroux, Noonday Press, 1973), p. 42.

28. Samuel Beckett, letter to Thomas McGreevy, August 3, 1934.

29. Mollie Roe, Sheila Page; and Samuel Beckett, letter to Thomas McGreevy, August 3, 1934.

30. Samuel Beckett, letter to Thomas McGreevy, September 8, 1934.

31. *Ibid.*

32. "Censorship in the Saorstat," unpublished manuscript now in Baker Library, Dartmouth College. Not listed in *F & F*, mentioned in Harvey, *Poet and Critic*. Harvey incorrectly dates it as 1936, but it was written in 1934 for *Bookman* and returned to Beckett when the magazine ceased publication.

33. Samuel Beckett, letter to Thomas McGreevy, September 8, 1934.

34. Patrick Magee, March 24, 1976, New Haven, Conn.

CHAPTER NINE 1935:

1. Samuel Beckett, letter to Thomas McGreevy, August 31, 1935.

2. Mollie Roe.

3. Samuel Beckett, letter to Thomas McGreevy, December 27, 1934.

4. Samuel Beckett, letter to Thomas McGreevy, January 1, 1935.

5. *Ibid.*

6. Samuel Beckett, letter to Thomas McGreevy, January 1 and 9, 1935.

7. Samuel Beckett, letter to Thomas McGreevy, January 9, 1935.

8. Samuel Beckett, letter to Thomas McGreevy, January 18 and 29, 1935.

9. Samuel Beckett, letter to Thomas McGreevy, February 8, 1935.

10. Samuel Beckett, letter to Thomas McGreevy, September 23, 1935.

11. Samuel Beckett, letter to Thomas McGreevy, March 10, 1935.

12. Alan Schneider, August 8, 1971, Hastings-on-Hudson, New York.

13. Samuel Beckett, letter to Thomas McGreevy, February 14, 1935.

14. Samuel Beckett, letter to Thomas McGreevy, January 29, 1935.

15. This information is based on Beckett's letters to Thomas McGreevy, and upon anonymous sources.

16. This and all other information about Beckett in Dublin is from his letters to Thomas McGreevy of April 25, May 5 and 15, and an undated letter probably of May 23, 1935.

17. Samuel Beckett, letter to Thomas McGreevy, May, 1935.

18. Samuel Beckett, letter to Thomas McGreevy, May 15, 1935.

19. Samuel Beckett, letter to Thomas McGreevy, May, 1935.

20. All information in this paragraph is from Samuel Beckett, letter to Thomas McGreevy, May 15, 1935.

21. Samuel Beckett, letter to Thomas McGreevy, May (probably 23), 1935.

22. All information about Samuel Beckett, theater, and film, from letter to Thomas McGreevy, May (probably 23), 1935.

23. Fletcher, *The Novels of Samuel Beckett* (London: Chatto and Windus, 1964), p. 45.

24. Samuel Beckett, letter to Thomas McGreevy, July 25 and 29, August 31, 1935.

25. Samuel Beckett, letter to Thomas McGreevy, July 25 and 29, 1935.

26. Samuel Beckett, letter to George Reavey, October 13, 1935.

27. Samuel Beckett, letter to Thomas McGreevy, September 8, 1935.

28. *Ibid.*

29. *Ibid.*

30. Samuel Beckett, letter to Thomas McGreevy, October 8, 1935.

31. These lectures were published as *Analytical Psychology, Its Theory and Practice* (New York: Pantheon Books, 1968). All references to this edition.

32. Reprinted in *Analytical Psychology* as Figure 4, p. 49.

33. Phrase used by George Reavey in notes for a diary, summer, 1935, following conversation with Thomas McGreevy, who commented on the propensity for Irishmen to perform services for and pay attentions to their mothers which are usually reserved for wives and sweethearts.

34. Beckett has discussed this with Peggy Guggenheim, Lawrence Harvey, Dr. A. G. Thompson and others.

35. *All That Fall,* in *Krapp's Last Tape and Other Short*

Dramatic Pieces. (New York: Grove Press, 1960), p. 82 ff. All references to this edition.

36. Samuel Beckett, letter to Thomas McGreevy, October 8, 1935.

37. Clancy Sigal, "Is This the Person to Murder Me?" *Sunday Times* (Color Magazine), March 1, 1964, pp. 17–22.

38. Thomas McGreevy, undated letter to George Reavey.

39. Samuel Beckett, letter to Thomas McGreevy, October 8, 1935.

40. Samuel Beckett, letter to Thomas McGreevy, December 31, 1935.

41. Samuel Beckett, letter to Thomas McGreevy, December 31, 1935 and January 10, 1936.

42. David Sutton, letter to DB, August 12, 1974.

43. Samuel Beckett, letter to Thomas McGreevy, January 29, 1936.

44. Maurice Sinclair, July 24, 1973, Paris.

45. Samuel Beckett, letter to Thomas McGreevy, December 31, 1935.

46. Samuel Beckett, letter to George Reavey, January 9, 1936.

47. Samuel Beckett, letter to George Reavey, May 2, 1936.

48. Samuel Beckett, letter to George Reavey, May 6, 1936; letter to Thomas McGreevy, June 9, 1936.

49. Samuel Beckett, letter to George Reavey, June 9, 1936.

50. *Ibid.*

51. Samuel Beckett, letter to George Reavey, May 6, 1936. *Thorns of Thunder,* published by Europa Press, distributed by Stanley Knott, 1936, London.

52. Samuel Beckett, letter to Thomas McGreevy, June 9, 1936.

CHAPTER TEN MURPHY:

'1. Dr. A. G. Thompson.

2. *Murphy*, p. 240.

3. This is one of two mathematical mistakes in all of Beckett's writings. Here he accounts for six of the seven scarves. In conversation, November 17, 1971, Beckett stated that this was an oversight:

he had intended to account for all seven but forgot one. When the mistake was called to his attention, he found it amusing and decided to leave it as it was.

4. Bim and Bom were in an early version of *Waiting for Godot,* and were called the "Stalinist comedians." This line was deleted in later editions because Beckett wanted the play to be timeless.

5. My interpretation of this game is based on the analysis of Vonn Scott Bair.

6. Samuel Beckett, letter to Thomas McGreevy, July 17, 1936.

7. *Ibid.*

8. Fletcher, *Novels of Samuel Beckett,* p. 55.

CHAPTER ELEVEN 1935–38:

1. Samuel Beckett, letters to Thomas McGreevy, May 3, June 5, July 17 and 26, 1936.

2. Mary Manning Howe; Samuel Beckett, letter to Thomas McGreevy, July 17, 1936.

3. *Watt,* p. 47.

4. Samuel Beckett, letter to Thomas McGreevy, August 7, 1936.

5. *Ibid.*

6. Published in *Dublin Magazine,* 1936, also in Calder and Boyars and Grove Press *Poems in English.* Original enclosed in letter to Thomas McGreevy, July 15, 1936.

7. Samuel Beckett, letter to Thomas McGreevy, May 3, 1936.

8. Samuel Beckett, letter to Thomas McGreevy, June 5, 1936.

9. Samuel Beckett, letter to Arland Ussher, September 9, 1936, HRC, Austin, Texas; Samuel Beckett, letter to George Reavey, n.d.

10. Samuel Beckett, letter to Arland Ussher, March 25, 1936, HRC, Austin, Texas.

11. Maurice Sinclair.

12. Samuel Beckett, letter to Thomas McGreevy, June 5, 1936.

13. *Ibid.*

14. Samuel Beckett, letter to Thomas McGreevy, March 6, 1936.

15. Samuel Beckett, letter to Thomas McGreevy, June 5, 1936.

16. Samuel Beckett, letter to Thomas McGreevy, June 5, 1936; letter to Arland Ussher, June 15, 1936, HRC, Austin, Texas. When Beckett went to Paris that autumn, he told Joyce about it. Joyce, whose financial situation was always critical, thought of applying for it himself, but decided not to because the area was noted for severe thunderstorms and he was terrified of them.

17. Samuel Beckett, letter to Thomas McGreevy, August 7, 1936.

18. Samuel Beckett, letter to Thomas McGreevy, July 26, 1936.

19. Samuel Beckett, letter to Thomas McGreevy, September 9, 1936.

20. Samuel Beckett, June 19, 1973, Paris.

21. Samuel Beckett, letters to Thomas McGreevy, March 25, April 9, July 26, August 7, and 19, 1936.

22. Samuel Beckett, letter to Thomas McGreevy, June 5, 1936.

23. Mary Manning Howe, August 14, 1974, Woodbridge, Conn.

24. Information about Beckett and Dublin theater from Mary Manning Howe, Dr. Andrew Ganly, Mervyn Wall, Dr. A. J. Leventhal, and anonymous sources.

25. Samuel Beckett, letter to Thomas McGreevy, June 5, 1936.

26. Samuel Beckett, letter to Thomas McGreevy, September 9, 1936.

27. Mary Manning Howe; Isabella Gardner Tate, June 19, 1974, Ojai, California; Betty Stockton Farley, Martha's Vineyard, Mass., June 20, 1974.

28. Mary Manning Howe, Dr. A. J. Leventhal, John Manning, Sean and Seumas Mandy, W. S. Maguinness, and Samuel Beckett's letters to George Reavey, Arland Ussher, Thomas McGreevy and others.

29. Samuel Beckett, letter to Thomas McGreevy, September 8, 1935.

30. Mary Manning Howe, Isabella Gardner Tate.

31. The woman in question wishes to remain anonymous.

32. Samuel Beckett, letter to Thomas McGreevy, September 19, 1936.

33. Samuel Beckett, letter to Thomas McGreevy, February 16, 1937.

34. Samuel Beckett, letter to Thomas McGreevy, October 10, 1936.

35. "The Expelled," *Stories and Texts for Nothing* (New York: Grove Press, 1967), p. 13.

36. George Reavey; Samuel Beckett, letter to Thomas McGreevy, October 10, 1936.

37. George Reavey.

38. Samuel Beckett, letter to George Reavey, December 20, 1936.

39. Samuel Beckett, letter to George Reavey, November 13, 1936.

40. Samuel Beckett, letter to George Reavey, December 27, 1936.

41. Samuel Beckett, letter to Thomas McGreevy, December 22, 1936.

42. Samuel Beckett, August 23, 1972, and January 14, 1975.

43. Samuel Beckett, letter to Thomas McGreevy, January 18, 1937.

44. *Ibid.*

45. *transition*, tenth anniversary, 27 (April-May, 1938), p. 33. In line 12, "Bollux" became "Bullock's." Line 13 was originally "you won't cure it you can't endure it," and he changed it to "you won't cure it—you won't endure it." In lines 14, 16, 17, 18 and 19 all commas were removed.

46. Samuel Beckett, letter to Thomas McGreevy, February 16, 1937.

47. George Reavey; Samuel Beckett, letter to Thomas McGreevy, February 16, 1937.

48. *Ibid.*

49. Samuel Beckett, letter to Thomas McGreevy, February 16, 1937.

50. Samuel Beckett, letter to George Reavey, February 15, 1937.

51. Richard Church, letter to George Reavey, January 12, 1937.

52. Hamish Hamilton, letter to George Reavey, April 9, 1937.

53. Samuel Beckett, letter to Thomas McGreevy, March 25, 1937.

54. Samuel Beckett, letter to Thomas McGreevy, March 7, 1937.

55. *Ibid.*

56. Samuel Beckett, letter to Thomas McGreevy, March 25, 1937.

57. Samuel Beckett, letter to Arland Ussher, on stationery of Hotel Leinfelder, München, June 26, 1937, HRC, Austin, Texas. (This date is in error: The letter was definitely written in Munich but Beckett left there at the end of March. On June 26 he was in Dublin.) He used this image in *Watt*, the novel he wrote several years later.

58. Sheila Page, Mollie Roe, Maurice Sinclair; and Samuel Beckett, letter to Thomas McGreevy, April 20, 1937.

59. Samuel Beckett, letter to Thomas McGreevy, April 20, 1937.

60. Samuel Beckett, letter to Mary Manning Howe, June 17, 1937.

61. Mollie Roe, Mary Manning Howe; Samuel Beckett, letter to Thomas McGreevy, October 6, 1937.

62. Samuel Beckett, letter to Joseph Maunsell Hone, July 3, 1937, HRC, Austin, Texas.

63. Samuel Beckett, letter to Arland Ussher, n.d. (internal evidence suggests July, 1937), HRC, Austin, Texas.

64. Samuel Beckett, letter to Mary Manning Howe, June 17, 1937.

65. *Ibid.*

66. Samuel Beckett, undated letter to Arland Ussher (July, 1937), and June 15, 1937.

67. Arland Ussher, January 22, 1974, Dublin; Samuel Beckett, letter to Thomas McGreevy, August 4, 1937.

68. Samuel Beckett, letter to Thomas McGreevy, April 20, 1937.

69. *Ibid.*

70. Samuel Beckett, letter to George Reavey, July 22, 1937.

71. Samuel Beckett, letter to Joseph Maunsell Hone, July 3, 1937, HRC, Austin, Texas.

72. Manuscript in possession of Ruby Cohn, who, with Samuel Beckett's permission, graciously made it available to me. All quotations from this manuscript.

73. Samuel Beckett, April 13, 1972, Paris.

74. Samuel Beckett, letter to George Reavey, August 6, 1937.

75. Samuel Beckett, letter to Thomas McGreevy, August 4, 1937.

76. Samuel Beckett, April 13, 1972, Paris.

77. John Fletcher, October 29, 1971, Paris; Raymond Federman, December 29, 1974, New York.

78. Samuel Beckett to DB and others.

79. George Reavey, Alan Schneider; Ruby Cohn, April 18, 1973, San Francisco; Samuel Beckett, April 13, 1972, Paris.

80. Samuel Beckett, letter to Thomas McGreevy, April 20, 1937.

81. Samuel Beckett, letter to Thomas McGreevy, June 7, 1937.

82. Samuel Beckett, letter to Arland Ussher, June 15, 1937, HRC, Austin, Texas.

83. Samuel Beckett, letter to Thomas McGreevy, August 14, 1937.

84. Samuel Beckett, letter to Joseph Maunsell Hone, July, 1937, HRC, Austin, Texas.

85. *Authors Take Sides on the Spanish Civil War*, ed. Nancy Cunard. Published by Left Review, London, 1937. Beckett's contribution appears on p. 6.

86. *As I Was Walking Down Sackville Street*. Oliver St. John Gogarty (London: Rich and Cowan, Ltd., 1936).

87. Maurice Sinclair.

88. Samuel Beckett, letter to Thomas McGreevy, May 14, 1937.

89. Samuel Beckett, letter to Thomas McGreevy, June 7, 1937.

90. Samuel Beckett, letter to Thomas McGreevy, July 23, 1937.

91. Samuel Beckett, letter to Arland Ussher, July 11, 1937, HRC, Austin, Texas.

92. Samuel Beckett, letter to Thomas McGreevy, August 4, 1937.

93. Samuel Beckett, letter to Thomas McGreevy, September 21, 1937.

94. Samuel Beckett, letter to Thomas McGreevy, August 23, 1937.

95. *Ibid.*

96. *Ibid.*

97. Samuel Beckett, letter to George Reavey, August 6, 1937.

98. Samuel Beckett, letter to Thomas McGreevy, September 21, 1937.

99. Samuel Beckett, letter to Thomas McGreevy, September 28, 1937.

100. Samuel Beckett, letter to Thomas McGreevy, September 28, October 6, 1937.

101. Samuel Beckett, letter to Thomas McGreevy, October 14, 1937.

102. Samuel Beckett, letter to Thomas McGreevy, October 6, 1937.

CHAPTER TWELVE 1938–39:

1. Samuel Beckett, letter to George Reavey, October 27, 1937, Paris.

2. Samuel Beckett, letter to Thomas McGreevy, November 1, 1937.

3. Ulick O'Connor, *Oliver St. John Gogarty: A Poet and His Times* (London: Jonathan Cape, 1964), p. 278.

4. Samuel Beckett's affidavit, taken September 13, 1937. No official transcript of the trial was kept by the Public Records Office. The only papers pertaining to the case of *Sinclair* vs. *Gogarty* may be found in Volume 300/P, 1937, in the Public Records Office at The Four Courts, Dublin. They consist only of a deposition of a witness who was unable to be present at the actual trial, a statement of claim by the plaintiff's solicitors, an account of the final settlement and, oddly, the affidavit of Samuel Beckett.

5. All quotations from the trial are from the account in the *Irish Times*, November 23–27, 1937.

6. Ulick O'Connor, August 7, 1972, Dublin.

7. Samuel Beckett, letter to Arland Ussher, April 6, 1938, HRC, Austin, Texas. Ulick O'Connor claims that Gogarty never forgave nor forgot Beckett's testimony. In 1956 he wrote to O'Connor, referring to a broadcast of *Waiting for Godot* on the BBC's Third Programme: "I am sorry you praised Beckett's play. It is nothing but a long wail."

8. Samuel Beckett, letter to Thomas McGreevy, December 10, 1937.

9. Maurice Sinclair.

10. Shenker, "Moody Man of Letters," Sec. 2, pp. x, 1, 3. Beckett is of course in error about the year he established residence in

Paris. It is possible that this may have led to his giving the wrong dates to Lawrence Harvey also, who echoes them in *Samuel Beckett, Poet and Critic*. In an interview, May 27, 1972, Harvey said that all dates throughout his book are based entirely on information given to him by Beckett, with no other verification. When Beckett was asked about the possible confusion of 1936 and 1937, he replied that it was "a very hazy period" for him. "Once I lived through it I forgot about it and got on with other things. I don't keep any records and it wasn't very important anyway. No doubt I was confused if my letters prove otherwise." (To DB, April 13, 1972.) His correspondence is extensive; some has been quoted here to verify his movements during this time.

11. The first check cleared the Bank of Ireland, College Green, on December 21, 1937. The second came to him at the time of publication, March 23, 1938. He received sixteen pounds twenty-eight shillings after he paid Reavey's fee. The cancelled checks are among the papers of the late George Reavey.

12. Samuel Beckett, letters to Thomas McGreevy, December 10 and 22, 1937.

13. Samuel Beckett, letter to Thomas McGreevy, November 3, 1937.

14. Samuel Beckett, letters to Thomas McGreevy, December 7 and 10, 1937.

15. Samuel Beckett, letter to Thomas McGreevy, December 22, 1937.

16. Descriptions are from Beckett's letters to Thomas McGreevy and from persons who have asked to remain anonymous.

17. *transition*, April-May, 1938.

18. Samuel Beckett, letter to Thomas McGreevy, December 22, 1937.

19. Robert Kastor. Samuel Beckett, letter to Thomas McGreevy, January 5, 1938.

20. Samuel Beckett, letter to Thomas McGreevy, January 5, 1938.

21. *Ibid.*

22. *Stories and Texts for Nothing* (New York: Grove Press, Evergreen Editions, 1967), p. 48.

23. Samuel Beckett, letter to Thomas McGreevy, January 5, 1938.

24. This was the expression many persons used to describe Joyce's manner toward Beckett during this period, among them Mrs.

William (Jennie) Bradley, Brian Coffey, George Reavey, Maria Jolas, Robert Kastor and others.

25. "Liam," in conversations and interviews, has asked in this one instance to remain anonymous.

26. Peggy Guggenheim, *Out of This Century: The Informal Memoirs of Peggy Guggenheim* (New York: Dial Press, 1946), p. 194.

27. *Ibid.*

28. Peggy Guggenheim, June 26, 1973, Venice.

29. Guggenheim, *Century*, p. 195.

30. *Ibid.*

31. At this point in her narration, Guggenheim's chronology is questionable. She claims that she did not see him for some time, but other events would seem to indicate that it could not have been later than December 27 or 28 that they met again.

32. Guggenheim, *Century*, p. 195.

33. Peggy Guggenheim, June 28, 1973, Venice.

34. Guggenheim, *Century*, p. 197.

35. Samuel Beckett, letter to Thomas McGreevy, January 21, 1938; Brian Coffey to DB.

36. Guggenheim, *Century*, p. 196.

37. *Ibid.*

38. *Ibid.*

39. *Ibid.*

40. Among those whose interviews helped me to form an interpretation of the stabbing incident are Brian Coffey, George Reavey, Peggy Guggenheim, Robert Kastor, Maurice Sinclair, Ann Beckett, Maria Jolas and others; also Samuel Beckett's letters to Thomas McGreevy, George Reavey and Arland Ussher.

41. Samuel Beckett, letter to Thomas McGreevy, January 12, 1938.

42. Letter to Giorgio and Helen Joyce, January 12, 1938; in *Selected Letters of James Joyce*, ed. Richard Ellmann (New York: The Viking Press, 1975), p. 390.

43. Samuel Beckett, letter to Thomas McGreevy, January 21, 1938.

44. *Ibid.*

45. Brian Coffey.

46. Reprinted in *F & F*, p. 96, n. 491.

47. Poem enclosed in letter to Thomas McGreevy, January 27, 1938. It was originally written in English, but Beckett says nothing about having written the poem for Peggy Guggenheim. Perhaps he

showed it to her and she assumed it was about her. He only mentions Peggy Guggenheim once in his letters to Thomas McGreevy: "Peggy Guggenheim has been here and I have seen quite a lot of her," January 5, 1938.

48. Samuel Beckett, letter to Thomas McGreevy, January 27, 1938.

49. *Irish Times*, January 8, 1938, p. 11; Ann Beckett to DB.

50. Samuel Beckett, letter to Thomas McGreevy, January 21, 1938.

51. Peggy Guggenheim to DB, June 28, 1973, Venice.

52. Peggy Guggenheim to DB; Samuel Beckett, letter to Thomas McGreevy, January 27, 1938.

53. Samuel Beckett, letter to Thomas McGreevy, January 21, 1938.

54. Samuel Beckett, letter to George Reavey, January 22, 1938.

55. The blurb reads:

MURPHY; By Samuel Beckett; Author of *More Pricks Than Kicks, Whoroscope, etc.*

To define some things is to kill them; no less this novel. Its meaning is implicit and symbolic, never concrete. To attempt to extract it would be to damp its spirit. And what spirit! What gusto! What hilarity! The reader is carried along on the wave of an abundant creative imagination expressing itself in scene after scene of superlative comedy, ironic situations that only the Irish genius could conceive.

Murphy is a character for whom the unseen is the real and the seen a necessary obstacle to reality. To get beyond that obstacle is his aim in life, and he neglects or despises the criteria of the substantial world, hence he moves in the lowest strata of society; he lives intermittently with a prostitute and her persuasions cannot move him to better his material prospects. He lives on the balance between the real charge for his lodgings and that which the landlady submits to his guardian who pays for them. He pretends to look for a job, but so long as he can devote some time of each day to exploring the inner life of the mind, that is all he is worried about. Ultimately he gets a job in an asylum, where he feels a certain kinship with the inmates and gets on with them. The other characters only try to find Murphy in order to nail him to life; but they are in at the death only. Identification of his body and distribution of the ashes after cremation are their only direct dealings with him.

But if the theme of the book defies description, not so the writing. The portrayal of the scenes is masterly; there is a diversity of simile which could only proceed from a mind well stocked with many seemingly antagonistic branches of knowledge, and the author possesses an encyclopedic vocabulary. The style is leavened with a Celtic waywardness which is as attractive as it is elusive and leaves the reader questioning the source of his enjoyment.

56. Samuel Beckett, letter to Thomas McGreevy, January 31, 1938.

57. John Kobler, September 24, 1971, New York.

58. Samuel Beckett, letter to Thomas McGreevy, February 21, 1938.

59. *Ibid.*

60. John Kobler.

61. Samuel Beckett, letter to Arland Ussher, March 27, 1938, HRC, Austin, Texas.

62. Samuel Beckett, letter to Arland Ussher, April 6, 1938, HRC, Austin, Texas.

63. *Times Literary Supplement*, March 12, 1938, p. 172, col. 1.

64. *F & F*, entries 1920–25, pp. 237–39.

65. *New English Weekly*, XII (March 17, 1938), pp. 454–455. All quotes from this review. Professor Lawrence Graver called this review to my attention.

66. Samuel Beckett, letter to George Reavey, March 23, 1938.

67. Samuel Beckett, letter to George Reavey, April 14, 1938.

68. Brian Coffey, letter to George Reavey, March 17, 1938.

69. Samuel Beckett, letter to Arland Ussher, March 27, 1938, HRC, Austin, Texas.

70. *Ibid.*

71. Samuel Beckett, letter to Arland Ussher, December 20, 1938, HRC, Austin, Texas.

72. Samuel Beckett, letter to Gwynned Vernon Reavey, April 14, 1938.

73. *Ibid.*

74. Samuel Beckett, letter to Thomas McGreevy, April 23, 1938.

75. Samuel Beckett, letters to Thomas McGreevy, April 3 and 22, 1938.

76. Samuel Beckett, letters to Thomas McGreevy, April 3, May 26, 1938, and to George Reavey, n.d., 1938.

77. Ellmann, *James Joyce*, p. 714.

78. *Soutes, Revue de culture revolutionnaire internationale*, 9, 1938, p. 41.

79. *F & F*, p. 38; Samuel Beckett, letter to Thomas McGreevy, April 3, 1938.

80. Samuel Beckett, letter to Thomas McGreevy, April 3, 1938.

81. *Les Temps Modernes*, No. 14, November, 1946, pp. 288–293. Also see *F & F*, p. 50.

82. Harvey, p. 183. It should be noted that Harvey's chronology is in error by approximately one year. (See note 13.)

83. George Reavey to DB, Samuel Beckett to George Reavey, April 22, 1938.

84. Brian Coffey, Marie Péron.

85. Guggenheim, *Century*, pp. 206–207. Lawrence Harvey, in *Poet and Critic*, p. 183, writes: "During his convalescence he came to know the girl who visited him at the hospital and who is now his wife." In an interview, May 27, 1972, Harvey stated that Beckett told him Guggenheim was referring to Suzanne Deschevaux-Dumesnil, now Madame Beckett.

86. George Reavey, Peggy Guggenheim.

87. Samuel Beckett, letter to Thomas McGreevy, June 15, 1938.

88. Samuel Beckett, letter to Thomas McGreevy, August 5, 1938.

89. Samuel Beckett, letter to Thomas McGreevy, May 26, 1938.

90. Samuel Beckett, letter to Thomas McGreevy, June 15, 1938.

91. Samuel Beckett, letter to George Reavey, August 5, 1938.

92. Samuel Beckett, letter to Thomas McGreevy, August 5, 1938.

93. *Ibid.*

94. Impressions of Samuel Beckett in Dublin based on interviews with Alan Thompson, A. J. Leventhal, Arland Ussher, Mary Manning Howe, Andrew Ganly and others who wish to remain anonymous.

95. Samuel Beckett, letters to George Reavey, June 20, 1938 and Thomas McGreevy, August 5, 1938; and Peggy Guggenheim.

96. Peggy Guggenheim.

97. Now in Baker Library, Dartmouth College. It has never been published. Beckett gave the typescript to Lawrence Harvey in the spring of 1962 and told Harvey the following: "written about 1942. One of the earliest French texts. I showed it to a sculptor who disappeared in the war. I left Paris in 1942, so it must have been then, no later." Harvey then states that Federman and Fletcher mention

it in the bibliography, p. 108, n. 612, under *Known Unpublished Works,* and quote Beckett as saying it was "written in 1938 or 1939 at the latest." Harvey says he is inclined to accept their dating, "as thorough and determined bibliographers, they pressed Beckett harder, I am sure, than I did." In an interview, January, 1974, Madame Marie Péron said that she can state with assurance that this is the text Beckett and her late husband worked on during Beckett's 1938 visit, and if not the actual text, a variant of it. She does know that Beckett was actually writing in French during this time. This is also attested to by Georges Belmont, Brian Coffey and George Reavey. Peggy Guggenheim remembers that he wrote in French because he often spoke of it to her, one moment thrilled with the ease and facility of it, the next depressed at the difficulty because he could not take certain thoughts directly into French without first passing through English.

98. Brian Coffey.

99. Lawrence Harvey appended this comment to the typescript in Baker Library, Dartmouth.

100. Samuel Beckett, letter to George Reavey, September 27, 1938.

101. Ellmann, *James Joyce,* p. 723.

102. Samuel Beckett, letter to Arland Ussher, December 20, 1938, HRC, Austin, Texas.

103. *Ibid.*

104. Stanley William Hayter, July 9, 1973, Paris.

105. Samuel Beckett, letter to George Reavey, February 19, 1939.

106. Samuel Beckett, letter to George Reavey, March 5, 1939.

107. *F & F,* p. 97, n. 492.

108. Mollie Roe, January 28, 1974.

CHAPTER THIRTEEN 1939–42:

1. Samuel Beckett, letter to George Reavey, September 26, 1939.

2. This is the expression most of the people I interviewed used when they spoke of Beckett at this time.

3. Ellmann, *James Joyce*, p. 741.

4. *Ibid.*

5. George Reavey.

6. Ellmann, *James Joyce*, p. 741.

7. Samuel Beckett, letter to George Reavey, December 6, 1938.

8. *JJ Letters*, Vol. III, pp. 465–66.

9. Robert Kastor to DB, December 12, 1974, Long Branch, New Jersey.

10. Mme. Péron, January, 1974.

11. Ellmann, *James Joyce*, p. 745.

12. George Reavey to DB.

13. In general, this is the account given in Lawrence Harvey, *Poet and Critic*, p. 348 ff. It was verified by Samuel Beckett, April, 1972, and elaborated upon by George Reavey and others.

14. George Reavey, interview January 5, 1972.

15. August 19, 1940. The letter was signed by P. J. O'Byrne for the Legation d'Irlande en Espagne.

16. Ellmann, *James Joyce*, n., p. 747.

17. Samuel Beckett as quoted in John Kobler's unpublished article, written for the *Saturday Evening Post* in September, 1964, graciously made available by the author.

18. Alan Simpson, *Beckett & Behan and a Theatre in Dublin* (London: Routledge and Kegan Paul, 1962), p. 64.

19. John Fletcher, *Novels of Samuel Beckett*, p. 59.

20. Foot, M.R.D., *S.O.E. in France: An Account of the Work of the British Special Operations Executive in France, 1940–44* (London: Her Majesty's Stationery Office, 1966), p. 198.

21. Marie Granet, *Ceux de la Résistance (1940–44)* (Paris: Les Éditions de Minuit, 1964), p. 26. In several authoritative studies of Resistance activity, Péron is listed as having been a member of several *réseaux*, operating at the same or different times. His widow, Madame Marie Péron, says, however, that Péron's actual work was only with *Étoile*, that his meetings with others had been confused as membership rather than the simple assistance that it was.

22. Information about Beckett's activity in the Resistance is from interviews with Samuel Beckett, Gabrielle Buffet-Picabia and Jeannine Picabia, January 10, 1974, Paris, Marie Péron and others. Jeannine Picabia is listed in both French and British accounts as having worked directly with Armel Guerne, but as far as she can recall, she never worked directly with *Prosper*, the large British S.O.E. unit, nor did anyone in *Gloria*. For one trying to square Beckett's

movements with official accounts of *Gloria*, the difficulty is compounded because the activities of the *réseau* are often confused with Jeannine Picabia's activities, since her code name was the same. At one time or another, the *réseau Gloria* was in contact with *Prosper*, *Étoile*, *Interallie* (an S.O.E. group composed mainly of Polish intellectuals in exile), and several other lesser-known *réseaux*.

23. This may not have been his real name, but it was the only one Jeannine Picabia knew.

24. The stamp is now in possession of Jeannine Picabia.

25. Gabrielle Buffet-Picabia.

26. Lucie Léon, *James Joyce and Paul L. Léon: The Story of a Friendship* (New York: The Gotham Book Mart, 1948), p. 31.

27. *Ibid.*

28. *Ibid.*, p. 32.

29. Gabrielle Buffet-Picabia.

30. Marie Péron, Jeannine Picabia.

31. Adrien Dansette, *Histoire de la Libération de Paris* (Paris: Fayard, 1946), p. 42.

32. Henri Noguères, en collaboration avec M. Degliame-Fouché et J.-L. Vigier, *Histoire de la Résistance en France de 1940–45* (Paris: Éditions Robert Laffont, 1969), Vol. II, p. 138, témoignage de Michel Brault, Ier part, chap. 6.

33. E. H. Cookridge (pseud. of Edward Spiro), *Set Europe Ablaze* (New York: Thomas Y. Crowell Co., 1967), p. 215. (Originally published as *Inside S.O.E.* [London: Arthur Barker Ltd.].)

34. Foot, *S.O.E. in France*, p. 144.

35. Henri Michel, *Les Mouvements Clandestins* (Paris: Presses Universitaires, 1961), p. 77.

36. Foot, *S.O.E. in France*, pp. 319–320.

37. As an example of the difference in records, the British insist that Suttill's arrest took place in July, 1942, while the French do not record his arrival in France until October, 1942. As a purely subjective reaction to the value of the intellectuals' contribution to Resistance effort, Professor Leslie Beck, one of the senior British officials in charge of coordinating French and British activity, insists that "intellectuals were not specially fitted for unpleasant underground work. The greater their 'genius' the lesser their ability as a rule" (to DB, June 25, 1974). Professor Beck also stated that he himself kept no unofficial records of Resistance activity, and most of the British papers are still classified and will probably be unavailable for public inspection for many years. As far as he can recall, he never

encountered the name of Samuel Beckett in any circumstance, either with S.O.E. or French Resistance groups.

38. Jeannine Picabia, Marie Péron.

39. Cookridge, *Set Europe Ablaze*, pp. 97–98.

40. Robert Alesch was arrested at the end of the war, brought to trial in 1947 and sentenced to death by hanging. The execution took place in the yard of the Prison de la Santé.

41. Jeannine Picabia, January 11, 1974, Paris.

42. Fletcher, *Novels of Samuel Beckett*, p. 59.

43. Marie Péron, January, 1974, Paris.

44. Marie Péron.

45. John Calder, January 24, 1974, London.

46. John Kobler, March 27, 1972, New York; Jack MacGowran, July 9, 1971, Lennox, Massachusetts.

47. re: Passeur: Les abus de certains [Passeurs] de la ligne de démarcation—tout un scénario avait été monté des attaques simulées pour faire croire à ceux qui fuyaient la Zone Sud, et en particulier, aux Juifs, que le danger était immense, afin de les convaincre de payer des sommes énormes.—Granet, *Ceux de la Résistance*, p. 25.

48. Laurence Wylie, letter to DB, December 13, 1973.

49. Samuel Beckett, Jeannine Picabia.

50. I am grateful to Jeannine Picabia, who first told me of this award, and to General Pierre Renauld, French Army (Ret.), who provided me with a copy of this citation, and to Elizabeth and Charles Edwards, who translated it.

51. I asked everyone I interviewed who might have shared Beckett's confidence in the postwar years if they knew of any award he might have received for his Resistance activity, and only Jeannine Picabia knew that he had received the *Croix de Guerre*. Madame Péron, who would likely have known, knew nothing about it, nor did any member of the Beckett family.

CHAPTER FOURTEEN 1942–45:

1. This information is in the *mairie*, or city hall, in Roussillon. A handwritten notation indicates that Beckett departed at the end of the war without making the proper formalities. I am grateful to

Professor Laurence Wylie of Harvard University, who most graciously allowed me to use the materials he has accumulated over the years dealing with Beckett's time in Roussillon.

2. Madame Escoffier is still alive, though very old. This information from Professor Laurence Wylie to DB, letter of December 13, 1973.

3. Josette Hayden.

4. Josette Hayden, Maurice Sinclair, Laurence Wylie, Roger Blin, and others.

5. Josette Hayden.

6. *Ibid.*

7. In the first draft manuscript of *Krapp's Last Tape* (HRC, Austin, Texas), and in several subsequent drafts, Beckett called Miss McGlone, who sings in a strong Connaught accent, Miss Beamish.

8. Professor Laurence Wylie.

9. These lines, with the subsequent word play on the name Vaucluse are omitted in the English translation.

10. Professor Laurence Wylie.

11. Caroline Beckett Murphy, Ann Beckett, Josette Hayden, and others.

12. Josette Hayden, Maurice Sinclair.

13. Simone de Beauvoir, *The Mandarins* (Huntington, New York: Fontana Modern Novels, 1960), p. 46.

14. Harvey, *Poet and Critic*, p. 222.

15. Information about Beckett's breakdown is from exiles, villagers and personal friends who have asked to remain anonymous. I have been greatly helped in writing this account by Dr. Barbara Poteat, Dr. Richard Cooper, Dr. A. G. Thompson, and by R. D. Laing's *The Divided Self: An Existential Study in Sanity and Madness* (Harmondsworth, England: Penguin Books, 1969). The chapters "Psychotic Developments" and "The Self and the False Self in a Schizophrenic" were especially helpful.

16. I base much of the following analysis on Laing, *The Divided Self*, p. 163.

17. *Watt*, p. 254.

18. Letter to Arland Ussher, March, 1937, HRC, Austin, Texas; conversation with George Reavey; used in *Watt*, pp. 13–15.

19. For example, Fletcher, *Novels of Samuel Beckett*, p. 99.

20. Letters to Reavey, conversation with DB and others.

21. *Watt*, p. 215.

22. *Ibid.*, p. 227.

23. Raymond Federman, *Journey to Chaos: Samuel Beckett's Early Fiction* (Berkeley and Los Angeles: University of California Press, 1965), p. 156.

24. *Watt*, p. 247 ff.

25. *Ibid.*, p. 247.

26. One of these paintings hangs in Madame Hayden's house in Reuil-en-Brie.

27. Arms and ammunition were dropped into the Vaucluse and the Gard. A *réseau* called *Monk* was active there from 1942 until D Day, and American successes after 1944 were largely due to this circuit. Information from Cookridge, *Set Europe Ablaze*, p. 214. Beckett, who was only an *agent de liaison*, i.e., an occasional volunteer, is not listed among the members of *Monk*.

28. Laurence Wylie, December 13, 1973.

29. Laurence Wylie.

30. Josette Hayden.

31. Laurence Wylie.

32. Josette Hayden.

33. Samuel Beckett to DB, Paris, April 13, 1972. Beckett's anger with Routledge increased when he discovered quite by accident that the unsold copies of *Murphy* had been remaindered *before* the war, *not* after, as he was told in 1945. In conversation (to DB, April, 1972) he said the note in Federman and Fletcher, p. 21, is not correct and he has asked them to change it in subsequent editions.

34. Samuel Beckett thanks her for it in a letter of June 21, 1945.

35. Jeannine Picabia.

36. Caroline Beckett Murphy.

37. From Beckett's correspondence with McGreevy.

38. Suzanne returned safely to the apartment in May, 1945, where she discovered that Geer and Lisl van Velde had been living there for some time, although they had very little to sustain them, as "Sam must have taken it all with him when he left." (Geer van Velde, letter to Gwynned Vernon Reavey, May 2, 1945.) Actually, the apartment had been ransacked, and some of Beckett's books and papers were taken, along with other household possessions.

39. Ann Beckett.

40. Freda Young, Killiney, August 9, 1972.

41. Brian Coffey.

42. Thomas Wall, Liam O'Brian, Mervyn Wall, Alan Thompson and others.

43. Samuel Beckett, letter to Thomas McGreevy, January 31, 1938; *Jack B. Yeats, An Appreciation and an Interpretation*, by

Thomas McGreevy (Dublin: Victor Waddington Publications, 1945). Beckett's review appeared in the *Irish Times* on August 4, 1945, p. 2.

44. *Irish Times*, June 9, 1945, p. 2.

45. George Reavey, Brian Coffey.

46. Dr. Andrew Ganly.

47. Mary B. Murphy, General Secretary of the Irish Red Cross Society, in a letter to David Sutton, July 26, 1974.

48. Dr. Alan Thompson.

49. Matron Mary Crowley graciously gave me a copy of this book.

50. First published in *Cahiers des Saisons*, no. 2, October, 1955, pp. 115–116.

51. Darley seemed to be recovered after several months in the tuberculosis ward and actually did become a working member of the staff, but he died shortly after returning to Ireland when the hospital was turned over to the French Red Cross. This information from Miss Mary Crowley, former matron, Irish Red Cross hospital, St. Lô.

52. *Irish Times*, June 24, 1946, p. 5. The poem provoked several letters to the editor, among them one from a bewildered reader who quoted the same lines by Byron about Coleridge that had appeared about Beckett in the TCD Miscellany in 1929: "I wish he would explain his explanations."

53. The following information is from Matron Mary Crowley, Dublin, November 4, 1974.

CHAPTER FIFTEEN 1946–48:

1. Maurice Sinclair, Jack MacGowran, John Montague and others.

2. Fletcher, *Samuel Beckett's Art*, p. 20. Beckett gave what he called "one of [his] last remaining typescripts" to Lawrence Harvey. It is now in Baker Library, Dartmouth College.

3. Manuscript in HRC, Austin, Texas.

4. Samuel Beckett, June 19, 1973.

5. *La Fin,* translated by Richard Seaver in *Stories and Texts for Nothing.*

6. *Ibid.,* p. 72.

7. George Reavey, January 5, 1972; Samuel Beckett, August 23, 1972.

8. Professor W. S. Maguinness, January 24, 1974.

9. Leslie Daiken, letter to George Reavey, May 22, 1946.

10. A copy of the letter from Devin A. Garrity, dated August 7, 1946, is in possession of George Reavey.

11. A. J. Leventhal, Mervyn Wall, Hilary Heron Greene, Basil Rakoszi.

12. Fletcher, *Samuel Beckett's Art,* p. 82.

13. Hilary Heron Greene, October 31, 1974, Dalkey, Ireland.

14. Manuscript in HRC, Austin, Texas.

15. John Montague.

16. As quoted in Hugh Kenner, *Reader's Guide to Samuel Beckett,* p. 198, n. 13.

17. The source of this quotation wishes to remain anonymous.

18. Marie Péron.

19. Professor W. S. Maguinness.

20. *F & F,* pp. 49–50, n. 252.1.

21. Beckett is not sure of the chronology of his postwar writings, since many manuscripts were not dated. He tried to cooperate with Federman and Fletcher and with other scholars who pressed him for an accurate listing, but he confided (to DB and others) that in many cases it was impossible for him to do more than guess.

22. Perhaps "Irishness" is the best term to describe the qualities Beckett found especially troublesome in this novel. Vivian Mercier, in *Beckett/Beckett* (New York: Oxford University Press, 1977), notes that *Mercier and Camier* is, "Of all the works written in French . . . the one most unmistakably set in Ireland. True, no Irish place names are mentioned, nor is there to my knowledge a Saint-Ruth Square in any Irish City, but Marshal St. Ruth died in Ireland at the Battle of Aughrim, as every Irish schoolboy knows. Many of the surnames—Madden, Conaire, Joly, Hamilton—are Irish or to be found in Ireland. As for the names of the title characters, Beckett must have known E. D. Camier at either Portora or Trinity and by 1946 was probably aware of me as a Portora and Trinity alumnus. . . . The coins and the drinks—stout, J. J.—are Irish, too, but the clinching details come on pp. 165–68 of the French, where Mercier and Camier are walking on the Old Military Road (*l'ancien chemin des armées*), see the city below them, and notice a simple cross out

on the bog. They can't remember why it's there, but the narrator tells us that a patriot was executed there by the enemy, or at any rate his body was left there. '*Il s'appellait Masse.*' Irishmen with longer memories than Mercier and Camier will recall that the patriot was named Noel Lemass: his family, though now Catholic, are of Huguenot descent. The unpretentious monument is now a familiar landmark to those who walk over the Dublin Mountains, though motorists may miss it unless they stop to admire the view." I am grateful to Professor Mercier for allowing me to quote an earlier version of his discussion than that which appears in the book on pp. 41–42.

Also, Charles Jasper Joly was Andrews Professor of Astronomy and Astronomer Royal of Ireland from 1897 till 1906. His work was largely a continuation of Sir William Rowan Hamilton's work on quaternions. (From Bailey, *History of TCD*, pp. 211–212.) Beckett, with his interest in astronomy, was no doubt familiar with the work of both men.

23. "The Expelled," in *Stories and Texts for Nothing*, p. 9.

24. Maurice Sinclair.

25. Maurice Sinclair, Josette Hayden; Samuel Beckett, letter to Arland Ussher, HRC, Austin, Texas.

26. *Fontaine*, X, December, 1946–January, 1947, pp. 684–708.

27. Gabrielle Buffet-Picabia, Jeannine Picabia, Kay Boyle.

28. Maurice Sinclair, Edward Beckett, Josette Hayden, Jeannine Picabia, Gabrielle Buffet-Picabia, Marie Péron.

29. Kay Boyle, Gabrielle Buffet-Picabia.

30. Josette Hayden.

31. Patrick Magee, March 26, 1976, New Haven, Conn.

32. Cohn, *Back to Beckett*, p. 70.

33. "The Calmative," *Stories and Texts for Nothing* (New York: Grove Press, 1967), p. 27.

34. Cohn, *Back to Beckett*, p. 72.

35. Samuel Beckett, letter to George Reavey, May 14, 1947; Toni Clerkx, née Jacoba van Velde, a novelist and the sister of Bram and Geer, was then a literary agent. In late 1946, she took over Reavey's prewar function. She was responsible for Bordas's accepting the French translation of *Murphy*.

36. Samuel Beckett, June 19, 1973.

37. "La Fin," "Le Calmant," "L'Expulsé" and "Premier Amour." When he wrote them, Beckett intended for all four to be published together. Shortly after, he changed his mind and withheld "Premier Amour," which was published in separate book form in French in 1970 and in English in 1974.

38. Kobler, unpublished *Saturday Evening Post* article.

39. Samuel Beckett, letter to Arland Ussher, February 17, 1947, HRC, Austin, Texas.

40. Alan Schneider, Barney Rosset.

41. To DB, April 13, 1972. In one form or another, it is the same remark he has made to a number of his friends and scholars, among them Ruby Cohn, John Montague, John Fletcher, Alan Schneider.

42. Typescript of *Éleuthéria* is in Baker Library, Dartmouth College.

43. To Arland Ussher, December 20, 1938 (HRC, Austin, Texas), Beckett wrote: ". . . you will always be welcome in 6 Rue des Favorites (formerly Impasse des Favorites), not far from the still existing Impasse de l'Enfant Jésus . . ."

44. Manuscript in HRC, Austin, Texas.

45. Samuel Beckett, letter to George Reavey, May 14, 1947.

46. *Ibid.*

47. Samuel Beckett, letter to George Reavey, June 25, 1947.

48. The sources wish to remain anonymous.

49. Samuel Beckett, letter to George Reavey, May 14, 1947.

50. Alan Thompson, Andrew Ganly.

51. Samuel Beckett, letter to George Reavey, August 15, 1947.

52. *Ibid.*

53. *Ibid.*

54. *Ibid.*

55. Janvier, *Beckett par Lui-Même*, p. 21, my translation.

56. Cohn, *Back to Beckett*, p. 112.

57. *Ibid.*, p. 78.

58. Marie Péron.

59. John Fletcher has noted the division in *Molloy,* in which the two parts of the novel seem derived separately from two previous experiments, the *Quatre Nouvelles* and *Mercier et Camier,* as if Beckett had not clearly conceived *Molloy* to be a novel from the beginning, but only a continuation of the *Quatre Nouvelles.* Fletcher, *Novels of Samuel Beckett,* p. 129.

60. *Molloy,* in *Three Novels,* pp. 164–165.

61. Ann Beckett, Hilary Heron Greene, Caroline Murphy.

62. Mrs. Peggy Beckett, August 10, 1972.

63. *Molloy,* in *Three Novels,* p. 39.

64. Fletcher, *Novels of Samuel Beckett,* p. 127.

65. Samuel Beckett, letter to Thomas McGreevy, January 14, 1948.

66. *Ibid.*

67. "Trois Poèmes," *transition 48*, June 2, 1948, pp. 96–97.

68. Samuel Beckett, letter to Thomas McGreevy, March 13, 1948.

69. *Molloy* (Paris: Les Éditions de Minuit, 1951), p. 9.

70. *Molloy*, in *Three Novels*, p. 8.

71. *Malone Dies*, in *Three Novels*, p. 8.

72. *Ibid.*, p. 264.

73. *Ibid.*, pp. 199, 207, 216, 180.

74. Fletcher, *Novels of Samuel Beckett*, p. 175.

75. *Proust*, in *Proust and Three Dialogues*, p. 48.

76. Maurice Sinclair.

77. Joan Mitchell, January 12, 1974, Vetheuil, France; Maria Jolas, July 12, 1973, Paris; Elizabeth Ryan, Mary Manning Howe, George Reavey and others.

78. Samuel Beckett, letter to George Reavey, July 8; no year, but internal evidence confirms 1948.

79. Samuel Beckett, letter to George Reavey, July 8, 1948.

80. Samuel Beckett, letters to Thomas McGreevy, George Reavey and others.

81. Hilary Heron Greene.

82. Josette Hayden, Hilary Heron Greene, Maurice Sinclair.

CHAPTER SIXTEEN WAITING FOR GODOT:

1. Roger Blin, July 5, 1973.

2. Colin Duckworth, "The Making of Godot" in *Casebook on Waiting for Godot*, ed. Ruby Cohn (New York: Grove Press, 1967), p. 89.

3. *Ibid.*

4. John Fletcher afterword and notes to *Waiting for Godot* (London: Faber and Faber, 1971), p. 108.

5. Samuel Beckett, June, 1973.

6. Samuel Beckett, August 23, 1972, Paris.

7. Roger Blin.

8. Ruby Cohn, April 10, 1973, San Francisco.

9. A. J. Leventhal.

10. Samuel Beckett to Alan Schneider and many others.

11. Samuel Beckett to Harold Hobson.

12. Samuel Beckett to DB and others.

13. *Ibid.*

14. Samuel Beckett to DB, John Montague, Alan Schneider, Roger Blin and others.

15. Roger Blin.

16. In interviews with friends and professional associates who knew him before and after his great fame, this comment recurs repeatedly in any detailed analysis of Beckett and his attitude toward his writing.

17. Duckworth, "The Making of Godot," p. 95. Dr. Duckworth's article is an excellent comparison of *Mercier et Camier* and *Waiting for Godot,* and discussion of how Beckett has used the earlier work in the later.

18. *En Attendant Godot,* Éditions de Minuit, p. 9. *Waiting for Godot,* Grove Press, p. 7.

19. The following description of conversations between Beckett and Suzanne comes from unsolicited comments made by close friends and associates in separate interviews. This impression of Beckett and Suzanne seems to have been shared by persons who know them best, and knew them well at the time he wrote this play.

20. *Waiting for Godot,* p. 9.

21. John Fletcher and John Spurling, *Beckett: A Study of His Plays* (New York: Hill and Wang, 1972), p. 39. The authors note that Beckett was not wholly successful at avoiding definition, quoting the fifth *Text for Nothing:* "Why did Pozzo leave home, he had a castle and retainers." *Stories and Texts for Nothing,* p. 96.

22. *Waiting for Godot,* p. 9.

23. Letters to George Reavey, Arland Ussher, Mary Manning Howe, Thomas McGreevy and others.

24. Fletcher, Cohn, Adam Tarn, et al.

25. Samuel Beckett, November 17, 1971.

26. Samuel Beckett, letter to Arland Ussher, July 11, 1937, HRC, Austin, Texas.

27. *transition 48,* 4 (January, 1949), pp. 19–21.

28. "F——," p. 21.

29. *Molloy,* p. 176.

30. John Manning, Mary Manning Howe, Sean and Seumas Mandy.

31. *Waiting for Godot*, p. 37.

32. Cohen, *Back to Beckett*, p. 133.

33. The only extant photo of William Beckett shows him sitting in the stands at Leopardstown racetrack in a hat and coat similar to those worn by Vladimir and Estragon. Reproduced here following p. 000.

34. I am indebted to John Montague, Roger Blin and Adam Tarn, who discussed Beckett's use of language with me, and helped me to formulate these ideas.

35. Vivian Mercier, "The Mathematical Limit," *The Nation*, CLXXXVIII (Feb. 14, 1959), pp. 144–145.

36. Roger Blin, A. J. Leventhal and others.

CHAPTER SEVENTEEN 1949–50:

1. Gabrielle Buffet-Picabia, "Apollinaire," *transition 50*, 6 (October, 1950), ed. Georges Duthuit, Paris, pp. 110–126. Not listed in *F & F*.

2. *transition 48*, 1, p. 6.

3. Pierre Schneider, January 14, 1974, Paris.

4. Pierre Schneider.

5. *transition 49*, 5 (December 1949), pp. 97–103.

6. *F & F*, p. 24.

7. *Proust and Three Dialogues*, p. 120.

8. *Ibid.*

9. *Ibid.*, p. 121.

10. *Ibid.*, p. 125.

11. Mollie Roe, November 12, 1974, Guildford, Surrey, England.

12. Arland Ussher, George Reavey, A. J. Leventhal, Jack MacGowran and others.

13. Andrew Ganly.

14. Norris Davidson, November 2, 1974, Dublin.

15. Alan Thompson, Andrew Ganly.

16. Adam Tarn, October 19, 1973, Ottawa, Canada.

17. Roger Blin.

18. *F & F*, n. 496, p. 98.

19. Octavio Paz, letter to DB, July 29, 1974; Gerald Brenan, letter to DB, January 28, 1975.

20. *transition 49*, 5 (December 1949), p. 104.

21. *Envoy* I (January 1950), pp. 11–19.

22. Gabrielle Buffet-Picabia.

23. Mahood is one of many variants of the name Mahomet, who was called the "false prophet of God" in the Middle Ages.

24. *The Unnamable*, in *Three Novels* (New York: Grove Press, 1955), p. 305.

25. *Ibid.*

26. *Ibid.*

27. *Ibid.*, p. 298. "Baile atha Clathe" is the Gaelic name for Dublin.

28. *Ibid.*, p. 302.

29. *Ibid.*, pp. 303–304.

30. I quote from the article "Moody Man of Letters" by Israel Shenker in the *New York Times*, May 6, 1956. I use Shenker's quote because it is the most apt phrasing of this thought, repeated to me in part by Beckett and in my interviews with others. I am cautious to ascribe these words directly to Beckett, since Shenker, in his letter to me, states that he said nowhere in the article that Beckett gave him an interview, but relies on journalistic devices throughout.

31. Jung, *Analytical Psychology*, p. 82.

32. *The Unnamable*, p. 396.

33. *Ibid.*, pp. 395–396.

34. *Ibid.*, p. 391.

35. *Ibid.*

36. Alfred Alvarez, *Samuel Beckett* (New York: The Viking Press, Modern Masters Series, 1973), p. 63.

37. *The Unnamable*, p. 393.

38. This information from Roger Blin, July 3 and 5, 1973, Paris.

39. Roger Blin.

40. *Ibid.*

41. Roger Blin, July 12, 1974.

42. Geoffrey Thompson.

43. *transition 50*, 6 (October, 1950), pp. 103–105.

44. *Krapp's Last Tape*, pp. 19–20.

45. Caroline Beckett Murphy.

46. The following information is from Jerome Lindon, June 19, 1973, Paris.

47. Jerome Lindon. This is the language of the contract.

48. This was Beckett's description to Ussher, Reavey, Sinclair, Leventhal and others.

49. Samuel Beckett to DB and others. Octavio Paz, in a letter to DB, July 29, 1974, said he did not collaborate with Beckett in the translation, though occasionally, not more than two or three times, he clarified some obscure allusions in one baroque poem. He and Beckett met several times in a cafe, where Beckett explained that he had taken the job because he, too, needed the money. Beckett told Paz that he did not know Spanish well, but was relying on his French, a grasp of Latin and *the help of a friend who knew Spanish well*. In his letter, Paz was angry that he had been asked to comment on the circumstances of this translation, saying he wanted nothing further to do with it.

50. Gerald Brenan, letter to DB, January 28, 1975.

51. *F & F*, p. 132.

52. Samuel Beckett, letter to George Reavey, December 11, 1950.

53. Samuel Beckett, letter to George Reavey, November 9, 1961.

54. Samuel Beckett, letter to George Reavey, December 11, 1950.

CHAPTER EIGHTEEN 1951–53:

1. Samuel Beckett, letter to Roger Blin, January 15, 1951.

2. Jerome Lindon, June 19, 1973.

3. Caroline Beckett Murphy.

4. Jerome Lindon. The photo is reproduced in *Samuel Beckett at Sixty*, facing p. 25.

5. Samuel Beckett, letter to Thomas McGreevy, 1948.

6. The letter is in possession of Roger Blin.

7. Roger Blin.

8. Adam Tarn.

9. None of Beckett's novels has ever sold more than 10,000 copies in France except for *Molloy*, which sold 35,000 copies in the Minuit edition and 50–55,000 copies in the 10–18 series. The plays

have consistently sold out in repeated printings.——Jerome Lindon to DB, June 19, 1973.

10. *Les Temps Modernes* VII (September, 1951), 385–416.

11. Samuel Beckett, Jerome Lindon, Roger Blin.

12. *F & F*, pp. 239–241.

13. Jerome Lindon.

14. Samuel Beckett to George Reavey, Brian Coffey and others.

15. Jerome Lindon.

16. Georges Neveaux, letter to Roger Blin, January 29, 1952. My translation.

17. Roger Blin.

18. Roger Blin, July 3, 1973. The letter is from an actor who wishes to be anonymous.

19. *Studio de club d'essai, de la radio*, February 17, 1952, 15 h. 15.

20. Roger Blin; Richard Seaver, September 24, 1971, New York.

21. Josette Hayden, January, 1974. The text was later published in *Cahiers d'Art—Documents*, November 22, 1955.

22. Vivian Mercier, April 29, 1974.

23. Published in 1955.

24. Reference to this translation, unnamed, is in a letter to Thomas McGreevy, September 19, 1952. It is not listed in *F & F*, and either was forgotten by Beckett or else he did not consider it significant enough to mention to his bibliographers.

25. Pierre Schneider.

26. Caroline Beckett Murphy, January 17, 1974, Killiney.

27. Roger Blin, John Montague and others.

28. Samuel Beckett, letter to George Reavey, May 12, 1953.

29. Roger Blin, July 15, 1973.

30. Caroline Beckett Murphy, January 17, 1974, Killiney.

31. Madeleine Montague, July 9, 1973, Paris; also John Montague, Pierre Schneider, A. J. Leventhal, Mervyn Wall and anonymous sources.

32. Samuel Beckett, letter to Roger Blin, August 25, 1952.

33. Roger Blin, July 15, 1973, Paris.

34. Jerome Lindon.

35. Roger Blin.

36. Sergio Gerstein, June 22, 1976, New York.

37. Roger Blin.

38. Sergio Gerstein.

39. Information about set construction is from Sergio Gerstein.

40. Jean Martin, May 12, 1976, New York.

41. Jean Martin.

42. Sergio Gerstein, Roger Blin.

43. In the now relatively rare first edition, the passage appears on p. 56. In the definitive edition, the line preceding the exchange, "*Charmante soirée*," is changed from Estragon to Vladimir.

44. Act II, pp. 106–107 in Les Éditions de Minuit; pp. 48–49 in Grove Press edition.

45. P. 49 in the Grove Press edition.

46. Samuel Beckett, July 3, 1973.

47. Samuel Beckett, letter to Roger Blin, January 9, 1953.

48. *Ibid.*

49. Geneviève Serreau, July 11, 1973, Paris; Roger Blin, Sergio Gerstein.

50. *La Libération*, January 7, 1953.

51. *Arts #400*, January 27, 1953.

52. *Ibid.* The reviews quoted above all appear in *Casebook on Waiting for Godot*, ed. Ruby Cohn.

53. Martin Esslin, "Is it All Gloom and Doom?" *The New York Times*, Sunday, September 24, 1967, sec. D, p. 3.

CHAPTER NINETEEN 1953–54:

1. Samuel Beckett, letter to George Reavey, May 12, 1953.

2. Account of the publication of *Watt* is from interviews with Richard Seaver, September 24, 1971, and Richard and Jeannette Seaver, January 27, 1975, New York; Christopher Logue, November 11, 1974, London; Alexander Trocchi, November 15, 1974, London; Maurice Girodias, April 11, 1974, New York; Iris Owens, May 13, 1974, New York.

3. Alexander Trocchi.

4. This is Iris Owens's description of Beckett.

5. Maurice Girodias.

6. *Ibid.*

7. *Watt* was banned on October 22, 1954. *Molloy* was banned in all English editions, but not in French, on January 20, 1956. As of

1968, the final listing of publications banned in Ireland, both had not been removed. The only other of Beckett's writings to be officially banned was *More Pricks Than Kicks*, on October 23, 1934.

8. Maurice Girodias; Samuel Beckett, letter to Jean Wright Beckett, June 27, 1953.

9. *Nimbus*, II (Autumn, 1953), pp. 61–62.

10. "Samuel Beckett," *Spectator*, October 23, 1953, pp. 458–459.

11. This expression, in one form or another, was used by Beckett and his critics to describe this period of time.

12. December 14, 1953.

13. Samuel Beckett, letter to Jean Wright Beckett, June 27, 1953.

14. *Ibid.*

15. Madeleine Renaud, July 6, 1973, Paris.

16. Samuel Beckett, June 19, 1973; Edward Beckett, January 25, 1974, London.

17. Jerome Lindon.

18. Samuel Beckett, letter to George Reavey, May 12, 1953.

19. Barney Rosset, March 29, 1974, New York; John Calder, January 24, 1974, London; and Marion Boyars, December 10, 1972, Westport, Conn. All agree with this interpretation.

20. Barney Rosset, letter to his staff, September 28, 1953.

21. Barney Rosset, letter to his staff, September 19, 1953.

22. Richard Seaver.

23. *Ibid.*

24. Patrick Bowles, translator's note to Frederich Dürrenmatt, *The Visit* (New York: Grove Press, 1962).

25. Barney Rosset and Samuel Beckett, correspondence of September, 1953.

26. Samuel Beckett, letter to Barney Rosset, September 1, 1953.

27. Barney Rosset to DB, March 29, 1974.

28. He continued to do so until 1968, when he allowed Agnes and Ludovic Janvier to render *Watt* into English.

29. Samuel Beckett, letter to Thomas McGreevy, September 27, 1953.

30. Roger Blin, July 14, 1973, Paris.

31. Samuel Beckett, letter to George Reavey, September 29, 1953.

32. This observation and those following were made in almost every interview conducted for this book; thus I will not single out separate individuals for citation.

33. Samuel Beckett, letter to Thomas McGreevy, December 14, 1953.

34. Ian MacMillan, January 16, 1974, Dublin.

35. Roger Blin and others.

36. Roger Blin, A. J. Leventhal, Josette Hayden.

37. Caroline Beckett Murphy.

38. No. II, April, 1954, pp. 619–620.

39. Samuel Beckett, letter to Thomas McGreevy, March 1, 1954.

40. Samuel Beckett, November 17, 1971, April 13, 1972, June 19, 1973, Paris. Beckett told this writer that he would not talk about Joyce again, to anyone, for any reason. Richard Ellmann would not consent to be interviewed for this book.

41. Beckett claims not to recall all the offensive passages because there were so many changes made by him and Blin and by others at that time, such as Rosset, who were concerned with the printed text. It was a period of heavy revision, when he spent as much time as he could at Ussy, and he claims that all the objections from all quarters have blurred in his mind through the passage of time. To DB, November 17, 1971.

42. Samuel Beckett to A. G. Thompson, Alan Thompson. The following account is based on interviews with Mary Manning Howe, Caroline Beckett Murphy, Ann Beckett, Edward Beckett, Mrs. Harriet Chance and others.

43. Samuel Beckett, letter to Jean Beckett, November 24, 1954.

44. Ludovic Janvier, *Beckett par Lui-Même*. The manuscript and three typescripts of successive versions are in the Ohio State University Library.

45. Samuel Beckett, undated letter to Roger Blin.

CHAPTER TWENTY 1955–57:

1. The following account is based on information from Roger Blin and Beckett's correspondence with Jean Wright Beckett.

2. The following information is based on interviews with

Robert Kastor, conversations with Maria Jolas, Beckett's correspondence with Thomas McGreevy and George Reavey.

3. Published in November, 1955.

4. *From an Abandoned Work*, in *First Love and Other Shorts* (New York: Grove Press, 1974), all quotations from this edition.

5. Peter Bull, *I Know the Face, But . . . .* (London: Peter Davies, Ltd., 1959), pp. 169–170.

6. Milton Shulman, *"Last Night's Theatre, Duet for Two Symbols,"* the *Evening Standard*, London, August, 1955.

7. *Punch*, August 10, 1955.

8. W. A. Darlington, "Obscure Play is Oddly Moving; West End Transfer," the *Daily Telegraph*, London, August, 1955.

9. Samuel Beckett, letter to Thomas McGreevy, August 7, 1955.

10. Kenneth Tynan, "New Writing," *The Observer*, August 7, 1955, p. 11.

11. Harold Hobson, "Tomorrow," *The Sunday Times*, London, August 7, 1955.

12. Samuel Beckett, letter to H. O. White, October 10, 1955, in Trinity College Library, Dublin.

13. Alan Simpson, *Beckett and Behan and a Theatre in Dublin*, p. 67.

14. *Evening Herald*, Dublin.

15. Samuel Beckett, letter to Thomas McGreevy, November 16, 1955.

16. Alan Schneider, "Waiting for Beckett: A Personal Chronicle," *Chelsea Review*, No. 2, September, 1958.

17. The following is from interviews with Alan Schneider and Samuel Beckett.

18. William Heron to Anne Chisholm Davie, March 9, 1975. The following is from interviews conducted for DB by Mrs. Davie.

19. Geoffrey Thompson.

20. Geoffrey Thompson unfortunately cannot remember their exact words.

21. Olive Maguinness, January 24, 1974, London.

22. Samuel Beckett, letter to Thomas McGreevy, December 16, 1955.

23. Samuel Beckett, letter to Alan Schneider, December 27, 1955.

24. The following information is based on interviews with Samuel Beckett, Alan Schneider, John Lahr and Barney Rosset; telephone conversations with Herbert Berghof and Thornton Wilder; from Alan Schneider's "Waiting for Beckett: A Personal Chronicle"; and John Lahr's *Notes on a Cowardly Lion* (New York: Ballantine Books, 1969).

25. Thornton Wilder, July 15, 1971, Hamden, Conn.

26. *Anastasia; The Remarkable Mr. Pennypacker*.

27. Lahr, *Cowardly Lion*, p. 303.

28. *Ibid.*, p. 312.

29. *Ibid.*, p. 313.

30. *Ibid.*, p. 303.

31. "Beckett's Letters on Endgame," *The Village Voice Reader*, ed. Daniel Wolf and Edwin Fancher (Garden City, N.Y.: Doubleday, 1962), p. 183.

32. As quoted in *The New York Times*, "Why They Wait for Godot," September 21, 1958, p. 36 ff.

33. Barney Rosset; Marilynn Meeker, January 5, 1972, New York.

34. Samuel Beckett, letter to Thomas McGreevy, April 27, 1956.

35. The manuscript is in Ohio State University Library, Columbus, Ohio.

36. John and Beryl Fletcher, *Fin de partie* (London: Methuen, 1970), p. 9.

37. Typescripts are also in Ohio State University Library.

38. Samuel Beckett, letter to Alan Schneider, June 21, 1956. Published in *The Village Voice Reader* as "Beckett's Letters on Endgame," p. 183. Alan Schneider persuaded Beckett to allow the letters to be published in the hope that it would bolster audience interest in the first American production (Alan Schneider to DB, July 8, 1971).

39. Information about Beckett and Cissie Sinclair is from Ann Beckett and Maurice Sinclair. Beatrice, Lady Glenavy, gives a version of this in *Gossip*, p. 178.

40. The Irish writer wishes to be anonymous. I am also indebted to Vonn Scott Bair, who provided me with information about chess in this chapter.

41. Kay Boyle, Gabrielle Buffet-Picabia, Josette Hayden, the anonymous Irish writer and others.

42. Arturo Schwarz, *The Complete Works of Marcel Duchamp* (New York: Harry N. Abrams, Inc., 1970), p. 70.

43. *Ibid.*

44. *Ibid.*, p. 62. The Irish author discussed Duchamp's book with Beckett.

45. *Ibid.*, pp. 62–63.

46. *Ibid.*, pp. 63–64.

47. Cohn, *Back to Beckett*, p. 152.

48. A. J. Leventhal, Barney Rosset, Richard Seaver.

49. Cohn, *Back to Beckett*, p. 152.

50. Jean Martin, Roger Blin, Patrick Magee, Jack MacGowran.

51. Patrick Magee. Ruby Cohn, in *Back to Beckett*, gives a slightly different wording. I use here the exact words of persons cited in interviews.

52. Jean Martin, Roger Blin, Jack MacGowran, Patrick Magee.

53. Cohn, *Back to Beckett*, p. 152.

54. *Ibid.*, p. 153.

55. *Ibid.*, p. 154.

56. *Ibid.*

57. Jean Martin.

58. Harold Hobson, untitled review of *Fin de partie*, directed by Graham Murray for the 69 Theatre Company, Shaw Theatre, London. *The Sunday Times*, London, July 15, 1973.

59. Samuel Beckett, letter to Alan Schneider, December 29, 1957. In *Village Voice Reader*, p. 185.

60. Samuel Beckett, letter to Nancy Cunard, April 4, 1956, HRC, Austin, Texas.

61. Samuel Beckett, letter to Thomas McGreevy, April 27, 1956.

62. Samuel Beckett, letter to Nancy Cunard, April 4, 1956, HRC, Austin, Texas.

63. *Ibid.*

64. Vivian Mercier, letter to DB, May 23, 1974.

65. *Ibid.*

66. Samuel Beckett, letter to Jean Wright Beckett, November 24, 1956.

67. Jean Martin, Roger Blin, Josette Hayden.

68. Among them the University of Texas, Ohio State and Washington University, St. Louis. With few exceptions, most of Beckett's manuscripts are in American collections. Several are in private hands, but these are usually jettisoned bits and pieces, usually

no more than a few pages, which were given by Beckett as gifts. One of the more notable "missing" manuscripts is *Murphy*, which Beckett will only say is "in private hands in London."

69. "Beckett's Letters on *Endgame*," p. 183.

70. Samuel Beckett, letter to Vivian Mercier, May 15, 1956.

71. Samuel Beckett, letter to Thomas McGreevy, June 4, 1956.

72. Barney Rosset; Samuel Beckett, letter to Thomas McGreevy, June 30, 1956.

73. Samuel Beckett, letter to Thomas McGreevy, June 4, 1956.

74. *Ibid.*

75. Samuel Beckett, letter to Thomas McGreevy, June 30, 1956.

76. Samuel Beckett, letter to Thomas McGreevy, July 30, 1956.

77. "Beckett's Letters on *Endgame*," p. 183.

78. *Trinity News: A Dublin University Weekly*, III, June 7, 1956, p. 4.

79. Marilynn Meeker, Barney Rosset, Richard Seaver.

80. Samuel Beckett, letter to Nancy Cunard, July 5, 1956, HRC, Austin, Texas.

81. Samuel Beckett, letter to Thomas McGreevy, July 30, 1956.

82. Samuel Beckett, letter to Thomas McGreevy, October 18, 1956.

83. Samuel Beckett, letter to Thomas McGreevy, November 16, 1956.

84. Samuel Beckett, letter to Thomas McGreevy, June 4, 1956.

85. Aidan Higgins and John Montague.

86. Samuel Beckett, letter to Thomas McGreevy, October 18, 1956.

87. *Ibid.*

88. *Ibid.*

89. Samuel Beckett, letter to Nancy Cunard, September 23, 1956, HRC, Austin, Texas.

90. "Beckett's Letters on *Endgame*," p. 184.

91. Samuel Beckett to John Montague, Maurice Sinclair, Marion Leigh, Bettina Jonic.

92. Samuel Beckett, letter to Thomas McGreevy, March 3, 1957.

93. Caroline Beckett Murphy.

94. Ann Beckett, Caroline Beckett Murphy, Maurice Sinclair.

95. Josette Hayden.

96. Roger Blin.

97. Samuel Beckett, letter to Thomas McGreevy, March 3, 1957.

98. Samuel Beckett, undated letter to Roger Blin.

99. Brian 'Coffey.

100. *Les Lettres Nouvelles*, V (March, 1957), pp. 321–351.

101. The following opinions are based on extensive interviews with the persons named, and with many others who were in Paris at the time and knew all the parties mentioned. Thus, I do not single out specific persons for attribution and do not list all the sources.

102. Wyn Henderson to Anne Chisholm Davie, March, 1974.

103. A. J. Leventhal.

104. John Montague, Jean Martin, Roger Blin.

105. This information is from the woman in question, who wishes to remain anonymous.

106. Samuel Beckett, letter to Thomas McGreevy, March 23, 1957.

107. Jack B. Yeats, letter to Samuel Beckett, December, 1956.

108. Samuel Beckett, letter to Thomas McGreevy, April 5, 1957.

109. Samuel Beckett, letter to H. O. White, April 15, 1957, Trinity College Library, Dublin.

110. Jean Martin, Roger Blin.

111. John Fletcher, October 31, 1971, Paris.

112. Roger Blin, July 13, 1973.

113. A. J. Leventhal.

114. Jean Martin, Roger Blin.

115. Samuel Beckett, letter to Thomas McGreevy, April 5, 1957.

116. "Beckett's Letters on *Endgame*," p. 185.

117. *Ibid.*

118. Samuel Beckett, letter to Thomas McGreevy, July 30, 1957.

119. "Beckett's Letters on *Endgame*," p. 184.

120. Alan Schneider.

121. For Schneider's thoughts about the production of *Endgame*, see "Waiting for Beckett: A Personal Chronicle," *op. cit.*

122. Roger Blin, Jean Martin.

123. Samuel Beckett, letter to Thomas McGreevy, November 27, 1957.

124. *Ibid.*

125. Pierre Schneider.

126. The following information is from Joan Mitchell, Pierre Schneider, John Montague, Madeleine Montague, Stanley William Hayter, and others.

CHAPTER TWENTY-ONE 1958–60:

1. Barney Rosset, March 29, 1974.

2. Samuel Beckett to DB and others.

3. Typescripts of *Krapp's Last Tape* are in the HRC, Austin, Texas. In a letter to Jake Schwartz, March 15, 1958, also in HRC, Beckett states that he had "4 stages, in typescript with copious and dirty corrections, of a short stage monologue I have just written (in English) for Pat Magee. This was composed on the machine from a tangle of old notes, so I have not the MS to offer you." Beckett, as of 1974, still retained the original version.

4. Alec Reid, *All I Can Manage, More Than I Could* (New York: Grove Press, 1971), p. 21.

5. *Krapp's Last Tape*, in *Krapp's Last Tape and Other Short Dramatic Pieces*, p. 28.

6. Eileen O'Casey, October 30, 1974, Dublin.

7. John Calder.

8. John Kobler, July 2, 1972. The incident in the Falstaff took place in the summer of 1965.

9. Samuel Beckett, letter to Jake Schwartz, March 15, 1958, HRC, Austin, Texas.

10. *Ibid.*

11. Samuel Beckett to DB, R.B.D. French, A. J. Leventhal and others.

12. Samuel Beckett, letter to Jake Schwartz, April 5, 1958, HRC, Austin, Texas.

13. *Ibid.*

14. Samuel Beckett, letter to Thomas McGreevy, June 2, 1958.

15. *Ibid.*

16. *Ibid.*

17. *Purgatorio,* IV, 106–109; Samuel Beckett, letter to Thomas McGreevy, April 21, 1958.

18. Pierre Schneider.

19. Samuel Beckett, letter to Jake Schwartz, August 10, 1958, HRC, Austin, Texas.

20. Samuel Beckett, letter to Thomas McGreevy, October 19, 1958.

21. *Ibid.*

22. Information about Samuel Beckett in London is from Jocelyn Herbert, John Calder, Bettina Jonic, Jean Martin, Roger Blin and others.

23. Samuel Beckett, letter to Nancy Cunard, October 27, 1958, HRC, Austin, Texas.

24. *The Observer,* November 2, 1958, p. 19.

25. Ann Beckett, Caroline Beckett Murphy, Edward Beckett, Hilary Heron Greene.

26. Samuel Beckett, letter to Jake Schwartz, February 15, 1959, HRC, Austin, Texas.

27. Samuel Beckett, letter to H. O. White, February 3, 1959, TCD Library.

28. Samuel Beckett, letter to DB, July 24, 1971.

29. This information is from all three of Beckett's publishers, numerous associates in the theater, personal friends and from Beckett's correspondence as well.

30. Translation by Dr. A. J. Leventhal, from the Latin text spoken by the public orator in Trinity College, Dublin, at the conferment of the Doctor of Letters, honoris causa, on Samuel Beckett, July 2, 1959.

31. *Les Lettres Nouvelles,* I (March 4, 1959), pp. 5–13.

32. Samuel Beckett to Martin Esslin, Barney Rosset, John Calder and others.

33. Marcel Mihalovici, "My Collaboration with Samuel Beckett," in *Beckett at Sixty,* pp. 20–22.

34. Samuel Beckett, undated letter to Thomas McGreevy.

35. Mihalovici, "My Collaboration," p. 22.

36. Samuel Beckett, letter to Thomas McGreevy, May 17, 1959.

37. Samuel Beckett, letter to Thomas McGreevy, October 29, 1959.

38. Christopher Logue.

39. Alec Reid.

40. Samuel Beckett, letter to Thomas McGreevy, April, 1959.

41. Samuel Beckett, letter to Thomas McGreevy, May 17, 1959.

42. *Ibid.*

43. Samuel Beckett, letter to Thomas McGreevy, July 19, 1959.

44. *Ibid.*

45. The following information is from Caroline Beckett Murphy.

46. The following information is from Sheila and Donald Page, January 28, 1974, Compton, Surrey.

47. Samuel Beckett, letter to Thomas McGreevy, September 21, 1959.

48. *Embers* won the 1959 Prix Italia for literary or dramatic works, with or without music. It was first broadcast on BBC Third Programme, June 24, 1959; produced by Donald McWhinnie.

49. Samuel Beckett, letter to Thomas McGreevy, September 21, 1959.

50. Samuel Beckett, letter to Thomas McGreevy, November 30, 1959.

51. *Ibid.*

52. Samuel Beckett, letter to Jake Schwartz, November 5, 1959, in possession of William York Tindall.

53. Samuel Beckett, letter to Thomas McGreevy, 1937.

54. The following observations on theater are from conversations between Samuel Beckett and DB, Paris, 1971, 1972, 1973.

55. Samuel Beckett to DB, June 19, 1973.

56. Samuel Beckett, letter to Thomas McGreevy, February 9, 1960.

57. Alan Schneider, August 7, 1971.

58. A. J. Leventhal.

59. "Rebuke to Nihilism," *Christian Century*, LXXVII (March 2, 1960), 256–257.

60. "Krapp and a Little Claptrap," *New Republic*, CXLIII (February 22, 1960), 21–22.

61. A. J. Leventhal.

62. Samuel Beckett, letter to Thomas McGreevy, February 9, 1960.

63. *X: A Quarterly Review*, I (November, 1959), pp. 35–37.

64. Samuel Beckett, letter to John Calder, March 17, 1960, HRC, Austin, Texas.

65. Samuel Beckett, letter to Thomas McGreevy, February 9, 1960; Jerome Lindon to DB, June 19, 1973.

66. Samuel Beckett, letter to Thomas McGreevy, February 9, 1960.

67. Herbert Blau, "Meanwhile, Follow the Bright Angels," *Tulane Drama Review*, V (September, 1960), 90–91.

68. Pierre Schneider.

69. The manuscript of *Happy Days* is at Ohio State University. These impressions were gained in an interview with Ruby Cohn, San Francisco, April 20, 1973.

70. Edward Beckett, January 25, 1974, London.

71. *Evergreen Review*, V (March-April, 1961), 47–60.

72. Roger Blin.

73. Samuel Beckett, letter to Thomas McGreevy, August 15, 1960; Roger Blin to DB, July 12, 1973.

74. *Irish Times*, March 30, 1960. This letter and the entire correspondence between Beckett and Connolly Cole is in the Berg Collection, the New York Public Library.

75. Samuel Beckett to Connolly Cole, March 23, 1960, Berg Collection.

76. Eileen O'Casey to DB, October 20, 1974, Dublin.

77. Amy Gibson to DB, November 12, 1974, London.

78. Shivaun O'Casey Kenig, November 9, 1974, London.

79. Eileen O'Casey.

80. Ann Beckett.

81. Peter Beckett.

82. Ann Beckett.

83. Jerome Lindon.

84. This is John Fletcher's translation from the French *Comment C'est*, as it appears in *The Novels of Samuel Beckett*, p. 214. The English *How It Is*, translated by Beckett, pp. 11–12, is not as revealing.

85. Driver, "Beckett by the Madeleine," pp. 21–25.

86. *Ibid.*

87. *Ibid.*

88. Samuel Beckett, letter to Thomas McGreevy, Edward Beckett to DB, n.d.

89. Samuel Beckett, letter to John Calder, July 24, 1960, HRC, Austin, Texas.

90. Notebook in possession of Samuel Beckett.

91. Samuel Beckett, letter to Thomas McGreevy, November 10, 1960.

CHAPTER TWENTY-TWO 1961–62:

1. Samuel Beckett, letter to Thomas McGreevy, January 9, 1961. Leventhal's book was to be a collection of personal photographs of Beckett and his family, some unpublished poems and fragments of prose, and a long essay, part criticism and part biography. Beckett was never in favor of the book, but told Leventhal to proceed with it if he needed the commission. Leventhal finally abandoned the project because he sensed Beckett's aversion to it.

2. Samuel Beckett, letter to Alan Schneider, January 2, 1961.

3. Samuel Beckett, letter to Thomas McGreevy, January 9, 1961.

4. John Montague.

5. Harold Pinter to DB, November 14, 1974, London. By chance, in the little-used Westminster Library in Bermondsey, Pinter found a copy of *Murphy* in the original 1938 Routledge edition. Since the pages were still uncut and no other reader had ever checked it out, Pinter decided the book was meant to be his, and he kept it.

6. Roger Blin.

7. Harold Pinter, November 14, 1974, London.

8. Harold Pinter.

9. *Ibid.*

10. *Ibid.*

11. A. J. Leventhal.

12. The following account of Samuel Beckett's marriage is from Alan Schneider, Barney Rosset, A. J. Leventhal, Ann Beckett and others. Also, Samuel Beckett's correspondence to McGreevy, Schneider, Schwartz, Calder and others.

13. Sheila Page.

14. Ann Beckett.

15. Certificate of an entry of marriage, General Registrar Office, St. Catherine's House, London.

16. Jean Reavey, April 19, 1975, New York.

17. There is no mention of the award in letters to the friends who sent congratulations, among them Thomas McGreevy, Adam Tarn, George Reavey and others. Roger Blin, Geneviève Serreau, Madeleine Renaud and others are the sources for verbal expressions of congratulation.

18. *L'Express*, May 4, 1961, p. 38.

19. The following information is from Jean Martin, Roger Blin, Josette Hayden, A. J. Leventhal, Marion Leigh and others.

20. Samuel Beckett, letter to Thomas McGreevy, May 30, 1961.

21. Samuel Beckett to DB, November 17, 1971.

22. Henry Wenning, July 14, 1971, New Haven; Samuel Beckett to DB, November 17, 1971.

23. Samuel Beckett to DB, November 17, 1971.

24. Henry Wenning.

25. Samuel Beckett, undated letter to Jacob Schwartz; internal evidence suggests January, 1961, HRC, Austin, Texas.

26. Samuel Beckett, undated letter to Thomas McGreevy; also Samuel Beckett, letter to Sylvia Beach, March 27, 1961, in Princeton University Library.

27. Patric Farrell, October 9, 1974, New York; James Stern, November 14, 1974, London.

28. Samuel Beckett, letter to Thomas McGreevy, July 17, 1961.

29. I am grateful to Alan Schneider for the following information.

30. John Calder; Bettina Jonic, November 12, 1974, London.

31. Samuel Beckett, letter to Thomas McGreevy, July 17, 1961.

32. *Ibid.*

33. Edward Beckett.

34. Samuel Beckett, letter to Thomas McGreevy, October 15, 1961.

35. Edward Beckett.

36. Samuel Beckett, letter to Thomas McGreevy, October 15, 1961.

37. *Ibid.*

38. Alan Schneider.

39. Avigdor Arikha, October 30, 1971, Paris, and December 18, 1972, New York; and Samuel Beckett to DB, November 17, 1971, Paris.

40. Samuel Beckett, letter to Thomas McGreevy, October 23, 1961.

41. Samuel Beckett, letter to Sylvia Beach, October 22, 1961, in Princeton University Library.

42. Samuel Beckett, letter to Ethel deKeyser, December 10, 1961, HRC, Austin, Texas.

43. John Montague.

44. Samuel Beckett, letter to Thomas McGreevy, March 3, 1962.

45. *F & F*, n. 271.1, p. 70.

46. Alec Reid.

47. *Cascando and other short dramatic pieces* (New York: Grove Press, n.d., first printing), p. 13.

48. Jerome Lindon.

49. Jack MacGowran, July 9, 1971, Lennox, Mass.

50. A. J. Leventhal, John Montague; Samuel Beckett to Thomas McGreevy.

51. John Montague.

52. Roger Blin.

53. John Montague.

54. Samuel Beckett, letter to Thomas McGreevy, March 31, 1962.

55. Lawrence Harvey, May 27, 1972, Hanover, New Hampshire.

56. All are now in Baker Library, Dartmouth College, Hanover, New Hampshire.

57. Lawrence Harvey.

58. Which subsequently became part of *Samuel Beckett: Poet and Critic*.

59. Samuel Beckett, letter to Thomas McGreevy, May 5, 1962.

60. Samuel Beckett, letter to Thomas McGreevy, May 5, 1962; Lawrence Harvey to DB.

61. Samuel Beckett, letter to Thomas McGreevy, April 7, 1962.

62. A. J. Leventhal.

63. Lawrence Harvey.

64. A. J. Leventhal.

65. Samuel Beckett, letter to Thomas McGreevy, May 31, 1962.

66. Robert Craft, *Stravinsky: Chronicle of a Friendship, 1948–1971* (New York: Alfred A. Knopf, 1972), pp. 153–154. Craft quoted Beckett as saying he did not agree with John Butler Yeats, that of his two sons, Jack B. Yeats was the greater talent. In fact, it is just the opposite: Beckett said that he did consider Jack B. Yeats the greater talent than W. B. (to DB, August, 1973).

67. Samuel Beckett, letter to Thomas McGreevy, June 4, 1962.

68. Samuel Beckett, letter to Thomas McGreevy, July 22, 1962.

69. *Play, Cascando and other short dramatic pieces* (New York: Grove Press, 1963), pp. 46, 47.

70. Samuel Beckett, letter to Thomas McGreevy, July 22, 1962.

71. Josette Hayden.

72. Maria Jolas; Samuel Beckett, letter to Thomas McGreevy, July 22, 1962.

73. John Montague.

74. Jean Reavey, unpublished diaries, June 30, 1962.

75. Samuel Beckett, letter to Jean Reavey, August 6, 1962.

76. *Ibid.*

77. Alan Schneider.

78. Jean Reavey, unpublished diaries, August, 1962.

79. George Reavey.

80. Jean Reavey, unpublished diaries, August, 1962.

81. Samuel Beckett, letter to Thomas McGreevy, September 30, 1962.

82. *Ibid.*

83. The following information is from interviews with Jack MacGowran, Melanie Carvill, Gloria MacGowran, Samuel Beckett, John Calder.

84. Jack MacGowran.

85. On February 23, 1965, *Beginning to End* was broadcast by the BBC-TV *Monitor* program, and further revisions were made. (See *F & F*, n. 503, p. 103, in which Beckett's letter to John Fletcher is quoted, stating that he was informed of textual changes in the *Monitor* program and accepted them.)

86. Samuel Beckett to DB, November 17, 1971.

87. Jack MacGowran.

88. Jack MacGowran; José Ferrer, October 10, 1976, New York.

89. Mollie Roe.

90. Ulick O'Connor, *Brendan Behan* (London: Coronet Books, 1972), p. 292.

91. Samuel Beckett, letter to H. O. White, December 6, 1961, Trinity College, Dublin.

92. Samuel Beckett, letter to Roger Blin, December 17, 1972, in possession of DB.

93. Adam Tarn, October 19, 1973, Ottawa.

CHAPTER TWENTY-THREE 1963–65

1. Samuel Beckett, letter to Shivaun O'Casey Kenig, April 1, 1963, saying he was sending money; also Jack MacGowran to DB.

2. Samuel Beckett, letter to Thomas McGreevy, May 11, 1963.

3. Samuel Beckett, letters to William York Tindall, January 15 and 22, 1963.

4. The following observations are based on conversations with Samuel Beckett, Alan Schneider, Roger Blin, Herbert Blau, John Calder, Madeleine Renaud, Simone Benmusa, Ruby Cohn and many others.

5. Samuel Beckett, letter to Thomas McGreevy, May 11, 1963.

6. Samuel Beckett to DB and others.

7. Roger Blin.

8. *Ibid.*

9. *Ibid.*

10. *Ibid.*

11. *Ibid.*

12. R.B.D. French.

13. Madeleine Renaud, Roger Blin, Jean Martin, R.B.D. French, and others.

14. R.B.D. French.

15. Alan Schneider.

16. Roger Blin.

17. Jocelyn Herbert.

18. *Samuel Beckett Exhibition*, Reading University Library, 1971, p. 92.

19. Samuel Beckett to DB, June 19, 1973.

20. Jocelyn Herbert, Billie Whitelaw and Bettina Jonic.

21. Samuel Beckett, letter to Jack MacGowran, May 27, 1964, HRC, Austin, Texas. Also, Geneviève Serreau, July 11, 1973, Paris; Simone Benmusa, July 2, 1973, Paris.

22. Alan Simpson, *Beckett and Behan and a Theatre in Dublin*, p. 63.

23. Philippe Staib, "A Propos Samuel Beckett," in *Beckett at Sixty*, p. 89.

24. Samuel Beckett, letter to Thomas McGreevy, June 9, 1964.

25. Jack MacGowran.

26. Samuel Beckett, letter to Thomas McGreevy, June 9, 1964.

27. Samuel Beckett to DB, November, 1971.

28. The following information from Barney Rosset, Alan Schneider, Richard Seaver.

29. Alan Schneider, "On Directing *Film*," in *Film by Samuel Beckett* (New York: Grove Press, 1969), p. 67.

30. Alan Schneider to DB, August 7, 1971.

31. Schneider, "On Directing," p. 68.

32. *Ibid.*, pp. 67–68.

33. *Ibid.*, p. 68.

34. Barney Rosset.

35. Schneider, "On Directing," p. 71.

36. *Ibid.*, p. 72.

37. *Ibid.*, p. 73.

38. For an excellent discussion of the problems encountered, see Schneider's essay on *Film*.

39. Kenneth Koch, telephone conversation, January 3, 1972.

40. Alan Schneider.

41. Barney Rosset.

42. Jean Reavey, unpublished diaries, August, 1964; Kay Boyle, George Reavey, Samuel Beckett to DB.

43. John Kobler graciously made the article available to me. Unfortunately it was never published, as the *Saturday Evening Post* ceased publication shortly after.

44. Jean and Alan Schneider, May 13, 1975, Hastings-on-Hudson, N.Y.

45. Barney Rosset.

46. Shivaun O'Casey Kenig.

47. Adam Tarn.

48. See *Angels of Darkness* (London: George Allen & Unwin, 1972), p. 16 ff.

49. *Ibid.*, p. 17.

50. *Ibid.*

51. Samuel Beckett, letter to Shivaun O'Casey Kenig, January 13, 1965, Paris.

52. William O'Sullivan, November 12, 1971, Dublin.

53. Adam Tarn.

54. Each of the above statements is based on interviews with individuals who benefited from Beckett's kindness and generosity. In the interest of their privacy, I have not cited the sources of these remarks, with the exception of Mrs. Kenig and Mr. Tarn who wanted to make a statement about Beckett's kindness.

55. Samuel Beckett, letter to Thomas McGreevy, January 30, 1965.

56. Roger Blin.

57. "F——," *transition 48*, 4 (January, 1949), pp. 19–21.

58. Anonymous.

59. Samuel Beckett, letter to Thomas McGreevy, March 8, 1965.

60. Simone Benmusa.

61. Duckworth, *Darkness*, p. 19.

62. Samuel Beckett, letter to Thomas McGreevy, May 17, 1965.

63. McGreevy amassed a great number of pages dealing with his boyhood in Tarbert, County Limerick. Unfortunately, at his death in 1967, he had not yet written of his friendships with Joyce, Beckett, Aldington, Cunard and all the friends of the halcyon Paris days, nor of his long continuing correspondence with T. S. Eliot, Wallace Stevens, Marianne Moore, and others.

64. Samuel Beckett, letter to Thomas McGreevy, August 31, 1965.

65. Samuel Beckett, letter to Shivaun O'Casey Kenig, June 5, 1965, Paris.

66. Fanny Howe, August 8, 1974, Woodbridge, Conn.

67. Professor and Mrs. Maguinness.

68. Niall Montgomery, January 21, 1974, Dublin.

69. Melanie Carvill.

70. Elizabeth Ryan.

71. Alan Schneider, June 25, 1972, Hastings-on-Hudson, N.Y.

72. Patric Farrell, October 19, 1974, New York; *The New York Times* carried a story on June 16, 1965, which gave a long itinerary of places to which Beckett was supposed to guide Farrell and deBrun, but he never actually took them anyplace but Fouquet's.

73. Caroline Beckett Murphy, Edward Beckett.

74. Samuel Beckett, letter to Thomas McGreevy, August 31, 1965.

75. John Montague, Harold Pinter.

76. Samuel Beckett, letter to Patric Farrell, December 25, 1965.

77. Samuel Beckett, letter to Thomas McGreevy, December 25, 1965.

78. *Ibid.*

79. *Ibid.*

CHAPTER TWENTY-FOUR 1966–69:

1. Samuel Beckett, letter to William York Tindall, January 6, 1966.

2. A. J. Leventhal, John Montague.

3. Samuel Beckett, letter to John Montague, November 15, 1968.

4. Samuel Beckett, letter to John Montague, February 16, 1966.

5. Samuel Beckett, letter to Ruby Cohn, as quoted in her article, "Acting For Beckett," *Modern Drama*, IC, 1966, p. 237.

6. *Poems by Samuel Beckett I*, selected and introduced by John Fletcher, produced by Martin Esslin, transmitted Wednesday, March 9, 1966, BBC Third Programme, featuring *Whoroscope*, "Eneug I," "Serena II," "Alba," "Cascando," "St. Lô," "My way is in the sand flowing," "What would I do without this world, faceless, incurious," and "I would like my love to die." *Poems by Samuel Beckett II* was broadcast Thursday, November 24, 1966, BBC Third Programme, and included "The Vulture," "Serena III," "Echo's Bones," "Serena I," the first addenda from *Watt*, "Da Tagte es," "Sanies I," and "Who may tell the tale of the old man" (also from *Watt*).

7. Samuel Beckett, letter to Patric Farrell, December 15, 1965.

8. The following analysis is based on conversations with actors, directors and other associates in the theaters of the three countries under discussion. Because the list is lengthy, I cite none here in order to avoid confusion by citing some and not others.

9. The following account is from Adam Tarn.

10. Shown on April 13, 1966, on Suddeutscher Rundfunk Stuttgart, with Deryk Mendel as Joe and Nancy Illig as the Voice.

11. Samuel Beckett, letter to *Hermathena*, May 11, 1966, TCD Library.

12. BBC-2, July 4, 1966. Beckett was assisted by Alan Gibson in directing this performance. Michael Bakewell was the producer.

13. Elizabeth Ryan.

14. Samuel Beckett, letter to Thomas McGreevy, September 13, 1966.

15. Raymond Federman, December 27, 1975, New York; and John Fletcher, October 19, 1971, Paris.

16. John Fletcher.

17. Manuscript in possession of Samuel Beckett, details in *Samuel Beckett, an Exhibition*, Reading University Library, p. 118.

18. My translation, from R. U. L., p. 118.

19. John Kobler, John Montague, A. J. Leventhal and others.

20. He wrote this same message to many friends; thus I single no one out here.

21. A. J. Leventhal.

22. Jean Reavey.

23. This statement was repeated to many of his friends, so none is singled out here.

24. Josette Hayden.

25. Ruby Cohn.

26. John Kobler.

27. Among them *Le Monde*, September 28, 1967, p. 5.

28. Roger Blin.

29. Samuel Beckett, letter to John Kobler, March 6, 1968.

30. Samuel Beckett, letter to John Knowlson, February 8, 1971, in Reading University Library, p. 106.

31. Barney Rosset and Alan Schneider.

32. Joanna Richardson, *Enid Starkie* (New York: Macmillan Publishing Company, Inc., 1973), p. 266.

33. Caroline Beckett Murphy and Ann Beckett.

34. Ann Beckett, A. J. Leventhal.

35. Kay Boyle, April 15, 1973, San Francisco.

36. Adam Tarn.

37. *Ibid.*

38. My emphasis. Alec Reid kindly gave me a copy of the original script, given to him by Samuel Beckett. The printed version is from *Oh! Calcutta!* (New York: Grove Press, 1969), p. 9.

39. Samuel Beckett to DB, November 17, 1971.

40. *Ibid.*

41. Kenneth Tynan, telephone conversation, November 11, 1974, London.

42. Samuel Beckett to DB, November 17, 1971.

43. A. J. Leventhal, Josette Hayden and others.

44. This account of Beckett's Nobel Prize is based on interviews with Adam Tarn, John Kobler, Barney Rosset, Roger Blin, Jerome Lindon, Josette Hayden, A. J. Leventhal, John Montague, John Calder, Jean Martin and many others. I cite those who have actually discussed the situation at the time he learned of the award with Beckett or Madame Beckett.

CHAPTER TWENTY-FIVE 1969–73:

1. Kjell Stromberg, "The 1969 Prize," *Nobel Prize Library* (New York: Helvetica Press, Inc., 1971), p. 71.

2. *Ibid.*, p. 72.

3. Citation of the Swedish Academy for the 1969 Nobel Prize in Literature to Samuel Beckett.

4. Alec Reid to DB.

5. Alec Reid, "Reluctant Prizeman," p. 63.

6. *Life* magazine, November 7, 1969, p. 91.

7. *Ibid.*

8. Information about Beckett in Nabeul and Cascais is from Samuel Beckett's letters: to Adam Tarn, November 2, 1969; to George Reavey, December 21, 1969, January 13, 1970; and from interviews with Jerome Lindon, Barney Rosset, Richard Seaver, John Calder, Bettina Jonic, Roger Blin, John Kobler and others.

9. Among those he wrote to October 22 and 23, were John Montague, A. J. Leventhal, Adam Tarn, Barney Rosset.

10. He repeated this remark verbally to Lawrence Harvey, John Fletcher, A. J. Leventhal, John Montague and others.

11. Samuel Beckett, letter to Adam Tarn, November 2, 1969.

12. A. J. Leventhal and John Montague.

13. The book finally appeared in November, 1976, as *I Can't Go On, I'll Go On*, edited and with an introduction by Richard Seaver, featuring selections from Beckett's entire canon. This information from Barney Rosset, Fred Jordan, Richard Seaver, and from correspondence in the files of Grove Press.

14. *Premier Amour* (Paris: Éditions de Minuit, 1970).

15. Patrick Magee, April 24, 1976, New Haven, Conn.

16. John Calder. Beckett called his translation *First Love*. Calder and Boyars published it in 1973, Grove Press in 1974.

17. Information about the Samuel Beckett Theatre is from Francis Warner, letter to DB, June 11, 1975; *Parade* magazine, November 26, 1972, p. 2; Samuel Beckett, letter to Francis Warner, June 1, 1967; from interviews and conversations with Samuel Beckett, Alan Schneider, Barney Rosset, John Calder, Jerome Lindon and others, and from interviews conducted for DB by Professor J. D. O'Hara in England during summer, 1977.

18. Samuel Beckett, letter to Barney Rosset, July, 1969; related correspondence from Grove Press files.

19. Information about Samuel Beckett's eye surgery is from Beckett's correspondence with Barney Rosset, Richard Seaver, John Montague, Vivian Mercier and George Reavey, and from interviews with Josette Hayden, Desirée Moorehead Hayter, Stanley William Hayter, Bettina Jonic, John Calder, A. J. Leventhal and others.

20. Beckett's correspondence with Jack MacGowran, among others, HRC, Austin, Texas.

21. Beckett's description of the hospital to Adam Tarn, Barney Rosset, Alan Schneider, Jack MacGowran, Bettina Jonic Calder and others.

22. Samuel Beckett, letter to Jack MacGowran, November 5, 1970, HRC, Austin, Texas.

23. Samuel Beckett, letter to Jack MacGowran, December 24, 1970, HRC, Austin, Texas.

24. Samuel Beckett's telegram to Barney Rosset, November 31, 1970; Samuel Beckett, letter to George Reavey, December 1, 1970; John Calder and Bettina Jonic.

25. Samuel Beckett, letter to Jack MacGowran, HRC, Austin, Texas; and to Desirée Moorehead Hayter.

26. Samuel Beckett, letter to George Reavey, April 15, 1971.

27. Desirée Moorehead Hayter, July 9, 1973, Paris.

28. Ann Beckett.

29. Samuel Beckett, letter to George Reavey, May 24, 1971.

30. Photo by Jean Reavey. Reproduced here following p. 562.

31. Samuel Beckett, letter to Jack MacGowran, February 7, 1971, HRC, Austin, Texas.

32. *Ibid.*

33. This information from Melanie Carvill, Barney Rosset, Richard Seaver, and from Beckett's correspondence with MacGowran, now in HRC, Austin, Texas.

34. John Kobler, Barney Rosset, John Unterecker and others.

35. Adam Tarn, October 19, 1973, Ottawa, Canada.

36. Samuel Beckett, letter to George Reavey, August 7, 1971.

37. The following information is from Samuel Beckett to DB, November 17, 1971; and Samuel Beckett, letter to George Reavey, August 30, 1971.

38. Melanie Carvill.

39. This phrase figures in his correspondence and conversation with so many persons that I cite none here rather than omit one inadvertently.

40. Samuel Beckett, letter to George Reavey, August 30, 1971.

41. Samuel Beckett, letter to George Reavey, October 20, 1971.

42. This is a phrase used by Beckett himself and by his few close associates and friends.

43. Samuel Beckett, letter to George Reavey, December 18, 1971.

44. Samuel Beckett, letter to Barney Rosset, December 8, 1971; Samuel Beckett, letters to Jack MacGowran, November 19, 23, and December 2, 1971, HRC, Austin, Texas.

45. Liam Miller, Moira Miller, Alec Reid.

46. Samuel Beckett, letter to Barney Rosset, December 8, 1971.

47. Samuel Beckett, letter to Jack MacGowran, April 16, 1971, HRC, Austin, Texas.

48. Samuel Beckett, letter to Fred Jordan, September 2, 1971; Fred Jordan, letter to Samuel Beckett, April 20, 1972.

49. Samuel Beckett, letter to Fred Jordan, April 12, 1972; Fred Jordan, letter to Samuel Beckett, April 20, 1972.

50. Samuel Beckett to George Reavey in conversation, July, 1973, Paris.

51. Samuel Beckett, letter to Jean Reavey, March 18, 1972.

52. A phrase which he has used to many people in describing the previously written works issued in the 1970's.

53. Manuscript in the Beckett Collection, Reading University, England.

54. Aidan Higgins, "Beckett in Berlin," *Atlantis*, no. 1 (March, 1970), p. 54.

55. This remark was attributed to James Knowlson, in conversation with Avigdor Arikha, by Professor Stanley E. Gontarski in "The Voice of One Crying in the Wilderness: The Emergence of *Not I*," Modern Languages Association Special Session; "Samuel Beckett: The Writings of the Last Ten Years, 1966–76," December 29, 1976, New York.

56. Samuel Beckett, April 13, 1972, Paris.

57. *Time*, December 11, 1972, p. 122.

58. Clive Barnes, "A World Premiere of Beckett's *Not I*," *The New York Times*, Friday, November 24, 1972.

59. Samuel Beckett to DB, Alan Schneider, Billie Whitelaw, A. J. Leventhal and others.

60. Adam Tarn.

61. Samuel Beckett, *Still*, with six etchings by Stanley William Hayter and notes by A. J. Leventhal. (Milan: M'Arte Edizioni, 1975). Printed in an edition of 160 copies, with prices ranging from $300 to $450.

62. Samuel Beckett, letter to George Reavey, August 9, 1972.

63. Information about the American Beckett Festival is from Alan Schneider, Barney Rosset, and Jessica Tandy and Hume Cronyn, June 29, 1977, New Haven, Conn.

64. All information about *Not I* is from Jessica Tandy.

65. Hume Cronyn.

66. Samuel Beckett, letter to DB, October 17, 1972.

67. Samuel Beckett, letter to George Reavey, November 13, 1972.

68. Samuel Beckett, letter to DB, December 14, 1972.

69. Samuel Beckett, letter to DB, October 17, 1972.

70. Samuel Beckett, letter to George Reavey, December 25, 1972.

71. The following information is from interviews with Billie Whitelaw, November 17, 1974, London; Jocelyn Herbert, November 10, 1974; Anthony Page, telephone conversation, July 24, 1975, New York; Harold Pinter, November 14, 1974, London; Samuel Beckett, June 19, 1973.

CHAPTER TWENTY-SIX 1973–:

1. Samuel Beckett, letter to John Kobler, July 6, 1972.
2. (London and New York: Petersburg Press, 1977.)
3. (New York, The Gotham Book Mart Master Series, 1976.)
4. Edited and with an introduction by James Knowlson and Felix Leakey (Reading: Whiteknights Press, 1976).
5. Bertrand Poirot-Delpech, "Beckett—the Galactic Whim," the *Guardian*, November 14, 1976.
6. By Calder and Boyars, general editor James Knowlson.
7. Calvin Israel, undated letter to J. D. O'Hara.
8. Samuel Beckett's note attached to a letter to Barney Rosset from Arlene Donovan (Zero Mostel's representative), January 17, 1973.
9. Samuel Beckett's undated note appended to Estelle Parson's letter to him in care of Barney Rosset.
10. Barney Rosset.
11. Samuel Beckett, letter to Barney Rosset, July 11, 1973.
12. *Ibid.*
13. Samuel Beckett, letter to George and Jean Reavey, April 10, 1975. Because the Reaveys asked him a second time for permission for the Mabou Mines Company to perform *Cascando,* he gave it again, even though he was unhappy with their variations. He met the members of the company in Berlin in the fall of 1976, but he refused to view their production.
14. Samuel Beckett, letter to George Reavey, February 7, 1974.
15. Samuel Beckett, letter to Barney Rosset, February 10, 1974.
16. *Ibid.*
17. Samuel Beckett, letter to Adam Tarn, April 25, 1973.
18. Undated letter to Mary Manning Howe.
19. Undated letter to Adam Tarn.
20. Samuel Beckett, letter to George Reavey, January, 1974.
21. John Montague, December 10, 1975, Woodbridge, Connecticut.
22. Samuel Beckett, letter to George Reavey, January 8, 1975.
23. Samuel Beckett, letter to George Reavey, March 23, 1975.
24. Samuel Beckett, letter to George Reavey, April 14, 1975.
25. *Ibid.*
26. Samuel Beckett, letter to George Reavey, December 7, 1975.
27. George Reavey, December 19, 1975.

28. Correspondence with Rosset, Reavey, Schneider and others.

29. These opinions came from James and Tania Stern, Brian Coffey, Alan Schneider, Michael and Anne Chisholm Davie, and others.

30. *London Sunday Times*, May 23, 1976. All subsequent quotes from this review.

31. Robert Cushman, "In a Hellish Half Light," London *Observer*, May 23, 1976. All subsequent quotes from this review.

32. Mel Gussow, "Beckett Continues to Refine His Vision," *The New York Times*, Sunday, December 26, 1976, pp. D1, D27.

33. For obvious reasons, I shall not identify the persons who were so open and candid in their discussions with me unless they have given me express permission to quote.

34. The following comments were made by scholars attending the Modern Languages Association special session No. 613, "Samuel Beckett: The Last Decade 1966–76," December 29, 1976, New York.

35. *The Nation*, February 19, 1977, p. 216 ff.

36. Published in London by Calder and Boyars, and in New York by Grove Press.

37. Patrick Magee.

38. Samuel Beckett, letter to Patrick Magee, December 15, 1975.

39. *The Nation*, p. 217.

40. Paul Grey, "Words of the Bard of the Bitter End," *Time*, February 7, 1977, pp. 84–85.

41. Samuel Beckett, letter to DB, July 20, 1971.

42. Samuel Beckett to DB, November 17, 1971.

43. In one form or another, he had made this remark to DB and others.

INDEX

Blin, Rogers, (*Cont.*)
    Waiting for Godot and, 382, 384,
      388, 398, 402–05, 409–30 *passim*,
      436, 439, 440, 444, 447, 472, 480,
      486, 506, 512–13, 548, 632
Bloomsday (Joyce), 492
Blunden, Edmund, 600
Bonnelly (farmer in Roussillon), 324–
    25
Bookman, 182–83, 191, 232
Borges, Jorge Luis, 532
Bosquets de Bondy, Les, see *Groves
    of Bondy, The*
Botteghe Oscure, 437
Bowles, Patrick, 431, 438–39, 447
Bowra, C. M., 410
Boyle, Kay, 81, 238, 302, 357, 541, 574
Bradley, Jennie, 78
Bradley, William, 78
Bray, Barbara, 586
"Breath," 602–03
Brecht, Bertolt, 592
Brenan, Gerald, 398, 409–10
Breton, André, 52, 116, 142, 143
Breuer, Lee, 633–34
Brion, Marcel, 535
Bronowski, Jacob, 130, 154
Brown, Curtis, 505
Browne, Gareth, 589
Bruce, Brenda, 554
Brueil, Mr. (teacher), 32
Bruller, Jean, 406
Brun, Elsa de, 584
Bruno, Giordano, 76, 90
Brustein, Robert, 515
Buckland-Wright, John, 298–99
Buckland-Wright, Mary, 298
Budgen, Frank, 69
Bull, Peter, 450, 453
Burroughs, William, 434
Burton, Richard, 611–12
Butor, Michel, 590
Byrne, Davy, 46

Caetani, Princess Marguerite, 437
Cagney, Sean, 166, 172, 240
Cahiers d'Art, 347
Cahiers de l'Herne, 631
Calder, Bettina, 537, 614
Calder, John, 493, 500, 516, 537, 557,
    611, 614, 639
Calder and Boyars, 524, 541, 620
"Calmative, The," 358–59
Campbell College, 56–57
Candide (Voltaire), 92
Capuchin Annual, 339
Caretaker, The (Pinter), 527
Carlier, Robert, 406–07
Carvill, Melanie, 583
Cascando, 541–42, 543, 548, 559, 576
"Cascando," 230, 231

"Case in a Thousand, A," 182, 183–84
Casement, Tom, 509
Cat and the Moon, The (Yeats), 383
Céline, Louis-Ferdinand, 165, 249, 275
Censorship in the Saorstat, 217
Cent-vingt Jours de Sodom, Les (de
    Sade), 282–83
Ce Soir, 465
Chalbert, Pierre, 591
Chamberlain, Neville, 295, 296
Chaplin, Charlie, 48, 570, 605
Char, René, 332, 373
Chatto and Windus, 106, 109, 162, 172,
    186, 206, 230, 234, 247–48
Chauffard, R. J., 517
Cheriane, Madame, 313
"Che Sciagura," 92–93
Chester Cycle, 199
Chevaliers de la table ronde, Les (Coc-
    teau), 279
Chicago *Tribune*, 130
Church, Richard, 247–48
Churchill, Winston, 323
Claddagh Records, 589
Clarke, Austin, 46, 119, 182, 232, 292
Clarke, Charles C., 49, 55
Clerkx, Toni (pen name of Jacoba van
    Velde), 322, 359, 367, 408
Clooney, Rosemary, 556
Cocteau, Jean, 279
Coffey, Brian, 182, 199, 205, 217, 231,
    234, 270, 277, 279, 285, 291, 292,
    295, 299, 339, 396, 479, 582
Coffey, Bridget, 299
Coffey, Joe, 572–73, 574
Coghlan, John, 194
Cogley, Madame, 46
Cohn, Ruby, 257, 359, 466–67
Cole, Connolly, 518
Colum, Padraic, 119
Comédie, see *Play*
Come and Go, 580, 590, 593
Comisso, Giovanni, 99
Comment c'est, see *How It Is*
*Comment Proust a composé son ro-
    man* (Feuillerat), 181
"Concentrisme, Le," 50
Connoisseur, 176
Connolly, Cyril, 198–99, 378
Constable (publisher), 230
Contempo, 179
Corneille, Pierre, 124, 127
Costello, Nuala, 153
Cousine Bette (Balzac), 199
Covici-Friede, 234
Craft, Robert, 547
Crane, Hart, 78
Cremin, Constantine, 443
Crevel (poet), 52, 116, 143, 178
Criterion, 181
Cronyn, Hume, 624–26